BUSINESS ETHICS
Roles and Responsibilities

BUSINESS ETHICS
Roles and Responsibilities

Joseph L. Badaracco, Jr.
Harvard Business School

Chicago · Bogota · Boston · Buenos Aires · Caracas
London · Madrid · Mexico City · Sydney · Toronto

Senior sponsoring editor:	Kurt L. Strand
Editorial coordinator:	Michele Dooley
Senior marketing manager:	Kurt Messersmith
Project editor:	Paula M. Buschman
Production manager:	Laurie Kersch
Cover designer:	Jeanne M. Rivera/Annette Spadoni
Art studio:	Steadman and Gibson Corporate Design, Inc.
Art coordinator:	Heather Burbridge
Compositor:	Graphic World, Inc.
Typeface:	10/12 Times Roman
Printer:	R. R. Donnelley & Sons Company

Library of Congress Cataloging-in-Publication Data

Badaracco, Joseph.
    Business ethics : roles and responsibilities / Joseph L. Badaracco.
        p.   cm.
    ISBN 0-256-14946-1
    1. Business ethics. I. Title.
    HF5307.B3 1995
    174'.4—dc20   94–27615

Printed in the United States of America

1 2 3 4 5 6 7 8 9 0 DO 1 0 9 8 7 6 5 4

For John Shad

Preface

Business managers have enormous power in modern industrial societies. With this power come responsibilities. These are important moral, legal, and practical obligations that often clash with each other and create serious personal and organizational dilemmas.

The case studies and readings in this book concentrate on three basic questions:

1. What moral responsibilities do men and women take when they become business executives?
2. What are the common ways in which these responsibilities can conflict with each other and with managers' personal moral convictions?
3. How can managers and companies resolve these conflicts in practical and responsible ways?

This book offers both a practical and conceptual perspective on these fundamental questions of business ethics. The case studies it presents focus on the practical ethical issues that managers face in their daily work. These case studies are particularly valuable for undergraduate and graduate students, because many of the cases focus on young men and women confronting difficult ethical issues in the early, vulnerable years of their careers.

In addition, the cases focus heavily on contemporary management problems. Several of them examine recent controversies—over RU 486, the so-called French abortion pill, the Treasury securities scandal at Salomon Brothers, and the establishment of maquiladora plants in Mexico by U.S. firms. Many cases involve issues of "diversity"—situations in which gender, race, national background, or religious preference matter significantly. Others focus on ethical issues involving contemporary figures, such as Ross Perot, Malcolm X, and Thomas Monaghan, the founder of Domino's Pizza. In addition, an entire section of the book deals with the ethical issues that managers face when their organizations are involved in strategic alliances or in other relationships linking companies with other stakeholders.

This book is designed to place the practical issues of business ethics in a unique conceptual framework, one that focuses explicitly on the roles and responsibilities of business managers. The framework is based on powerful ideas drawn from important moral philosophers, economists, psychologists, business historians, and experts on management. The book includes many extended excerpts from the writings of a wide range of seminal thinkers, contemporary and classic, to enable students to examine important ideas and arguments in the authors' own words.

To further clarify the conceptual framework, the book also includes several comparative case studies. These focus on the ethical responsibilities of attorneys, medical personnel, and government officials and enable students to compare the role obligations of business managers with those of other professionals.

For managers, the best ethical frameworks are practical. They help managers recognize and analyze important issues and help them find responsible, practical ways of resolving them. The ideas, principles and concepts presented in this book were all chosen and developed to be useful—both for grappling with the case studies presented here and with the high stakes and real world issues of business ethics that are an inescapable part of managers' work.

ACKNOWLEDGMENTS

This book reflects important contributions by many individuals. Dean John McArthur, other senior faculty members of the Harvard Business School, and the school's generous alumni provided me with the time and resources that this work required. John Shad's support and guidance have been especially vital to this endeavor, and the book is dedicated to him, with deep gratitude for his generous and far-sighted contributions.

I am also especially indebted to Kenneth Andrews and the late John Matthews, who were pioneers in business ethics at the Harvard Business School, and to three of their successors, Mary Gentile, Kenneth Goodpaster, and Thomas Piper. During the mid-1980s, his group devoted its talents and energy to the creation of Decision Making and Ethical Values, the first required MBA course in business ethics in the school's history. I was fortunate to be able to work with them in the early years of their effort, and I learned a great deal from doing so, much of which is reflected in this book.

During the last several years, I have also had the opportunity to work with the wider circle of colleagues who have taught Decision Making and Ethical Values and contributed to its development: James Austin, Michael Beer, Thomas Bonoma, Raymond Corey, Dwight Crane, Gregory Dees, Robert Hayes, William McLennan, Cynthia Montgomery, Lynn Sharp Paine, Sharon Parks, Howard Stevenson, and Shoshana Zuboff.

Many of these colleagues also helped me, through their advice and suggestions, to develop the MBA course, Moral Dilemmas of Management, on which this book is based. The course is also based heavily on what I learned by participating in the Harvard University Program on Ethics in the Professions. Among other things, the program introduced me to Dennis Thompson and Kenneth Winston, who contributed significantly to the conceptual framework of the Moral Dilemmas of Management course and of this book.

I also want to thank the colleagues who have given me permission to include cases of theirs in this book. These are Thomas Piper for "ProTech," Bart van Dissel for "Martha McCaskey," Kenneth Goodpaster for "International Drilling Corporation" and for "H. J. Heinz," Lynn Sharp Paine for "The Procters' Problem" and for "Lotus MarketPlace," Mary Gentile for "Laura Wollen," Dwight Crane for "Salomon and the Treasury Securities Auction," Richard Tedlow for "James Burke: A Career in American Business," Willis Emmons for "Burroughs Wellcome & AZT," Greg Dees for "BayBank Boston," David Upton for "Australian Paper Manufacturers," and Lou Wells for "Bribery and Extortion in International Business."

I am especially indebted to two outstanding research associates, Allen Webb and Jerry Useem, who helped write many of the cases in this book. I also want to thank Kurt Strand and Paula Buschman of Richard D. Irwin for their friendly encouragement in guiding this book through the editorial process. Eugenie Moriconi contributed both professional skill and patience to the tasks of producing many of the case studies and other documents in this book and to helping orchestrate the complicated process of getting all of this material in one place in the right order.

Finally, I am deeply grateful to my wife, Patricia O'Brien, for the countless ways, large and small, in which she has contributed to this book.

Contents

PART I

Introduction

The cases and other readings in this book serve three basic objectives. The first two are practical. One is to help graduate and undergraduate students understand the ethical issues that business managers often must resolve. The other is to help prepare students, to the extent possible in a classroom, to deal effectively and responsibly with the ethical dilemmas, uncertainties, pressures, temptations, opportunities, and tests of character that they will face, if they choose careers as business managers. The third objective is intellectual. This text is designed to help students place the practical issues of business ethics in a powerful conceptual and historical context. Hence, the cases and readings draw heavily on works of moral philosophy, history, economics, psychology, and management to provide a firm conceptual basis for analyzing the ethical issues that managers face and for evaluating alternative ways of resolving these issues.

Business ethics is a complex subject because it affects business operations in so many ways. Ethical issues arise for managers in every functional area of a company—in marketing, finance, production, accounting, and human resource management. At the same time, these issues are also a fundamental concern of senior executives.[1] The way in which a company's leaders define ethical issues and resolve them strongly influences their ability to guide and lead others, and it shapes the cultural and ethical climate of their organizations.

---

[1] This book uses the term *managers* to describe the people in business organizations who have responsibility for organizing and guiding the work of other people. In other words, a manager may be responsible for a department with only two or three other people or for an entire firm employing thousands. The book uses the terms *executive* and *senior executive* to refer to the managers in the company who hold senior positions and who are responsible for the management of the entire firm or for major parts of it. Thus, the manager in charge of all of a firm's marketing would be referred to as an "executive," as would be a manager in charge of a division of a company.

1

Business ethics is also complex because the moral responsibilities of business executives do not stop at the boundaries of their firms. In today's interdependent world, business managers' decisions have serious and sometimes profound effects on many stakeholder groups—in their local communities, their nations, and often around the world. As a result, business ethics often involves issues of conflict or misunderstanding among different political or ethnic groups, communities, cultures, or nations.

Business ethics is also a vital personal matter for managers and executives, who typically devote a great deal of their life and energy to their jobs. Through the way they work, managers reveal, define, and shape their personal values. Their professional successes and failures, their challenges and frustrations, and their relationships with coworkers are an important source of meaning and value in managers' lives.

This book allows teachers and students to explore a wide range of these issues or to focus in greater depth on one or more of them. It provides a large, varied collection of case studies and readings. The case studies, set in the United States, Europe, Japan, and several developing countries, describe episodes in managers' early careers, in middle-management positions, as well as issues facing senior executives. Most of the cases can be analyzed at the level of personal ethics, organizational culture and values, and the relationship between a company and its various stakeholders in society.

No one should underestimate the stakes involved when business executives confront serious ethical issues. Chester Barnard, one of the most important management theorists of the 20th century and a leading business executive in his own right, wrote in his classic work *The Functions of the Executive:* "It seems to me inevitable that the struggle to maintain cooperation among men should as surely destroy some men morally as battle destroys some physically."[2]

YOUNG MANAGERS' DILEMMAS

Many of the cases in this book focus on issues that managers confront in the early stages of their careers. During these first years, and especially during the initial three to five years, young men and women can easily find themselves in confusing, stressful, high stakes situations in which the right thing to do, both practically and ethically, is especially difficult to discern. In many situations, the young managers feel strong pressure from organizations or even from their immediate supervisors to do things that seem to them sleazy, unethical, or even illegal. Many of the cases, concepts,

---

[2]Chester Barnard, *The Functions of the Executive* (Cambridge, Mass.: Harvard University Press, 1982), p. 278.

and frameworks in this book are designed to help young managers understand these situations better and avoid their hazards. In short, this material takes "the view from the trenches" as a critical perspective on business ethics.

DILEMMAS

Most of the cases in this book focus on situations in which a manager faces a dilemma involving difficult ethical and administrative considerations. This focus on dilemmas is deliberate. Challenging dilemmas raise important questions of ethical analysis and action, and thereby provide students with opportunities to learn by practicing the concepts and frameworks presented in the text. At the same time, discussions of difficult conflicts of responsibility help students understand and reexamine the values and assumptions that they will bring to their own careers.

Students will also find that their peers often think about moral dilemmas in ways that differ from their own, even though everyone has analyzed the same set of facts.[3] Understanding others' viewpoints — particularly their moral perspectives and their judgments about what is really important in a management situation, and what sort of action will be effective — is a valuable educational experience. Above all, this experience helps students prepare for working in and eventually leading diverse organizations in which thoughtful people differ significantly about a wide range of important issues.

A GENERAL MANAGEMENT PERSPECTIVE

This book's approach to business ethics is designed to help students understand the work of general managers in business organizations. The book does not make the commonplace and mistaken assumption that ethical issues and managerial issues fall in separate categories. Typically, these issues are closely intertwined. Professor C. Roland Christensen of the Harvard Business School has described the talents of outstanding business managers in the following words, and his emphasis on management responsibility underlies the basic philosophy of this book:

> The uniqueness of a good general manager lies in one's ability to lead effectively organizations whose complexity he or she can never fully understand, where

---

[3]Throughout this book, the terms *ethical* and *moral* are used interchangeably. While this is a common practice, it is important to note that some people reserve the word "moral" for issues involving personal beliefs and values, and they use the word "ethical" to describe principles of right and wrong or justice and fairness governing social conduct.

the capacity to control directly the human and physical forces comprising that organization is severely limited, and where he or she must make or review and assume ultimate responsibility for present decisions which commit concretely major resources to a fluid and unknown future.[4]

FRAMEWORKS FOR ANALYSIS AND ACTION

This book is organized around two basic frameworks. The first is designed to help students *analyze* the ethical issues that managers often confront. The second framework focuses on issues of *action* and helps in the development of practical, responsible plans for resolving difficult ethical dilemmas.

These frameworks draw heavily on fundamental ideas from moral philosophy, business history, modern economics, and other disciplines, and they are designed to help students and managers understand and analyze the basic issues of business ethics in a disciplined fashion. The rest of this introduction provides an overview of these two frameworks and explains how they shape the basic structure of this book.

A FRAMEWORK FOR ANALYSIS: SPHERES OF RESPONSIBILITY

Before taking action on an ethical issue, a manager needs to understand its basic dimensions. In many cases, the problem involves conflicts among different responsibilities. Some of these are responsibilities that human beings have simply because they are human beings. Others "come with the territory"—that is, they are responsibilities that men and women take when they become business managers.

The analytical framework of this book is organized around the basic idea that the moral dilemmas of managers often arise from conflicts among or within different *spheres of responsibility*.[5] Each sphere is a coherent and compelling set of ethical claims that emphasizes the moral aspects of

---

[4]Joseph L. Bower et al., *Business Policy: Text and Cases* (Homewood, Ill.: Richard D. Irwin, 1991), p. x.

[5]This analytical framework draws heavily on ideas developed by the political philosopher Michael Walzer. In his book *Spheres of Justice,* Walzer analyzes the concept of justice by dividing the social life of human beings into different spheres of activities. Each of these is centered on some different human good, such as education, beauty, health, or wealth. Walzer believes that each of these goods should be distributed according to moral standards; but, on Walzer's analysis, the appropriate criteria are not universal and absolute. Rather, they originate in the values and meanings associated with a particular good in a certain community at a particular point in its history. See Michael Walzer, *Spheres of Justice* (New York: Basic Books, 1993), pp. 3–30.

certain human relationships, guiding principles, duties, norms of behavior, and personal aspirations.

Executives' responsibilities can be divided into four spheres: personal ethical values, responsibilities as economic agents, responsibilities as organization leaders, and responsibilities in cooperative capitalism. Together, these four spheres provide a map of the moral territory of business management. The next several pages briefly introduce each of these sources of managerial responsibility.

PERSONAL ETHICAL VALUES

In simplest terms, the sphere of personal ethical values consists of the duties, commitments, and ideals that shape and guide individuals' lives. In many respects, the sphere of private ethics seems to be primary, to represent morality in its truest and most profound sense. It seems quite natural, after all, to think that people are first and foremost individual moral agents and only secondarily take on social roles and responsibilities as executives, attorneys, or physicians. The personal sphere can be described abstractly in terms of a few basic principles: obey the law, keep promises, tell the truth, be true to one's values, and so forth.

In reality, however, individual morality is richer and more complex than any set of abstract principles can indicate. Individual morality often differs in important ways from person to person, reflecting factors that are individual and sometimes highly particular. For many people, personal morality is strongly influenced by their religious beliefs, while others find guiding principles and aspirations in the example of their parents or other people they admire, in literature, in philosophy, or in convictions developed through their own lives and reflection. For some people, personal ethics revolve heavily around commitments to their families; others are committed to work, or to political reform, or to friendships.

These differing approaches to individual morality are not, however, simply matters of subjective, personal preference. Most individuals' ethical beliefs are firmly embedded in norms and assumptions—some examined and some implicit—that originate with their families, communities, and the cultural and historical traditions that shape their early lives and education.

From the time of the ancient philosophers, in Greece as well as in China and India, a handful of questions have been asked, answered, and reanswered by men and women seeking to understand the foundations of personal morality. What distinguishes a good life from a bad life? What distinguishes a good person from an evil one? How can individuals gain a sense of purpose, coherence, and wholeness in their lives? In the Western world, such questions have defined individual morality ever since Socrates, Plato, and Aristotle began asking them 2,500 years ago.

The readings and cases in Part II of the book present in-depth perspectives on several important ways of defining and analyzing the ethical obligations of individuals. The aim of these readings is not to make students into professional moral philosophers. Nor are the readings and cases intended to display the rich complexities of various philosophical systems. Only years of study could accomplish either of these aims. Rather, the goal is to present, as clearly as possible, the fundamental principles of several important traditions of moral philosophy, and to do so in ways that encourage rigorous analysis and practical insight into the ethical challenges of management life.

Consequences.   One of these traditions, which is typically called "utilitarianism," focuses on the morality of consequences. Jeremy Bentham and John Stuart Mill crystallized this set of ideas during the early and middle years of the 19th century. Their basic concept was that the morally correct action for individuals were the actions that would do the most good and the least harm for everyone affected by the act.

Rights and Duties.   A second tradition focuses on rights and duties. In general terms, this tradition starts with the fundamental idea that all human beings, simply because they are human beings, have certain rights, and that other human beings have duties to respect those rights. For example, human beings have a right to life, and others have a duty not to injure or kill innocent human beings. Many philosophers—as well as political theorists and theologians—have contributed to this way of thinking about ethical issues. One of its foremost philosophical advocates was Immanuel Kant, the 18th-century European philosopher.

Character and Virtue.   A third perspective, sometimes called the "ethics of virtue and character," originated, in the Western tradition, in the writings of the ancient Greek philosophers, particularly Aristotle. Its central tenet is that human beings can make the right moral judgments if they practice basic human virtues, such as courage, temperance, prudence, and fairness, if they are members of communities whose standards and practices express and reinforce these virtues, and if they pay careful attention to the particular, distinctive features of the situations they face.

Beyond Individual Morality.   As the introduction to Part II of this book will make clear, each of these ways of defining the central principles of individual morality offers powerful insights. At the same time, each has limitations. And while none of them has emerged as the single right way for individuals to resolve the ethical dilemmas they face, each crystallizes a vital element in sound ethical deliberation.

Many people think, quite naturally, these basic principles of morality exhaustively define the ethical obligations of business executives. So, one might ask: Do business executives really have any responsibilities or obligations beyond those defined by utilitarianism, by the ethics of rights and duties, and by the ethics of character and virtue? The answer to this question is "yes," and the following elements of the analytical framework focus on the other spheres of responsibility that create powerful moral claims for business executives.

Role Obligations

Men and women take on additional responsibilities when they become business executives—just as they do when they become physicians, attorneys, or members of other professions. These responsibilities, sometimes called "role obligations," are, in essence, duties that come with the job. Attorneys, for example, have an obligation to zealously defend the interests of their clients. Physicians have obligations to safeguard and contribute to the health of their patients. (As the U.S. health system evolves, physicians may take on other duties, such as responsibly managing and allocating the health care resources they control.)

What are the role obligations of business executives? Unfortunately, these duties cannot be summarized in a single succinct phrase like "the zealous defense of a client's interests." And there are different ways of describing the role responsibilities of business executives, as well as controversy about precisely what these obligations are. As a consequence, this book does not define the role obligations of business executives in a single proposition or principle. Rather, it describes and analyzes these obligations through a broad, encompassing framework designed to reflect the wide range of work situations in which business managers find themselves. These situations vary—in terms of the ownership of a company, the legal framework in which its managers are operating, and the traditions, cultures, and histories of different countries. As a result, the basic framework of this book describes *three* differing spheres of responsibility that are often—though not always—important elements of a business manager's role obligations.

This distinction between personal ethics and role obligations is not hard and fast. Indeed, business executives' personal values shape their ways of defining their role obligations. And the converse is also true: The role obligations and the daily work of business management also shape the personal values of individual managers. It is important to remember, then, that the discussions of different spheres of responsibility in this book are ways of indicating different but interrelated sets of ethical principles and obligations. The four spheres of managers' responsibilities are not ways of defining airtight categories, and it would be seriously misleading to oversimplify and strictly compartmentalize the ethical responsibilities of business executives.

RESPONSIBILITIES AS ECONOMIC AGENTS

Part III of this book focuses on the role obligations that business managers have as economic agents. In the Anglo-American legal tradition, a basic tenet of corporate law is that managers have a fiduciary duty to serve the interests of their company's shareholders. Professor Robert Clark, the dean of Harvard Law School, has written that "Case law on managers' fiduciary duty of care can fairly be read to say that a manager has an affirmative, open-ended duty to maximize the beneficiaries' [i.e., the shareholders'] wealth, regardless of whether this is specified in any actual contract."[6]

This duty is typically both a legal and an ethical obligation. The ethical duty involves a promise, which may be implicit or explicit, to use the owners' resources in the ways that the owners want them used. For most publicly held companies in the United States, majority ownership is held by pensions, insurance companies, and other so-called institutional investors. These shareholders seek—and are generally obligated by law to seek—high or maximum rates of return on the funds they have invested.

For some economists, corporate attorneys, business executives, and philosophers this is too narrow a definition of managers' economic obligations. Instead, they define the duties of economic agents in broader terms than simply serving shareholder interests. Part III provides an opportunity to analyze and evaluate several of these other ideas, such as the idea that, as economic agents, managers are also obligated to compete fairly and vigorously. Evidence indicating that at least some shareholders want managers to pursue other objectives, in addition to high and secure financial returns, is also presented. Finally, Part III places the economic responsibilities of business managers in a broad historical context, showing the roots of these ideas in long-standing concerns about individual liberty, freedom, and property rights.

RESPONSIBILITIES AS ORGANIZATION LEADERS

Many business executives, as well as many thoughtful observers and analysts of managers' work, believe that modern business executives have

---

[6]Robert C. Clark, "Agency Costs versus Fiduciary Duties," in *Principals and Agents: The Structure of Business,* ed. John W. Pratt and Richard J. Zeckhauser (Boston: Harvard Business School Press, 1985), pps. 71–79.

a second important set of professional responsibilities: their obligations as leaders of the semipermanent communities that are conventionally called "companies." Within these organizations, business managers exercise enormous power. In particular, their decisions and actions have significant consequences for the lives, livelihoods, and well-being of their employees. With this power comes responsibility.

Part IV of this book presents cases and readings that explore the business executives' responsibilities as organization leaders. In part, these responsibilities entail managing a company in ways that achieve a basic threshold of decency and that demonstrate respect for the rights and dignity of employees and other managers.

But this merely sets a base level of responsibility: It says only "do no harm." There are, however, other organizational responsibilities that merit careful attention. Most managers and employees devote a great deal of their lives, time, and energy to their work. For many people, employment does not simply provide a paycheck, as important as this is. Their jobs are also a source of meaning, purpose, and value. The culture and ethical climate that managers create in a company can significantly enhance or diminish the personal well-being of other managers and employees in their firms.

The cases in Part IV focus in particular on the tools available to managers for influencing the ethical climate, norms, and standards of their organizations. The roles of recruiting, promotion, measurement and incentives, and the example of senior executives are all examined in detail.

RESPONSIBILITIES IN COOPERATIVE CAPITALISM

Part V of this book departs from a familiar, long-standing but misleading view of companies—the idea that companies have fairly well-defined boundaries and that the ethical responsibilities of business executives stop at the boundaries of their firms. Part V examines the important managerial responsibilities that come into view once this assumption is loosened or abandoned altogether.

The traditional theory of the firm treats companies as discrete and almost isolated economic entities. Each firm has its own senior executives, management hierarchy, shareholders, fully owned assets, and employees. The classic view is that managers' judgments and powers govern decisions—including ethical decisions—within a company's boundaries. Outside the firm, beyond its boundaries, decisions are governed by the impersonal forces of competitive markets and the law.

During the past quarter-century, two powerful forces have seriously undermined the view that a firm is, in the phrase of one economist, "an island of managerial authority surrounded by a sea of market relationships."[7] These forces have led many executives and observers of modern business to seek different ways of describing firms. John Welch, the chairman of General Electric Corporation, has coined the term *boundarylessness* to describe his vision of the dominant organizational form of the future. From this perspective, traditional functional areas "inside" a firm, such as marketing, production, and R&D, are no longer separate from each other but work closely together; at the same time, outside groups, such as customers, suppliers, local communities, government agencies, and other stakeholders are no longer kept at arm's length from a firm but collaborate closely with it.

Company–Community Interdependence. The first driving force altering company boundaries has been the gradual acknowledgment — by managers, firms, government officials, and others — of the power that companies have over the economic and social health of the communities in which they operate. Unfortunately, some of the most compelling evidence of the interdependence between companies and their communities has been newspaper headlines about cities or towns devastated by plant closings, bankruptcies, or the improper disposal of hazardous wastes. On the positive side, many companies have been lauded for aggressive steps to improve education, training, and environmental conditions in their local communities.

During the last decade, many companies have discovered that their relationship with local communities is a two-way street. That is, the health and vitality of local communities can affect the competitiveness of firms just as much as firms can affect their communities. Successful companies depend heavily on high-caliber local infrastructure in the form of roads, ports, and telecommunications; and, to attract the right managers and workers, firms need local communities offering good schooling, affordable housing, and public safety.

Strategic Alliances. The second trend that has shattered the old-fashioned notion of clearly defined company boundaries has been the widespread creation of strategic alliances. A large body of data demonstrates how frequently companies are now joining forces with suppliers, customers, labor unions, and sometimes competitors and government agencies. These alliances take many different forms: joint ventures, research consortiums, informal buyer–supplier collaboration, minority equity investments, and so forth.

Whatever their form, alliances have the same consequences: They blur the boundaries of the firm by creating joint responsibility for important

---

[7]G. B. Richardson, "The Organization of Industry," *Economic Journal,* October 1972, p. 883.

decisions and, in many cases, for the management of a factory, a sales force, or a research lab. This shared responsibility makes it far more difficult to say just where the ethical responsibilities of one firm stop and those of its partner begin. This is a second important reason why the responsibilities of business executives extend beyond the traditional boundaries of the firm.

A FRAMEWORK FOR ACTION

A common but mistaken idea is that the ethical issues of management differ in significant ways from conventional management problems. And while this may be true in certain superficial respects, the underlying similarities are deep and important. In particular, when managers confront a difficult ethical challenge or a conventional management problem, they must do more than simply analyze the problem. What distinguishes outstanding managers, on both ethical and nonethical issues, is their ability to devise and implement plans of action that deal effectively with the issue at hand.

Ethical issues present particularly daunting implementation challenges. As most of the cases in this book indicate, ethical issues are often intertwined with complicated business problems. The business issues themselves—whether in marketing, manufacturing, or finance—are often quite difficult. And, typically, these business issues must be resolved in the process of dealing with the ethical problem. But the ethical elements in a particular situation usually raise the degree of difficulty managers face.

Differing Judgments.   Often, different managers will view the same ethical situation in a different light—reflecting differences in their own values, experiences, and responsibilities. Managing these differences in judgment and perspective can be quite difficult.

"Hot Buttons."   Many ethical problems are "hot button" issues. People have strong feelings about them and readily personalize discussion and analysis. As a result, ethical issues within companies are more likely to become minefields than accounting or engineering problems.

Crucibles for Leadership.   Ethical issues often become crucial tests of a manager's leadership ability and management style. When other people in a company observe how a manager or executive deals with an ethical issue, they do not simply assess his or her analytical ability or business judgment. Often they also assess what kind of person the manager is and the degree to which they will trust this person in the future. At the same time, many ethical issues are turning points for entire organizations. By choosing one or another of a vexing dilemma, executives take stands in favor of one set of values and one approach to a problem, rather than another. For all these reasons, action planning on ethical issues is a subtle, difficult, critical matter.

The readings and cases in Part II of this book provide basic guidelines designed to help managers think through various ways of resolving an ethical dilemma. Thus, Part II not only shows how principles of moral philosophy are useful analytical tools for understanding the sphere of individual ethics, it also provides a framework for evaluating alternative plans of action in response to ethical challenges.

The framework for action, like the framework for analysis, is not based on a single work of philosophy or a single ethical perspective. Rather, it seeks to present a synthesis of four fundamental ideas about the best way to think through difficult ethical issues. In this way, the framework enables students, teachers, and managers to emphasize certain ethical criteria more heavily in one situation than in another, depending on distinctive aspects of a problem, the culture and values of a particular company, the personalities and values of the individuals making the decision, and the social, political, and economic context in which the company operates.

At the risk of oversimplification, the framework for action can be distilled into four questions:

- Which course of action will do the most good and the least harm?
- Which alternative best serves others' rights, including shareholders' rights?
- What plan can I live with? Which plan is consistent with the basic values and commitments of my organization?
- Which course of action is feasible in the world as it is?

These questions must be asked and answered at the same time because they balance and correct each others' deficiencies. Enshrining any one of them as "the answer" to all ethical dilemmas is dangerous.

For example, the question "Which course of action is feasible in the world as it is?" can be a useful way of grounding a plan of action in concrete realities. However, using this question as a sole perspective on complex issues can lead a manager in the direction of sleazy opportunism and amoral pragmatism. Hence, this question must be balanced by the explicitly ethical concerns of the other three questions. Similarly, asking "What can I live with?" or "What can we live with in this organization?" is a way of rooting plans of action in the abiding values of particular individuals and institutions. But this approach can also be dangerous if relied on exclusively. It can, for example, open the door to prejudiced, self-interested judgments. So this question also must be balanced by concern for the consequences of a decision for other people and for the rights at stake in a particular situation.

THE HISTORICAL PERSPECTIVE

Placing the problems and issues confronting contemporary managers in a larger historical context leads to a deeper understanding of business ethics. The basic structure of this book provides this historical perspective. Each of the four major parts of the book not only describes an important sphere of managers' obligations, but also serves as an individual chapter in the story of the evolution of the complex roles and responsibilities of contemporary business managers.

"Prebusiness" Ethics.   Part II of this book lays the historical foundation. In focusing on individual ethics, the text addresses issues raised by ancient philosophers, historians, and political leaders long before clusters of economic activity were ever conceived of as businesses or the notion of a business manager came into being.

Entrepreneurial Capitalism.   Part III examines the moral responsibilities of business executives as economic agents—a subject that did not emerge as an issue until millennia later, after the Industrial Revolution had begun in Great Britain roughly 200 years ago. Classical economists, such as Adam Smith and John Stuart Mill, then began to define the moral obligations of business executives in terms of property rights, market discipline, and competition. What they saw emerging was the world of entrepreneurial capitalism, an economic system in which small owner-managed companies compete in large markets that they cannot influence.

Managerial Capitalism.   Roughly 100 years ago, the economic landscape changed again, and managers' responsibilities grew more complex. The reason was the rise of managerial capitalism. Large, sometimes gigantic, firms had now appeared on the economic horizon and dominated much of it. For railroads, oil companies, steel firms, and many other large firms, competition was oligopolistic. That is, these firms avoided direct competition on price and cooperated with each other, either tacitly or explicitly, to divide markets, avoid overinvestment, and influence government policies in ways that favored the well-being of the major firms in an industry.

These large firms also employed thousands or tens of thousands of people on a long-term basis, and the decisions of their managers powerfully affected the lives and livelihoods of these employees. Executives began, in effect, to create and shape the power structures and social and ethical norms inside their companies. The cases and readings of Part IV of this book deal explicitly with the new set of ethical obligations that arose in the era of managerial capitalism.

Cooperative Capitalism.   Finally, during this century, and particularly during the last 30 years, many firms have evolved into even more complex forms. They have started international operations—raising the question of whether managers should adopt one set of ethical practices for their entire worldwide organizations or customize these practices to the cultures and laws of different countries. Also, many firms have begun to create close, complex relationships—so-called strategic alliances—with government agencies, labor unions, customers, suppliers, and even their competitors. Many firms have become, in essence, the centers of global networks. Their boundaries are unclear, their workforces increasingly diverse, and these companies are now simultaneously subject to the laws of many nations—or, according to some critics, to the laws of none. This new corporate form—the global network organization—creates yet another set of ethical responsibilities for business managers. Their responsibilities to other stakeholders in the system of cooperative capitalism are the principal focus of Part V.

Varieties of Capitalism. This most recent phase in the evolution of managers' responsibilities places a spotlight on yet another difficult set of ethical issues. As American companies have competed more frequently with their counterparts from Japan, as well as from countries in Asia, Europe, and other parts of the world, managers have become increasingly aware that capitalism is not a single monolithic economic and social system.

For business managers, there is almost no such thing as capitalism, but only varieties of capitalism. Each version of capitalism is, in many critical ways, a distinctive economic system with its own particular mix of legal obligations, implicit cultural norms, and distinctive relationships among business, government, and other stakeholders; each also has its own set of implicit and explicit rules that shape the ethical obligations of business executives.

The old saying, "When in Rome, do as the Romans do," is a very simple way of addressing this complex issue. It acknowledges that the rules of the managerial game—in ethical, legal, and competitive terms—can differ dramatically, depending on whether a business executive is operating in Japan, Germany, Mexico, or one of the emerging economies of Eastern Europe. Several of the cases and readings in Part V of this book present important managerial issues that distinguish the major varieties of capitalism in the world today.

It is important to remember that each successive economic and organizational development in this long story creates greater complexity and additional responsibilities for business managers. The rise of cooperative capitalism does not erase or replace the other obligations that managers have—as individuals, as economic agents, or as leaders of semipermanent human communities. Instead, each set of additional obligations is added to the others, modifies them, and complicates the ethical and managerial challenges facing business executives and their companies.

OVERVIEW OF INTRODUCTORY CASES

The cases in this introductory section provide an overview of the basic issues that the other parts of the book explore in detail. The first case—"The Lake Pleasant Bodies Case"—is quite unusual because it does not deal with a business issue but presents a classic case in legal ethics. In essence, it raises the question of what obligations a man or woman takes when he or she becomes an attorney, and it shows how these role obligations can readily conflict with individuals' personal moralities. Indirectly, the case raises the question of what responsibilities men and women assume when they take the social role of business executive.

The next three cases—"The Analyst's Dilemma," "Steve Findley," and "Susan Woods"—provide opportunities to consider answers to this question. Each of the cases focuses on a difficult dilemma confronting a young manager. In each case, the young manager must analyze a range of possible ethical responsibilities and, like the attorney in "The Lake Pleasant Bodies Case," decide which of them has a higher priority.

The section ends with a brief, open-ended, and provocative passage from the play *Dirty Hands* by the French philosopher Jean-Paul Sartre. Implicit in the passage are several powerful ways of framing the situations in which business managers, as well as others in positions of power, face complicated ethical dilemmas.

THE LAKE PLEASANT BODIES CASE (A)

Frank Armani hoped that the man across the desk from him didn't notice his shaking hands as he reached for a cigarette. Daniel Petz had traveled to Armani's Syracuse law office in September 1973 after reading newspaper accounts linking the disappearance of his daughter Susan earlier that summer to Armani's client, Robert Garrow. Although Armani had tried to prepare himself for the meeting with Petz, it wasn't easy to remain calm as the man began to plead with him for help in locating his missing daughter. Armani knew all too well that Petz's 20-year-old daughter had been brutally murdered just one month earlier. In fact, Armani himself had climbed down into an abandoned mine shaft and photographed the dead girl's body.

Initial Contacts with Robert Garrow

Frank Armani's first contact with Robert Garrow was in August 1972 when Garrow sought legal advice from Armani after a minor auto accident. At that time, Armani was aware that Garrow had served eight years in prison for the rape of a teenage girl. Since his release from prison in 1968, Garrow had compiled an excellent record as a family man, neighbor, and employee. The New York State Crime Com-

---

This case was prepared by Ellen West under the direction of Professor Joseph Badaracco, Jr.

Copyright © 1990 by the President and Fellows of Harvard College.

Harvard Business School case 390–212. (Revised October 1991).

mission had even studied Garrow as an example of a convict who had broken the typical pattern of recidivism among released prisoners.

In November 1972, Garrow called Armani from the Syracuse Public Safety building after being charged with unlawful imprisonment and possession of a dangerous drug. Garrow had allegedly held two Syracuse University students hostage at gunpoint and then tied them up. The students refused to press charges after it was determined that the drugs found in Garrow's car belonged to them, and Garrow was released. Armani had worked hard to obtain the court's subsequent dismissal of the charges so Garrow would not be held in violation of his parole and sent back to prison.

Seven months later, in June 1973, Armani was notified by the police that they had Garrow in custody for allegedly molesting two young girls, aged 10 and 11. Although he began to wonder about his client, Armani felt that the two girls had been coached to produce their statements against Garrow. Armani never got the opportunity to defend his client on these charges, however. After being arraigned and released on bail, Garrow failed to show up for trial on July 23, 1973. Armani managed to obtain a three-day postponement of the trial date, but Garrow again failed to appear and a warrant was issued for his arrest.

The Lake Pleasant Murders

On the afternoon of July 29, 1973, Armani received a call from an investigator with the state Bureau of Criminal Investigation (BCI). Eighteen-year-old Philip Domblewski had been murdered that morning while camping with friends in the Adirondack Mountains near Lake Pleasant, New York. Domblewski's three companions had positively identified Garrow as the man who led them into the woods, tied them to trees, and then stabbed their friend to death. Garrow had fled into the woods after one of the campers managed to escape and return with help.

One of the largest manhunts in the state's history was now under way, and the BCI wanted Armani's help in assessing just how dangerous Garrow was. The investigators suspected that Garrow was responsible for the disappearance and murder of other young people in the Lake Pleasant area. The body of 21-year-old Daniel Porter had been recovered nine days before, but police had been unable to locate the young man's camping companion, Susan Petz. Believing that the Boston College student might still be alive, police wanted to capture Garrow alive in the hope that he would reveal her whereabouts.

The search, which was costing taxpayers over $50,000 a day, continued into the second week in August. The protracted manhunt had a devastating impact on the summer tourist season in the Adirondacks. The governor kept constant pressure on the BCI to bring Garrow in. Frank Armani even appeared on television, issuing a plea to his client: "Running away will do you no good, Robert. I'm willing to help. Come on in, and you won't get hurt."

On August 9, police staked out the area near the home of Garrow's sister and spotted Garrow's nephew carrying food into the woods. State troopers and conservation officers moved in to flush Garrow out of the woods into a line of armed officers. Despite orders to take Garrow alive, one of the officers opened fire with a high-powered rifle. Garrow was struck in the back, arm, and leg. A second round of fire nearly tore Garrow's left foot off. As word of Garrow's capture spread, hand-painted signs appeared throughout the Adirondacks expressing gratitude to the troopers for apprehending him.

That evening Armani received a call from Garrow's wife, Edith. She had been able to speak with her husband before he went into surgery, and he had asked her to call Armani.

Garrow wanted Armani to represent him. Reluctant to accept the job before he was sure he could handle it, Armani told Edith he would have to speak with Garrow about his representation.

After learning that police had already tried unsuccessfully to question Edith, Armani cut their conversation short and told her to call him the following day. During the manhunt he had noticed unmarked police cars following both him and Edith Garrow, and now he thought it was possible that the phones were tapped.

When he hung up the phone, Armani's wife, Mary, confronted him, asking why he had to be the one to defend Garrow. Armani reminded her that he hadn't officially taken the case yet; he said he owed it to Garrow as a client to go to the hospital and speak with him. Mary replied that she was worried that the case was "out of his league." After all, because his legal practice consisted mostly of liability work, Armani had never handled a murder defense before.

An irritated Armani explained to his wife that, because Garrow didn't have the resources to hire a private attorney, the court would appoint a public defender for him. Given his limited criminal defense experience, Armani said it was unlikely that the court would appoint him to represent Garrow. He didn't really want the case, he conceded; but because Garrow would not talk to anyone else at the moment, Armani really didn't see how he could refuse to visit him.

On the evening of August 10, Armani made the five-hour drive to the hospital in Plattsburg. Garrow, his left arm and left foot in casts, told Armani he was in a lot of pain. He claimed that in the ambulance on the way to the hospital, the police had begun to question him about Susan Petz's disappearance. When he didn't answer them, Garrow said they twisted his arm and foot until he passed out. Garrow also maintained that the doctors at the hospital refused to treat him until he spoke with the police. Garrow claimed that the harassment was continuing, and he said he had been subjected to constant questioning and deprived of food and water.

With tears in his eyes, Garrow pleaded with Armani to help him. Armani responded that the court would appoint a public defender for him, but Garrow persisted: "I don't want any other lawyer. I want you to represent me, Frank. Take everything I've got. But please, Frank, you gotta stay with me on this one."

Armani promised to see what he could do and cautioned Garrow against talking with anyone else, even Edith.

As he left the hospital, the police, believing that Susan Petz might still be alive, asked Armani to let them know if Garrow revealed anything about her whereabouts. Armani replied, "I'll see what I can do," but he wasn't sure how to resolve the potential conflict. On the one hand, he had a duty to preserve in confidence any information disclosed by Garrow. However, he also felt strongly that he had a duty to save Susan Petz's life if he could and thereby prevent the commission of a murder.

The following morning Armani went to see the district judge who was slated to try the case. The judge told Armani that he heard about Garrow's refusal to speak with any other lawyer. Because Garrow trusted Armani, the judge felt that Armani could do the best job defending him and he therefore appointed Armani as Garrow's public defender. Armani tried to protest, saying that he had never before defended a murder suspect. The judge assured him that he would be able to defend his client admirably and asked Armani if his time would allow him to take the case. Armani replied that he would be able to work the case in.

Back at the hospital that afternoon, Armani tried to get his client to talk about the Domblewski murder. Denying that he had killed anyone, Garrow claimed to have a difficult time remembering what had happened on July 23. He had had another one of his terrible headaches that morning. Frustrated with his client, Armani explained to Garrow that unless he told him all that had transpired, Armani would not be able to mount a successful defense. Armani pressed on for another seven hours, but Garrow continued to claim that he could not remember what happened.

A few days later Armani ran into Francis Belge, an old friend and Syracuse colleague with substantial criminal-defense experience. He confided in Belge that he was having a difficult time getting his client to speak about the charges against him. Garrow's cat-and-mouse game was beginning to wear him out, Armani said. If he pressed his client too hard, Garrow's face contorted and reddened with rage. At these times Armani wanted to run from the hospital room.

Armani told Belge that he planned to use an insanity defense—if Garrow couldn't be proved insane, no one could. The case would be complicated and Armani needed help. He asked Belge to join him as co-counsel. Belge refused, saying that Garrow didn't stand a chance of getting a fair trial in the small mountain community where the Domblewski murder had occurred. Belge brushed aside Armani's suggestion that they ask the court for a change of venue to another New York town, arguing that the local people would want to get revenge against Garrow.

Belge then took Armani to task for appearing on television during the manhunt. Belge felt strongly that Armani's action was tantamount to admitting his client's guilt. Armani saw it differently. He felt that he had been obligated to try to convince Garrow to surrender so he could be processed by a judicial system that would ideally presume him innocent until proven guilty. Belge needled Armani for thinking a jury in the Adirondacks would presume Garrow to be innocent.

Armani asked Belge one more time to join him on the case, but Belge refused. As Armani faced the prospect of defending Garrow single-handedly, he couldn't fight the feeling that he had overcommitted himself.

Preparing a Defense

Armani was convinced that Garrow had killed Philip Domblewski and that his only defense was to plead innocent by reason of insanity. The first step would be to convince the judge at a pretrial hearing that Garrow was mentally unfit to stand trial. If, however, his client was declared competent to stand trial, Armani would then be faced with the task of convincing a jury that Garrow did not comprehend the nature or consequences of his actions.

Armani set out to establish that his client had a lifelong history of aberrant behavior. He first interviewed Garrow's neighbors and an employer in Syracuse, all of whom portrayed him as a model husband, family man, and employee. However, after Frank Armani began to probe more deeply into Garrow's history, another side of his client's personality was revealed. Garrow's sisters described the physical and verbal abuse he had suffered at the hands of their alcoholic father. Garrow's mother was also abusive, beating him regularly with whatever implement was at hand. When Garrow was five, his mother knocked him unconscious with a piece of firewood, and on another occasion she split her son's head open with a crowbar.

At the age of seven, Armani learned, Garrow was boarded out to a neighboring farm where he lived a lonely, isolated existence for seven years. By the time he was 11 years old, he was regularly molesting farm animals and drinking their blood. At age 15, Garrow was sentenced to reform school for two years after a fight with his father.

When he was 17, Garrow walked in on his girlfriend making love to a long-haired man. The betrayal drove Garrow to enlist in the Air Force, although he spent most of his two years of military service in the stockade for a variety of offenses. He returned to northern New York, married Edith, and settled in Albany. Garrow was 25 years old and the father of two children when he was convicted in 1960 for raping a teenage girl and knocking her boyfriend unconscious.

Armani interviewed several psychiatrists, including the one who had examined Garrow at the time of his rape conviction. The doctor felt that Garrow's sexual aberrations and violent rages were connected; Garrow would accost a couple, get angry at the man, and then rape the woman. The doctor also felt that it was likely that Garrow's headaches were the result of his 1972 car accident.

The psychiatric evaluations and his own investigations convinced Armani that his client was insane. Under New York law, defendants judged innocent by reason of insanity are committed to a mental institution until a panel of psychiatrists judges them sane enough to return to society. The improbability that Garrow would ever become well enough to be released was important to Armani in his pursuit of the insanity defense. Armani was extremely disturbed by the thought that, by acting as effective counsel for Garrow, by doing everything he could to protect his client's rights, he could make Garrow a free man.

As he became consumed with Garrow's defense, Armani's work for his other clients suffered. He began to turn over many of his files to the three other attorneys in his office. Armani felt a certain amount of guilt at not being able to handle his clients' matters personally. He also knew that, by taking on the time-consuming Garrow case, he was reducing the profits to be shared by the firm's partners.

Although Armani felt he had been thorough in his preparation for the trial, he was still unsure of his ability to defend Garrow in the courtroom. In addition, he was facing the prospect of further involvement with Garrow as the police began to build cases against Garrow for the Porter murder and the Petz disappearance. Garrow was also implicated in the disappearance of a 16-year-old high school student, Alicia Hauck, who had been missing since July. Although Garrow called Armani constantly to request visits, he was not forthcoming with useful information about any of the crimes.

Faced with these pressures, Armani approached Belge again late in August of 1973. Belge suggested that, to gain Garrow's cooperation, Armani had to convince him that information regarding additional crimes could be used to plea bargain with the district attorney for a judgment of not guilty by reason of insanity, which would allow Garrow to be sentenced to a psychiatric hospital.

This time, Belge agreed to accompany Armani to the hospital for a visit with Garrow. Inflamed by the harassment of the troopers guarding Garrow's room, Belge decided to act as co-counsel. Garrow, however, was suspicious of the new addition to his defense team, and the two lawyers were again unable to get any useful information out of their client that evening.

The following morning Armani persuaded his client to submit to hypnosis. Armani stressed how important it was that he and Belge know as much as possible to construct an effective defense. During the hypnotic session, Armani planted the suggestion that Garrow should cooperate fully during an afternoon interview with Belge.

As Belge entered Garrow's room that afternoon, he turned on the television and a portable fan because he was sure that Garrow's room was bugged. Belge prefaced his questioning by telling Garrow that his best shot at a successful insanity plea was as part of a pretrial bargain with the district attorney.

Under Belge's questioning, Garrow first described picking up Alicia Hauck hitchhiking, raping her, and then stabbing her to death in a Syracuse cemetery as she tried to escape. When Belge pressed for information about Susan Petz, Garrow described his encounter with Daniel Porter and Petz. He said he stabbed Porter to death during a struggle and then took Susan Petz to a wooded area near his parents' home. He kept her in a tent with him for three days, raping her repeatedly. After she tried to escape, Garrow stabbed Susan Petz to death. Garrow then described the abandoned mine shaft where he had hidden Susan Petz's body. After denying involvement in any other crimes, he told Belge where he could find the body.

Checking Garrow's Story

That afternoon the two lawyers first traveled to the area where Garrow told them he had hidden Susan Petz's body in an abandoned mine shaft. Armani and Belge both hoped that their client had made up his gruesome tales to allow his attorneys to plea bargain. En route they noticed that they were being followed by an unmarked police car. After switching cars with a friend of Belge's, they lost the tail and proceeded to the mine shaft.

With Armani holding him, Belge leaned into the shaft. After Belge peered into the darkness using a flashlight, he demanded that Armani pull him up. Armani noted the tears in his partner's eyes as Belge told him he had seen Susan Petz's body. Armani then grabbed his Polaroid; with Belge holding on, he lowered himself into the shaft to photograph the body.

Armani's first reaction after locating Susan Petz's body was to tell someone what they'd found. He told Belge that the girl's parents had

to know. Belge replied that unless Garrow gave them permission to do so, they could not reveal to anyone what they had seen. Still, Armani could not help but imagine how he would feel if it were his daughter's body lying in the mine shaft.

The next morning the two lawyers searched the Syracuse cemetery where Garrow said he had left Alicia Hauck's body. Unable to locate the remains in the dense underbrush, they returned to Plattsburgh to have Garrow draw a map for them. They immediately made the five-hour return trip to Syracuse but still could not find Alicia Hauck's body where Garrow said it would be. Armani, satisfied that Garrow had killed Alicia Hauck, was concerned that they would be spotted if they continued to search for the girl's body. He didn't think it was necessary to view her remains. The next day, however, Belge returned to the cemetery, located Alicia Hauck's body, and photographed it.

Making a Decision

The night before Mr. Petz's visit, Armani sat alone in his office looking through his files on the Garrow case. He looked at the photographs of Susan Petz and Alicia Hauck from missing-persons bulletins and was struck by their similarity in appearance. Both young women also bore some resemblance to Garrow's wife Edith, a woman camping companion of Philip Domblewski and, most significantly, the girlfriend that 17-year-old Garrow had caught in bed with another man.

As Garrow's attorneys, Armani knew he and Belge had a duty of confidentiality to their client. Armani, however, did not find it as easy as Belge to accept the consequences of this duty:

> He tried to imagine what it must be like for the parents of Alicia Hauck and Susan Petz—how they must be praying for their daughters' safety,

---

EXHIBIT 1

Constitution of the United States of America
Amendment V

No person shall be held to answer for a capital, or otherwise infamous crime, unless on a presentment or indictment of a Grand Jury, except in cases arising in the land or naval forces, or in the militia, when in actual service in time of war or public danger; nor shall any person be subject for the same offense to be twice put in jeopardy of life or limb; nor shall be compelled in any criminal case to be a witness against himself, nor be deprived of life, liberty, or property, without due process of law; nor shall private property be taken for public use without just compensation.

Amendment VI

In all criminal prosecutions, the accused shall enjoy the right to a speedy and public trial, by an impartial jury of the State and district wherein the crime shall have been committed, which district shall have been previously ascertained by law, and to be informed of the nature and cause of the accusation; to be confronted with the witnesses against him; to have compulsory process for obtaining witnesses in his favor, and to have the assistance of counsel for his defense.

Amendment IX

The enumeration in the Constitution, of certain rights, shall not be construed to deny or disparage others retained by the people.

Amendment XIV

1. All persons born or naturalized in the United States, and subject to the jurisdiction thereof, are citizens of the United States and of the State wherein they reside. No State shall make or enforce any law which shall abridge the privileges or immunities of citizens of the United States; nor shall any State deprive any person of life, liberty, or property, without due process of law; nor deny to any person within its jurisdiction the equal protection of the laws.

---

how they must be hoping against hope that their daughters would turn up alive one day soon and give this nightmare a happy ending. Armani tried to imagine the pain he and his wife would feel if one of his daughters were missing. He tried to imagine how badly he and Mary would want any news, even if the news might be that their missing daughter was dead.

He thought back to 1962, the year his younger brother, his only brother, had disappeared while flying an Air Force reconnaissance mission over the North Sea. Harry Armani's body had never been recovered. Armani remembered well the pain his parents had suffered from not knowing for certain what had happened to their son. His mother had never completely recovered from that loss.[1]

Torn between his duty to his client and his empathy for the victims' families, Armani sought the right words to speak to the desperate father seated before him.

---

[1]Alibrandi and Armani, *Privileged Information,* pp. 91–92.

THE ANALYST'S DILEMMA (A)

During the spring of 1989, I faced an ethical dilemma that forced me to choose between my moral duty to respect my best friend's right to confidentiality and my obligation to my employer. I was working in investment banking at the time at Bullard & Bartell (B&B).

The loyalty and commitment that investment bankers, particularly analysts, feel toward their employers is difficult for many to understand. At B&B, a medium-sized firm with about 150 investment bankers in New York, we understood that our loyalty to our career and to our employer was, with few exceptions, our first priority. There exists almost a cult mentality in these organizations, and those who stay accept that one's loyalty to the firm, in many instances, takes precedence over one's health, family, and friends. It was this loyalty that made my dilemma so difficult.

While working at B&B, I was living with my best friend Lori, who was an analyst in the capital finance group at Universal Bank, a large commercial bank with more than $20 billion in assets. Lori was one of four Universal bankers who were working on the leveraged buyout of Suntech Corporation, which was in the frozen foods business. B&B was orchestrating the Suntech leveraged buyout. In addition to providing the short-term financing for the transaction through a bridge loan, B&B had arranged to purchase 65 percent of the Suntech stock and hold it on a long-term basis. Universal, the agent bank on the deal, structured and underwrote the loan for the senior debt. Not only did I know the entire B&B team working on the deal, but the vice president, Steven—the second in command on the team— was my adviser and friend.

I had always felt strongly that my personal life was my business and that when I walked into my apartment at night I took my B&B hat off. Although we couldn't discuss the specifics of our business transactions, Lori and I often discussed issues that we faced at work and solicited advice from one another. As analysts, we had both been advised of our duty to respect the confidentiality of the information to which we would be privy. For example, I knew that she was working on "igloo" with the B&B team; eventually, I became aware that "igloo" was the code name for Suntech. For a long time, however, I hadn't known the identity of "igloo" nor would I ask. I respected the confidential nature of the business. Neither one of us was offended by the other using the code name for a company; it wasn't that we didn't trust each other, but rather that we respected our duties to preserve confidentiality.

One Friday evening, I came home very late from work and Lori was still awake and obviously upset. She told me that she couldn't talk to me about her problem. I found this very hard to believe because we had always told each other everything. Eventually, Lori said that she really needed to talk to me about her problem but explained that it might put me in a difficult situation. She asked me to promise that I would keep what she was about to tell me in confidence; I agreed, assuming that it must be a personal problem. She told me that she had lost her job that day because Universal was dissolving its capital finance group. My first concern was for Lori and the fact that she would be unemployed within a couple of weeks. We spent a great deal of time discussing her options in a difficult economic environment;

This case was prepared by Jerry Useem under the direction of Professor Joseph Badaracco, Jr.

Harvard Business School case 394-056.

many people in the financial community were losing their jobs and having a very difficult time finding new opportunities. Later, I asked about Suntech, and we discussed the potentially disastrous ramifications that Universal's decision would have upon this deal. We both knew that a last-minute pullout by one of the major players in a leveraged buyout could put a deal in serious jeopardy. Little problems can prevent a deal from happening on Wall Street, and this was a big problem.

In dissolving its capital finance group, Universal would be selling off its entire loan portfolio to other banks. Because the Suntech deal had not been completed, however, Universal was going to back out of the Suntech loan agreement altogether, and B&B would have to find a new agent bank. Universal's sudden withdrawal left B&B in an extremely precarious position. Although the tender offer had already been made, the deal would not be complete until a sufficient number of Suntech stockholders sold their shares. In the meantime, B&B had put $112 million on the line in bridge financing until the stock purchase could be refinanced with high-yield bonds. Most problematic was the fact that Bill, the senior banker from Universal on the deal, was out of the country, and his team intended to wait until he returned to New York to inform the B&B deal team of the situation. He would be back on Monday at the earliest.

My primary concern was that the news of the event would be leaked to the press over the weekend before the B&B team had a chance to reassure the high-yield market, and that the uncertainty concerning the agent bank would scare away potential investors. If B&B could not raise money immediately on the high-yield market, several bad scenarios could ensue. In the worst case, the bonds would not be sold and the deal would fall apart. A delay in selling the bonds was a more likely scenario, but this possibility would have serious consequences as well. B&B would have to maintain its bridge

loan during this period, thereby tying up almost all of the bank's lending money and preventing it from transacting other deals. In either case, the cost to B&B's reputation would be severe: if the market found out about Universal's withdrawal from this high-profile deal before B&B did, the people on the B&B team would look foolish. Individual careers and the firm as a whole might be damaged badly.

The success of the high-yield bond issue was not my only concern. The less time B&B had to line up a new agent bank, the greater the likelihood the new agent bank would take advantage of Suntech's compromised position to tighten the terms of the loan agreement in a way that would be detrimental to Suntech. The Suntech management had haggled for months with Universal to obtain the loan terms it needed to pursue its high-growth strategy. Now, because it desperately needed an agent bank to finance the leveraged buyout, Suntech might be forced into hastily accepting terms that would impede this strategy. In addition, higher uncertainty (and therefore higher risk) surrounding the deal might require Suntech to borrow at higher interest rates. The increased interest payments could create liquidity problems within the company that, in turn, would make a high-growth strategy difficult. If Suntech could not grow as quickly as it had planned, B&B's 65 percent equity in the company would be worth less.

The main issue was that, if the B&B team could have the next few days to line up a well-respected agent bank and prepare responses to the market's concern, both the deal and B&B's reputation could be saved. I wanted to tell Steven the next day out of a sense of loyalty to the firm and to him; however, I had given my word to Lori that I would not repeat what she had told me.

As my official "mentor" at the firm, Steven had become a good friend. He and Lori had also gotten to know each other well while working together on the Suntech deal. In contrast to some of the other bankers who seemed to be obsessed with living out the image of the cold 80s investment banker, Steven was a genuinely nice, normal person who showed more of a human side than most. For example, every evening at six o'clock, B&B would bring food into the office so people could take a short break. As we congregated in the hall to eat cookies and chat, Steven sometimes would notice that I looked like I was under a lot of stress and would invite me into his office to sit down and talk. We would discuss the pressure and deadlines that I was facing, but we also would talk about other matters, such as our families, or where I wanted to go to business school.

Often, Steven would tell me to leave the investment banking business before I burned out. He was glad that his sister, who was about my age, had quit investment banking after working on Wall Street for a year. Steven himself was in his early 30s, and he explained that people who stayed in the business as long as he did reached a point where it became difficult to change professions; they became "sucked in" by the money, he said, and found that they weren't trained to do anything else. "Get out before it's too late," he would warn me. "You're young, go to business school, go do something different." The dilemma that I now faced was precisely the type of situation in which I would have asked Steven for advice. Unfortunately, going to him in this instance was obviously out of the question. How I solved the dilemma, furthermore, might have a serious impact on Steven: if the deal fell apart, Steven would probably lose part of his annual bonus and possibly have a harder time finding a job at another bank if he ever chose to leave B&B.

My obligations to Lori were the other half of my dilemma. Lori and I had been best friends since my freshman year in college. She was a year older than I, but we both had been finance majors and members of the same sorority. Lori was the kind of person who would do anything for me. There were times in college when I would be worrying about an accounting exam I had the next day, and Lori would put aside her own work to stay up until one in the morning helping me understand balance sheets and income statements. Lori also had a lot to do with my plans after college. When I was looking for a job my senior year, she got me interested in B&B by putting me in touch with a friend of hers who worked there. Even before I got the job at B&B, we had been planning to live together in New York once I graduated.

Lori was not an investment banker and could not quite understand why work had come to dominate my life so completely. Lori worked hard, but she would be home by six or seven o'clock every night and did not work weekends. The mentality at B&B, on the other hand, was that you lived, ate, and breathed your work. I would come home from the office after Lori was in bed and leave before she was awake; sometimes she wouldn't see me for days at a time. Because Lori did not work in the same kind of high-pressure culture, she viewed work responsibilities differently than I. From my own perspective inside the charged environment of B&B, matters such as the Suntech deal were all-absorbing and seemed to be of astronomical importance. But from Lori's viewpoint on the outside, my degree of devotion to B&B—not to mention the number of hours I worked—simply did not make sense. As a result, I knew it would be difficult for my roommate to grasp how important it was to me to save the Suntech deal.

I was extremely uncomfortable. I realized that compromise was essential and that there seemed to be no course of action that would leave me feeling good about myself. Clearly, from a utilitarian perspective, I should have told Steven and the B&B team. The employees of B&B, the "owners" of its parent company, the employees of Suntech, the bondholders and equity holders would all have been much better off if this deal were completed successfully. However, I felt a personal obligation to honor my word to my best friend.

I had grown up with a very strong sense of what was right and wrong, so it had never taken me long to figure out what to do in difficult situations such as this one. It came naturally to me to do the honest thing. But for the first time, I found myself in circumstances in which the definitions of right and wrong were blurry. I had been privy to information in the past that could have benefited others, but I had always made my decision based on the law. In this case, I didn't have the law to guide me; I had to base my decision on my personal code of ethics. It was also the first time that I faced a dilemma with such potentially huge ramifications: if the problem were handled improperly, the deal could fall apart. If the B&B team realized that I could have helped to prevent this disaster, I could find myself in the ranks of the unemployed.

While I understood Universal's rationale in deciding to wait for Bill to get back to the country so he could handle the matter in person, I felt this valuable time could truly make or break the deal. In fact, I felt the Universal team had made an unethical decision in deciding not to disclose this valuable information immediately to B&B. I also realized they had put their loyalty to one person (their boss) above their business obligation to B&B. Was I prepared to do the same thing?

I also wondered if I was using my obligation to Lori as a way of avoiding a very difficult situation. It certainly would have been easier to stay out of the situation entirely and pretend that I had never heard a thing; however, if the deal did not close I would have to live with the fact that I could have possibly prevented the disaster. I struggled with the situation and searched for a perspective and course of action with which I could live. I reasoned that, since I had been in my apartment when I heard about the situation and had been acting in the capacity of a "private citizen," B&B was not entitled to the information. Somehow, though, I felt that this was a copout. Perhaps, as an analyst, I felt an unusually strong sense of commitment to my employer. I spent 90 percent of my waking hours at the office and had given up most of my outside interests and pleasures in life to work at this company; I was "brought up" to believe that one's commitment to the company came first.

The fact that I was even considering breaking my word to my best friend made me wonder if my perspective had become warped over the last couple of years. I could imagine situations in which I would definitely break my word to a friend to "do the right thing," but all of these situations involved saving other people from physical harm, rather than economic harm. This situation did not seem to have a comfortable solution. I had only a few choices. Unfortunately, Lori was extremely reluctant to inform her group that she had told me about Universal's situation and pleaded with me to keep my promise. We had always been careful in the past not to share confidential information to avoid situations such as this.

STEVE FINDLEY

Two months after graduating from Harvard College and starting work as a financial analyst at Putnam & Peters in September 1985, Steve Findley found this message on his desk. It was from Michael Gordon, a managing director of the firm:

Findley, please see me ASAP. Wetstone and Brown have an oral presentation to the Delaware Resource Redemption Authority tomorrow. Webster has to go to St. Louis. We need to know if you can take his place.

This case presents, in Steve Findley's own words, his reaction to the message and the steps he took after receiving it.

* * * * *

The message was a major surprise. Putnam and Peters (P&P), a major investment banking firm headquartered in New York, had an unwritten policy against including analysts in any oral presentations or client meetings. Moreover, the Delaware Resource Redemption Authority (DRRA) was a potential client that was selecting bond underwriting managers for its multiyear bond issue program. This request from the head of the department sounded almost too good to be true. Rob Wetstone and Pete Brown were vice presidents in the utilities group and I was a first-year analyst in the general markets group. Moreover, I knew very little about resource recovery, which was a fairly specialized area of municipal finance.

While I was elated at the chance to quickly impress my superiors, I wanted to completely understand why I was selected for this opportunity over the four analysts and three associates in the utilities group. I decided to discuss the situation with Andrew Webster, a vice president in the general markets area and good friend over the past two years.

Andrew Webster

Andrew Webster was the highest-ranking black professional at Putnam & Peters. He was a second-year vice president. These two facts alone conveyed the limited opportunities that historically had been available for minorities at the major investment banks.

Black investment bankers were rare until the early 1980s. Their numbers had steadily increased during the first half of the decade due to an increase in numbers of blacks attending business school and the rise of a summer internship program for gifted minority students started by a nonprofit organization called the Sponsors for Educational Opportunity (SEO). Still, the absolute and relative numbers remained small and were overrepresented in the lower rungs of the professional ladder (analysts, who were college graduates, and associates, who were freshly minted business school graduates).

One area of investment banking was becoming very progressive with regard to black professionals: municipal finance. Unlike corporate finance, which involved the issuance of stocks and bonds for corporations, municipal finance focused on structuring and issuing bonds for governmental entities. Over the past 10 years, blacks had been elected or appointed to an increasing number of high-ranking political offices, and they could influence the selection of investment bankers, just as corporate treasurers and CEOs traditionally influenced the selection of investment banking

---

This case is based upon a paper written by a recent MBA graduate of the Harvard Business School, and it has been partially disguised. The case was prepared by Professor Joseph Badaracco, Jr.

firms in corporate finance. Recognizing an opportunity both to add talented professionals and capitalize on a political trend, the top firms started to increase their hiring of black professionals.

Mr. Webster and I had become good friends in 1983 when I participated in the SEO Wall Street intern program the summer between my sophomore and junior years of college. I was randomly assigned to P&P's municipal finance department that year and had returned to work there the following summer. In August 1985, upon graduation, I started full-time work at the firm. Andrew had been my mentor during the two summers, though I rarely worked with him on any projects during the second summer. Since my initial summer, I also had worked frequently with Mike Gordon and Steve Glick, the head of the department and second-in-charge, respectively, and had become good friends with them. To the consternation of many other analysts and associates, I was frequently selected to work with them on some of the department's most important projects. This trend had continued on my return in 1985.

"Webby, what's the deal with DRRA? Did you know that Mike asked me to go to the orals?" I asked him anxiously. I was hoping that he would tell me that Mike simply had decided to accelerate the progress of "Golden Boy" (as I had been called by another summer intern the previous year).

"Steve," he responded, "let me tell you what's happening. Look at us. What similarities are there? Let me tell you that the new state treasurer of Delaware also is black.

"Listen, I hate for you to be introduced to this side of the business so soon. The state treasurer wants to see at least one black professional or the firm has no chance of being named a manager. I'm used to these situations, but if you feel uncomfortable, you don't have to go. I'll either try to reschedule with St. Louis or neither of us will go. If you decide to go, Brown will tell you what part they want you

to give. It's your decision, but I'll support you either way."

That explanation confirmed my suspicions. While I may have been Gordon's "Golden Boy," I still was black and that carried certain burdens and responsibilities in the investment banking field. Andrew was correct; I was not used to this type of situation and had never thought about how I would respond. As I sat in his office, I realized that this was a real dilemma.

If I accepted, I had to justify this decision to myself and define the role I wanted to play in the presentation. If I rejected this request, I certainly needed to rationalize my decision to Mike and Steve, who were white and might not understand why a first-year analyst refused to be a "team player." Furthermore, it would be necessary to justify this decision to myself in light of the potential career risk. Given the imminence of the presentation, to respond within the hour.

Background

Both of my parents were high achievers. My mother attended Radcliffe College and my father earned his doctoral degree in history from Harvard University. When they obtained their education in the early 1950s, one could count the number of black students at Harvard on two hands. As a result of their achievements, they preached advancement through hard work and personal development. They refused to accept any excuses for failure or laziness.

While they did not pressure their only child to pursue any particular career path or extracurricular activities, they believed in "doing" rather than "protesting" or "complaining." During the Civil Rights movement, for example, they were active members of the NAACP and National Urban League and believed in advancement through equal educational opportunities and racial integration.

Their philosophy of "action over words" also influenced their day-to-day actions. In

1960, when my father was teaching at the University of California at Davis, they attempted to go to dinner at a local restaurant, which reputedly refused to serve blacks. Having made reservations under my father's name, they showed up at the establishment and were told that there was some mistake and their reservations must have been lost. Although the restaurant was virtually empty, the hostess would not seat them because they had no reservation. My mother realized the establishment could have knowingly canceled the reservation because my father was very well known in Davis, having grown up there and starred athletically for the local high school and college.

Instead of complaining or staying home, my mother went home and made another reservation at the restaurant under her maiden name. Since she has a Boston accent, there was no suspicion on the part of the restaurant. When they returned to the restaurant an hour later, they were seated by the same hostess without a problem.

While I never confronted the blatant racism experienced by my parents, I did encounter several situations where race was clearly an important factor in another person's actions. In each instance, I chose to adopt their philosophy of "action over words." The following are several examples of such occasions:

• In 1980, I was selected to attend the Wilkes-Johnson Memorial Cancer Institute summer science program for highly qualified high school juniors and seniors. My application was pushed strongly by a black chemistry teacher at my high school and I became the first black to be admitted to this program. As a result, there were questions in my mind, and in the minds of the admissions committee as I later discovered, about my "true" qualifications. This required a decision about whether I wanted to go as a possible "token."

• During my senior year in high school, while I was pitching for my high school team against a rural school in upstate New York, several of their players consistently heckled me with cries of "watermelon picker." There was nothing that could be done to stop these comments, but my coach gave me the choice of either continuing as pitcher, changing positions, leaving the game, or filing a protest with the league after the game.

• During the spring of my senior year in high school, the Knights of Columbus, a civic group in Buffalo that sponsors an award luncheon for all of the valedictorians of the area high schools, offered to present me with an award for being the salutatorian of my high school. This was highly unusual, since no other salutatorians were given this opportunity. The organization may have been asked by the school system to do so because I was the first black to achieve either honor in that area in recent years. Again, I had to make a decision about whether this type of award was an honor or patronizing.

Almost every racial dilemma that I have confronted concerns the recognition of achievement, rather than blatant rejection due to race. In each instance, I chose to accept the challenge or award as a method of instilling self-discipline and confidence.

My experiences and upbringing were characterized by an ethic of hard work and achievement. I was highly competitive, sometimes impatient, and always self-confident. This self-confidence had been reinforced greatly by success in several areas and disciplines. Like my parents, I wanted to reject any external reasons for failure and believed that one could accomplish almost anything through dedication and talent.

My First Job

I had two summers of experience at Putnam & Peters before returning full time in August 1985. I considered and treated Mike Gordon, Steve Glick, and Andrew Webster like older brothers or mentors. Consequently, I had a tremendous amount of loyalty to these individuals and had turned down a greater amount of money from another major investment bank to return to the firm.

I was apparently well-positioned within the department. I also believed that this job met all of my medum-term career requirements. It was fast-paced and very competitive. Furthermore, the industry rewarded performance very well. In addition to a high starting salary and huge potential bonuses, I could possibly earn a business school scholarship from P&P if I was a top performer. Most important, I believed that investment banking was becoming increasingly color-blind as the desire for profit drove every firm to recruit the most talented individuals available. Municipal finance investment banking in particular seemed to offer blacks the most immediate opportunity for long-term advancement. Given these trends, I was sure that my talents would be judged fairly and equally.

September 1985

I took a look at the glorious view from Andrew Webster's office, turned to the door, and walked back to my own little cubicle. At least two conflicting impulses surged through me. One was to walk straight to Mike Gordon's office and either make up an excuse why I could not go ("too much work") or simply tell him that this was not acceptable. ("Surely," I thought, "given our relationship, he'll understand.") Another was to stop making such a big issue of this and be a team player. (Part of me was saying, "Stop fooling yourself, just make the best of it.") I picked up the phone to dial my father's office, before remembering he and my mother were at a meeting of the American Historical Association in Honolulu. Even if they had been around, I'm not sure they could have helped me. This decision had to come from within.

SUSAN WOODS

Susan Woods, an analyst in the corporate finance department at a major investment bank, stopped by Ron Capwell's office on her way home Monday evening. Susan had been working with Ron, a managing director, on a major acquisition for Harco Industries and the deal was finally coming to a close after several months of intense effort. After Susan finished reviewing final details of the transaction with Ron, he reminded her that Harco was hosting a celebratory luncheon on Friday afternoon in recognition of the efforts of the bankers and lawyers. Ron asked Susan if she had ever been to the Gotham Club, the prominent men's club where the luncheon was scheduled to take place. When Susan replied that she hadn't,

Ron explained to her that women were not allowed to enter the club through the front door, so she would have to come in through the back entrance. Sensing her dismay, Ron told Susan that she had better get used to the way business was done in the investment banking industry. Everyone made sacrifices to keep the client happy, Ron said, and, if she found

---

This case was prepared by Ellen E. West under the direction of Professor Joseph Badaracco, Jr.

Copyright © 1990 by the President and Fellows of Harvard College.

Harvard Business School case 391-059 (Revised November 1991).

this difficult, she would be in for some real surprises further down the road.

As she rode the subway home that evening, Susan tried to think through the situation. Perhaps she had been naive to be shocked by Ron's attitude. This sort of thing probably happened to every woman in business. Yet she still felt uncomfortable. What were her alternatives? How could she maintain self-respect and also get ahead in the business world? What would her decision say about the kind of person she was?

Later, Susan found herself thinking over many aspects of the situation and her background:

It seems I'm always trying to find the middle ground between charging ahead to change society and playing it safe. I am outspoken about things I believe in, but I also have a tendency to try to keep everyone happy. I wanted to be accepted, to have people like me.

In my family, I am the stubborn child. People often say I take after my father in that respect. He and I fought often as I sought to establish my independence. I remember when, at age 13, I decided to become a vegetarian. My father demanded an explanation. I told him that meat was an inefficient source of nutrition because too many resources were used to feed a fraction of the world's population. I don't think my father bought my argument, but he didn't interfere with my decision.

I usually made a "big deal" out of not doing things I didn't want to do. At a fairly young age, for example, I felt disillusioned with institutionalized religion. I was raised in a liberal Jewish tradition, but I didn't understand why my parents forced me to go through rituals that had no meaning for me. At services, I would refuse to recite words if I didn't know what they meant. My attitude didn't disturb my parents, who seemed to be satisfied with my attendance.

Because I did well in school, my parents trusted my judgment. They would never tell me that something couldn't be achieved. The general attitude was that, if you keep working at something, eventually, you'll succeed. According

to my father, there are concerned, liberal democrats and then there was "everyone" else. He was particularly vehement in his criticisms of Nixon and people of "that type." I think he felt it was better to be vocal about causes, even if you turned out to be wrong or ineffective, than to be apathetic.

I never expected to be confronted with discrimination. I grew up in a particularly egalitarian home. Although my parents made some distinctions along traditional role lines in their treatment of my two brothers and my younger sister and I, no one in my family or circle of friends ever implied that my opportunities were limited by my gender. I never questioned the assumption that I would pursue a professional career. I had the example of my parents, both of whom earned the same salary as researchers at the National Institutes of Health and my grandmother, who had graduated from law school in 1928. I admired people like Golda Meir and Jimmy Carter, but my mother and my grandmother were my real sources of inspiration.

I grew up in Alexandria, Virginia, a progressive suburb of upper-middle-class professionals just outside of Washington, D.C. At the public high school I attended, as many women as men pursued courses in math and science. Like my older brother, I always wanted to be a doctor. I was very strong in science and never stopped to question whether I would enjoy a career in medicine.

The Ivy League college I went to was like an extension of high school. Most of my friends shared my liberal attitudes. Students were rewarded according to performance and it seemed that women did just as well as men academically. Looking back, I can see that my college experience was very insulated. I had not been aware of differences that had existed. Most of my professors were men. There were all-male clubs at the college, but no counterpart organizations for women. I often went to events at the men's clubs, but always as the guest of a man. Now I wish I had done something about it.

I was aware that there was a "women's movement," but I never saw it as having an impact on my life. At college, I knew about the women's groups on campus, but I never considered joining them. I didn't see equality for women as requiring a "big battle." I figured that I would solve any problems as I faced them, but I really didn't expect to encounter many difficulties.

By the end of my freshman year at college, I realized that I wasn't enjoying the pre-med courses I was taking and switched my major to economics. In my sophomore year, I became involved with the college's student concession agency, United Student Agencies (USA), which published student course evaluation guides, ran the laundry and dry-cleaning services in the dormitories, and managed various other student-run businesses on campus. No one in my family had ever been in business and I had no conception of what business did before working with USA. The fact that only one woman had served as president of USA in its 30 years of existence made me aware for the first time that being a woman might limit my advancement. In my senior year, however, I was elected president of USA. I felt that most of the unique concerns that might be faced by a woman president of USA had probably been resolved already.

My direct supervisor at USA was a woman general manager. She looked at USA as a business, pure and simple, and didn't think she should have to take into account the academic pressures faced by the student employees of USA. As the elected president of USA, I felt it was my responsibility to speak for the students in the organization. The relationship between the manager and me deteriorated rapidly. As the situation became increasingly unpleasant, I consulted my parents, roommates, and friends.

Finally, I decided that I could not continue to fight it out with her every day, even though I felt that her policies were damaging morale at USA. I served out the final six months of my term as president without engaging in further battles. I actually think that the students, my friends, and my parents were relieved that I had decided not to make a "scene."

I can see now that my handling of the situation at USA fit a pattern. I would fight against what I viewed as injustices until I wore myself out. Eventually, the cause still not won, I would have to take six months "off," to rest and recover my energies for the next battle.

Despite the problems with the general manager, I had enjoyed my experience at USA and I decided to look for a job in business after graduation. I knew that I wanted a fair degree of autonomy, because eventually I hoped to work in my own company. I interviewed on campus with companies in a wide range of industries. I chose investment banking because it appeared to be glamorous and challenging and I couldn't find anything else with the same appeal. Friends of mine who had entered investment banking a year earlier confirmed that there was no other job where you could learn as much.

I had not been very concerned about what it would be like as a woman to work at an investment bank. I had heard that there weren't too many women at the firm I chose to join and was conscious that the people at the firm seemed to fit a certain "type" in terms of appearance and background. When the firm offered me a job, I wondered whether I hadn't fooled them. After all, I didn't look on the outside like what I was on the inside.

During my first month at the firm, I noticed that the women analysts were getting a lot of client-oriented assignments and not as much of the quantitative work as the men we had started with. I was worried because I knew that, if an analyst didn't develop essential quantitative skills within her first six months at the firm, none of the senior people would want her staffed on their projects.

For the first time in my life, I felt I was being treated differently because I was a woman and that the situation was out of my control. There was no support network among the women in the department to which I could turn for advice. One woman had just been made managing director and there were three other women at the associate and vice president levels. Out of 30 analysts in the department, only 5 were women. I often went out socially with two of the women analysts in my department, but generally there was no camaraderie among the women analysts.

I went to the associate in charge of assignments, who happened to be a woman, and explained that I needed an opportunity to develop quantitative skills. The next project I was assigned to was the Harco Industries deal, which involved a lot of quantitative work. I felt that, to prove my dedication and capability to the other members of the team, I had to work much harder than a man at my level. I put in long hours on the project, working nights and weekends for months. I am proud of my work and the luncheon is an important opportunity to strengthen my relationship with one of the firm's most valuable clients. As a member of the firm's Harco Industries team, I'm going to be assigned to all future projects for Harco.

I really want to talk this over with my roommates. All four of us work at investment banks and we often share our work experiences. I don't think, though, that any of them have faced an issue like this before. Maybe my mother has experienced similar things in medicine, particularly when she had entered the profession 30 years ago. What compromises did she make to further her career? When my grandmother was told that she would have to learn to type and take shorthand to get a job in a law firm, she decided not to pursue a career with an established firm, preferring to work independently as an attorney for friends and family. Can I find an independent road to travel?

DIRTY HANDS

The passage below is from the play *Dirty Hands* by Jean-Paul Sartre.[1] These words are spoken by a Communist leader named Hoederer in an argument with a younger comrade.

How you cling to your purity, young man! How afraid you are to soil your hands! All right, stay pure! What good will it do? Why did you join us? Purity is an idea for a yogi or a monk.... To do nothing, to remain motionless, arms at your sides, wearing kid gloves. Well, I have dirty hands. Right up to the elbows. I've plunged them in filth and blood. But what do you hope? Do you think you can govern innocently?

---

[1]Source: Jean-Paul Sartre, "Dirty Hands," in *No Exit and Three Other Plays,* translated by Lionel Abel (New York: Vintage International, 1989), p. 218.

This case was prepared by Joseph Badaracco, Jr.
Copyright © 1990 by the President and Fellows of Harvard College.
Harvard Business College case 390-213 (Revised 1991).

PART II

The Sphere of Personal Ethics

For many people, personal morality is the essence of ethics. The duties, aspirations, commitments, and values of human beings seem, quite naturally, to be the foundation on which all morality rests. While the frameworks of this book are based on the idea that business executives, like other professionals, have responsibilities that originate in several ethical spheres, individual obligations and values are the most important tools for *analyzing* the ethical problems managers face and for evaluating different ways of *resolving* these problems. Hence, this first major part of the book focuses on the sphere of individual ethics.

Personal ethics is *not* exclusively an individual matter. Individuals' values originate in, and in most cases are strongly influenced by, the social groups in which individuals grow up and live. A person's moral values and principles are typically embedded in social norms and assumptions, in slowly evolving commitments and responsibilities, and in the enveloping ways of life, of families, friends, and various communities. One can only really understand what a person means when he or she says "These are my basic values" or "These are the ethical principles by which I try to live," by considering the rich and complex background of social influences.

This part of the book presents cases and readings that define and explain the central elements of the sphere of personal ethics. The next three parts of the book then define and examine the ethical responsibilities that originate in and are shaped by the social roles of business executives.

AN OVERARCHING FRAMEWORK FOR INDIVIDUAL ETHICS

The framework sketched in the following paragraphs is the most important conceptual element in this book. It is significant, first, because it defines the sphere of personal ethics and provides basic analytical perspectives that can help managers carefully assess the ethical dilemmas they face.

Second, this framework is a valuable device for evaluating different ways of resolving an unethical dilemma. In short, the framework cuts through both analytical and action issues raised by managers' moral dilemmas.

The third reason this framework is so important is historical: The four basic components of the framework summarize a long tradition of serious thought about power and responsibility that originated millennia ago when human beings first began to reflect on moral issues. The four components in the personal ethics framework represent, in effect, some of the most powerful and incisive voices in a long conversation, spanning many generations, many cultures, and a wide range of social, political, and economic conditions.

The basic elements in this framework can be summarized in these questions:

1. Which course of action will do the most good and the least harm?
2. Which alternative best serves others' rights, including shareholders' rights?
3. What plan can I live with? Which is consistent with the basic values and commitments of my company?
4. Which course of action is feasible in the world as it is?

The Ethics of Consequences.   The first fundamental question about individual ethics is this: What course of action in a particular situation will do the most good and the least harm for everyone affected by it? This question focuses on the morality of consequences. In essence, it defines the ethically "right" approach to a problem as the one that does the greatest good and the least harm. Philosophers use the term *utilitarianism* to describe this approach to moral philosophy. Although some have argued that utilitarian ideas were anticipated by the early Greek philosophers or by such 18th-century figures as David Hume, it was a pair of 19th-century British thinkers, Jeremy Bentham and John Stuart Mill, who are credited with crystallizing the basic tenets of utilitarianism. For this reason, one of the first readings in this part of the book is a lengthy excerpt from Mill's classic work, *Utilitarianism*, which was first published in 1861.

One of the strengths of the utilitarian way of thinking is that it is consistent with much of our ordinary, everyday thinking about ethical issues. People typically view an action as "right" or "good" if it brings about benefits to other people; by the same token, "bad actions" hurt others. Moreover, the utilitarian way of thinking does not limit its assessment of benefits and costs to those that can be counted or translated into monetary terms. Rather, the tradition of utilitarian thought emphasizes that the full range of human aspirations, pleasures, and satisfactions—art, music, and the pleasures of the ordinary amusements of life, as well as food, clothing, and the satisfaction of other basic needs—are all among the consequences that count in a utilitarian analysis.

Utilitarianism is also attractive to business people and many government officials because it accords with much of the thinking that they do in their professional roles. Cost-benefit analysis and cost-risk analysis are standard tools of both public and private decision making.

When used as a managerial guideline, utilitarianism asks business executives to examine the full range of consequences at stake in a dilemma. This can be accomplished by breaking down the basic question of consequences into several subquestions:

1. Which groups and individuals will benefit from different ways of resolving a dilemma?
2. How greatly?
3. Who will be put at risk or suffer?
4. How severe will the suffering be?
5. In what ways can the risk and harm be alleviated?

These questions, inevitably, can only serve as starting points for what is often a long process of fact gathering and analysis. The questions are not a formula or algorithm for reaching conclusions. Moreover, there are no universal definitions of harm or good, nor are there any hard and fast ways of measuring and trading off harms and benefits against each other. Much depends on particular circumstances, institutions, and specific legal and social arrangements. But the basic guiding question remains: Which course of action is likely to do the most good and the least harm?

Act and Rule Utilitarianism. Utilitarianism has been the topic of many complex and subtle philosophical analyses, and some of these have direct bearing on managers' decisions. For example, philosophers distinguish between what they call "act" utilitarianism and "rule" utilitarianism.

Act utilitarianism is based on the idea that each decision should be judged on its overall consequences. In contrast, rule utilitarianism avoids a macro-assessment of every particular action and, instead, searches for general guidelines, such as "Repay your debts" or "Keep your promises," which, if followed, would promote the greatest good for the greatest number.

For a manager faced with a difficult ethical issues, act utilitarianism would suggest thinking about the full range of consequences resulting from different ways of resolving an issue, which, if followed, would promote the greatest good for the greatest number. A rule utilitarian, on the other hand, would turn to relevant general principles, such as "Tell the truth" or "Compete vigorously and honestly," on the grounds that the greatest good would be achieved by following such guidelines.[1]

Various ways of specifying the consequences are available for a utilitarian analysis. The classic version is to define consequences in terms of the greatest happiness for the greatest number. A close alternative is to think in terms of the greatest good for the greatest number. A more precise and contemporary interpretation relies upon cost-benefit analysis. This analysis defines the morally right decision in a particular situation as the one that creates the greatest set of benefits, weighed against the net of costs involved in creating those benefits. Other versions introduce a concept of risk, since a cost or a benefit that is unlikely should not be weighted as heavily as one that is almost certain to occur.

The Ethics of Rights and Duties.   For many philosophers, theologians, and other thinkers, actions are wrong if they violate a moral duty and are right if they conform to a moral duty. Most people are familiar with such duties. They include, for example, obligations to avoid harming innocent people, to keep promises, to tell the truth, to respect others' rights, and to behave justly.

This approach to ethics differs dramatically from the morality of consequences. It rejects the idea of reducing ethical issues to some grand, means–end calculation. Instead, it views certain acts, such as killing an innocent human being, as simply wrong, in and of themselves. This remains true, even if killing the innocent person might lead to significant benefits for many other people—for example, by making it possible to transplant the dead person's organs into several dangerously ill people, thereby saving their lives.

On this view of morality, motives are critical. If someone gives money to a homeless person to impress others, she is *not* performing a moral act; but, if she gives money to meet her duty to alleviate suffering, she *is*. While the consequences for the poor person are the same in both cases, the morality of the action is not. Thus, morally good actions are motivated by a desire to perform one's duty because it is the right thing to do, and not because of the consequences that result from the action.

Traditional religious beliefs often rely heavily on the ethics of duty and appropriate motives. In other words, members of many religious groups are expected to act in certain ways because it is God's will that they do so. Human duties originate in divine commandments, and a believer should follow these commandments *because* they are God's will and because they are fundamentally right, and not because of the consequences they

---

[1]Some philosophers have argued vigorously that the distinction between act and rule utilitarianism is flimsy. See R. M. Hare, *Freedom and Reason* (Oxford: Oxford University Press, 1963). Other books and articles in the suggested readings for this section provide analysis and criticism of the contemporary philosophical arguments about utilitarianism.

produce. Abraham's willingness to sacrifice his son Isaac, in obedience to God's wishes, is a powerful example of this approach to ethics.

Other thinkers ground the ethics of duties and rights in respect for other persons — for their lives and values, their autonomy, their dignity as human beings — as the basic justification of this approach to morality. On this view, the reason it is morally wrong to lie to innocent people or to harm them or to violate their rights is that these actions deny others the respect we owe them as human beings. Moreover, violations of duties are wrong regardless of their consequences. Even if actions produce positive results, they are still wrong, simply because it is morally wrong to treat other human beings in certain ways.

The ethics of rights and duties was crystallized by various thinkers in the 17th and 18th centuries. The philosopher Immanuel Kant, for example, argued strongly that adherence to duty and principle was the core of ethics (an excerpt from one of his most important works appears later in this chapter). Another example is Thomas Jefferson's draft of the Declaration of Independence, which stated bluntly that human beings had inalienable rights to life, liberty, and the pursuit of happiness. People generally accept similar ideas in their everyday life, believing that people have the rights to be treated with respect, to have promises kept, to be told the truth, and to be spared unnecessary injury.

Acceptance of such rights leads, in turn, to accepting certain duties as part of individual morality. In effect, rights and duties are the flip sides of the same coin. It would mean little to say that a person had a particular right — for example, the right to be treated with respect — without saying that other people had a duty to respect this right. Therefore, when business executives and managers face a difficult moral issue, a second fundamental question is: What important rights are at stake in this situation? Or, phrased in terms of duties, the question becomes: What important duties are you obligated to meet in this situation?

The Ethics of Virtue and Character.   The third important element in thinking about individual ethics is captured in the following set of questions: What decision and course of action can I live with, given my personal values? Which decisions and actions best serve my commitments and aspirations in life? And for business managers in a particular company: What decisions and actions are most consistent with the kind of human organization we are trying to create?

The roots of these questions can be traced to the ancient Greek philosophers, in particular Aristotle, to Confucius in the Eastern tradition, as well as to the other founders of the world's great religious traditions.

This view of morality differs from the moralities of consequences and duties in two principal ways. First, it focuses on the character of the person who acts, as well as the rightness or wrongness of particular actions. It is only partially misleading to say that, according to this view of morality, the right action in a situation is the one that a person with moral integrity decides is best after serious reflection. Second, this approach does not view moral decision making as an exercise in the logical application of abstract universal principles to specific situations. Instead, it affirms the judgment-based and sometimes intuitive ways in which people commonly make moral decisions. Sound ethical judgments, according to this view, are the result of practical wisdom guided by personal integrity, not rationalistic calculations about consequences or duties. These judgments reflect not only the duties that obligate a person but the commitments and aspirations that guide a person's life.

Unlike the morality of consequences and the morality of duties, this approach to ethical issues does not lend itself to a clear and precise statement in terms of a single basic principle. There is, of course, a short list of commonsense ethical considerations—tell the truth, keep promises, and so forth—which are widely accepted as guidelines for virtuous living and for the development of good character. However, these simple principles are only highly abstract versions of the actual morality of individuals' commitments, ideals, and aspirations. When these are examined closely, the ethics of character and virtue reveals itself as a very complex matter.

"Who Am I?"   Some of this complexity arises because the ethics of character and virtue takes the question "Is this decision or action right or wrong?" and places it in the context of the particular values, norms, and commitments through which particular individuals find meaning and purpose in their life. It also focuses on the norms and values of specific communities at particular points in their histories. This third approach to individual ethics introduces issues of "Who am I?," "What kind of person should I aspire to become?," and "What are the important values and standards of my community?" As a result, this approach to morality tends to single out *differences* among individuals and communities, rather than seeking ethical principles that apply universally.

Another factor that makes the morality of ethics and character quite complex is its emphasis on the implicit and intuitive aspects of ethical decision making. Often, an individual's basic values are clearest in retrospect, when people reflect on the patterns underlying their past actions. Indeed, few people have the skills and the inclinations—so highly prized in academia—to translate the implicit morality of their lives into clear and precise systematic terms.

For some people, such rational articulation can even be a betrayal of the essence of ethics, a denial of Blaise Pascal's observation that the heart has its reasons that reason does not know. People can usually give reasons for what they do and what they think. Often, they can give reasons for these reasons. But at some point, the chain of reasoning becomes difficult or vanishes altogether, and people can say little more about why they made a particular decision. Or they will say something quite unsatisfying to philosophers and other systematic thinkers, roughly along the lines of "Well, those are my reasons and I've tried to explain my reasoning as best I can. This just seems right to me. Given who I am, this is what I must do."

What the abstract views of ethics leave out—in their focus on universal principles involving either consequences or duties—is that people devote their lives to many different aims and ends, not simply to one overriding central concern. Therefore, to try to reduce personal morality to a simple and grand moral precept—such as "do the greatest good for the greatest number"—is to ignore the variety and particularity of the specific commitments and values that guide people's lives and decisions.

Another difficulty in precisely defining the ethics of virtue and character is that the moral norms and instincts of any particular individual rarely take the form of a harmonized and integrated whole. More typically, personal morality involves contradictory impulses, ambiguous or shifting goals, as well as admirable values—such as honesty and compassion—which can easily conflict with each other in particular situations. Hence, in trying to understand the moral values of particular individuals it is helpful to ask not only about abiding values and commitments but also for points of tension and contradiction or ambiguity.

Further complexity finds its way into the ethics of character and virtue because the sources of individual identity and values are not purely personal but are also social. Philosopher Alasdair MacIntyre explains:

> I am someone's son or daughter, someone else's cousin or uncle; I am a citizen of this or that city, a member of this or that guild or profession; I belong to this clan, that tribe, this nation. Hence what is good for me has to be good for one who inhabits these roles. As such, I inherit from the past of my family, my city, my tribe, my nation, a variety of debts, inheritances, rightful expectations, and obligations. These constitute the given of my life, my moral starting point. This is in part what gives my life its own moral particularity.[2]

The Role of Objectivity. This emphasis on the particular and personal, and sometimes intuitive aspects of morality, should not be construed as an escape from objective ethical criteria, such as the concepts of basic human rights and duties or the assessment of consequences discussed above. These objective standards are ways of assessing and testing the ways of life to which individuals are committed and the values and practices by which they make their decisions. They are, in effect, in a kind of objective "view from nowhere" that encourages individuals to take an impartial and objective perspective on the difficult ethical situations. These

---

[2]Alasdair MacIntyre, *After Virtue* (Notre Dame, Ind.: University of Notre Dame Press, 1984), p. 33.

view-from-nowhere criteria are ways of helping individuals overcome the natural human tendency to bias decisions in one's own self-interest and to analyze situations through the screen of their own perceptions. Objective ethical criteria serve a crucial role in balancing the viewpoints and biases of particular people in specific situations, who may easily become captives of "the view from somewhere."[3]

Objectivity is, of course, difficult to define. In part, this is because it is so difficult for people to look through the screens and filters of their own biases and self-interests. The contemporary philosopher John Rawls has devised a test, which is a crucial element in his theory of justice, that can also be used to develop an objective perspective on ethical issues. In essence, Rawls asks people to think about difficult issues from behind what he calls a "veil of ignorance." Rawls describes this approach in the following words:

> Among the essential features of this situation is that no one knows his place in society, his class position or social status, nor does anyone know his fortune in the distribution of natural assets and abilities, his intelligence, strength, and the like. . . . The principles of justice are chosen behind a veil of ignorance. This ensures that no one is advantaged or disadvantaged in the choice of principles by the outcome of natural chance or the contingency of social circumstances. Since all are similarly situated and no one is able to design principles to favor his particular condition, the principles of justice are the result of a fair agreement or bargain.[4]

Ethics and Practicality.   The 15th-century Florentine statesman and political philosopher Niccolo Machiavelli crystallized the fourth element of individual ethics. This can be summarized in a single pragmatic question: What will work in the world as it is?

In any situation, there may be several options that could, in theory, meet some or all of the competing demands of consequences, rights and duties, and personal integrity. Machiavelli's question calls attention to another dimension of these options by asking which of them are actually feasible. In the case of a business manager facing an ethical dilemma, it asks which option is practical, given his or her power in an organization, the company's competitive, financial, and political positions, the likely costs and risks of various plans of action, and the time available for action.

For some people, this approach to ethical issues is amoral or even worse. It focuses on means, not ends, and it fails to examine the morality of either the means or the ends. But this criticism fails to hit the mark.

---

[3]See Thomas Nagel, *The View from Nowhere* (Oxford: Oxford University Press, 1986).
[4]John Rawls, *A Theory of Justice* (Cambridge, Mass.: Harvard University Press, 1971), p. 12.

Machiavelli would not be remembered today for simply having made the obvious point that unscrupulous people often get ahead in life. Machiavelli prided himself for thinking as a realist, as a statesman, and as a philosopher who was preoccupied with practical events and the necessities of power, with what leaders must do so their organizations can at least survive and perhaps prosper in the world *that one actually found,* not the world one hoped for. Isaiah Berlin, one of this century's foremost interpreters of Machiavelli, wrote that Machiavelli believed that:

> what ought to be done must be defined in terms of what is practicable, not imaginary; statecraft is concerned with action within the limits of human possibility, however wide; men can be changed, but not to a fantastic degree. To advocate ideal measures, suitable only for angels, as previous political philosophers seemed to him to often to have done, is visionary and irresponsible and leads to ruin.[5]

In short, this fourth element in individual ethics states that, for men and women with real responsibility, good intentions are not good enough. The pragmatic perspective on business ethics need not be an invitation to the cautious measures of the "organization man." The question of what is practical is used most effectively by a resourceful, persistent, imaginative, bold manager or leader who does not shun risk. But a plan of action for resolving an ethical dilemma, however high-minded its creator may be, will accomplish little or nothing if it is not practical.

JUDGMENT AND BALANCING ACTS

It is natural to ask which of the four perspectives is the right way to think about an ethical issue. Should one consider principally the consequences of a situation, or the rights and duties at stake, or the ethics of virtue and character, or the realistic practical concerns facing a business manager or anyone confronting an ethical dilemma? The basic answer, which is unsettling to many but often quite accurate, is that it all depends. There are some situations in which consequences are decisive. In other cases, rights and duties are of paramount concern. In still other situations in which neither consequences nor duties define the final answer, an individual can and must make a decision on the basis of his or her own values, or those of a company, or in view of powerful practical considerations.

In effect, the four long traditions of thinking about ethical issues cannot be harmonized in some simple superprinciple that specifies when and how

---

[5]Isaiah Berlin, "The Originality of Machiavelli," in Isaiah Berlin, *Against the Current* (New York: Viking Press, 1980), p. 46.

to weigh consequences, duties, character, and practicalities. The desire to find a single overarching principle is quite natural, and it is one of the compeling forces that have led philosophers, theologians, and others to develop many of the ideas sketched in this section of the book. And while many of these people think they have found precisely such a principle, they run directly into difficulties when confronted with someone else who is equally convinced that he or she has found another decisive principle. Former U.S. Supreme Court Justice Oliver Wendell Holmes suggests both the power of this quest for certainty as well as its frustrations:

> I would not give a fig for the simplicity on this side of complexity, but I would give my life for the simplicity on the other side of complexity.[6]

While there is no formula for definitively resolving dilemmas that involve conflicting ethical principles, several important guidelines can help managers and others make better decisions in these situations. These guidelines reflect an important tradition in moral philosophy, one whose origins are usually traced to Aristotle, that focuses on "practical reason" or "practical wisdom." The guidelines can be stated as a series of questions:

1. Have all the relevant, significant facts been brought forward and examined carefully? Have facts been distinguished from opinions and preferences?

2. Have all viewpoints on the issue been clearly expressed? Has there been a good faith effort to understand the views of groups and individuals whose ideas may be unorthodox, critical, or disruptive to accepted ways of doing things?

3. Have the relevant ethical principles been stated clearly and applied rigorously to the facts of the situation and to the alternative ways of viewing the situation?

4. Have the individuals involved in making the decision examined the underpinnings of their instincts and inclinations? Can they articulate the reasons behind their intuitive judgments? Have they tried to look beyond their biases and ways of filtering reality?

5. Have similar or analogous situations been examined carefully to see how conflicts of principle were resolved and to see how well or poorly these other dilemmas were handled? What, in other words, are the useful or illuminating precedent cases?

None of these guidelines will provide the simplicity or certainty that Oliver Wendell Holmes and others have desired. They will, however, load the dice in favor of more responsible decisions.

---

[6]James O'Toole, *The Executive's Compass* (New York: Oxford University Press, 1993), p. 12.

OVERVIEW OF CASES AND READINGS

The cases and readings in this part of the book focus on each of the four basic perspectives on individual ethics. The first case, "Truman and the Bomb," places President Truman's decision about using nuclear weapons to end WWII in context of the ethics of consequences and the ethics of rights and duties. Truman's final decision, as well as the range of alternatives that he and his advisers might have considered, provide opportunities to analyze, test, and understand the implications of these two ways of analyzing ethical issues and plans of action.

This historic case is followed by two readings, one from the writings of John Stuart Mill and the other by Immanuel Kant, which introduce some of the fundamental reasoning behind the ethics of consequences and the ethics of rights and duties. Next, two cases — "International Drilling Corporation" and "The Serpent Was There" — provide opportunities to apply these fundamental principles. One case involves a young manager and the other a medical team working in a developing country.

The following series of cases and readings concentrate on the issues of individual ethics, character, and personal integrity. The introductory reading, entitled "Morality and Character," presents extended excerpts from the writings of Aristotle, Confucius, and Nietzsche, as well as from important interpreters of their writings.

The first three cases that follow focus on issues of personal integrity facing young managers. "Taro Yoshida" deals with the choice that a young Japanese manager must make between continuing his education in the United States and returning to Japan to fulfill a variety of weighty duties. "The Procters' Problem" examines the issues that a young couple face as they decide how to balance their responsibilities at work with their responsibilities to their children. In doing this, they must come to terms with questions about their own priority of values and commitments. "Chris Miller" deals with a business plan, venture capital, and, of all things, a pregnancy.

These cases are followed by two that are essentially moral biographies — of H. Ross Perot and of Thomas Monaghan, the founder of Domino's Pizza. Each of these cases provides an opportunity to understand how an individual's values and commitments evolved over the course of their lifetime and, in particular, through certain crucial moments or turning points in their lives. These cases also provide an opportunity for illuminating comparisons and contrasts, because they represent a diverse range of religion, culture, race, and socioeconomic background.

The final cases and reading in this section deal with the issue of ethics and practicality. The reading is one of the most important chapters in *The Prince* by Machiavelli. The case that follows consists of an extended excerpt from a famous essay by the Pulitzer Prize-winning historian Richard Hofstadter. He raises, in explicit terms, the question of whether Lincoln was essentially a Machiavellian, especially in his public statements as a political candidate and his presidential decisions on the issues of slavery and race.

Having analyzed Abraham Lincoln's philosophy of action and his approach to pragmatic political change, it is important to examine a dramatically different approach to Machiavelli's question of what is practical in the world as it is. The final case in this section of the book consists principally of excerpts from *The Autobiography of Malcolm X,* which tells the story of a man whose uncompromising, direct, confrontational style of leadership propelled him from prison-bound obscurity to national prominence. This case sharply defines an alternative approach to practical action on ethical issues—one that is paralleled in many companies' situations by the direct, confrontational approach taken by whistle-blowers. At the same time, the "Malcolm X" case is a fitting conclusion to this section because his ideas and actions can be assessed in terms of consequences, rights and duties, and the remarkable evolution of his own thinking and ethical values.

SUGGESTIONS FOR ADDITIONAL READING

Aristotle, *Nicomachean and Ethics,* trans. by Terence Irwin (Indianapolis: Hackett Publishing, 1985).

Chester I. Barnard, *The Functions of the Executive* (Cambridge, Mass.: Harvard University Press, 1982), pp. 258–84.

Isaiah Berlin, "The Originality of Machiavelli," in Isaiah Berlin, *Against the Current* (New York: Viking Press, 1980), pp. 25–79.

William K. Frankena, *Ethics* (Englewood Cliffs, N.J.: Prentice Hall, 1973).

Stuart Hampshire, *Morality and Conflict* (Cambridge, Mass.: Harvard University Press, 1983).

William James, *Pragmatism* (Buffalo, N.Y.: Prometheus Books, 1991).

Albert R. Johnsen and Stephen Toulmin, *The Abuse of Casuistry* (Berkeley: University of California Press, 1988).

Walter Kaufmann, *Nietzsche: Philosopher, Psychologist, Antichrist* (Princeton, N.J.: Princeton University Press, 1974), chaps. 1 and 10.

David Luban, *Lawyers and Justice* (Princeton, N.J.: Princeton University Press, 1988), pp. 104–47.

Niccolo Machiavelli, *The Prince* (London: Penguin Classics, 1988).

Alexander Mehamas, *Nietzsche: Life as Literature* (Cambridge, Mass.: Harvard University Press, 1985) pp. 141–234.

Martha C. Nussbaum, "The Discernment of Perception: And Aristotelian Conception of Private and Public Rationality," in *Love's Knowledge: Essays on Philosophy and Literature* (New York: Oxford University Press, 1990).

John Rawls, *A Theory of Justice* (Cambridge, Mass.: Harvard University Press, 1971), pp. 1–53.

J. J. C. Smart and Bernard Williams, *Utilitarianism For and Against* (Cambridge, Mass.: Cambridge University Press, 1986).

Michael Walzer, "Political Action: The Problem of Dirty Hands," *Philosophy and Public Affairs,* Winter 1972, pp. 160–80.

TRUMAN AND THE BOMB

The presidency of the United States carries with it a responsibility so personal as to be without parallel.

Very few are ever authorized to speak for the President. No one can make decisions for him. No one can know all the processes and stages of his thinking in making important decisions. Even those closest to him, even members of his immediate family, never know all the reasons why he does certain things and why he comes to certain conclusions. To be President of the United States is to be lonely, very lonely at times of great decisions.

Harry S Truman[1]

Hiroshima[2]

The Reverend Mr. Tanimoto got up at five o'clock that morning. He was alone in the parsonage, because for some time his wife had been commuting with their year-old baby to spend nights with a friend in . . . a suburb to the north. Of all the important cities of Japan, only two, Kyoto and Hiroshima, had not been visited in strength by B-san, or Mr. B, as the Japanese-. . . called the B-29; and Mr. Tanimoto, like all his neighbors and friends, was almost sick with anxiety. . . . Mr. Tanimoto had been carrying all the portable things from his church, in the close-packed residential district . . . to a house . . . two miles from the center of town. . . . That is why he had risen so early.

Mr. Tanimoto had studied theology at Emory College, in Atlanta, Georgia; he had graduated in 1940; he spoke excellent English; he dressed in American clothes; he had corresponded with many American friends right up to the time the war began. . . . In compensation, to show himself publicly a good Japanese, Mr. Tanimoto had taken on the chairmanship of his

---

[1] Harry S Truman, *Memoirs by Harry S Truman, vol. I: Year of Decisions* (Garden City, N.Y.: Doubleday, 1955), p. ix. Reprinted by permission of Doubleday & Company. Used by permission of Margaret Truman Daniel.

[2] From *Hiroshima* by John Hersey. Copyright 1946, © 1985 by John Hersey. Copyright renewed 1973 by John Hersey. Reprinted by permission of Alfred A. Knopf, Inc.

This series of excerpts has been reprinted with permission. It was prepared by Ellen West under the direction of Joseph Badaracco, Jr.

local tonarigumi, or Neighborhood Association, and to his other duties and concerns this position had added the business of organizing air-raid defense for about 20 families. . . .

Before six o'clock that morning, Mr. Tanimoto started for [the] house. . . . A few minutes after [he] started, the air-raid siren went off—a minute-long blast that warned of approaching planes but indicated to the people of Hiroshima only a slight degree of danger, since it sounded every morning at this time, when an American weather plane came over . . . . Hiroshima was a fan-shaped city . . . its main commercial and residential districts, covering about four square miles in the center of the city, contained three-quarters of its population, which had been reduced by several evacuation programs from a wartime peak of 380,000 to about 245,000. Factories and other residential districts, or suburbs, lay compactly around the edges of the city. . . . A rim of mountains runs around the other three sides of the delta.

As [he] started up a valley away from the tight-ranked houses, the all-clear sounded. (The Japanese radar operators, detecting only three planes, supposed that they comprised a reconnaissance.) . . . Then a tremendous flash of light cut across the sky . . . it travelled from east to west, from the city toward the hills. It seemed a sheet of sun. [He] reacted in terror—and [he] had time to react (for [he was] 3,500 yards, or two miles, from the center of the explosion). . . . Mr. Tanimoto took four or five steps and threw himself between two big rocks in the garden. . . . He felt a sudden pressure, and then splinters and pieces of board and fragments of tile fell on him. He heard no roar.

When he dared, Mr. Tanimoto raised his head and saw that the . . . house had collapsed. He thought a bomb had fallen directly on it. Such clouds of dust had risen that there was a sort of twilight around. In panic . . . he dashed out into the street. . . . In the street, the first thing he saw was a squad of soldiers who had been burrowing into the hillside opposite, making one of the thousands of dugouts in which the Japanese apparently intended to resist invasion, hill by hill, life for life; the soldiers were coming out of the hole, where they should have been safe, and blood was running from their heads, chests, and backs. They were silent and dazed.

Under what seemed to be a local dust cloud, the day grew darker and darker. . . . He reflected that, although the all-clear had sounded and he had heard no planes, several bombs must have been dropped. He thought of a hillock in the . . . garden from which he could get a view of . . . the whole of Hiroshima . . . and he ran back up to the estate.

From the mound, Mr. Tanimoto saw an astonishing panorama. Not just a patch of [the neighborhood], as he had expected, but as much of Hiroshima as he could see through the clouded air was giving off a thick, dreadful miasma. Clumps of smoke, near and far, had begun to push up through the general dust. He wondered how such extensive damage could have been dealt out of a silent sky; even a few planes, far up, would have been audible. Houses nearby were burning, and, when huge drops of water the size of marbles began to fall, he half thought they must be coming from the hoses of firemen fighting the blazes. (They were actually drops of condensed moisture falling from the turbulent tower of dust, heat, and fission fragments that had already risen miles into the sky above Hiroshima.) . . .

He had thought of his wife and baby, his church, his home, his parishioners, all of them down in that awful murk. Once more he began to run in fear—toward the city. . . . He was the only person making his way into the city; he met hundreds and hundreds who were fleeing, and every one of them seemed to be hurt in some way. The eyebrows of some were burned off and skin hung from their faces and hands.

Others, because of pain, held their arms up as if carrying something in both hands. Some were vomiting as they walked. Many were naked or in shreds of clothing. On some undressed bodies, the burns had made patterns—of undershirt straps and suspenders and, on the skin of some women (since white repelled the heat from the bomb and dark clothes absorbed it and conducted it to the skin), the shapes of flowers they had had on their kimonos. Many, although injured themselves, supported relatives who were worse off. Almost all had their heads bowed, looked straight ahead, were silent, and showed no expression whatever.

. . . Mr. Tanimoto saw, as he approached the center, that all the houses had been crushed and many were afire. Here the trees were bare and their trunks were charred. He tried at several points to penetrate the ruins, but the flames always stopped him. Under many houses, people screamed for help, but no one helped; in general, survivors that day assisted only their relatives or immediate neighbors, for they could not comprehend or tolerate a wider circle of misery. The wounded limped past the screams, and Mr. Tanimoto ran past them. As a Christian he was filled with compassion for those who were trapped, and as a Japanese he was overwhelmed by the shame of being unhurt. . . .

Mr. Tanimoto's way around the fire took him across the East Parade Ground, which, being an evacuation area, was now the scene of a gruesome review: rank on rank of the burned and bleeding. Those who were burned moaned, "Mizu, mizu! Water, water!" Mr. Tanimoto found a basin in a nearby street and . . . he began carrying water to the suffering strangers. When he had given drink to about 30 of them, he realized he was taking too much time. . . . He went to the river again, the basin in his hand, and jumped down onto a sandspit. There he saw hundreds of people so badly wounded that they could not get up to go

further from the burning city. . . . Two or three small boats were ferrying hurt people across the river from Asano Park, and, when one touched the spit, Mr. Tanimoto . . . jumped into the boat. It took him across to the park. There, in the underbrush, he found some of his charges of the Neighborhood Association.

When Mr. Tanimoto . . . reached the park, it was very crowded, and to distinguish the living from the dead was not easy, for most of the people lay still, with their eyes open. . . . He decided to try to get back to his church . . . but he did not get far; the fire along the streets was so fierce that he had to turn back. He walked to the riverbank and began to look for a boat in which he might carry some of the most severely injured across the river from Asano Park and away from the spreading fire. Soon he found a good-sized pleasure punt drawn up on the bank. . . . He worked the boat upstream to the most crowded part of the park and began to ferry the wounded. . . . He worked several hours that way. . . .

Mr. Tanimoto found about 20 men and women on the sandspit. He drove the boat onto the bank and urged them to get aboard. They did not move and he realized that they were too weak to lift themselves. He reached down and took a woman by the hands, but her skin slipped off in huge, glovelike pieces. He was so sickened by this that he had to sit down for a moment. Then he got out into the water and, though a small man, lifted several of the men and women, who were naked, into his boat. Their backs and breasts were clammy, and he remembered uneasily what the great burns he had seen during the day had been like: yellow at first, then red and swollen, with the skin sloughed off, and finally, in the evening, suppurated and smelly. . . . On the other side, at a higher spit, he lifted the slimy living bodies out and carried them up the slope away from the tide. He had to keep consciously repeating to himself, "These are human beings."

Henry L. Stimson[3]

The policy adopted and steadily pursued by President Roosevelt and his advisers was a simple one. It was to spare no effort in securing the earliest possible successful development of an atomic weapon. The reasons for this policy were equally simple. The original experimental achievement of atomic fission had occurred in Germany in 1938, and it was known that the Germans had continued their experiments. In 1941 and 1942 they were believed to be ahead of us, and it was vital that they should not be the first to bring atomic weapons into the field of battle. Furthermore, if we should be the first to develop the weapon, we should have a great new instrument for shortening the war and minimizing destruction. At no time from 1941 to 1945 did I ever hear it suggested by the president, or by any other responsible member of the government, that atomic energy should not be used in the war. All of us of course understood the terrible responsibility involved in our attempt to unlock the doors to such a devastating weapon; President Roosevelt particularly spoke to me many times of his own awareness of the catastrophic potentialities of our work. But we were at war, and the work must be done. I therefore emphasize that it was our common objective throughout the war to be the first to produce an atomic weapon and use it. The possible atomic weapon was considered to be a new and tremendously powerful explosive, as legitimate as any other of the deadly explosive weapons of modern war. The entire purpose was the production of a military weapon; on no other ground could the wartime expenditure of so much time and money have been justified.

. . . As time went on it became clear that the weapon would not be available in time for use in the European theater, and the war against Germany was successfully ended by the use of what are now called conventional means. But in the spring of 1945 it became evident that the climax of our prolonged atomic effort was at hand. By the nature of atomic chain reactions, it was impossible to state with certainty that we had succeeded until a bomb had actually exploded in a full-scale experiment; nevertheless it was considered exceedingly probable that we should by midsummer have successfully detonated the first atomic bomb. This was to be done at the Alamogordo Reservation in New Mexico. It was thus time for detailed consideration of our future plans.

Martin J. Sherwin[4]

. . . Stimson, for one, began to ponder seriously the revolutionary aspects of the atomic bomb during the winter of 1944–45. By March he was convinced that its development raised issues that "went right down to the bottom facts of human nature, morals, and government." And yet this awareness of its profound implications apparently did not lead him to raise the sort of questions that might naturally seem to follow from such awareness. He never suggested to Roosevelt or Truman that its military use might incur a moral liability (an issue the secretary did raise with regard to the manner in which conventional weapons were used), or that

---

[3] Henry L. Stimson (1867–1950), secretary of war under President Roosevelt from July 1940 to April 1945 and under President Truman from April to September 1945, was in overall charge of the United States atomic development program. Selections by Stimson are excerpted from "The Decision to Use the Atomic Bomb" as it appeared in *Harper's Magazine*, later incorporated in the chapter "The Atomic Bomb and the Surrender of Japan" in *On Active Service in Peace and War*, by Henry L. Stimson and McGeorge Bundy. Copyright 1948 by Henry L. Stimson and McGeorge Bundy. Copyright renewed 1976 by McGeorge Bundy. Reprinted by permission of HarperCollins Publishers, Inc.

[4] Selections from Sherwin are excerpted from *A World Destroyed: The Atomic Bomb and the Grand Alliance*, by Martin J. Sherwin (New York: Alfred A. Knopf, 1975). Copyright © 1973, 1975 by Martin J. Sherwin. Reprinted by permission of Alfred A. Knopf, Inc.

chances of securing Soviet postwar cooperation might be diminished if Stalin did not receive a commitment to international control prior to an atomic attack on Japan. . . . Yet it must be pointed out that Bush and Conant[5] never seriously questioned the assumption of the bomb's use either. Like Niels Bohr,[6] they made a clear distinction between, on the one hand, its military application, which they took to be a wartime strategic decision, and, on the other, its moral and diplomatic implications, which bore on the longer-range issues of world peace and security and relations among nations. . . .

The preoccupation with winning the war obviously helped to foster this dichotomy in the minds of these men. But a closer look at how Bohr and Stimson respectively defined the nature of the diplomatic problem created by the bomb suggests that for the Secretary of War and his advisers (and ultimately for the President they advised) the dichotomy was, after all, more apparent than real. As a scientist, Bohr apprehended the significance of the new weapon even before it was developed, and he had no doubt that scientists in the Soviet Union would also understand its profound implications for the postwar world. He also was certain that they would convey the meaning of the development to Stalin, just as scientists in the United States and Great Britain had explained it to Roosevelt and Churchill. Thus the diplomatic problem, as Bohr analyzed it, was not the need to convince Stalin that the atomic bomb was an unprecedented weapon that threatened the life of the world, but the need

to assure the Soviet leader that he had nothing to fear from the circumstances of its development. It was by informing Stalin during the war that the United States intended to cooperate with him in neutralizing the bomb through international control, Bohr reasoned, that it then became possible to consider its wartime use apart from its postwar role.

Stimson approached the issue differently. Without Bohr's training and without his faith in science and in scientists, atomic energy in its undeveloped state had a different meaning for him. Memoranda and interviews could not instill in a nonscientist with policymaking responsibilities the intuitive understanding of a nuclear physicist whose work had led directly to the Manhattan Project.[7] The very aspect of the atomic bomb on which Bohr placed so much hope for achieving a new departure in international affairs—its uniqueness—made it unlikely that nonscientists would grasp its full implications and therefore act on his proposals. . . .

It was only after Bohr's proposal[8] was rejected . . . in September 1944 that events forced Stimson to think deeply about the weapon under his charge. Beginning with the fixed assumption that the bomb would be used in the war, he developed a view of the relationship between it and American diplomacy that reinforced that assumption, or at least gave him no cause to question it. For he could not consider an untried weapon an effective diplomatic bargaining counter; on the contrary, its diplomatic value was related to, if not primarily dependent on, its demonstrated worth as a military force. . . .

---

[5] Dr. Vannevar Bush, director of the Office of Scientific Research and Development and president of the Carnegie Institution of Washington, and Dr. James B. Conant, chairman of the National Defense Research Committee and president of Harvard University.

[6] Danish physicist who escaped to England from Nazi-occupied Denmark in September 1943 and was greatly concerned with the development of an atomic arms race after the war.

---

[7] The code name for the U.S. effort to develop an atomic bomb.

[8] In the summer of 1944, Bohr tried to convince Roosevelt and Churchill that an agreement for international control could be accomplished only by inviting Soviet participation in postwar atomic energy planning, **before** the bomb was a certainty and **before** the war was over.

The need for assurance that the bomb would work raises the central question: Did Stimson's understanding that the bomb would play an important diplomatic role after the war actually prevent him from questioning the assumption that the bomb ought to be used during the war? It must be stressed, in considering this question, that Stimson harbored no crude hatred or racial antagonism for the Japanese people. Nor was he blind to moral consideration that might affect world public opinion.

Stimson

On March 15, 1945, I had my last talk with President Roosevelt. My diary record of this conversation gives a fairly clear picture of the state of our thinking at that time. . . .

. . . I went over with him the two schools of thought that exist in respect to the future control after the war of this project, in case it is successful, one of them being the secret close-in attempted control of the project by those who control it now, and the other being the international control based on freedom both of science and of access. I told him that those things must be settled before the first projectile is used and that he must be ready with a statement to come out to the people on it just as soon as that is done. He agreed to that. . . .

This conversation covered the three aspects of the question which were then uppermost in our minds. First, it was always necessary to suppress a lingering doubt that any such titanic undertaking could be successful. Second, we must consider the implications of success in terms of its long-range postwar effect. Third, we must face the problem that would be presented at the time of our first use of the weapon, for with that first use there must be some public statement.

I did not see Franklin Roosevelt again.[9] The next time I went to the White House to discuss atomic energy was April 25, 1945, and I went to explain the nature of the problem to a man whose only previous knowledge of our activities was that of a senator who had loyally accepted our assurance that the matter must be kept a secret from him. Now he was President and Commander-in-Chief, and the final responsibility in this as in so many other matters must be his. . . .

Memorandum discussed with President Truman April 25, 1945:

1. Within four months we shall in all probability have completed the most terrible weapon ever known in human history, one bomb of which could destroy a whole city.

2. Although we have shared its development with the U.K., physically the United States is at present in the position of controling the resources with which to construct and use it and no other nation could reach this position for some years.

3. Nevertheless it is practically certain that we could not remain in this position indefinitely.

 a. Various segments of its discovery and production are widely known among many scientists in many countries, although few scientists are now acquainted with the whole process which we have developed.

 b. Although its construction under present methods requires great scientific and industrial effort and raw materials, which are temporarily mainly within the possession and knowledge of the United States and the U.K., it is extremely probable that much easier and cheaper methods of production will be discovered by

---

[9] President Franklin D. Roosevelt died on April 12, 1945, and Vice President Harry S Truman succeeded him.

scientists in the future, together with the use of materials of much wider distribution. As a result, it is extremely probable that the future will make it possible for atomic bombs to be constructed by smaller nations or even groups, or at least by a larger nation in a much shorter time.

4. As a result, it is indicated that the future may see a time when such a weapon may be constructed in secret and used suddenly and effectively with devastating power by a willful nation or group against an unsuspecting nation or group of much greater size and material power. With its aid even a very powerful unsuspecting nation might be conquered within a very few days by a very much smaller one. . . .

5. The world in its present state of moral advancement compared with its technical development would be eventually at the mercy of such a weapon. In other words, modern civilization might be completely destroyed.

6. To approach any world peace organization of any pattern now likely to be considered, without an appreciation by the leaders of our country of the power of this new weapon, would seem to be unrealistic. No system of control heretofore considered would be adequate to control this menace. Both inside any particular country and between the nations of the world, the control of this weapon will undoubtedly be a matter of the greatest difficulty and would involve such thoroughgoing rights of inspection and internal controls as we have never heretofore contemplated.

7. Furthermore, in the light of our present position with reference to this weapon, the question of sharing it with other nations and, if so shared, on what terms, becomes a primary question of our foreign relations. Also our leadership in the war and in the development of this weapon has placed a certain moral responsibility on us which we cannot shirk without very serious responsibility for any disaster to civilization which it would further.

8. On the other hand, if the problem of the proper use of this weapon can be solved, we would have the opportunity to bring the world into a pattern in which the peace of the world and our civilization can be saved.

The next step in our preparations was the appointment of . . . the Interim Committee,[10] [which] was charged with the function of advising the President on the various questions raised by our apparently imminent success in developing the atomic weapon. I was its chairman.

Sherwin

. . . On May 16 [Stimson] reported to Truman that he was anxious to hold the Air Force to "precision bombing" in Japan because "the reputation of the United States for fair play and humanitarianism is the world's biggest asset for peace in the coming decades."[11] But

---

[10] Members of the Interim Committee included James F. Byrnes (then a private citizen) as personal representative of the president; Ralph A. Byrd, under secretary of the Navy; William L. Clayton, assistant secretary of state; Dr. Vannevar Bush; Dr. Karl Compton, chief of the Office of Field Service in the Office of Scientific Research and Development and president of the Massachusetts Institute of Technology; and Dr. James B. Conant. The committee was assisted by a scientific panel whose members included Dr. A.H. Compton, director of the atomic energy project at the University of Chicago; Dr. J. R. Oppenheimer, director of the atomic energy project at Los Alamos; Dr. E. O. Lawrence, director of the atomic energy project at the University of California, Berkeley; and Dr. Enrico Fermi.

[11] On March 9–10, 1945, the Air Force launched its first incendiary raids on the Tokyo area. Hundreds of bombers took part and hundreds of tons of incendiaries were dropped. A quarter of the city of Tokyo was destroyed, 83,000 persons were killed, and 40,000 were injured. Similar successive raids burned out a great part of the urban area of Japan. Stimson, with a long-standing aversion to urban area bombing, was the one senior official who questioned the fire raids.

his concern here, it is evident, was not with the use as such of weapons of mass destruction, but simply with the manner in which they were used. "The same rule of sparing the civilian population should be applied as far as possible to the use of any new weapon," he wrote in reference to the bomb. The possibility that its extraordinary and indiscriminate destructiveness represented a profound qualitative difference, and so cried out for its governance by a higher morality than guided the use of conventional weapons, simply did not occur to him. On the contrary, the problem of the bomb as he perceived it was how to effectively subsume its management under the existing canons of international behavior.

. . . Stimson consciously considered two diplomatic effects of a combat demonstration of the atomic bomb: first, the impact of the attack on Japan's leaders, who might be persuaded thereby to end the war; and second, the impact of that attack on the Soviet Union's leaders, who might then prove to be more cooperative. It is likely that the contemplation together of the anticipated effects on both Japanese and Soviet leaders was what turned aside any inclination to question the use of the bomb.

In addition, however, to the diplomatic advantages policymakers anticipated, there were domestic political reactions they feared, and these, too, discouraged any policy other than the most devastating and rapid use of the bomb. Everyone involved in administering the atomic energy program lived with the thought that a congressional inquiry was the penalty he might pay for his labors. . . .

Beyond reasons directly related to the war, to postwar diplomacy, or to domestic policies, there was another, more subtle consideration moving some advisers to favor a combat demonstration of the bomb. Stimson informed [a] news commentator . . . in February 1974:

> President Conant has written me that one of the principal reasons he had for advising me

that the bomb *must be used* was that that was the only way to awaken the world to the necessity of abolishing war altogether. No technological demonstration, even if it had been possible under the conditions of war—which it was not—could take the place of the actual use with its horrible results. . . . I think he was right and I think that was one of the main things which differentiated the eminent scientists who concurred with President Conant from the less realistic ones who didn't.

On May 31, 1945 . . . the Interim Committee submitted a formal recommendation that the atomic bomb be used without warning against Japan. The Committee had met officially on three previous occasions . . . [y]et the question of whether the bomb should be used at all had never actually been discussed. The minutes of the Interim Committee suggest why. The committee members had come together as advocates, the responsible advisers of a new force in world affairs, convinced of the weapon's diplomatic and military potential, aware of its fantastic cost, and awed by their responsibilities. They were also constrained in their choices by several shared but unstated assumptions reinforced for scientists and policymakers alike by the entire history of the Manhattan Project: First, that the bomb was a legitimate weapon that would have been used against the Allies if Germany had won the race to develop it. Second, that its use would have a profound impact upon Japan's leaders as they debated whether or not to surrender. Third, that the American public would want it used under the circumstances. And fourth . . . that its use ultimately would have a salutary effect on relations with the Soviet Union. These assumptions suggested, at least obliquely, that there were neither military, diplomatic, nor domestic reasons to oppose the use of the weapon. On the contrary, four years of war and the pressures to end it, four years of secrecy and the prospect of more; $2 billion and the question "For what?", Japan's tenacious resistance and America's commitment to un-conditional surrender; Soviet behavior and the need for international control—all these factors served to bolster the accepted point of view.

...There is no suggestion...in the questions the secretary placed before the assembled group, that his memory was serving him well when he wrote in his autobiography: "The first and greatest problem [for the Interim Committee] was the decision on the use of the bomb—should it be used against the Japanese, and if so, in what manner?" The fact is that a discussion of this question was placed on the agenda only after it was raised casually in the course of conversation during lunch.

...Compton recalls that he asked Stimson whether it might not be possible to arrange something less than a surprise atomic attack that would so impress the Japanese that they would see the uselessness of continuing the war.... Various possibilities were brought forward, but were discarded one after the other....

After considerable discussion of types of targets and the desired effect, Stimson expressed the conclusion, on which there was general agreement, that the Japanese would not be given any warning; and that the bombing would not concentrate on a civilian area, but that an attempt would be made to make a profound psychological impression on as many Japanese as possible. Stimson accepted Conant's suggestion that the most desirable target would be a vital war plant employing a large number of workers and closely surrounded by workers' homes. No member of the Committee spoke to the contradiction between this conclusion and their earlier decision not to concentrate on a civilian area.

This critical discussion on the use of the bomb was over. It had not only confirmed the assumption that the new weapon was to be used, but that the *two* bombs that would be available early in August should be used.

Stimson

The Interim Committee and the scientific panel also served as a channel through which suggestions from other scientists working on the atomic project were forwarded to me and to the president. Among the suggestions thus forwarded was one memorandum which questioned using the bomb at all against the enemy. On June 16, 1945, after consideration of that memorandum, the scientific panel made a report, from which I quote the following paragraphs:

The opinions of our scientific colleagues on the initial use of these weapons are not unanimous: they range from the proposal of a purely technical demonstration to that of the military application best designed to induce surrender. Those who advocate a purely technical demonstration would wish to outlaw the use of atomic weapons, and have feared that if we use the weapons now our position in future negotiations will be prejudiced. Others emphasize the opportunity of saving American lives by immediate military use, and believe that such use will improve the international prospects, in that they are more concerned with the prevention of war than with the elimination of this special weapon. We find ourselves closer to these latter views: we can propose no technical demonstration likely to bring an end to the war; we see no acceptable alternative to direct military use.

...The ultimate responsibility for the recommendation to the president rested upon me, and I have no desire to veil it. The conclusions of the committee were similar to my own, although I reached mine independently. I felt that to extract a genuine surrender from the Emperor and his military advisers, they must be administered a tremendous shock which would carry convincing proof of our power to destroy the Empire. Such an effective shock would save many times the number of lives, both American and Japanese, that it would cost.

The facts on which my reasoning was based and steps taken to carry it out now follow.

The principal political, social, and military objective of the United States in the summer of 1945 was the prompt and complete surrender of Japan. Only the complete destruction of her military power could open the way to lasting peace.

Japan, in July 1945, had been seriously weakened by our increasingly violent attacks. It was known to us that she had gone so far as to make tentative proposals to the Soviet government, hoping to use the Russians as mediators in a negotiated peace. These vague proposals contemplated the retention by Japan of important conquered areas and were therefore not considered seriously. There was as yet no indication of any weakening in the Japanese determination to fight rather than accept unconditional surrender. If she should persist in her fight to the end, she had still a great military force.

In the middle of July 1945 . . . [t]he total strength of the Japanese Army was estimated at about five million men. . . . The Japanese Army was in much better condition than the Japanese Navy and Air Force. The Navy had practically ceased to exist except as a harrying force against an invasion fleet. The Air Force had been reduced mainly to reliance upon kamikaze, or suicide, attacks. These latter, however, had already inflicted serious damage on our seagoing forces, and their possible effectiveness in a last ditch fight was a matter of real concern to our naval leaders.

As we understood it in July, there was a very strong possibility that the Japanese government might determine on resistance to the end, in all the areas of the Far East under its control. In such an event the Allies would be faced with the enormous task of destroying an armed force of 5 million men and 5,000 suicide aircraft, belonging to a race which had already demonstrated its ability to fight literally to the death.

The strategic plans of our armed forces for the defeat of Japan as they stood in July had been prepared without reliance on the atomic bomb, which had not yet been tested in New Mexico. We were planning an intensified sea and air blockade and greatly intensified strategic air bombing through the summer and early fall, to be followed on November 1 by an invasion of the southern island of Kyushu. This would be followed in turn by an invasion of the main island of Honshu in the spring of 1946. The total U.S. military and naval force involved in this grand design was of the order of 5 million men; if all those indirectly concerned are included, it was larger still.

We estimated that if we should be forced to carry this plan to its conclusion, the major fighting force would not end until the latter part of 1946, at the earliest. I was informed that such operations might be expected to cost over a million casualties, to American forces alone. Additional large losses might be expected among our allies, and, of course, if our campaign were successful and if we could judge by previous experience, enemy casualties would be much larger than our own.

It was already clear in July that, even before the invasion, we should be able to inflict enormously severe damage on the Japanese homeland by the combined application of "conventional" sea and air power. The critical question was whether this kind of action would induce surrender. It therefore became necessary to consider very carefully the probable state of mind of the enemy, and to assess with accuracy the line of conduct which might end his will to resist.

With these considerations in mind, I wrote a memorandum for the president, on July 2, which I believe fairly represents the thinking of the American government as it finally took shape in action. . . .

Memorandum for the President, July 2, 1945, on proposed program for Japan:

. . . A question then comes: Is there any alternative to such a forceful occupation of Japan which will secure for us the equivalent of an unconditional surrender of her forces and a permanent destruction of her power again to strike an aggressive blow at the "peace of the Pacific"? I am inclined to think that there is enough such chance to make it well worthwhile our giving them a warning of what is to come and a definite opportunity to capitulate. As above suggested, it should be tried before the actual forceful occupation of the homeland islands is begun and furthermore the warning should be given in ample time to permit a national reaction to set in.

We have the following enormously favorable factors on our side — factors much weightier than those we had against Germany:

Japan has no allies.

Her navy is nearly destroyed and she is vulnerable to a surface and underwater blockade which can deprive her of sufficient food and supplies for her population.

She is terribly vulnerable to our concentrated air attack on her crowded cities, industrial, and food resources.

She has against her not only the Anglo-American forces but the rising forces of China and the ominous threat of Russia.[12]

We have inexhaustible and untouched industrial resources to bring to bear against her diminishing potential.

We have great moral superiority through being the victim of her first sneak attack.

The problem is to translate these advantages into prompt and economical achievement of our objectives. . . . It is therefore my conclusion that a carefully timed warning be given to Japan by the chief representatives of the United States, Great Britain, China, and, if then a belligerent, Russia by calling on Japan to surrender and permit the occupation of her country in order to insure its complete demilitarization for the sake of the future peace.

This warning should contain the following elements:

The varied and overwhelming character of the force we are about to bring to bear on the islands.

The inevitability and completeness of the destruction which the full application of this force will entail.

The determination of the Allies to destroy permanently all authority and influence of those who have deceived and misled the country into embarking on world conquest.

The determination of the Allies to limit Japanese sovereignty to her main islands and to render them powerless to mount and support another war.

The disavowal of any attempt to extirpate the Japanese as a race or to destroy them as a nation.

A statement of our readiness, once her economy is purged of its militaristic influence, to permit the Japanese to maintain such industries, particularly of a light consumer character, as offer no threat of aggression against her neighbors, but which can produce a sustaining economy, and provide a reasonable standard of living. . . .

The withdrawal from their country as soon as the above objectives of the Allies are accomplished, and as soon as there has been established a peacefully inclined government, of a character representative of the masses of the Japanese people. I personally think that if in saying this we should add that we do not exclude a constitutional monarchy under her present dynasty, it would substantially add to the chances of acceptance.

. . . Success of course will depend on the potency of the warning which we give her. She has an extremely sensitive national pride and, as we are now seeing every day, when actually locked with the enemy will fight to the very death. For that reason the warning must be tendered before the actual invasion has occurred and while the impending destruction, though clear beyond peradventure, has not yet reduced her to fanatical despair. If Russia is part of the threat, the Russian attack, if actual, must not have progressed too far. Our own bombing should be confined to military objectives as far as possible.

_____

[12] Joseph Stalin had given his word at Yalta in February 1945 that the Soviet Union would enter the war against Japan two or three months after the end of war in Europe.

... It will be noted that the atomic bomb is not mentioned in this memorandum. On grounds of secrecy the bomb was never mentioned except when absolutely necessary, and furthermore, it had not yet been tested. It was of course well forward in our minds as the memorandum was written and discussed that the bomb would be the best possible sanction if our warning were rejected.

Truman[13]

The historic message of the first explosion of an atomic bomb was flashed to me in a message from Secretary of War Stimson on the morning of July 16. The most secret and the most daring enterprise of the war had succeeded. We were now in possession of a weapon that would not only revolutionize war but could alter the course of history and civilization. This news reached me at Potsdam the day after I had arrived for the conference of the Big Three.[14]

Preparations were being rushed for the test atomic explosion at Alamogordo, New Mexico, at the time I had to leave for Europe, and on the voyage over I had been anxiously awaiting word on the results. I had been told of many predictions by the scientists, but no one was certain of the outcome of this full-scale atomic explosion. As I read the message from Stimson, I realized that the test not only met the most optimistic expectation of the scientists but that the United States had in its possession an explosive force of unparalleled power. . . .

We reviewed our military strategy in the light of this revolutionary development.[15] We were not ready to make use of this weapon against the Japanese, although we did not know as yet what effect the new weapon might have, physically or psychologically, when used against the enemy. For that reason the military advised that we go ahead with the existing military plans for the invasion of the Japanese home islands. . . .

On July 24, I casually mentioned to Stalin that we had a new weapon of unusual destructive force. The Russian premier showed no special interest. All he said was that he was glad to hear it and hoped we would make "good use of it against the Japanese." . . .

The final decision of where and when to use the atomic bomb was up to me. Let there be no mistake about it. I regarded the bomb as a military weapon and never had any doubt that it should be used. The top military advisers to the president recommended its use, and when I talked to Churchill he unhesitatingly told me that he favored the use of the atomic bomb if it might aid to end the war.

In deciding to use this bomb I wanted to make sure that it would be used as a weapon of war in the manner prescribed by the laws of war. That meant that I wanted it dropped on a military target. I had told Stimson that the bomb should be dropped as nearly as possibly [sic] on a war production center of prime military importance.

Stimson's staff had prepared a list of cities in Japan that might serve as targets. Kyoto, though favored . . . as a center of military activity, was eliminated when Secretary Stimson pointed out that it was a cultural and religious shrine of the Japanese.

Four cities were finally recommended as targets: Hiroshima, Kokura, Niigata, and Nagasaki. They were listed in that order as targets for the first attack. The order of selection was in accordance with the military importance of these cities, but allowance would be given for weather conditions at the time of the bombing. Before the selected targets were approved as proper for military purposes, I personally went

---

[13] Harry S Truman, *Memoirs by Harry S Truman, vol. I: Year of Decisions* (Garden City, N.Y.: Doubleday, 1955).

[14] The alliance of the United States, the United Kingdom, and the Soviet Union.

[15] When General Dwight D. Eisenhower, as the victorious Allied commander in Europe, learned about Alamogordo from Henry Stimson at Potsdam, he hoped that "we would never have to use such a thing."

over them in detail with Stimson, Marshall, and Arnold, and we discussed the matter of timing and the final choice of the first target.

General Spaatz, who commanded the Strategic Air Forces, which would deliver the bomb on the target, was given some latitude as to when and on which of the four targets the bomb would be dropped. . . . The War Department was given orders to instruct General Spaatz that the first bomb would be dropped as soon after August 3 as weather would permit.

With this order the wheels were set in motion for the first use of an atomic weapon against a military target. I had made the decision. I also instructed Stimson that the order would stand unless I notified him that the Japanese reply to our ultimatum was acceptable.

Stimson

There [had been] much discussion in Washington about the timing of the warning to Japan. The controling factor in the end was the date already set for the Potsdam meeting of the Big Three. It was President Truman's decision that such a warning should be solemnly issued by the United States and the U.K. from this meeting, with the concurrence of the head of the Chinese government, so that it would be plain that **all** of Japan's principal enemies were in entire unity. This was done, in the Potsdam ultimatum of July 26, which very closely followed the above memorandum of July 2, with the exception that it made no mention of the Japanese emperor.

On July 28 the Premier of Japan, Suzuki, rejected the Potsdam ultimatum by announcing that it was "unworthy of public notice." In the face of this rejection we could only proceed to demonstrate that the ultimatum had meant exactly what it said when it stated that, if the Japanese continued the war, "the full application of our military power, backed by our

resolve, will mean the inevitable and complete destruction of the Japanese armed forces and just as inevitably the utter devastation of the Japanese homeland."

For such a purpose the atomic bomb was an entirely suitable weapon. . . .

Hiroshima was bombed on August 6, and Nagasaki on August 9. These two cities were active working parts of the Japanese war effort. One was an army center; the other was naval and industrial. Hiroshima was the headquarters of the Japanese Army defending southern Japan and was a major military storage and assembly point. Nagasaki was a major seaport and it contained several large industrial plants of great wartime importance. We believed that our attacks had struck cities which must certainly be important to the Japanese military leaders, both army and navy, and we waited for a result. We waited one day.

. . . After a prolonged Japanese cabinet session in which the deadlock was broken by the emperor himself, the offer to surrender was made on August 10. It was based on the Potsdam terms, with a reservation concerning the sovereignty of the emperor. While the Allied reply made no promises other than those already given, it implicitly recognized the emperor's position by prescribing that his power must be subject to the orders of the allied supreme commander. . . . Our great objective was thus achieved, and all the evidence I have seen indicates that the controling factor in the final Japanese decision to accept our terms of surrender was the atomic bomb.

The two atomic bombs which we had dropped were the only ones we had ready, and our rate of production at the time was very small. Had the war continued until the projected invasion on November 1, additional fire raids of B-29s would have been more destructive of life and property than the very limited number of atomic raids which we could have executed in the same period. But the atomic bomb was more than a weapon of terrible destruction; it was a psychological weapon. . . . On August 6 one B-29 dropped a single atomic weapon on Hiroshima. Three days later a second bomb was dropped on Nagasaki and the war was over. So far as the Japanese could know, our ability to execute atomic attacks, if necessary by many planes at a time, was unlimited. As Dr. Karl Compton has said, "It was not one atomic bomb, or two, which brought surrender; it was the experience of what an atomic bomb will actually do to a community, *plus the dread of many more,* that was effective."

Hiroshima

Mr. Tanimoto, after his long run and his many hours of rescue work, dozed uneasily. When he awoke, in the first light of dawn, he looked across the river and saw that he had not carried the festered, limp bodies high enough on the sandspit the night before. The tide had risen above where he had put them; they had not had the strength to move; they must have drowned. He saw a number of bodies floating in the river.

[Later,] [s]tatistical workers gathered what figures they could on the effects of the bomb. They reported that 78,150 people had been killed; 13,983 were missing; and 37,425 had been injured. . . . As the months went by and more and more hundreds of corpses were dug up from the ruins . . . the statisticians began to say that at least a hundred thousand people had lost their lives in the bombing. Since many people died of a combination of causes, it was impossible to figure exactly how many were killed by each cause, but the statisticians calculated that about 25 percent had died of direct burns from the bomb, about 50 percent from other injuries, and about 20 percent as a result of radiation effects. The statisticians' figures on property damage were more reliable: 62,000 out of 90,000 buildings destroyed, and 6,000 more damaged beyond repair. In the heart of the city, they found only five modern buildings that could be used again without major repairs.

Scientists swarmed into the city. Some of them measured the force that had been necessary to shift marble gravestones in the cemeteries, to knock over 22 of the 47 railroad cars at Hiroshima station, to lift and move the concrete roadway on one of the bridges, and to perform other noteworthy acts of strength, and concluded that the pressure exerted by the explosion varied from 5.3 to 8.0 tons per square yard. Others found that mica, of which the melting point is 900° C., had fused on granite gravestones 380 yards from the center; that telephone poles of Cryptomeria japonica, whose carbonization temperature is 240° C., had been charred at 4,400 yards from the center; and that the surface of gray clay tiles of the type used in Hiroshima, whose melting point is 1,300° C., had dissolved at 600 yards; and, after examining other significant ashes and melted bits, they concluded that the bomb's heat on the ground at the center must have been 6,000° C.

MORALITY AND CONSEQUENCES

Utilitarianism is one of the most important and influential of all moral theories. It judges the rightness and wrongness of actions on the basis of their consequences.

By itself, an act is neither good nor bad. Its consequences are the determining factor. An action is morally right if it produces more benefits than harm for all the parties it affects. The best actions morally are those that maximize benefits to all affected and minimize harms they suffer or the costs they incur. The morality of consequences often finds expression in economics and other social sciences and in public policy decision procedures, such as cost-benefit analysis.

Three British philosophers—David Hume (1711–1776), Jeremy Bentham (1748–1832), and John Stuart Mill (1806–1873)—developed the intellectual foundations of utilitarianism. The passages below are by Mill. In them, he defines the basic principle of utilitarianism, explains the consequence—happiness—that morally good actions promote, and outlines the justification for this approach to moral decisions.

> The creed which accepts as the foundation of morals, Utility or the Greatest Happiness Principle, holds that actions are right in proportion as they tend to promote happiness, wrong as they tend to produce the reverse of happiness. By happiness is intended pleasure, and the absence of pain; by unhappiness, pain and the privation of pleasure.
>
> Now, such a theory of life excites in many minds, and among them in some of the most estimable in feeling and purpose, inveterate dislike. To suppose that life has (as they express it) no higher end than pleasure—no better and nobler object of desire and pursuit—they designate as utterly mean and grovelling; as a doc-

trine worthy only of swine, to whom the followers of Epicurus were, at a very early period, contemptuously likened.

> But there is no known Epicurean theory of life which does not assign to the pleasures of the intellect, of the feelings and imagination, and of the moral sentiments, as much higher value as pleasures than to those of mere sensation.
>
> Few human creatures would consent to be changed into any of the lower animals; for a promise of the fullest allowance of a beast's pleasures, no intelligent human being would consent to be a fool, no instructed person would be an ignoramus, no person of feeling and conscience would be selfish and base, even though they should be persuaded that the fool, the dunce, or the rascal is better satisfied with his lot than they are with theirs. . . . It is better to be a human being dissatisfied than a pig satisfied; better to be Socrates dissatisfied than a fool satisfied.
>
> I must again repeat, what the assailants of utilitarianism seldom have the justice to acknowledge, that the happiness which forms the utilitarian standard of what is right in conduct, is not the agent's own happiness, but that of all concerned. As between his own happiness and that of others, utilitarianism requires him to be as strictly impartial as a disinterested and benevolent spectator. In the golden rule of Jesus of Nazareth, we read the complete spirit of the ethics of utility. To do as one would be done by, and to love one's neighbor as oneself, constitutes the ideal perfection of utilitarian morality.

*   *   *   *   *

These passages are taken from *Utilitarianism*, first published in 1861. This case was prepared by Joseph Badaracco, Jr.

When . . . it is . . . positively asserted to be impossible that human life should be happy, the assertion, if not something like a verbal quibble, is at least an exaggeration. If by happiness be meant a continuity of highly pleasurable excitement, it is evident enough that this is impossible. A state of exalted pleasure lasts only moments, or in some cases, and with some intermissions, hours or days, and is the occasional brilliant flash of enjoyment, not its permanent and steady flame. Of this the philosophers who have taught that happiness is the end of life were as fully aware as those who taunt them. The happiness which they meant was not a life of rapture; but moments of such, in an existence made up of few and transitory pains, many and various pleasures, with a decided predominance of the active over the passive, and having as the foundation of the whole, not to expect more from life than it is capable of bestowing. A life thus composed, to those who have been fortunate enough to obtain it, has always appeared worthy of the name of happiness. And such an existence is even now the lot of many, during some considerable portion of their lives. The present wretched education, and wretched social arrangements, are the only real hindrance to its being attainable by almost all.

*   *   *   *   *

The only proof capable of being given that an object is visible, is that people actually see it. The only proof that a sound is audible, is that people hear it; and so of the other sources of our experience. In like manner, I apprehend, the sole evidence it is possible to produce that anything is desirable, is that people do actually desire it. If the end which the utilitarian doctrine proposes to itself were not, in theory and in practice, acknowledged to be an end, nothing could ever convince any person that it was so. No reason can be given why the general happiness is desirable, except that each person, so far as he believes it to be attainable, desires his own happiness. This, however, being a fact, we have not only all the proof which the case admits of but all which it is possible to require, that happiness is a good: that each person's happiness is a good to that person, and the general happiness, therefore, a good to the aggregate of all persons. Happiness has made out its title as *one* of the ends of conduct, and consequently one of the criteria of morality.

Source: *Utilitarianism and Other Essays,* Alan Ryan (New York, Viking Penguin, 1987), pp. 278, 281, 284, 307.

MORALITY AND DUTIES

For many philosophers, theologians, and other thinkers, actions are morally wrong if they violate a moral duty and morally right if they conform to a duty. Most people are familiar with such duties. They include, for example, obligations to avoid harming innocent people, to keep promises, to tell the truth, to respect others' rights, and to behave justly.

For this view of morality, motives matter critically. If someone gives money to a homeless person to impress others, she is not performing a moral act. If she gives to meet her duty to alleviate suffering, she is. While the consequences for the poor person are the same in both cases, the morality of the action is not. Morally good actions are motivated by a desire to perform one's duty because it is the right thing to do.

This case was prepared by Joseph Badaracco, Jr.
Copyright © 1990 by the President and Fellows of Harvard College.
Harvard Business School case 390-207 (Revised 1991).

Respect for other persons—for their lives and values, their autonomy, their dignity as human beings—is the basic justification of this approach to morality. The reason it is morally wrong to lie to innocent persons or to harm them or to violate their rights is that these actions deny others the respect we owe them as human beings. Moreover, violations of duties are wrong regardless of their consequences. Even if actions produce positive results, they are still wrong, simply because it is morally wrong to treat other human beings in certain ways.

In the passage below, Immanuel Kant states this view—a position that has profoundly influenced moral philosophy since Kant began publishing his ideas in the late 18th century.

Nothing in the world—indeed nothing even beyond the world—can possibly be conceived which could be called good without qualification except a good will. Intelligence, wit, judgment, and the other talents of the mind, however they may be named, or courage, resoluteness, and perseverance as qualities of temperament, are doubtless in many respects good and desirable. But they can become extremely bad and harmful if the will, which is to make use of these gifts of nature and which in its special constitution is called character, is not good. It is the same with the gifts of fortune. Power, riches, honor, even health, general well-being, and the contentment with one's condition which is called happiness, make for pride and even arrogance if there is not a good will to correct their influence on the mind and on its principles of action so as to make it universally conformable to its end.

* * * * *

Some qualities seem to be conducive to this good will and can facilitate its action, but, in spite of that, they have no intrinsic unconditional worth. They rather presuppose a good will, which limits the high esteem which one otherwise rightly has for them and prevents their

being held to be absolutely good. Moderation in emotions and passions, self-control, and calm deliberation not only are good in many respects but even seem to constitute a part of the inner worth of the person. But however unconditionally they were esteemed by the ancients, they are far from being good without qualification. For without the principle of a good will they can become extremely bad, and the coolness of a villain makes him not only far more dangerous but also more directly abominable in our eyes than he would have seemed without it.

The good will is not good because of what it effects or accomplishes or because of its adequacy to achieve some proposed end; it is good only because of its willing, i.e., it is good of itself.

* * * * *

If then there is a supreme practical principle or, in respect of the human will, a categorical imperative, it must be one which, being drawn from the conception of that which is necessarily an end for everyone because it is an end *in itself,* constitutes an objective principle of will, and can therefore serve as a universal practical law. The foundation of this principle is: rational nature exists as an end in itself. Man necessarily conceives his own existence as being so; so far then is it a subjective principle of human actions. But every other rational being regards its existence similarly, just on the same rational principle that holds for me; so that it is at the same time an objective principle from which as a supreme practical law all laws of the will must be capable of being deduced. Accordingly the practical imperative will be as follows: *So act as to treat humanity, whether in thine own person or in that of any other, in every case as an end withal, never as means only.*

These passages appear in the first and second sections of *The Fundamental Principles of the Metaphysic of Morale,* first published in 1785. Reprinted with the permission of Macmillan College Publishing Co. from *Foundations of the Metaphysics of Morals* by Immanual Kant, translated by Lewis White Beck. Copyright © 1990 by Macmillan College Publishing Company, Inc.

INTERNATIONAL DRILLING CORPORATION (A)

Don Taylor sat at his typewriter and sweated. It was hot. Nine months ago, when he had moved his family to Dallas, they had told him the nights would be cool. But this night Taylor was hot. He was chain-smoking again as he bent over to reread what he had written. It was almost dawn and Taylor had been writing all night. The wastebasket was full of discarded papers.

In May of 1971 Don Taylor accepted a job with the International Drilling Corporation (IDC). Taylor was 27 years old and had graduated from the Harvard Business School in 1968. After receiving his MBA, Taylor spent two years in the Peace Corps. He then worked in New York City for a division of one of the largest industrial concerns in America. Frustrated by what he considered to be "bad management" and "office politics," Don Taylor had quit his New York job. A close friend and Harvard classmate had suggested he write to Robert Dumont, chairman of the board of IDC, a rapidly growing oil and gas company with headquarters in Dallas, Texas. "Dumont's a real entrepreneur," his friend remarked, "and there should be plenty of room for you to test yourself."

Taylor liked the idea of working in a smaller company, and both he and his wife wanted to leave the New York area. After flying to Dallas to interview IDC executives, Taylor was hired as assistant to the president of IDC. Jeff Williams, IDC's president, had been hired in February of 1971. He was 38 years old and had been a successful stockbroker. Robert Dumont, who founded IDC and still owned over 30 percent of the company, had been impressed with Williams' knowledge of the investment markets and had convinced him to leave the brokerage business and join IDC. Jeff Williams had no experience in managing a natural resources company. When Don Taylor was hired, Williams spoke expansively of "running a tight ship" and "cleaning house," but admitted he hardly knew where to begin. Williams told Taylor in May of 1971 that his primary function would be to help "straighten out the company's internal operations."

IDC's Business

The International Drilling Corporation was engaged in the marketing of limited partnership interests in oil and gas drilling ventures. The company had an established sales force of 25 people who functioned as wholesalers to members of the investment community. Broker-dealers then sold the limited partnership interests to investors. These interests were similar to shares in a common stock mutual fund. Unlike mutual funds, however, the IDC drilling funds were set up as a series of partnerships that started each quarter. IDC's first fund, for example, was 1966–4, meaning it was opened in the final quarter of 1966. Investors put up a minimum of $2,500 each and, at the end of the quarter, if at least $200,000 had been raised, the partnership was closed and a new one opened. Investors were not allowed to take out their profits for 10 years (unless they reached age 65). Instead, profits were automatically reinvested in subsequent partnerships. Each year IDC was required to file a detailed prospectus with the Securities and Exchange Commission (SEC) describing its drilling programs.

Persons who purchased shares of IDC's drilling funds were limited partners, as defined

This case was written by Professor Kenneth E. Goodpaster of the University of St. Thomas.

Copyright © 1981 by the President and Fellows of Harvard College.

Harvard Business School case 382-111 (Revised 1983).

under the limited partnership laws of Texas. They had limited liability and could not influence the management of the drilling program. Management of all the ventures was vested in IDC, and IDC received a 25 percent "profits interest" for its management efforts. IDC's prospectus disclosed that IDC would charge each partnership for all of the direct expenses incurred on behalf of the partnership (e.g., salaries of the geologists and managers, overhead expenses, and the like). Under the IDC plan, an investor could "cash out" of a partnership by writing to IDC. IDC published quarterly reports of the "cash surrender value" of each of the partnerships formed under the plan. According to the prospectus, these "cash surrender values" were determined by evaluating all of the drilling activities of each partnership. Independent engineers were required to be used to arrive at the current cash surrender value of each drilling program.

Robert Dumont considered himself the pioneer of this concept. He proudly explained that, through his IDC vehicles, the opportunities of investing in oil and gas, formerly enjoyed only by the very wealthy, were made available to the average individual. Oil and gas drilling were afforded special treatment under the United States tax laws. The expenditures required to locate a potential oil field and drill a well were deductible by the investor for tax purposes, and, if oil or gas were ever produced, a portion of the income generated was also exempt from taxation.

IDC's advertising literature stated that for every $10,000 invested, a $7,500 or $8,000 tax deduction could be expected in the first year. Assuming an investor in the 50 percent tax bracket, the advertising went on to say that "up to $4,000 of tax savings" were to be had. Thus, for a "cost" of only $6,000, an investor could have $10,000 "working for him" in the IDC drilling program.

The IDC drilling programs were extremely popular. When Don Taylor joined the company in May 1971, 18 partnerships had been formed. The initial partnership was formed with $375,000 of investor capital. The first 1971 partnership (closed on March 31, 1971) had $9,500,000 of investor capital.

Aside from its 25 wholesalers, IDC employed a staff of geologists, land men, field managers, and support personnel. The company had sales offices in 12 cities in the United States and operations offices in Dallas, Midland, Tulsa, and Calgary.

Robert Dumont was thought to be one of the wealthiest citizens of Dallas. He was on the board of a large local bank and was reputed to have "close" political connections "in Washington."

The IDC Organization

Don Taylor's first impressions of the IDC organization were very favorable. In spite of Jeff Williams' warnings about "cleaning house," Taylor was impressed with the energy and enthusiasm of the IDC employees. Robert Dumont was held in the highest esteem by everyone Taylor spoke to during his first months on the job. Dumont was seldom seen in the Dallas offices, but it was said that all major decisions affecting IDC were made by him. IDC's common stock had appreciated in price dramatically since the firm went public in 1968, and the rise in value was generally attributed to Dumont's creative ideas and forceful promotional efforts. From its beginnings as an oil exploration enterprise, IDC had diversified and expanded its operations, until by 1971 it was involved in many aspects of international natural resource development. Exhibit 1 presents a corporate description from the 1970 annual report.

There was no formal organization chart and Don Taylor soon learned that Dumont abhorred such formalization. "We are a free-form organization," he was told by Brian Rosenberg, an IDC vice president thought to be

EXHIBIT 1   International Drilling Corporation (A)

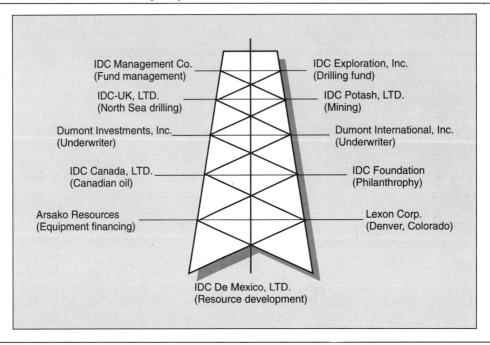

IDC Management Co. (Fund management)	IDC Exploration, Inc. (Drilling fund)
IDC-UK, LTD. (North Sea drilling)	IDC Potash, LTD. (Mining)
Dumont Investments, Inc. (Underwriter)	Dumont International, Inc. (Underwriter)
IDC Canada, LTD. (Canadian oil)	IDC Foundation (Philanthrophy)
Arsako Resources (Equipment financing)	Lexon Corp. (Denver, Colorado)
IDC De Mexico, LTD. (Resource development)	

Source: 1970 annual report.

particularly close to Dumont. "Everyone has plenty to do and we don't worry about charts. . . ." In spite of the lack of written guidelines, Taylor was able to observe an informal hierarchy at IDC. The sales and marketing staffs had large and richly furnished offices on one floor of the IDC office building in downtown Dallas. The operations staff was officed in comparatively plain surroundings on a separate floor. The office of the president, Jeff Williams, was on the same floor as the sales and marketing personnel. Dumont's offices (on yet another floor) were the most luxurious Taylor had ever seen. There were a group of executives characterized by Jeff Williams as the "brain trust" whose offices were located close to Dumont's. Taylor was told that these executives had been with IDC "from the start" and that they were an instrumental part of the

company's rapid expansion and recent success. After several weeks with IDC, Taylor could include in the "brain trust" the following men: Brian Rosenberg, Bill Halpern, and Dave Ford (all vice presidents), Steve Stein, and Tom Lowe (both lawyers), and Frank Souring (described as a "special assistant" to Dumont). Except for Lowe and Souring, who were in their early 60s, all of the members of the "brain trust" were in their late 30s. Don Taylor was impressed with their intelligence and their enthusiasm for IDC.

Don Taylor's First Eight Months

Jeff Williams, IDC's president, lived in Los Angeles. When Taylor arrived in Dallas and reported for work, he learned that Mr. Williams was "not going to be in the office this week." Williams commuted to and from Dallas from his Los Angeles home (using an IDC executive jet) and spent much of his time at the IDC sales office in Los Angeles. He had left instructions for Taylor to "get acquainted with things."

Taylor's initial disappointment over the lack of direction given him by Williams soon gave way to enthusiasm. The young MBA found a number of minor projects that needed attention and that allowed him to apply analytic techniques acquired at business school. Several members of the brain trust had staff members and assistants who were Taylor's age and they were more than happy to let Taylor help them with analyses, reports, and cost studies.

Taylor particularly liked Art Weaver, personnel director, and Wendel Toms, one of Brian Rosenberg's assistants. In June of 1971, Taylor was assigned responsibility for the physical distribution of IDC's sales literature. The mailroom had long been the object of criticism from the IDC sales force. Taylor learned that mailing expenses had exceeded $100,000 in the first five months of 1971, and sales materials were consistently being lost or delayed. He found himself working 12 hours a day to correct the distribution problems.

After six weeks, Taylor had trimmed mailing costs by 75 percent. He had reorganized mailroom policies so that by utilizing bulk storage and shipping procedures all sales offices were receiving the required sales literature in a timely manner. Even the most particular of the IDC salesmen were complimentary. Although Taylor was proud of the job he had done, he was upset when he overheard Bill Halpern refer to him as "the new mailboy."

In September, Taylor was given a large office adjoining that of Jeff Williams. Although Williams never gave his assistant a list of duties and responsibilities, Taylor soon found himself in the midst of a dozen new projects. He was asked to fly (usually aboard one of the IDC executive jets) to New York, Los Angeles,

Denver, or San Francisco to "check out" new ventures or potential acquisitions. Jeff Williams began to ask Taylor to represent the president in various staff meetings and Taylor was given a 20 percent raise in his salary on October 15, 1971.

On October 30, 1971, a meeting was held in Mr. Williams' office that startled and upset Don Taylor. "I want you to listen and take notes," Jeff Williams explained, "but keep your mouth shut." During the meeting Brian Rosenberg, Steve Stein, and a lawyer Taylor had never seen before discussed with Williams certain activities that had occurred in 1969 that were in violation of the securities laws. It seems that three broker-dealers were paid commissions for selling partnership interests in excess of what was allowed and disclosed in the prospectus. It was described as a "minor" and "technical" violation and Rosenberg assured Williams that IDC's "tracks were covered."

Williams made a few comments during the meeting. After the others had left he told Taylor he might as well destroy his notes. "The whole mess is so stupid," he remarked, "but there's nothing we can do about it now . . . and there's no sense in making a big deal out of it." Taylor took his notes home and filed them in a desk drawer.

In November, Taylor was put in charge of a companywide budgeting program. He welcomed the opportunity to creatively use his business school education and to learn more about the various IDC departments. However, before the program was a week old, Taylor was assigned to analyze a major acquisition. Mr. Dumont wanted to purchase a large mutual fund management company. Taylor worked directly with Brian Rosenberg and, for the first time since joining IDC, felt he was part of the brain trust. After the acquisition study was complete, Taylor asked Williams if he could return to the budgeting program. Williams informed him that Dumont had "killed" the idea.

Taylor was greatly disappointed. On his own he had begun to devise a standard cost control system for Dumont Investments and Dumont International, the two underwriting subsidiaries that sold IDC's partnerships. He felt confident a simple system of budgets and monthly reports could help reduce corporate overhead and sales expenses. Jeff Williams had often complained that these were "exorbitant."

The aborted budgeting project had also stimulated Taylor to draft several memos for Jeff Williams' signature, requesting more detailed operating information from IDC Exploration and IDC Management Company. Regular computerized MIS reports were virtually nonexistent, and those that came to Williams were poorly organized and often inaccurate. Taylor, who prided himself on his skill with numbers, was at a loss to decipher most of the computer reports. His draft memos would have required each of the department heads to write Jeff Williams a summary of each month's activities and expenditures. When the budgeting project was stopped, Williams handed the drafts back to his young assistant: "Good ideas, Don, but we'll have to wait."

It seemed to Taylor that IDC's rapid growth had led to undue confusion in the accounting departments. Mr. Williams would ask Taylor to "check on that figure" or "find out who authorized that expenditure" and Taylor would be unable to get the required information. A disturbing pattern was emerging. The IDC controller and his assistants seemed helpful and cooperative, but the data, they explained, was "in the computer" or "unavailable." Jeff Williams didn't seem surprised when Taylor reported his failures. "This whole place is a mess," the young president would remark, "and I think Dumont likes it that way."

Taylor also learned from Wendel Toms that Robert Dumont and members of the brain trust were heavily invested in oil and gas ventures. Toms said he had seen a summary of these investments and "they were very profitable. . . .

Dumont doesn't always invest in the same properties that the IDC partnerships do." Taylor wondered if there was a conflict of interest.

The IDC drilling partnership that "closed" on October 30 was the largest in the company's history, amounting to over $13 million. During the spring and summer of 1971, IDC had acquired several more small companies. One was involved in equipment leasing, one was a recreational land development company, and one was an electronics firm. IDC's common stock was selling at an all-time high of $80 per share.

During their first summer in Dallas, the Taylors had become close friends with Mike and Sheila Hull. Mike Hull was editor of a large Dallas newspaper and he and Don Taylor enjoyed playing tennis together. "One of these days, Don, you're going to have to tell me about IDC. Dumont's a mystery here in town. Nobody really knows how he makes all that money." Don Taylor heard himself reply that he, too, was often mystified by IDC's success.

The December Meeting

In December, Robert Dumont called a special meeting to review the financial position of all of the IDC subsidiaries. The meeting was to be held on a Sunday and Jeff Williams called Don Taylor on Friday night to ask him to attend the meeting in his absence. "Rosenberg, Stein, and Halpern are getting all the figures together. All you have to do is show up, listen, and report back to me. Dumont won't be there." Taylor was flattered and excited to be included in such a high-level session. On Sunday morning Stein, Rosenberg, and Halpern were in jocular moods, but Taylor immediately recognized that their joking was a sign of nervousness. One after another IDC's operations were reviewed. Surprisingly, all seemed to be in great need of working capital. Halpern, a CPA, rapidly recited the facts and figures. Even while reporting increasing profits, almost all operating entities were short of cash. Taylor was shocked. He was acting as the informal secretary of the meeting and, after almost two hours of discussion, sadly announced that almost $20 million would be needed by January 30 if IDC was to continue operating as it had in the past. The current oil and gas partnership was not selling well. Only $900,000 had been raised to date and the recent $13 million partnership was, in actuality, only $4 million. Robert Dumont had personally invested almost $8 million to "boost" the figure to record levels.

Taylor also learned that many of the IDC drilling programs had experienced very poor operating performances. Little oil and gas was being pumped and more and more investors were requesting that IDC "buy them out." In the past, IDC had "bought out" old partners with funds raised for new partnerships. This practice was disclosed in the prospectus, but it required that new partnerships be ever larger so sufficient money would be available to buy out old partnership interests as well as to drill new wells. Brian Rosenberg explained the crisis: "We now have almost $1 million of partnership interests to be bought out. If our current partnership is closed with, say $2 million, then 50 percent of the money will have to go toward buying out old interests. The tax deductions have already been taken on these old interests, so the current partnerships will have a terrible tax shelter potential. Investors will only get a 30 percent write-off. We'll be dead!"

Don Taylor asked why the old partnerships were valued so high, if so little oil and gas were being discovered and pumped. "Well," smiled Halpern, "the 'cash surrender values' may be a bit overstated. But that's what investors look at when they decide to invest. The higher the cash surrender values on past partnerships, the more credibility the current program will have." Taylor shook his head in disbelief.

Rosenberg, Halpern, Stein, and Taylor met for eight hours that Sunday. Once the basic

figures were out on the table and Taylor announced the $20 million "cash need," a feeling of camaraderie was felt by the four men. Halpern told Taylor that this was the first time many of these summary figures had ever been discussed at IDC. "Bob Dumont never allowed any one of us to have access to all the facts. That's how IDC has been run. None of the salesmen, for example, really knows how the partnerships are performing. And none of the oil guys knows how the money is raised."

When Taylor returned home at dinnertime, he was exhausted. He had agreed to write a summary report outlining the specific cash needs of each subsidiary. The other three executives had also asked him to write a brief report of their recommendations concerning a basic reorganization of IDC. Halpern, Rosenberg, and Stein believed that less emphasis should be placed on "promoting" oil and gas ventures and more placed on operating the ventures themselves. They also recommended that tighter financial controls be established and that Dumont delegate more responsibility to the operating heads of the various subsidiaries and divisions. Although he had not mentioned it at the meeting, Taylor was sure his recent ideas for improved control and reporting would go a long way toward solving these problems.

After thinking about the meeting, Taylor sat down after dinner and organized his thoughts. He was still in a state of shock, but there was more to it than just the financial crisis. Dumont's brain trust had carefully reviewed the cash needs and had concluded that, by cutting back in certain areas and drawing on IDC's commercial lines of credit, the necessary funds could be made available. And their willingness to recommend organizational changes was encouraging. He was excited about the possibilities of implementing his reporting system. But, Taylor realized, they had completely ignored the more basic moral implications of the meeting's disclosures. Taylor listed the items that bothered him the most:

• Cash surrender values were "a bit overstated" (remark by Halpern).

• Dumont personally commingled his own funds with those of his IDC companies, often lending them money or borrowing from them (a handwritten footnote to one of Halpern's financial statements where he admitted that even he didn't have up-to-date and complete figures on these "particular transactions").

• Partnership funds were "temporarily" used by other IDC operations from time to time. One of the partnerships formed in 1971 was still "owed" $4 million by the newly acquired IDC real estate company. (When Rosenberg stated this fact in the meeting, Stein had mumbled that "he didn't want to hear about that sort of thing.")

• Partnerships were buying more and more of their oil and gas properties from a little-known IDC subsidiary, which was "marking up" the properties as much as 100 percent. (This remark was made by Rosenberg and both he and Halpern refused to discuss it further when Taylor casually asked them to explain how this operated.)

On Tuesday, when Jeff Williams flew in from Los Angeles, Taylor showed him a draft of the meeting report. "Dumont will never go for the reorganization," he stated. "You guys must have had a ball." Taylor asked if he could have dinner with Williams "to go over some other things that were discussed." Jeff Williams smiled and asked, "Did you get into the ripoffs? Is that what's worrying you? Yeah, let's have dinner."

Over dinner that night, Taylor described his impressions of "the facts behind the facts" to his boss. Mr. Williams admitted that he was aware of many of the "questionable" dealings and conflicts of interest. "This kind of thing goes on all the time in the oil business. One company sells another a dog; six months later it does the other company a favor and it all evens out. Dumont knows what he's doing and he calls the shots around here." Williams stated that his main concern was to protect the investors who were being "screwed" in the IDC drilling funds. "When I first joined IDC, George Hart (manager of the Tulsa operations office) came to me and described the way Dumont ran the company. I figured I could clean it up a little and we would be OK. But Dumont and his brainboys still make all the decisions. I can't seem to stop them from ripping off the partnerships, but I can limit the ripoff." Williams then explained how he had occasionally vetoed an intercompany deal that was especially "rotten." Dumont, he explained, had backed down when Williams threatened to resign. "Dumont wants to go out for another public offering of IDC stock and he knows that if I quit he'll have trouble getting a decent underwriter."

Taylor was disappointed with Jeff Williams' response to Taylor's disclosures. The president had voiced only mild indignation and portrayed himself as being virtually powerless to correct matters. However, at one point he had been quite firm. "Don, if you and I can tackle the problem of the lack of decent information around here, maybe we can *do* something! Your ideas about new reports and budgets might be the answer." Taylor wondered how other IDC employees felt. For the next 10 days he tried to engage other IDC executives in conversations about some of the practices he had learned about at the December meeting. As Taylor explained to his wife, "I'm beginning to think a lot of people either don't know about what's going on or know and just don't care."

Ten days after the Sunday meeting, Brian Rosenberg delivered the final draft of the report to Robert Dumont. He called Taylor the following day and said, "He's mad as hell at us for even discussing some of the topics.

None of our recommendations will be implemented and I'm supposed to collect and destroy all of our notes on the meeting. Let's just say the meeting never happened ... OK?"

Taylor felt completely let down and wondered if he should resign. He thought back to some of the comments Art Weaver had made: "Look, Don, they know what they're doing. I'm sure there's no real problem ... you just don't know all the facts. Stop worrying about things that you don't know about."

Dave Ford and Mr. Souring had taken another tack: "There's nothing to bother about that a little belt-tightening and money-raising won't cure. You and Jeff should stop looking for trouble and start selling IDC! Tell Williams to get out there and promote ... that's what we need."

Taylor remembered Jeff Williams' response to these comments: "Those two live in a fairy world. Stick around, Taylor, and help me fight that kind of thinking. Maybe we can tackle Dumont and keep him from ruining all of the partnerships."

But Taylor had little confidence in Jeff Williams' ability to reform IDC or Robert Dumont. "I don't doubt his sincerity," he sighed to his wife, "but Dumont won't ever let him make any *real* changes. Hell, Dumont is making too much money the way things are!"

Don Taylor was under great pressure. He knew he was backing himself into an uncomfortable corner. From one point of view his job was becoming a real challenge. He was anxious to try out his management ideas. From another point of view, it was turning sour. Too many people were too ignorant of too many transactions. The thought of leaving another job after only nine months added to his feeling of panic. He realized that he had few "hard facts" to confirm his suspicions of corporate wrongdoing, but it seemed that he ought to do something. His wife put it very bluntly: "If there is that kind of hanky-panky going on, you are a part of it. You can't just look the other way.... Can you?"

On the night of January 20, 1972, Taylor decided to write a report describing his suspicions of unethical IDC corporate behavior. At least writing it down would enable him to organize his thoughts. He had no idea whom the report would be for: The SEC? The IRS? A local DA? A newspaper? The IDC board of directors? Jeff Williams? Bob Dumont? Himself? Taylor swore silently to himself as he sat at his typewriter.

THE SERPENT WAS THERE

In 1979, a young woman who later graduated from the Harvard Business School was an unwitting participant in a medical tragedy in Trinidad and Tobago. This case first describes the accident and then explains how the woman and her co-workers reacted to it. It is told in her own words.

In 1981, I faced a serious ethical dilemma that arose from a failed surgical procedure.

It was an incident I will remember for the rest of my life. To this day I reflect on the

This case is based on a paper written by a recent MBA graduate of the Harvard Business School, and it has been partially disguised. It was prepared by Joseph Badaracco, Jr.

outcome and hope that the correct decision was made.

I was a nurse supervisor in charge of training an operating room hospital staff of locals in Trinidad and Tobago for World Health, Inc. This is a nonprofit American organization whose chief purpose is to provide modern treatment for surgical disorders suffered by residents of developing countries.

It was late on a Friday afternoon. The intense heat of the August day was finally dissipating when an elderly woman was wheeled into the operating room for a cataract removal, our last surgical procedure in an exhausting week.

The patient lay before us in the center of the sterile, green operating room. The tiles may have been what made the room appear deceivingly cool. Perhaps it was the empty quality of the room itself; only an instrument table and stark aluminum lamp, jutting out from the center ceiling, were visible. No back-up generator existed; it was a very primitive operating room. There was a damp quality to the air, like that of a closed basement on a humid summer day.

Dark and deeply furrowed like the soil she tilled, the patient's face reflected years of hardship. She had obviously never seen such a clean and modern medical facility before. Beneath the uncertainty and fear, her expression revealed years of oppression and severe poverty. Yet she radiated a sense of dignity that I could only appreciate but never fully comprehend.

Speaking Spanish, the highly trained young American surgeon gently assured the woman that this was a routine, simple, and painless operation; it would be over shortly. The student nurse reached for the woman's hand as the doctor promised that the sight in her left eye would soon be restored.

The surgeon, straddling a small black stool at the head of the surgical table, glanced at the instrument tray to his left. Hand outstretched, he paused for a moment, looked up, and asked where the local anesthetic was. The student nurse turned toward me; I nodded. She walked out of the operating room into a small stock room next door. Seconds later she returned with a small bottle. Resuming her position alongside me, she handed me a bottle whose label read "Lidocaine." I passed it to the surgeon for a third verification. I held the bottle up so the surgeon could withdraw the Lidocaine into a sterile syringe. He then injected the clear liquid through the long, needled syringe deeply into the patient's left tear duct.

Only the sound of a whirring fan broke the silence in that room. I felt a stream of tropical air brush my face momentarily as it rotated in its arc. I closed my eyes for an eternal moment.

The fan whirled by me again. Suddenly the woman began groaning and writhing in pain while lifting herself off the table. Purely out of reflex, I grabbed her upper arms — thinking how ironic it was that her arms were as slender as the stalks of sugar cane she spent her days harvesting. My thumb and forefinger touched while strongly encircling these arms. I forced her to resume a reclining position. She turned her head from side to side mumbling in Spanish. We tried to restrain her as she continued to shake her head frantically. Something was seriously wrong.

The fan continued in the wave of its arc, but now it was spreading a distinctive smell throughout the musty room. In an instant the young surgeon's eyes met mine, and mirrored the panic and fear there.

The surgeon froze. "Do you smell something?" I remember his question vividly.

"Formaldehyde." I replied without thinking.

The syringe slipped from the surgeon's grasp to the floor. "Irrigate her eye," he said in a quiet yet controling way. I ripped the seal from the sterile solution bottle and poured it into her eye. As he held her head firmly, I kept the colorless fluid gushing into her eye. It was no use; the intervening seconds were too long to save the eye from the sightless glaze that had now hardened over it.

The surgeon grasped the small bottle of Lidocaine, now lying empty on the tray. Pulling off his mask he held the bottle under his nose and then let it drop back alongside the unused instruments. We looked at each other, unable to move. This woman would never see again out of that eye. Her other eye remained shuttered by its cataract. We had injected formaldehyde directly into her eye. How could formaldehyde have gotten into the Lidocaine bottle?

I watched the surgeon pick up the phone and dial the familiar number of the chief surgeon's home residence. We stood in the now-empty operating room. Even the instrument tray was gone; no evidence pertaining to the recent events existed. I studied the surgeon's expression as the conversation ensued with our boss, aware of the cool tiles pressed against the bare skin on the back of my neck and legs as I leaned against the wall.

The circle of orange settled on top of the peaked mountains; sunlight was dimming and, hence, the heat diminished. The surgeon and I were silent as we drove up the winding, bumpy roads to the outskirts of the city. As we climbed higher our separation from the true existence of the people our work was designed to help grew. The surroundings were now beautiful; only the scent of flamingo trees in full bloom could be detected. We passed high forbidding iron gates, barely able to detect the exquisite colored tiles on the Victorian-styled rooftops nestled behind. We paused at the most impressive gate and honked. An armed guard ran toward us, paused, then unlocked the gate; we were allowed to enter the residence of the chief surgeon.

The sunset was magnificent from the veranda. The peaked mountains were blackened by the shadows. The sun had slipped behind them and left an orange disappearing rainbow.

How deceiving the beauty was. The sunset had blackened the poverty, one could not focus on what really lay below us in the city.

Following dinner, we became silent while the servant refilled our coffee cups. The chief surgeon nodded, and his wife quickly left through the ceiling-high French doors. He did not speak until her footsteps on the marble floor could no longer be heard. I watched and listened closely. Here was a man, highly trained in the States, board certified, and still teaching part-time at a medical school in Milwaukee. He knew of poverty; he understood poverty, but would not accept it as being inevitable. He had grown up in the city that we could no longer see clearly from this view. He understood this oppressive country, its culture, heritage, and the complexity of its leaders and people; his people. I could not imagine what those deep-set brown eyes had seen in their 60 years of existence; 60 years of unselfish dedication.

His words were quiet and firm. We all knew that someone on the clinic staff had made a gross mistake and mislabeled a bottle. He said that we could not undo the tragic mishap of that afternoon, but that we would have to think how best to handle the situation. He felt that no matter what course of action we took, in no way should we put ourselves or the continued practice of providing safe and clean surgery to locals at risk. We had restored the sight of hundreds of people and would help perhaps thousands more. The young surgeon and I did not say a word, knowing that, if this had occurred in the United States, our careers could well be over before they ever started. The three of us were dedicated to helping people, yet we had taken the eye of a woman.

We discussed the complexity of the day's tragedy late into the night. If the error were made public, there was a chance that the people who most desperately needed our care would stay away. The trust that had taken so long to establish would be broken. We also recognized that acknowledging the tragic incident could put our training program in jeopardy, thus denying local citizens the opportunity to learn medical skills. We considered the successes of our education program and the direct impact that we had made in improving both the health care system and the economy of Trinidad and Tobago. If made public, the reputation of the chief surgeon as well that of World Health, Inc., could be irreversibly damaged, through a mistake that we still did not have a full understanding of. The government had been trying to obstruct our teachings; they would now have reason to end the training program that was fully under way.

The toughest issue for each of us was that of honesty. By not admitting the tragic mistake to the woman or the community, in essence we were lying. This violated values that we all held dear. Yet we knew what might happen if we told the truth. Honesty seemed inconsistent with our dedication to providing outstanding medical care to all. Somehow, we had already made a grave error; would we make it worse or better by lying about it?

Together that night we made the difficult decision, one that we would live with for the rest of our lives, that we would let the incident pass without further comment. We agreed that halting our work would be a far greater tragedy than what occurred in that operating room.

As the formaldehyde was destroying her eye, in her agony the woman had cried out in Spanish, "Why is the serpent causing me so much pain?"

In voodoo, the serpent is the devil. Maybe in a sense the woman was right; the serpent was there that Friday afternoon. The woman will always believe this, as will the others in her village. Perhaps she was right. It could be that the serpent dwells in human errors and carelessness. It may be that the devil feeds on the lofty expectation placed on the most careful, highly trained, and ethical medical professionals. The serpent reminds us that they are human, too, and make errors from time to time. Should their careers be therefore ruined? Should their capacity for good vanish because the serpent appears from time to time? That seems to me to be a far greater evil than what happened in the operating room in Trinidad and Tobago that day. If fear of failure ends human attempts to do good, the devil will have won.

MORALITY AND CHARACTER

The passages in this note present fundamental ideas about the role of character, commitment, and self-creation in morality and ethical decision making. The viewpoints and arguments differ significantly from those presented in the

This note was prepared by Allen P. Webb and Joseph Badaracco, Jr.

Copyright © 1992 by the President and Fellows of Harvard College.

Harvard Business School note 393-037 (Revised 1993).

notes "Morality and Consequences" and "Morality and Duties." Many of the passages in this note are taken from the classic works of Aristotle and Confucius; others are drawn from the powerful, provocative writings of Friedrich Nietzsche.

Aristotle

The torch of classical Greek philosophy passed first from Socrates to Plato, who founded his academy in Athens, and then to Aristotle

(384–322 B.C.), who became a member of Plato's academy at the age of 17. Upon Plato's death in 347 B.C., Aristotle departed for Macedon, where he tutored Alexander the Great. Then in 334 B.C., he returned to Athens to found a school of his own.

Unlike Plato, who immortalized Socrates' dialogues in *The Republic* and other works, Aristotle often disagreed with his mentor. Aristotle was particularly critical of Plato's belief that reason alone was sufficient to attain virtue. The passages below, from *Nicomachean Ethics,* emphasize the role that intuition, experience, habit, and integrity play both in moral development and in the cultivation of prudence, justice, courage, and temperance, which were Aristotle's four virtues.

Virtue, then, is of two sorts, virtue of thought and virtue of character. Virtue of thought arises and grows mostly from teaching, and hence needs experience and time. Virtue of character results from habit [ethos]; hence its name "ethical," slightly varied from "ethos."[1]

. . . . If something arises in us by nature, we first have the capacity for it, and later display the activity. This is clear in the case of the senses; for we did not acquire them by frequent seeing or hearing, but already had them when we exercised them, and did not get them by exercising them.

Virtues, by contrast, we acquire, just as we acquire crafts, by having previously activated them. For we learn a craft by producing the same product that we must produce when we have learned it, becoming builders, for example, by building and harpists by playing the harp; so also, then, we become just by doing just actions, temperate by doing temperate actions, brave by doing brave actions.[2]

To sum up, then, in a single account: A state of character arises from the repetition of similar activities. Hence we must display the right activities, since differences in these imply corresponding differences in the states. It is not unimportant, then, to acquire one sort of habit or another, right from our youth; rather, it is very important, indeed all-important.[3]

* * * * *

. . . Both excessive and deficient exercises ruin strength; and likewise, too much or too little eating or drinking ruins health, while the proportionate amount produces, increases, and preserves it.

The same is true, then, of temperance, bravery, and the other virtues. For if, for example, someone avoids and is afraid of everything, standing firm against nothing, he becomes cowardly, but if he is afraid of nothing at all and goes to face everything, he becomes rash. Similarly, if he gratifies himself with every pleasure and refrains from none, he becomes intemperate, but if he avoids them all, as boors do, he becomes some sort of insensible person. Temperance and bravery, then, are ruined by excess and deficiency but preserved by the mean. . . . Refraining from pleasures make us become temperate, and when we have become temperate we are most able to refrain from pleasures. And it is similar with bravery; habituation in disdaining what is fearful and in standing firm against it makes us become brave, and when we have become brave we shall be most able to stand firm.[4]

. . . We must take the intermediate that is relative to us. For if, for example, 10 pounds are a lot for someone to eat, and 2 pounds a little, it does not follow that the trainer will prescribe 6, since this might also be either a little or a lot for the person who is to take it—for Milo [the athlete] a little, but for the beginner in gymnastics a lot; and the same is true for running and wrestling. In this way every scientific expert avoids excess and deficiency and seeks and chooses what is intermediate—but intermediate relative to us, not in the object.[5]

[1] Aristotle, *Nicomachean Ethics,* trans. by Terence Irwin (Indianapolis: Hackett Publishing Company, 1985), p. 33.
[2] Ibid., p. 34.
[3] Ibid., p. 35.
[4] Ibid., pp. 35–7.
[5] Ibid., p. 43.

Hence it is hard work to be excellent, since in each case it is hard work to find what is intermediate; e.g., not everyone, but only one who knows, finds the midpoint in a circle. So also getting angry, or giving and spending money, is easy and anyone can do it; but doing it to the right person, in the right amount, at the right time, for the right end, and in the right way is no longer easy, nor can everyone do it. Hence doing these things well is rare, praiseworthy, and fine.[6]

In summary, then, if we do these things we shall best be able to reach the intermediate condition. But no doubt this is hard, especially in particular cases, since it is not easy to define the way we should be angry, with whom, about what, for how long; for sometimes, indeed, we ourselves praise deficient people and call them mild, and sometimes praise quarrelsome people and call them manly. Still, we are not blamed if we deviate a little in excess or deficiency from doing well, but only if we deviate a long way, since then we are easily noticed.[7]

All this makes it clear, then, that in every case the intermediate state is praised, but we must sometimes incline towards the excess, sometimes toward the deficiency; for that is the easiest way to succeed in hitting the intermediate condition and doing well.[8]

Martha Nussbaum, university professor at Brown University, is a modern interpreter and proponent of Aristotle's ideas. The passages below are from her essay, "The Discernment of Perception: An Aristotelian Conception of Private and Public Rationality."

A great part of *rational* deliberation will be concerned with questions about whether a certain course of action here and now really counts as realizing some important value (say, courage or friendship) that is a prima facie part of her idea of the good life; or even whether a certain way of acting (a certain relationship — type or

particular) really counts as the sort of thing she wants to include in her conception of a good life at all. Whether this friendship, this love, this courageous risk, really is something without which her life will be less valuable and less complete. For this sort of question, it seems obvious that there is no mathematical answer; and the only procedure to follow is (as we shall see) to imagine all the relevant features as well and fully and concretely as possible, holding them up against whatever intuitions and emotions and plans and imaginings we have brought into the situation or can construct in it. There is really no shortcut at all; or none that is not corrupting. The most we have by way of a theory of correct procedure is the account of good deliberation given by Aristotle himself, which is deliberately thin, referring for its content to the account of character. It not only does not tell us how to compute the mean, it tells us that there is no general true answer to this question. Beyond this, the content of rational choice must be supplied by nothing less messy than experience and stories of experience. Among stories of conduct, the most true and informative will be works of literature, biography, and history; the more abstract the story gets, the less rational it is to use it as one's only guide. Good deliberation is ike theatrical or musical improvisation, where what counts is flexibility, responsiveness, and an openness to the external; to rely on an algorithm here is not only insufficient, it is a sign of immaturity and weakness.[9]

. . . Frequently, leaders, like private citizens, will be confronted with unpalatable moral choices, choices in which there is no loss-free, and perhaps even no guilt-free, course available. We want leaders who will be able to make tough necessary choices in such situations, preferring *A* to *B* or *B* to *A*. We do not want the presence of a recognized dilemma to prevent

---

[6] Ibid., p. 51.
[7] Ibid., p. 52.
[8] Ibid., p. 53.

---

[9] Martha C. Nussbaum, "The Discernment of Perception: An Aristotelian Conception of Private and Public Rationality," in *Love's Knowledge: Essays on Philosophy and Literature* (New York: Oxford University Press, 1990), p. 74. Copyright © 1990 by Martha C. Nussbaum. Reprinted by permission of Oxford University Press, Inc.

them from evincing a preference. But we also want them to preserve and publicly display enough of the Aristotelian intuitions of the ordinary private person that they will say, here is a situation in which we are violating an important human value. . . . I believe, with Aristotle, that . . . superior clarity and simplicity does not make things better; that rising above a human problem does not solve it. . . .[10]

* * * * *

Aristotle illustrates the idea of ethical flexibility in a vivid and famous metaphor. He tells us that a person who makes each choice by appeal to some antecedent general principle held firm and inflexible for the occasion is like an architect who tries to use a straight ruler on the intricate curves of a fluted column. No real architect does this. Instead, following the lead of the builders of Lesbos, he will measure with a flexible strip of metal, the Lesbian Rule, that "Bends to the shape of the stone and is not fixed.". . . Good deliberation, like the Lesbian Rule, accommodates itself to the shape that it finds, responsibly and with respect for complexity. . . . Excellent choice cannot be captured in general rules, because it is a matter of fitting one's choice to the complex requirements of a concrete situation, taking all of its contextual features into account. . . .[11]

. . . Aristotle has no objection to the use of general guidelines of this sort for certain purposes. They have a useful role to play so long as they keep their place. Rules and general procedures can be aids in moral development, since people who do not yet have practical wisdom and insight need to follow rules that summarize the wise judgments of others. Then, too, if there is not time to formulate a fully concrete decision in the case at hand, it is better to follow a good summary rule or a standardized decision procedure than to make a hasty and inadequate contextual choice. . . . But Aristotle's point in all these cases is that the rule or

algorithm represents a falling off from full practical rationality, not its flourishing or completion. . . . [12]

* * * * *

Good perception is a full recognition or acknowledgment of the nature of the practical situation; the whole personality sees it for what it is. The agent who discerns intellectually that a friend is in need or that a loved one has died, but who fails to respond to these facts with appropriate sympathy or grief, clearly lacks a part of Aristotelian virtue. It seems right to say, in addition, that a part of discernment or perception is lacking. This person doesn't really, or doesn't fully, *see* what has happened, doesn't recognize it in a full-blooded way or take it in. We want to say that she is merely saying the words. "He needs my help," or "she is dead," but really doesn't yet fully *know* it, because the emotional part of cognition is lacking. And it isn't just that sometimes we need the emotions to *get to* the right (intellectual) view of the situation; this is true, but not the entire story. Neither is it just that the emotions supply extra, praiseworthy elements external to cognition but without which virtue is incomplete. The emotions are themselves modes of vision, or recognition. Their responses are part of what is knowing, that is truly recognizing or acknowledging, *consists in.*[13]

Stuart Hampshire is a professor of philosophy at Stanford University. In the passages below, he draws heavily upon Aristotle's ideas to explain morality in terms of individual integrity, defined in terms of abiding personal commitments to particular virtues and ways of life.

This is the approved practice of the people to whom I belong, and to whom I am committed, and I find nothing harmful in it: This is an essential part of the way of life to which I am

---

[10] Ibid., pp. 65–6.
[11] Ibid., pp. 69–71.

[12] Ibid., p. 73.
[13] Ibid., p. 79.

committed and it is not an evil way of life: This has always been our practice, and, properly understood, it is not unfair, and it is important in our way of life: This is how I feel, and how I have always felt: To change now would be to repudiate my past, and I find nothing unjust or harmful in the practice. These are justifications in a moral context, all of which appeal to the agent's sense of his own identity and character as a person and of his history, which partially determines his sense if identity: This is my ground and I must stand on it: I do not claim that everyone everywhere must do what I must do: but this is my character, and, because it is, I must act in this way. Such justifications are sometimes spoken of as appeals to integrity, a distinct virtue to be ranked with justice and benevolence.[14]

* * * * *

There are extreme situations, not rare in this century, in which the subject reasonably sees himself as confronted with a choice between two different ways of life, which cannot be combined into one; and this great choice may be concentrated, and usually is concentrated, in a particular conflict of duties on a particular occasion, and it may never come up for consideration in an abstract way and as a general issue.[15]

The notion of commitment has its place here. The young man is required to choose between the commitment to a life, or to a considerable part of a life, as a resister, as a member of a revolutionary movement, and as the servant of an overriding political cause, and on the other side the commitment to a life of decent usefulness and of family loyalty. The first commitment will demand the virtues of courage above all, of dedication, selflessness, also of loyalty; it will also call for violence, skill in deceit, readiness to kill, and probably also false friendship and occasional injustice. The second will demand the

virtues of friendship and affection, gentleness, justice, loyalty, and honesty; it will also call for acquiescence in public injustice, some passivity in the face of the suffering of others, some lowering of generous enterprise and energy because of political repression. These are two different ways of life, because they demand different dispositions and habits of mind, different social settings, and different ends of action. The young man has to choose between two possible types of person, each with his own set of virtues and defects, now incompatible sets.[16]

* * * * *

The implication is that the correct behavior should not be the outcome of careful and laborious calculation and reflection; it should be immediate, spontaneous, governed by intuition. Something similar would be claimed for the proper command of a language; one should be able to speak spontaneously and intuitively, and to select the right word without reflection and without recourse to dictionary or grammar. Also the swift and intuitive choice of the right words is often a matter of good manners and sometimes also a moral matter; for instance, as clearly expressing the right feeling.[17]

Aristotle allowed very little difference in this respect between morality and good manners. Both should be fully internalized as stable dispositions which lead, effortlessly and immediately, to reasonable conduct and to reasonable assessments of situations demanding action, and to making the assessments without too much brooding and effort.[18]

Confucius

The writings of Confucius and his students critically influenced political, social, and economic thought in China for more than 2,000 years. The excerpts below were drawn from three of the "Four Books" of Confucian thought. The *Analects,* a record of

---

[14] Stuart Hampshire, *Morality and Conflict* (Cambridge, Mass.: Harvard University Press, Copyright © 1983), p. 8. Reprinted by permission.
[15] Ibid., p. 33.

[16] Ibid., p. 33.
[17] Ibid., p. 103.
[18] Ibid., pp. 103–4.

conversations between Confucius and his colleagues, is the oldest of the four. It was probably written sometime soon after Confucius's death in 479 B.C. Scholars believe that Tsŭ-ssŭ, Confucius's grandson, and Tsêng Shên, another disciple, wrote two of the other books, *The Doctrine of the Mean* and *The Great Learning,* respectively. In the 12th century A.D., Chu Hsi formally compiled the Four Books. Beginning in 1313, the Four Books became the basis for questions on the state civil service examination, a status they retained until 1919, in somewhat modified form.[19] A number of themes run through the Four Books. Among them are the necessity of each individual finding and living consistently with his or her own "Mean" or "Way" and the importance of community.

Confucius said to Zichan, a famous prime minister of the state of Zheng, "The way of exemplary people is fourfold. They are deferential in their own conduct, respectful in their service of employers, generous in taking care of people, and just in employing people."[20]

Thus it is that the superior man is quiet and calm, waiting for the appointments of *Heaven,* while the mean man walks in dangerous paths, looking for lucky occurrences. The Master said, "In archery we have something like the way of the superior man. When the archer misses the centre of the target, he turns round and seeks for the cause of his failure in himself."[21]

It is said in the Book of Poetry, "Looked at in your apartment, be there free from shame as being exposed to the light of heaven." Therefore, the superior man, even when he is not moving, has *a feeling of* reverence, and while he speaks not, he has *the feeling of* truthfulness.[22]

Confucius said, "People make mistakes according to their individual type. When you observe their errors, you can tell if people are humane."[23]

* * * * *

The duties of universal obligation are five, and the virtues wherewith they are practised are three. The duties are those between sovereign and minister, between father and son, between husband and wife, between elder brother and younger, and those belonging to the intercourse of friends. Those five are the duties of universal obligation. Knowledge, magnanimity, and energy, these three, are the virtues universally binding. And the means by which they carry *the duties* into practice is singleness. Some are born with the knowledge of *those duties;* some know them by study; and some acquire the knowledge after a painful feeling of their ignorance. But the knowledge being possessed, it comes to the same thing. Some practice them with a natural ease; some from a desire for their advantages; and some by strenuous effort. But the achievement being made, it comes to the same thing.[24]

The ancients who wished to illustrate illustrious virtue throughout the kingdom, first ordered well their own States. Wishing to order well their States, they first regulated their families. Wishing to regulate their families, they first cultivated their persons. Wishing to cultivate their persons, they first rectified their hearts. Wishing to rectify their hearts, they first sought to be sincere in their thoughts. Wishing to be sincere in their thoughts, they first extended to the utmost their knowledge. Such extension of knowledge lay in the investigation of things.

---

[19] Li Fu Chen and Shih Shun Liu (translator), *The Confucian Way* (London: Unwin Brothers, Ltd., 1986), pp. 1–4. Arthur Waley (translator), *The Analects of Confucius* (New York: Vintage Books, 1989), pp. 13–17.

[20] *Analects,* Book V, Chapter 16. Translation by Thomas Cleary in *The Essential Confucius* (New York: Harper San Francisco of Harper Collins, Publishers, 1992), p. 31. Copyright © 1992 by Thomas Cleary. Reprinted by permission of Harper Collins Publishers, Inc.

[21] *The Doctrine of the Mean,* Chapter XIV.4-.5. Translation by James Legge in *Confucius: Confucian Analects, The Great Learning & The Doctrine of the Mean* (New York: Dover Publications, 1971), p. 395.

---

[22] *The Doctrine of the Mean,* Chapter XXXIII.3 in Legge, p. 432.

[23] *Analects,* Book IV, Chapter 7 in Cleary, p. 95.

[24] *The Doctrine of the Mean,* Chapter XX.8-9 in Legge, pp. 406–7.

Things being investigated, knowledge became complete. Their knowledge being complete, their thoughts were sincere. Their thoughts being sincere, their hearts were then rectified. Their hearts being rectified, their persons were cultivated. Their persons being cultivated, their families were regulated. Their families being regulated, their States were rightly governed. Their States being rightly governed, the whole kingdom was made tranquil and happy.

From the Son of Heaven down to the mass of the people, all must consider the cultivation of the person the root of *everything besides.*[25]

Tu Wei-Ming is a professor of Chinese history and philosophy at Harvard University. His book *Centrality and Commonality* focuses on only one of the Four Books, *The Doctrine of the Mean* (or *Chung-yung*). In his work, Tu Wei-Ming emphasizes the interaction in Confucian thought of individual moral development and the sound community.

The multiplicity of its ["The Way's"] models as well as the complexity of its rules and procedures renders it unrealistic even to attempt to formulate an all-embracing pattern of behavior universally applicable to those aspiring to become profound.[26] . . . the Way of the profound person can be conceived in terms of two interrelated dimensions—conscientiousness (chung) within and altruism (shu) without.[27]

*　*　*　*　*

For the traditional Confucian, ancestral worship by filial sons may be taken as the microcosm of an ideal society. . . . To respect the old and to honor the dead is to show special concern for the common origin of all. . . . Society so conceived is not an adversary system consisting of pressure groups but a fiduciary community based on mutual trust.[28]

Since a person in the Confucian tradition is always conceived as a center of relationships, the more one penetrates into one's inner self, the more one will be capable of realizing the true nature of one's human-relatedness. Accordingly, "self-watchfulness when alone," as a spiritual cultivation, far from being a quest for the idiosyncrasy of an atomized individual, is intended to reach levels of that reality which underlies common humanity. The profound person does not practice self-watchfulness for the intrinsic value of being alone. In fact, he sees little significance in solitariness, unless it is totally integrated into the structure of social relations.[29] . . . Human relatedness is certainly an integral part of self-cultivation, but one's ability to maintain continuous association with other human beings is predicated on an ever-deepening realization of one's inner morality.[30]

The profound person, through a long and unceasing process of delving into his own ground of existence, discovers his true subjectivity not as an isolated selfhood but as a great source of creative transformation. As the inner sincerity of the profound person brings forth an unflagging supply of moral and spiritual nourishment for the people around him, the Confucian ideal of society (the fiduciary community) gradually comes into being. The continuous well-being of such a society depends on the cultivation of the profound person in an ever-broadening net of human relations, for self-realization in *Chung-yung's* view necessarily involves a process of fulfilling the nature of others. Thus, the great foundation and the universal path of the world are both centered on the transforming influence of the profound person. The hidden and subtle way by which the brilliant virtue of the profound person radiates outward is colorless and shapeless, but, like the fecundity of heaven and earth, its creative power is visible and manifest everywhere. Yet, as *Chung-yung* strongly maintains,

---

[25] *The Great Learning,* "The Text of Confucius," part 4 in Legge, pp. 357–8.
[26] Tu Wei-Ming, *Centrality and Commonality: An Essay on Confucian Religiousness* (Albany: State University of New York Press, 1989), p. 32.
[27] Ibid., p. 34.

[28] Ibid., p. 48.
[29] Ibid., p. 27.
[30] Ibid., p. 51.

reality in its all-embracing fullness authenticates the concrete manifestation of common human existence as well as the most mysterious function of the universe. And it is through self-knowledge derived from ordinary experience that the most profound wisdom unfolds.[31]

* * * * *

The Confucians take the Greek dictum that an unexamined life is not worth living one step further and contend that an uncultivated life is disrespectful of oneself and dehumanizing to others. . . . A good Confucian must not take the human way for granted. Following our Heaven-ordained nature requires strenuous effort at self-transformation.[32] . . . Confucian religiousness begins with the phrase "ultimate self-transformation," which implies a critical moment in a person's life as well as a continuous process of spiritual cultivation.[33]

Nietzsche

Friedrich Nietzsche (1844–1900) was a German philosopher whose life and work have generated great controversy and exerted enormous influence over modern Western thought. Although Nietzsche never completed his dissertation or qualifying exams, he became a full professor at the University of Basel at the age of 26. After 20 years of prolific writing, Nietzsche became insane in 1889 and remained so until his death.

During this period, his sister Elisabeth planted the seeds of his association with German nationalism and, eventually, Nazism. Elisabeth was married to Bernhard Förster, a highly visible anti-Semitic agitator. Nietzsche was repulsed by Förster's activities, and once in a letter warned his sister against connecting him in any way with her husband's work: "It is a matter of honor to me to be absolutely clean and unequivocal regarding anti-Semitism, namely opposed, as I am in my writings."[34]

After becoming insane, however, Nietzsche was unable to defend either himself or his work. Elisabeth cobbled together passages from his private notebooks to produce *The Will to Power,* first published in 1901 and significantly expanded in 1906. Nietzsche had further refined many of the ideas from his notebooks in other works; Elisabeth's compilation clouded the world's perception of his views, particularly because she tried to pass it off as his magnum opus. Later, she ". . . doggedly persuaded the Nazis to accept her brother as their philosopher. . ."[35] By selectively quoting passages taken grossly out of their proper context, Nazi "intellectuals," such as Alfred Bäumler, Heinrich Härtle, and Richard Oehler, painted Nietzsche's work as scholarly justification for the Third Reich. A fair reading of Nietzsche would have revealed that he violently opposed racism, anti-Semitism, arch-nationalism, and pan-Germanism—the standard components of Nazi ideology.

The wrongful appropriation of Nietzsche by a few Nazi philosopher-quacks should not obscure his role in the development of Western thought. Nietzsche's ideas about power, religion, and human nature were startlingly original. Perhaps Nietzsche's most enduring legacy was his contribution to the existentialist movement in European philosophy. By emphasizing that everything is, in one way or another, an interpretation of reality, Nietzsche paved the way for future existential philosophers, artists, and deconstructionist literary critics. The passages below display Nietzsche's typical style,

---

[31] Ibid., pp. 90–91.
[32] Ibid., p. 100.
[33] Ibid., p. 116.

---

[34] Walter Kaufmann, *Nietzsche: Philosopher, Psychologist, Antichrist* (Princeton, N.J.: Princeton University Press, 1974), p. 45. This brief sketch of Nietzsche draws upon chapters 1 and 10 of Kaufmann's book, as well as on Kaufmann's biographical sketch in *The Encyclopedia of Philosophy,* volumes 5 and 6, ed. Paul Edwards (New York: Collier-Macmillan and the Free Press, 1972), pp. 504–13.
[35] Kaufmann, 1974, p. 46.

which relied on short, suggestive, often provocative statements open to varied interpretation. The first is perhaps the most famous of all Nietzsche's statements.

> Thus spoke the devil to me once: "God, too, has his hell: that is his love of man." And most recently I heard him say this: "God is dead; God died of his pity for man."[36]

* * * * *

> Against positivism, which halts at phenomena—"There are only *facts*"—I would say: No, facts is precisely what there is not, only interpretations. We cannot establish any fact "in itself": perhaps it is folly to want to do such a thing.[37]

* * * * *

> "This is *my* way; where is yours?"—thus I answered those who asked me "the way." For *the* way—that does not exist.[38]

* * * * *

> Oh, my friends, that your self be in your deed as the mother is in her child—let that be *your* word concerning virtue.[39]

* * * * *

> Whether one does not have the right to account all great men *evil?* This cannot be shown in a pure state in all individual cases. Often they have been capable of masterly dissimulation and assumed the outward forms and gestures of great virtues. Often they honored virtue seriously and with a passionate hardness against themselves, but out of cruelty: seen from a distance this is deceptive. Many misunderstood themselves; not infrequently a great task calls forth great qualities, e.g., justice. The essential point is: the greatest perhaps also possess

great virtues, but in that case also their opposites. I believe that it is precisely through the presence of opposites and the feelings they occasion that the great man, *the bow with the great tension,* develops.

> The highest man would have the greatest multiplicity of drives, in the relatively greatest strength that can be endured. Indeed, where the plant "man" shows himself strongest one finds instincts that conflict powerfully (e.g., in Shakespeare), but are controlled.[40]

* * * * *

> Zarathustra* replied: "Why should that frighten you? But it is with man as it is with the tree. The more he aspires to the height and light, the more strongly do his roots strive earthward, downward, into the dark, the deep—into evil."[41]

* * * * *

> *One thing is needful.* —To "give style" to one's character—a great, a rare art! It is practiced by those who survey all the strengths and weaknesses of their nature and then fit them into an artistic plan until every one of them appears as art and reason and even weaknesses delight the eye. Here a large mass of second nature has been added; there a piece of original nature has been removed—both times through long practice and daily work at it. Here the ugly that could not be removed is concealed; there it has been reinterpreted and made sublime. Much that is vague and resisted shaping has been saved and exploited for distant views; it is meant to beckon toward the far and immeasurable. In the end, when the work is finished, it becomes evident how the constraint of a single taste governed and formed everything large and small. Whether this taste was good or bad is less

---

[36] *Thus Spoke Zarathustra,* Second Part, "On the Pitying."

[37] *The Will to Power,* Book III, 481.

[38] *Thus Spoke Zarathustra,* Third Part, "On the Spirit of Gravity."

[39] *Thus Spoke Zarathustra,* 2nd Part, "On the Virtuous."

[40] *The Will to Power,* Book IV, 966–7.

* Zarathustra was the central figure in Nietzsche's monumental *Also Sprach Zarathustra* (Thus Spoke Zarathustra). Essentially a mouthpiece for Nietzsche, Zarathustra was said to have descended to earth in order to tell men how to live.

[41] *Thus Spoke Zarathustra:* First Part, "On the Tree on the Mountainside."

important than one might suppose, if only it was a single taste!⁴²

What is it, fundamentally, that allows us to recognize *who has turned out well?* That a well-turned-out person pleases our senses, that he is carved from wood that is hard, delicate, and at the same time smells good. He has a taste only for what is good for him; his pleasure, his delight cease where the measure of what is good for him is transgressed. He guesses what remedies avail against what is harmful; he exploits bad accidents to his advantage; what does not kill him makes him stronger. Instinctively, he collects from everything he sees, hears, lives through, *his* sum: he is a principle of selection, he discards much. He is always in his own company, whether he associates with books, human beings, or landscapes; he honors by *choosing,* by *admitting,* by *trusting.*⁴³

* * * * *

For *that* is what I am through and through: reeling, reeling, reeling in, raising up, raising, a raiser, cultivator, and disciplinarian, who once counseled himself, not for nothing: Become who you are!⁴⁴

Alexander Nehamas, a professor of philosophy at the University of Pennsylvania, has devoted much of his career to the study of Nietzsche. His book *Nietzsche: Life as Literature,* from which the passages below are drawn, is a modern reinterpretation of Nietzsche's ideas. Nehamas argues that Nietzsche looked at the world in a manner similar to how one might read and interpret literature, and that he sought, through his work, to create himself as a literary figure.

The self, according to Nietzsche, is not a constant, stable entity. On the contrary, it is

something one becomes, something, he would even say, one constructs. A person consists of absolutely everything one thinks, wants, and does. But a person worthy of admiration, a person who has (or is) a self, is one whose thoughts, desires, and actions are not haphazard but are instead connected to one another in the intimate way that indicates in all cases the presence of style. A self is just a set of coherently connected episodes, and an admirable self, as Nietzsche insists again and again, consists of a large number of powerful and conflicting tendencies that are controlled and harmonized. Coherence, of course, can also be produced by weakness, mediocrity, and one-dimensionality. But style, which is what Nietzsche requires and admires, involves controlled multiplicity and resolved conflict. It still, however, does not seem to require what we generally consider moral character.⁴⁵

* * * * *

The free spirits know that their mode of life is their own creation and that it is not the only mode that is necessary or even possible. They therefore do not want to impose it on others, and they do not try to cling to it once it has outlived its usefulness: "The view that *truth is found* and that ignorance and error are at an end is one of the most potent seductions there is. Supposing it is believed, then the will to examination, investigation, caution, experiment is paralyzed: it can even count as criminal, namely as *doubt* concerning truth." . . . The free spirits do not believe in "the" truth . . . and they therefore do not believe that it can be found once and for all. They will therefore refuse to privilege the practices in which they are engaged. Aware that nothing about them need remain the same over time, and that nothing about the world will, the free spirits are "at home, or at least . . . guests, in many countries of the spirit;

---

⁴² *The Gay Science,* Book IV, 290.

⁴³ *Ecce Homo,* "Why I am so Wise," 2.

⁴⁴ *Thus Spoke Zarathustra,* Fourth Part, 1, in Alexander Nehamas, *Nietzsche: Life as Literature* (Cambridge, Mass.: Harvard University Press, 1985), p. 168.

⁴⁵ Reprinted by permission of the publishers from *Nietzsche: Life as Literature* by Alexander Nehamas (Cambridge, Mass.: Harvard University Press, 1985), p. 7. Copyright © 1985 by the President and Fellows of Harvard College.

having escaped again and again from the musty agreeable nooks into which preference and prejudice, youth, origin, the accidents of people and books or even exhaustion from wandering seemed to have banished us. . . ."[46]

* * * * *

Nietzsche believed that the goal of every philosophical view is to present a picture of the world and a conception of values which makes a certain type of person possible and which allows it to prosper and to flourish. As we have already seen, he wrote: "We seek a picture of the world in that philosophy in which we feel freest; i.e., in which our most powerful drive feels free to function. This will also be the case with me!" . . . He believed that the evaluation of philosophical views is to a very great extent an evaluation of this type of agent. And he thought that, though all philosophers aim at presenting such a type, only he was aware of that fact.[47]

* * * * *

Thus we identify ourselves differently over time. And though, as is often the case with the voice of this state, the "I" always seems to refer to the same thing, the content to which it refers and the interests for which it speaks do not remain the same. It is constantly in the process of changing. . . . Amelie Rorty has used this same metaphor for the self. She urges that we think of the self not as a contemporary city built on a regular grid but more as a city of the Middle Ages, with many semi-independent neighborhoods, indirect ways of access from one point to another, and without a strong central municipal administration. She writes, "We can regard the agent self as a loose configuration of habits, habits of thought and perception and motivation and action, acquired at different stages, in the service of different ends."

The unity of the self, which therefore also constitutes its identity, is not something given

but something achieved, not a beginning but a goal.[48]

* * * * *

Becoming who one is, in Nietzsche's terms, excludes such complacency altogether: "All those who are 'in the process of becoming' must be furious when they perceive some satisfaction in this area, an impertinent 'retiring on one's laurels' or 'self-congratulation.'" . . . The creation of the self is not a static episode, a final goal which, once attained, forecloses the possibility of continuing to change and to develop.[49]

* * * * *

More important, however, is the fact that so long as we are alive, we are always finding ourselves in new and unforeseen situations; we constantly have new thoughts and desires, we continue to perform new actions. In their light we may at any point come to face the need to reinterpret, to reorganize, or even to abandon earlier ones. . . . It is not to cultivate stable character traits that make my reactions predictable and unsurprising. It is not simply to age, though aging is certainly connected with it: the young still have "the worst of tastes, the taste for the unconditional" and have not yet learned "to put a little art in their feelings and rather to risk trying even what is artificial — as the real artists of life do." Rather, it is to become flexible enough to use whatever I have done, do, or will do as elements within a constantly changing, never finally completed whole.[50]

* * * * *

What one is, then, is just what one becomes. In counseling himself to become who he is, Zarathustra becomes able to want to become what in fact he does become and not to want anything about it, about himself, to be different. To become what one is, we can see, is not to reach a specific new state and to stop becoming — it is

---

[46] Ibid., p. 70.
[47] Ibid., p. 128.

[48] Ibid., p. 182.
[49] Ibid., p. 188–9.
[50] Ibid., pp. 189–90.

not to reach a state at all. It is to identify one-self with all of one's actions, to see that everything one does (what one becomes) is what one is. In the ideal case it is also to fit all this into a coherent whole and to want to be everything that one is: it is to give style to one's character; to be, we might say, becoming.[51]

---

[51] Ibid., p. 191.

TARO YOSHIDA

I departed Boston on July 12 to Tokyo via Chicago. The Northwest flight from Chicago to Tokyo seemed the longest and gloomiest I had ever had.

I arrived at Tokyo International Airport without a minute of sleep. I found myself terribly nervous. It happened to be the notorious "Friday, the 13th." As soon as I finished check-out at the airport, I made a phone call to the personnel department. I made an appointment at 9 A.M. the next Monday the 16th. I was already so tense. As soon as I arrived at my home in Tokyo, I immediately went to bed.

Since my early age, I have always had a special feeling about teaching. I always wanted to become a teacher when I grew up. I guess that is because of my parents' influence. They both had been teachers. I find it funny to recall that I was confident to think that I could teach classes much better than my teacher when I was in my first grade. Since I started learning English in my seventh grade, I had been attracted by this entirely new Western language and decided to become an English teacher in the future. That dream brought me to study abroad in my 12th grade as an exchange student at a high school in New York for one year. However, having been exposed to a totally different culture, my interest was geared toward people and society, rather than merely learning a language.

In college, I majored in political science to understand different social structures of various countries, and I was actually encouraged by several of my professors to go to graduate school right after graduation. Notwithstanding, I was reluctant to follow that path, because graduate work in Japan is rather isolated from real society. There are not many interactions between the ivory tower and the real world, even in such a practical field as business. At that time, I was interested in business–government relations, and I thought I needed to have some industry experience. I decided to get a job instead of doing my masters degree right away. My rationale was that I could always go back to school later, whereas I could not join any big Japanese company after my graduate work because of the company's recruiting policy of hiring young BA holders.

The Japan Sangyo Bank (JSB) was the ideal choice for me because of its significant role as a leader of industrial finance. It has historically played a role as a coordinator between government and industry in Japan, and is one of the most respected financial institutions. Considering its corporate culture of valuing the big picture and strategic thinking, I firmly believe that JSB was the best place to work.

This case was prepared by Joseph Badaracco, Jr.

Copyright © 1991 by the President and Fellows of Harvard College.

Harvard Business School case 391-143.

I was assigned to the international business department, where I was engaged in trade finance and investment for the first two years. Then I was transferred to a newly opened branch in Osaka to generate business strategy to penetrate the conservative market as a new entrant and to engage in sales management of bank debentures. In spite of my initial academic interest, I became more and more inclined to actual business activities during this four-year period.

One day, my boss suggested that I take the examination for studying abroad with a two-year company sponsorship. Although I was enjoying my current work very much, study abroad appeared also attractive, because I was hoping to eventually work in one of the overseas branches. I could not help recalling my college days in which I was dreaming to study in the United States.

The in-house examination was very tough and competitive. The first day was English and a written exam on business and economics. Those who passed the first stage took the second day exams. They consisted of an interview with executives, performance appraisal, recommendations from your boss, and a physical exam. Selected were 15 candidates out of 150. I decided to apply for business school so that my study would be useful in my later business career at JSB. Harvard was my first choice, and I was accepted. My boss encouraged me "to absorb as much knowledge and skill as possible in order to become a future leader of the international division at JSB." I was grateful to my boss and my company for providing me with such a great educational opportunity and was determined to do my best.

As soon as I arrived in Boston, I attended Harvard Summer School to take financial accounting and statistics. What a beautiful campus it is! I remembered I had visited here once when I was a sophomore student, dreaming to study here someday. The dream came true. I appreciated my company again, especially when thinking that all my colleagues are working very hard day and night. I was determined to work as hard as my colleagues in Japan.

Business school started in September. Incredible pressure. How could a modest and reserved Japanese student ever compete with these most aggressive and competent sectionmates? After a while, as I got used to such a learning environment, the more I appreciated intellectual stimulation. Day by day, I felt my understanding become more solid, and my classroom participation felt more comfortable.

As I continued my study, I found myself being confused in terms of my career. Being in an academic environment have surely evoked my adoration toward academia, which had been dormant for years.

First, I was stimulated by the life style and performance of the academic people at the school. Business school professors have strong interface with the real world, either as consultants or as field researchers. I was quite impressed with the way American academics are truly in the field of business.

Second, I was unconsciously influenced by the attitudes of my sectionmates toward their career building. They came to the business school to try to find the best career for them. They seemed to build their own careers on their own responsibility. This was totally fresh for a Japanese like myself, being used to having our careers managed by the personnel department.

Third, I found it fascinating to study business phenomena from the sociological perspective. Such fields as multicultural management, organizational behavior in an international context, and comparative study of business and society deserved my investing my entire energy.

Conflict between the two forces—personal value and reality—emerged in my mind. I rediscovered myself at Harvard. And I felt emancipated in terms of my career decision. On the other hand, I was sponsored by my company and expected to return to Japan to work in banking. I was expected to concentrate in the finance-accounting area. Probably organizational behavior and general management areas are the last things the company wants me to concentrate on. I still remember clearly the encouragement my bosses and my colleagues gave me. I felt myself selfish, especially when I recalled some of my colleagues who could not study abroad but still wished me the best.

Should I be honest with myself, or should I withhold myself?

What is my duty as a corporate-employed Japanese MBA student? As an employee, the prime duty is to do my best in my job assignment. And my current assignment is to study at Harvard Business School. Although there is no written contract between me and my company regarding my obligation after graduation, I strongly felt an implicit moral duty such as *"on"* (a debt of gratitude) and *"giri"* (moral obligation), so as not to betray my bosses' expectation of my coming back to the company and eventually leading the international business area.

These are the implicit moral grammar, the supreme virtues of traditional communities in Japan. My company did a very nice thing for me; it gave the opportunity to have a wonderful experience other employees could not have. Once given very favorable treatment, *on* for me was to show loyalty and commitment to the community on a long-term basis. In Japan, people can do *on wo ada de kaesu* if they receive *on* and have moral indebtedness and return *ada,* which is literally betrayal, returning evil for good. This is morally bad in the very, very classical tradition. *Giri* is almost the same but more broad. Some one is very *giri-gatai* if he doesn't forget indebtedness and he always responds to someone's favor. In traditional Japan, if you don't conform to this norm, you are expelled from the community, even though you are living in it still. I found myself very worried about *giri* and *on* when I considered what my colleagues and bosses responses would

be. Will they be saying I have no *giri* and *on*? But, honestly, modern capitalism is not the same as traditional, closed villages so I had a mixed feeling.

Would my resignation from my job in the midst of my scholarship have a strong impact on my company? How shocking would it be? Would it effect any change in the company's overseas training system in the near future? Would such news have a negative effect on morale of my colleagues who have been working hard while I was studying? Although all of these seemed possible, there was no way I could tell.

In my life, I received a strong influence from my family since my childhood. The supreme value my parents had was to contribute to society through education. Since my sister followed their suit by entering the graduate school of education, I have been the only family member in a profit-making organization.

My decision was further complicated by taking into account social norms peculiar to Japan. As a member of society, you have to respect and conform to its custom and culture to a certain extent. In Japan, people usually stay in one company once they get a job. They tend to regard a company as a community which in fact constitutes the large part of their lives. They do not usually regard their companies merely as the place to receive their salaries. Companies are truly a large part of their lives. Therefore, getting a job is considered almost as significant as getting married, with no exaggeration. Although things may be changing recently, the majority of Japanese businesspersons still think that way, in my opinion.

In addition to such psychological aspects, cost-benefit analysis of switching jobs answers "no" to the potential job-hoppers. If one tries to move from one company to another, one encounters tremendous disadvantages at least in terms of one's own status, knowledge and skill, salary, personal network, company culture, and credibility. The following are the concise description of all these constraints which I found inevitable.

The first constraint is status. Unlike the United States, they have to climb up the status ladder all over again once they moved into other firms unless they were head-hunted with favorable conditions. Moreover, one distinct characteristic of Japanese corporations lies in its *"doki"* concept. *Doki* literally means the same generation, and actually means a group of employees who entered the company the same year, mostly right after college. The *doki* relations are pretty solid, and often the best friends and even the spouses are found among this group. Each member of the *doki* group holds equal relationships to each other, as opposed to the vertical relations with *sempai* (seniors) or *kohai* (juniors). While they are very friendly and egalitarian to each other, everybody in the company is extremely sensitive to his relative position among the *doki* and is also to other *doki* members' promotion. A fierce competition exists among them. And this phenomenon can be found in any company in Japan. In such a circumstance, how could any job-hopper possibly be accepted?

The second constraint is the knowledge and skill. Largely because of the result of on-the-job training, some of the employees' skill and knowledge are company-specific, rather than universal and convertible across company borders. This requires retraining for any newcomers from other companies.

The third constraint is a salary, which is largely based on seniority. This salary structure obviously makes it beneficial for employees to stay in the same company.

The fourth constraint is a personal network. Along with the *doki* described above, the personal network is the key element of business in Japan. Staying in one organization for decades makes you acquainted with key persons in the corporation. The importance of this can never be emphasized enough when considering the fact that a large part of important business decisions are made based on informal relationships with colleagues. The notorious after-five drinking party is a very important function in Japan. For this reason, it is a tremendous disadvantage to switch jobs.

The fifth constraint is a company culture. My sectionmate, with a spiteful tongue, was right in describing Japanese corporate culture a "cult." Every employee is thoroughly infused of the company culture since the very first day through training program and dormitory life. My two-year living experience at the company dormitory gave a revolutionary impact on me. It is quite doubtful for outsiders to acquire it at later stages.

The sixth constraint is credibility. In Japan, it is still perceived that changing a job is not favorable. In some occasions, people who switch jobs are even questioned on their credibility, on the grounds that they are rebels to the traditional society. For instance, in some traditional regions, young women's parents usually do not want their daughters to marry young men with job-changing records unless they have good reasons to do so.

In comparison to the United States, in which people can switch jobs several times until they finally find what the most suitable job for them is, the Japanese are quite unfortunate in such a sense that they have to decide their life-long occupation while being students even without working experiences beforehand. It is as if you married a woman or man without even dating. As touched on before, the two biggest choices in life are getting jobs and getting married in Japan. And they should be just "two." It should not be more than two. That certainly discourages any career change at a later stage in life.

People in Japan have a strong sense of what the appropriate ages are to do various things. For example, a woman in her late 20s tends to be worried about missing the *tekirei*, or appropriate age for marriage. Undergraduate students are in their early 20s, and graduate students are not any older than 30. In such a social norm, returning to graduate school and doing a doctoral study in his early 30s is quite a deviant behavior. I was impressed to have met a couple of professors at Harvard who did their PhDs in their 40s.

Japanese companies are close communities. Even one's private human relations are based on a company community. People in the company are the "insiders," and others the "outsiders." Therefore, leaving a company means not only leaving one's job but also leaving the community. A tremendous uneasiness of whether one can maintain one's personal relations even after one leaves the company remain.

Currently, two types of job mobility are increasing in number, although they are still minor trends. The first type is the foreign exchange dealers trained in major Japanese banks getting head-hunted to many American and European banks' Tokyo branches. This reflects the rapid growth of Tokyo international financial market. The second type is the MBA returnees in major Japanese corporations moving to either U.S. companies or other Japanese companies with a favorable offer. It is an extremely sensitive issue, since it is not only unfavorable to the Japanese companies, which originally sent their employees abroad for an MBA, but also threatening to the existing employees for losing their privilege of the "promotions from within." Recently, more companies demand an explicit contract with the employees studying for an MBA, stipulating the obligation of working for them for a certain time after graduation, which resembles the U.S. companies. However, again, these trends are still of limited weight. Most Japanese businesspeople firmly believe the benefit of staying in their same companies.

CHRIS MILLER

Chris Miller turned down the radio and began to concentrate on a pressing dilemma. Chris was 10 minutes away from the downtown office building where the second board meeting of the newly formed Boston Benefits Group (BBG) was about to be held. Chris was a member of the board and had advised the two founders — Linda Gibbons and Ellen Ravisson — on the start-up of their benefits consulting firm.

Linda and Ellen had met at a larger firm in the benefits consulting business where they both worked as benefits consultants, helping

This case was prepared by Michael J. Roberts.

Copyright © 1992 by the President and Fellows of Harvard College.

Harvard Business School case 393-076 (Revised 1993).

large firms purchase and provide benefit plans for their employees. The two had both quit when the management of this firm had demanded that everyone sign a noncompete agreement, forbidding them from going into the benefits consulting business on their own, or from trying to woo any existing clients. While Linda and Ellen had no thoughts of doing so, they felt that the noncompete was overly restrictive. They refused to sign it and had been fired as a result. Thus, they decided that they would go into business on their own. The women had — with Chris's considerable help — developed a business plan that indicated that the business could be quite successful.

Chris had been involved in the venture because Linda was a close friend, and because

Chris's experience as a financial consultant was valued by the two founders. All had gone smoothly until two weeks ago, when—in a conversation about the business—Linda related that Ellen had just discovered that she was two months pregnant.

Over the past month, Chris had helped the two develop their business plan and projections and had negotiated the start-up financing they would need. At this afternoon's meeting, the closing would occur, and BBG would receive $80,000 in start-up financing from John Blackwell, a local and wealthy physician, who happened to be Drew Gibbons' partner in a cardiology practice. (Drew was Linda Gibbons's husband.) Linda and Ellen had decided that they did not want to tell Blackwell of Ellen's pregnancy:

> He's a male chauvinist and he'll think that Ellen won't be able to be actively involved in the business. He'll back out of his financing commitment. Ellen will just take two months off, and while she's home, she'll work.

Indeed, Chris was inclined to agree with their assessment of Blackwell. At an early meeting to hammer out the details of the financing, Blackwell had flatly stated: "Be sure you girls get life insurance in case you get hit by a bus or get pregnant or something."

Yet, for all his blustering, Blackwell was giving the two women the money on extremely favorable terms. The $80,000 was essentially a loan that could be paid out of profits; Blackwell wasn't really participating in the business's upside. Chris was sure that Blackwell was being so generous because of his relationship with Linda and her husband. Blackwell would also be a member of the board, yet his involvement in the business seemed destined to be extremely passive.

Chris had asked Linda and Ellen to be available half an hour before the scheduled start of the board meeting so the three could discuss the situation. Chris intended to offer the two strong advice to tell Blackwell of Ellen's condition, yet, as the hour approached, things seemed more and more confusing. Chris wondered what the right thing to do was, how strongly those views should be presented to Ellen and Linda, and also whether the board membership that Chris held imposed any additional obligations with respect to fellow board member Blackwell.

Chris guided the Volvo into the underground garage and immediately spotted Linda and Ellen exiting from their car. They waved eagerly and Chris walked over to meet them.

THE PROCTERS' PROBLEM

Elizabeth screamed. Selina and Ken Procter opened their eyes groggily. Ken said, "I'll get her." Selina responded, "It's OK. It's my turn." She glanced at the clock and saw it was 3:30 AM. Elizabeth clutched her ear and continued

---

This case is a modified version of "Selina Procter: Parent and Professional," case material of the Darden Graduate Business School Foundation, Charlottesville, Virginia. The case was prepared by Lynn Sharp Paine.

to cry as Selina held her close and tried to comfort her. Selina guessed that Elizabeth, who was 18 months old, was probably suffering from yet another ear infection—the fourth this winter. A healthy, robust child, Elizabeth nevertheless seemed to wage a continuous battle against ever more serious ear infections.

As she stood there gazing at the whimpering child, Selina's thoughts abruptly turned to practicalities. Her first thought was that she would have to get Elizabeth to the doctor early in the morning. The pediatrician had told Selina that permanent damage to the ear drum could result from failure to treat the infection, and he would want to know how Elizabeth had reacted to the new medicine she had been taking for the last two weeks. But it was not only fear of injury that motivated Selina; she simply couldn't bear to see her child in such distress.

As Selina reflected on Elizabeth's condition, she remembered the meeting scheduled for 9:00 A.M. the next morning. Selina and a senior partner in her law firm were to represent one of the firm's clients in discussions about the terms on which they would be willing to settle a $20 million lawsuit brought against the client and five other defendants. Because of the number of defendants, the meeting had been difficult to arrange. At last, after delays of several weeks, the meeting was set. Selina had prepared memoranda for the senior partner and was to make a presentation to all the defendants concerning the costs of failing to reach a prompt settlement.

Selina began to plan the next morning's activities. She quickly realized that she couldn't possibly take Elizabeth to the doctor and get to work in time for the meeting. The doctor's office wouldn't open for calls until 8:00 AM, the earliest appointment was at 9:00 AM, and in all likelihood that appointment would not be available. Unfortunately, Ken had to catch a plane at 7:30 AM for a two-day trip.

On most work days, things went fairly smoothly. Selina usually left the house for work around 7:30 AM, and the sitter would arrive half an hour later to look after Elizabeth for the day. Ken and four-year-old Jonathan would then set out for nursery school together, except for the several times each month when consulting assignments took him out of town. After delivering Jonathan and greeting his teacher, Ken would head for work. He was usually at his desk by 8:30 AM.

As a lawyer, Selina could generally set her own schedule. She worked about 30 hours a week under her firm's part-time work policy for parents. In some weeks, however, she had worked as many as 40 hours. This schedule gave her the time she felt she wanted and should have with her children. Despite the forebodings of her law school classmates and some of the older, conservative partners in the firm, she believed she was making progress toward partnership. In fact, much to her own surprise and satisfaction, her salary increases had kept in step with those of her full-time colleagues during her three years at the firm.

Selina was ambitious at work and knew that her children would outgrow their need for her. Her clients liked her, and a number of other attorneys at the firm had told her that her future there was bright. Her only concern was the occasional suggestion, sometimes made kiddingly, that a full-time commitment might brighten her prospects. Sometimes Selina wondered whether this wasn't true, and she felt disappointed that she might be closing the door somewhat on her career opportunities.

Ken's job at a major consulting firm was considerably less flexible, often requiring 60 or more hours a week. His firm did offer a limited flex-time policy, but he wasn't comfortable asking for it. None of his friends had done so, and he had felt awkward about being the first.

Because of her part-time schedule, Selina could usually fit doctors' appointments in after work or on days off. (On a few occasions, Ken had been able to take the children to the doctor.) Anticipating the difficulties of being working parents, Selina and Ken had chosen to live near good public transportation. They were also lucky to live near a relative who was willing to help out with the children in a crisis. Aunt Lydia lived alone and seemed to relish the companionship of the children when she was with them. Selina wished that Aunt Lydia were not in Florida just now.

Selina lay down with Elizabeth on the bed in the guest room. She really didn't know what to do in the morning, but she knew she would probably be awake the rest of the night ministering to Elizabeth, working out possible plans for the morning, and, once again, mulling over her own situation and that of other young professional women with children.

An excellent student at her Ivy League university, Selina had majored in art history and graduated near the top of her class. While in college, she had worked hard to get the most from her education. Selina had met Ken in her junior year, and they were married shortly after graduation. When Ken took a job teaching in a college preparatory school, Selina began taking classes for a doctorate in history. After two years of course work (and two years of relative poverty as a graduate student and the wife of a school teacher), Selina decided that a career in law would suit her talents and interests and provide them with a good living. Ken set his sights on business school, and together they pursued professional degrees. For two years they were students, and then Ken got his MBA. A year later, Selina graduated from law school and was awarded a prestigious fellowship that allowed her (along with Ken) to travel around the world for a year.

During the year, they decided to start a family, and Jonathan was born shortly after their return. For the next year, Selina was fully engrossed in the new experiences of motherhood. In fact, she was exhilarated by her new responsibilities and her love for Jonathan. Child care help several mornings a week gave her time to read and attend a seminar on recent legal developments, as well as teach a class on tort law at a local law school. Selina enjoyed her new opportunities to meet other mothers. She also understood for the first time the important role played by stay-at-home mothers who looked after the schools and other community concerns.

After a year, however, Selina wanted to begin practicing law. Throughout law school, she had been excited at the prospect of working as an attorney, and she was confident she would excel in the profession. As an educated woman and mother, she also believed that the law would enable her to make a public contribution to her community—while also encouraging other women who would be following along in college and graduate school.

On the other hand, she strongly believed that Jonathan and Ken deserved a considerable portion of her time. After all, Selina thought, being a parent is not like being an employee in an organization. An organization doesn't need you personally; it needs someone who can perform a job. Your child does need you personally. Parenthood is more than a set of functions; it's a personal commitment, like marriage. You couldn't hire someone to perform all your wifely functions and still be a wife, and you can't hire someone to perform all your parental functions and still be a parent.

Selina also loved Jonathan and attributed to him a transformation of her own perspectives. His appreciation of nature and his cheerful awakening every morning had given her a reawakened love of life. Now each day had its own identity. She occasionally felt sorry for those "successful" people—mostly men but increasingly women—confined to routines and patterns of existence that gradually shut them off more and more from the essence of life.

Selina had discussed her views with Ken, as well as with some of their friends, several of whom had children. While everyone seemed to agree with her conclusions, few people had thought about the issues to the extent she had.

Selina and Ken's solution to her concerns was for her to take a part-time job with a prestigious Washington, D.C., firm. Through careful planning, things had worked out well. When Elizabeth was born, after Selina had been with the firm for a year and a half, she took a three-month maternity leave. Now, with two children—and especially with Elizabeth's ear infections and with Jonathan's growing list of friends and birthday parties—things were getting more complicated. Selina's philosophy of parenthood seemed more and more correct to her. Jonathan was asking serious questions—about life, death, God, truth—and she felt she wanted to answer them. No babysitter, no matter how good, would give the answers she wanted to give. Anyway, in Selina's view, the very act of answering such questions was what was important.

Selina had found it difficult to find a babysitter who shared her values and whom she could fully trust. So far she had been lucky. The sitter she and Ken had hired seemed to share their basic values. She and Ken thought their children benefitted from being close to someone other than their parents, someone like their sitter, who was a good person and yet who had some different ideas.

Selina and Ken had rejected full-time day care for their children. They believed that too much institutionalization at an early age was undesirable. They wondered what effects it might have on self-reliance and individual creativity. On the other hand, spending a few mornings at nursery school or day care was all to the good. No matter how creative or self-reliant you are, you still have to get along with others.

Friendship was a relationship Selina valued highly. She wanted her children to be able to make and have good friends. Ironically, she felt this was another reason she should not work full-time. She wanted her children to be able to invite friends home to play after school. And then there were lessons, sports events, and just time to talk together uninterrupted by the mechanics of living—cooking, eating, errands. All these activities required time.

Selina might have chosen to stay home full time, but she believed that it was important for women to work and for men and women to have economic equality. She had vowed in childhood that she would always protect her capacity to be economically self-sufficient. Also, Selina liked her work and excelled at it. It was a refreshing change from household—as distinguished from child care—responsibilities.

Selina felt that the difficulties she faced while the children were young could be somewhat alleviated if Ken were more flexible about his work and committed more energy to child care and household tasks. She couldn't tell whether his consulting requirements were really as demanding as he claimed. She also suspected that he might be able to work more efficiently and cut his hours somewhat, if he put his mind to it. She was aware that some of the younger male associates in her law firm claimed they had to work 12 hours a day to stay in the running for partnership. Selina knew this wasn't true. She believed their devotion to the firm disguised the deeper reality that they were avoiding themselves or their families, or simply lacked confidence in themselves.

Ken and Selina had talked about parenthood before their marriage; but both agreed, when they talked more recently, that it had been very difficult to anticipate the actual day-to-day experience of parenthood and careers. Ken believed women were fully as capable as men in every way of importance in today's world; but, in Selina's view, he didn't fully appreciate the demands of parenthood. When Ken and Selina discussed these issues, he said he wanted to do his share. He tried to pitch in after work and often expressed his sympathy when Selina "had to take care of Elizabeth's needs once again" and he couldn't help out. Ken hoped that things would change once he was promoted and had more control over his time.

In fact, Selina was the only one who had really developed a "philosophy of parenthood." Selina believed that men should and could share equally in parenthood. While she knew that many men claimed to be equal partners in parenthood, she saw little real evidence that this was the case. She wondered why Ken didn't seem to think about the children as much as she did. He wanted to fit them to his life, rather than to adapt and to learn from them.

Selina had never missed an important appointment or meeting because of childcare responsibilities. She had always been able to work things out to accommodate her clients, her employer, and her children, though the price she paid—in terms of stress, anxiety, and last-minute juggling—was high. Selina was both amused and disgusted by the lawyers who worried that part-timers were likely to miss important meetings. Busy lawyers were always missing important meetings; you can only be in one place at a time, and busy lawyers have numerous clients clamoring for their attention all the time. Scheduling seemed to become a controversial issue only if children were involved. Even a conflicting tennis game or a car problem received more respect from some

attorneys than a child's needs when offered as a scheduling constraint.

Nevertheless, Selina did not want to miss tomorrow's meeting. She had worked on her presentation, and the meeting could not easily be rescheduled.

Selina thought about how tired she would be in the morning. She was reluctant to ask the sitter to take Elizabeth to the doctor. The sitter did not know the doctor, and he would likely have questions that only Selina could answer. She also remembered the attention her own mother had lavished on her as a sick child.

It was 5:30 AM; Elizabeth had dozed off. Selina was growing weary of her thoughts. She had been through them so many times before. The cumulative stress of these concerns, day after day, was wearing on her, and she knew that something had to change.

H. ROSS PEROT

Talking about myself is sort of a waste of time. I've only lived one life. It's been overdocumented. Half of it is truth. Half of it is myth. I would think readers are probably sick of it. I'm sick of it.

Henry Ross Perot[1]

Morton Meyerson, the 45-year-old president of Electronic Data Systems Corporation (EDS), walked into the office of EDS chairman and

[1] N.R. Kleinfield, "The 'Irritant' They Call Perot," *The New York Times,* April 27, 1986, section 3, p. 1.

This case was prepared by Ellen E. West under the direction of Joseph Badaracco, Jr. This case draws heavily from *Irreconcilable Differences* (Boston: Little, Brown, 1989) by Doran P. Levin and other sources cited in the endnotes.

Copyright © 1990 by the President and Fellows of Harvard College.

Harvard Business School case 390-210 (Revised 1992).

founder, Henry Ross Perot. Meyerson was deeply disturbed by his meeting the day before with General Motors (GM) chairman Roger Smith and GM's executive vice president for finance, Alan Smith. "Ross, I've thought about what happened and I'm not sure we should do a deal with GM," Meyerson said.

Since GM's pursuit of an acquisition of EDS had become public news, the two companies had faced intense pressure to decide what form any transaction would take. In late May, Meyerson flew to Detroit for a scheduled negotiating session. Perot had not yet given up the idea that EDS could sign up GM as a customer without having to be acquired by the automaker. Meyerson had begun to explain to the GM executives how much EDS's independence meant to the people who worked there and, in particular, to Ross Perot.

Roger Smith had been furious, Meyerson now reported to Perot. He had blown up at Meyerson, disparaging EDS and its negotiating tactics. Meyerson had waited until the tirade ended, told Smith "I don't think we have anything further to discuss," and prepared to leave. Smith approached Meyerson and asked him to stay and continue the discussions. Meyerson finished the day's meeting and returned to Dallas that evening.

"Now, Mort, we've all had bad days," Perot began, "... GM overnight can at least double the revenue numbers it took us 22 years to build." He tried to convince Meyerson that any deal would ensure that GM could not go back on its pledge to maintain EDS's independence.

"Ross, given what happened with Roger, I think you should have someone else negotiate with GM," Meyerson replied.[2]

Early Years in Texarkana

Henry Ross Perot was born on June 27, 1930, in Texarkana, Texas. His great-grandfather Perot had immigrated to Louisiana from France before the Civil War. Perot's grandfather, in turn, had made his way upriver and overland to a small town near Texarkana where he had hacked out a clearing in the wilderness and built a trading post and general store.[3]

Although Perot's father, Gabriel Ross Perot, provided a comfortable living for his family,

using his skills as a cotton broker and horse trader, Perot's childhood was shaped by the hardships of the Great Depression.[4] His mother, Lulu May, emphasized to Ross and his sister Bette the importance of sharing with those who were less fortunate. When Lulu May's practice of distributing meals from the Perots' back door led hobos to mark the curb next to the house, young Ross asked his mother whether he should clean it off. She told him not to.[5]

Lulu May was a sweet, strong, spiritual woman, although she didn't wear her Methodist beliefs on her sleeve. She read the Bible each morning and insisted on honesty, uprightness, and perfect manners from her children.[6] If her children misbehaved, she did not hit them and she did not yell. It was said she looked them in the eye, told them what to do, and they simply could not bring themselves to continue to make her unhappy.[7]

From an early age, Perot was fascinated with his father's work and would often tag along when his father "visited" with cotton planters around Texarkana.[8] Perot recalled:

> I spent my entire boyhood involved in the very basics of what business is. My father dealt with the farmer who raised the cotton. He taught me as a small boy that buying cotton from a man *once* had very little value unless you developed a personal relationship with him, unless you treated him fairly, unless he trusted you. Otherwise, he won't come back to you next year.[9]

---

[2] Doran P. Levin, *Irreconcilable Differences* (Boston: Little, Brown, 1989), pp. 101–04.

[3] John Brooks, *The Go-Go Years* (New York: Weybright and Talley, 1973), p. 15.

[4] Levin, *Irreconcilable Differences,* p. 16.

[5] Albert Lee, *Call Me Roger* (Chicago, Contemporary Books, 1987), p. 148.

[6] Levin, *Irreconcilable Differences,* p. 17.

[7] Ken Follett, *On Wings of Eagles* (New York: William Morrow, 1983), p. 51.

[8] Levin, *Irreconcilable Differences,* p. 18.

[9] Fred Powledge, "H. Ross Perot Pays His Dues," the *New York Times Magazine,* February 2, 1970, section VI, pp. 16, 17.

The elder Perot was also an enthusiastic horse breeder, trainer, and trader:[10]

> A farmer would drive up to our place, knock on the door, and tell my daddy, "Gabe, I've got that horse you always wanted." No matter how much he wanted the horse, Daddy would reply, "What horse?" The fella would have brought his horse 25 miles, and he didn't want to go home yet. "How much do you want?" my daddy would ask. "Three hundred dollars," the farmer would say. "Don't believe I want him." "Dammit, Gabe, aren't you going to look at him?" He'd go outside, make some elaborate compliments about the animal, but say he didn't want to buy it. A few days later they'd settle for $225 and everybody was happy.[11]

Despite Lulu May's objections, Ross Sr. loved lifting his young son onto the backs of untamed horses and teaching him how to break the animals for riding.[12] Perot later remembered breaking horses as early as the age of six. "I got a dollar or two for every horse. The job was incentive-oriented. When I got on a horse and it didn't buck, I was paid."[13]

Perot's father was not all business, however. He would employ people he did not need, just because they didn't have a job. Every year the Perot family car would go to the county fair crammed with black employees, each of whom was given a little money to spend and a Perot business card to show if anyone tried to give him a hard time.

One of Ross Sr.'s former employees had once ridden a freight train to California and, upon being arrested for vagrancy, had shown the Perot business card. The sheriff had replied, "We don't care who you are, we're throwing you in jail." The employee called Ross Sr., who wired the train fare for the man to come back. When the man reached Texarkana, Ross Sr. gave him back his job.[14]

Perot belonged to a tight group of friends throughout his childhood. Although smaller than his peers, Perot was determined to succeed at anything he tried. One summer he decided to learn a back flip from the high diving board at Texarkana Country Club. A friend watched in amazement as Perot spent hours perfecting his technique. Over and over Perot plunged into the water, wearing a T-shirt to protect his back against the water's sting.[15]

As a youngster, Perot sold War Bonds, garden seeds, used saddles, Christmas cards, and subscriptions to the *Saturday Evening Post*. When Perot was 12, he decided to take on a newspaper delivery route for the *Texarkana Gazette*. The only route available was in Texarkana's black community.[16] Perot woke each day at 3:30 A.M. to travel his 20-mile delivery route on horseback before school.[17]

Once, Ross Sr. became ill and Perot had to leave Texarkana to visit him for a few days in Shreveport. Since he could find no one to relieve him, Perot went from house to house along his route explaining the situation. His customers told him that if he saved the papers and delivered them when he returned, they would pay him.[18]

For many years, Perot was more interested in his business ventures than in his schoolwork. He finally met his match in his 11th-grade teacher. "It's just too bad you're not as smart as your friends," she told him, pointing to their superior grades as evidence.[19] With that challenge in front of him, Perot quickly improved his grades. He told her he would make straight

---

[10] Levin, *Irreconcilable Differences*, p. 16.

[11] Arthur M. Louis, "The Fastest Richest Texan Ever," *Fortune*, November 1968, p. 228.

[12] Levin, *Irreconcilable Differences*, pp. 16–17.

[13] Christopher S. Wren, "Ross Perot: Billionaire Patriot," *Look*, March 24, 1970, p. 30.

[14] Follett, *On Wings of Eagles*, p. 99.

[15] Levin, *Irreconcilable Differences*, pp. 17–18.

[16] Levin, *Irreconcilable Differences*, p. 20.

[17] Wren, "Ross Perot: Billionaire Patriot," p. 30.

[18] Lee, *Call Me Roger*, p. 148.

[19] Levin, *Irreconcilable Differences*, p. 19.

A's for the next six weeks and proceeded to make them for the rest of his high school career.[20]

The Naval Academy

When the boy who had been Perot's idol throughout high school went to the United States Naval Academy after graduation, Perot decided that was the place for him, too, although he had never seen the ocean. He attended Texarkana Junior College for two years and sent countless letters to Texas's senators and congressmen until he received the coveted appointment to the Naval Academy.

Perot arrived at Annapolis in June 1949 and graduated four years later. While he was ranked only 454th out of 925 in his class academically, he was voted best all-around midshipman, life president of his class, and head of the honor committee. The Academy yearbook noted: "What Ross lacked in physical size he more than replaced by his capacity to win friends and influence people."[21]

After completing his four years of required service, Perot did not find the decision about his future difficult:

> I loved the Navy, loved the sea, loved ships.
> But I always find that whatever I'm doing,
> I'm thoroughly involved in it. In the Navy, the
> promotion system and the seniority system
> and the waiting-in-line-concept were just sort of
> incompatible with my desire to be measured
> and judged by what I could produce.[22]

IBM's Super Salesman

One of Perot's duties aboard a Navy aircraft carrier had been to escort visitors touring the vessel. A visiting IBM executive had turned to Perot at the end of one such tour and invited him to interview with IBM if he decided to leave the Navy. Perot followed up on the advice and it didn't take IBM long to decide to offer Perot a position as a salesman in Dallas. While at the Naval Academy, Perot had met Margot Birmingham on a blind date and had married her in 1956. The young couple packed their belongings and headed for Dallas.

If the Navy wasn't Perot's kind of place, it certainly seemed that IBM was. While most salespeople spent the first 45 minutes of their day drinking coffee and planning the rest of their day, Perot was already calling on customers.[23] At first, Perot was too intense to be a natural salesman and had to be told to lighten up.[24] He then quickly joined IBM's 100% Club for salesmen who achieved their yearly sales quota.[25]

In order to make his job more interesting and to earn higher commissions, Perot asked to be given the toughest accounts and was successful with them. The more he achieved at IBM, however, the more frustrated he became. In 1961, the company began to experiment with its sales incentives system, forming sales teams that paired strong salesmen with weaker ones. The territories of successful salesmen were cut back and compensation was increasingly tied to seniority to alleviate the jealousy of managers earning less than their salesmen. Perot became discouraged as the company's focus moved away from individual attainment.[26] Of the 20 accounts Perot and his partner Dean Campbell shared, Campbell covered 18 and Perot covered the two most difficult. When Perot landed one of the large accounts, he claimed that Campbell was not entitled to a share of the commission, even though Campbell would have to share in the loss if Perot

---

[20] Follett, *On Wings of Eagles,* p. 57.
[21] Jon Nordheimer, "Billionaire Texan Fights Social Ills," *New York Times,* November 28, 1969, p. 41.
[22] Powledge, "H. Ross Perot Pays His Dues," p. 19.

[23] Levin, *Irreconcilable Differences,* p. 24.
[24] Todd Mason, *Perot* (Homewood, Ill.: Dow Jones-Irwin, 1990), p. 37.
[25] Levin, *Irreconcilable Differences,* p. 24.
[26] Ibid.

failed to deliver on the contract. IBM backed Perot.[27]

In 1962, with his territory and quota reduced, Perot was able to meet his annual quota by January 19. With little monetary incentive to work hard, he would go to the local YMCA to swim during his lunch hour. As a subtle form of protest, he usually left his suit and towel on top of his desk throughout the day.[28]

Electronic Data Systems Corporation

Perot thought he could revive his enthusiasm for IBM by helping it launch an entirely new line of business. Corporations spent millions of dollars for computer hardware but lacked the expertise to harness the computers' abilities. Perot believed that IBM should start a computer services division, which would help customers get the most out of their hardware. IBM was not interested.

Perot felt stifled. He claimed that his moment of inspiration came while he was sitting in a barber's chair, looking through a *Reader's Digest.* He came across the following line from Thoreau: "The mass of men lead lives of quiet desperation." Perot knew then that he had to leave IBM.

On June 27, 1962, his 32nd birthday, Perot capitalized Electronic Data Systems Corporation with $1,000. Lulu May, who had encouraged him to start his own business, joined Margot and Ross's sister Bette on EDS's board. His first two employees were Milledge A. ("Mitch") Hart III and Thomas J. Marquez, both the sons of east Texas cattle traders and former colleagues at IBM.[29]

Perot's strategy was to tell customers to concentrate on what they did best and to leave the data processing to EDS. EDS could do it faster and cheaper and customers would be told in advance how much EDS's services would cost.[30] The first step for any EDS account was a full-scale feasibility study. While the study usually recommended that the client hire EDS, it had the effect of getting cash into the company at the start.[31] IBM responded to Perot's efforts by forming a "Stop EDS" team, which shadowed Perot's team and reminded potential customers that EDS had no track record.[32]

Until Perot could sign up his first captive data processing customer, he worked to sell the excess computer capacity of some of his former IBM customers. Although EDS landed its first facilities-management contract in 1963, the company made profits of only $4,100 on revenue of $400,000 in fiscal 1964.[33]

EDS's business took off in 1965, however, with the passage of Medicare and Medicaid legislation. Federal and state agencies needed assistance in setting up systems to process and pay millions of claims. By 1968, EDS had $7.7 million in revenues, 25 percent of which came from Medicare and Medicaid contracts. Profits had climbed to a 20 percent aftertax rate, compared with a 2 percent rate four years earlier.[34]

As his business grew, Perot realized he needed additional capital, but he had a mistrust of borrowing. Perot had been reluctant to go public because he liked the advantages a private company enjoyed over publicly held competitors and because he was afraid that some of his employees might become euphoric with their paper profits and slack off. Perot later told the press that he had become seriously interested in going public only after an employee mentioned to him that he'd like to know what his EDS shares were worth. Perot had

[27] Mason, *Perot,* pp. 36–40.
[28] Ibid.
[29] Louis, "Fastest Richest Texan Ever," p. 170.

[30] Levin, *Irreconcilable Differences,* p. 27.
[31] Mason, *Perot,* p. 44.
[32] Ibid, p. 29.
[33] Ibid, p. 30.
[34] Ibid.

summoned a meeting of the other stockholders, all of them employees, and had found a majority in favor of an offering.[35]

The stock market was soaring in 1968 and investment banks were beating down Perot's door. Perot rejected the enticements of older, more established investment banks in favor of a small firm. While other firms had offered to sell EDS stock at 30, 50, or 70 times current annual earnings, R. W. Pressprich & Company offered a multiple of 100 times earnings.[36]

Perot, it was said, played naive country boy throughout the negotiations, pretending to be baffled by Wall Street's rituals while actually learning to turn them to his own advantage. He suggested that the original buyers of EDS stock be offered a 90-day, money-back guarantee and tried to write his own prospectus ("All alone, against overwhelming odds, with little money . . .").[37]

Pressprich & Company underwrote the initial public offering of EDS stock on September 12, 1968, at $16.50 per share, or 118 times earnings. Only 675,000 of the 17.5 million authorized shares were offered, and 325,000 of those were Perot's.[38] EDS stock continued to rise in 1969 and 1970, reaching $160 per share in March 1970.[39] Perot got so enthusiastic about his company that he often made claims that experts in the industry considered preposterous: "There's a greater body of knowledge in EDS on how to effectively use a computer in a commercial company, than in any other company in the world. . . . EDS some day is going to be one of the country's great corporations."[40]

Corporate Culture

From the beginning, Perot modeled his company after IBM. EDS would be different from IBM, however, in one significant way. Perot planned to pay close attention to the ideas of the people who worked with him, regardless of their rank.[41] As Perot later put it: "When you consider the impact that his work has on him and his family, the company has a moral obligation to be an exciting place for an employee."[42]

Perot wrote the 12-page EDS Code of Conduct, which every employee had to sign.[43] The all-purpose code reminded employees that "your character, integrity, and behavior, both on and off the job, determine the image of EDS in the community. Therefore, your standards of conduct must, at all times, be above approach."[44] EDS employees did not fulfill their obligations merely by obeying the law. A prohibition against bribery said, for example:

> A determination that a payment or practice is not forbidden by law does not conclude the analysis. . . . It is always appropriate to make further inquiry into the ethics. . . . Could you do business in complete trust with someone who acts the way you do? The answer must be YES.[45]

Appearance and dress codes were strict. Men were to have short hair. Beards and mustaches were forbidden. Women were not allowed to wear slacks or short skirts and, at one time, the duties of a female EDS treasurer included measuring the other women employees' skirts to ensure proper length. No loud ties were permitted, nor were shoes with buckles

---

[35] Louis, "Fastest Richest Texan Ever," pp. 168, 169.
[36] Brooks, *Go-Go Years,* p. 17.
[37] Ibid, p. 18.
[38] John Whitmore, "H. Ross Perot—Business with a Social Thrust," *Finance,* August 1971, pp. 6, 11.
[39] Levin, *Irreconcilable Differences,* p. 33.
[40] "Texas Breeds New Billionaire," *Business Week,* August 30, 1969, p. 74.

---

[41] Levin, *Irreconcilable Differences,* p. 27.
[42] Powledge, "H. Ross Perot Pays His Dues," p. 19.
[43] Follett, *On Wings of Eagles,* p. 97.
[44] Lee, *Call Me Roger,* pp. 150–51.
[45] Follett, *On Wings of Eagles,* p. 97.

or tassels.[46] Since EDS employees worked with executives of top companies, they had to dress as well as their customers. "You might call this camouflage in the corporate jungle," joked Perot.[47]

Drinking alcohol at lunch or discussing salaries were grounds for immediate dismissal.[48] Perot allegedly fired employees for having extramarital affairs, because, if they were being unfaithful at home, they might be unfaithful to their work.[49] One former EDS employee was told by her supervisor that she would be fired if the company found out that she was living with a man to whom she wasn't married.[50]

EDS recruiting efforts were designed to weed out the uncommitted.[51] Its philosophy was captured by a plaque on the wall in Perot's office: "Eagles don't flock, you have to find them one at a time." [52] Many EDS employees had been lured away from IBM. Beginning in 1968, EDS recruiters had given priority to Vietnam veterans, a policy begun for patriotic reasons and continued when Perot found that the vets often made first-class managers.[53] At the end of the Vietnam War, about 15 percent of the company's annual recruits were former military officers and, in 1977, the figure was still at 10 percent.[54]

To find people who met EDS standards, the firm avoided hiring from prestigious Ivy League schools. Instead, Perot's recruiters focused on universities closely tied to the Mormon church and small rural schools, such as East Texas State University.[55] Perot looked for people who had proved themselves in some field, whether it was music, athletics, or computer science. Perot loved kids who worked their way through school. He looked for people who had been in battle, whether at the state piano-playing contest, the finals of the chess tournament, or in Khe Sanh. He admired toughness born of conflict. "Find people who love to win," he lectured the recruiters. "If you can't find people who love to win, then find some people who hate to lose."[56]

Only 1 out of every 30 applicants was hired and, once offered a job, had to accept or decline on the spot.[57] Employees who accepted an offer from EDS signed a contract that forbade negotiating with other computer companies during and after employment at EDS[58] and required them to reimburse the company for their training costs if they left within three years.

New employees were subjected to a grueling training and trial period, which lasted as long as two years. EDS employees estimated that 25 percent of the trainees didn't survive the company's boot camp.[59] After a year on the job, employees attended a 10-week session of technical training and indoctrination. Said one head of EDS recruiting: "Other [company] classes are 'I'm O.K., you're O.K.' Ours is intensively competitive. It's deliberately intense because we're looking for character. We're not a legion of workaholics, but this is where we drive that part of the culture home."[60]

---

[46] Laurie P. Cohen and Charles F. McCoy, "Perot's Singular Style Raises Issue of How He'll Fit at GM," *Wall Street Journal,* July 2, 1984, p. 17.

[47] Powledge, "H. Ross Perot Pays His Dues," p. 26.

[48] Cohen and McCoy, "Perot's Singular Style," p. 17.

[49] Whitmore, "Business with a Social Thrust," p. 11.

[50] Cohen and McCoy, "Perot's Singular Style," p. 17.

[51] Ibid.

[52] Follett, *On Wings of Eagles,* p. 90.

[53] Ibid, p. 55.

[54] "H. Ross Perot's New Game Plan at EDS," *Business Week,* April 11, 1977, pp. 92, 94.

[55] Ibid.

[56] Levin, *Irreconcilable Differences,* p. 86.

[57] Wren, "Ross Perot: Billionaire Patriot," p. 32.

[58] Ron Rosenbaum, "Ross Perot to the Rescue!" *Esquire,* December 1980, pp. 60, 65.

[59] Cohen and McCoy, "Perot's Singular Style," p. 17.

[60] "Wheels of the Future," *Newsweek,* June 17, 1985, pp. 64, 68.

After 1975, EDS headquarters were situated on the grounds of a former country club in North Dallas. Uniformed armed guards stood at the entrance gate 24 hours a day. The 77-acre compound, surrounded by a barbed-wire fence, had its own jogging tracks, pool, tennis courts, and nine-hole golf course. The company encouraged employees to spend as much leisure time as possible within the secure enclosure.[61]

Perot insisted that everyone in a customer's data processing department become EDS employees, subject to the EDS code.[62] Data processing personnel at California Blue Shield said EDS's takeover began with an announcement over the public address system telling everyone to report to the company cafeteria. Higher-salaried employees were grouped on one side of the room, lower-salaried ones on the other. A former woman employee recalled:

> We were told that EDS had taken over and that we were all working for them. The dress code was explained. . . . If you didn't go along there was no place for you. Either you signed the new contract by the next day or you had to leave the premises. Immediately. There wasn't even an arrangement for personal property. You couldn't go back to your desk and get your personal articles . . . and it kept going downhill; anyone who even discussed salaries got fired.
> It was just like a concentration camp. They ruled by fear.[63]

From the beginning, Perot had felt strongly that EDS should belong to the people who built it. He motivated his employees with stock incentives so they would have a stake in EDS's future.[64] A small group of top people received large financial rewards. Of the company's 600 employees in 1969, 25 were paper millionaires.[65]

Further down the organization, however, the rewards were less spectacular. Entry-level workers were paid the industry average. Said a data processor who interviewed at other companies, "People couldn't believe how little I make." Other data processing companies had successfully raided EDS for employees, and other EDS workers quit from burnout. Outsiders who didn't understand the company's culture couldn't figure out why EDS employees worked so hard for so little.[66]

Many EDS managers spoke of Perot with reverence. Stories of Perot's demonstrations of loyalty ranged from simple gestures of thoughtfulness to seemingly Herculean undertakings. One day early in EDS's struggling days, Perot disappeared from the team effort for most of the day, in itself unusual. When the team members got home that night, they learned that Perot had visited each of their spouses to apologize for their long hours at the office. He had given each spouse 100 shares of EDS stock and his personal thank you.

When Perot heard indirectly that an employee's son had a learning difficulty, he arranged for the boy to see specialists immediately to work out a learning plan. Another employee had been on the job only a couple of months when his back was broken in a hiking accident. Perot took care of the medical bills and set up an annuity so that the young man would receive support for the rest of his life.

Mort Meyerson told of the time his wife got a bit of Drano in her eye. Local doctors said she would probably lose sight in the eye, but Perot stepped in without being asked, found out who was the best ophthalmologist in the

---

[61] Rosenbaum, "Ross Perot to the Rescue!" pp. 60, 65, 67.

[62] Levin, *Irreconcilable Differences,* p. 56.

[63] Robert Fitch, "H. Ross Perot: America's First Welfare Billionaire," *Ramparts,* pp. 42, 47–48.

[64] Powledge, "H. Ross Perot Pays His Dues," p. 19.

[65] "Texas Breeds New Billionaire," *Business Week,* August 30, 1969, p. 73.

[66] Cohen and McCoy, "Perot's Singular Style," p. 17.

country, and flew her to Johns Hopkins in a rented jet. "Ross saved my wife's sight," Meyerson said. "You can imagine how I feel about Ross after that."[67]

An EDS recruiter would later recall the obverse of Perot's intense loyalty to his employees. Each year, EDS had named a "Recruiter of the Year" and engraved the person's name on a plaque at headquarters. When a winner left the company, Perot wanted his name erased from the plaque. It was almost as if Perot took it as a personal insult that someone would want to work elsewhere.[68]

Perot the Common Man

The stock market plunged in April 1970 and EDS stock went with it, falling in price by a third. While Perot was still worth close to $1 billion on paper, his loss exceeded in actual purchasing power what J.P. Morgan was worth at the time of his death and was probably more than any man had ever lost in a single day.[69] Perot's reaction to seeing his EDS holdings fall in value by over $450 million: "This bothered me less than if one of my children had broken a finger. It's a nonevent."[70]

Perot claimed that "the day I made Eagle Scout was more important to me than the day I discovered I was a billionaire."[71] A year after becoming a multimillionaire, Perot was still living in a relatively modest four-bedroom home in North Dallas and driving a four-year-old Lincoln Continental. The family drove to their country lake house in a 10-year-old Ford. The Perots had no live-in maids, no chauffeurs, no live-in nannies. Perot did his own shopping, frequently at K-mart, Sears, and J.C. Penney and bought his suits off the rack

at Neiman-Marcus.[72] He didn't drink or smoke, not out of a religious conviction, but "because it never appealed to me."[73]

Perot insisted that he would not leave any significant portion of his wealth to his children so as not to "deny them the same chances I had." He planned to spend the bulk of his fortune finding ways to remedy social problems and improve the quality of life for all Americans.[74] He refused to take personal income tax deductions on his charitable contributions on the ground that morally he owed the tax money to a country that had done so well by him.[75]

There was a method to his philanthropy. He wanted to set up each program as a model, test it, and if it worked, get it enacted into law.[76] He donated $2.5 million to the Dallas public schools to finance an experimental school for disadvantaged minority children. He contributed $1 million to the Boy Scouts of America with a stipulation that the organization investigate ways to take scouting into the ghetto. He purchased land in Texas for a Girl Scout summer camp with a suggestion that the facility be used during the rest of the year as a boarding school for poor children. Though he was a Presbyterian, he gave $50,000 a year to help support a Jesuit high school in Dallas that had a large Mexican-American student body.[77]

By instinct Perot involved himself in moral confrontations in which, in his terms, he was always the winner. Once in 1969, a group of young West Coast radicals came to ask him to finance "the revolution." Rather than avoid them or send them away, Perot took the

---

[67] Lee, *Call Me Roger,* p. 152–54.

[68] Follett, *On Wings of Eagles,* p. 95.

[69] Brooks, *Go-Go Years,* p. 2.

[70] Levin, *Irreconcilable Differences,* p. 39.

[71] "Ross Perot: Dallas Crusader," *Newsweek,* April 13, 1970, p. 69.

[72] Lee, *Call Me Roger,* p. 145; Wren, "Ross Perot: Billionaire Patriot," p. 31.

[73] Nordheimer, "Billionaire Texan Fights Social Ills," p. 41.

[74] Ibid.

[75] Brooks, *Go-Go Years,* pp. 19–20.

[76] Wren, "Ross Perot: Billionaire Patriot," p. 32.

[77] Nordheimer, "Billionaire Texan Fights Social Ills," p. 41.

opportunity to give them an object lesson. In his most businesslike manner he asked, "How long will it take and what will it cost?" The radicals were speechless.[78]

Perot and the POWs

In the fall of 1969, Perot had funded a trip to Paris by the wives of prisoners of war so they could ask the North Vietnamese for information about their husbands. When the wives returned, one of them came by to thank Perot for his help. She brought her 4½-year-old son. Perot recalled:

> This little boy had never seen his dad. He was born after his dad was missing in action. When I was 4½ years old I had been with my dad several hours a day every day of my life. He was my best friend. We had a particularly close association. So I was particularly sensitive to what that little boy was giving up. And I decided right then.[79]

Within three weeks Perot put together a team of EDS executives, which formed an organization named United We Stand. United We Stand spent about $1 million on 300 newspaper ads, 30 million postcards, and a half-hour television show, which expressed support for President Nixon's Vietnam policies.[80] In December 1969, United We Stand chartered two Boeing jets and Perot announced a mission to deliver traditional Christmas dinners, medical supplies, and family messages to American prisoners of war held by the North Vietnamese.

Perot would later recall consulting his mother, Lulu May, about his forthcoming mission. Colleagues at EDS had pointed out that if he put his life in danger the price of EDS stock might fall. He was faced with a moral dilemma: Did he have the right to make shareholders suffer, even for the best of causes? Lulu May's

answer had been unhesitating: "Let them sell their shares."[81]

The North Vietnamese government denied Perot permission to enter the country and told him to send the gifts by ordinary channels through Moscow. On December 21 he took off for Bangkok in the jet he had named "Peace on Earth" with a cargo of supplies, Red Cross officials, clergymen, and reporters. After an unsuccessful meeting with North Vietnamese officials in Laos, Perot conceded that he had failed in efforts to fly supplies to the prisoners. He was not giving up, however. He had asked permission to fly on to Moscow and send the supplies through "official" channels.

"Peace on Earth" then flew to Anchorage where more than 1,000 residents volunteered to break down the supplies into individual packages as required by the North Vietnamese. The Soviets denied Perot a visa, however, and the plane headed back to Dallas after logging over 35,000 miles on its mission. Three months later, Perot returned to Vientiane in a plane full of journalists in another unsuccessful attempt to meet with North Vietnamese officials.

The Wall Street Journal questioned whether efforts such as Perot's were worth the attention they received and noted that Perot "keenly appreciates the value of publicity, not only for his causes and his company but also for himself."[82] Perot had spent $2 million on the POW cause, but he would later estimate that the publicity would have cost $60 million to buy.[83] The paper did go on to quote friends who thought Perot's motives were sincere: "Ross truly believes that the North Vietnamese would turn over U.S. prisoners and start meaningful peace negotiations, if he could

---

[78] Brooks, *Go-Go Years,* p. 20.
[79] Powledge, "H. Ross Perot Pays His Dues," p. 24.
[80] Ibid.

[81] Follet, *On Wings of Eagles,* p. 52.
[82] Norman Pearlstein, "Mr. Perot and His Quixotic Mission," *The Wall Street Journal,* December 31, 1969, p. 4.
[83] Follett, *On Wings of Eagles,* p. 58.

just talk to them and show them the light."[84]

Perot insisted that his mission had not been a failure:

> The purpose of the Christmas trip was not to take packages to prisoners, but to put the North Vietnamese in the position where they had to talk. We wanted to create a pressure-cooker situation where they had to see us. They didn't have to love us, but they had to see us.[85]

Perot offered the following facts as "tangible proof" that his efforts had not been in vain: the amount of mail received by prisoners had increased dramatically, prisoners had received better medical care, and the identities of more prisoners had been revealed.[86] These facts were later corroborated by released POWs.

Perot had also accomplished his secondary purpose of educating the American people on the plight of POWs.[87] Perot continued to meet with POW families, provided support to community efforts to publicize the issue, and gave speeches on behalf of the prisoners' cause wherever he was invited.[88] After the United States signed a cease-fire agreement providing for the return of all prisoners, Perot disclosed that he had been paying cash for almost four years, working through a shadowy world of "intermediaries" for information about and pictures of POWs. Men working for Perot, including EDS employees, met 47 times with Pathet Lao, North Vietnamese, and Vietcong representatives around the world.[89] Perot also contributed money to more problematic missions, including an armed expedition into Laos from Thailand in 1983. Not only was it unsuccessful, it halted official talks with the

Laotians for a year and may have violated the Logan Act, which prohibits private citizens from negotiating for the United States.[90]

Although Perot denied receiving support or encouragement from the White House for his efforts, a *Wall Street Journal* editorial pointed out that North Vietnamese suspicions that the Nixon administration was behind the project were not exactly contradicted by Perot's personal and political background. Perot had been a substantial contributor to Nixon's 1968 presidential campaign and 10 to 15 members of EDS management had worked on the Nixon campaign while on the company's payroll.[91] Perot also served as a trustee of the foundation that would build Nixon's presidential library.[92] Perot himself would later claim that Secretary of State Henry Kissinger had requested his help in publicizing the POW issue.[93]

Perot always described himself as a political independent and claimed to support Republican and Democratic candidates with contributions and his vote. Despite his propensity to speak out on public issues, Perot asserted that he would be a failure as a politician. "I'm a direct, action-oriented person and I'd be terrible in public office," he said.[94] He characterized his role as that of a catalyst: "I'm just the grain of sand in the oyster that makes the pearl."[95]

The Wall Street Experiment

Between 1964 and 1969, EDS revenues and earnings doubled each year.[96] To continue such spectacular growth in the face of increasing

---

[84] Pearlstein, "Quixotic Mission," p. 4.
[85] Powledge, "H. Ross Perot Pays His Dues," p. 25.
[86] Ibid.
[87] Ibid.
[88] Whitmore, "Business with a Social Thrust," p. 12.
[89] Levin, *Irreconcilable Differences,* p. 37.

[90] Mason, *Perot,* pp. 238, 243.
[91] Pearlstein, "Quixotic Mission," p. 4.
[92] *The New York Times,* May 13, 1969, pp. 1, 20.
[93] Levin, *Irreconcilable Differences,* p. 34.
[94] Nordheimer, "Billionaire Texan Fights Social Ills," p. 41.
[95] Wren, "Ross Perot: Billionaire Patriot," p. 32.
[96] Nordheimer, "Billionaire Texan Fights Social Ills," p. 41.

competition, EDS focused on the creation of broad-based "industry centers." After working with a small number of pilot companies, EDS designed a system to meet an industry's data processing needs from remote computer installations. In 1969, EDS was operating "industry centers" for insurance and food distribution companies, and future "centers" were planned for banks, utilities, and brokers."[97]

During the late 1960s, trading volume on Wall Street increased dramatically. Because brokerages lacked systems capable of processing the higher volume of transactions, their "back rooms" were strangled by massive amounts of disorganized paperwork. Perot thought that the troubles on Wall Street represented a huge opportunity for EDS.

In July 1970, EDS purchased the computer operations of F.I. duPont, Glore Forgan & Company, the nation's third-largest brokerage house, for EDS stock worth about $3.8 million.[98] EDS simultaneously received an eight-year facilities management contract with duPont worth at least $8 million annually. Perot denied any connection between the transactions, but, just a week earlier, duPont management had offered another computer services firm a back-office contract on the condition that the company put $4 million to $5 million into duPont. EDS's competitor had declined the offer.[99]

Perot became what some called the self-styled savior of Wall Street.[100] In numerous speeches to investment analysts, Perot, telling patriotic anecdotes and often accompanied by uniformed veterans, told Wall Street that its business practices were substandard. He suggested boldly that he and EDS might be the antidote to Wall Street's illness.[101]

Perot remained in Dallas and sent 37-year-old Mitch Hart, the president of EDS, and Morton Meyerson, an EDS vice president, to make an intensive study of duPont's finances.[102] The veterans quickly discovered that duPont was in much worse shape than Perot or EDS had thought when they signed the data processing contract.[103]

In late November 1970, the New York Stock Exchange (NYSE) confirmed that it had engaged EDS to evaluate the exchange's data processing and communications facilities.[104] Several days later, duPont revealed that it would receive a capital infusion from Perot.[105] Perot had been approached by Attorney General John Mitchell, Treasury Secretary John Connally, and members of a crisis committee formed by the NYSE. Perot was told that in rescuing duPont he would be performing a great service to his country.[106] Perot said:

> I felt that if ... duPont went under, Wall Street would be in serious danger of crumbling.... And if this mechanism — Wall Street — failed, there would have to be wholesale nationalization of capital-hungry industries. In turn, the taxpayer would then be expected to provide money for these industries.[107]

Although Perot later said that his decision to invest an additional $10 million in duPont was based 10 percent on economics and 90 percent on national interest,[108] he had

---

[97] "Texas Breeds New Billionaire," *Business Week*, August 30, 1969, p. 74; Whitmore, "Business with a Social Thrust," p. 6.

[98] *Business Week*, December 5, 1970, p. 78.

[99] *Business Week*, March 27, 1971, p. 74.

[100] Alan J. Mayer, "Savior or Swindler?" *Newsweek*, July 14, 1975, p. 64.

[101] Levin, *Irreconcilable Differences*, p. 41.

[102] Arthur M. Louis, "Ross Perot Moves in," *Fortune*, July 1971, pp. 90, 93.

[103] Levin, *Irreconcilable Differences*, p. 40.

[104] David McClintick, "Big Board Sets Study of Its Communications and Data Processing," *The Wall Street Journal*, November 24, 1970, p. 4.

[105] *The New York Times*, November 26, 1970, p. 65.

[106] Levin, *Irreconcilable Differences*, p. 42.

[107] Whitmore, "Business with a Social Thrust," p. 9.

[108] Ibid, p. 8.

contacted other major brokerage houses to ensure that his interest in duPont would not prevent EDS from receiving other back-office contracts.[109] Five Medicare subcontracts to EDS, which had been held up for a year or more, were approved by the Social Security Administration within six months after Perot's investment in duPont. Perot vigorously denied any connection between the events.[110]

In exchange for the loan, PHM Corporation, a privately held corporation formed by Perot, Hart, and Meyerson, received the right to acquire 51 percent or more of the stock of an incorporated duPont. PHM would receive additional equity if the duPont partners failed to provide a $15 million capital infusion within 90 days. The exchange overlooked the fact that the 90-day subordinated loan violated NYSE guidelines requiring a one-year minimum period for capital contributions.[111]

Perot soon became the center of controversy on Wall Street. What was his true character? Was Perot a ruthless bounty hunter and scalper taking advantage of well-mannered gentlefolk in temporary distress or was he a long-suffering and public-spirited citizen willing to endure appalling financial sloppiness and to put huge sums of his own money at risk for the country? In truth, it was a perfect Perot moral situation, of precisely the sort he had been drawn into, or perhaps created for himself, on many occasions over the years, in which he could make what he did a virtue and a virtue of what he did.[112]

As the March deadline approached and the partners' contribution failed to materialize,

rumors circulated that Perot would not renew the $10 million loan made in November.[113] The actual negotiations between the PHM group and the duPont partners were quite acrimonious. The duPonts resented what they saw as the unreasonable demands for equity made by Perot, and Perot was concerned that the funds he injected into the firm would be withdrawn by the partners. Perot was infuriated at what he considered the ingratitude of the duPont family, and he surmised that they wanted him to buy them off. Perot, who liked to relate how he came up the hard way, also resented "these people who have never worked."[114]

By May 14, 1971, Perot's group raised its total investment in duPont to $40 million in return for 80–88 percent of the firm's equity and a $15 million indemnification from the NYSE. The Federal Reserve Board granted a special exemption from its margin rules to allow PHM to borrow more against EDS stock.[115] NYSE chairman Bernard J. Lasker praised Perot, who was now the single biggest investor on Wall Street:

> . . . as long as there is a Wall Street we will owe a tremendous debt of gratitude to Ross Perot . . . I for one will be, as long as I live, forever grateful. . . . I think Ross Perot did something for the country, for the economy, for the investor, for confidence, for the industry, for the stock exchange, and for the firm's 180,000 customers.[116]

Others on Wall Street, however, questioned the motives of an investor who also had services to sell.[117] Some claimed that Perot had threatened to pull out of duPont if certain demands were not met, including a demand that he or his companies be allowed to invest in other

[109] *Business Week,* March 27, 1971, p. 76.

[110] Michael C. Jensen, "Texas Tornado Hits Wall Street," *The New York Times,* March 25, 1973, section III, pp. 1, 5.

[111] *Business Week,* December 19, 1970, p. 39.

[112] Brooks, *Go-Go Years,* p. 341.

[113] *The Wall Street Journal,* March 12, 1971, p. 4.

[114] Louis, "Ross Perot Moves in," p. 113.

[115] *New York Times,* April 3, 1971, p. 39; *The Wall Street Journal,* April 5, 1971, p. 7.

[116] *Business Week,* March 27, 1971, p. 72.

[117] *Business Week,* January 26, 1974, pp. 60, 61.

brokerages.[118] Rumors persisted that Perot had sought assurances that he would be compensated for taking over duPont by having much of the data processing business of the exchange community directed to his company.[119] Perot was convinced that the criticism was attributable to competitors who felt threatened by duPont: "They suddenly view duPont as a huge potential competitor and that's why you see the rash of snippy little stories."[120]

Perot insisted that he personally would not be on the board of the new corporation. "It would be a mistake for me to come in and dominate the firm," he said.[121] Although he was neither an officer nor a director of duPont, Perot conducted what amounted to an evangelical crusade within the firm. He traveled across the country in an effort to visit all 112 duPont offices, carrying the team philosophy personally to every duPont employee:[122] "We tell them we just don't want any whiners around—and the reaction has been thrilling."[123]

Perot wanted to do away with what he saw as Wall Street's hierarchical distinctions:

> There will be no back office or cage at du-Pont. Anyone who puts those names on important parts of the business is asking for trouble. We want this to be the most respected company in the brokerage business, to recruit the best possible people, and we want one class of employee at duPont.[124]

"I want people to identify with me, to create a closely knit team, rather than the lone wolves that characterize Wall Street,"

asserted Perot;[125] but his vocal patriotism didn't play well at duPont. New York was an intellectual center, Democratic, and hostile to the U.S. war effort. Many brokers and traders favored beards, long hair, bell-bottomed trousers, and colorful ties. Seeing these as symptoms of slackness that had caused duPont's monumental losses, Perot imposed EDS standards. The stockbrokers, however, balked at lockstep regimentation and crew-cut discipline.[126]

> The first day we got there we were all told to get short haircuts. Two blacks with Afros quit immediately. We were told to wear dark suits and bow ties. No mustaches. We took a course in how to sleep. How are you supposed to sleep? First you shake one arm, then the other arm, then both arms. Then you shake one leg, then the other leg, then both legs.[127]

In a speech before financial writers, Perot acknowledged that his tightly disciplined, aggressive approach to business was not always popular: "It's like a cold shower. You're either attracted by it or repelled by it. If you don't like it, there are a lot of other opportunities."[128]

Although only 33 years old and without any experience in the securities industry, Mort Meyerson was named president of duPont.[129] When Meyerson had joined EDS in 1965 it had seemed to him, the grandson of a Jewish tailor from the Lower East Side of New York, that everyone at EDS was a Perot clone: white, Protestant, and ex-Naval Academy. Although Meyerson fit only one of these categories, Perot found his offbeat, creative style complementary. Perot could always count on Meyerson to

[118] *New York Times,* May 2, 1972, Section F, p. 9.
[119] Ibid.
[120] Michael C. Jensen, "DuPont Walston Failure Is First Defeat for Perot," *The New York Times,* January 22, 1974, p. 55.
[121] *Business Week,* March 27, 1971, p. 74.
[122] Louis, "Ross Perot Moves in," p. 91.
[123] Whitmore, "Business with a Social Thrust," p. 9.
[124] *Business Week,* March 27, 1971, p. 76.

[125] *Time,* June 4, 1973, pp. 82, 84.
[126] Levin, *Irreconcilable Differences,* pp. 44, 46.
[127] Richard E. Rustin, "Foundering Firm," *The Wall Street Journal,* February 26, 1974, p. 4.
[128] John J. Abele, *The New York Times,* September 10, 1971, p. 45.
[129] *The Wall Street Journal,* April 19, 1971, p. 8.

give him a slightly oblique approach to solving a problem.[130]

Meyerson, described by a duPont partner as "a young man in a hurry," said, "I look on this firm as a sleeping giant that we've got to wake up. We want to look like a hard-charging outfit." He instituted daily 8:00 A.M. meetings for department heads.[131] Meyerson and his team reorganized many departments and established a "meaningful" internal reporting system.[132] The firm closed its books every night. Meyerson formed a surveillance group to educate the firm's employees about securities regulations and to police their activities.[133] EDS executives were assigned as administrative aides to duPont people.[134]

Meyerson's inexperience and his tendency to surround himself with "yes men" resulted in what one former duPont salesman referred to as "lousy management."[135] The celebrated 8:00 A.M. meetings were discontinued when early high attendance fell off. Newly recruited duPont executives complained of constant politicking.[136] Critics noted that no significant cutbacks were made in the number of branch offices, allowing EDS to continue to receive revenues for processing the firm's trades.[137]

In late August 1971, an audit revealed that the firm had unresolved differences of $86 million in its accounts due to such problems as missing securities, bad debts, and incorrect dividend payments. PHM increased its cash investment by $35 million.

Although Perot could not duplicate the character of the EDS work force at duPont overnight, he could affect change through new recruits.[138] In September 1971, Meyerson was joined by a former Marine Corps recruiter who had left his position as head of EDS recruiting to coordinate recruiting efforts for duPont.[139] Veterans, especially the gung-ho types who filled EDS's ranks, would be welcome.[140] Perot set up a $14 million-a-year training school in Beverly Hills, which offered a six-month course for securities salesmen. In between classes in salesmanship in the mornings and studying for their stockbrokers' licenses in the evening, the recruits made cold calls for the United Way to sharpen their telephone skills.[141]

Recruiting ex-military men didn't work as well in brokerage sales as it had in EDS's computer operations, however. A man who thrived on the tight order and teamwork of a combat unit didn't necessarily possess the initiative and interpersonal skills to develop retail brokerage accounts.[142] In making clear his distrust of old-time employees, and in trying to force the staff into a paramilitary mold, his critics said, Perot succeeded only in destroying one of the firm's major strengths: its crackerjack sales organization.[143]

With the firm operating in the black for the first 10 months of 1971, Perot was asserting that there had been a "dramatic turnaround" in duPont's operations since his group assumed control.[144] In April 1972, however, a recapitalization plan was completed with Perot

[130] Levin, *Irreconcilable Differences,* p. 51.
[131] "How Perot Operates duPont, Glore Forgan," *Business Week,* October 21, 1971, p. 72.
[132] *The Wall Street Journal,* August 23, 1971, p. 5.
[133] *Fortune,* July 1971, p. 115.
[134] Mason, *Perot,* p. 110.
[135] *Business Week,* January 26, 1974, pp. 60, 62.
[136] Art Detman, "Can Ross Perot Change Wall Street?" *Dun's,* March 1973, p. 49.
[137] *Business Week,* January 26, 1974, pp. 60, 62.

[138] Levin, *Irreconcilable Differences,* p. 44.
[139] *Business Week,* October 2, 1971, p. 72.
[140] Levin, *Irreconcilable Differences,* p. 44.
[141] Mason, *Perot,* p. 112.
[142] Levin, *Irreconcilable Differences,* pp. 46–47.
[143] Rustin, "Foundering Firm," p. 1.
[144] Richard E. Rustin, and Wayne E. Green, *The Wall Street Journal,* November 24, 1971, p. 4.

providing an additional $9 million in capital. The exchange also provided the $15 million indemnification previously promised. Mort Meyerson declared, "The firm's capital problems are now history."[145]

In July 1972, after a year and a half of discussions, Perot invested $5 million in Walston & Company, Inc. as part of a refinancing program that could ultimately give him a one-third interest in the firm. Although the NYSE had amended its constitution to allow Perot to make loans to more than one member firm,[146] the investment was made by a concern formed by Perot and his wife Margot to ward off potential Justice Department objections.[147] EDS simultaneously signed a 10-year data processing contract with Walston.

By spring 1973, Perot had assumed operational control at duPont, despite having denied any intention to do so when he first took over the firm. Perot personally hired all duPont recruits. He sought out personal exposure, including television talk-show guest spots and speeches before investment industry and business groups. Said Perot: "Wall Street needs flesh-and-blood identification. They have to identify with someone. Everywhere I go people stop me to talk about the securities business."[148]

Perot, like many others on Wall Street, believed that the fundamental problem was the flight of the small investor from the market. Perot wrote the copy and approved the layouts for a duPont ad campaign in April 1973, which featured a drawing of Perot's face and outlined his investment philosophy.[149]

Institutional investors, however, dominated the stock market and created the most profitable commission business for brokers. The individual investors sought by duPont were not really "the little guys," according to a former duPont salesman:

We were told to go after the elephants, Mr. Perot's term for fat cats, big investors, company presidents, guys like that. We were told the little guy wasn't at all important. He gives you too much trouble, you can't make any money off him. The elephants already were established with other brokers. They weren't sitting around doing nothing: Believe me, they were pretty hard to find.[150]

A partial consolidation of Walston and duPont was completed in July 1973, creating the second-largest brokerage firm in the United States.[151] Perot gained voting control of Walston without increasing his $10 million investment in the firm. Antitrust objections were overcome by invoking the "failing firm" doctrine, and critics claimed that the move had been necessary to prevent the collapse of duPont.[152] Perot had also bought significant earnings for EDS, with contracts from duPont and Walston estimated to bring in 18 percent of EDS's 1973 revenues.[153]

Perot never gained the acceptance of the Wall Street "club" that couldn't forget or forgive the hard bargain he struck with the duPont partners.[154] Edmond duPont brought a lawsuit, alleging that Perot breached his fiduciary relationship with the partnership while EDS computer programmers had access to the books. The widow of Walston's founder also

---

[145] John J. Abele, "Dupont Firm Gets New Net Capital," *The New York Times,* April 7, 1972, p. 45.
[146] *Business Week,* April 3, 1979, p. 74.
[147] Detman, "Can Ross Perot Change Wall Street?" p. 49.
[148] *Business Week,* May 26, 1973, p. 64.
[149] Ibid.

[150] Rustin, p. 1.
[151] *New York Times,* February 14, 1974, p. 61.
[152] *Business Week,* September 29, 1973, pp. 32. 33.
[153] Detman, "Can Ross Perot Change Wall Street?" p. 48.
[154] *Business Week,* January 26, 1974, pp. 60, 61.

brought suit, to nullify the consolidation of the two firms because duPont had failed to disclose what bad shape it was in.

The situation at duPont continued to deteriorate. It was estimated that over 10 percent of the firm's salespeople had left the firm between July 1973 and January 1974.[155] In the two years since Perot had taken over duPont, the firm had lost $32 million and Walston was also losing money. Meanwhile, Perot had poured another $12.8 million into duPont and another $5 million into Walston, for a total investment in the two firms of $92 million. The expected rush of data processing business had never materialized, with only two other firms having signed up for EDS's data processing services.

By late January 1974, Perot had had enough. DuPont Walston, the nation's second-largest brokerage, announced that it would attempt to sell its retail brokerage operations and liquidate the rest of its operations. EDS stock traded at $18 3/8 per share. Perot's estimated fortune fell to $160 million.

Perot told associates that he felt like a cotton farmer who lost his crop to the bugs just as he was about to bring it in. He claimed that the environment on Wall Street was so dismal during the period when he and his aides were attempting to make duPont profitable that it could hardly have succeeded no matter how skilled the management.[156] After all, NYSE firms collectively had lost $80 million in 1973 after showing a profit of $787 million in 1972.[157]

"Whatever else you say about them, you have to give the Perot people credit for working their tails off — 80 hours a week wasn't unusual," said a Wall Street executive.[158] Although Perot's team had cleared up a monumental back-office mess at duPont, there were those who felt that other reasons contributed to the problems:

> They [the Perot people] failed because they didn't recognize that although duPont's back office was really screwed up in 1968 and 1969, the firm's producing parts were in excellent condition. If they had let the production people continue to run without interference and had been content to put in capital, I think the firm would have made it easily. But they considered that everyone who had been associated with the partnership was incompetent.[159]

Another Wall Street executive commented:

> There's no doubt that Perot saved duPont from certain failure and maybe averted a major crisis in the industry, although, don't forget, it was a good thing for EDS, too. What I'm tired of, though, is his holier-than-thou attitude. He acts like he's going to save the industry, but he doesn't know beans about Wall Street.[160]

After Wall Street

EDS had lost sales momentum in the early 1970s as attention focused on duPont. Competition increased and margins dropped. EDS stock fell to less than $11 per share in late 1974.[161]

Meyerson returned to Dallas and EDS in 1975 without a defined role but determined to prove himself. Perot asked him to find out what was wrong with EDS's faltering Medicaid and Medicare business. Meyerson asked Ken Riedlinger, then a promising manager in EDS's Columbus, Ohio, office, to be the regional manager in charge of selling contracts in the eastern United States.[162]

---

[155] *Business Week,* January 26, 1974, p. 63.
[156] Jensen, "DuPont Walston Failure," p. 55.
[157] *Time,* February 4, 1974, p. 69.
[158] Rustin, p. 4.

[159] *The Wall Street Journal,* February 26, 1974, pp. 1, 31.
[160] Detman, "Can Ross Perot Change Wall Street?" p. 48.
[161] Levin, *Irreconcilable Differences,* pp. 49–50.
[162] Ibid, pp. 50–52.

Beginning in 1971, state and federal investigators questioned the nature of EDS contracts to process state Medicare and Medicaid claims. EDS's persistent refusal to open its books to government auditors resulted in charges that the company was trying to hide excessive profits made from government health programs. Perot maintained EDS profits were in line with those in major industries and that estimates putting EDS profit margins in the 100–200 percent range were wild exaggerations by biased bureaucrats. He would open his books, he said, when the government required it of all private subcontractors and stopped "zeroing in" on EDS.[163]

Investigations also covered Perot's earliest activities at EDS. Perot had run the Texas Blue Shield (TBS) computer department on a part-time basis after leaving IBM, and one of his first deals for EDS was to sell the excess computer capacity of another former IBM client, Southwestern Mutual Life, to TBS.[164] In 1965, EDS received a data processing subcontract for the new Medicare program from TBS. The claims processing system used by EDS had been developed by TBS at government expense.[165]

Critics also complained that EDS got many of its contracts even though it was not the lowest bidder and that Perot used his political clout to get contracts. In 1973, a storm of controversy surrounded the awarding of a $125,000 consulting contract to EDS in New York when it was revealed that Perot had met personally with Governor Nelson Rockefeller after EDS had previously been rejected from the competition.

In August 1974, it was divulged that Mitch Hart and an EDS vice president had secretly funneled $100,000 through dummy committees into the 1972 presidential campaign of Representative Wilbur Mills of Arkansas. At the time, Mills was head of the House Ways and Means Committee and was expected to have a guiding influence on any national health insurance plan.[166]

Although EDS often countered that its superior capabilities warranted higher fees, EDS's performance was not immune to criticism. Within six months of EDS's takeover of the Illinois Medicare system in April 1979, the backlog of unprocessed claims mushroomed and the error rate on processed claims was 25 percent. EDS failed all five major performance standard tests during the contract's first year and paid contractual penalties of almost $700,000. A public outcry led to full-scale HEW and GAO investigations and a Congressional Health Care subcommittee inquiry.[167]

EDS maintained that the government seemed bent on running EDS out of the Medicare and Medicaid-processing business. According to Perot and other EDS officials, some federal employees were sponsoring their own programs instead of the one developed and marketed by EDS. "My people painted a Rembrandt," Perot said of EDS's work for the government's insurance carriers. "And now they're being criticized by people who couldn't whitewash a fence."[168]

Riedlinger was determined to help Meyerson turn EDS around. If EDS needed more time, he tried to delay bid deadlines. If EDS was ready but its competition needed more time,

[163] Francis X. Clines, "Perot: Supersalesman in Relief Controversy," *The New York Times*, September 24, 1973, p. 35.

[164] "Shrinkage?" *Forbes*, June 15, 1972, p. 25.

[165] Fitch, "America's First Welfare Billionaire," pp. 43–44.

[166] *The New York Times*, August 2, 1974.

[167] Rosenbaum, "Ross Perot to the Rescue!" p. 69.

[168] "Ross Perot's Problem Child," *Newsweek*, February 18, 1974, p. 77.

he tried to convince health care commissioners to move the date up.[169]

Riedlinger's aggressive tactics won numerous contracts for EDS. When EDS lost out in bidding for renewal of its Texas Medicaid contract in July 1980, Perot called Riedlinger back in to lead the fight. Riedlinger's strategy was to make sure that anything that compromised the reputation of the winning bidder, Bradford National Corporation of New York, appeared on TV and in the newspapers. After Perot made personal visits to three of its members, the Texas State Board of Human Resources called for an evaluation of the award by independent consultants.[170]

The consultants affirmed the original decision, but Perot sued to block the awarding of the contract. Riedlinger sent a private jet to bring a New York state senator to Texas to publicly criticize Bradford's professional competence in its performance on a similar contract with New York state. Stories about alleged attempted bribery by Bradford appeared in papers across the country. In January 1981, the board announced that it would start the bidding process all over again. By the time bidding was reopened in 1982, Bradford had completely dropped out of the Medicaid business and EDS won the contract unopposed.[171]

Riedlinger loved working with Perot in the heat of battle, and to him, the victory over Bradford was an emotional event that further bound him to Perot and EDS. While Riedlinger's actions hadn't precisely squared with the noble ideals of his youth, he tried to put the reservations out of his mind.[172]

Adventure in Iran

For nearly a decade after his stock exchange escapade, Perot avoided the spotlight, slowly shed his eccentric image, and settled down to business.[173] In a 1979 interview, Perot said that he'd like everybody to forget about him and his curious adventures and focus on EDS. "EDS is always represented as a dismal failure, and I'm seen as a businessman who lost a billion dollars."[174]

In November 1976, EDS moved overseas, signing a $41 million contract with the Iranian government to computerize the country's social security and national health insurance programs. By December 1978, as revolutionary turmoil spread through Iran, the Iranian government was six months and $5 million behind on its payments to EDS. Perot decided to stop operations and evacuate his employees from the country.

On December 28, 1978, Iranian authorities responded to EDS's pullout by arresting and imprisoning EDS's country manager for Iran and his assistant. Although no charges had been brought against them, bail for the two men was set at $12.75 million. The two men were later charged with bribing Iranian officials to obtain the EDS contract with the government, but Perot maintained that the men were being held hostage to coerce EDS into continuing to run the social security computers.

Perot first tried to use his network of connections in Washington to pressure the Iranian government, but he quickly became impatient with the lack of results. In a later interview, Perot recalled:

> Now the turning point was . . . my mother was dying of cancer. She knew the men were being

---

[169] Levin, *Irreconcilable Differences,* p. 53.
[170] Ibid, p. 63.
[171] Ibid, p. 64.
[172] Ibid.

[173] Rosenbaum, "Ross Perot to the Rescue!" p. 60.
[174] Elizabeth Bailey, "Getting EDS into Washington," *Forbes,* May 14, 1979, p. 178.

held hostage. I laid the whole thing out to her and I said, "What do you think we ought to do?" And she said, "I don't think there's any question but that you have to go rescue them. That's it."[175]

Perot put together a squad of eight EDS executives with military backgrounds and asked retired Green Beret colonel Arthur D. "Bull" Simons to train and lead them. In 1970, Simons had led an unsuccessful raid on a North Vietnamese POW camp and an admiring Perot had organized a reunion party for the raiders and the POWs in 1973.

On January 13, 1979, Perot secretly went into Iran at great personal risk to make one last attempt at a negotiated solution. The negotiations failed, however, and on January 18, the two men were transferred to a different, more heavily fortified prison, rendering useless the squad's planned rescue operation. Perot went to the prison to visit the two men to boost their morale.

On February 11, 1979, the prison was stormed by a mob, and thousands of inmates, including the two EDS executives, poured out into the streets. Simons and one team of EDS commandos took the two men overland through Iran to the Turkish border, where they met up with the other members of the squad. Perot was waiting with a leased 707 in Istanbul to take the team back to Dallas. Perot would always say later that he had arranged for the raid on the Iranian prison, which he called "the largest jailbreak in history." In 1981, Perot hired Ken Follett, the best-selling author of spy thrillers, to memorialize the rescue of the EDS executives. *On Wings of Eagles* became a best-seller and was the basis for a 1986 television movie.

Later, when U.S. embassy personnel were seized in Iran, a country-and-western song titled "Where Are You Now When We Need You, Ross Perot?" got considerable airplay. The day after the failure of the U.S. commando rescue mission, *The Dallas Morning News* ran a story that was headlined, in apparent astonishment, PEROT NOT CONSULTED ON RAID.[176]

GM Comes to Call[177]

On April 2, 1984, Perot took a call from John Gutfreund, the chairman of Salomon Brothers, a major New York investment bank. The following day, Gutfreund was in Perot's legendary Dallas office. There was a copy of a Frederic Remington sculpture, "The Spirit of '76" painting of the Yankee Doodle dandies, and numerous paintings by Norman Rockwell. Displayed along with abundant photographs of Margot and their five children was a framed canceled $1,000 check, the initial capitalization for EDS in 1962.

Meyerson, whom Perot had named president of EDS in 1979, joined the meeting. Gutfreund relayed a message from his client, General Motors, that it would like to acquire EDS in a friendly transaction. Perot and Meyerson had been prepared for a potential offer, but they were stunned that it was coming from General Motors.

Both Perot and Meyerson recognized the potential business for EDS in meeting the huge computer service needs of General Motors. GM owned over 200 IBM mainframes, more than 200,000 terminals, and used several CAD/CAM systems. In 1984, GM spent approximately $6 billion on data processing. The

---

[175] Richard Shenkman, "Rescue by the Private Sector," *National Review,* May 30, 1980, pp. 652, 653.

[176] Rosenbaum, "Ross Perot to the Rescue!" p. 62.
[177] This section and the following one are taken largely from Levin except where noted otherwise.

paperwork for GM's health care programs alone amounted to 40 million claims each year from GM employees, families, and retirees. GM's health care costs averaged $450 per car in 1983.

One week later, Perot called Gutfreund and asked for a get-acquainted meeting with Roger Smith and General Motors in Detroit. While Perot didn't think that GM's interest would result in a full-fledged merger offer, he was flattered at their interest in his company.

As Meyerson and Perot flew over GM facilities in a helicopter, they were impressed by the huge scale on which GM operated. Once inside the headquarters of General Motors' data processing division, however, Meyerson noticed outdated equipment and saw people applying the computers in ways that struck him as rather quaint, compared with applications by some of EDS's customers.

Over lunch, Roger Smith explained his vision of what General Motors could accomplish with EDS's computer expertise. GM would become a "paperless" company, with engineering, designing, manufacturing, sales, and financing all handled by one computer network. As he talked of his plans for GM, Smith became increasingly excited. He used expressions like "Holy Toledo!" and "Gee whiz!" He was sincere and likable, and he was funny, Perot and Meyerson thought.

A week later, Roger Smith and F. Alan Smith, GM's chief financial officer, paid a reciprocal visit to EDS headquarters. The two men saw that what they had read of Perot and his company was true. While some of the rigid rules had been relaxed, (e.g., pastel-colored shirts and mustaches were now permitted), the EDS organization was still a disciplined team of highly motivated individuals.

Within a few days, a small team from GM, Salomon, and the law firm Skadden, Arps, Meagher and Flom arrived in Dallas. Once GM had completed its financial due diligence investigation of EDS, Meyerson headed a team

of a dozen EDS employees dispatched to Detroit to figure out what EDS could do for GM. After three days of discussions with GM engineers, the team members presented the results of their study to Alan Smith.

By May 1984, the secrecy surrounding the exploratory talks between GM and EDS had begun to evaporate. Dan Dorfman, a financial journalist with his own cable program, called Mort Meyerson to ask if EDS was in merger negotiations with anyone. Meyerson denied that anything was going on.

The Genesis of Class E Stock

The cover story for the visiting teams of executives had been that GM was evaluating a potential data processing contract with EDS. For Perot and Meyerson, the cover story constituted their true version of reality. They understood that GM wanted to acquire EDS, but they believed that a giant data processing contract, or perhaps a joint venture, was most desirable for both companies.

Perot tried to explain to Roger Smith why acquiring EDS was a self-defeating idea during a series of one-on-one meetings in Dallas: "Our people are extremely independent, and they're given an extraordinary amount of freedom on the job. They can't be under the authority of the people they're trying to help. It won't work." GM executives, however, were adamant that whoever had access to and control over GM's most sensitive information had to be part of GM and not an outside contractor.

Perot also noted the disparity in the compensation systems of the two companies. While GM had a generous bonus program, it could not match the opportunities offered to valued EDS employees to participate in the company's stock price appreciation.

By early May, the two sides were at an impasse over the issues of compensation and independence. One night, over dinner at a Chinese restaurant in Dallas, the GM team

EXHIBIT 1 Summary Financial Information for the Years Ended June 30, 1970–1979 ($ in thousands)

	1970	1971	1972	1973	1974	1975	1976	1977	1978	1979
Operating results:										
Revenues	$47,617	$75,226	$90,955	$111,882	$118,734	$123,896	$132,952	$164,188	$217,837	$274,298
Net income	7,214	10,671	12,603	15,200	15,349	14,648	13,602	16,428	19,666	23,702
Earnings per share	0.30	0.44	0.52	0.64	0.64	0.60	0.55	0.66	0.77	0.91
Financial position:										
Total assets	40,558	63,129	78,941	98,501	114,849	96,753	101,846	112,893	130,431	175,620
Long-term debt	4,493	2,848	1,054	102	3,486	3,034	2,249	3,695	2,638	11,144
Stockholders' equity	23,310	38,905	52,814	66,145	82,901	66,884	76,149	87,242	97,628	120,076
Other information:										
Employees		2,898	3,168	3,428	3,499	3,660	3,942	6,386	6,399	9,343

113

came up with the outline for a solution. GM would create a new class of stock whose dividend would be tied to the performance of EDS. The Class E (E for EDS) stock would technically be GM stock, but in reality would represent ownership rights in only a small part of GM. A major hurdle to be faced was the NYSE policy of opposing multiple classes of common stock. GM would be transferring profits from GM common stock, trading at a multiple of six times its earnings, to a stock that traded at 16 times earnings.[178]

On Wednesday, May 16, 1984, Dan Dorfman reported that EDS was in "exploratory merger talks" that could lead to the acquisition of EDS by a "giant U.S. corporation." As its share price continued to rise in response to the rumors, EDS was forced to acknowledge that talks were taking place, although it did not identify its suitor. Perot was disappointed that word was out, because he still wasn't absolutely sure what, if anything, he wanted to do about GM. The following day, however, Perot confirmed to a *Wall Street Journal* reporter that GM had approached EDS. In a separate interview, Meyerson told *The Wall Street Journal* that investors should not assume the inevitability of a GM acquisition of EDS. GM and EDS might form a joint venture or work out a data service contract, with GM taking an equity position in EDS.

---

[178] Mason, *Perot,* p. 136.

TOM MONAGHAN:
IN BUSINESS FOR GOD

Late in 1990, Tom Monaghan, the owner and founder of Domino's Pizza, Inc., announced that he was interested in selling his successful pizza-delivery chain to give himself more time to spend on his various philanthropies. Monaghan, 54, had led Domino's from a single pizza store to the largest pizza-delivery business in the world. The Ann Arbor, Michigan-based Domino's achieved a record $2.5 billion in sales in its 5,185 franchises in 1990.

A devout Roman Catholic, Monaghan had also enjoyed the things that money could buy.

He fulfilled a childhood dream in 1984, for example, when he bought the Detroit Tigers. During two decades, the Detroit press contrasted two sides of his character, but Monaghan had seen no conflicts; in 1986, he wrote:

> I never confuse these sides of my makeup. So I see no contradiction between, on the one hand, sitting down at home to a simple meal that my wife spoons out of the pots it was cooked in and, on the other, insisting that the meals in the executive dining room at Domino's headquarters be of five-star quality, impeccably served, with white linen tablecloths, fine china designed by Frank Lloyd Wright, silverware, and crystal glasses.[1]

This case was prepared by Stephen J. Sallah under the direction of Joseph Badaracco, Jr.

Copyright © 1992 by the President and Fellows of Harvard College.

Harvard Business School case 392-079.

---

[1] Thomas S. Monaghan, *Pizza Tiger* (New York: Random House, 1986), p. 7.

Tom Monaghan's Early Years

Tom Monaghan was born in Ann Arbor, Michigan, in 1937; his brother Jim was born two years later. Their father, Francis Monaghan, had worked as a hay baler on a local farm and later drove a tractor trailer for the Interstate Company. Their mother, Anna (Geddes) Monaghan, left nurses' training to raise the boys.

Tom was four years old when Francis Monaghan died on Christmas Eve, at age 39, of peritonitis. Anna Monaghan took her two sons to the wake. When Tom saw his dead father, he was frightened and pulled away from his mother, jumped on his father's chest, and screamed, "Wake up, Daddy, wake up!" Most of what Monaghan learned about his father came from a diary his mother kept, but he still harbored memories of his father and his untimely death. Monaghan wrote:

> Our little house in the country near Ann Arbor, Michigan, seemed empty to me from then on. I have many memories of that place and the yard around it, where I used to play. My earliest recollection is of running after Dad when I was about two years old; I wanted to be with him wherever he went. I remember watching him at work outside the house and wondering why he used three nails instead of one to fasten a board.[2]

Anna Monaghan used the $2,000 that she received from her husband's life insurance to pay off the house and property. Unable to afford the expenses of raising two boys, she put them into foster homes. In addition, Tom was a difficult child, strong and restless; as a single mother, Anna Monaghan felt overwhelmed. She planned to finish nursing school, get a job, and bring the boys back home.

After short stays at several foster homes, Monaghan and his brother were sent first to live with an elderly couple, Mr. and Mrs. Frank Woppman. The couple maintained strict rules, but keeping the house clean and quiet proved difficult for the hyperactive Tom. He and his brother were soon sent to a Catholic orphanage in Jackson, Michigan, run by nuns. It was there that Monaghan first developed his love for architecture. The orphanage was an old Victorian mansion, and its large cupola commanded a view of the terrace.

> I learned how big that yard was when I had to push one of the dozens of lawnmowers the nuns kept stored behind the latticework of the rambling old porches. I learned a lot of other things in the orphanage, too: how to scrub and polish floors and iron shirts and trousers by the hundreds. I became the fastest ironer in the place. In addition to these chores, every boy had an assigned duty. Mine was to clean the carved banisters of the soaring main staircase. I was fascinated by the way the stairs were constructed. They were at least eight feet wide; they would accommodate all the boys in the orphanage as a grandstand from which to watch movies. But their most striking feature was a tall newel post topped by a large statue of St. Joseph.[3]

Monaghan spent six and a half years at St. Joseph's. He was a good student for the first two years and credited this to the attention and encouragement he received from one particular nun:

> Sister Berarda always encouraged me, even when my ideas seemed far-fetched. I remember telling the class that when I grew up I wanted to be a priest, an architect, and a shortstop for the Tigers. The other kids laughed and said that it was impossible to do all three. Sister Berarda quieted them down and said, "Well, I don't think it's ever been done before, Tommy, but if you want to do it, there's no reason you can't." That was inspiring.[4]

---

[2] Ibid, p. 22.

[3] Ibid, p. 27.
[4] Ibid, p. 30.

Anna Monaghan visited the boys fairly often and always spoke of bringing them home. She had moved to Traverse City in northern Michigan, working on the nursing staff of a local hospital. When Tom and his brother were in the sixth grade, they went to live with their mother.

Monaghan remembered "how exciting it was to be free, to be able to come and go . . . to be allowed to have money in my pocket, to be able to make money."[5] But the relationship with his mother was never good, and he stayed away as much as possible to avoid arguing with her. He attended school during the day and worked in the evenings. Unfortunately, the problems with his mother worsened and, within a year, she turned him back to the state foster care system. Jim remained with his mother.

The rest of Tom's childhood was spent on farms, one of which was owned by Mr. and Mrs. Edwin Crouch. The soil was especially difficult to work, and the reason that the Crouches took in foster children was immediately apparent to Tom. They treated him well and, despite the rocky soil, Tom enjoyed the chores. He was given a small windowless room with no heat or lights, and he read by a crack in the wall where daylight entered. Inspired that Abe Lincoln could become president by reading in such circumstances, Monaghan became a regular patron of the public library. He read all its architecture books, especially the ones about his idol, Frank Lloyd Wright, and he spent hours daydreaming about Tom Monaghan, famous architect, or Tom Monaghan, teenage tycoon.

Religion became increasingly important as he entered high school. He never missed Mass on Sundays and, as an altar boy, he became friendly with the parish priest, Father Passeno. The two had long discussions about relationships and Father Passeno helped Tom cope

with the misunderstandings with his mother. As a show of gratitude, Monaghan used his earnings from an entire summer to buy the priest a Lalique glass statue of the Virgin Mary.

In the spring of his freshman year of high school, Monaghan decided he had a religious vocation:

> I'll never forget that moment of revelation, because it came when I was on the Crouch farm shoveling manure. The symbolism of the situation was overpowering: Standing up to my ankles in muck, I saw that I had been wallowing in crass, worldly thoughts when I should have been concentrating on my spiritual quest. I decided then and there that I would become a priest. I remember what I had told Sister Berarda, and I intended to make good on it.[6]

Father Passeno helped him apply to the seminary in Grand Rapids. The priest warned him that the adjustment would be difficult and that he was already a year behind; but when Monaghan was accepted, he felt elated and decided to attend.

Monaghan didn't make it through the first year. He was called to the rector's office and told that he "lacked the vocation" to become a priest. No other setback devastated him like this one. Looking back, he felt that the similarities between the seminary and the orphanage were difficult to deal with and kept him sidestepping the rules. Once he developed a bad reputation among the upperclassmen, who acted as proctors, it was difficult to stay out of the rector's office.

When he returned home, his mother was furious and the bickering started immediately. To make matters worse, Monaghan found that he and his brother had grown apart. So he rarely went home and instead set pins at the local bowling alley for meals, attending school everyday but never studying. One day the county sheriff drove alongside Monaghan on

---

[5] Ibid, p. 31.

[6] Ibid, p. 35.

his way to the bowling alley and announced he was going to take him to the detention home. Monaghan recalled:

> I was in shock. It was like some awful nightmare. I had committed no crime. I had never been delinquent in any way. Yet here I was being locked up like a common thief. The custodian's wife told me my mother had signed the order; she just couldn't put up with me any longer. I didn't know how I would face the other kids at school after they learned I was in the detention home with juvenile delinquents and some real criminals.[7]

Monaghan, embarrassed by his predicament, began taking a circuitous route to and from school that took him through his mother's neighborhood. This way he kept his secret from his classmates. The only person who knew was his basketball coach, Joe Kraupa. Monaghan became friendly with Kraupa, who kept his secret and treated him decently.

Life at the detention home was "void of compassion." Monaghan was appalled at the stealing and other criminal behavior, and the way the other kids seemed to accept it. Monaghan quickly made friends with the custodians and with one of the policemen and his wife. Sometimes he would even "talk to a kid by hand" for the custodians. Monaghan had always been a good boxer and admitted to enjoying a good fight from time to time.

Within six months, Monaghan's Aunt Peg, his father's sister, found out about the situation and was irate. She took him home with her to Ann Arbor. Monaghan loved the family atmosphere there, especially sitting around at night and hearing stories of Monaghan's father as a boy.

Monaghan attended St. Thomas High School. He also worked as a soda jerk, earning 55 cents an hour. Monaghan strove to be the fastest in town. He continued setting pins at night and worked as a busboy on weekends. He couldn't settle down as a student, however, and graduated 44th in a class of 44. His yearbook picture bore the following caption: "The harder I try to be good, the worse I get; but I may do something sensational yet."[8]

After graduation, Monaghan wanted to attend college. His aunt and uncle explained that they needed his room and he was forced to get lodging elsewhere. His grades were too low for the University of Michigan, so he attended Ferris State College in Grand Rapids, which was affordable and had an architectural trade program. With this degree and nine years of field experience, he could become a licensed architect. This was his only chance of fulfilling his life-long dream.

His grades were excellent at Ferris and he was soon accepted to the University of Michigan. Unfortunately, unable to find a job in Detroit that paid enough to support himself and his education, he never accepted the offer.

Frustrated, Monaghan hitchhiked to Chicago. He found a room in an inexpensive hotel and a job setting pins at a bowling alley. Concerned about his emerging career as a pin setter, Monaghan walked into what he thought was an Army recruiter's office and enlisted. The next day, during his physical, he asked one of the recruits if the ball-and-anchor symbol on the wall was an Army symbol. The man responded, "It's the Marines, you dummy!" At the time, Monaghan didn't believe there was much difference, but he soon changed his thinking.

The discipline and rigor of the Marines were not difficult for Monaghan, who was a natural athlete and accustomed to a structured environment. He was shocked, however, at the drill instructors' foul language. He had heard language like this before but never from someone in authority. Eventually, though, what seemed

---

[7] Ibid, p. 38.

[8] Alson and Greenwalt, p. 106.

at first like constant harassing and berating started to make sense to him:

> This is what leadership is built on. The Corps appears to be powering over individuals when, in fact, it is empowering them, teaching them self motivation. This is the source of the Marines' famous *esprit de corps* . . . my perspective has changed. If I had a son, the best advice I could give him would be to serve a hitch in the Marines before going into business.[9]

After boot camp and advanced infantry training, Monaghan was sent to Okinawa. He spent most of his free time at the base library reading every book that he thought could help him improve himself, including all the works of Dale Carnegie and Norman Vincent Peale. He also started to dream about his life: building a house in the country and farming his own food. Reading up on different regions of the country to determine where he would settle down, he began to envision himself rich and successful, which drove him to study even more.

While in transit from Japan to the Philippines, Monaghan reflected on his life and developed the first version of his Five Personal Priorities:

> Now I was pulled up short by the realization that the exciting scenarios I'd been creating— which I had no doubt would someday be realized—could turn out to be empty and meaningless if they lacked consideration for others and for God. I asked myself what good a lot of money would be to me if I didn't have friends, a good marriage, continued good health, or I didn't go to heaven. . . . I was certain that no matter how elaborate or grandiose my daydreams got, I would never get to the point where I would violate my Catholic upbringing. From these kinds of thoughts I developed my priorities.[10]

Monaghan said his priorities guided every aspect of his life, including the building and management of Domino's Pizza. (The Appendix presents a later version of the Five Personal Priorities.)

Just before leaving the Marines, Monaghan met an oilman, John Patrick Ryan, during a liberty call in Las Vegas. It was 1960 and Ryan talked of the big oil strikes in Texas. Fascinated at all the high-powered transactions in which Ryan had been involved, Monaghan gave him $500 in cash, and Ryan promised to triple his investment in 90 days. This money was quickly used up and, to protect his investment, Monaghan wired Ryan the rest of his bank account. He never heard from John Patrick Ryan again.

After losing his savings from the Marines, Monaghan was again unable to attend the University of Michigan. He stayed with his brother in Ann Arbor, who was working for the post office. His brother also held odd jobs, one of which was working nights at DomiNick's Pizza Parlor in Ypsilanti. Tom opened a newsstand and started a *New York Times* paper route, the first of its kind west of the Allegheny Mountains. He got the idea from the large number of professors in the area who regularly bought the newspaper.

Jim wanted to buy DomiNick's Pizza Parlor and take turns running it with Tom. The price was $500 plus the assumption of $3,000 in debt. This seemed like a lot of money, but Monaghan reasoned that, since it was only open seven hours a day, he and his brother would only have to work three and a half hours each. Jim could keep his job at the post office, and Tom could keep his newsstand. With $75 in cash and a note from the bank, the brothers were in business.

Domino's Pizza, Inc.

On December 1, 1960, Tom and Jim Monaghan reopened the doors of DomiNick's Pizza, which had been closed for six months. Unable to

---

[9] *Pizza Tiger,* p. 44.
[10] Ibid, p. 47.

depend on a regular customer base, Monaghan hired two unemployed men to deliver pizza, paying each 10 cents per delivery plus a 10 percent commission. Because the delivery business, mostly to the university, was very successful, the brothers decided to focus on delivery, rather than on a normal sit-down crowd. Initially, business boomed; but when school broke for the summer, they realized how much they depended on the college: sales plummeted 75 percent. Furthermore, the business took more time than anticipated, and the Monaghans had to make a career choice. Tom decided to sell the newsstand, and Jim decided to continue at the post office. Jim wanted nothing for his half of the business but Tom, unable to offer him cash, insisted that he take his car.

Monaghan made a firm commitment to become a "pizza man." He was captivated by the art of pizza-making and began experimenting immediately. From the previous owner, Dominic DiVarti, he learned that the secret of a good pizza is the sauce. Monaghan began visiting other pizza sellers and, if he liked their sauce, asked for a recipe. Surprisingly, most obliged.

His business and confidence booming, Monaghan opened a second store, Pizza King, located near Central Michigan University in Mount Pleasant. It met with instant success. Unable to manage both stores, Monaghan hired Jim Gilmore to manage DomiNick's, while he established operations in the second store. Gilmore, an experienced restauranteur, was also an admitted alcoholic. However, Monaghan was convinced that Gilmore had recovered and could handle the Ypsilanti operation. Without asking for any money, he made Gilmore an equal partner in DomiNick's.

On a delivery for Pizza King, Monaghan met his future wife, Margie Zybach, a student at Central Michigan. He had been especially shy with girls when he was growing up, but was attracted to her smile. Although Margie was a Lutheran, their wedding ceremony was held in a Catholic Church. Monaghan hoped to convert his wife to Catholicism, but never succeeded.

After their wedding, the young couple moved into a trailer, and Margie began to help with the store, continuing after their first daughter was born. Meanwhile, the search for better pizza sauces continued. Every Monday, the family loaded into the car and ventured to two or three pizza parlors looking for the perfect recipe.

During one stop, Monaghan filled in for a cook. The kitchen was located next to a large picture window and, to the delight of the owner, Monaghan, who had become a master pizza maker, quickly drew a crowd on the busy street by tossing, spinning, and flipping the dough in the air. It wasn't all pleasure for Monaghan, however, who picked up tips to improve his own operation.

He continued to expand by borrowing money from banks and by selling portions of successful operations to employees. Monaghan used a "divide and conquer" strategy of locating in the same area but outside the delivery range of his existing stores, thereby providing economies in advertising without cannibalizing the sales of each store. It also set the stage for Monaghan's commissary system. The commissary was a central location where pizza dough and other ingredients were prepared and sold to each store. Monaghan could utilize high-speed mixing and cutting equipment at the commissary, thereby increasing the productivity of all the stores.

Jim Gilmore then approached Monaghan with an idea of buying a sit-down, full-menu restaurant in Ann Arbor, and Monaghan agreed. Because of his history, Gilmore was unable to get credit and Monaghan put the restaurant's assets in his own name. Many things bothered Monaghan about Gilmore's new operation, but when Gilmore asked to get out of their partnership, Monaghan obliged, giving him $20,000 plus the Pizza King and the new restaurant. His dealings with Gilmore weren't over, however, since Gilmore had resumed drinking, and both stores and all debt were still in Monaghan's name.

During the same period, Dominic DiVarti asked Monaghan to discontinue the use of the name DomiNick's, since DiVarti intended to open another restaurant. An employee suggested the Domino's name, which Monaghan thought sounded sufficiently Italian. An advertising agent designed the logo, a domino with three dots, one for each pizza store in operation.

Monaghan insisted on high standards from his employees, meeting weekly with his store managers to discuss strategy. They committed themselves to using only the highest quality and freshest ingredients and implemented a 30-minute delivery guarantee, a bonus for drivers, and a driver-of-the-week award. Local competitors in Ann Arbor (and, later, around the country) responded with their own 30- and sometimes 29-minute guarantees. While his managers focused on the day-to-day operations, Monaghan concentrated on improving the efficiency of the operation. By improving the layout and bringing in high-speed ovens, he increased the capacity of the three stores and set the groundwork for franchising, modeling his operation after McDonald's.

The franchising plans were shattered in November 1966 when Jim Gilmore filed for bankruptcy. Monaghan was saddled with $75,000 of debt. Urged by his attorney to file for bankruptcy, Monaghan refused. He didn't want to lose his pizza operations, and he wanted to pay each creditor 100 cents on the dollar. He reasoned that he had succeeded to this point by treating everyone fairly and vowed to continue. He negotiated with each creditor individually and convinced them that they would receive all their money — and he made good on his promise.

With this problem cleared up, Monaghan returned his attention to franchising. The early franchises were started by ex-Domino's employees and were located near large colleges. The franchisee would provide capital and about 5.5 percent of sales to Domino's as a royalty, while Monaghan offered management training and advertising support. In addition, Monaghan maintained 25 percent ownership in each franchise.

Helped by the increasing popularity of both pizza and franchising, Domino's began to grow quickly. In fact, Monaghan soon had a difficult time keeping track of all the operations. There was no accounting system in place, and managing the franchises was taking all of his time. The commissary operation deteriorated, and franchisees were complaining about the price, quality, and delivery. In addition, Monaghan was opening stores in residential areas and forcing growth, believing that a high growth rate would impress the financial markets and make possible an initial public offering. To support these objectives, he opened one new store per week.

By spring 1970, Monaghan once again found himself unable to pay his bills. Not only were residential stores far more expensive to operate, the residential areas were not as receptive to delivery as college campuses. The average college store brought in about $6,000 per week while the average residential store generated only $700. Domino's offices above the Ypsilanti store had employed a dozen salaried personnel, but the crisis forced Monaghan to lay off everyone except his wife and a secretary. Unfortunately, this wasn't enough. On May 1, 1970, Monaghan lost control of Domino's. Creditors forced him to assign 51 percent of Domino's stock to Ken Heavlin, a turnaround specialist. Monaghan kept the presidency but had no authority.

Everyone, except Monaghan, felt that bankruptcy was inevitable. To make matters worse, a group of Domino's franchisees, upset with a deterioration in commissary operations (Heavlin made them profit centers and service dropped off drastically), stopped paying their royalties and filed a class action suit against Monaghan. At this point, most of Monaghan's cash was coming from royalties.

Within a year, Heavlin decided to leave. Monaghan bought back his shares in exchange for a company-owned store. Monaghan continued to reduce his debts, traveling around the country to persuade the franchisees, one-by-one, to drop their suit. A few decided to leave, and Monaghan bought their units and controlled them as company stores. He closed down many of the residential stores.

As things started to look up, Monaghan reviewed what caused the crisis. He foreswore expansion for its own sake and started to inspect and evaluate each franchise. He implemented strict codes of conduct and purchased a mobile home unit that went around the country with a group of field inspectors. He recalled:

> You don't get what you expect unless you inspect . . . when a store is running smoothly, visiting it seems like a waste of time. But just stop visiting that store for a few months, and it will deteriorate dramatically. I learned that lesson the hard way, through experience.[11]

During a flight to visit a franchise, Monaghan read *Try Giving Yourself Away* by David Dunn. During the early 1930s, Dunn, an evangelical Christian, developed the philosophy of "giving yourself away." He wrote, "Almost everything in the world can be bought for money—except the warm impulses of the human heart. They have to be given." Monaghan realized that *he* was most happy when he was giving, rather than getting, and he felt that got to the heart of what Domino's service was all about. Dunn's ideas showed Monaghan how to apply "Christian philosophy in a nondenominational way, to

the day-to-day business of Domino's."[12] Most importantly, he credited his wife with applying these principles throughout all of their troubles: "Margie had put up with my long hours without a vacation, giving her time and effort freely and cheerfully. I would never have gotten back on my feet if it hadn't been for her."[13]

By 1973, with 76 stores in 13 states, Domino's was finally profitable, and the company was never again in the red. Domino's success even generated a buyout offer from Pizza Hut, which Monaghan rejected. Monaghan also found a new method of expansion. He encouraged franchisees to allow their best managers to open their own stores, giving each person in the chain a percentage of the profits. While this reduced royalties from each store, it ensured more successful recruitment and retention of employees.

In December 1974, Monaghan once again felt overwhelmed by the magnitude of the operation and hired Russ Hughes, a formal and impersonal man who stressed systems, rather than personal relations. While Monaghan found him difficult to communicate with, he recognized Hughes' capabilities and began to turn more and more company control over to him. Things were going well until Hughes expressed an interest in buying Monaghan out, presenting him with a detailed business plan. Monaghan fired Hughes on the spot. "I had given this man everything he'd asked for to help him do his job, I had increased his salary to $50,000 plus bonuses, a chunk of stock worth about $150,000, and a car, but he hasn't been working for me at all, I thought, he's been working strictly for himself!"[14]

The problems that Monaghan assumed when he fired Hughes included no growth in 1975 and a trademark lawsuit filed by Amstar

---

[11] Ibid, p. 170.

[12] Ibid, p. 174.
[13] Ibid, p. 183.
[14] Ibid, p. 198.

Corporation for infringement on the Domino's Sugar name. The low growth was attributed to Hughes' lengthy store approval process and Monaghan began immediately to rebuild the relationships with his franchises and soon the business regained momentum.

After he lost the first court battle with Amstar, Monaghan filed an appeal. If he lost again, most of his franchise contracts would be invalid since he could no longer offer the Domino's name. The appeal continued until 1980, when the judge ruled that the name Domino's Pizza was not likely to be confused with Domino's Sugar.

Monaghan "suddenly felt free of an unseen weight," and again focused on operations. He hired consultants to do time-motion studies of pizza making. Continuing to travel throughout the country, he challenged store employees to beat his own best time for pizza making, 11 seconds flat. To improve speed and efficiency, he also established Domino's Olympics, which consisted of events replicating the duties of backroom pizza operations. Franchisees sent their best people, and the winners brought back cash prizes for themselves and their franchise.

Monaghan expanded rapidly through the 1980s, and started to sell to "outsiders" (i.e., non-Domino's people). By keeping the business simple and by improving the budgeting and accounting systems, he improved the firm's standing in the financial community. In addition, he formed a finance subsidiary to help franchisees get started. By the late 1980s, Domino's was adding three franchises per day. With greater and greater economies in marketing, sales in each store were growing by over 15 percent per year. By 1989, Domino's had over 5,000 franchises.

Monaghan's Personal Life

Monaghan's wealth increased dramatically as Domino's became the largest pizza maker in the world. In 1990, it sold over 19 percent of the pizzas consumed in the United States. Throughout this period, he devoted his considerable wealth and growing free time to his hobbies and his charities.

In 1984, he bought the Detroit Tigers and watched the team win the World Series that year. He bought dozens of antique cars and sometimes brought them to Tiger Stadium before games.

Monaghan's interest in Frank Lloyd Wright never waned; he continued to collect Wright furniture, china, and crystal and even helped design the Domino's headquarters building, using classic Frank Lloyd Wright "lines." He spent his vacations visiting Wright masterpieces, such as the Imperial Hotel in Japan, and sponsored 30 awards for the world's best architects.

Concerned about the plight of the farmer, Monaghan teamed up in the late 1980s with Booker T. Whatley, a specialty farmer, who ran a diversified farm operation. Whatley grew any vegetable that his soil allowed and, for a fee, members picked fresh vegetables as needed. Monaghan, a fitness and nutrition fanatic, was intrigued by the farm as well as the nutritional benefits of this arrangement, so he sponsored a program to help spread Whatley's methods all over the country.

On a trip to a possible franchise location in Honduras, Monaghan visited a children's mission. Monaghan was impressed by the caring approach of the priest in charge, and he immediately became a sponsor. Noting the importance of religion as well as daily sustenance to these children, he began to sponsor other charities in Latin America, with a goal of building one chapel for each Domino's store in Latin America.

After an audience with Pope John Paul II, Monaghan donated $100,000 to the Vatican to buy a computer system to improve the accounting records. In addition, during this visit with the pope, Monaghan had the "closest thing to a calling that a lay person can have."

EXHIBIT 1   Legatus

Legatus is an international organization of Roman Catholic lay men and women, with their spouses, drawn from the top levels of corporate leadership in the business world.

The organization's name comes from the Latin word for "ambassador," and describes the Legatus mission — to be ambassadors of Christ in the business world.

Membership is limited to practicing Catholics who are chief executive officers, presidents, managing directors, or the top-ranked individual in companies with at least 50 employees and $4 million in annual sales. These criteria help to ensure a common spirit among its members.

Legatus provides its members with the opportunity to support one another in actively living out the Catholic faith, and to apply the Church's ethical and moral teaching to their lives in a practical way.

In addition to regular monthly chapter meetings, Legatus sponsors a national and an international conference each year, holds a series of retreats for its members, and publishes a monthly newsletter.

Legatus was founded in 1987 by Tom Monaghan after meeting Pope John Paul II. In three years, the organization has grown to include almost 600 members. Legatus has local chapters in 11 major U.S. cities, as well as in a number of foreign countries.

Legatus is a nonprofit organization, and does not endorse or carry out projects of any kind. As a sign of their love for the church, 10 percent of Legatus' dues are given each year to the support of the Holy See.

He decided that establishing an organization of Catholic CEO's to be ambassadors of Christ in the business world was a worthy calling. In 1987, he founded Legatus for this purpose. (Exhibit 1 presents its charter.)

Some of his philanthropies proved controversial. Although he disavowed membership in the Word of God, an ecumenical, charismatic Christian group, Monaghan was an active contributor. In addition, a large portion of Domino's upper management were members. The group had been called a "cult" by the Detroit press, and the names Domino's and Monaghan seemed to appear in conjunction with it frequently.

In 1989, the National Organization for Women (NOW) called for a boycott of Domino's because of Monaghan's contributions to anti-abortion activities. His beneficiaries included Right to Life of Michigan and several anti-abortion candidates, including the Michigan governor. Monaghan was also accused of supporting Operation Rescue, a charge he vehemently denied. Jan Ben-Dor, president of Michigan NOW, made her feelings about Monaghan clear in March 1990:

> Monaghan is lying. We have state election records showing that he gave $106,000 to anti-choice. He owns the house where the Ann Arbor Operation Rescue is based, and Domino's headquarters is a thicket of sexism, cultism, and intrigue. He's a self-defeating, tragic figure. There are people that are mad at him for just about everything. He even ruined the [Detroit] Tigers — and you have to work really hard to lose the support of baseball fans. Besides, his pizza tastes like cardboard.[15]

A number of franchises around the country were hurt badly by the boycotts, and some owners took out paid advertisements explaining that they were not responsible for Monaghan's anti-abortion campaign. Although Monaghan was pressured to end the boycott, he did not meet with any of the abortion rights groups.

---

[15] Alex Prud'Homme, "Is There Life after Pizza," *Business Month,* March 1990, p. 52.

Monaghan claimed that the boycott had not hurt sales and said that, even if it did, "it wouldn't change my mind. I can't stand by and watch innocent people murdered."[16]

The abortion issue caused Monaghan problems at home, as well. His wife supported the abortion rights movement and disagreed with Monaghan's outspoken pro-life convictions. She said, "If men had babies, there would be no laws against abortion."[17]

Requirements for Domino's employees caused trouble as well. Beards were not allowed. Women could wear not slacks, only skirts of a specified length. Monaghan was sued for many of these regulations; a Sikh man, for example, went to court over the no-beard policy. Monaghan argued that the policy had been in place before the man assumed employment. Monaghan also encouraged his employees to follow his clean-living and hard-working example, and almost half of the company's staff people joined health clubs. Monaghan even had the elevators slowed in his corporate headquarters to encourage employees to use the stairs. He paid one of his senior managers, also a close friend, $100,000 when he completed a marathon and won a bet he had made with Monaghan.

Another source of controversy for Monaghan and Domino's was the 30-minute-delivery guarantee, which included free or discounted pizza if delivery took longer than 30 minutes. This policy was implicated in 39 traffic fatalities nationwide, and drivers had also been accused of driving recklessly to avoid penalties for late delivery. Groups formed in communities all over the country to support legislation to restrict all delivery promises. Monaghan and the company resisted dropping the delivery guarantee, considered a key factor in Domino's success. (Domino's biggest competitor, Pizza Hut, offered 30-minute service in only its rural areas.) In the 1988 Domino's annual report, Monaghan wrote that "failing to honor the 30-minute-delivery guarantee was one of the big disappointments of 1987 . . . delivery performance is still totally unacceptable and therefore must be our biggest priority in 1988 . . . not fulfilling a promise is inexcusable, it not only goes against everything we believe in, but it's also bad business."[18]

Joseph Kinney, an official at the National Safe Workplace Institute, a group that monitored job hazards, claimed that Domino's driver-death rate was inexcusably high: as high as the rate for job-related deaths in the mining industry. He cited a Domino's employee death rate of 50 per 100,000, as compared with 30 per 100,000 in the mining and construction industry.[19] Kinney urged a boycott of Domino's on college campuses and urged students not to work as drivers for the company, as well.[20]

Concerned about driver accidents, Monaghan mandated that the franchises change the policy so the driver was not penalized for being late. The free-pizza policy was also scaled down to discounting the next order. Monaghan ran advertisements in many newspapers, explaining the new policy and its origins. Monaghan acknowledged a high accident rate for Domino's drivers but maintained that it was not due to the 30-minute-guarantee but rather to a variety of causes, such as bad weather, falling asleep at the wheel, and inexperienced drivers. Subsequently, he instituted safe driving courses and bonuses.

Some less-controversial activities have led to trouble. His annual, $1 million Christmas light

---

[16] Alson and Greenwalt, p. 111.

[17] Ibid, p. 111.

[18] Eric N. Berg, "Fight on Quick Pizza Delivery Grows," *The New York Times,* August 29, 1989, p. D6.

[19] Ibid, p. D6.

[20] Anonymous, "Critics Charge That Domino's Is Making Pizza to Die for," *People Weekly,* September 25, 1989, p. 105.

extravaganza drew both praise and criticism. While people came from all over Michigan to see the display, it has caused interstate accidents and traffic jams as people slowed their cars to see it. The township was suing for these accidents, claiming that the display was too large and gaudy.

A brand-new headquarters building, leaning 16 degrees off level, gained Domino's even more notoriety. Monaghan called it the "leaning tower of pizza," but the State of Michigan called it an eyesore not zoned to be a leaning building. Monaghan maintained that most of this attention only helped Domino's grow.

By the late 1980s, profits in the pizza chain were eroding. Many competitors had entered the market, including Pizza Hut, and they forced Domino's to cut prices, increase marketing costs, and run expensive promotions to maintain market share. Monaghan's goal—not profitability but to be "number one in every market in which we operate"—had become costly. In 1989, profits slid to only 0.2 percent of sales.

Looking Ahead

Through the years, Monaghan had often reflected on Sister Berarda, his "greatest inspiration," and how she taught him the Golden Rule, the Catholic faith, and a "deep-rooted respect for the Lord."

> I think religion is the most important thing in the world. It gives you a pretty clear guide on how to behave. But it was always the fear of hell, rather than the desire for heaven, that kept me in tow. I might want to have a different woman every night, or I might want to practice contraception, but I can't. We're not here to squeeze as much pleasure into life as possible; what we do here determines where we spend the hereafter.[21]

As he began to look ahead to life beyond Domino's, he reflected on the materialism of his past. "A lot of the things I purchased were lifelong dreams, but maybe not very good ones. Material things don't mean much to me anymore." He always wanted to be an example for others by "showing that you can be successful and wealthy and still live honestly and as a Christian." Instead of showing this, he said, "my material possessions just made me look rich and egotistical . . . I've always been inspired by people, rather than textbooks, so I am concerned with how people view me."

He recently started keeping two notebooks, one listing his material acquisitions, the other his spiritual quests. Monaghan had also begun to eat nothing but bread and water two days a week. His last material pleasure, a summer home for him and Margie to retire, in, had been scaled down from his original plan.

Monaghan planned to fill the second notebook with giving. He believed his most important mission after selling Domino's would be to build Legatus into a much larger worldwide organization, thereby having the greatest impact in spreading God's word. He continued to fund missions in Latin America and announced an aggressive plan to build Catholic missions in underdeveloped countries. The free time gained by selling Domino's would allow him to visit them.

Appendix: Five Personal Priorities[22]

Spiritual

My background makes concern about spiritual matters as natural to me as breathing. I grew up Catholic, and for a short time I attended a seminary, with every intention of becoming a priest. My religious faith is strong. I know I can never be a success on this earth unless I am on good terms with God. I know I would

---

[21] Prud'Homme, p. 49.

[22] Excerpted from *Pizza Tiger*, pp. 8–18.

not have been able to build Domino's without the strength I gained from my religious faith. In the earlier years, I was hit by a series of difficulties. Each one seemed like a knockout blow. But I was able to get off the floor every time and come back stronger than ever. That's the power of faith. I use it every day. No matter how tense or tired I get, I can take time out to pray or say a rosary and feel refreshed. That's a tremendous asset.

I've always told Domino's employees and franchisees that all they have to do to be successful is have a good product, give good service, and apply the Golden Rule. Those elements alone will make any company stand out above its competitors and will generate better public relations than high-powered PR campaigns. . . .

The biggest little thing you can do is simply be nice to people. I've often remarked in speeches that my objective is to have everyone say that Domino's Pizza people are nice. Not brilliant or charming or models of efficiency, just *nice.* How can that be achieved? Simply by getting employees to take every opportunity to be friendly, to smile at the customer and say "please" and "thank you" and "sir" and "ma'am."

Social

A loving wife and family are, to me, essential for a happy and productive life.

My wife, Margie, was in my corner through all those tough battles of the early years in Domino's. To say I couldn't have succeeded without her would be a tremendous understatement.

. . . After our first two daughters were born, Margie helped me in the Ypsilanti store. Our babies slept in cardboard boxes in the corner while Margie answered telephones and did the bookkeeping. She still works in Domino's accounting department and personally hands out paychecks to every employee in our headquarters.

After family on my scale of social relationships come friends. Nobody can succeed in business without the help of friends. And that probably goes double in franchising, where trust is the grease that keeps the working parts from binding. . . .

Community involvement is another important part of my social priority. I believe a business has an obligation to participate in programs to help the community that supports it. The Jaycees have provided a reliable vehicle for me to get involved in community work over the years, and that relationship also has been a great help to me in times of need. For example, in 1968, after fire destroyed our headquarters, the Ypsilanti Jaycees pitched in and donated many hours of manual labor to clean up the mess, and they helped me find temporary office space.

Mental

The key factor in maintaining a healthy mind is a clear conscience. This means you have done your best to live up to your own expectations. A clear conscience fosters self-esteem, a positive attitude, and an optimistic outlook, all of which promote success in business. I believe the mind needs exercise, that it will grow in capacity and thinking ability if it is forced to by constant questioning and the desire for new information.

My questioning sometimes irritates people. A former top executive in Domino's used to get red-faced and say I was driving him crazy, because no matter what he told me, I would always ask "Why?" or "Why not?" I was just trying to learn from him, and I'll do that with anyone who has something worth knowing, and that's everybody.

Physical

It may sound corny, but I subscribe to the idea that the body is the temple of the soul. As a living edifice, it needs proper fuel and good maintenance. If I lost my health, I'd give every penny I had to get it back, and I don't know anyone who wouldn't.

I know how tough it is to lose weight because I'm naturally a big eater. If I let myself, I could polish off a large pizza and any dessert put in front of me and ask for seconds. But I'm religious about counting calories. Every Friday and Monday, or on any day that my weight has moved up over 163 pounds when I get on the scale in the morning, I limit myself to 500 calories. I eat dessert only 11 times a year: Christmas, Easter, Thanksgiving, just before Lent, St. Patrick's Day, and six family birthdays. I call these my "pig-out" days. But despite calorie counting, I couldn't keep my weight under control without exercise.

Six days a week, I do 45 minutes of floor exercises, including 150 consecutive pushups, followed by a six-and-a-third-mile run. Twice a week, I end my run in the fitness center at our new headquarters, Domino's Farms, and work out for an hour. . . .

Financial

The financial priority is last on my list, because it arises from the others. I know that, if I attend to the first four properly, financial success will follow as surely as day follows night.

I view money in much the same way P. T. Barnum did: it's important only for things it can allow you to do. Hamilton Basso wrote of Barnum that he wanted money because it allowed him to reach for "the larger hope, the more compeling dream, which for him was fame." My dreams are different, but achieving them is the reason I want to make more and more money.

MORALITY AND REALISM

Niccolò Machiavelli (1469–1527) was a Florentine. At the time of his birth, the city was a prosperous textile manufacturing center and one of the capitals of European commerce. Florence was also the political, economic, and military epicenter of the wealthy north-Italian city states (Pisa, Siena, Prato, Pistoia, Lucca, and San Gimignano), which comprised Tuscany. Cosimo, Piero, and Lorenzo de Medici—father, son, and grandson—dominated Florence's ostensibly representative government through most of the 15th century.

This note was prepared by Allen P. Webb and Joseph Badaracco, Jr.

Copyright © 1992 by the President and Fellows of Harvard College.

Harvard Business School note 393-036.

Machiavelli came of age at a turbulent juncture in Florentine history, when this stable and prosperous old order was overturned. France had invaded the Italian peninsula in 1494, touching off a chaotic period of alliances, betrayals, and battles among and between both Italian cities and foreign powers. Lorenzo de Medici's son Pietro was ill-suited to lead Florence when his father died in 1492. The city exiled Pietro and adopted a republican government soon afterward. Like most Italian city-states, the Florentine republic relied increasingly on Swiss, German, and eastern European mercenaries amidst the chaos. The republic also allied itself closely with France, which proved to be its undoing in 1512 when France withdrew from Italy. At this point, Giuliano de Medici, assisted by his brother

Pope Leo X and the Spanish army, assumed leadership of Florence.

The return of the Medici was disastrous for Machiavelli's career. He had served as a member of the republican diplomatic corps from 1498, at the age of 29, until its fall in 1512. During these years, he both represented Florence abroad and assumed important managerial duties in the home office. Machiavelli, a patriot who once wrote a friend that he loved Florence "more than his own soul," was also a violent opponent of Florence's dependence on foreign mercenaries. He therefore organized the local militia forces, whose defeat at the hands of Spanish regulars touched off the fall of the republic. None of this endeared him to the returning Giuliano de Medici. The new government stripped Machiavelli of his position, briefly tortured him as a suspect in an anti-Medici plot, and finally put him out to pasture in the Tuscan countryside. It was there that Machiavelli wrote *The Prince* in 1513. In a desperate (and futile) attempt to regain a diplomatic post, "even," he wrote a friend, "if they start me off by rolling stones," Machiavelli dedicated his book to Giuliano.[1]

The Prince intersperses Machiavelli's commentary with a multitude of historical and contemporary anecdotes about the acquisition, maintenance, and application of power. Many of the tales described the success of leaders who behaved treacherously. Machiavelli did not claim that underhanded behavior was desirable or morally acceptable. ". . . [I]t cannot

be called talent," he wrote, "to slay fellow-citizens, to deceive friends, to be without faith, without mercy, without religion; such methods may gain empire, but not glory." But Machiavelli found that the historical record presented him with inescapable evidence that deception often worked and was, at times, an indispensable instrument of state. This line of reasoning has caused many to view Machiavelli as an amoral creature, and *The Prince* as a dangerous work.

Sympathetic critics, however, have emphasized that, although he rejected traditional Christian ethics, Machiavelli put forth a vision for an alternative society, "a society geared to ends just as ultimate as the Christian faith, a society in which men fight and are ready to die for (public) ends which they choose for their own sake."[2] Implicit in such a world is the denial that morally valuable ends can always be pursued with morally pure means and that there is a single "correct" way of life for all people and societies.[3] The passage below is Chapter 15 of *The Prince*. It emphasizes the importance of realism and practicality in policy making and embodies this then-radical denial. It shows why this book, written before the Protestant Reformation and the Enlightenment, marked a critical shift in the history of Western political thought.

> It remains now to see what ought to be the rules of conduct for a prince towards subject and friends. And as I know that many have written on this point, I expect I shall be considered presumptuous in mentioning it again, especially as in discussing it I shall depart from the methods of other people. But, it being my intention to write a thing which shall be useful to him who apprehends it, it appears to me more appropriate to follow up the real truth of a matter than the imagination of it; for many have pictured republics and principalities which

---

[1] All biographical and background information from Robert M. Adams, ed., *The Prince: A New Translation, Backgrounds, Interpretations, Peripherica* (New York: W.W. Norton, 1977), pp. vii–xvi. Machiavelli's love of Florence is described in Isaiah Berlin, "The Originality of Machiavelli," in *Against the Current: Essays in the History of Ideas* (New York: Viking Press, 1980), p. 54. Machiavelli's statement about rolling stones, from the introduction to *The Prince*, Peter Bondanella, ed. and trans., and Mark Musa, trans. (Oxford: Oxford University Press, 1984), p. xi.

[2] Berlin, 1980, p. 54.
[3] Ibid., p. 76.

in fact have never been known or seen, because how one lives is so far distant from how one ought to live, that he who neglects what is done for what ought to be done, sooner effects his ruin than his preservation; for a man who wishes to act entirely up to his professions of virtue soon meets with what destroys him among so much that is evil.

Hence it is necessary for a prince wishing to hold his own to know how to do wrong, and to make use of it or not according to necessity. Therefore, putting on one side imaginary things concerning a prince, and discussing those which are real, I say that all men when they are spoken of, and chiefly princes for being more highly placed, are remarkable for some of those qualities which bring them either blame or praise; and thus it is that one is reputed liberal, another miserly, using a Tuscan term (because an avaricious person in our language is still he who desires to possess by robbery, whilst we call one miserly who deprives himself too much of the use of his own); one is reputed generous, one rapacious; one cruel, one compassionate; one faithless, another faithful; one effeminate and cowardly, another bold and brave; one affable, another haughty; one lascivious,

another chaste; one sincere, another cunning; one hard, another easy; one grave, another frivolous; one religious, another unbelieving, and the like. And I know that every one will confess that it would be most praiseworthy in a prince to exhibit all the above qualities that are considered good; but because they can neither be entirely possessed nor observed, for human conditions do not permit it, it is necessary for him to be sufficiently prudent that he may know how to avoid the reproach of those vices which would lose him his state; and also to keep himself, if it be possible, from those which would not lose him it; but this not being possible, he may with less hesitation abandon himself to them. And again, he need not make himself uneasy at incurring a reproach for those vices without which the state can only be saved with difficulty, for if everything is considered carefully, it will be found that something which looks like virtue, if followed, would be his ruin; whilst something else, which looks like vice, yet followed brings him security and prosperity.[4]

----

[4] Niccolò Machiavelli, *The Prince,* trans. by W. K. Marriott (London: J. M. Dent & Sons, 1925), chap. 15.

ABRAHAM LINCOLN AND THE SELF-MADE MYTH

I happen, temporarily, to occupy this White House. I am a living witness that any one of your children may look to come here as my father's child has.

Abraham Lincoln, *to the 166th Ohio Regiment*

The Lincoln legend has come to have a hold on the American imagination that defies

----

comparison with anything else in political mythology. Here is a drama in which a great man shoulders the torment and moral burdens

----

Allen P. Webb prepared this note under the direction of Joseph Badaracco, Jr.
Harvard Business School note 393-049.

of a blundering and sinful people, suffers for them, and redeems them with hallowed Christian virtues—"malice toward none and charity for all"—and is destroyed at the pitch of his success. The worldly wise John Hay, who knew him about as well as he permitted himself to be known, called him "the greatest character since Christ," a comparison one cannot imagine being made of any other political figure of modern times.

If the Lincoln legend gathers strength from its similarity to the Christian theme of vicarious atonement and redemption, there is still another strain in American experience that it represents equally well. Although his metier was politics and not business, Lincoln was a preeminent example of that self-help which Americans have always so admired. He was not, of course, the first eminent American politician who could claim humble origins, nor the first to exploit them. But few have been able to point to such a sudden ascent from relative obscurity to high eminence; none has maintained so completely while scaling the heights the aspect of extreme simplicity; and none has combined with the attainment of success and power such an intense awareness of humanity and moral responsibility. It was precisely in his attainments as a common man that Lincoln felt himself to be remarkable, and in this light that he interpreted to the world the significance of his career. Keenly aware of his role as the exemplar of the self-made man, he played the part with an intense and poignant consistency that gives his performance the quality of a high art. The first author of the Lincoln legend and the greatest of the Lincoln dramatists was Lincoln himself. . . .

Early Career

If historical epochs are judged by the opportunities they offer talented men to rise from the ranks to places of wealth, power, and prestige, the period during which Lincoln grew up was among the greatest in history, and among all places such opportunities were most available in the fresh territory north and west of the Ohio River—the Valley of Democracy.

Abraham Lincoln was 19 years old when Andrew Jackson was elected president. Like most of the poor in his part of the country, Thomas Lincoln was a Jacksonian Democrat, and his son at first accepted his politics. But some time during his 18th or 19th year, Abraham went through a political conversion, became a National Republican, and cast his first vote, in 1832, for Henry Clay.

The National Republican (later Whig) Party was the party of internal improvements, stable currency, and conservative banking; Lincoln lived in a country that needed all three. Doubtless there were also personal factors in his decision. If the Democrats spoke more emphatically about the equality of man, the Whigs, even in the West, had the most imposing and affluent men. That an ambitious youth should look to the more solid citizens of his community for political guidance was natural and expedient; the men Lincoln most respected in the Indiana town of his boyhood were National Republicans, great admirers of Henry Clay; and as Dennis Hanks mournfully recalled, Lincoln himself "allways Loved Hen Clay's speaches. . . ."

After a few years of stagnation Lincoln advanced with the utmost rapidity in his middle 20s. While many of the stories about the hardships of his youth celebrated in Lincoln legendary are true, it is noteworthy that success came to him suddenly and at a rather early age. At 24 he was utterly obscure. At 28 he was the leader of his party in the Illinois House of Representatives, renowned as the winner of the fight to bring the state capital to Springfield, extremely popular in both Sangamon County and the capital itself, and partner of one of the ablest lawyers in the state. Of his first years in Springfield, Herndon writes: "No man ever had an easier time of it in his early days than Lincoln. He had . . . influential and financial friends to help him; they almost fought each other for the privilege of assisting Lincoln. . . . Lincoln was a pet . . . in this city."

From this time to the end of his life — except for the years between 1849 and 1854, when his political prospects were discouraging — Lincoln was busy either as officeholder or officeseeker. In the summer of 1860, for a friend who wanted to prepare a campaign biography, he wrote in the third person a short sketch of his political life up to that time: 1832 — defeated in an attempt to be elected to the legislature; 1834 — elected to the legislature "by the highest vote cast for any candidate"; 1836, 1838, 1840 — re-elected; 1838 and 1840 — chosen by his party as its candidate for Speaker of the Illinois House of Representatives, but not elected; 1840 and 1844 — placed on Harrison and Clay electoral tickets "and spent much time and labor in both those canvasses"; 1846 — elected to Congress; 1848 — campaign worker for Zachary Taylor, speaking in Maryland and Massachusetts, and "canvassing quite fully his own district of over 1,500 for General Taylor"; 1852 — placed on Winfield Scott's electoral ticket, "but owing to the hopelessness of the cause in Illinois he did less than in previous presidential canvasses"; 1854 — ". . . his profession had almost superseded the thought of politics in his mind, when the repeal of the Missouri Compromise aroused him as he had never been before"; 1856 — "made over 50 speeches" in the campaign for Frémont; prominently mentioned in the Republican national convention for the vice presidential nomination.

The rest of the story is familiar enough. . . .

Thoroughly humbled by his depressing obscurity in Congress, he turned with reluctance to the law, overcome by a melancholy "so profound," says Beveridge, "that the depths of it cannot be sounded or estimated by normal minds. Certainly political disappointment had something to do with his despondency." His ambitions were directed toward public life; he had no legal aspirations, lucrative though his practice was. Years later, when the two were preparing their study of him, Herndon objected to Jesse Weik's desire to stress Lincoln's legal eminence: "How are you going to make a *great* lawyer out of Lincoln? His soul was afire with its own ambition and that was not law. . . ."

. . . In the fall of 1854, hungering for the Senatorial nomination and fearing to offend numerous old-line Whigs in Illinois, he fled from Springfield on Herndon's advice to avoid attending a Republican state convention there. One of his most terrible fits of melancholy overcame him when he failed to get the nomination the following year. "That man," says Herndon (whose adoration of Lincoln assures us we are listening to no hostile critic), "who thinks Lincoln calmly gathered his robes about him, waiting for the people to call him, has a very erroneous knowledge of Lincoln. He was always calculating and planning ahead. His ambition was a little engine that knew no rest." With all his quiet passion Lincoln had sought to rise in life, to make something of himself through his own honest efforts. It was this typically American impulse that dominated him through the long course of his career before he became interested in the slavery question. It was his understanding of this impulse that guided his political thought.

Like his father, Lincoln was physically lazy even as a youth, but unlike him had an active forensic mind. When only 15 he was often on stumps and fences making political speeches, from which his father had to haul him back to his chores. He was fond of listening to lawyers' arguments and occupying his mind with them. Herndon testifies that "He read specially for a special object and thought things useless unless they could be of utility, use, practice, etc."[1] When Lincoln read he preferred to read aloud. Once when Herndon asked him about it he answered: "I catch the idea by two senses, for when I read aloud I *hear* what is read and I see it . . . and I remember it better, if I do not understand it better." These are the reading habits of a man who is preparing for the platform. . . .

As an economic thinker, Lincoln had a passion for the great average. Thoroughly middle-class in his ideas, he spoke for those millions of Americans who had begun their lives as hired workers—as farm hands, clerks, teachers, mechanics, flatboat men, and rail-splitters—and had passed into the ranks of landed farmers, prosperous grocers, lawyers, merchants, physicians, and politicians. Theirs were the traditional ideals of the Protestant ethic: hard work, frugality, temperance, and a touch of ability applied long and hard enough would lift a man into the propertied or professional class and give him independence and respect if not wealth and prestige. Failure to rise in the economic scale was generally viewed as a fault in the individual, not in society. It was the outward sign of an inward lack of grace—of idleness, indulgence, waste, or incapacity. . . .

. . . His own rather conventional version of the self-help ideology is expressed with some charm in a letter written to his feckless stepbrother, John D. Johnston, in 1851:

> Your request for eighty dollars I do not think it best to comply with now. At the various times when I have helped you a little you have said to me, "We can get along very well now";

but in a very short time I find you in the same difficulty again. Now, this can only happen by some defect in your conduct. What that defect is, I think I know. You are not lazy, and still you are an idler. I doubt whether, since I saw you, you have done a good whole day's work in any one day. You do not very much dislike to work, and still you do not work much, merely because it does not seem to you that you could get much for it. This habit of uselessly wasting time is the whole difficulty.

Lincoln advised Johnston to leave his farm in charge of his family and go to work for wages.

> I now promise you, that for every dollar you will, between this and the first of May, get for your own labor . . . I will then give you one other dollar. . . . Now if you will do this, you will soon be out of debt, and, what is better, you will have a habit that will keep you from getting in debt again. . . . You have always been kind to me, and I do not mean to be unkind to you. On the contrary, if you will but follow my advice, you will find it worth more than 80 times $80 to you.

Given the chance for the frugal, the industrious, and the able—for the Abraham Lincolns if not the John D. Johnstons—to assert themselves, society would never be divided along fixed lines. There would be no eternal mud-sill class. "There is no permanent class of hired laborers among us," Lincoln declared in a public address. "Twenty-five years ago I was a hired laborer. The hired laborer of yesterday labors on his own account today, and will hire others to labor for him tomorrow. Advancement—improvement in condition—is the order of things in a society of equals." For Lincoln the vital test of a democracy was economic—its ability to provide opportunities for social ascent to those born in its lower ranks. This belief in opportunity for the self-made man is the key to his entire career; it explains his public appeal; it is the core of his criticism of slavery. . . .

---

[1] For years Herndon kept on their office table the *Westminster Review,* the *Edinburgh Review,* other English periodicals, the works of Darwin, Spencer, and other English writers. He had little success in interesting Lincoln. "Occasionally he would snatch one up and peruse it for a little while, but he soon threw it down with the suggestion that it was entirely too heavy for an ordinary mind to digest."

. . . One of the reasons why I am opposed to slavery is just here. What is the true condition of the laborer? I take it that it is best for all to leave each man free to acquire property as fast as he can. Some will get wealthy. I don't believe in a law to prevent a man from getting rich; it would do more harm than good. So while we do not propose any war upon capital, we do wish to allow the humblest man an equal chance to get rich with everybody else. When one starts poor, as most do in the race of life, free society is such that he knows he can better his condition; he knows that there is no fixed condition of labor for his whole life. . . . That is the true system.

Lincoln's simplicity was very real. He called his wife "mother," received distinguished guests in shirtsleeves, and once during his presidency hailed a soldier out of the ranks with the cry: "Bub! Bub!" But he was also a complex man, easily complex enough to know the value of his own simplicity. With his morbid compulsion for honesty he was too modest to pose coarsely and blatantly as a Henry Clay or James G. Blaine might pose. (When an 1860 campaign document announced that he was a reader of Plutarch, he sat down at once to validate the claim by reading the *Lives.*) But he did develop a political personality by intensifying qualities he actually possessed.

Even during his early days in politics, when his speeches were full of conventional platform bombast, Lincoln seldom failed to strike the humble manner that was peculiarly his. "I was born and have ever remained," he said in his first extended campaign speech, "in the most humble walks of life. I have no popular relations or friends to recommend me." Thereafter he always sounded the theme. "I presume you all know who I am—I am humble. Abraham Lincoln. . . . If elected I shall be thankful; if not it will be all the same. . . . " But self-conscious as the device was, and coupled even as it was with a secret confidence that Hay called "intellectual arrogance," there was still

no imposture in it. It corresponded to Lincoln's own image of himself.

There was always this pathos in his plainness, his lack of external grace. "He is," said one of Mrs. Lincoln's friends, "the *ungodliest* man you ever saw." His colleagues, however, recognized in this a possible political asset and transmuted it into one of the most successful of all political symbols—the hard-fisted rail-splitter. At a Republican meeting in 1860 John Hanks and another old pioneer appeared carrying fence rails labeled: "Two rails from a lot made by Abraham Lincoln and John Hanks in the Sangamon Bottom in the year 1830." And Lincoln, with his usual candor, confessed that he had no idea whether these were the same rails, but he was sure he had actually split rails every bit as good. The time was to come when little Tad could say: "Everybody in this world knows Pa used to split rails. . . ."

Slavery: Early Views

His later career as an opponent of slavery extension must be interpreted in the light of his earlier public indifference to the question. Always moderately hostile to the South's "peculiar institution," he quieted himself with the comfortable thought that it was destined very gradually to disappear. Only after the Kansas-Nebraska Act breathed political life into the slavery issue did he seize on it as a subject for agitation; only then did he attack it openly. His attitude was based on justice tempered by expediency—or perhaps more accurately, expediency tempered by justice. . . .

During his boyhood days in Indiana and Illinois Lincoln lived in communities where slaves were rare or unknown, and the problem was not thrust upon him. The prevailing attitude toward Negroes in Illinois was intensely hostile. Severe laws against free Negroes and runaway slaves were in force when Lincoln went to the Springfield legislature, and there is no evidence of any popular movement to liberalize them. Lincoln's experiences with slavery on his journeys to New Orleans in 1828 and 1831 do not seem to have made an impression vivid enough to change his conduct. Always privately compassionate, in his public career and his legal practice he never made himself the advocate of unpopular reform movements.

While Lincoln was serving his second term in the Illinois legislature the slavery question was discussed throughout the country.... The Illinois legislature turned the subject over to a joint committee, of which Lincoln and his Sagamon County colleague, Dan Stone, were members. At 28 Lincoln thus had occasion to review the whole slavery question on both sides. The committee reported proslavery resolutions, presently adopted, which praised the beneficent effects of white civilization upon African natives, cited the wretchedness of emancipated Negroes as proof of the folly of freedom, and denounced abolitionists.

Lincoln voted against these resolutions. Six weeks later—the delay resulted from a desire to alienate no one from the cause that then stood closest to his heart, the removal of the state capital from Vandalia to Springfield—he and Stone embodied their own opinions in a resolution that was entered in the Journal of the House and promptly forgotten. It read in part: "They [Lincoln and Stone] believe that the institution of slavery is founded on injustice and bad policy, but that the promulgation of abolition doctrines tends to increase rather than abate its evils." (Which means, the later Lincoln might have said, that slavery is wrong but that proposing to do away with it is also wrong because it makes slavery worse....)

In 1845, not long before he entered Congress, Lincoln again had occasion to express himself on slavery, this time in a carefully phrased private letter to a political supporter who happened to be an abolitionist.

I hold it a paramount duty of us in the free States, due to the Union of the States, and perhaps to liberty itself (paradox though it may seem), to let the slavery of the other states alone; while, on the other hand, I hold it to be equally clear that we should never knowingly lend ourselves, directly or indirectly, to prevent that slavery from dying a natural death—to find new places for it to live in, when it can not longer exist in the old.

Throughout his political career he consistently held to this position.

After he had become a lame-duck congressman, Lincoln introduced into Congress in January 1849 a resolution to instruct the committee on the District of Columbia to report a bill abolishing slavery in the District.... Lincoln himself added a section requiring the municipal authorities of Washington and Georgetown to provide "active and efficient means" of arresting and restoring to their owners all fugitive slaves escaping into the District. (This was six years before he confessed that he hated "to see the poor creatures hunted down.") Years later, recalling this fugitive-slave provision, Wendell Phillips referred to Lincoln somewhat unfairly as "that slavehound from Illinois." The bill itself, although not passed, gave rise to a spirited debate on the morality of slavery, in which Lincoln took no part.

The Making of a President

When Lincoln returned to active politics the slavery issue had come to occupy the central position on the American scene.... The Republican Party, built on opposition to the extension of slavery, began to emerge in small communities in the Northwest. Lincoln's ambitions and interests were aroused, and he proceeded to rehabilitate his political fortunes.

His strategy was simple and forceful. He carefully avoided issues like the tariff, internal improvements, the Know-Nothing mania, or prohibitionism, each of which would alienate important groups of voters. He took pains in all his speeches to stress that he was not an abolitionist and at the same time to stand on the sole program of opposing the extension of slavery. On October 4, 1854, at the age of 45, Lincoln *for the first time in his life* denounced slavery in public. In his speech delivered in the Hall of Representatives at Springfield (and later repeated at Peoria) he declared that he hated the current zeal for the spread of slavery: "I hate it because of the monstrous injustice of slavery itself." He went on to say that he had no prejudice against the people of the South. He appreciated their argument that it would be difficult to get rid of the institution "in any satisfactory way." "I surely will not blame them for not doing what I should not know how to do myself. If all earthly power were given me, I should not know what to do as to the existing institution. My first impulse would be to free all the slaves and send them to Liberia, to their own native land." But immediate colonization, he added, is manifestly impossible. The slaves might be freed and kept "among us as underlings." Would this really better their condition?

> What next? Free them, and make them politically and socially our equals. *My own feelings will not admit of this,* and if mine would, we well know that those of the great mass of whites will not.

And yet nothing could justify an attempt to carry slavery into territories now free, Lincoln emphasized. For slavery is unquestionably wrong. "The great mass of mankind," he said at Peoria, "consider slavery a great moral wrong. [This feeling] lies at the very foundation of their sense of justice, and it cannot be trifled with. . . . No statesman can safely disregard it." The last sentence was the key to Lincoln's growing radicalism. As a practical politician he was naturally very much concerned about those public sentiments which no statesman can safely disregard. It was impossible, he had

learned, safely to disregard either the feeling that slavery is a moral wrong or the feeling— held by an even larger portion of the public— that Negroes must not be given political and social equality.

He had now struck the core of the Republican problem in the Northwest: how to find a formula to reconcile the two opposing points of view held by great numbers of white people in the North. Lincoln's success in 1860 was due in no small part to his ability to bridge the gap, a performance that entitles him to a place among the world's great political propagandist. . . .

If the Republicans were to succeed in the strategic Northwest, how were they to win the support of both Negrophobes and antislavery men? Merely to insist that slavery was an evil would sound like abolitionism and offend the Negrophobes. Yet pitching their opposition to slavery extension on too low a moral level might lose the valued support of the humanitarians. Lincoln, perhaps borrowing from the old free-soil ideology, had the right formula and exploited it. He first hinted at it in the Peoria speech:

> The whole nation is interested that the best use shall be made of these Territories. *We want them for homes of free white people. This they cannot be, to any considerable extent, if slavery shall be planted within them.* Slave States are places for poor white people to remove from, not to remove to. New free States are the places for poor people to go to, and better their condition. For this use the nation needs these Territories.

. . . Lincoln took the slavery question out of the realm of moral and legal dispute and, by dramatizing it in terms of free labor's self-interest, gave it a universal appeal. To please the abolitionists he kept saying that slavery was an evil thing; but for the material benefit of all Northern white men he opposed its further extension.

The importance of this argument becomes increasingly clear when it is realized that Lincoln used it in every one of his recorded speeches from 1854 until he became the president-elect. . . .

These efforts, together with his strategy of appealing to abolitionists and Negrophobes at once, involved him in embarrassing contradictions. In northern Illinois he spoke in one vein before abolition-minded audiences, but farther south, where settlers of Southern extraction were dominant, he spoke in another. It is instructive to compare what he said about the Negro in Chicago with what he said in Charleston.

Chicago, July 10, 1858:

Let us discard all this quibbling about this man and the other man, this race and that race and the other race being inferior, and therefore they must be placed in an inferior position. Let us discard all these things, and unite as one people throughout this land, until we shall once more stand up declaring that all men are created equal.

Charleston, September 18, 1858:

I will say, then, that I am not, nor ever have been, in favor of bringing about in any way the social and political equality of the white and black races [applause]; that I am not, nor ever have been, in favor of making voters or jurors of negroes, nor of qualifying them to hold office, nor to intermarry with white people. . . .

And inasmuch as they cannot so live, while they do remain together there must be the position of superior and inferior, and I as much as any other man am in favor of having the superior position assigned to the white race.

It is not easy to decide whether the true Lincoln is the one who spoke in Chicago or the one who spoke in Charleston. Possibly the man devoutly believed each of the utterances at the time he delivered it; possibly his mind, too, was a house divided against itself. In any case it is easy to see in all this the behavior of a professional politician looking for votes. . . .

. . . In the ensuing elections the Republican candidates carried a majority of the voters and elected their state officers for the first time. Douglas returned to the Senate only because the Democrats, who had skillfully gerrymandered the election districts, still held their majority in the state legislature. Lincoln had contributed greatly to welding old-line Whigs and antislavery men into an effective party, and his reputation was growing by leaps and bounds. . . .

Conduct of the War

Before Lincoln took office, the issues on which he was elected had become obsolete. Seven states of the deep South had seceded. The great question was no longer slavery or freedom in the territories, but the nation itself. . . .

There need be no doubt about how Lincoln saw the conflict; he had innumerable occasions to state his view of it to Congress, to the country, even to foreign workingmen. It was, of course, a war to preserve the Union; but the Union itself was a means to an end. The Union meant free popular government, "government of the people, by the people, for the people." But popular government is something deeper and more valuable than a mere system of political organization: it is a system of social life that gives the common man a chance. Here Lincoln returns again to his favorite theme — the stupendous value to mankind of the free-labor system. "This," he asserts gravely in his first extended message to Congress,

is essentially a people's contest. On the side of the Union it is a struggle for maintaining in the world that form and substance of a government whose leading object is to elevate the condition of men — to lift artificial weights from all shoulders; to clear the paths of laudable pursuit for all; to afford all an unfettered start, and a fair chance in the race of life . . . this is the leading object of the government for whose existence we contend.

Such popular government has often been called an experiment, he went on, but two phases of the experiment have already been successfully concluded: the establishing and administering of it. There remains a final test—"its successful maintenance against a formidable internal attempt to overthrow it." The people must now demonstrate to the world that those who can fairly win an election can defeat a rebellion, and that the power of government which has been honestly lost by ballots cannot be won back by bullets. "Such will be a great lesson of peace: teaching men that what they cannot take by an election, neither can they take it by a war; teaching all the folly of being the beginners of a war."

Then there was his superb formulation of an everlasting problem of republican politics: "Must a government, of necessity, be too strong for the liberties of its own people, or too weak to maintain its own existence?"

Thus, skillfully, Lincoln inverted the main issue of the war to suit his purpose. What the North was waging, of course, was a war to save the Union by denying self-determination to the majority of Southern whites. But Lincoln, assisted by the blessed fact that the Confederates had struck the first blow, presented it as a war to defend not only Union but the sacred principles of popular rule and opportunity for the common man.

Here is a war aim couched in the language of Lincoln's old ideal, the language that had helped to make him president. Notice that while it is politically on the radical or "popular" side of the fight, it is historically conservative: it aims to preserve a long-established order that has well served the common man in the past. The Union is on the *defensive,* resisting "a war upon the rights of all working people." . . .

Bring the South back, save the Union, restore orderly government, establish the principle that force cannot win out, and do it with the least cost in lives and travail—there is the Lincoln program. The tremendous forces of social revolution storm about his head, and in the end he bows to them. But not without doubt and hesitation. Not even without a struggle against his own destiny to become the symbol of freedom. . . .

The Emancipation Proclamation

As the conflict wore on, the difficulties of fighting a war against a slave power without fighting slavery became painfully evident. Fugitive slaves began to make their way into the Union lines. How were the generals to deal with them? In August 1861, the abolitionist General Frémont, sorely tried by guerrilla warfare in Missouri, declared martial law and proclaimed that all slaves of local owners resisting the United States were freemen. After failing to induce Frémont to revoke his proclamation voluntarily, Lincoln promptly countermanded it. Later he overruled an order of General David Hunter freeing slaves in Georgia, Florida, and South Carolina. . . .

. . . Lincoln had genuine constitutional scruples, but his conservatism in everything pertaining to slavery was also dictated by political and strategic considerations.

He was determined to hold the loyalty of the four border states, Maryland, Kentucky, Missouri, and Delaware, all of which were unwilling to participate in an antislavery crusade. The three larger states, as a glance at the map will show, were vital to Union strategy and to the safety of the capital itself. They were also contributing soldiers to the cause. Frémont's action, Lincoln reported, had had an extremely unfavorable effect on the Kentucky legislature, and in the field a whole company of volunteers upon hearing it had thrown down their arms and disbanded. Further, a great section of conservative Northern opinion was willing to fight for the Union but might refuse to support a war to free Negroes, and kept insisting that the war would become more bitter if the South saw that it was fighting avowed abolitionism. In everything he did, Lincoln had to reckon with the political potential of this sentiment, and he well understood its power, for it was a piece with the old anti-Negro feeling he had always known in Illinois politics. . . .

. . . As the war lengthened, Radical sentiment became stronger. Lincoln was in no position to thrust aside the demands of the very element in the country that supported the war most wholeheartedly. Men who had never thought of attacking the South's peculiar institution before secession were now ready to destroy it in the most abrupt and ruthless way if by so doing they could hasten the end of the war. They argued that it was self-contradictory to fight the war without smashing slavery and with it the South's entire social structure. . . .

Lincoln surveyed the scene with his extraordinary brooding detachment, and waited. (He had, reported Charles Francis Adams, Jr., "a mild, dreamy, meditative eye, which one would scarcely expect to see in a successful chief magistrate in these days of the republic.") He listened to the protests and denunciations of the Radicals and their field agents throughout the country, and politely heard abolition delegations to the White House. Like a delicate barometer, he recorded the trend of pressures, and as the Radical pressure increased he moved toward the left. To those who did not know him, it seemed that he did so reluctantly. The Radicals watched his progress with grim satisfaction—with the feeling, as Wendell Phillips expressed it, that, if Lincoln was able to grow, "it is because we have watered him." But it is significant that such a haughty and impatient abolitionist as Senator Charles Sumner developed a deep respect and affection for Lincoln. According to one report, Lincoln said one day to Sumner: "We'll fetch 'em; just give

us a little time. . . . I should never have had votes enough to send me here, if the people had supposed I should try to use my veto power to upset slavery. . . ."

It was all in keeping with his profound fatalism. He had always believed—and in conversations at Springfield had often told Herndon of his faith—that events are governed (the words are Herndon's) "by certain irrefragable and irresistible laws, and that no prayers of ours could arrest their operation in the least—. . . that what was to be would be inevitable. . . ." Looking back on events in 1864, Lincoln could say with a profound modesty: "I claim not to have controlled events but confess plainly that events have controlled me." As the Radicals gained in strength, he conducted a brilliant strategic retreat toward a policy of freedom. . . .

His program flowed from his conception that his role was to be a moderator of extremes in public sentiment. It called for compensated emancipation. . . . To a member of the senate he wrote in 1862 that the cost of freeing with compensation all slaves in the four border states and the District of Columbia, at an average price of $400 per slave, would come to less than the cost of 87 days of the war. Further, he believed that taking such action would shorten the war by more than 87 days and "thus be an actual saving of expense." Despite the gross note of calculation at the end (one rescues 432,000 human beings from slavery and it turns out to be a saving of expense), the proposal was a reasonable and statesmanlike one, and it is incredible that the intransigence of all but one of the states involved should have consigned it to defeat.

The alternative idea of colonizing the Negroes abroad was and always had been pathetic. . . . By 1860 its fantastic character must have been evident to every American who was not determined to deceive himself. Nevertheless, when a deputation of colored men came to see Lincoln in the summer of 1862, he tried to persuade them to set up a colony in Central America, which, he said, stood on one of the world's highways and provided a country of "great natural resources and advantages." "If I could find 25 able-bodied men, with a mixture of women and children," he added, with marvelous naiveté, "... I could make a successful commencement...."

When Lincoln at last determined, in July 1862, to move toward emancipation, it was only after all his other policies had failed. The Crittenden Resolution had been rejected, the border states had quashed his plan of compensated emancipation, his generals were still floundering, and he had already lost the support of great numbers of conservatives. The Proclamation became necessary to hold his remaining supporters and to forestall—so he believed—English recognition of the Confederacy." "I would save the Union," he wrote in answer to Horace Greeley's cry for emancipation. "... If I could save the Union without freeing any slave, I would do it; and if I could do it by freeing all the slaves, I would do it." In the end, freeing all the slaves seemed necessary....

The Emancipation Proclamation of January 1, 1863, had all the moral grandeur of a bill of lading. It contained no indictment of slavery, but simply based emancipation on "military necessity." It expressly omitted the loyal slave states from its terms. Finally, it did not in fact free any slaves. For it excluded by detailed enumeration from the sphere covered in the Proclamation all the counties in Virginia and parishes in Louisiana that were occupied by Union troops and into which the government actually had the power to bring freedom. It simply declared free all slaves in "the States and parts of States" where the people were in rebellion—that is to say, precisely where its effect could not reach. Beyond its propaganda value the Proclamation added nothing to what Congress had already done in the Confiscation Act.

Seward remarked of the Proclamation: "We show our sympathy with slavery by emancipating the slaves where we cannot reach them and holding them in bondage where we can set them free." The London *Spectator* gibed: "The principle is not that a human being cannot justly own another, but that he cannot own him unless he is loyal to the United States."

But the Proclamation was what it was because the average sentiments of the American Unionist of 1862 were what they were. Had the political strategy of the moment called for a momentous human document of the stature of the Declaration of Independence, Lincoln could have risen to the occasion. Perhaps the largest reasonable indictment of him is simply that in such matters he was a follower and not a leader of public opinion....

The Price of the Presidency

Lincoln was shaken by the presidency....

Lincoln's rage for personal success, his external and worldly ambition, was quieted when he entered the White House, and he was at last left alone to reckon with himself. To be confronted with the fruits of his victory only to find that it meant choosing between life and death for others was immensely sobering....

The presidency was not something that could be enjoyed. Remembering its barrenness for him, one can believe that the life of Lincoln's soul was almost entirely without consummation. Sandburg remarks that there were 31 rooms in the White House and that Lincoln was not at home in any of them. This was the house for which he had sacrificed so much!

As the months passed, a deathly weariness settled over him. Once when Noah Brooks suggested that he rest, he replied: "I suppose it is good for the body. But the tired part of me is *inside* and out of reach." There had always been a part of him, inside and out of reach, that had looked on his ambition with detachment and wondered if the game was worth the candle. Now he could see the truth of what he had long dimly known and perhaps hopefully suppressed—that for a man of sensitivity and compassion to exercise great powers in a time of crisis is a grim and agonizing thing. Instead of glory, he once said, he had found only "ashes and blood." This was, for him, the end product of that success myth by which he had lived and for which he had been so persuasive a spokesman. He had had his ambitions and fulfilled them, and met heartache in his triumph.

MALCOLM X

I've never been one for inaction. Everything I've ever felt strongly about, I've done something about.

I firmly believe that Negroes have the right to fight against these racists, by any means that are necessary.

Malcolm X

Introduction

The man who came to be known as Malcolm X was born as Malcolm Little in 1925 in Omaha, Nebraska. His father, Earl Little, was a Baptist minister and disciple of Marcus Garvey, the Universal Negro Improvement Association leader who espoused black-race purity and exhorted blacks to return to their African homeland. One day, after he had moved his family to a plot of land outside East Lansing, Michigan, Earl Little angrily stormed out of the house and was not seen again until he was found dead that night, his skull bashed in and his body cut nearly in two. Although the exact circumstances of his death have been a matter of dispute, Malcolm—who was six at the time—believed that his father was killed by white racists who attacked him and laid him in front of a streetcar.

The family eventually fell into extreme poverty and Malcolm's mother drifted into insanity. When she was finally sent to a state mental hospital, her eight children were split up as dependents of the state. Malcolm ended up in a detention home near Lansing for his record of bad behavior, but he nonetheless displayed much promise by exceling in his junior high classes. At the end of eighth grade, however, restless and suddenly disillusioned by the racism of one of his teachers, he dropped out of school and moved to the Roxbury neighborhood of Boston, where his half-sister Ella lived.

In Roxbury, he entered the hip world of black bars and swinging dance halls, newly clad in outrageously colored zoot suits. He was known on the street as "Red," because of the reddish

Jerry Useem and Allen Webb prepared this case under the direction of Joseph Badaracco, Jr. It is based on *The Autobiography of Malcolm X* by Malcolm X, with the assistance of Alex Haley. Copyright © 1964 by Alex Haley and Malcolm X and copyright © 1965 by Alex Haley and Betty Shabazz. Reprinted by permission of Random House, Inc.; and Marshall Frady, "The Children of Malcolm," *New Yorker*, October 12, 1992, pp. 64–81.

Copyright © 1993 by the President and Fellows of Harvard College.

Harvard Business School case 394-078.

color of his hair, or as "Detroit Red," because of his Michigan roots. After he landed a job as a sandwich vendor on the train running between Boston and New York, he shifted his base to Harlem. Soon, he was gambling, steering men to prostitutes, using drugs, then selling drugs, and brandishing an automatic pistol in stickups. Returning to Boston, he ran a burglary ring out of Harvard Square with the aid of his white girlfriend Sophia. His reckless style finally got him arrested, and at age 20 he was sentenced to 8–10 years in prison.

It was here — at "the very bottom of the American white man's society," as he later put it — that Malcolm converted to Islam. The conversion came through several of his siblings, who told him in letters and visits that they had found the "natural religion for the black man." They had become members of the Nation of Islam, or the "Black Muslims," led by the diminutive and mysterious Elijah Muhammad. They explained that Allah had specially ordained Elijah Muhammad to uplift the blacks of North America by revealing to them the truth that the white man was (literally) the devil. This revelation was like a "blinding light" to Malcolm; he quickly adopted the ascetic lifestyle of a devout Muslim — which included prohibitions on dating, sports, and eating more than one meal a day — and resolved to spend the rest of his life telling the white man about his true nature. He spent his remaining years in prison in an intense effort at self-education — reading serious books for the first time, sharpening his arguing skills in prison debates, and studying the doctrines of Elijah Muhammad. Emerging on parole in 1952, he replaced the slave name Little with an X representing his long-lost African surname.

Because of Malcolm X's intelligence, powerful persona, and intense devotion to the Nation of Islam, Elijah Muhammad appointed him minister of Temple Number Seven in Harlem. Malcolm X thereafter became an informal chief spokesman for the entire national organization. In Harlem, he would hold crowds of 15,000 spellbound at street rallies for up to four hours. With his fiery yet controlled oratory attracting national attention, the Nation of Islam expanded from an obscure, Chicago-based Islamic sect of about 400 people to a national ministry with some 10,000 registered members. It had its own schools, a network of more than 30 radio stations, and a militia of black-suited guards known as the Fruit of Islam.

In preaching a gospel of enlightenment, liberation, and empowerment for black Americans, Malcolm X simultaneously expressed a raw, uncompromising racial hatred that outraged many whites. He also drew fire from civil rights leaders who sought nonviolent integration. Martin Luther King, Jr., said he disapproved of Malcolm X's "demagogic oratory" and his "litany of articulating the despair of the Negro without offering any positive, creative alternative."[1] Finally, Malcolm X ran into conflict with other Black Muslims. There was increasing tension within the Nation of Islam over Malcolm's growing national prominence; he had, in fact, come to embody the Black Muslims for most of America, and was one of the most sought-after speakers in the country. In addition, Malcolm X felt constricted and isolated by the organization's rigid and sometimes bizarre racial ideology, and he was incensed by the discovery that Elijah Muhammad had fathered several illegitimate babies with Muslim women.

In early 1964, Malcolm X announced his startling separation from the Nation of Islam. Accused of being a traitor by his former Muslim brothers — and the subject of death threats from some of them — he organized the Muslim Mosque, Inc., and then the nonreligious Organization of Afro-American Unity.

---

[1] Quoted in Marshall Frady, "The Children of Malcolm," *The New Yorker,* October 12, 1992, p. 71.

Malcolm X spent the next year struggling to redefine his philosophy. After he made a religious pilgrimage to Mecca in the spring of 1964, there were some signs that he was moderating his virulent antiwhite sentiment. He also returned from this trip with a new Muslim name: El-Hajj Malik El-Shabazz.

This case consists principally of excerpts from Malcolm X's only substantial written work: *The Autobiography of Malcolm X,* which he wrote with the assistance of Alex Haley.

Childhood

In the chapter entitled "Mascot," Malcolm X recalled the man and woman who ran the detention home in Mason, Michigan, to which he was sent at age 13.

They were good people. Mrs. Swerlin was bigger than her husband, I remember, a big, buxom, robust, laughing woman, and Mr. Swerlin was thin, with black hair, and a black mustache and a red face, quiet and polite, even to me.

They liked me right away, too. Mrs. Swerlin showed me to my room, my own room—the first in my life. It was in one of those huge dormitory-like buildings where kids in detention were kept in those days—and still are in most places. I discovered next, with surprise, that I was allowed to eat with the Swerlins. It was the first time I'd eaten with white people—at least with grown white people—since the Seventh Day Adventist country meetings. It wasn't my own exclusive privilege, of course. Except for the very troublesome boys and girls at the detention home, who were kept locked up—those who had run away and been caught and brought back, or something like that—all of us ate with the Swerlins sitting at the head of the long tables.

They had a white cook helper, I recall—Lucille Lathrop. (It amazes me how these names come back, from a time I haven't thought about for more than 20 years.) Lucille

treated me well, too. Her husband's name was Duane Lathrop. He worked somewhere else, but he stayed there at the detention home on the weekends with Lucille.

I noticed again how white people smelled different from us, and how their food tasted different, not seasoned like Negro cooking. I began to sweep and mop and dust around in the Swerlins' house, as I had done with Big Boy at the Gohannases'.[2]

They all liked my attitude, and it was out of their liking for me that I soon became accepted by them—as a mascot, I know now. They would talk about anything and everything with me standing right there hearing them, the same way people would talk freely in front of a pet canary. They would even talk about me, or about "niggers," as though I wasn't there, as if I wouldn't understand what the word meant. A hundred times a day, they used the word "nigger." I suppose that in their own minds, they meant no harm; in fact, they probably meant well. It was the same with the cook, Lucille, and her husband, Duane. I remember one day when Mr. Swerlin, as nice as he was, came in from Lansing, where he had been through the Negro section, and said to Mrs. Swerlin right in front of me, "I just can't see how those niggers can be so happy and be so poor." He talked about how they lived in shacks, but had those big, shining cars out front.

And Mrs. Swerlin said, me standing right there, "Niggers are just that way. . . ." That scene always stayed with me.

It was the same with the other white people, most of them local politicians, when they would come visiting the Swerlins. One of their favorite parlor topics was "niggers." One of them was the judge who was in charge of me in Lansing.

---

[2] The Gohannases were an older couple who briefly took care of Malcolm after his mother was committed to the mental institution; "Big Boy" was their nephew.

He was a close friend of the Swerlins. He would ask about me when he came, and they would call me in, and he would look me up and down, his expression approving, like he was examining a fine colt, or a pedigreed pup. I knew they must have told him how I acted and how I worked.

* * * * *

Then, in the second semester of the seventh grade, I was elected class president. It surprised me even more than other people. But I can see now why the class might have done it. My grades were among the highest in the school. I was unique in my class, like a pink poodle. And I was proud; I'm not going to say I wasn't. In fact, by then, I didn't really have much feeling about being a Negro, because I was trying so hard, in every way I could, to be white. Which is why I am spending much of my life today telling the American black man that he's wasting his time straining to "integrate." I know from personal experience. I tried hard enough.

"Malcolm, we're just so *proud* of you!" Mrs. Swerlin exclaimed when she heard about my election. It was all over the restaurant where I worked. Even the state man, Maynard Allen, who still dropped by to see me once in a while, had a word of praise. . . .

The topmost scholastic standing, I remember, kept shifting between me, a girl named Audrey Slaugh, and a boy named Jimmy Cotton. . . . And then one day, just about when those of us who had passed were about to move up to 8-A, from which we would enter high school the next year, something happened which was to become the first major turning point of my life.

Somehow, I happened to be alone in the classroom with Mr. Ostrowski, my English teacher. He was a tall, rather reddish white man and he had a thick mustache. I had gotten some of my best marks under him, and he had always made me feel that he liked me. He was,

as I have mentioned, a natural born "adviser," about what you ought to read, to do, or think about any and everything. We used to make unkind jokes about him: why was he teaching in Mason instead of somewhere else, getting for himself some of the "success in life" that he kept telling us how to get?

I know that he probably meant well in what he happened to advise me that day. I doubt that he meant any harm. It was just in his nature as an American white man. I was one of his top students, one of the school's top students but all he could see for me was the kind of future "in your place" that almost all white people see for black people.

He told me, "Malcolm, you ought to be thinking about a career. Have you been giving it thought?"

The truth is, I hadn't. I never have figured out why I told him, "Well, yes, sir, I've been thinking I'd like to be a lawyer." Lansing certainly had no Negro lawyers—or doctors, either—in those days, to hold up an image I might have aspired to. All I really knew for certain was that a lawyer didn't wash dishes, as I was doing.

Mr. Ostrowski looked surprised, I remember, and leaned back in his chair and clasped his hands behind his head. He kind of half smiled and said, "Malcolm, one of life's first needs is for us to be realistic. Don't misunderstand me, now. We all here like you, you know that. But you've got to be realistic about being a nigger. A lawyer—that's no realistic goal for a nigger. You need to think about something you *can* be. You're good with your hands—making things. Everybody admires your carpentry shop work. Why don't you plan on carpentry? People like you as a person—you'd get all kinds of work.

The more I thought afterwards about what he said, the more uneasy it made me. It just kept treading around in my mind.

What made it really begin to disturb me was Mr. Ostrowski's advice to others in my class—

all of them white. Most of them had told him they were planning to become farmers. But those who wanted to strike out on their own, to try something new, he had encouraged. Some, mostly girls, wanted to be teachers. A few wanted other professions, such as one boy who wanted to become a county agent; another, a veterinarian; and one girl wanted to be a nurse. They all reported that Mr. Ostrowski had encouraged what they had wanted. Yet nearly none of them had earned marks equal to mine.

It was a surprising thing that I had never thought of it that way before, but I realized that whatever I wasn't, I was smarter than nearly all of those white kids. But apparently I was still not intelligent enough, in their eyes, to become whatever *I* wanted to be.

It was then that I began to change—inside.

I drew away from white people. I came to class, and I answered when called upon. It became a physical strain simply to sit in Mr. Ostrowski's class.

Where "nigger" had slipped off my back before, wherever I heard it now, I stopped and looked at whoever said it. And they looked surprised that I did.

I quit hearing so much "nigger" and "What's wrong?"—which was the way I wanted it. Nobody, including the teachers, could decide what had come over me. I knew I was being discussed.

In a few more weeks, it was that way, too, at the restaurant where I worked washing dishes, and at the Swerlins'.

Roxbury

Without telling anyone why, Malcolm wrote his half-sister Ella in Roxbury to ask if he could come live with her. The week he finished eighth grade, Malcolm boarded a Greyhound bus for Boston. "No physical move in my life has been more pivotal or profound in its repercussions," he recalled in the Autobiography. *In the chapter entitled "Homeboy," he described his first reaction to black society in Roxbury.*

So I went gawking around the neighborhood—the Waumbeck and Humboldt Avenue Hill section of Roxbury, which is something like Harlem's Sugar Hill, where I'd later live. I saw those Roxbury Negroes acting and living differently from any black people I'd ever dreamed of in my life. This was the snooty black neighborhood; they called themselves the "Four Hundred," and looked down their noses at the Negroes of the black ghetto, or so-called "town" section where Mary, my other half-sister, lived.

What I thought I was seeing there in Roxbury were high-class, educated, important Negroes, living well, working in big jobs and positions. Their quiet homes sat back in their mowed yards. These Negroes walked along the sidewalks looking haughty and dignified, on their way to work, to shop, to visit, to church. I know now, of course, that what I was really seeing was only a big city version of those "successful" Negro boot blacks and janitors back in Lansing. The only difference was that the ones in Boston had been brainwashed even more thoroughly. They prided themselves on being incomparably more "cultured," "cultivated," "dignified," and better off than their black brethren down in the ghetto, which was no further away than you could throw a rock. Under the pitiful misapprehension that it would make them "better," these Hill Negroes were breaking their backs trying to imitate white people.

Any black family that had been around Boston long enough to own the home they lived in was considered among the Hill elite. It didn't make any difference that they had to rent out rooms to make ends meet. Then the native-born New Englanders among them looked down upon recently migrated Southern home owners who lived next door, like Ella. And a big percentage of the Hill dwellers were in

Ella's category—Southern strivers and scramblers, and West Indian Negroes, whom both the New Englanders and the Southerners called "Black Jews." Usually it was the Southerners and the West Indians who not only managed to own the places where they lived but also at least one other house, which they rented as income property. The snooty New Englanders usually owned less than they.

In those days on the Hill, any who could claim "professional" status—teachers, preachers, practical nurses—also considered themselves superior. Foreign diplomats could have modeled their conduct on the way the Negro postmen, Pullman porters, and dining car waiters of Roxbury acted, striding around as if they were wearing top hats and cutaways.

I'd guess that 8 out of 10 of the Hill Negroes of Roxbury, despite the impressive-sounding job titles they affected, actually worked as menials and servants. "He's in banking," or "He's in securities." It sounded as though they were discussing a Rockefeller or a Mellon—and not some gray-headed, dignity-posturing bank janitor, or bond-house messenger. "I'm with an old family" was the euphemism used to dignify the professions of white folks' cooks and maids who talked so affectedly among their own kind in Roxbury that you couldn't even understand them. I don't know how many 40- and 50-year-old errand boys went down the Hill dressed like ambassadors in black suits and white collars, to downtown jobs "in government," "in finance," or "in law." It has never ceased to amaze me how so many Negroes, then and now, could stand the indignity of that kind of self-delusion.

*   *   *   *   *

Malcolm was befriended by a street-smart hipster named Shorty, who was also originally from Lansing and did not suspect that Malcolm was about 10 years younger than he. Announcing to Malcolm "I'm going to school you to the happenings," Shorty introduced him to Roxbury's exuberant night life.

The first liquor I drank, my first cigarettes, even my first reefers, I can't specifically remember. But I know they were all mixed together with my first shooting craps, playing cards, and betting my dollar a day on the numbers, as I started hanging out at night with Shorty and his friends. Shorty's jokes about how country I had been made us all laugh. I still was country, I know now, but it all felt so great because I was accepted. . . .

Shorty soon decided that my hair was finally long enough to be conked. He had promised to school me in how to beat the barbershops' three- and four-dollar price by making up congolene, and then conking ourselves.

I took the little list of ingredients he had printed out for me, and went to a grocery store, where I got a can of Red Devil lye, two eggs, and two medium-sized white potatoes. Then at a drugstore near the poolroom, I asked for a large jar of Vaseline, a large bar of soap, a large-toothed comb and a fine-toothed comb, one of those rubber hoses with a metal spray-head, a rubber apron and a pair of gloves. "Going to lay on that first conk?" the drugstore man asked me. I proudly told him, grinning, "Right!"

Shorty paid six dollars a week for a room in his cousin's shabby apartment. His cousin wasn't at home. "It's like the pad's mine, he spends so much time with his woman," Shorty said. "Now, you watch me—"

He peeled the potatoes and thin-sliced them into a quart-sized Mason fruit jar, then started stirring them with a wooden spoon as he gradually poured in a little over half the can of lye. "Never use a metal spoon; the lye will turn it black," he told me.

A jelly-like, starchy-looking glop resulted from the lye and potatoes, and Shorty broke in the two eggs, stirring real fast—his own conk and dark face bent down close. The congolene turned pale yellowish. "Feel the jar," Shorty said. I cupped my hand against the outside, and snatched it away. "Damn right, it's hot, that's the lye," he said. "So you know it's going to burn when I comb it in—it burns *bad*. But the longer you can stand it, the straighter the hair."

He made me sit down, and he tied the string of the new rubber apron tightly around my neck, and combed up my bush of hair. Then, from the big Vaseline jar, he took a handful and massaged it hard all through my hair and into the scalp. He also thickly Vaselined my neck, ears, and forehead. "When I get to washing out your head, be sure to tell me anywhere you feel any little stinging," Shorty warned me, washing his hands, then pulling on the rubber gloves, and tying on his own rubber apron. "You always got to remember that any congolene left in burns a sore into your head."

The congolene just felt warm when Shorty started combing it in. But then my head caught fire.

I gritted my teeth and tried to pull the sides of the kitchen table together. The comb felt as if it was raking my skin off.

My eyes watered, my nose was running. I couldn't stand it any longer; I bolted to the washbasin. I was cursing Shorty with every name I could think of when he got the spray going and started soap-lathering my head.

He lathered and spray-rinsed, lathered and spray-rinsed, maybe 10 or 12 times, each time gradually closing the hot water faucet, until the rinse was cold, and that helped some.

"You feel any stinging spots?"

"No," I managed to say. My knees were trembling.

"Sit back down, then. I think we got it all out okay."

The flame came back as Shorty, with a thick towel, started drying my head, rubbing hard. *Easy, man, easy!* I kept shouting.

"The first time's always worst. You get used to it better before long. You took it real good, homeboy. You got a good conk."

When Shorty let me stand up and see in the mirror, my hair hung down in limp, damp strings. My scalp still flamed, but not as badly; I could bear it. He draped the towel around my shoulders, over my rubber apron, and began again vaselining my hair.

I could feel him combing, straight back, first the big comb, then the fine tooth one.

Then, he was using a razor, very delicately, on the back of my neck. Then, finally, shaping the sideburns.

My first view in the mirror blotted out the hurting. I'd seen some pretty conks, but when it's the first time, on your *own* head, the transformation, after the lifetime of kinks, is staggering.

The mirror reflected Shorty behind me: We both were grinning and sweating. And on top of my head was this thick, smooth sheen of shining red hair—real red—as straight as any white man's.

How ridiculous I was! Stupid enough to stand there simply lost in admiration of my hair now looking "white," reflected in the mirror in Shorty's room. I vowed that I'd never again be without a conk, and I never was for many years.

Red

Malcolm found a job as a shoeshiner at the Roseland Ballroom, where he was mesmerized by such music greats as Benny Goodman and Duke Ellington who played there and sometimes graced his shoeshine chair. Most of the dances were for whites only, although on some nights there were dances for blacks. On his first night at the ballroom, Malcolm learned from an experienced shoeshiner named Freddie.

Freddie then said for me to pay close attention, that he was going to be busy and for me to watch but not get in the way, and he'd try to get me ready to take over at the next dance, a couple of nights later.

As Freddie busied himself setting up the shoeshine stand, he told me, "Get here early . . . your shoeshine rags and brushes by this footstand . . . your polish bottles, paste wax, suede brushes over here . . . everything in place, you get rushed, you never need to waste motion. . . ."

While you shined shoes, I learned, you also kept watch on customers inside, leaving the urinals. You darted over and offered a small white hand towel. "A lot of cats who ain't planning to wash their hands, sometimes you can run up with a towel and shame them. Your towels are really your best hustle in here. Cost you a penny apiece to launder—you always get at least a nickel tip."

The shoeshine customers, and any from the inside rest room who took a towel, you whisk-broomed a couple of licks. "A nickel or a dime tip, just give 'em that," Freddie said. "But for two bits, Uncle Tom a little—white cats especially like that. I've had them to come back two, three times a dance" . . . .

"But, look, you ever shined any shoes?" He laughed when I said I hadn't, excepting my own. "Well, let's get to work. I never had neither."

Freddie got on the stand and went to work on his own shoes. Brush, liquid polish, brush, paste wax, shine rag, lacquer sole dressing . . . step by step, Freddie showed me what to do.

"But you got to get a whole lot faster. You can't waste time!" Freddie showed me how fast on my own shoes. Then, because business was tapering off, he had time to give me a demonstration of how to make the shine rag pop like a firecracker. "Dig the action?" he asked. He did it in slow motion. I got down and tried it on his shoes. I had the principle of it. "Just got to do it faster," Freddie said. "It's a jive noise, that's all. Cats tip better, they figure you're knocking yourself out!"

By the end of the dance, Freddie had let me shine the shoes of three or four stray drunks he talked into having shines, and I had practiced picking up my speed on Freddie's shoes until they looked like mirrors. After we had helped the janitors to clean up the ballroom after the dance, throwing out all the paper and cigarette butts and empty liquor bottles, Freddie was nice enough to drive me all the way home to Ella's on the Hill in the second-hand maroon Buick he said he was going to trade in on his Cadillac. He talked to me all the way. "I guess it's all right if I tell you, pick up a couple of dozen packs of rubbers, two bits apiece. You notice some of those cats that came up to me around the end of the dance? Well, when some have new chicks going right, they'll come asking you for rubbers. Charge a dollar, generally you'll get an extra tip."

He looked across at me. "Some hustles you're too new for. Cats will ask you for liquor, some will want reefers. But you don't need to have nothing except rubbers—until you can dig who's a cop."

"You can make $10, $12 a dance for yourself if you work everything right," Freddie said, before I got out of the car in front of Ella's. "The main thing you got to remember is that everything in the world is a hustle. So long, Red."

*　　*　　*　　*　　*

Malcolm's next job was selling sandwiches on the train between New York and Boston.

That sandwich man I'd replaced had little chance of getting his job back. I went bellowing up and down those train aisles. I sold sandwiches, coffee, candy, cake, and ice cream as fast as the railroad's commissary department could supply them. It didn't take me a week to learn that all you had to do was give white people a show and they'd buy anything you offered them. It was like popping your shoe-shine rag. The dining car waiters and Pullman porters knew it, too, and they faked their Uncle Tomming to get bigger tips. We were in that world of Negroes who are both servants and psychologists, aware that white people are so obsessed with their own importance that they will pay liberally, even dearly, for the impression of being catered to and entertained. . . .

The regular "Yankee Clipper" sandwich man, when he came back, was put on another train. He complained about seniority, but my sales record make them placate him some other way. The waiters and cooks had begun to call me "Sandwich Red."

By that time, they had a laughing bet going that I wasn't going to last, sales or not, because I had so rapidly become such an uncouth, wild young Negro. Profanity had become my language. I'd even curse customers, especially servicemen; I couldn't stand them. I remember that once, when some passenger complaints had gotten me a warning, and I wanted to be careful, I was working down the aisle and a big, beefy, red-faced cracker soldier got up in front of me, so drunk he was weaving, and announced loud enough that everybody in the car heard him, "I'm going to fight you, nigger." I remember the tension. I laughed and told him, "Sure, I'll fight, but you've got too many clothes on." He had on a big Army overcoat. He took that off, and I kept laughing and said he still had on too many. I was able to keep that cracker stripping off clothes until he stood there drunk with nothing on from his pants up, and the whole car was laughing at him, and some other soldiers got him out of the way. I went on. I never would forget that. . . .

Prison

Following a lengthy downward cycle of dope-peddling, burglary, and running from both the law and several underworld enemies, Malcolm was apprehended, tried, and sent to prison in Massachusetts.

I served a total of seven years in prison. Now, when I try to separate that first year—plus that I spent at Charlestown—it runs all together in a memory of nutmeg and the other semidrugs, of cursing guards, throwing things out of my cell, balking in the lines, dropping my tray in the dining hall, refusing to answer my number—claiming I forgot it—and things like that. I preferred the solitary that this behavior brought me. I would pace for hours like a caged leopard, viciously cursing aloud to myself. And my favorite targets were the Bible and God. But there was a legal limit to how much time one could be kept in solitary. Eventually, the men in the cellblock had a name for me: "Satan." Because of my antireligious attitude.

After several of his brothers and one of his sisters puzzled Malcolm by telling him in letters to stop eating pork and smoking cigarettes, Malcolm's brother Reginald visited him in prison to explain.

He said, finally, as though it had just happened to come into his mind, "Malcolm, if a man knew every imaginable thing that there is to know, who would he be?"

Back in Harlem, he had often liked to get at something through this kind of indirection. It had often irritated me, because my way had always been direct. I looked at him. "Well, he would have to be some kind of a god."

Reginald said, "There's a *man* who knows everything." I asked, "Who is that?" "God is a man," Reginald said. "His real name is Allah."

Allah. That word came back to me from Philbert's letter; it was my first hint of any connection. But Reginald went on. He said that God had 360 degrees of knowledge. He said that 360 degrees represented "the sum total of knowledge."

To say I was confused is an understatement. I don't have to remind you of the background against which I sat hearing my brother Reginald talk like this. I just listened, knowing he was taking his time in putting me onto something. And if somebody is trying to put you onto something, you need to listen.

"The devil has only 33 degrees of knowledge—known as Masonry," Reginald said. I can so specifically remember the exact phrases since, later, I was going to teach them so many times to others. "The devil uses his Masonry to rule other people."

He told me that this God had come to America, and that he had made himself known to a man named Elijah—"a black man, just like us." This God had let Elijah know, Reginald said, that the devil's "time was up." I didn't know what to think. I just listened. "The devil is also a man," Reginald said. "What do you mean?" With a slight movement of his head, Reginald indicated some white inmates and their visitors talking, as we were, across the room.

"Them," he said. "The white man is the devil." He told me that all whites knew they were devils—"especially Masons." I never will forget: my mind was involuntarily flashing across the entire spectrum of white people I had ever known; and for some reason it stopped on Hymie, the Jew, who had been so good to me. Reginald, a couple of times, had gone out with me to that Long Island bootlegging operation to buy and bottle up the bootleg liquor for Hymie. I said, "Without any exception?" "Without any exception."

"What about Hymie?" "What is it if I let you make $500 to let me make $10,000?" After Reginald left, I thought. I thought. Thought. I couldn't make of it head, or tail, or middle. The white people I had known marched before my mind's eye. From the start of my life. The state white people always in our house after the other whites I didn't know had killed my father . . . the white people who kept calling my mother "crazy" to her face and before me and my brothers and sisters, until she finally was taken off by white people to the Kalamazoo asylum . . . the white judge and others who had split up the children . . . the Swerlins, the other whites around Mason . . . white youngsters I was in school there with, and the teachers—the one who told me in the eighth

grade to "be a carpenter" because thinking of being a lawyer was foolish for a Negro. . . .

My head swam with the parading faces of white people. The ones in Boston, in the white-only dances at the Roseland Ballroom where I shined their shoes . . . at the Parker House where I took their dirty plates back to the kitchen . . . the railroad crewmen and passengers . . . Sophia.

The whites in New York City—the cops, the white criminals I'd dealt with . . . the whites who piled into the Negro speakeasies for a taste of Negro *soul* . . . the white women who wanted Negro men . . . the men I'd steered to the black "specialty sex" they wanted. . . . Boston cops . . . Sophia's husband's friend, and her husband, whom I'd never seen, but knew so much about . . . Sophia's sister . . . the Jew jeweler who'd helped trap me[3] . . . the social workers . . . the Middlesex County Court people . . . the judge who gave me 10 years . . . the prisoners I'd known, the guards and the officials. . . .

Reginald, when he came to visit me again in a few days, could gauge from my attitude the effect that his talking had had upon me. He seemed very pleased. Then, very seriously, he talked for two solid hours about "the devil white man" and "the brainwashed black man."

When Reginald left, he left me rocking with some of the first serious thoughts I had ever had in my life: that the white man was fast losing his power to oppress and exploit the dark world; that the dark world was starting to rise to rule the world again, as it had before; that the white man's world was on the way down, it was on the way out.

"You don't even know who you are," Reginald had said. "You don't even know, the white devil has hidden it from you, that you are a

---

[3] The jeweler had cooperated with the police to arrest Malcolm when he brought a stolen watch to the jeweler's shop to be fixed.

race of people of ancient civilizations, and riches in gold and kings. You don't even know your true family name, you wouldn't recognize your true language if you heard it. You have been cut off by the devil white man from all true knowledge of your own kind. You have been a victim of the evil of the devil white man ever since he murdered and raped and stole you from your native land in the seeds of your forefathers. . . ."

Many a time, I have looked back, trying to assess, just for myself, my first reactions to all this. Every instinct of the ghetto jungle streets, every hustling fox and criminal wolf instinct in me, which would have scoffed at and rejected anything else, was struck numb. It was as though all of that life merely was back there, without any remaining effect, or influence. I remember how, sometime later, reading the Bible in the Norfolk Prison Colony library, I came upon, then I read, over and over, how Paul on the road to Damascus, upon hearing the voice of Christ, was so smitten that he was knocked off his horse, in a daze. I do not now, and I did not then, liken myself to Paul. But I do understand his experience.

I have since learned—helping me to understand what then began to happen within me—that the truth can be quickly received, or received at all, only by the sinner who knows and admits that he is guilty of having sinned much. Stated another way: only guilt admitted accepts truth. The Bible again: the one people whom Jesus could not help were the Pharisees; they didn't feel they needed any help.

The very enormity of my previous life's guilt prepared me to accept the truth. . . .

I did write to Elijah Muhammad. He lived in Chicago at that time, at 6116 South Michigan Avenue. At least 25 times I must have written that first one-page letter to him, over and over. I was trying to make it both legible and understandable. I practically couldn't read my handwriting myself; it shames even to remember it. My spelling and my grammar were as bad, if not worse. Anyway, as well as I could

express it, I said I had been told about him by my brothers and sisters, and I apologized for my poor letter.

Mr. Muhammad sent me a typed reply. It had an all but electrical effect upon me to see the signature of the "Messenger of Allah." After he welcomed me into the "true knowledge," he gave me something to think about. The black prisoner, he said, symbolized white society's crime of keeping black men oppressed and deprived and ignorant, and unable to get decent jobs, turning them into criminals.

He told me to have courage. He even enclosed some money for me, a $5 bill. Mr. Muhammad sends money all over the country to prison inmates who write to him, probably to this day. Regularly my family wrote to me, "Turn to Allah . . . pray to the East."

The hardest test I ever faced in my life was praying. You understand. My comprehending, my believing the teachings of Mr. Muhammad had only required my mind's saying to me, "That's right!" or "I never thought of that."

But bending my knees to pray—that *act*—well, that took me a week.

You know what my life had been. Picking a lock to rob someone's house was the only way my knees had ever been bent before.

I had to force myself to bend my knees. And waves of shame and embarrassment would force me back up.

For evil to bend its knees, admitting its guilt, to implore the forgiveness of God, is the hardest thing in the world. It's easy for me to see and to say that now. But then, when I was the personification of evil, I was going through it. Again, again, I would force myself back down into the praying-to-Allah posture. When finally I was able to make myself stay down—I didn't know what to say to Allah.

For the next years, I was the nearest thing to a hermit in the Norfolk Prison Colony. I never have been more busy in my life. I still marvel at how swiftly my previous life's thinking pattern slid away from me, like snow off a roof. It is as though someone else I knew of had lived by hustling and crime. I would be startled to catch myself thinking in a remote way of my earlier self as another person.

The things I felt, I was pitifully unable to express in the one-page letter that went every day to Mr. Elijah Muhammad. And I wrote at least one more daily letter, replying to one of my brothers and sisters. Every letter I received from them added something to my knowledge of the teachings of Mr. Muhammad. I would sit for long periods and study his photographs.

I've never been one for inaction. Everything I've ever felt strongly about, I've done something about. I guess that's why, unable to do anything else, I soon began writing to people I had known in the hustling world, such as Sammy the Pimp, John Hughes, the gambling house owner, the thief Jumpsteady, and several dope peddlers. I wrote them all about Allah and Islam and Mr. Elijah Muhammad. I had no idea where most of them lived. I addressed their letters in care of the Harlem or Roxbury bars and clubs where I'd known them.

I never got a single reply. The average hustler and criminal was too uneducated to write a letter. I have known many slick, sharp-looking hustlers, who would have you think they had an interest in Wall Street; privately, they would get someone else to read a letter if they received one. Besides, neither would I have replied to anyone writing me something as wild as "the white man is the devil."

What certainly went on the Harlem and Roxbury wires was the Detroit Red was going crazy in stir, or else he was trying some hype to shake up the warden's office.

Nation of Islam

After his release from prison, Malcolm X helped build the Nation of Islam into a potent organization. In the chapter entitled "Minister Malcolm X," he recounted an important evening in the history of the Black Muslims.

I mentioned, you will remember, how in a big city, a sizable organization can remain practically unknown, unless something happens that brings it to the general public's attention. Well, certainly no one in the Nation of Islam had any anticipation of the kind of thing that would happen in Harlem one night.

Two white policemen, breaking up a street scuffle between some Negroes, ordered other Negro passers-by to "Move on!" Of these bystanders, two happened to be Muslim brother Johnson Hinton and another brother of Temple Seven. They didn't scatter and run the way the white cops wanted. Brother Hinton was attacked with nightsticks. His scalp was split open and a police car came and he was taken to a nearby precinct.

The second brother telephoned our restaurant. And with some telephone calls, in less than half an hour about 50 of Temple Seven's men of the Fruit of Islam were standing in ranks-formation outside the police precinct house.

Other Negroes, curious, came running, and gathered in excitement behind the Muslims. The police, coming to the station house front door, and looking out of the windows, couldn't believe what they saw. I went in, as the minister of Temple Seven, and demanded to see our brother. The police first said he wasn't there. Then they admitted he was, but said I couldn't see him. I said that until he was seen, and we were sure he received proper medical attention, the Muslims would remain where they were.

They were nervous and scared of the gathering crowd outside. When I saw our Brother Hinton, it was all I could do to contain myself. He was only semiconscious. Blood had bathed his head and face and shoulder. I hope I never again have to withstand seeing another case of sheer police brutality like that.

I told the lieutenant in charge, "That man belongs in the hospital." They called an ambulance. When it came and Brother Hinton was taken to Harlem Hospital, we Muslims followed, in loose formations, for about 15 blocks along Lenox Avenue, probably the busiest thoroughfare in Harlem. Negroes who never had seen anything like this were coming out of stores and restaurants and bars and enlarging the crowd following us.

The crowd was big, and angry, behind the Muslims in front of Harlem Hospital. Harlem's black people were long since sick and tired of police brutality. And they never had seen any organization of black men take a firm stand as we were.

A high police official came up to me, saying "Get those people out of there." I told him that our brothers were standing peacefully, disciplined perfectly, and harming no one. He told me those others, behind them, weren't disciplined. I politely told him those others were his problem.

When doctors assured us that Brother Hinton was receiving the best of care, I gave the order and the Muslims slipped away. The other Negroes' mood was ugly, but they dispersed also, when we left. We wouldn't learn until later that a steel plate would have to be put into Brother Hinton's skull. (After that operation, the Nation of Islam helped him to sue; a jury awarded him over $70,000, the largest police brutality judgment that New York City has ever paid.)

For New York City's millions of readers of the downtown papers, it was, at that time, another one of the periodic "Racial Unrest in Harlem" stories. It was not played up, because of what had happened. But the police department, to be sure, pulled out and carefully studied the files on the Nation of Islam, and appraised us with new eyes. Most important, in Harlem, the world's most heavily populated black ghetto, the *Amsterdam News* made the whole story headline news, and for the first time the black man, woman, and child in the streets was discussing "those Muslims."

Interaction with the Media

In late 1959, the television program was aired. "The Hate That Hate Produced"—the title— was edited tightly into a kaleidoscope of "shocker" images . . . Mr. Muhammad, me, and others speaking . . . strong-looking, set-faced black men, our Fruit of Islam . . . white-scarved, white-gowned Muslim sisters of all ages . . . Muslims in our restaurants, and other businesses . . . Muslims and other black people entering and leaving our mosques. . . .

Every phrase was edited to increase the shock mood. As the producers intended, I think people sat just about limp when the program went off.

In a way, the public reaction was like what happened back in the 1930's when Orson Welles frightened America with a radio program describing, as though it was actually happening, an invasion by "men from Mars."

No one now jumped from any windows, but in New York City there was an instant avalanche of public reaction. It's my personal opinion that the "Hate . . . Hate . . ." title was primarily responsible for the reaction. Hundreds of thousands of New Yorkers, black and white, were exclaiming "Did you hear it? Did you see it? Preaching *hate* of white people!"

Here was one of the white man's most characteristic behavior patterns—where black men are concerned. He loves himself so much that he is startled if he discovers that his victims don't share his vainglorious self-opinion. In America for centuries it had been just fine as long as the victimized, brutalized and exploited black people had been grinning and begging and "Yessa, Massa" and Uncle Tomming. But now, things were different. First came the white newspapers—feature writers and columnists: "Alarming" . . . "hate messengers" . . . "threat to the good relations between the races" . . . "black segregationists" . . . "black supremacists," and the like.

And the newspapers' ink wasn't dry before the big national weekly news magazines started: "Hate teachers" . . . "violence seekers" . . . "black racists" . . . "black fascists" . . . "anti-Christian" . . . "possibly Communist inspired. . . ."

It rolled out of the presses of the biggest devil in the history of mankind. And then the aroused white man made his next move.

Since slavery, the American white man has always kept some handpicked Negroes who fared much better than the black masses suffering and slaving out in the hot fields. The white man had these "house" and "yard" Negroes for his special servants. He threw them more crumbs from his rich table, he even let them eat in his kitchen. He knew that he could always count on them to keep "good massa" happy in his self-image of being so "good" and "righteous." "Good massa" always heard just what he wanted to hear from these "house" and "yard" blacks. "You're such a good, *fine* massa!" Or, "Oh, massa, those old black nigger fieldhands out there, they're happy just like they are; why, massa, they're not intelligent enough for you to try and do any better for them, massa—"

Well, slavery time's "house" and "yard" Negroes had become more sophisticated, that was all. When now the white man picked up his telephone and dialed his "house" and "yard" Negroes—why, he didn't even need to instruct the trained black puppets. They had seen the television program; had read the newspapers. They were already composing their lines. They knew what to do.

I'm not going to call any names. But if you make a list of the biggest Negro "leaders," so-called, in 1960, then you've named the ones who began to attack us "field" Negroes who were sounding *insane,* talking that way about "good massa."

"By no means do these Muslims represent the Negro masses." That was the first worry, to reassure "good massa" that he had no reason to be concerned about his fieldhands in the ghettos. "An irresponsible hate cult," . . . "an unfortunate Negro image, just when the racial picture is improving."

They were stumbling over each other to get quoted. "A deplorable reverse racism" . . . "Ridiculous pretenders to the ancient Islamic doctrine" . . . "Heretic anti-Christianity—"

The telephone in our then small Temple Seven restaurant nearly jumped off the wall. I had a receiver against my ear five hours a day. I was listening, and jotting in my notebook, as press, radio, and television people called, all of them wanting the Muslim reaction to the quoted attacks of these black "leaders." Or I was on long distance to Mr. Muhammad in Chicago, reading from my notebook and asking for Mr. Muhammad's instructions. I couldn't understand how Mr. Muhammad could maintain his calm and patience, hearing the things I told him. I could scarcely contain myself.

My unlisted home telephone number somehow got out. My wife Betty put down the phone after taking one message, and it was ringing again. It seemed that wherever I went, telephones were ringing.

The calls naturally were directed to me, New York City being the major news media headquarters, and I was the New York minister of Mr. Muhammad. Calls came, long distance from San Francisco to Maine . . . from even London, Stockholm, Paris. I would see a Muslim brother at our restaurant, or Betty at home, trying to keep cool; they'd hand me the receiver, and I couldn't believe it, either. One funny thing in all that hectic period, something quickly struck my notice: the Europeans never pressed the "hate" question. Only the American white man was so plagued and obsessed with being "hated." He was so guilty, it was clear to me, of hating Negroes.

"Mr. Malcolm X; why do you teach black supremacy, and hate?" A red flag waved for me, something chemical happened inside me, every time I heard that. When we Muslims had talked about "the devil white man" he had been relatively abstract, someone we Muslims rarely actually came into contact with, but now here was that devil-in-the-flesh on the phone — with all of his calculating, cold-eyed, self righteous tricks and nerve and gall. The voices questioning me became to me as breathing, living devils.

"The guilty, two-faced white man can't decide *what* he wants. Our slave foreparents would have been put to death for advocating so-called integration with the white man. Now when Mr. Muhammad speaks of 'separation,' the white man calls us 'hate teachers' and 'fascists'!

"The white man doesn't *want* the blacks! He doesn't *want* the blacks that are a parasite upon him. He doesn't *want* this black man whose presence and condition in this country expose the white man to the world for what he is! So why do you attack Mr. Muhammad?"

I'd have *scathing* in my voice; I *felt* it.

"For the white man to ask the black man if he hates him is just like the rapist asking the *raped,* or the wolf asking the *sheep,* 'Do you hate me?' The white man is in no moral *position* to accuse anyone else of hate!

"Why, when all of my ancestors are snake-bitten, and I'm snake-bitten, and I warn my children to avoid snakes, what does that *snake* sound like accusing *me* of hate-teaching?"

"Mr. Malcolm X," those devils would ask, "why is your Fruit of Islam being trained in judo and karate?" An image of black men learning anything suggesting self-defense seemed to terrify the white man. I'd turn their question around: "Why does judo or karate suddenly get so ominous because black men study it? Across America, the Boy Scouts, the YMCA, even the YWCA, the CYP, PAL — they *all* teach judo! It's all right, it's fine until *black men* teach it! Even little grammar school classes, little girls, are taught to defend themselves."

"How many of you are in your organization, Mr. Malcolm X? Right Reverend Bishop T. Chickenwing says you have only a handful of members"

"Whoever tells you how many Muslims there are doesn't know, and whoever does know will never tell you—"

The Bishop Chickenwings were also often quoted about our "anti-Christianity." I'd fire right back on that:

> Christianity is the white man's religion. The Holy Bible in the white man's hands and his interpretations of it have been the greatest single ideological weapon for enslaving millions of non-white human beings. Every country the white man has conquered with his guns, he has always paved the way, and salved his conscience, by carrying the Bible and interpreting it to call the people "heathens" and "pagans"; then he sends his guns, then his missionaries behind the guns to mop up. . . .

I can remember those hot telephone sessions with those reporters as if it were yesterday. The reporters were angry. I was angry. When I'd reach into history, they'd try to pull me back to the present. They would quit interviewing, quit their work, trying to defend their personal white devil selves. They would unearth Lincoln and his freeing of the slaves. I'd tell them things Lincoln said in speeches, *against* the blacks. They would drag up the 1954 Supreme Court decision on school integration.

"That was one of the greatest magical feats ever performed in America," I'd tell them. "Do you mean to tell me that nine Supreme Court judges, who are past masters of legal phraseology, couldn't have worked their decision to make it stick as *law?* No! It was trickery and magic that told Negroes they were desegregated — Hooray! Hooray! — and at the same time it told whites 'Here are your loopholes.'"

The reporters would try their utmost to raise some "good" white man whom I couldn't refute as such. I'll never forget how one practically lost his voice. He asked me did I feel *any* white men had ever done anything for the black man in America. I told him, "Yes, I can think of two. Hitler, and Stalin. The black man in America couldn't get a decent factory job until Hitler put so much pressure on the white man. And then Stalin kept up the pressure — "

But I don't care what points I made in the interviews, it practically never got printed the way I said it. I was learning under fire how the press, when it wants to, can twist, and slant. If I had said "Mary had a little lamb," what probably would have appeared was "Malcolm X Lampoons Mary."

Even so, my bitterness was less against the white press than it was against those Negro "leaders" who kept attacking us. Mr. Muhammad said he wanted us to try our best not to publicly counterattack the black "leaders" because one of the white man's tricks was keeping the black race divided and fighting against each other. Mr. Muhammad said that this had traditionally kept the black people from achieving the unity which was the worst need of the black race in America.

But instead of abating, the black puppets continued ripping and tearing at Mr. Muhammad and the Nation of Islam until it began to appear as though we were afraid to speak out against these "important" Negroes. That's when Mr. Muhammad's patience wore thin. And with his nod, I began returning their fire.

"Today's Uncle Tom doesn't wear a handkerchief on his head. This modern, 20th-century Uncle Thomas now often wears a top hat. He's usually well-dressed and well-educated. He's often the personification of culture and refinement. The 20th-century Uncle Thomas sometimes speaks with a Yale or Harvard accent. Sometimes he is known as Professor, Doctor, Judge, and Reverend, even Right Reverend Doctor. This 20th-century Uncle Thomas is a *professional* Negro . . . by

that I mean his profession is being a Negro for the white man."

Never before in America had these hand-picked so-called leaders been publicly blasted in this way. They reacted to the truth about themselves even more hotly than the devilish white man.

Before very long, radio and television people began asking me to defend our Nation of Islam in panel discussions and debates. I was to be confronted by handpicked scholars, both whites and some of those PhD "house" and "yard" Negroes who had been attacking us. Every day, I was more incensed with the general misrepresentation and distortion of Mr. Muhammad's teachings; I truly think that not once did it cross my mind that previously I never had been *inside* a radio or television station, let alone faced a microphone to audiences of millions of people. Prison debating had been my only experience speaking to anyone but Muslims.

From the old hustling days I knew that there were tricks to everything. In the prison debating, I had learned tricks to upset my opponents, to catch them where they didn't expect to be caught. I knew there were bound to be tricks I didn't know anything about in arguing on the air.

I knew that if I closely studied what the others did, I could learn things in a hurry to help me to defend Mr. Muhammad and his teachings.

I'd walk into those studios. The devils and black PhD puppets would be acting so friendly and "integrated" with each other — laughing and calling each other by first names, and all that; it was such a big lie it made me sick in my stomach. They would even be trying to act friendly toward me — we all knowing they had asked me there to try and beat out my brains. They would offer me coffee. I would tell them "No, thanks," to please just tell me where was I supposed to sit. Sometimes the microphone sat on the table before you, at other times a smaller, cylindrical microphone was hung on a cord around your neck. From the start, I liked those microphones better; I didn't have to keep constantly aware of my distance from a microphone on the table.

The program hosts would start with some kind of dice-loading, nonreligious introduction for me. It would be something like "and we have with us today the fiery, angry chief Malcolm X of the New York Muslims. . . ." I made up my own introduction. At home, or driving my car, I practiced until I could interrupt a radio or television host and introduce myself.

"I represent Mr. Elijah Muhammad, the spiritual head of the fastest-growing group of Muslims in the Western Hemisphere. We who follow him know that he has been divinely taught and sent to us by God Himself. We believe that the miserable plight of America's 20 million black people is the fulfillment of divine prophecy. We also believe the presence today in America of The Honorable Elijah Muhammad, his teachings among the so-called Negroes, and his naked warning to America concerning her treatment of these so-called Negroes, is all the fulfillment of divine prophecy. I am privileged to be the minister of our Temple Number Seven here in New York City which is a part of the Nation of Islam, under the divine leadership of The Honorable Elijah Muhammad—"

I would look around at those devils and their trained black parrots staring at me, while I was catching my breath—and I had set my tone.

They would outdo each other, leaping in on me, hammering at Mr. Muhammad, at me, and at the Nation of Islam. Those "integration"-mad Negroes—you know what they jumped on. *Why* couldn't Muslims *see* that "integration" was the answer to American Negroes' problems? I'd try to rip that to pieces.

No *sane* black man really wants integration! No *sane* white man really wants integration! No sane black man really believes that the white man ever will give the black man anything more than token integration. No! The Honorable Elijah Muhammad teaches that for the black man in America the only solution is complete *separation* from the white man!

Anyone who has ever heard me on radio or television programs knows that my technique is nonstop, until what I want to get said is said. I was developing the technique then.

The Honorable Elijah Muhammad teaches us that since Western society is deteriorating, it has become overrun with immorality, and God is going to judge it, and destroy it. And the only way the black people caught up in this society can be saved is not to *integrate* into this corrupt society, but to *separate* from it, to a land of our *own*, where we can reform ourselves, lift up our moral standards, and try to be godly. The Western world's most learned diplomats have failed to solve this grave race problem. Her learned legal experts have failed. Her sociologists have failed. Her civil leaders have failed. Her fraternal leaders have failed. Since all of these have *failed* to solve this race problem, it is time for us to sit down and *reason!* I am certain that we will be forced to agree that it takes *God Himself* to solve this grave racial dilemma.

Every time I mentioned "separation," some of them would cry that we Muslims were standing for the same thing that white racists and demagogues stood for. I would explain the difference.

No! We reject *segregation* even more militantly than you say you do! We want *separation,* which is not the same! The Honorable Elijah Muhammad teaches us that *segregation* is when your life and liberty are controlled, regulated, *by someone else.* To *segregate* means to control. Segregation is that which is forced upon inferiors by superiors. But *separation* is that which is done voluntarily, by two equals for the good of both! The Honorable Elijah Muhammad teaches us that as long as our people here in America are dependent on the white man, we will always be begging him for jobs, food, clothing, and housing. And he will always control our lives, regulate our lives, and have the power to segregate us. The Negro here in America has been treated like a child. A child stays within the mother until the time of birth! When the time of birth arrives, the child must be separated, or it will *destroy* its mother and itself. The mother can't carry that child after its time. The child cries for and needs its own world!

Anyone who has listened to me will have to agree that I believed in Elijah Muhammad and represented him 100 percent. I never tried to take any credit for myself.

I was never in one of those panel discussions without some of them just waiting their chance to accuse me of "inciting Negroes to violence." I didn't even have to do any special studying to prepare for that one.

The greatest miracle Christianity has achieved in America is that the black man in white Christian hands has not grown violent. It is a miracle that 22 million black people have not *risen up* against their oppressors in which they would have been justified by all moral criteria, and even by the democratic tradition! It *is a miracle* that a nation of black people has so fervently continued to believe in a turn-the-other-cheek and heaven-for-you-after-you-die philosophy! It is a miracle that the American black people have remained a peaceful people, while catching all the centuries of hell that they have caught, here in white man's heaven! The *miracle* is that the white man's puppet Negro 'leaders,' his preachers and the educated Negroes laden with degrees, and others who have been allowed to wax fat off their black poor brothers, have been able to hold the black masses quiet until now.

I guarantee you one thing—every time I was mixed up in those studios with those brainwashed, "integration"-mad black puppets, and those tricky devils trying to rip and tear me down, as long as the little red light glowed "on the air," I tried to represent Elijah Muhammad and the Nation of Islam to the utmost.

* * * * *

Except for all-black audiences, I liked the college audiences best. The college sessions sometimes ran two to four hours—they often ran overtime. Challenges, queries, and criticisms were fired at me by the usually objective and always alive and searching minds of undergraduate and graduate students, and their faculties. The college sessions never failed to be exhilarating. They never failed in helping me to further my own education.

I never experienced one college session that didn't show me ways to improve upon my presentation and defense of Mr. Muhammad's teachings. Sometimes in a panel or debate appearance, I'd find a jam-packed audience to hear me, alone, facing six or eight student and faculty scholars—heads of departments, such as sociology, psychology, philosophy, history, and religion, and each of them coming at me in his specialty.

At the outset, always I'd confront such panels with something such as: "Gentlemen, I finished the eighth grade in Mason, Michigan. My high school was the black ghetto of Roxbury, Massachusetts. My college was in the streets of Harlem, and my master's was taken in prison. Mr. Muhammad has taught me that I never need fear any man's intellect who tries to defend or to justify the white man's criminal record against the nonwhite man—especially the white man and the black man here in North America."

It was like being on a battlefield with intellectual and philosophical bullets. It was an exciting battling with ideas. I got so I could feel my audiences' temperaments. I've talked with other public speakers; they agree that this ability is native to any person who has the "mass appeal" gift, who can get through to and move people. It's a psychic radar. As a doctor, with his finger against a pulse, is able to feel the heart rate, when I am up there speaking, I can *feel* the reaction to what I am saying. . . .

The white liberal may be a little taken aback to know that from all Negro audiences I never have had one challenge, never one question that defended the white man. That has been true even when a lot of those "black bourgeoisie" and "integration"-mad Negroes were among the blacks. All Negroes, among themselves, admit the white man's criminal record. They may not know as many details as I do, but they know the general picture.

But, let me tell you something significant: This very same bourgeois Negro who, among Negroes, would never make a fool of himself in trying to defend the white man—watch that same Negro in a mixed black and white audience, knowing he's overheard by his beloved "Mr. Charlie." Why, you should hear those Negroes attack me, trying to justify, or forgive the white man's crimes! These Negroes are people who bring me nearest to breaking one of my principal rules, which is never to let myself become overemotional and angry. Why, sometimes I've felt I ought to jump down off that stand and get *physical* with some of those brainwashed white man's tools, parrots, puppets. At the colleges, I've developed some stock put-downs for them: "You must be a law student, aren't you?" They have to say either yes, or no. And I say, "I thought you were. You defend this criminal white man harder than he defends his guilty self!"

One particular university's "token-integrated" black PhD associate professor I never will forget; he got me so mad I couldn't see straight. As badly as our 22 millions of educationally deprived black people need the help of any brains he has, there he was looking like some fly in the buttermilk among white "colleagues" and he was trying to *eat me up!* He was ranting about what a "divisive demagogue" and what a "reverse racist" I was. I was racking my head, to spear that fool; finally, I held up my hand, and he stopped. "Do you know what white racists call black PhDs?" He said something like, "I believe that I happen

not to be aware of that"—you know, one of these ultra-proper-talking Negroes. And I laid the word down on him, loud: *"Nigger!"*

On the Civil Rights Movement

Let some civil rights "leader" make some statement, displeasing to the white public power structure, and the reporters, in an effort to whip him back into line, would try to use me. I'll give an example. I'd get a question like this: "Mr. Malcolm X, you've often gone on record as disapproving of the sit-ins and similar Negro protest actions—what is your opinion of the Montgomery boycott that Dr. King is leading?"

Now my feeling was that, although the civil rights "leaders" kept attacking us Muslims, still they were black people, still they were our own kind, and I would be most foolish to let the white man maneuver me against the civil rights movement.

When I was asked about the Montgomery boycott, I'd carefully review what led up to it. Mrs. Rosa Parks was riding home on a bus and at some bus stop the white cracker bus driver ordered Mrs. Parks to get up and give her seat to some white passenger who had just got on the bus. I'd say, "Now, just *imagine* that! This good, hard-working, Christian-believing black woman, she's paid her money, she's in her seat. Just because she's *black,* she's asked to get up! I mean, sometimes even for me it's hard to believe the white man's arrogance!"

Or I might say, "No one will ever know exactly what emotional ingredient made this relatively trivial incident a fuse for those Montgomery Negroes. There had been *centuries* of the worst kind of outrages against Southern black people—lynchings, rapings, shootings, beatings! But you know history has been triggered by trivial-seeming incidents. Once a little nobody Indian lawyer was put off a train, and fed up with injustice, he twisted a knot in the

British lion's tail. *His* name was Mahatma Gandhi!"

Or I might copy a trick I had seen lawyers use, both in life and on television. It was a way that lawyers would slip in before a jury something otherwise inadmissible. (Sometimes I think I really might have made it as a lawyer, as I once told that eighth grade teacher in Mason, Michigan, I wanted to be, when he advised me to become a carpenter.) I would slide right over the reporter's question to drop into his lap a logical-extension hot potato for him.

"Well, sir, I see the same boycott reasoning for Negroes asked to join the Army, Navy, and Air Force. Why should we go off to die somewhere to preserve a so-called democracy that gives a white immigrant of one day more than it gives the black man with 400 years of slaving and serving in this country?"

Whites would prefer 50 local boycotts to having 22 million Negroes start thinking about what I had just said. I don't have to tell you that it never got printed the way I said it. It would be turned inside out if it got printed at all. And I could detect when the white reporters had gotten their heads together; they quit asking me certain questions.

If I had developed a good point, though, I'd bait a hook to get it said when I went on radio or television. I'd seem to slip and mention some recent so-called civil rights "advance." You know, where some giant industry had hired 10 showpiece Negroes; some restaurant chain had begun making more money by serving Negroes; some Southern university had enrolled a black freshman without bayonets – like that. When I "slipped," the program host would leap on that bait: "Ahhh! Indeed, Mr. Malcolm X — you can't deny *that's* an advance for your race!"

I'd jerk the pole then. "I can't turn around without hearing about some 'civil rights advance'! White people seem to think the black man ought to be shouting 'hallelujah'! Four hundred years the white man has had his foot-long knife in the black man's back and now the white man starts to *wiggle* the knife out, maybe six inches! The black man's supposed to be *grateful?* Why, if the white man jerked the knife *out,* it's still going to leave a *scar!*"

*   *   *   *   *

Not long ago, the black man in America was fed a dose of another form of the weakening, lulling, and deluding effects of so-called integration. It was that "Farce on Washington," I call it.

The idea of a mass of blacks marching on Washington was originally the brainchild of the Brotherhood of Sleeping Car Porters' A. Philip Randolph. For 20 or more years the March on Washington idea had floated around among Negroes. And, spontaneously, suddenly now, that idea caught on.

Overalled rural Southern Negroes, small town Negroes, Northern ghetto Negroes, even thousands of previously Uncle Tom Negroes began talking "March!"

Nothing since Joe Louis had so coalesced the masses of Negroes. Groups of Negroes were talking of getting to Washington any way they could — in rickety old cars, on buses, hitch-hiking — walking, even, if they had to. They envisioned thousands of black brothers converging together on Washington — to lie down in the streets, on airport runways, on government lawns — demanding of the congress and the White House some concrete civil rights action.

This was a national bitterness; militant, unorganized, and leaderless. Predominantly, it was young Negroes, defiant of whatever might be the consequences, sick and tired of the black man's neck under the white man's heel.

The white man had plenty of good reasons for nervous worry. The right spark — some unpredictable emotional chemistry — could set off a black uprising. The government knew that thousands of milling, angry blacks not only could completely disrupt Washington but they could erupt in Washington.

The White House speedily invited in the major civil rights Negro "leaders." They were asked to stop the planned March. They truthfully said they hadn't begun it, they had no control over it—the idea was national, spontaneous, unorganized and leaderless. In other words, it was a black powder keg.

Any student of how "integration" can weaken the black man's movement was about to observe a master lesson.

The White House, with a fanfare of international publicity, "approved," "endorsed," and "welcomed" a March on Washington. The big civil rights organizations right at this time had been publicly squabbling about donations. *The New York Times* had broken the story. The N.A.A.C.P. had charged that other agencies' demonstrations, highly publicized, had attracted a major part of the civil rights donations while the N.A.A.C.P. got left holding the bag, supplying costly bail and legal talent for the other organizations' jailed demonstrators.

It was like a movie. The next scene was the "big six" civil rights Negro "leaders" meeting in New York City with the white head of a big philanthropic agency. They were told that their money wrangling in public was damaging their image. And a reported $800,000 was donated to a United Civil Rights Leadership council that was quickly organized by the "big six."

Now, what had instantly achieved black unity? The white man's money. What string was attached to the money? Advice. Not only was there this donation, but another comparable sum was promised, for sometime later on, after the March . . . obviously if all went well.

The original "angry" March on Washington was now about to be entirely changed.

Massive international publicity projected the "big six" as March on Washington leaders. It was news to those angry grass-roots Negroes steadily adding steam to their March plans. They probably assumed that now those famous "leaders" were endorsing and joining them.

Invited next to join the March were four famous white public figures: one Catholic, one Jew, one Protestant, and one labor boss.

The massive publicity now gently hinted that the "big 10" would "supervise" the March on Washington's "mood," and its "direction."

The four white figures began nodding. The word spread fast among so-called liberal Catholics, Jews, Protestants, and laborites: it was "democratic" to join this black March. And suddenly, the previously March-nervous whites began announcing *they* were going.

It was as if electrical current shot through the ranks of bourgeois Negroes—the very so-called middle-class and upper-class who had earlier been deploring the March on Washington talk by grass-roots Negroes.

But white people, now, were going to march.

Why, some downtrodden, jobless, hungry Negro might have gotten trampled. Those "integration"-mad Negroes practically ran over each other trying to find out where to sign up. The "angry blacks" March suddenly had been made chic. Suddenly it had a Kentucky Derby image. For the status seeker, it was a status symbol. "Were you *there?*" You can hear that right today.

It had become an outing, a picnic.

The morning of the March, any rickety carloads of angry, dusty, sweating small-town Negroes would have gotten lost among the chartered jet planes, railroad cars, and air-conditioned buses. What originally was planned to be an angry riptide, one English newspaper aptly described now as "the gentle flood."

Talk about "integrated"! It was like salt and pepper. And, by now, there wasn't a single logistics aspect uncontrolled.

The marchers had been instructed to bring no signs—signs were provided. They had been told to sing one song: "We Shall Overcome." They had been told *how* to arrive, *when, where* to arrive, *where* to assemble, when to *start* marching, the *route* to march. First aid stations were strategically located—even where to *faint!*

Yes, I was there. I observed that circus. Who ever heard of angry revolutionists all harmonizing "We Shall Overcome . . . Suum Day . . . " while tripping and swaying along arm-in-arm with the very people they were supposed to be angrily revolting against? Who ever heard of angry revolutionists swinging their bare feet together with their oppressor in lily-pad park pools, with gospels and guitars and "I Have a Dream" speeches?

And the black masses in America were and still are having a nightmare. . . . And, inevitably, the black man's anger rekindled, deeper than ever, and there began bursting out in different cities, in the "long, hot summer" of 1964, unprecedented racial crises.

The JFK Assassination

No one needs to be reminded of who got assassinated in Dallas, Texas, on November 22, 1963.

Within hours after the assassination — I am telling nothing but the truth — every Muslim minister received from Mr. Elijah Muhammad a directive — in fact, *two* directives. Every minister was ordered to make no remarks at all concerning the assassination. Mr. Muhammad instructed that if pressed for comment, we should say: "No comment."

During that three-day period where there was no other news to be heard except relating to the murdered president, Mr. Muhammad had a previously scheduled speaking engagement in New York at the Manhattan Center. He canceled his coming to speak, and as we were unable to get back the money already paid for the rental of the center, Mr. Muhammad told me to speak in his stead. And so I spoke.

Many times since then, I've looked at the speech notes I used that day, which had been prepared at least a week before the assassination. The title of my speech was "God's Judgment of White America." It was on the theme, familiar to me, of "as you sow, so shall you reap," or how the hypocritical American white man was reaping what he had sowed.

The question and answer period opened, I suppose inevitably, with someone asking me, "What do you think about President Kennedy's assassination? What is your opinion?"

Without a second thought, I said what I honestly felt — that it was, as I saw it, a case of "the chickens coming home to roost." I said that the hate in white men had not stopped with the killing of defenseless black people, but that hate, allowed to spread unchecked, finally had struck down this country's chief of state. I said it was the same thing as had happened with Medgar Evers, with Patrice Lumumba, with Madame Nhu's husband.

The headlines and the news broadcasts promptly had it: *"Black Muslims' Malcolm X: 'Chickens Come Home to Roost.'"*

It makes me feel weary to think of it all now. All over America, all over the world, some of the world's most important personages were saying in various ways, and in far stronger ways than I did, that America's climate of hate had been responsible for the president's death. But when Malcolm X said the same thing, it was ominous.

My regular monthly visit to Mr. Muhammad was due the next day. Somehow, on the plane, I expected something. I've always had this strong intuition.

Mr. Muhammad and I embraced each other in greeting. I sensed some ingredient missing from his usual amiability. And I was suddenly tense — to me also very significant. . . .

"That was a very bad statement," he said. "The country loved this man. The whole country is in mourning. That was very ill-timed. A statement like that can make it hard on Muslims in general."

And then, as if Mr. Muhammad's voice came from afar, I heard his words: "I'll have to silence you for the next 90 days — so that Muslims everywhere can be dissociated from the blunder."

I was numb.

But I was a follower of Mr. Muhammad. Many times I had said to my own assistants that anyone in a position to discipline others must be able to take disciplining himself.

I told Mr. Muhammad, "Sir, I agree with you, and I submit, 100 percent."

After Mecca

The "chickens coming home to roost" incident was one of the sparks that led to Malcolm X's eventual separation from the Nation of Islam. In the turbulent period that followed, he sought new direction by traveling to the Islamic holy city of Mecca. He appeared at a press conference in the United States on his return.

I was asked about my "Letter From Mecca" — I was all set with a speech regarding that.

"I hope that once and for all my Hajj to the Holy City of Mecca has established our Muslim Mosque's authentic religious affiliation with the 750 million Muslims of the orthodox Islamic World. And I *know* once and for all that the Black Africans look upon America's 22 million blacks as long lost *brothers!* They *love* us! They *study* our struggle for freedom! They were so *happy* to hear how we are awakening from our long sleep — after so-called Christian white America had taught us to be *ashamed* of our African brothers and homeland!

"Yes — I wrote a letter from Mecca. You're asking me 'Didn't you say that now you accept white men as brothers?' Well, my answer is that in the Muslim World, I saw, I felt, and I wrote home how my thinking was broadened! Just as I wrote, I shared true, brotherly love with many white-complexioned Muslims who never gave a single thought to the race, or to the complexion, of another Muslim.

"My pilgrimage broadened my scope. It blessed me with a new insight. In two weeks in the Holy Land, I saw what I never had

seen in 39 years here in America. I saw all *races,* all *colors* — blue-eyed blondes to black-skinned Africans — in *true* brotherhood! In unity! Living as one! Worshipping as one! No segregationists — no liberals; they would not have known how to interpret the meaning of those words.

"In the past, yes, I have made sweeping indictments of all white people. I never will be guilty of that again as I know now that some white people *are* truly sincere, that some truly are capable of being brotherly toward a black man. The true Islam has shown me that a blanket indictment of all white people is as wrong as when whites make blanket indictments against blacks.

"Yes, I have been convinced that *some* American whites do want to help cure the rampant racism which is on the path to *destroying* this country!

"It was in the Holy World that my attitude was changed, by what I experienced there, and by what I witnessed there, in terms of brotherhood — not just brotherhood toward me, but brotherhood between all men, of all nationalities and complexions, who were there. And now that I am back in America, my attitude here concerning white people has to be governed by what my black brothers and I experience here, and what we witness here — in terms of brotherhood. The *problem* here in America is that we meet such a small minority of individual so-called good or brotherly white people. Here in the United States, notwithstanding those few 'good' white people, it is the *collective* 150 million white people whom the *collective* 22 million black people have to deal with!

"Why, here in America, the seeds of racism are so deeply rooted in the white people collectively, their belief that they are 'superior' in some way is so deeply rooted, that these things are in the national white subconsciousness. Many whites are even actually unaware of their own racism, until they face some test, and then their racism emerges in one form or another.

"Listen! The white man's racism toward the black man here in America is what has got him in such trouble all over this world, with other nonwhite peoples. The white man can't separate himself from the stigma that he automatically feels about anyone, no matter who, who is not his color. And the nonwhite peoples of the world are sick of the condescending white man!" ...

The next day I was in my car driving along the freeway when at a red light another car pulled alongside. A white woman was driving and on the passenger's side, next to me, was a white man. *"Malcolm X!"* he called out—and when I looked, he stuck his hand out of his car, across at me, grinning. "Do you mind shaking hands with a white man?" Imagine that! Just as the traffic light turned green, I told him, "I don't mind shaking hands with human beings. Are you one?"

* * * * *

My thinking had been opened up wide in Mecca. In the long letters I wrote to friends, I tried to convey to them my new insights into the American black man's struggle and his problems, as well as the depths of my search for truth and justice.

"I've had enough of someone else's propaganda," I had written to these friends. "I'm for truth, no matter who tells it. I'm for justice, no matter who it is for or against. I'm a human being first and foremost, and as such I'm for whoever and whatever benefits humanity *as a whole.*"

Largely, the American white man's press refused to convey that I was now attempting to teach Negroes a new direction. With the 1964 "long, hot summer" steadily producing new incidents, I was constantly accused of "stirring up Negroes." Every time I had another radio or television microphone at my mouth. When I was asked about "stirring up

Negroes" or "inciting violence," I'd get hot.

"It takes no one to stir up the sociological dynamite that stems from the unemployment, bad housing, and inferior education already in the ghettoes. This explosively criminal condition has existed for so long, it needs no fuse; it fuses itself; it spontaneously combusts from within itself...."

They called me "the angriest Negro in America." I wouldn't deny that charge. I spoke exactly as I felt. "I *believe* in anger. The Bible says there is a *time* for anger." They called me "a teacher, a fomenter of violence." I would say point blank, "That is a lie. I'm not for wanton violence, I'm for justice. I feel that if white people were attacked by Negroes—if the forces of law prove unable, or inadequate, or reluctant to protect those whites from those Negroes—then those white people should protect and defend themselves from those Negroes, using arms if necessary. And I feel that when the law fails to protect Negroes from whites' attack, then those Negroes should use arms, if necessary, to defend themselves."

"Malcolm X Advocates Armed Negroes!"

What was wrong with that? I'll tell you what was wrong. I was a black man talking about physical defense against the white man. The white man can lynch and burn and bomb and beat Negroes—that's all right: "Have patience" ... "The customs are entrenched" ... "Things are getting better."

Well, I believe it's a crime for anyone who is being brutalized to continue to accept that brutality without doing something to defend himself. If that's how "Christian" philosophy is interpreted, if that's what Gandhian philosophy teaches, well, then, I will call them criminal philosophies.

I tried in every speech I made to clarify my new position regarding white people—"I don't speak against the sincere, well-meaning, good white people. I have learned that there *are* some. I have learned that not all white people are racists. I am speaking against and my fight is against the white *racists*. I firmly believe that Negroes have the right to fight against these racists, by any means that are necessary."

But the white reporters kept wanting me linked with that word "violence." I doubt if I had one interview without having to deal with that accusation.

"I *am* for violence if nonviolence means we continue postponing a solution to the American black man's problem just to *avoid* violence. I don't go for nonviolence if it also means a delayed solution. To me a delayed solution is a nonsolution. Or I'll say it another way. If it must take violence to get the black man his human rights in this country, I'm *for* violence exactly as you know the Irish, the Poles, or Jews would be if they were flagrantly discriminated against. I am just as they would be in that case, and they would be for violence no matter what the consequences, no matter who was hurt by the violence."

Epilogue

On page two of his Autobiography, *Malcolm X wrote that "It has always been my belief that I, too, will die by violence."*

On the afternoon of February 21, 1965, Malcolm X walked onto the stage of Harlem's Audubon Ballroom to deliver a speech to a black audience of about 400 people. As he greeted the crowd, there was a disturbance in the eighth row, and Malcolm X raised both hands to say, "Hold it! Hold it! Don't get excited. Let's cool it,

brothers." While his security guards turned toward the distraction, three men approached the platform, one bearing a sawed-off shotgun, the other two pistols. The first shotgun blast hit Malcolm X in the chest and threw him backward. The three gunmen—all of them connected with the Nation of Islam—then opened fire on him where he lay, leaving his body riddled with 16 bullets and shotgun pellets. "It looked like a firing squad," one witness remembered.[4]

Three years after the slaying of Malcolm X, Martin Luther King, Jr., was shot down by an assassin's bullet in Memphis, Tennessee. His death touched off a string of race riots across the country, which affected 125 cities. In some places the National Guard and even the Army had to be called in to subdue the violence. Two months later, New York Senator and presidential candidate Robert F. Kennedy was assassinated by Sirhan Sirhan, a young Arab who was apparently outraged by certain pro-Israeli statements of the senator. In the fall of 1969, eight radicals known as the Chicago Eight went on trial for conspiring to incite riots during the Democratic Convention of 1968. There was so much disorder in the courtroom that defendant Bobby Seale, leader of the black militant organization the Black Panthers, was ordered bound and gagged. Another Black Panther leader, Fred Hampton, was killed in December 1969 during a Chicago police raid.

---

[4] Quoted in Frady, 78.

The Ethical Responsibilities of Economic Agents

Quite naturally, many people think the principal moral obligations of human beings are those that we have simply because we are human beings. While philosophers, theologians, novelists, poets, and others may disagree strongly about the right way of defining or prioritizing these obligations, there is wide agreement that the moral responsibilities described in the introduction to Part II provide the principal foundation for ethical behavior.

Part III offers a different way of thinking about ethical obligations, particularly those shouldered by business executives. Because its approach is controversial in two ways, it is important to be very clear from the outset about what this section does and does not assume.

Assumption One: Role Obligations. The first assumption is that people take on additional moral obligations when they perform certain roles in society. That is, a person who becomes a physician, attorney, educator, parent, or business executive takes on certain responsibilities. People who do not assume these roles do not have these responsibilities.[1]

Some philosophers and other analysts take issue with this view. In effect, they believe all human beings have the same ethical obligations. People should, for example, try to do the greatest good for the greatest number or fulfill their basic human duties, regardless of their social roles. And, at a high level of generalization or abstraction, it may be correct to say that ethics is about basic human obligations, rather than role-based obligations.

---

[1] An excellent, extended analysis of the role obligations of attorneys, physicians, business executives, and judges is Allen H. Goldman, *The Moral Foundations of Professional Ethics* (Totowa, N.J.: Rowman and Littlefield, 1980).

If, however, one examines the ethical issues that managers face in a more concrete fashion, it can be both illuminating and useful to suppose that managers, in fact, have certain ethical obligations that come with their position or role in society. In the first place, business executives and other professionals often believe firmly that their social roles bring them obligations. Often they describe the ethical issues they face as conflicts between these role obligations and their obligations as human beings. In other words, the assumption that managers and others *have* role obligations seems to help them make sense of and describe the ethical challenges they face.

In addition, laws as well as professional codes typically describe specific obligations that lawyers, physicians, and other professionals must meet. The cases in Part I (the introduction to this book) all involved conflicts between professional and personal obligations. For example, Frank Armani, the attorney in "The Lake Pleasant Bodies" case, had to weigh his obligations as a father and fellow human being against his duties as an attorney and the requirements of the lawyers' code of ethics. Similarly, the young managers in the other introductory cases had to balance personal responsibilities to friends and others against obligations to their employers.

In short, while the assumption that professionals have responsibilities that derive from their professional roles can be a topic of controversy among philosophers, it also serves as a valuable perspective—in both practical and conceptual terms—for understanding and mapping the ethical territory of business management.

Assumption Two: Ethical Obligations to Shareholders.   The second controversial aspect of this section (for at least some readers) is the idea that business executives have ethical obligations to serve shareholders' interests and that, in the Anglo-American legal tradition, this view translates into an ethical obligation to maximize returns to shareholders. This argument does not necessarily hold that maximizing shareholders' returns is the only ethical obligation of business executives, nor that it is always a manager's principal obligation, nor that this obligation can be defined in simple once-and-for-all terms that are universally applicable. The argument, however, suggests, as a topic for careful analysis and extended discussion, that business managers *may* have a strong ethical obligation to maximize the returns to a company's shareholders.

The readings and cases in this part enable students to examine in detail the intellectual, historical, and managerial reasons for thinking that managers have strong and clear obligations to maximize shareholders' returns. Other cases and readings suggest some of the conceptual problems and historical biases implicit in this view and provide social and political arguments for modifying or disagreeing with it.

THE RATIONALE FOR MANAGERS' ECONOMIC OBLIGATIONS

The economic obligations of business executives derive from three different sources. Most analysts who believe that business executives have these obligations rely on one or more of these ways of thinking. And it is important to note that each of the three approaches depends heavily on the ethical principles discussed in Part II. This is another way of emphasizing that these economic responsibilities of business executives are indeed moral obligations.

RIGHTS AND DUTIES

The ethics of rights and duties can be used as a rationale for managers' economic obligations in two different ways.

The Role of Promises.   The first rights and duties justification for managers' economic obligations is this: Shareholders own the investments they make in a company and are entitled to have their wishes followed with respect to the disposition of what is their property; at the same time, managers promise or commit themselves, whether implicitly or explicitly, to serve the interests of these owners. In legal terms, they have fiduciary obligations to a company's shareholders. Hence, managers have an ethical obligation to uphold this commitment and keep their promise, just as they would any other commitment or promise.

Put differently, the managers are agents; the owners are principals; and, as agents, managers are obligated to serve the interests of the principals. In the United States, the principals are typically so-called institutional investors, the trust departments of banks, pension funds, insurance companies, and their beneficiaries, rather than individuals who buy and sell stock for their own accounts.

In most cases, owners and investors want managers to earn high and sustained financial returns and to do so within appropriate risk levels. Institutional investors are generally obligated by law and regulation to seek such returns. Owners expect managers to obey the law and to respect the broad, basic ethical traditions and practices of society. However, within the limits of the law and accepted ethical practices, most investors seek high financial returns and, in a competitive market, will entrust their investments to companies and managers that offer the best prospects for achieving these returns.

During the 1980s, the language and concept of shareholders' *rights* was commonly used in hostile takeover battles. Implicit here was an ethical argument: that self-serving or incompetent managers had failed to meet their obligations to shareholders and, therefore, had to be replaced.

The Duty to Obey the Law.   A second underpinning of a manager's economic obligations is also founded on the principle of rights and duties. This rationale, however, invokes a much broader obligation: the duty that all citizens have to obey the legitimate laws of the societies in which they live. The clear, basic thrust of U.S. corporate law, as it governs executives' legal obligations, was described by Professor Robert Clark, dean of the Harvard Law School, in these terms: "Case Law on managers' fiduciary duty of care can be fairly read to say that the manager has an affirmative, open-ended duty to maximize the beneficiaries' wealth regardless of whether this is specified in any actual contract."[2]

The laws obligating managers to serve shareholders' interests are deeply woven into the legal fabric of commercial life in the United States and many other countries. These laws reflect the preferences and considered judgments of these societies. They have been enacted by legitimate government bodies, and they have been reviewed, modified, and affirmed over decades or even longer periods by legislatures and judicial bodies. Hence, they create strong moral claims—just as the other legitimate laws of a society do—on the decisions and actions of business executives.

At the same time, the duty to serve shareholders' interests and to respect their rights is not a trump card that overrides all other rights and duties. The following are the central reasons why managers cannot simply act as automatons programmed to maximize shareholders' interests:

1. Difficulties arise for managers when their fiduciary obligation clashes with other ethical obligations, such as those described in Parts II, IV, and V.

2. Recent changes in the laws of a few states provide some leeway for boards of directors and for managers to consider the interests of other stakeholders when they make strategic decisions.

3. As several of the cases and readings in this section show, countries with different legal traditions do not define managers' responsibilities in the same way as Anglo-American tradition.

4. Some studies of shareholders' preferences indicate that financial returns are only one among several important considerations. One recent study found, for example, that shareholders ranked the efforts to stop pollution and to improve product safety *ahead* of higher dividends as objectives for corporate managers.[3]

---

[2] Robert C. Clark, "Agency Costs versus Fiduciary Duties," in *Principals and Agents: The Structure of Business,* ed. John W. Pratt and Richard J. Zeckhauser (Boston: Harvard Business School, 1985), pp. 71–79.

[3] See Marc J. Epstein, "The Annual Report Report Card," *Business and Society Review,* Spring 1992, p. 83.

Consequences.   The second key element in the framework of managers' economic obligations rests on the utilitarian approach to ethics, described in Part II. As the readings in this section show, its basic tenet is that society benefits when managers and companies compete vigorously with each other and seek to serve the interests of their shareholders.

For many, this is a controversial proposition. The failures and limits of capitalist economies have been well and frequently chronicled. And, to be sure, serious social problems coexist with market systems and are often caused or exacerbated by them. Yet to acknowledge that markets can and do fail is not a denial of a basic moral contribution that market systems make — the provision of a material base for the well-being and happiness of many people. Much of the wealth that flows from the capitalist cornucopia directly alleviates human suffering and provides pleasure, security, health, and prosperity for many members of a society.

Some people instinctively dismiss these consequences as material or (merely) economic. However, as Part II emphasized, the fundamental insight of British philosopher John Stuart Mill, one of the intellectual godfathers of utilitarianism, was that good actions — that is, *morally* good actions — were those that brought the greatest happiness to the greatest number of people. Joseph Schumpeter, one of the leading economists of the 20th century, made the following observation about a fundamental tendency of capitalist systems, a feature of these economies that underscores their utilitarian claim to moral benefit. Schumpeter wrote that:

> there are no doubt some things available to the modern workman that Louis XIV himself would have been delighted to have — modern dentistry, for instance... the capitalist process, not by coincidence but by virtue of its mechanism, progressively raises the standard of life of the masses.[4]

Note how firmly this way of thinking is grounded in the morality of consequences. The utilitarian argument for executives' moral obligations acknowledges that investors and managers are typically motivated by self-interest and often by greed or other morally dubious motives. Profit maximization need not be an intrinsically moral criteria — comparable to a physician's obligation to safeguard and promote a patient's health. Nevertheless, the utilitarian argument runs, by encouraging companies and managers to compete vigorously to meet consumers' demand and serve owners' interests, the market system channels nonmoral or even corrupting motives into actions that serve the common good.

Markets and Individual Freedom.   A third underpinning of managers' economic obligations also draws on the ethical principles described in the introduction to Part II. And, like the other two foundations of this obligation, it is also the subject of complex and important disputes.

---

[4] Joseph Schumpeter, *Capitalism, Socialism, and Democracy* (New York: Harper Colophon/ Harper & Row, 1975), pp. 67–68, 83.

This third rationale draws heavily on basic ideas about rights and freedom. Its basic thrust is that managers' obligation to serve shareholders' interests is a key element in a complex system of vital economic rights. These economic rights are, in turn, deeply entwined with a larger class of fundamental human rights. These economic and human rights form the foundation—socially, intellectually, and politically—on which modern democracies rest. In short, market systems reflect, express, and celebrate vital human freedoms.

In the ideal market system, individuals choose the work they will do, the products and services they wish to buy, and the ways they will invest their savings. Vigorous competition expands the range of choices in the markets for labor, goods, and capital. When people make these choices and fashion their lives around their preferences, they are exercising their rights as autonomous human beings.

Put differently, market systems rest on bedrock moral beliefs about the autonomy of individuals, the value of freedom and consent, and the centuries-long struggle to free individuals from the power of the state and various churches. In the words of Robert Nozick, a prominent contemporary philosopher (whose ideas on this issue are described later in this section), market transactions are "capitalist acts between consenting adults."[5]

This line of argument suggests it is hardly an accident that many countries around the world, which have overthrown either communist or authoritarian tyranny, are now simultaneously embracing various combinations of individual rights, competitive markets, property rights, and democratic politics. Human freedom and the opportunity for individual choice and self-expression are part of a complex social and political structure; a crucial part of its undergirdings are the economic freedoms that business executives practice and respect in meeting their obligations to shareholders.

QUESTIONS ABOUT THE FRAMEWORK

The cases and readings that follow, both in this part of the book and the next two, provide opportunities to understand and critique the framework of economic obligations discussed above. The questions that emerge crystallize a tradition of critical analysis and social reform that started when the Industrial Revolution first began to alter the social, political, and economic life of Great Britain nearly 200 years ago. Thus, the idea that economic agents have moral responsibilities and the counteridea that these ideas can too easily be exaggerated or misconstrued is hardly a recent

---

[5] Robert Nozick, *Anarchy, State, and Utopia* (New York: Basic Books, 1974), p. 163.

phenomenon. Questions about the economic responsibilities of business executives have deep roots in the Western political tradition, and the issues of business ethics that contemporary managers face are only the most recent exchanges in a long and controversial discussion extending back for well over a century.

These are some of the major lines of questioning and criticism that this part of the book introduces:

1. How well do market systems actually serve utilitarian objectives? That is, how well will the overall good of society be served if markets are imperfect, as they almost inevitably are? How well can markets help individuals and societies meet their true needs when markets—through new product development, marketing, and advertising—may *create* needs that do not reflect important human values? How well can markets promote the greatest good for the greatest number if income is distributed unevenly among consumers? And if income is unevenly distributed, will markets tend to correct or exacerbate these differences?

2. Do the rights of shareholders and the duties of managers (to serve shareholders' interests, to maximize profits, and to obey corporate law) constitute a moral principle appropriate for guiding all of the varied ethical decisions that business executives must resolve? Does this definition of managers' duties reflect a now outdated Darwinian view of capitalism?

Or, to the contrary, are the basic principles of property rights, free competition, and managers' fiduciary duties the central tenets of the economic reform movements now sweeping many nations of the world?

3. Are managers, who follow the traditional definition of their economic obligations, reducing their stature as human beings by seeking to act as if they were merely profit-maximizing androids, rather than human beings who should bring to their work a full range of human passions, commitments, and values?

Or, on the other hand, is it prudent for a democratic society to encourage business executives, men and women who wield enormous economic power, to indulge their own personal values and interests at work? Shouldn't these people confine the pursuit of their personal interests and values to their private time and pursue a more limited set of objectives—those defined above as managers' economic responsibilities—while they are on the job?

4. To what extent must the Anglo-American definition of managers' economic responsibilities be altered when managers do business in other countries? How do the varieties of capitalism differ among regions of the world and among countries? Are these differences disappearing as some sort of "global capitalism" spreads around the world? Or, instead, is the Asian variety of capitalism, with its own distinctive definition of managers' responsibilities, now demonstrating its superiority to the other versions?

5. Even if one agrees that business executives have a moral obligation to maximize profits, should this be viewed as their principal or exclusive obligation? What responsibilities do managers have to the people in their organization whose livelihoods depend on executives' decisions and actions? To what extent to managers' responsibilities extend to people in groups outside the traditional boundaries of the firm? And how should these responsibilities be balanced against managers' economic duties? (This last set of questions is noted here because it is one of the fundamental issues addressed throughout this book. However, Parts IV and V provide cases and readings that address these issues in depth.)

OVERVIEW OF CASES AND READINGS

This part begins with a long conceptual note. The first, "The Moral Responsibilities of Economic Agents," consists of excerpts from philosophers, economists, political thinkers, and others who flesh out the logic of the argument that managers' principal responsibility is to serve their shareholders' interests.

The first case study that follows these readings is "The Smoke Wars." It examines several of the many controversies that fall under the broad umbrella of concerns about smoking, health, national health care costs, smokers' rights, and company responsibilities. In addition, it provides an opportunity for students to contrast and evaluate two very different rationales for regulating smoking as well as for *limiting* such regulations. One rationale is based heavily on the ethics of consequences; the other on the ethics of rights and duties.

"The Individual and the Corporation" examines the potential conflicts between, on the one hand, managers' basic human rights to self-expression and free speech, guaranteed by most political democracies, and on the other hand, their obligations as corporate officers. Both cases help sharpen the set of issues referred to in the third question above. This classic case is followed by a highly contemporary one, "Tom Reese," which describes the dilemma faced by a young, gay consultant assigned to work for a client who relishes gay-bashing comments. Reese must balance his obligations as a shareholder's agent with his own personal integrity and values.

"ProTech, Inc.," focuses on another tension between managers' economic obligations and other moral imperatives. In this case, responsibilities for truth telling and the responsibility to obey the law seem to conflict with an executive's responsibilities to uphold confidentiality, to maintain the viability of a business, and to bring it to the point where it can earn profits. "Kathryn McNeil" focuses on the dilemma managers face in trying to respond to internal competitive pressures while, at the same time, creating workplaces that are hospitable to employees with families. Finally, the "Martha McCaskey" case describes the dilemma facing a young consultant who is reluctant to gather certain information on behalf of a client, even though the client and her employer will benefit if she does so.

The last case, "The IBM–Fujitsu Dispute," focuses on the issue of how managers' responsibilities vary under different forms of capitalism. The case concentrates on the long-standing intellectual property dispute between IBM and Fujitsu, its largest Japanese competitor. The case issues unfold against the background of two very different systems for defining managers' economic responsibilities and for structuring the relationships between companies and other institutions in society.

SUGGESTIONS FOR FURTHER READING

Chester Barnard, *The Functions of the Executive* (Cambridge, Mass.: Harvard University Press, 1982), pp. 258–84.

Norman Bowie, "New Directions in Corporate Responsibility," *Business Horizons,* July–August 1991, pp. 56–65.

Richard T. DeGeorge, *Business Ethics* (New York: Macmillan, 1982), pp. 109–27.

Thomas Donaldson, *Corporations and Morality* (Englewood Cliffs, N.J.: Prentice Hall, 1982).

Peter F. Drucker, *The Unseen Revolution: How Pension Fund Socialism Came to America* (New York: Harper & Row, 1976).

Amitai Etzioni, *The Moral Dimension* (New York: Free Press, 1988).

Milton Friedman, *Capitalism and Freedom* (Chicago: University of Chicago Press, 1962).

John Kenneth Galbraith, "The Affluent Society" (Boston: Houghton Mifflin, 1958).

Robert Heilbroner, "Controlling the Corporation," in Heilbroner, ed., *In the Name of Profit* (Garden City, N.J.: Doubleday, 1972).

Paul Heyne, *The Economic Way of Thinking* (Chicago: Science Research Associates, 1976).

George C. Lodge, *The New American Ideology* (New York: Alfred A. Knopf, 1977).

Robert F. O'Neil, "Corporate Social Responsibility and Business Ethics: A European Perspective," *International Journal of Social Economic,* Spring 1986, pp. 64–76.

Charles Phillips, "What Is Wrong with Profit Maximization?" in *Issues in Business and Society,* ed. W. T. Greenwood (Boston: Houghton Mifflin, 1977).

John W. Pratt and Richard J. Zeckhauser, *Principles and Agents: The Structure of Business* (Boston: Harvard Business School Press, 1985).

THE MORAL RESPONSIBILITIES OF ECONOMIC AGENTS

This note presents long excerpts from the writing of philosophers, political economists, and other thinkers. Each passage presents ideas and arguments that help to answer a single fundamental question: What are the basic moral responsibilities of business executives?

The excerpts are both historical and contemporary. The older passages are taken from some of the most important works in the Western tradition of political and economic thought. The recent passages give modern interpretations of the classic ideas. Taken together, the excerpts show the origins and evolution of the central ideas that undergird modern capitalism and help define the responsibilities of executives within this system.

Thomas Hobbes

Hobbes was an English philosopher and political theorist who lived from 1588 to 1679. He shocked many of his contemporaries by arguing that human beings were basically selfish and motivated by fear and desire for power. This passage is from his most famous work, *Leviathan.*

> Whatsoever therefore is consequent to a time of war, where every man is enemy to every man, the same is consequent to the time wherein men live without other security than what their own strength and their own invention shall furnish them withal. In such condition there is no place for industry, because the fruit thereof is uncertain: and consequently no culture of the earth; no navigation, nor use of the commodities that may be imported by sea;

This note was prepared by Ilyse Barkan under the direction of Joseph Badaracco, Jr.

Harvard Business School note 390-167 (Revised 1991).

no commodious building; no instruments of moving and removing such things as require much force; no knowledge of the face of the earth; no account of time; no arts; no letters; no society; and which is worst of all, continual fear, and danger of violent death; and the life of man, solitary, poor, nasty, brutish, and short.

John Locke

John Locke, sometimes called "the intellectual ruler of the 18th century," lived from 1632 to 1704 and wrote works on philosophy, psychology, education, and politics. Thomas Jefferson drew on Locke's ideas when he wrote the Declaration of Independence. All the passages below come from his *Two Treatises on Civil Government,* except for the last, which comes from his *Letter Concerning Toleration.*

> Though the earth and all inferior creatures be common to all men, yet every man has a "property" in his own "person." This nobody has any right to but himself. The "labour" of his body and the "work" of his hands, we may say, are properly his. Whatsoever, then, he removes out of the state that Nature hath provided and left it in, he hath mixed his labour with it, and joined to it something that is his own, and thereby makes it his property. It being by him removed from the common state Nature placed it in, it hath by this labour something annexed to it that excludes the common right of other men. For this "labour" being the unquestionable property of the labourer, no man but he can have a right to what that is once joined to, at least where there is enough, and as good left in common for others.
>
> He that is nourished by the acorns he picked up under an oak, or the apples he gathered from the trees in the wood, has certainly appropriated them to himself. Nobody can deny but the nourishment is his. I ask, then, when did they begin to be his? when he digested? or when

he ate? or when he boiled? or when he brought them home? or when he picked them up? And it is plain, if the first gathering made them not his, nothing else could. That labour put a distinction between them and common. That added something to them more than Nature, the common mother of all, had done, and so they became his private right.

* * * * *

It will, perhaps, be objected to this, that if gathering the acorns or other fruits of the earth, etc., makes a right to them, then any one may engross as much as he will. To which I answer, Not so. The same law of Nature that does by this means give us property, does also bound that property, too. "God has given us all things richly." Is the voice of reason confirmed by inspiration? But how far has He given it us— "to enjoy?" As much as any one can make use to any advantage of life before it spoils, so much he may by his labour fix a property in. Whatever is beyond this is more than his share, and belongs to others. Nothing was made by God for man to spoil or destroy.

* * * * *

The supreme power cannot take from any man any part of his property without his own consent. For the preservation of property being the end of government, and that for which men enter into society, it necessarily supposes and requires that the people should have property, without which they must be supposed to lose that by entering into society which was the end for which they entered into it; too gross an absurdity for any man to own. Men, therefore, in society having property, they have such a right to the goods, which by the law of the community are theirs, that nobody hath a right to take them or any part of them, from them without their own consent; without this they have no property at all. For I have truly no property in that which another can by right take from me when he pleases against my consent.

Now of those good things which Nature hath provided in common, every one hath a right (as hath been said) to as much as he could use;

and had a property in all he could effect with his labour; all that his industry could extend to, to alter from the state Nature had put it in, was his. He that gathered a hundred bushels of acorns or apples had thereby a property in them; they were his goods as soon as gathered. He was only to look that he used them before they spoiled, else he took more than his share, and robbed others. And, indeed, it was a foolish thing, as well as dishonest, to hoard up more than he could make use of. If he gave away a part to anybody else, so that it perished not uselessly in his possession, these he also made use of. And if he also bartered away plums that could have rotted in a week, for nuts that could last good for his eating a whole year, he did no injury; he wasted not the common stock; destroyed no part of the portion of goods that belonged to others, so long as nothing perished uselessly in his hands. Again, if he would give his nuts for a piece of metal, pleased with its colour, or exchange his sheep for shells, or wool for a sparkling pebble or a diamond, and keep those by him all his life, he invaded not the right of others; he might heap up as much of these durable things as he pleased; the exceeding of the bounds of his just property not lying in the largeness of his possession, but the perishing of anything uselessly in it.

And thus came in the use of money; some lasting thing that men might keep without spoiling, and that, by mutual consent, men would take in exchange for the truly useful but perishable supports of life.

* * * * *

It is labour indeed that puts the difference of value on everything; and let anyone consider what the difference is between an acre of land planted with tobacco or sugar, sown with wheat or barley, and an acre of the same land lying in common without any husbandry upon it, and he will find that the improvement of labour makes the far greater part of the value. I think it will be but a very modest computation to say, that of the products of the earth useful to the life of man, nine-tenths are the effects of labour. Nay, if we will rightly estimate things as they come to our use, and cast up the several expenses about them—what in them is purely owing to Nature and what to labour—we shall find that in most of them 99 hundredths are wholly to be put on the account of labour.

* * * * *

Political power is that power which every man having in the state of Nature has given up into the hands of society, and therein to the governors whom the society hath set over itself, with this express or tacit trust, that it shall be employed for their good and the preservation of their property. Now this power, which every man has in the state of Nature, and which he parts with to the society in all such cases where the society can secure him, is to use such means for the preserving of his own property as he thinks good and a Nature allows him; and to punish the breach of the law of Nature in others so as (according to the best of his reason) may most conduce to the preservation of himself and the rest of mankind; so that the end and measure of this power, when in every man's hands, in the state of Nature, being the preservation of all of his society—that is, all mankind in general—it can have no other end or measure, when in the hands of the magistrate, but to preserve the members of the society in the lives, liberties, and possessions, and so cannot be an absolute, arbitrary power over their lives and fortunes, which are as much as possible to be preserved; but a power to make laws, and annex such penalties to them as may tend to the preservation of the whole, by cutting off those parts, and those only, which are so corrupt that they threaten the sound and healthy, without which no severity is lawful. And this power has its original only from compact and agreement and the mutual consent of those who make up the community.

* * * * *

The political society is instituted for no other end, but only to secure every man's possession of the things of this life. The commonwealth seems to me to be a society of men constituted only for the procuring, preserving, and advancing their own civil interests.

Civil interest I call life, liberty, health, and indolency of body; and the possession of outward things, such as money, lands, houses, furniture, and the like. The care of each man's soul and the things of heaven, which neither does belong to the commonwealth nor can be subjected to it, is left entirely to every man's self.

Adam Smith

Smith, a Scot, was the father of classical economics. He lived from 1723 to 1790 and published his most famous work, *The Wealth of Nations,* in 1776. The passages below are taken from this book.

But man has almost constant occasion for the help of his brethren, and it is in vain for him to expect it from their benevolence only. He will be more likely to prevail if he can interest their self-love in his favour, and shew them that is for their own advantage to do for him what he requires of them. Whoever offers to another a bargain of any kind, proposes to do this. Give me that which I want, and you shall have this which you want, is the meaning of every such offer; and it is in this manner that we obtain from one another the far greater part of those good offices which we stand in need of. It is not from the benevolence of the butcher, the brewer, or the baker, that we expect our dinner, but from their regard to their own interest. We address ourselves, not to their humanity but to their self-love, and never talk to them of their own necessities but of their advantages. Nobody but a beggar chuses to depend chiefly upon the benevolence of his fellow-citizens.

The produce of industry is what it adds to the subject or materials upon which it is employed. In proportion as the value of this produce is great or small, so will likewise be the profits of the employer. But it is only for the sake of profit that any man employs a capital in the support of industry; and he will always, therefore, endeavour to employ it in the support of the industry of which the produce is likely to be of the greatest value, or to exchange for the greatest quantity either of money or of other goods.

As every individual, therefore, endeavours as much as he can both to employ his capital in the support of domestic industry, and so to direct that industry that its produce may be of the greatest value; every individual necessarily labours to render the annual revenue of the society as great as he can. He generally, indeed, neither intends to promote the public interest, nor knows how much he is promoting it. By preferring the support of domestic to that of foreign industry, he intends only his own security; and by directing that industry in such a manner as its produce may be of the greatest value, he intends only his own gain, and he is in this, as in many other cases, led by an invisible hand to promote an end which was no part of his intention. Nor is it always the worse for the society than it was no part of it. By pursuing his own interest he frequently promotes that of the society more effectually than when he really intends to promote it. I have never known much good done by those who affected to trade for the public good.

*   *   *   *   *

All systems either of preference or of restraint, therefore, being thus completely taken away, the obvious and simple system of natural liberty establishes itself of its own accord. Every man, as long as he does not violate the laws of justice is left perfectly free to pursue his own interest, his own way, and to bring both his industry and capital into competition with those of any other man or order of men. The sovereign is completely discharged from a duty, in the attempting to perform which he must always be exposed to innumerable delusions, and for the proper performance of which no human wisdom or knowledge could ever be sufficient; the duty of superintending the industry of private people, and of directing it towards the employments most suitable to the interest of the society. According to the system of natural liberty, the sovereign has only three duties to attend to; three duties of great importance, indeed, but plain and intelligible to common understanding: first, the duty of protecting the

society from violence and invasion of other independent societies; secondly, the duty of protecting, as far as possible, every member of the society from the injustice or oppression of every other member of it, or the duty of establishing an exact administration of justice; and, thirdly, the duty of erecting and maintaining certain public works and certain public institutions which it can never be for the interest of any individual, or small number of individuals, to erect and maintain.

Commerce and manufactures can seldom flourish long in any state which does not enjoy a regular administration of justice, in which the people do not feel themselves secure in the possession of their property, in which the faith of contracts is not supported by law, and in which the authority of the state is not supposed to be regularly employed in enforcing the payment of debts from all those who are able to pay. Commerce and manufactures, in short, can seldom flourish in any state in which there is not a certain degree of confidence in the justice of government.

*   *   *   *   *

Wherever there is great property there is great inequality. For one very rich man there must be at least five hundred poor, and the affluence of the few supposes the indigence of the many. The affluence of the rich excites the indignation of the poor, who are often both driven by want, and prompted by envy, to invade his possessions. It is only under the shelter of the civil magistrate that the owner of that valuable property, which is acquired by the labour of many years, or perhaps of many successive generations, can sleep a single night in security. He is at all times surrounded by unknown enemies, whom, though he never provoked, he can never appease, and from whose injustice he can be protected only by the powerful arm of the civil magistrate continually held up to chastise it.

*   *   *   *   *

The uniform, constant, and uninterrupted effort of every man to better his condition, the principle from which public and national, as well as private opulence is originally derived, is frequently powerful enough to maintain the natural progress of things towards improvement, in spite both of the extravagance of government and of the greatest errors of administration. Like the unknown principle of animal life, it frequently restores health and vigour to the constitution, in spite, not only of the disease, but of the absurd prescriptions of the doctor.

* * * * *

Both productive and unproductive labourers, and those who do not labour at all, are all equally maintained by the annual produce of the land and labour of the country. This produce, how great soever, can never be infinite, but must have certain limits. According, therefore, as a smaller or greater proportion of it is in any one year employed in maintaining unproductive hands, the more in the one case and the less in the other will remain for the productive, and the next year's produce will be greater or smaller accordingly; the whole annual produce, if we except the spontaneous productions of the earth, being the effect of productive labour.

John Stuart Mill

Mill, who lived from 1806 to 1873, was one of the most important philosophers and economists of his century. He is also well known for having begun to study Greek at the age of three and for learning mathematics, logic, classical literature, and political economy by 14. The first two passages are from *On Liberty;* the last from *Principles of Political Economy.*

The sole end for which mankind are warranted, individually or collectively, in interfering with the liberty of action of any of their number, is self-protection. . . . The only purpose for which power can be rightfully exercised over any member of a civilised community, against his will, is to prevent harm to others.

* * * * *

As soon as any part of a person's conduct affects prejudicially the interests of others, society

has jurisdiction over it, and the question whether the general welfare will or will not be promoted by interfering with it, becomes open to discussion. But there is no room for entertaining any such question when a person's conduct affects the interests of no persons besides himself, or needs not affect them unless they like (all the persons concerned being of full age, and the ordinary amount of understanding). In all such cases, there should be perfect freedom, legal and social, to do the action and stand the consequences.

* * * * *

Nothing is implied in property but the right of each to his (or her) own faculties, to what he can produce by them, and to whatever he can get for them in a fair market; together with his right to give this to any other person if he chooses, and the right of that other to receive and enjoy it.

Charles Darwin

Darwin, a British naturalist, lived from 1809 to 1882. He caused a revolution in biological science and in many other fields with his theory of evolution through natural selection. This passage is from his principal work, *The Origin of Species.*

Compare the eye to an optical instrument, we ought in imagination to take a thick layer of transparent tissue, with spaces filled with fluid, and with a nerve sensitive to light beneath, and then suppose every part of this layer to be continually changing slowly in density, so as to separate into layers of different densities and thicknesses, placed at different distances from each other, and with the surfaces of each layer slowly changing in form. Further we must suppose that there is a power, represented by natural selection or the survival of the fittest, always intently watching each slight alteration in the transparent layers; and carefully preserving each which, under varied circumstances, in any way or in any degree, tends to produce a distinctive image. We must suppose each new state of the instrument to be multiplied by the million; each to be preserved until a better one is produced, and then the old ones to be all destroyed. In living bodies, variations will cause the slight alterations, generation will multiply them almost infinitely, and natural selection will pick out the unerring skill in each improvement. Let this process go on for millions of years; and during each year on millions of individuals of many kinds; and may we not believe that a living optical instrument might thus be formed as superior to one of glass, as the works of the Creator are to those of man?

Alfred Marshall
Mary Paley Marshall

Alfred Marshall, 1842 to 1924, was one of the leading economists of the past 100 years. With his wife, Mary, a political economist, he wrote *The Economics of Industry,* from which the first passage is taken. The second comes from Alfred Marshall's *Principles of Economics.*

We have next to examine the consequences of the fact that the management of a large capital in any trade almost always requires rarer natural abilities and a more expensive training than the management of a small capital requires. We have seen that a man who conducts a large business must look far ahead, and wide around him; and that he must be continually on the look out for improved methods of carrying on his business, while the man who manages a small business may be content to follow the lead that is given to him by his neighbours. The former pays subordinates to do the work on which the latter spends the greater part of his time; and devotes all his energies to planning, and organizing, to forecasting the future and preparing for it. He must have a knowledge of men and the power of managing them. He must select his subordinates well, and while keeping the control of the business in his own hands, he must give them the freedom which will call forth their energy and sense of responsibility. Those who cannot do this, are incapable of building up a large business, or even of keeping one together, if inheritance or other accident should put them in possession of it.

A man who has all the rare qualities that are required for managing a large business will, unless he is specially unlucky, make a high rate of profits on his capital. These profits will increase his capital, and will encourage him to devise and carry out bold plans on a broad basis. The confidence that others have in him will enable him to borrow capital easily; and thus, because he has the faculties which are one condition of getting high Earnings of Management, he will rapidly acquire that control of a large capital which is the other condition.

We see then, firstly, that higher faculties are required for the management of a large than of a small capital; and secondly, that there is a process of selection continually going on by which those who have some capital and great business power, soon get control over a large capital; while on the other hand those who have not business power will speedily dissipate a large capital if they happen to get control over it.

*   *   *   *   *

And in a world in which all men were perfectly virtuous, competition would be out of place; but so also would be private property and every form of private right. Men would think only of their duties; and no one would desire to have a larger share of the comforts and luxuries of life than his neighbours. Strong producers could easily bear a touch of hardship; so they would wish that their weaker neighbours, while producing less should consume more. Happy in this thought, they would work for the general good with all the energy, the inventiveness, and the eager initiative that belonged to them; and mankind would be victorious in contests with nature at every turn. Such is the Golden Age to which poets and dreamers may look forward. But in the responsible conduct of affairs, it is worse than folly to ignore the imperfections which still cling to human nature.

History in general, and especially the history of socialistic ventures, shows that ordinary men are seldom capable of pure ideal altruism for any considerable time together; and that the exceptions are to be found only when the masterful fervour of a small band of religious enthusiasts makes material concerns to count for nothing in comparison with the higher faith.

Joseph Schumpeter

Schumpeter, who lived from 1888 until 1950, was born in what is now Czechoslovakia and taught economics at the University of Berlin and, for his last 18 years, at Harvard. This excerpt is from *Capitalism, Socialism, and Democracy*.

As we have seen in the preceding chapter, the contents of the laborer's budget, say from 1760 to 1940, did not simply grow on unchanging lines but they underwent a process of qualitative change. Similarly, the history of the productive apparatus of a typical farm, from the beginnings of the rationalization of crop rotation, plowing, and fattening to the mechanized thing of today — linking up with elevators and railroads — is a history of revolutions. So is the history of the productive apparatus of the iron and steel industry from the charcoal furnace to our own type of furnace, or the history of the apparatus of power production from the overshot water wheel to the modern power plant, or the history of transportation from the mailcoach to the airplane. The opening up of new markets, foreign or domestic, and the organizational development from the craft shop and factory to such concerns as U.S. Steel illustrate the same process of industrial mutation — if I may use that biological term — that incessantly revolutionizes[1] the economic structure from within, incessantly destroying the old one, incessantly creating a new one. This process of Creative Destruction is the essential fact about capitalism. It is what capitalism consists in and what every capitalist concern has got to live in. . . .

. . . The capitalist engine is first and last an engine of mass production, which unavoidably

means also production for the masses, whereas, climbing upward in the scale of individual incomes, we find that an increasing proportion is being spent on personal services and on handmade commodities, the prices of which are largely a function of wage rates.

Verification is easy. There are no doubt some things available to the modern workman that Louis XIV himself would have been delighted to have yet was unable to have — modern dentistry for instance. On the whole, however, a budget on that level had little that really mattered to gain from capitalist achievement. Even speed of traveling may be assumed to have been a minor consideration for so very dignified a gentleman. Electric lighting is no great boon to anyone who has money enough to buy a sufficient number of candles and to pay servants to attend to them. It is the cheap cloth, the cheap cotton and rayon fabric, boots, motorcars, and so on that are the typical achievements of capitalist production, and not as a rule improvements that would mean much to the rich man. Queen Elizabeth owned silk stockings. The capitalist achievement does not typically consist in providing more silk stockings for queens but in bringing them within the reach of factory girls in return for steadily decreasing amounts of effort.

. . . The capitalist process, not by coincidence but by virtue of its mechanism, progressively raises the standard of life of the masses. It does so through a sequence of vicissitudes, the severity of which is proportional to the speed of the advance. But it does so effectively.

F. A. Hayek

Hayek, born in 1899, taught economics at the University of Vienna. He is a founder of modern monetary theory and won the Nobel Prize in economic science in 1974. This passage is from an essay entitled "The Uses of Knowledge in Society."

The peculiar character of the problem of rational economic order is determined precisely by the fact that the knowledge of the circumstances of which we must make use never exists in

---

[1] Those revolutions are not strictly incessant; they occur in discrete rushes, which are separated from each other by spans of comparative quiet. The process as a whole works incessantly, however, in the sense that there always is either revolution or absorption of the results of revolution, both together forming what are known as business cycles.

concentrated or integrated form, but solely as the dispersed bits of incomplete and frequently contradictory knowledge which all the separate individuals possess. The economic problem of society is thus not merely a problem of how to allocate "given" resources—if "given" is taken to mean given to a single mind which deliberately solves the problem set by these "data." It is rather a problem of how to secure the best use of resources known to any of the members of society, for ends whose relative importance only these individuals know, or, to put it briefly, it is a problem of utilization of knowledge not given to anyone in its totality.

In ordinary language we describe by the word "planning" the complex of interrelated decisions about the allocation of our available resources. All economic activity is in this sense planning; and in any society in which many people collaborate, this planning, whoever does it, will in some measure have to be based on knowledge which, in the first instance, is not given to the planner but to someone else, which somehow will have to be conveyed to the planner. The various ways in which the knowledge on which people base their plans is communicated to them is the crucial problem for any theory explaining the economic process. And the problem of what is the best way of utilizing knowledge initially dispersed among all the people is at least one of the main problems of economic policy—or of designing an efficient economic system.

If we can agree that the economic problem of society is mainly one of rapid adaptation to changes in the particular circumstances of time and place, it would seem to follow that the ultimate decisions must be left to the people who are familiar with these circumstances, who know directly of the relevant changes and of the resources immediately available to meet them. We cannot expect that this problem will be solved by first communicating all this knowledge to a central board which, after integrating all knowledge, issues its orders. We must solve it by some form of decentralization. But this answers only part of our problem. We need decentralization because only thus can we ensure

that the knowledge of the particular circumstances of time and place will be promptly used. But the "man on the spot" cannot decide solely on the basis of his limited but intimate knowledge of the facts of his immediate surroundings. There still remains the problem of communicating to him such further information as he needs to fit his decisions into the whole pattern of changes of the larger economic system.

Fundamentally, in a system where the knowledge of the relevant facts is dispersed among many people, prices can act to coordinate the separate actions of different people in the same way as subjective values help the individual to coordinate the parts of his plan.

The whole acts as one market, not because any of its members survey the whole field, but because their limited individual fields of vision sufficiently overlap so that through many intermediaries the relevant information is communicated to all. The mere fact that there is one price for any commodity—or rather that local prices are connected in a manner determined by the cost of transport, etc.—brings about the solution which (it is just conceptually possible) might have been arrived at by one single mind possessing all the information which is in fact dispersed among all the people involved in the process.

We must look at the price system as much as mechanism for communicating information if we want to understand its real function—a function which, of course, it fulfills less perfectly as prices grow more rigid.

The essential utility of the price system consists in inducing the individual, while seeking his own interest, to do what is in the general interest, the differences can indeed no longer be ascribed to political prejudice. The remaining dissent seems clearly to be due to purely intellectual, and more particularly methodological, differences.

An essential part of the phenomena with which we have to deal is the unavoidable imperfection of man's knowledge and the consequent need for a process by which knowledge is constantly communicated and acquired.

Milton Friedman

Friedman, an economist specializing in monetary theory, taught principally at the University of Chicago. He won the Nobel Prize in economic science in 1976. The first passage appears in *Capitalism and Freedom;* the second in an essay entitled "The Social Responsibilities of Business Is to Increase Its Profits."

... In summary, the organization of economic activity through voluntary exchange presumes that we have provided, through government, for the maintenance of law and order to prevent coercion of one individual by another, the enforcement of contracts voluntarily entered into, the definition of the meaning of property rights, the interpretation and enforcement of such rights, and the provision of a monetary framework.

... The heart of the liberal philosophy is a belief in the dignity of the individual, in his freedom to make the most of his capacities and opportunities according to his own lights, subject only to the proviso that he not interfere with the freedom of other individuals to do the same. This implies a belief in the equality of men in one sense; in their inequality in another. Each man has an equal right to freedom. This is an important and fundamental right precisely because men are different, because one man will want to do different things with his freedom than another, and in the process can contribute more than another, to the general culture of the society in which many men live.

The United States has continued to progress; its citizens have become better fed, better clothed, better housed, and better transported; class and social distinctions have narrowed; minority groups have become less disadvantaged; popular culture has advanced by leaps and bounds. All this has been the product of the initiative and drive of individuals cooperating through the free market. Government measures have hampered not helped this development. We have been able to afford and surmount these measures only because of the extraordinary fecundity of the market. The invisible hand has been more potent for progress than the visible hand for retrogression.

* * * * *

In a free enterprise, private property system, a corporate executive is an employee of the owners of the business. He has direct responsibility to his employers. That responsibility is to conduct the business in accordance with their desires, which generally will be to make as much money as possible while conforming to the basic rules of the society, both those embodied in law and those embodied in ethical custom.

Robert Nozick

Nozick is a professor of philosophy at Harvard University. This passage appears in *Anarchy, State, and Utopia,* published in 1974.[2]

For suppose a distribution favored by one of these nonentitlement conceptions is realized. Let us suppose it is our favorite one and let us call this distribution D_1; perhaps everyone has an equal share, perhaps shares vary in accordance with some dimension you treasure. Now suppose that Wilt Chamberlain is greatly in demand by basketball teams, being a great gate attraction. (Also suppose contracts run only for a year, with players being free agents.) He signs the following sort of contract with a team: In each home game, 25 cents from the price of each ticket of admission goes to him. (We ignore the question of whether he is "gouging" the owners, letting them look out for themselves.) The season starts, and people cheerfully attend his team's games; they buy their tickets, each time dropping a separate 25 cents of their admission price into a special box with Chamberlain's name on it. They are excited about seeing him play; it is worth the total admission price to them. Let us suppose that in one season 1 million persons attend his home games, and

---

[2] Robert Nozick, *Anarchy, State, and Utopia,* pp. 160–64. Copyright © 1974 by Basic Books, Inc. Reprinted by permission of BasicBooks, a division of HarperCollins Publishers, Inc.

Wilt Chamberlain winds up with $250,000, a much larger sum than the average income and larger even than anyone else has. Is he entitled to this income? Is this new distribution D_2, unjust? If so, why? There is no question about whether each of the people was entitled to the control over the resources they held in D_1; because that was the distribution (your favorite) that (for the purposes of argument) we assumed was acceptable. Each of these persons chose to give 25 cents of their money to Chamberlain. They could have spent it on going to the movies, or on candy bars, or on copies of *Dissent* magazine, or of *Monthly Review*. But they all, at least 1 million of them, converged on giving it to Wilt Chamberlain in exchange for watching him play basketball. If D_1 was a just distribution, and people voluntarily moved from it to D_2, transferring parts of their shares they were given under D_1 (what was it for if not to do something with?), isn't D_2 also just? If the people were entitled to dispose of the resources to which they were entitled (under D_1), didn't this include their being entitled to give it to, or exchange it with, Wilt Chamberlain? Can anyone else complain on grounds of justice? Each other person already has his legitimate share under D_1. Under D_1, there is nothing that anyone has that anyone else has a claim of justice against. After someone transfers something to Wilt Chamberlain, third parties still have their legitimate shares; their shares are not changed. By what process could such a transfer among two persons give rise to a legitimate claim of distributive justice on a portion of what was transferred, by a third party who had no claim of justice on any holding of the others before the transfer?

Why might someone work overtime in a society in which it is assumed their needs are satisfied? Perhaps because they care about things other than needs. I like to write in books that I read, and to have easy access to books for browsing at odd hours. It would be very pleasant and convenient to have the resources of Widener Library in my back yard. No society, I assume, will provide such resources close to each person who would like them as part of his regular allotment (under D_1). Thus, persons either must do without some extra things that they want, or be allowed to do something extra to get some of these things. On what basis could the inequalities that would eventuate be forbidden? Notice also that small factories would spring up in a socialist society, unless forbidden. I melt down some of my personal possessions (under D_1) and build a machine out of the material. I offer you, and others, a philosophy lecture once a week in exchange for your cranking the handle on my machine, whose products I exchange for yet other things, and so on. (The raw materials used by the machine are given to me by others who possess them under D_1, in exchange for yet other things, and so on. Each person might participate to gain things over and above their allotment under D_1. Some persons even might want to leave their job in socialist industry and work full time in this private sector.)

Private property even in means of production would occur in a socialist society that did not forbid people to use as they wished some of the resources they are given under the socialist distribution D_1. The socialist society would have to forbid capitalist acts between consenting adults.

The general point illustrated by the Wilt Chamberlain example and the example of the entrepreneur in a socialist society is that no end-state principle or distributional patterned principle of justice can be continuously realized without continuous interference with people's lives.

Robert C. Clark

Clark has been a professor of law at Harvard Law School and, since 1989, its dean. This excerpt comes from an article entitled, "Agency Costs versus Fiduciary Duties."[3]

---

[3] Reprinted by permission of Harvard Business School Press from *Principals and Agents: The Structure of Business,* ed. John W. Pratt and Richard J. Zeckhauser. Boston: 1985, 1991, pp. 73, 74. Copyright © 1985, 1991 by the President and Fellows of Harvard College.

.... Case law on managers' fiduciary duty of care can fairly be read to say that the manager has an affirmative, open-ended duty to maximize the beneficiaries' wealth, regardless of whether this is specified in any actual contract. But with respect to the fiduciary's rights, the law leans exactly the other way. These rights are bounded in a fairly definite way. Essentially, the fiduciary cannot take any compensation from the beneficiaries or any other advantage from his official position (even when doing so does not seem to deprive the beneficiaries of any value they would otherwise get) except to the extent provided in an above-board, actual contract or in accordance with explicit statutory provisions. Thus, top executives' compensation is supposed to be expressly approved by the board of directors acting for the corporation.

... When the corporation enters into a transaction with another party who is director or officer, or in whom or in which a director or officer has a personal interest, the director or officer must prove, if called on to do so in a derivative lawsuit, that the transaction was "fair" to the corporation. "Fairness" means in part that the transaction was at least as advantageous to the corporation as a comparable transaction in a reasonably competitive market or as a hypothetical arm's-length bargain.

Richard Dawkins

Dawkins is a prominent British zoologist. This passage appears in his book, *The Selfish Gene.*

The fundamental unit of selection, and therefore of self-interest, is not the species, nor the group, nor even, strictly, the individual. It is the gene, the unit of heredity.... At some point a particularly remarkable molecule was formed by accident, the Replicator ... it had the extraordinary property of being able to create copies of itself.... The primeval soup was not capable of supporting an infinite number of replicator molecules.... There was a struggle for existence among replicator varieties. They did not know they were struggling, or worry about it; the struggle was conducted without any hard feelings, indeed without feelings of any kind....

Replicators began not merely to exist, but to construct for themselves containers, vehicles for their continued existence. The replicators which survived were the ones which built *survival machines* for themselves to live in.... Natural selection favors replicators which are good at building survival machines, genes which are skilled in the art of controling embryonic development. In this, the replicators are no more conscious or purposeful than they ever were. The same old processes of automatic selection between rival molecules by reason of their longevity, fecundity, and copying fidelity, still go on as blindly and as inevitably as they did in the far-off days.

Four thousand million years on, what was to be the fate of the ancient replicators? They did not die out, for they are past masters of the survival arts. But do not look for them floating loose in the sea; they gave up that cavalier freedom long ago. Now they swarm in huge colonies, safe inside gigantic lumbering robots, sealed off from the outside world, communicating with it by tortuous indirect routes, manipulating it by remote control. They are in you and in me; they created us, body and mind; and their preservation is the ultimate rationale for our existence. They have come a long way, those replicators. Now they go by the name of genes, and we are their survival machines.

BIBLIOGRAPHIC NOTES

Thomas Hobbes, *Leviathan,* edited and with an introduction by C. B. Macpherson (Harmondsworth, England: Penguin, 1968), I, 13.

John Locke, *Treatise of Civil Government and a Letter Concerning Toleration,* edited by Charles L. Sherman (New York: D. Appleton-Century Co., 1937), II *Civil Government,* V, pp. 26–27, 30, 46–47, 40; *Letter Concerning Toleration; Civil Government XV,* 171.

Adam Smith, *An Inquiry into the Nature and Causes of the Wealth of Nations,* edited by Edwin Cannan (New York: Modern Library Edition, 1937), II, 14; IV, 2; V, 3; V; II, 3; II, 3.

John Stuart Mill, *On Liberty* (New York: Macmillan, 1926), I, IV.

———. *Principles of Political Economy* (from the 5th London edition, New York: D. Appleton and Company, 1897), 2 vols, Book II, II, 3.

Charles Darwin, *On the Origin of Species* (A facsimile of the first edition with an introduction by Ernst Mayr) (Cambridge, Mass.: Harvard University Press, 1964), VI.

Alfred Marshall and Mary Paley Marshall, *The Economics of Industry* (London: Macmillan, 1879), Bk. II, Ch. XII, §§3,4 [pp. 139, 140].

———. *Principles of Economics,* 9th edition (London: Macmillan and Co., Ltd.; New York: Macmillan, 1961), I, I, §4 [vol. I, p. 9 in this edition].

Joseph Schumpeter, *Capitalism, Socialism, and Democracy,* 3rd edition (New York: Harper Colophon/Harper & Row, 1975), pp. 67–68, 83.

F. A. Hayek, "The Use of Knowledge in Society," *The American Economic Review* 35, no. 4 (September 1945), pp. 519–30, at 519, 520, 524–525, 526, 529, 530.

Milton Friedman (with the assistance of Rose Friedman) *Capitalism and Freedom* (Chicago: University of Chicago Press, 1962), pp. 19–20, 27, 195, 199–200.

———. "The Social Responsibility of Business Is to Increase Its Profits," *New York Times Magazine,* September 13, 1970, reprinted in *Harvard Business Review,* p. 87.

Robert Nozick, *Anarchy, State, and Utopia* (New York: Basic Books, 1974), pp. 160–62, 163–64.

Robert C. Clark, "Agency Costs versus Fiduciary Duties," in *Principals and Agents: The Structure of Business,* ed. John W. Pratt and Richard J. Zeckhauser (Boston: Harvard Business School Press, 1985), pp. 73, 74.

Richard Dawkins, *The Selfish Gene* (New York and Oxford: Oxford University Press, 1976), pp. 12, 16, 20, 21, 25, by permission of Oxford University Press.

THE SMOKE WARS

The Case For and Against the Cigarette Industry

Early 1989 saw a wave of public policy activism on "the smoking issue." Ten major bills were introduced during the first month of the 100th U.S. Congress. These bills proposed to increase the cigarette excise tax, eliminate corporate tax deductions for tobacco advertising, ban smoking in federal buildings, and prohibit smoking on all public conveyances. Many corporations had imposed restrictions on smoking at work; some simply refused to hire smokers. In March 1988, the Civil Aeronautics Board banned smoking on flights of less than two hours, which was extended to six hours by February 1990. Smoking in public places was restricted in 41 states. A New York City law, put into effect in April 1988, restricted smoking in restaurants, stores, theaters, hospitals, museums, banks, and virtually all other public places.

"The new rules are sparking explosive confrontations on all fronts," reported *Time.*[1] The article added:

> Even those who would like very much to quit want to do so in their own sweet time – not under a legal gun. They are sick of having glasses of water dumped on their ashtrays or ashtrays dumped on their beds. . . .
> Having long been segregated on scheduled flights, smokers are indignant about the outright

[1] "All Fired Up over Smoke," *Time,* April 18, 1988, pp. 64–75.

This case was prepared by V. Kasturi Rangan. The author is thankful to Janice Hitchcock, director of research at the Kennedy School's Smoking Policy Institute, and Loy Sheflott, HBS MBA 1988, for the motivation and background research they provided on which this case is based.
Copyright © 1989 by the President and Fellows of Harvard College.
Harvard Business School case 590-040 (Revised 1992).

ban. "I think it's discriminatory," says John Collins, a Los Angeles telecommunications contractor and frequent flyer. "First they put all of us smokers way in the back of the plane. We took that OK. But now they tell us that we can't smoke at all. The whole thing has been aggravating as hell, especially when I can remember when you used to get on a plane and the stewardesses were handing out five packs of cigarettes."

Signs on office walls that used to smile **Thank You For Not Smoking** now growl **If You Smoke, Don't Exhale. . . .**

Smokers know, of course, that it is not quite that simple. "You can't blame people for not wanting to breathe smoke," says Kay Michael, a reporter for the Charleston, West Virginia, *Daily Mail,* "but I wish the antismokers would try to understand that there is a physical addiction here. They seem to think we smoke just to mess up the air or something."

The Tobacco Institute (a tobacco-industry-sponsored research and information group) offered the following perspective regarding the various restrictions on smoking:[2]

> The United States Constitution imposes various restrictions on the power of the federal and state governments to regulate the lives of our citizenry. Plaintiffs who have attempted to elevate their own personal antismoking crusades against public entities to constitutional dimensions have uniformly been rebuffed. The leading case is Gasper *v.* Louisiana Stadium. There a group of nonsmokers sued to compel the authorities who manage the Louisiana Superdome to prohibit smoking during sports and other public events. In support of their demand, the plaintiffs claimed a constitutional right to a smoke-free environment, relying on the First Amendment (freedom of speech); Fifth and Fourteenth Amendments (due process right to life and liberty); and Ninth Amendment

(which protects unspecific but so-called fundamental rights).

> The district court unequivocally rejected any constitutional basis for imposing restrictions on smoking in a decision that was in all respects affirmed by the court of appeals. Responding to the First Amendment claim, the court found that "the state's permissive attitude toward smoking in the Louisiana Superdome adequately preserved the delicate balance of individual rights without yielding to the temptation to intervene in purely private affairs." In rejecting the due process claim, the court concluded that to apply the Fifth and Fourteenth Amendments to prohibit smoking would be

> *to mock the lofty purposes of such amendments and broaden their penumbral protections to unheard-of boundaries. . . . To hold otherwise would be to invite government by the judiciary in the regulation of every conceivable ill or so-called right to our litigious-minded society. The inevitable result would be that type of tyranny from which our founding fathers sought to protect the people by adopting the first 10 amendments to the Constitution.*

Cigarette industry advocates further claimed that restrictions on the employment of smokers was a threat to black Americans. Since statistics revealed that more blacks smoked than whites, hiring bans directed at smokers, they argued, would disproportionately affect black employment. (See Figure 1 below for demographics on smokers by education, race, and age.) Research compiled by the U.S. Surgeon General showed that blacks smoked more than whites and that the more educated the people were, the less likely they were to smoke. *Currents* summed up the industry's case:[3]

> The signs outside personnel offices these days are very different than they were before 1964. Posters proclaiming "Blacks Need Not Apply"

---

[2] "An Assessment of the Current Legal Climate Concerning Smoking in the Workplace," prepared by the law firm of Covington and Burling for the Tobacco Institute, January 1987.

[3] "Toward a Civil Rights Approach to Smoking," Dr. Robert W. Etheridge and John C. Fox, *Currents,* April 1987.

FIGURE 1   The Demographics

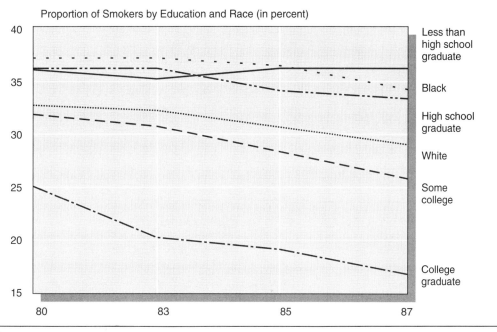

Proportion of Smokers by Education and Race (in percent)

Source: *Newsweek*, February 13, 1989.

Age group	12–17	18–19	20–25	26–35	36–74	75+	Total
No. of smokers (in millions)	3.3	1.6	9.7	13.7	27.0	1.0	56.3

Source: E.M. Lewit and D. Coate, *Journal of Health Economics*, 1982, pp. 62–87.

exist today largely only in museums as relics of a by-gone age. Yet new signs menacing to many blacks, but not mentioning race at all, are popping up across the country: "Smokers Need Not Apply." To the extent today's signs and the employment policies they represent exclude or disadvantage blacks in the workforce disproportionately compared to whites, they may well be as pernicious as their predecessors.

The battle regarding restrictions on "smoking" and "smokers" was only one among several that were being fought between the advocates and foes of the cigarette industry. The problem, of course, stemmed from the fact that,

since 1953, when the Sloan-Kettering Institute linked lung cancer with exposure to "tar" from cigarette smoking, scientific evidence had increasingly identified smoking as the leading cause of death in the United States. In his 1986 report, C. Everett Koop, the U.S. Surgeon General, reported:[4]

Smoking is now known to be causally related to a variety of cancers in addition to lung cancer, it is a cause of cardiovascular disease,

---

[4] The 1986 Report of the Surgeon General, U.S. Public Health Service.

particularly coronary heart disease, and is the major cause of the chronic obstructive lung disease. It is estimated that smoking is responsible for well over 300,000 deaths annually in the United States, representing approximately 15 percent of all mortality. . . . It is now clear that disease risk due to the inhalation of tobacco smoke is not limited to the individual who is smoking, but can extend to those who inhale tobacco smoke emitted into the air. [This was estimated at 5,000–6,000 lung cancer deaths annually.]

To offer a perspective to this otherwise abstract statistic on smoking mortality: "Consider that the death toll due to smoking is comparable to that which would result from three jumbo jet crashes a day, occurring every single day of the year."[5]

Thus the $35 billion (1988 retail cigarette sales) tobacco industry, which, according to a Chase Econometrics estimate,[6] contributed nearly $32 billion to the GNP, provided about $14 billion in federal and state taxes (split evenly), and employed close to one million people, was not without its detractors. Its critics pointed out that the health care costs attributed to smoking illnesses was about $22 billion, and productivity losses to the economy in the region of $30 billion-$40 billion.[7] Even though the incidence of adult smokers in the United States had dropped from 43 percent in 1965 to 26 percent in 1988, the advocates of the antismoking movement, nevertheless, pressed on with their battle to completely banish the smoking habit from the face of the earth.

---

[5] Dr. Kenneth E. Warner, "The Effects of Publicity and Policy on Smoking and Health," *Business and Health*, November 1984 (vol. 2, no. 1), pp. 7–14.

[6] "The Economic Impact" of the Tobacco Industry on the United States Economy," Bala Cynwyd, Penn.: Chase Econometrics, 1985.

[7] James M. Shultz, "Perspectives on the Economic Magnitude of Cigarette Smoking," *New York State Journal of Medicine*, July 1985.

The Combatants

The tobacco lobby was represented mainly by six cigarette companies and a jointly funded Tobacco Research Institute. In 1989, the six major tobacco companies in the United States were Philip Morris, R. J. Reynolds Tobacco (a division of RJR Nabisco), Brown and Williamson (a division of BATUS), Lorillard (a division of Loews Corporation), American Tobacco (a division of American Brands), and Liggett Group (owned by Bennett S. LeBow, a New York-based investor). The market shares of the six competitors and their leading brands are shown in Exhibit 1. Every one of these brands except Merit had been around for more than 20 years. By incurring over $2 billion dollars annually in advertising and promotional expenditure, the cigarette industry vastly outspent the antismoking group's consumer education programs (estimated to be in the region of $200 million to $300 million nationwide overall, agencies and organizations put together). In spite of the declining demand (approximately 2 percent annually), the cigarette industry's profitability for tobacco operations had either remained constant or improved. (See Exhibit 2 for aggregate trend of U.S. tobacco shipments and prices over the last 15 years.)

To continue their revenue growth, manufacturers were diversifying into other businesses and aggressively marketing cigarettes internationally. In 1985, for example, R. J. Reynolds merged with Nabisco Brands, and Philip Morris acquired General Foods. (Exhibits 3 to 6 provide a brief description of four leading cigarette manufacturers in the United States and their financial history for the periods 1985, 1986, and 1987.)

Battling this huge and powerful monolith called the tobacco industry was an assortment of agencies and actors loosely labeled the Anti-Smoking Movement.

Federal agencies, such as the Surgeon General's Office, Action on Smoking and Health

EXHIBIT 1 Market Shares of Leading Brands

		Market Share by Firm		
	1950	*1974*	*1979*	*1987*
Philip Morris	11.3	22.5	29.0	37.9
R.J. Reynolds	31.5	27.4	32.7	32.6
Brown and Williamson	5.2	17.4	14.5	10.8
Lorillard	5.5	8.2	9.6	8.2
American Brands	31.1	15.7	11.5	6.9
Liggett	18.6	4.6	2.7	3.6

		Market Share	
Brand	*Company*	*1980*	*1987*
1. Marlboro	Philip Morris	17.8	23.4
2. Winston	R.J. Reynolds	13.2	11.4
3. Salem	R.J. Reynolds	8.9	7.9
4. Kool	Brown and Williamson	8.9	5.7
5. Camel	R.J. Reynolds	4.3	4.3
6. Newport	Lorillard	3.0	4.2
7. Benson & Hedges	Philip Morris	4.6	4.0
8. Merit	Philip Morris	4.3	3.9
9. Vantage	R.J. Reynolds	3.9	3.3
10. Pall Mall	American Brands	3.9	3.1

Source: John C. Maxwell, industry analyst, and HBS "Note on the U.S. Cigarette Industry" (no. 183-046).

(ASH), and the Centers for Disease Control provided smoking-related consumer education, while the National Institutes of Health—comprising such agencies as the National Cancer Institute and the National Heart, Lung, and Blood Institute—provided funds for basic research.

The role of the government in regulating tobacco and tobacco products was limited; these products were specifically excluded from the Consumer Product Safety Act, the Toxic Substances Control Act, and the Food, Drug, and Cosmetic Act. The Federal Trade Commission, however, oversaw advertising and promotion practices and the enforcement of labeling requirements.

State and local governments also limited the distribution and use of tobacco products. Actions taken included restrictions on smoking in public places, minimum age of purchase laws, restrictions on sampling of products, and some advertising restrictions not covered by federal legislation. All 50 states and the District of Columbia added an excise tax on cigarettes, ranging from $0.02 a pack in North Carolina to $0.28 in Maine.

Three major national organizations were committed to research, public education, and communication on the risks associated with cigarettes: the American Cancer Society, the American Lung Association, and the American Heart Association. These entities created the

EXHIBIT 2 Historic Performance of U.S. Tobacco

	1972	1973	1974	1975	1976	1977	1978	1979	1980	1981	1982	1983
Product Data												
Value of shipments ($ mil.)	4,204	4,624	4,996	5,854	6,461	6,756	7,381	8,096	9,184	9,947	12,455	12,997
Cigarettes	3,589	4,004	4,380	5,209	5,830	6,098	6,660	7,323	8,315	8,991	11,434	11,941
Cigars	358	350	334	317	285	256	283	261	265	286	290	307
Chewing/smoking tobacco	258	270	282	328	346	401	438	512	604	671	731	749
Value of shipments (1982$)	11,627	12,363	12,268	12,780	12,948	12,255	12,104	12,111	12,152	12,047	12,455	11,455
Cigarettes	10,314	11,061	11,034	11,627	11,874	11,189	11,044	11,062	11,086	11,005	11,434	10,438
Cigars	583	559	504	458	402	349	357	316	298	299	290	305
Chewing/smoking tobacco	729	743	731	695	671	717	702	734	768	743	731	712
Shipments price index (1982 = 100)	35.4	36.8	40.3	45.5	49.7	55.0	60.9	66.8	75.5	82.5	100.0	113.5
Cigarettes	34.8	36.2	39.7	44.8	49.1	54.5	60.3	66.2	75.0	81.7	100.0	114.4
Cigars	61.3	62.7	66.2	69.2	70.9	73.5	79.3	82.7	89.0	95.5	100.0	100.8
Chewing/smoking tobacco	35.3	36.3	38.6	47.2	51.5	56.0	62.4	69.8	78.7	90.3	100.0	105.2
Trade Data ($ million)												
Value of imports	25.1	24.3	32.6	35.2	46.6	45.9	50.0	51.3	92.8	200	227	403
Cigarettes	0.6	0.7	1.7	2.1	2.6	3.1	3.9	5.6	6.9	7.5	7.9	11.1
Cigars	8.4	11.5	13.6	15.8	19.3	22.9	25.0	28.0	34.5	39.5	40.8	44.8
Chewing/smoking tobacco	16.1	12.1	17.3	17.3	24.7	19.9	21.1	17.7	51.4	153	178	348
Value of exports	240	289	361	401	536	637	763	959	1,082	1,259	1,287	1,169
Cigarettes	202	250	301	369	510	615	750	909	1,055	1,229	1,235	1,126
Cigars	3.0	3.7	4.0	4.6	5.7	5.5	7.7	8.8	9.9	11.0	10.5	8.5
Chewing/smoking tobacco	35.3	35.3	55.8	28.1	20.8	16.9	6.2	42.0	16.5	19.5	42.2	35.3
Average retail price per package (cents)	40.3	41.8	44.5	47.9	49.2	54.3	56.8	60.0	63.0	69.7	81.9	94.7
Average taxes (state plus federal) per package (cents)	20.0	20.0	20.0	20.0	20.0	20.0	20.0	20.0	21.0	21.0	21.0	31.4

Source: U.S. Industrial Outlook 1988 — Tobacco.
Source: Tobacco Institute: The Tax Burden on Tobacco, 1989.

EXHIBIT 3   Philip Morris

Philip Morris, Inc. (PM), the market leader since 1983, was the only company to have an increase in unit volume in 1987; its 37.9 percent market share was the highest obtained by any tobacco company since the 1930s. Marlboro, PM's flagship brand, accounted for 63 percent of its sales volume in 1987.

In addition to tobacco, PM engaged in two other business segments: beer and food products. The company owned and operated the Miller Brewing Company (Miller) and General Foods (GF) acquired in 1985. In 1988, the company acquired Kraft, Inc. These two acquisitions were a continuation of the company's 25-year strategy to use corporate resources to expand its earnings base internationally and through diversification.

	1987	1986	1985
Operating revenues ($ millions):			
Domestic tobacco	$ 7,640	$ 7,053	$ 6,611
International tobacco	7,004	5,638	3,991
Food	9,946	9,664	1,632
Beer	3,105	3,054	2,914
Financial services and real estate	488	474	303
Other	–	–	816
Total operating revenues	$28,183	$25,883	$16,267
Operating income ($ millions):			
Domestic tobacco	$ 2,715	$ 2,366	$ 2,047
International tobacco	582	492	413
Food	773	741	120
Beer	170	154	132
Financial services and real estate	68	32	66
Other	20	(10)	42
Operating companies income	$ 4,328	$ 3,775	$ 2,820

Source: Company annual reports.

Coalition on Smoking or Health in 1982. The coalition worked on initiatives ranging from imposition of excise taxes to regulating tobacco industry advertising and promotion practices.

Other health-related organizations adopted positions on smoking. The American Medical Association, for example, advocated a total ban on cigarette advertising. There were also a variety of advocacy groups dedicated to the elimination of smoking—for example, Americans for Nonsmokers' Rights and Ralph Nader's Common Cause.

Had all this made a difference? An article in *Business and Health* argued:[8]

Despite all the publicity on the health hazards of smoking, some 55 million Americans engage in the habit today, and their average daily consumption of more than 30 cigarettes per smoker is at an all-time high. Collectively,

---

[8] Dr. Kenneth E. Warner, "The Effects of Publicity and Policy on Smoking and Health," *Business and Health*, November 1984 (vol. 2, no. 1), pp. 7–14.

EXHIBIT 4 R. J. Reynolds Tobacco

RJR Nabisco, Inc. (RJR), formerly R. J. Reynolds Industries, increased its 1987 share of domestic sales to 32.6 percent, a 3 percent change from 1986 levels. RJR's portfolio of cigarette brands included Winston, Salem, Camel, Vantage, and Doral. Doral, the largest "branded generic," was RJR's first entry into the expanding price/value segment of the market. As the only generic in the top 10 brands in the United States, it was primarily responsible for the company's 38.6 percent market share within the price/value segment.

Having undergone significant restructuring between 1985 and 1987, RJR became one of the world's largest consumer products company; it includes Nabisco Brands, Inc., Del Monte Tropical Fruit Company, and R.J. Reynolds Tobacco Company.

These businesses produced a wide range of products, including cigarettes, cookies, crackers, nuts, snacks, confectionery products, processed fruits and vegetables, cereals, margarines, and fresh fruit.

	1987	*1986*	*1985*
Net sales ($ millions):			
Tobacco	$ 6,346	$ 5,866	$ 5,422
Food	9,420	9,236	6,200
Consolidated net sales	$15,766	$15,102	$11,622
Operating income ($ millions):			
Tobacco	$ 1,821	$ 1,659	$ 1,483
Food	915	820	549
Restructuring expense (1)	(250)	—	—
Corporate	(182)	(139)	(83)
Consolidated operating income	$ 2,304	$ 2,340	$ 1,949
Net sales ($ millions):			
United States	$11,721	$11,338	$ 9,095
Canada	850	1,060	830
Europe	2,361	2,055	1,125
Other geographic areas	1,387	1,217	996
Less transfers between geographic areas (1)	(553)	(568)	(424)
Consolidated net sales	$15,766	$15,102	$11,622
Operating income ($ millions):			
United States	$ 2,162	$ 2,026	$ 1,694
Canada	112	85	106
Europe	241	180	90
Other geographic areas	221	188	142
Restructuring expense (2)	(250)	—	—
Corporate	(182)	(139)	(83)
Consolidated operating income	$ 2,304	$ 2,340	$ 1,949

Source: Company annual reports.

EXHIBIT 5 Brown and Williamson

BATUS, founded in 1980, was the holding company for the United States business interests of B.A.T. Industries PLC (London, England). Founded in 1980, the company operated the Brown and Williamson Tobacco Corporation (B&W), the third-largest U.S. cigarette company. Kool, its flagship brand, was the fourth-largest-selling domestic cigarette brand. B&W brands included Kent, Lucky Strike, and Barclay, as well as several offerings in the price/value segment: Richland, a branded generic, and "GPC," an unbranded generic.

The company's two other business segments were retail and paper. Within retail, the company operated Saks Fifth Avenue, Marshall Field's, Ivey's, Brueners, and Thimbles. Appleton Papers, Inc., the world's largest producer of carbonless copy paper, manufactured specialty paper.

	1987	*1986*	*1985*
Sales (£ millions):			
UK	£ 4,179	£ 3,546	£3,465
Europe	5,077	5,480	4,242
North America	4,637	5,823	5,928
Australasia	531	554	485
Latin America	1,499	2,396	1,550
Asia	803	937	1,000
Africa	482	431	381
Total	£17,208	£19,167	£17,051
Profit (£ millions):			
UK	£295	£355	£275
Europe	223	186	113
North America	634	658	587
Australasia	36	40	31
Latin America	139	171	161
Asia	57	63	78
Africa	52	44	49
Total	£ 1,436	£ 1,517	£ 1,294
Sales (£ millions):			
Tobacco	£6,940	£8,339	£7,170
Retailing	3,948	4,762	4,671
Paper	1,692	1,755	1,499
Financial services	3,812	3,183	2,186
Other trading activities	816	1,128	1,525
Total	£17,208	£19,167	£17,051
Profit (£ millions):			
Tobacco	£722	£764	£738
Retailing	203	211	186
Paper	209	217	168
Financial services	267	291	137
Other trading activities	35	34	65
Total	£ 1,436	£ 1,517	£ 1,294

Source: Company annual reports.

EXHIBIT 6 American Tobacco Company

American Brands, Inc. (AB), was the holding company for the American Tobacco Company (ATC), the grandfather of the United States tobacco industry. Domestically, the company marketed three principal brands: Lucky Strikes and Carlton, both "low-tar," and Pall Mall, a nonfilter cigarette.

In 1986, AB celebrated the 20th anniversary of its diversification strategy. Capitalizing on its marketing and distribution strengths, the company invested over $2.6 billion, to become an international holding company of packaged consumer goods and financial services. Major lines in addition to tobacco included life insurance, hardware, and security (Master Lock and Pinkerton Securities Services), distilled beverages (Jim Beam Beverages), and food products (Sunshine Biscuits).

	1987	1986	1985
Net sales ($ millions):			
Tobacco products	$6,144.0	$5,169.4	$4,390.0
Distilled spirits	599.4	254.5	249.8
Hardware	291.6	302.6	256.9
Office products	508.6	346.9	336.7
Other	1,609.3	1,179.5	972.2
Total	$9,152.9	$7,252.9	$6,205.6
Operating income ($ millions):			
Tobacco products	$ 673.8	$ 498.6	$ 519.6
Distilled spirits	68.3	35.0	40.2
Hardware	42.1	40.6	40.1
Office products	26.5	(12.1)	17.1
Other	91.5	65.4	58.3
	902.2	627.5	675.3
Financial services	168.6	176.1	174.1
Total	$1,070.8	$ 803.6	$ 849.4
Business by geographic areas ($ millions):			
Net sales			
United States	$2,815.8	$2,390.6	$2,308.7
Europe	6,250.9	4,812.6	3,845.1
Other	86.2	49.7	51.8
Total	$9,152.9	$7,252.9	$6,205.6
Operating income ($ millions):			
United States	$ 577.9	$ 434.2	$ 516.1
Europe	315.0	194.7	158.8
Other	9.3	(1.4)	0.4
	902.2	627.5	675.3
Financial services (United States)	168.6	176.1	174.1
Total	$1,070.8	$ 803.6	$ 849.4

Source: Company annual reports.

Americans puff in excess of 600 billion cigarettes each year. Since the 1950s, millions of women have joined the smoking population and teenage girls have been particularly enthusiastic new recruits.

Figure 2 provides the trend of per capita cigarette consumption since the early 1900s, followed by a brief chronology of events.[9]

Recent Battles

The advocates and opponents of the tobacco lobby were locked in several major battles. While the demand for cigarettes declined nationwide, until the late 1980s the antismoking movement had hardly won any victories in direct confrontations between the two groups. This section outlines four of those battles.

The first, entitled *Free Speech or Marketing Ploy,* discusses the tobacco industry's vigorous defense to freedom of speech and advertising. The second battle, entitled *Wealth Is Not Health,* examines the tobacco industry's aggressive efforts to increase sales in global markets. The third battle, entitled *Of Mice and Men,* describes the outcome of a historic product liability suit against Liggett, a cigarette company; and finally the fourth battle, entitled *In Search of a Target,* reviews R. J. Reynolds' efforts to target new markets.

1. Free Speech or Marketing Ploy

Critics asserted that the cigarette industry used its marketing expertise to take advantage of unsuspecting consumers. The Health Advocacy Center reported that cigarette advertisers "prey on the insecurity of young people by providing them with sophisticated, self-

sufficient role models into which they think they can transform themselves simply by smoking." Further, the advertising images and brand positions, argued critics, were becoming more appealing to young smokers. A document the FTC obtained from Brown & Williamson explored how image projection advertising could be used to attract young people.[10]

> For the young smoker, the cigarette is not yet an integral part of life, of day-to-day life, in spite of the fact that they try to project the image of a regular, run-of-the-mill smoker. For them, a cigarette and the whole smoking process is part of the illicit pleasure category. . . . In the young smoker's mind a cigarette falls into the same category with wine, beer, shaving, wearing a bra (or purposely not wearing one), declaration of independence, and striving for self-identity. For the young starter, a cigarette is associated with the introduction to sex life, with courtship, with smoking "pot," and keeping late study hours.

The tobacco industry claimed that advertising was aimed at changing current smokers' brand loyalties, not at inducing nonsmokers, especially adolescents, to begin smoking. The International Advertising Agency supporting the tobacco industry's view argued:

> The reasons why people start smoking are complex and mostly concerned with the individual's psychology, background, and social context. He or she starts to smoke because of internal and external factors which have to do with the kind of person he or she is, with the example of parents and friends and with social influences exerted by peer groups. All that seems clear from the research that has been done. It is also clear that advertising plays no significant role in initiating the use of tobacco products. Such is the reasonable conclusion of serious, responsible researchers.

---

[9] For more information on the early history of the industry, see Susan Wagner, *Cigarette Country* (New York: Praeger Publishers, 1971); Maurice Corina, *Trust in Tobacco* (New York: St. Martin's Press, 1975); and Alfred Chandler and Richard Tedlow, *The Coming of Managerial Capitalism* (Homewood, Ill.: Richard D. Irwin, 1985).

---

[10] W. Meyers, "The Image Makers: Power and Persuasion of Madison Avenue," *New York Times Book,* 1984.

FIGURE 2 Adult per Capita Cigarette Consumption in the United States

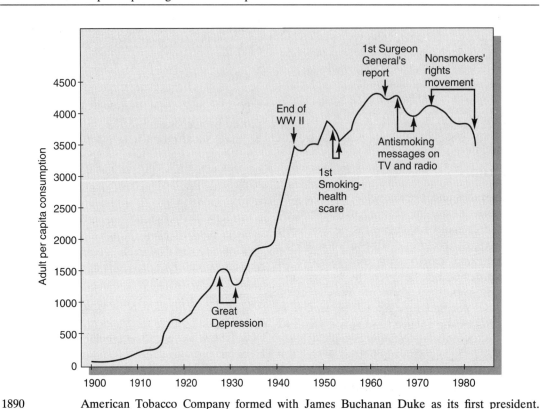

1890	American Tobacco Company formed with James Buchanan Duke as its first president.
1917 to 1919	During the First World War, per capita consumption increased from 337 to 426 cigarettes.
1939 to 1945	During the Second World War, per capita consumption soared from 1,779 to 3,457 cigarettes.
1953	Sloan-Kettering Institute linked lung cancer to cigarette smoking.
1955	Filter-tipped cigarettes introduced.
1964	U.S. Surgeon General identified cigarette smoking as a health problem and recommended health warnings and advertising restrictions.
	The cigarette industry adopted a voluntary code to discourage manufacturers from advertising and marketing to the youth market.
1965	Congress passed the Cigarette Labeling and Advertising Act, requiring warning labels to be printed on all cigarette packages.
1967	The Federal Communications Commission required that television and radio run antismoking advertising in parity with cigarette advertising.
1969	The cigarette industry voluntarily agreed to end all radio and television advertising. Congress banned these mediums in 1971.
1971	Low tar and nicotine cigarettes introduced.
	Per capita consumption started to decline steadily.
1986	Of the 55 million adult Americans who smoked, 15 million attempted to quit every year, and 1.5 million were actually successful.

Source: U.S. Department of Agriculture.

Critics disagree:[11]

> Their lips say "No, No," but the reality is Yes! Cigarette manufacturers do want young people to smoke. . . . Reality contradicts their claim. Cigarette advertisements depicting adults in their 20s in a myriad of athletic, adventurous, sexy pursuits appeal to a youthful audience. . . . One hardly needs to be an advertising executive to recognize that ads are aimed at attracting youth. Look at the Kool ads (and just who did they name the cigarette "Kool" to attract?) showing a male and female model, early 20s, blue jeans and T-shirts, leaning on a motorcycle looking, as the name implies, "Kool." . . . Of course, all cigarette advertising executives know of young women's obsession with their weight and the belief many hold that smoking will help them lose weight. Yes, Virginia, they're not called "Slims" for nothing.

In 1986, there were calls for a national ban on the advertising and promotion of cigarettes in all mediums. Cigarette companies' responses were typified by Philip Morris:[12]

> We believe that such proposals ignore the constitutional rights of our industry. Further, they seek to establish a precedent that could have very damaging consequences for many other products which are also legally sold, but which periodically attract public or legislative criticism. . . . We have spoken out vigorously against such prohibition, stressing the protection of commercial free speech under the First Amendment.

"Freedom of speech—a cherished freedom protected by the First Amendment of the American Constitution—is indeed the very cornerstone of our democracy; an America without it would be unthinkable," wrote two crusaders of the antismoking movement.[13] "This kind of zealous defense of the First Amendment is commendable, but in the context of tobacco advertising it is terribly misguided." They argued:

> Commercial speech is entitled to a far different standard of constitutional protection from the forms of speech that are classically protected by the First Amendment for the purpose of preserving political liberty.
>
> There is an excellent reason for according more constitutional protection to political speech than to commercial speech. The former relates to ideas, and it would be anathema to have the government tell us what ideas we may believe or listen to. We allow Nazis and Communists to speak because we know it is not possible to draw lines in deciding what are "good" and "bad" ideas. Even the most hated ideas must be tolerated to make sure that all ideas will always enjoy free expression. But commercial speech is not principally, if at all, intended to use or convey ideas. Rather, it is used to sell products and services. Although we do not want the government to protect us from "dangerous or unhealthy ideas," it is a fundamental duty of government to protect people from dangerous or unhealthy products. That is why it is perfectly consistent for the Constitution to prohibit Congress from passing any laws restricting freedom of speech while specifically authorizing Congress to regulate commerce, including advertising.

"Smoking is acceptable because smoking has been accepted by many individuals as a satisfying activity. Tobacco advertising is a result, not a cause, of that acceptance," argued the International Advertising Association:[14]

> When manufacturers of perfectly legal products are banned from advertising in certain media—or even from advertising at all—a completely different situation arises. It is the start of a process of restriction on the free flow of

[11] Julia Carol, "Cigarettes Advertisements and Youth," manuscript, Smoking Policy Institute Library, 1986.

[12] Philip Morris Company, *Annual Report,* 1986.

[13] Peter Hanauer and Michael Pertschuk, "Tobacco Advertising and the First Amendment," Smoking Policy Institute Library, 1986.

[14] "Tobacco and Advertising," a document prepared by the International Advertising Association, 1986.

competitive commercial information; a form of censorship which strikes at the very basis of a free economic society.

Many civil libertarians and advertising agencies flocked to the side of the cigarette companies, and nothing much came of a move to ban cigarette advertising and promotion completely. Paradoxically, while the cigarette companies vigorously defended their right to free speech, they were not entirely tolerant of dissenters, as the following story from *Time* illustrates:[15]

> Another victim of the smoking war retired from the field last week, this one suffering from an $84 million wound. The problem began when Northwest Airlines began to air TV ads announcing that smoking would soon be banned on all its domestic flights. During the commercial, the camera pans across passengers in the Northwest cabin, stopping to focus on a solitary smoker. When an announcer's voice proclaims the smoking ban, the passengers en masse — except for the smoker — burst into applause.
>
> Edward Horrigan, the vice chairman of RJR Nabisco, the tobacco and food giant, had a very different reaction as he watched the commercial. Considering his company's heavy involvement in cigarette manufacturing (among its brands: Camel, Winston, and Salem), Horrigan was annoyed by Northwest's tough stand against smokers. But he was enraged to learn that the spot had been created by Saatchi & Saatchi DFS Compton, the advertising agency that handled many of RJR's most familiar consumer staples, including Oreo and Fig Newton cookies and Life Savers candies.
>
> Two top RJR executives were dispatched to Saatchi's lower Manhattan headquarters to deliver some devastating news: RJR was firing Saatchi outright, snatching away in one swoop $84 million in annual billings and abruptly ending an 18-year business relationship. The action dramatically demonstrated, if anyone had

doubts, that the tobacco companies still wield considerable clout in the public debate about smoking. RJR executives clearly regarded Saatchi's Northwest ad as an affront to the firm's basic — and most profitable — business.

2. Wealth Is Not Health

"Like the North American manufacturers of another dangerous product (asbestos), the American tobacco industry has been trying, successfully, to expand in overseas (and not just Third-World) markets to offset a decline in sales at home," wrote *The Economist*.[16] Explaining the U.S. cigarette companies' efforts to break into export markets, the article added:

> The cigarette companies' first attempts to break into the Japanese market went up in smoke. Between 1981 and 1985, the Japanese reduced the import tariff on foreign cigarettes from 90 percent to 20 percent and, at the same time, slapped on a retail tax equivalent to 41 percent of the selling price of American cigarettes. During that time, despite $200 million spent on what is called "product development" and promotion in Japan, the Americans' market share rose from only 1.2 percent to 2 percent. That was when the tobacco industry called on its friends at the White House and in Congress to put pressure on the Japanese to open up its markets. . . .
>
> Japan has always been lax on cigarette advertising, particularly on television, and low-key on the health risks. Packets carry the innocuous, "For your health, don't smoke too much." But Japan Tobacco, Inc., a virtual monopoly before 1980, observed a voluntary limit on its television advertising not to encourage adolescents and women to smoke. In the early 1980s, 63 percent of Japanese men smoked, but only 12 percent of women did; in South Korea the figures were 68 percent and 7 percent; and in Hong Kong 37 percent and 5 percent. To the tobacco companies those disparities represent

---

[15] "All Fired Up over Smoke," *Time*, April 18, 1988, pp. 64–75.

[16] "The Trade Liberalization's Dark Shadow," *The Economist*, March 26, 1988. Copyright © 1988 The Economist Newspaper Group, Inc. Reprinted with permission.

millions of potential female customers who do not smoke. In 1987, in America, 27 percent of adult males smoked, and 24 percent of women.

The Americans brought a cigarette advertising boom to Japan. Advertisements are now frequently screened during family and children's shows, at times which would be illegal in America. . . .

Cigarette advertising, now second in value only to that for drink in Japan, seems to work. American cigarettes' market share in Japan has risen from 2 percent in 1985 to around 11 percent, worth around $3 billion in export revenues. It is still climbing. A recent survey showed that 17 percent of Japanese female college students now smoke, while only 3 percent of their mothers do.

Echoing the same theme, an article in the *National Journal* questioned, "Should the federal government's health policies jibe with its trade stance on tobacco?" The article continued:[17]

> After the first Surgeon General's report on smoking issued in January 1964, the American industry responded by expanding operations in Latin America. According to Philip L. Shepherd, an expert in Latin American tobacco marketing in Florida International University in Miami, U.S. cigarette companies "conquered the Latin market in three steps." After first breaking down the barriers that restricted the sale of foreign brands, U.S. firms saturated Latin consumers with advertising. Finally, Shepherd said, after carving out a niche in the market, the U.S. companies "began to buy out and take over most of the national cigarette firms in Latin America."
>
> According to industry critics, the principal cigarette producers, including Philip Morris International, R. J. Reynolds International, Inc., and American Tobacco, hope to repeat their

Latin American successes in Asia because the potential profits in the region are enormous. At a time when fewer than 30 percent of American males smoke, the rate is 63 percent for Japan and 70 percent for China; these figures make Japan the highest per capita and China the highest gross consumers of cigarettes on the planet.

> Industry spokesmen deny that American manufacturers are ramming tobacco down Asians' throats. "We are just striving to do as well there [in Asia] as we do in the United States and in Europe," said Donald Harris, director of communications for Philip Morris. "I would just point out that Japan, South Korea, and Taiwan are all producing cigarettes with no outside rivals. We're not out to convert [nonsmokers]; we're out to compete."
>
> Washington's negotiators, echoing the stance taken by the major tobacco houses and lobbying firms, say they view tobacco exports as principally an economic issue. "All we are asking is for equal treatment. We've been quite consistent on that point," said Peter F. Allgeir, assistant U.S. trade representative for Asia and the Pacific. "We are ready to abide by any and all laws as long as they apply to the domestic brands."
>
> According to Judith L. Mackay, the executive director of the Hong Kong Council on Smoking and Health, the trend toward franchising has already established what is essentially a "double standard of quality" in the Philippines and Indonesia. Popular brands produced by American firms in these countries have been found to have double and triple the average tar content of cigarettes manufactured in the United States, according to studies released by the Toronto-based Addiction Resources Center.
>
> "We are sending a message that Asian lungs are more expendable than American ones," said Representative Atkins, a member of the Foreign Affairs Subcommittee on Asian and Pacific Affairs. "Our government should not be bending over backwards to promote a product that we have *proved* leads to thousands of premature deaths every year." Atkins said that he and Levine are drafting legislation that would, among other things, require cigarette

---

[17] "When Health and Trade Policies Don't Jibe," *National Journal,* April 18, 1988. Copyright © 1988 by National Journal Inc. All Rights Reserved. Reprinted by permission.

manufacturers to comply with the safety restrictions "of the country of origin." Such legislation would require all exported U.S. cigarettes to carry warning labels; it could also prohibit U.S. tobacco houses from advertising their wares on foreign television.

In a related move, as an institutional investor in tobacco company stocks, Harvard University's Advisory Committee on Shareholder Responsibility wrote the following to its corporate committee, which was in charge of managing the university's funds.[18]

Harvard's traditional view is that companies in which we own stock should consider the social consequences of their activities. Given the medical data about cigarette smoking, a company engaged in that business must give serious thought to the health consequences of their profit-seeking efforts. As to cigarettes, it is possible to argue that the United States and many other industrialized countries have addressed the issues as a matter of democratic decision. The United States, for example, bans some advertising, taxes the product heavily, engages in public education, and—perhaps most importantly (though with disputed effectiveness)— insists that health warnings appear on packages and in advertising. In many underdeveloped countries, an overburdened political process has not effectively addressed the health consequences of cigarette smoking. There is little public education about the consequences of smoking, and government does not require warning notices. These countries are the large growth market for cigarette sales. Indeed, some analysts expect sales to fall in industrialized countries in the period ahead.

We believe that companies seeking to expand sales in the Third World should address in a serious way the social consequences of their actions. We think they should tell stockholders their reasons for not placing advertisements on packages and health warnings similar to those required in Europe and the United States.

. . . All "truth" and "knowledge" can be questioned, but at a given time in history some "facts" are regarded as proved according to the legitimate standards. We believe there is no reputable doubt that cigarette smoking contributes to cancer and heart disease. We therefore believe that a company selling cigarettes must consider its ethical responsibilities on the assumption that use of the product contributes to disease. For example, a cigarette company should consider whether it has a duty to inform buyers of health risks even in nations that do not impose a requirement of such warnings by law.

Some members of our committee also believe that Harvard, which refuses to own stock in some companies because it does not wish to be associated with particular economic activities (gambling, prostitution), should consider placing the production and sale of cigarettes in that category.

3. Of Mice and Men

In June 1988, the antismoking campaign claimed its first major legal victory in years. After the tobacco industry had beaten back over 300 smoker-death suits since the 1950s, without a single dime in damages, a jury awarded $400,000 to Antonio Cipollone, whose wife Rose died of lung cancer in 1984 after 40 years of heavy smoking. The following report concerning the award appeared in the *Boston Globe*.[19]

A federal jury in New Jersey last night dealt the tobacco industry a profound setback by finding, for the first time ever, that a cigarette company was liable for the death of a smoker. . . . It said Liggett, which produced the Chesterfield and L&M filter brands that Mrs. Cipollone smoked, misled the public through advertisements that portrayed its products as safe when it knew otherwise. . . .

Jurors said Mrs. Cipollone bore 80 percent of the responsibility for her own death.

---

[18] *Harvard Gazette,* October 28, 1988.

[19] "$400,000 Awarded in Death of Smoker," *Boston Globe,* June 14, 1988.

"The myth of invulnerability that protected the tobacco industry has been shattered," said Richard Daynard, a professor at Northeastern University Law School and a critic of smoking. "People now know tobacco companies can be held as accountable in a court of law as manufacturers of asbestos, Dalkon shields, and other dangerous products.

"There are going to be a tremendous number of cases filed as a result of this. . . . It is hard for me to see how the tobacco companies can cover the eventual expenses," said Daynard.

But Charles Wall, one of 14 full-time attorneys for cigarette firms in the New Jersey case, remained upbeat: "The ruling means that the tobacco company has maintained its record in the major issues dealing with conspiracy and fraud and misrepresentation. The verdict for the defendants on those issues sends a clear message to plaintiffs and plaintiffs' lawyers that there is not going to be money found in suing tobacco companies."

Plaintiffs "spent $3 million and got back $400,000, which is a lousy return on investment," he added in a telephone interview.

Wall said damages assessed against Liggett were "a compromise. I think jurors felt they needed to give Mr. Cipollone some money, they felt anybody who spent $4\frac{1}{2}$ years preparing this case and four months trying it, deserves something . . . and I think this whole thing will be overturned on appeal."

This was only the fourth smoking suit in recent years to reach a jury. But the Cipollone case was different: The widower's lawyers introduced secret tobacco company documents they said proved the firms had conspired and lied by proclaiming their products as safe when they were fully aware of the risks.

The case also had dramatic overtones: Mrs. Cipollone, who was 58, died a year after the suit was filed. Her husband, then 64, promised her he would carry on the fight. And this was the first case decided since Surgeon General C. Everett Koop reported a month earlier that cigarettes can be as addictive as heroin and cocaine.

What differentiated the Cipollone case from the 321 suits brought since 1954 was that the prior cases had been unable to demonstrate the industry's negligence in informing smokers about health risks. As a result, the cases rested on the individual's right to smoke and the personal responsibility associated with making that decision. The evidence in this case, according to antismoking activists, was "the first to suggest that the tobacco companies long ago privately acknowledged what they continue to deny—that is, that smoking is linked to cancer."[20] In a terse exchange, during the trial, the lawyers for the plaintiff questioned Mr. Kinsley Dey, Jr., Liggett's president, regarding an experiment in the early 1950s, where the company's researchers smeared the shaven backs of mice with tars from the cigarettes' condensed smoke. Cancerous tumors had sprouted on the mice's backs as a result.

Lawyer

What was the purpose of this?

Mr. Dey

To try to reduce tumors on the backs of mice.

Lawyer

It is nothing to do with the health and welfare of human beings? Is that correct?

Mr. Dey

That's correct.

Lawyer

How much did that study cost?

Mr. Dey

A lot. . . . Probably between $15 million and more.

Lawyer

And this was to save rats, right, or mice? You spend all this money to save mice the

---

[20] "Of Mice and Men," *The Economist,* April 16, 1988.

problem of developing tumors? Is that correct?

Mr. Dey

I've stated that we did.

4. In Search of a Target

R. J. Reynolds launched "Premier," a smokeless cigarette on October 1, 1988, in three test markets: St. Louis, Missouri, and Phoenix and Tucson, Arizona. The price per pack was about 30 cents higher than other cigarettes. The central advertising message was "Premier — the Cleaner Smoke." Marketing analysts speculated that R. J. Reynolds selected the test markets because the demographics in these cities indicated that they had numerous older, sophisticated smokers who might be trying to seek an alternative to quitting smoking. Antismoking activists and public health officials had denounced the new product as an attempt to numb the public to the dangers of smoking. They protested that the product went to market without being tested or approved by the Food and Drug Administration. Cigarettes were exempt from FDA regulations, except where health-related advertising claims were concerned. FDA, however, did regulate medical devices, and critics claimed that Premier was nothing but an instrument to vaporize nicotine, an addictive drug in cigarettes.

Much to the delight of the antismoking lobby, R. J. Reynolds announced on March 1, 1989, that it was officially withdrawing the brand from all test markets. The cigarette company said in a statement that "while smokers are very interested in the concept, the current product has not achieved adequate consumer acceptance."[21]

In January 1990, R. J. Reynolds attempted launching yet another new brand, "Uptown," targeted at blacks. The company chose the Uptown name because it scored highest on consumer surveys. The company planned to package the cigarettes with filters facing down instead of up because market research showed that many blacks opened cigarette packs from the bottom. Under attack from U.S. Secretary of Health and Human Services Louis Sullivan, the company abandoned its plans for the product launch. Sullivan had protested, "Uptown's message is more disease, more suffering, and more death for a group already bearing more than its share of smoking-related illness and mortality."

Newsweek, March 5, 1990, reported on R. J. Reynolds' plans for yet another new product, "Dakota."

> Last week, a marketing proposal leaked anonymously to an antismoking group revealed that Reynolds seemed to have another target in its sights: young (age 18–24), white, working-class women.
>
> Dubbed "virile females" in a campaign recommended by a marketing agency, these are among society's most vulnerable women — and most apt to fall for the new cigarette, to be called Dakota. With little education, they work in entry-level service or factory jobs and enjoy going to hot-rod and Monster Truck events with their boyfriends, according to the marketing plan.
>
> Oriented firmly in the present, they're unlikely to have absorbed information about smoking's long-term health risks to themselves — and, if pregnant, to their unborn.
>
> A cigarette company executive summarized her reactions: "Target market selection and segmentation form the basic building blocks of the marketing concept. What we are doing is what any sensible marketeer would do!"

What's All This Fuss about, Anyway?

"People who choose to gamble with their health should at least be required to cover their own bets. Otherwise, it's very difficult to take seriously all this thumb-sucking about 'soaring health costs,'" contend the nonsmokers.

---

[21] "Smokeless Cigarette Test Turns to Ashes," *Boston Globe,* March 1, 1989.

Consequently, there was a concerted effort to increase the excise tax from about 32 cents a pack to 48 cents a pack. At an average price of about $1.35/packet, that would represent a net price increase of a little over 10 percent. Some have argued that such an increase would encourage about 2 million persons to quit smoking or not to start. This was based on the price elasticities projected for the various age groups. The number of smokers in the 12- to 17-year group it was estimated would decline by 15 percent, the 18- to 19-year group by 9 percent, and the rest by about 4 percent. Some economists, however, opposed the idea of "sin" taxes because they unfairly punish the poor. They raise the question, "Why tax so heavily adult smokers who mainly harm themselves?" Nonsmokers, of course, reply, "Because taxpayers end up paying for it." The following excerpts from a scholarly article attempt to resolve this question of how much smokers really cost the rest of society.[22]

> Is there any way to associate a monetary value, an "economic worth," to the enhanced life expectancy that comes from quitting in time or from not smoking in the first place?
>
> There are two ways to formulate this question. They are sometimes called the prevalence approach and the incidence approach. The prevalence approach asks the question, what are the current annual costs inflicted on society, or on the economy, by the lifetime smoking practices of people who will be hospitalized this year, will be absent from work, or will die because of the consequences of current smoking. The incidence approach, on the other hand, examines the projected costs of hospitalization and other medical care, excess absenteeism, and premature death on account of current smoking practices.
>
> The first impact is the easiest to determine. Consider the smokers who lose more days of

work per year on account of illness than if they did not smoke. This results in lost production to the economy, unless employers can take up the slack with people who would otherwise work less or be unemployed; but most of what is lost to production is matched by the lost earnings of the workers. While nobody these days consumes exactly what he produces in a physical sense, most people and their families consume correspondingly more or less as their incomes go up or down. So the loss to the economy, or to the gross national product, lies mainly in the lost earnings, and, hence, consumption by those whose work schedules are impaired by their health. We may care about them and their consumption, just as we may care whether they die, but the cost falls on the economy mainly in the sense that they are themselves part of the economy. [Hence, under the prevalence approach, according to the author, there is no burden on society.]

> A particular simple illustration [of the incidence approach] can be built around an unmarried male who has cancer of the lung diagnosed at the median age for lung cancer diagnosis, age 65. He has—in the absence of his lung cancer—an average life expectancy of 16 years; he dies within the year and would, on average, have lived another 15. The average 65-year-old man has already retired. He draws $6,000 from a pension fund, and has some savings that yield interest or dividends, or possibly, a very modest home on which all mortgage payments have been completed. [The fraction of the labor force covered by private or government pension funds is well over half; the fraction of retired people drawing pension is smaller, but rising rapidly.] Had he lived, he would have paid $1,000 or $1,500 in federal and state income taxes and had $11,000 or $12,000 per year to spend. Dead, he relinquishes his claim to his Social Security and any retirement annuity. These are the transfers that he would have drawn had he lived. Discounting 15 years of these transfers at 6 percent yields a present value in excess of $100,000. The discounted value of his Social Security alone is $60,000. This, together with any financial assets or equity in his home, is what he leaves behind when he

[22] Thomas C. Schelling, "Economics and Cigarettes," *Preventive Medicine* 15(1986), pp. 549–60.

dies. In effect, he leaves a bequest of over $100,000 present value.

The idea that people who smoke and die 15 years early are net financial benefactors to the rest of society, by living most of a normal productive tax-paying life and dying before they can claim their retirement benefits, is momentarily surprising and somewhat paradoxical. But, we must not reverse the conclusion. If we begin by thinking that smokers in the aggregate inflict costs on the rest of us, and that is the reason why we should encourage them to quit or penalize them financially, then discovering that those who die leave behind more than they take from us might seem to suggest that we should happily let them smoke and relieve us of supporting them in their old age. But that would be a perverse and unnatural conclusion.

Not only was there increasing evidence that smokers were benefactors, not debtors, to society, but more recently questions had been raised regarding the net gain in life expectancy that would result as a consequence of a smoke-free society:[23]

> While decreasing age-adjusted death rates, the demise of tobacco use would alter the relative mix of diseases. Chronic obstructive lung disease, currently a major source of death and disability, would become relatively inconsequential, while other pulmonary diseases, including influenza and pneumonia in the elderly, might become more common.
>
> The dramatic decrease in lung cancers that would follow the demise of tobacco use undoubtedly would cause the age-adjusted cancer death rate to fall significantly, although it might be accompanied by increases in the [later] incidence of other cancers.
>
> While there is little evidence to support it, a second posited undesirable health consequence of the tobacco-free society might be substitution of other stress responses, including

deleterious habits ranging from alcohol or drug abuse to excessive consumption of food. The latter would bring the smoking-eating relationship full circle. . . . The net effect of freeing society from all the mortality caused by tobacco use would be life-expectancy increase of one to two years. To the lay public, this may not sound like much of a gain; to demographers and others familiar with vital statistics, it is dramatic.

A provocative article recently suggested that "drinking," not "smoking," should be the focus of society's demarketing efforts. The authors of that article concluded:[24]

> On balance, smokers probably pay their way at the current level of excise taxes on cigarettes; but one may, nonetheless, wish to raise those taxes to reduce the number of adolescent smokers. In contrast, drinkers do not pay their way: current excise taxes on alcohol cover only about half the costs imposed on others.

Echoing this viewpoint, a *Boston Globe* editorial argued:[25]

> Smoking does not cause people to rob their neighbors to support the habit, nor beat their spouses or children in a mood-altering frenzy, nor drive crazily, nor aid international drug cartels. Smoking does not endanger neighborhoods or contribute to street crime, clog courts, or fill prisons. Smoking does not take over a person's life to the exclusion of all else.
>
> Part of the popularity of antismoking crusades is based on smokers, despite their perverse habit, being otherwise rational and, therefore, generally more responsive to criticism than alcoholics and drug addicts are.
>
> For the right reasons, smokers should stop. But that goal is not advanced by equating smoking with drug abuse or alcohol abuse, nor should it divert attention from those ruinous addictions.

---

[23] Kenneth E. Warner, "Health and Economic Implications of a Tobacco-Free Society," *Journal of American Medical Association,* October 16, 1987 (vol. 258, no. 15).

[24] Willard G. Manning and others, "The Taxes of Sin: Do Smokers and Drinkers Pay Their Way?" *JAMA,* March 17, 1989 (vol. 261, no. 11).

[25] "The Smoking Equation," *Boston Globe,* May 19, 1988.

The Health Police Are Blowing Smoke

"Bolstered by bad science, the war on passive smoking is a trial run for a larger program of social manipulation," argued Bruce Biggs, writing in *Fortune*.[26] The article added:

> The war against smoking is turning into a "jihad" against people who smoke. Smokers are being exiled from public and private places and are facing discrimination in employment. The reason, we are told, is that tobacco is deadly not only to users, but also to innocents exposed to its noxious fumes.
>
> The truth is that America is suffering an epidemic of politically motivated hypochondria. Not only the liberty of smokers is threatened. Three decades ago the U.S. Public Health had apparently defeated its statutory enemy, communicable diseases, and decided to preserve itself by policing our private health. Smoking was the first target — a trial run in social manipulation. Sniffing victory in this skirmish, the feds are now turning their weapons on drinking, eating, and sex.
>
> But, you sputter, isn't the evidence conclusive that my smoke affects your health? Let me introduce you to the basics of scam science as generated for the feds. Smoking will be the example because it is the test case; but much of this mode of argumentation will be familiar to victims of the pollution, radiation, and toxic scams. All have their roots in the ambitions of the Public Health Service.
>
> Note first the duplicitous use of words: Toxic means poisonous, but does not specify at what dose. Everything is toxic if ingested in sufficient quantity. This magazine is toxic — eat enough copies and you will get sick. Anyone who describes a substance as toxic, without stating the dose level is engaging in flimflam; e.g., the Surgeon General informing us that cigarette smoke is "toxic." . . .
>
> Here's how the drill works: a toxie gets a government grant to terminate rats by all but drowning them in a suspect compound. He reports that whatzatapyrene is "carcinogenic." Because of the no-threshold principle, the feds can tell the public that "no safe dose level has been established." Next an epie gets a bigger grant to conduct a body count. He discovers that of 87,000 watzat workers over 30 years, 46 succumbed to cancer. But the epie has calculated 22.7 "expected" deaths of the cancer in a comparable normal group, so the relative risk of whatzatapyrene exposure is 2.03. The feds tell the press that whatzateers are "twice as likely to get cancer."
>
> Although the Public Health Service has been reticent about publicizing the fact, every study cited in support of the statement that "cigarette smoking causes cancer" reveals that a smoker is thoroughly unlikely to get cancer — only that he is statistically more likely to get it than a nonsmoker. No one can say precisely how much more likely.
>
> Perhaps this is why people continue to smoke despite the increasingly shrill scoldings they are subject to. So lately the feds have escalated the war. Their most ingenious weapon for converting private health into public health is the "determination" that second-hand smoke — or passive smoking, or in fed parlance environmental tobacco smoke (ETS) — harms the public at large. . . .
>
> More to the point, no industry is immune to the ravages of scam science. The feds are now trying to ban tobacco advertising in its surviving form. As the Surgeon General has said, "There is no safe cigarette." And no such thing as a safe automobile, a safe food, or a safe airline flight, or a safe ski, or safe cosmetic, or a safe condom. Nothing is safe as long as the authorities define private health as public health.

---

[26] Bruce B. Biggs, "The Health Police Are Blowing Smoke," *Fortune*, April 25, 1988. © 1988 Time Inc. All rights reserved.

THE INDIVIDUAL AND THE CORPORATION

In the 1830s, Alexis de Tocqueville, seeking to describe the social philosophy of the United States, put heavy emphasis on the new nation's reliance on individualism. He said, "Individualism is a novel expression, to which a novel idea has given birth." By the latter part of the same century, the rapid industrialization of the United States had contributed to the rise of large and increasingly powerful units of economic activity. As new and more complex forms of organization developed in all sectors of life, John D. Rockefeller was led to comment, "Individualism is gone, never to return."

This case concerns one aspect of the relationship between individuals and organizations. Its focus is on the problems that arose when a senior executive of a company wrote an article for a national magazine. The case information came from (1) Donald L. Singleton; (2) annual reports of Summit Petroleum, *Look* magazine, and other published sources; and Lawrence J. Mangum, a senior editor of *Look* magazine. All figures in the case are disguised. It will be evident from the material below that the case does not present the points of view of all the parties involved in the series of events described.

The Company

In the mid-1950s, a European-based oil company established a company called Summit Petroleum, Inc., in the United States. According to the new company's first annual report, Summit represented the European company's

This case was prepared by the late Professor John B. Matthews of the Harvard Business School.

Copyright © 1967 by the President and Fellows of Harvard College.

Harvard Business School, case 368-018 (Revised 1984).

first venture in the United States. Control was assured through ownership of more than 50 percent of the stock of Summit. Corporate headquarters was established in a large eastern city and operating offices were set up in Dallas, Texas. The latter were later to become Summit Petroleum of Texas.

Summit began actual operations after merging with another oil company. Within a short time, the company had a refinery, substantial resources of oil and natural gas, several thousand acres of undeveloped leaseholds, and over 200 gasoline stations located in four southwestern states.

The company continued to expand, both internally and through acquisitions, in subsequent years. The Summit trademark became increasingly well known in the Southwest and adjacent areas of the United States. By 1959, Summit had nearly 1,800 filling stations, and annual sales were approaching $70,000,000, including several billion cubic feet of natural gas. Most Summit retail gasoline stations were run by independent operators and supplied by independent jobbers; but in some cases, expansion was accelerated by the lease of company-owned stations to independent operators.

By the time the 1960 annual report was issued, Summit operated in nearly 20 states and had over 2,000 filling stations. Sales had increased more than 6 percent over 1959, as compared to an increase in consumer demand of approximately 1 percent in Summit's marketing territories. The annual report stated that "The effective advertising and sales promotion programs initiated in 1958 have been responsible in large measure for expanding consumer acceptance of [Summit] products." Although total company sales dipped slightly in 1962, gasoline sales reached an all-time high. In 1963, the acquisition of another oil company almost doubled the company's facilities, gave it an entry into petrochemicals, and added more than 1,000 retail gasoline stations. Many of the latter were immediately converted to Summit colors and station signs. By the end of 1963, the annual reports indicated, in brief, that net income had grown to almost $4.5 million in the comparatively short period of Summit's life, while gross operating income was over $150 million.

The Individual

The Dallas Morning News of April 17, 1964, carried a brief story stating that Summit Petroleum of Texas had confirmed the resignation of Mr. Donald L. Singleton from the Summit organization. The story identified Mr. Singleton as the senior vice president in charge of marketing, refining, pipelines, transportation, and crude oil purchasing for Summit of Texas, and as a vice president and member of the board of directors of Summit Petroleum, Inc. Mr. Singleton had joined the Texas company in Dallas in 1957 as marketing manager. In 1958, he became vice president for marketing of all refined products. By 1962, he had become the senior vice president of the Texas firm. In addition, from 1960 through 1963, the annual reports of Summit Petroleum, Inc., listed Mr. Singleton as vice president of marketing and a member of the board.

Donald Singleton was born in Santa Barbara, California, in 1922 where his father was a sales manager for an oil company in the Los Angeles area. After attending high school at St. Joseph's Academy, Singleton went to St. Mary's College and later transferred to the University of Washington. He graduated in 1943 as a foreign trade major. During his college career, Singleton served as business manager of the university's daily newspaper, belonged to the naval ROTC, and managed a filling station. On subsequent active duty with the U.S. Navy, he saw action in the Southwest Pacific and the Philippine Islands, was wounded, and received a Bronze Star.

At the end of World War II, Singleton decided to go into business for himself. He returned to the Philippines and set up an import-export business. The business prospered, reaching an annual volume of $12 million within a six-year period. Singleton and his wife then decided to return to the United States. Their oldest boy was ready for school, and the Singletons preferred an American school. Mr. Singleton also preferred to develop his business career in the United States. Using part of the proceeds from the sale of his import-export business, he established a firm in California that specialized in financing home builders. In addition, after a few months, he decided to enter the oil business. He set up the Singleton Oil Company, became an independent distributor for a major oil company, and phased out his finance business.

Singleton's company doubled his supplier's volume in its territory. In addition, he introduced a line of tires, batteries, and accessories (TBA). Intrigued by the possibilities of innovation in the merchandising and marketing fields, he purchased some old school busses, renovated them, and turned them into "rolling stores" for his TBA lines. In less than three years, Singleton's TBA volume in his rolling stores was $150,000.

Singleton's interest in management and innovation led him to look for an expanding company whose resources and activities would permit a greater degree of experimentation and opportunity for progression. Summit Petroleum appeared to offer such an opportunity, and in 1957 he joined Summit as marketing manager, taking a $10,000 cut in income to join the company.

Singleton prospered at Summit. His family and personal background in oil jobbing helped him establish good working relationships with the company's independent jobbers and retailers, and he showed a flair for merchandising, promotion, and station design. He was especially interested in design and promotion. The Summit brand attained wide publicity, both in its area and throughout the oil industry, when Singleton developed a new approach in service station design. In a busy industrial section of Dallas, Summit put up a service station that consisted of separate islands offering gasoline, service, and customer facilities. Each island was distinguished by a 30-foot concrete tower of mushroom design. The customer island had a patio and rest areas, and Summit installed air conditioning, floor-to-ceiling drapes, oriental tile, and Florida red marble. The station received considerable attention in Dallas and was written up in a number of industry publications. Singleton had also been instrumental in the development of mobile self-powered service stations that offered "Summit a la Carte"; the stations were written up in *Fortune, Business Week,* and other magazines and trade papers.

Summit's Azure Ozone (fictitious name) advertising campaign was originated by Singleton. In the early 1960s, an additive war reflected the keen competition in the oil industry, as company after company introduced special additives to gasoline to gain competitive advantage. The first additives introduced by the major oil companies attained great prominence, but later ones did not because of conflicting claims and duplication. Singleton and Summit investigated the possibilities of an additive for Summit gasoline. Singleton decided, however, that the use of an additive would be prohibitively expensive, and would be only another me-too type of promotion. In his opinion, the industry suffered from too much "me-too-ism" in its advertising and promotion.

As a result, Singleton developed the idea of spoofing gasoline additives as a promotional technique. Together with Summit's advertising agency, he worked out a campaign. The general idea of the promotion was that Summit gasoline had all the additives a car could possibly use. So did all the other Summit products, with the exception of the air that Summit stations put in customers' tires. Summit would, therefore, get to work immediately on the ultimate additive and, under the Summit Five-Year Plan, have Azure Ozone available for tires on May 12, 1966; the time was set for 4:30 in the afternoon of that day, because some Summit trucks "don't get around until late in the afternoon." In the meantime, "to help customers through the difficult withdrawal period from regular air, Summit offered azure balloons, azure valve caps, azure asphalt, azure credit cards (for special customers), and Azure Air Room Freshener." The latter was also promoted and sold by a Dallas department store and achieved national publicity.

The Azure Ozone campaign was concentrated in newspaper advertisements throughout Summit's marketing area and aided by various kinds of promotion at the service station level. For example, azure-colored asphalt aprons were installed at some stations, and various contests and promotional devices were tied to the concept.

The Azure Ozone approach was praised in trade and advertising journals, and it was the least expensive major campaign ever conducted by the company. Consumers found its newness and gentle spoofing interesting. The trade recognized it as an effective promotional device, and it won a number of advertising awards. Singleton himself was in great demand as a speaker before oil industry and advertising media groups.

Thus, by the end of 1963, Summit's promotional campaigns had been extremely successful. Mr. Singleton's contributions to the company's marketing efforts had been substantial, and these and other accomplishments seemed attested to by the steady broadening of his responsibilities and his recognition by various industry journals. For example, in January 1954, *Southwest Advertising and Marketing* said:

Probably one of the reasons for Summit's phenomenal growth is its aggressive and imaginative young senior vice president [Donald L. Singleton]. Even though he is in direct charge of the company's major operations—refining, marketing, transportation, crude oil acquisition, and other departments—[Singleton] handles the company's advertising personally.

The Assassination of President Kennedy

On November 22, 1963, President John Kennedy was assassinated in Dallas. Lawrence J. Mangum (fictitious name), a senior editor of *Look* magazine, was sent from New York to cover the assassination and subsequent developments. Mangum talked to many prominent Dallas citizens, among them government, professional, and business leaders, and he was struck by what seemed to him to be an attitude of defensiveness about Dallas. Attacks on the city itself had not yet begun to appear in any volume, but many of those to whom Mangum talked seemed to him to behave and speak as if the city itself were in some way guilty of the presidential assassination and the shooting of Lee Harvey Oswald.

A few days after the assassination, Mr. Mangum met the president of the advertising firm that handled Summit's account. During a discussion of events in Dallas, the agency president suggested that Mangum ought to talk with "Don Singleton, an impressive young guy from the oil industry." He described Singleton as a man who had been a registered Republican in California, an Eisenhower supporter in 1952, a Stevenson man in 1956, and a registered Democrat in Texas "because there was no point in being anything else." The advertising executive said that Singleton had something on his mind, and that it was probably quite different from what Mangum had been encountering.

Singleton's *Look* Article

Mr. Mangum was favorably impressed by Don Singleton. At a dinner meeting, he found that Singleton had strong feelings about the president's death. Singleton showed Mangum a copy of a letter that he had sent to one of the two leading papers in Dallas, setting forth what he believed should be the city's sense of shame and suggesting that the city erect a suitable memorial to the late president. The letter had not been printed, and Singleton told Mangum that he believed this was because the Dallas papers chose to print only those communications that praised the city itself while condemning acts of violence as isolated events unrelated to its general atmosphere. At the time of his initial meeting with Mangum, Singleton and the advertising agency president were preparing a newspaper advertisement for which Singleton would pay the full cost—the ad would express his feelings about the loss of the president and his dissatisfaction with his own failure to act as a responsible member of the community, and suggest that Dallas itself should erect a memorial appropriate to the memory of Mr. Kennedy.

Mr. Mangum told the casewriter that he had said to Singleton that *Look* sometimes ran articles by nonprofessional writers. He had said that the odds were against publication, but that Singleton could prepare an article if he wished to do so. Singleton's reaction was favorable, and Mangum was impressed by what seemed to be Singleton's desire to help his city reassess its attitudes and actions.

As Mr. Singleton later described his activities to the casewriter, he wrote his article during the next two weeks, spending part of his time in a Dallas hotel. Although carrying on his responsibilities at Summit of Texas, he did not tell anyone at Summit of Texas or Summit Petroleum, Inc., about the article. He considered it a personal venture and the expression of a personal viewpoint that did not concern his company or his fellow employees. He emphasized that neither in the article nor in subsequent statements did he identify the name of his company. In conversations with his wife and Mangum, Singleton had indicated an awareness that the expression of his ideas might have some repercussions. Nevertheless, he went ahead with the preparation of the article. In statements made subsequent to the publication of his article, he said that two factors had prompted him to do so. In regard to President Kennedy, he said:

It wasn't just that I agreed with most of his policies and his plans for the future; it was his manner and his exuberance and his dignity which made our national government all the more exciting and important.

Singleton's other major reason had to do with Dallas:

I also believe strongly that open reasoned dialogue on any subject this side of perfection is more likely to produce good results than a monolithic "everything is fine, and even if it isn't don't stir things up" attitude. Before the assassination I was willing to go along with this mystique. . . . I think we should have not only expressed regret at the assassination of President Kennedy, but at the same time should have conceded that the past ugly incidents[1] may have encouraged extremist elements here. It is only human for many outsiders to suspect our motives when they hear nothing but disclaimers that anything at all has ever been amiss.

After Singleton finished his article, Mr. Mangum and his staff documented it.[2] The article was published in the March 24, 1964, issue of *Look.* Excerpts from it are reproduced below;

the omissions do not detract materially from the substance of the article, and in no case do they represent excisions of the author's ideas.

MEMO from a Dallas Citizen[3]

By Donald L. Singleton

We are rich, proud Dallas, "Big D" to Texas and we have never wanted a lesson in humility from any man. Not even from a murdered President of the United States. We have lived for three months with national tragedy, and I won't be popular for bringing this subject up now. But somebody must. To say nothing, more important, to do nothing, only says to the rest of the world that, as they have read, we shrugged the whole thing off.

* * * * *

. . . The tragedy would not go away. Day after day, I drove down to the slopes in front of the Texas School Book Depository, and always, no matter when I got there, or whether it rained or snowed, groups of people stood as at a shrine among the madonnas put up by children and the fresh flowers brought by nameless citizens. It still goes on. As I write this, not so much as a street, let alone a stone monument, has been dedicated to Kennedy, but the people have built their own memorial out of their patient presence.

Now, some of our ablest citizens have begun to understand that we can't make sense out of the future until we confront the past. Kennedy's death is a fact. I hope that out of our many arguments will come a memorial that is more than a statue. If we are to learn the lessons that President Kennedy came to teach, we must build a living, searching memorial. We could, for instance, buy the Texas School Book Depository, from which the fatal shots were fired, and rebuild it for a better purpose. It would become

---

[1] Singleton referred here to incidents involving Adlai Stevenson and Lyndon Johnson.

[2] In this context, the word *documented* refers to the process of checking on factual statements. For example, Mangum checked on the question of a Kennedy memorial in Dallas and learned there was strong sentiment for what he called a "modest marker" at the site of the assassination, with the bulk of the contributions going to the Kennedy Library in Boston, Massachusetts. An ad hoc commission had been established in Dallas to study the question of a fitting memorial.

---

a civic research center, under Southern Methodist University, dedicated to study of the urban evils that lead to violence and hatred.

*   *   *   *   *

. . . I think Dallas feels shame, not guilt. Many people here are ashamed to have been caught acting like fools—as they have been doing for many months—at the moment when the nation, and their President, needed the best they could give in thought, action and coherent criticism. He came to tell us so. Leaders must be guided by learning and reason, he planned to say, "or else those who confuse rhetoric with reality and the plausible with the possible will gain the popular ascendancy with their seemingly swift and simple solutions to every world problem." He never got to deliver his address, but his death, more than his life, shocked people out of the hysterics they had worked themselves into. Big D's penance for its silly years should lead to a meaningful memorial to its dead teacher. Or his death will be, for Dallas, in vain.

You had to live here in recent years to make sense out of today's confusion. None of us can claim to be blameless. For six years I have been helping build an oil business, a successful one, but at church, civic functions, and parties, I have sat on the sidelines like a foreign observer at a tribal rite. I even got so I didn't pay much attention to the "Impeach Earl Warren" stickers on the bumpers in my neighborhood. They were not, it seemed then, much more of an affectation than the genuine alligator cowboy boots and mink chaps worn by people who had every other luxurious distraction our nation can offer.

*   *   *   *   *

A Texan with a cause is formidable, and a Texan doing the work of the Lord is awesome. It was almost as if these people had set up a new religion. They put God aside, for the emergency. . . .

Outsiders make the mistake of thinking that the prominent businessmen of Dallas led the Birch chapters, the National Indignation Conference, and the other political equivalents of a college panty raid. Not so. The Dallas leaders,

the bankers, and businessmen who set up the Citizens Council are an intelligent and dedicated group. They have given the city an efficient government, an honest (if not always efficient) police force, a low tax rate, and a booming economy. But they view their leadership in a narrow sense. . . .

*   *   *   *   *

Then it happened. I was sitting over a eight-ounce steak at the Trade Mart, where the President was to speak. When the news came, the first reaction around my table was the one I heard over and over in the next few hours: "I hope the killer didn't come from Dallas." But Dallas was elected by Providence to stand in the hard light of tragedy.

I'll never forget the rest of that terrible day. At the first telephone booth, I called a business friend to cancel an appointment. The telephone operator was sobbing, so I comforted her. She said, "That wonderful man—why did it have to happen in Dallas?" Next, my friend's secretary said, "Oh, Mr. Singleton, I'm broken-hearted. It *must* have been somebody from out of town; nobody in Dallas would do such a thing." My friend said, "Well, they finally got what they wanted." He didn't have to explain to me—or anybody else in town—who he was talking about. I said, "Yes, but suppose it turns out to be a Communist or a Black Muslim?" His answer was loyal Dallasite: "Well, I sure as hell hope that whoever he is, he's from out of town".

*   *   *   *   *

Basically, I suppose, the things that are wrong with Dallas are the things that are wrong with a world whose technology has raced beyond man's ability to shape it to his needs. We know how to get a man into orbit, but we can't find a good way to get to and from work. We can teach machines to think, but not our children. We have shining cities that false-front for stinking, crime-breeding slums; only a very rich society could afford so much poverty. We develop the greatest communications medium mankind has ever dreamed of, and then devote it to trivia and violence. And so on: Make up your own list. It will do, as long as it does not just pass the blame to somebody else—the UN, Washington, the Communist conspiracy, anybody. We can't pass the buck. We have work to do.

In one sense, those who say, "It could have happened anywhere," are quite right. But somehow Big D doesn't derive much comfort from that, nor is it possible. For I'm afraid the record shows all too clearly that, in addition to having the world's ills, Dallas has managed to develop a few special complications. For all I know, other cities have our disease, too, but the epidemic broke out *here*. Maybe the President could have caught it anywhere, but he caught it *here*. Here is where the quarantine sign is, and I don't think it will ever really come down until we take it down ourselves.

Will we do it? The answer now is: maybe. Thousands of us are taking inventory of our civic faults. The assassination shocked us into our reappraisal, so our search for solutions should, in justice, be a memorial to the man who died here. A civic research center in Kennedy's name could bring the best minds to help us, to keep up the momentum of the work. It won't happen automatically. We still have many who want the whole thing to blow away in the next dust storm.

We need help. If you who don't live here will see the difference between the guilt we don't feel and the shame many of us *do* know, we can succeed. We can bring pride, a better pride, back to Dallas, and make the School Book Depository more than a murderer's sanctuary.

One thing is sure: Thanks to the world's searchlight, we have a magnificently illuminated operating room. Never again will we be able to see our city, its good and bad, as clearly as we do now. We have the opportunity, bought by a great man's life, to treat what ails Dallas and, maybe, the "anywhere" where it didn't happen.

Aftermath

Mr. Singleton told the casewriter that shortly after the March 24 issue of *Look* was published, the president of Summit of Texas and Singleton discussed the latter's article. For a few weeks thereafter, nothing further was said on the subject. Things were less quiet on other fronts, however. Singleton said that he received over 800 letters and 500 phone calls, about 90 percent of which praised his position. He did not know how many other letters or calls were received elsewhere in the company, but he believed that the number was large and that the balance of their sentiment was less favorable to him. He knew that a certain number of Summit's credit cards were returned to the company.

On Monday, April 13, another conversation took place between Singleton and Summit's Texas president. The next day, Singleton signed a statement of resignation, which he told the casewriter had been presented to him.

The parent company's board meeting was scheduled for mid-April. As a board member, Singleton had had hotel and plane reservations for some time. Because he was "physically and emotionally tired and thought that a trip might help me unwind," and "just to see what would happen," Singleton went East, but did not visit the board meeting. No one from Summit got in touch with him.

On April 14, the *Dallas Morning News* stated that Summit of Texas had confirmed Singleton's resignation. In a story dated April 17, *Advertising Age* carried the information that Summit's advertising agency had resigned the Summit account, which reportedly amounted to more than $750,000 of commissionable advertising. The story quoted the agency president:

> One of the few privileges you have in the agency field is deciding whose money you want to accept. We just decided that we didn't want Summit's any longer.

The casewriter learned that some time after Singleton's departure from Summit, he and Lawrence Mangum had looked back at the events and forces that might have been involved in his situation. They considered the

EXHIBIT 1 The Individual and the Corporation

Texas Press Clipping Bureau – Dallas

Borger, Texas
NEWS HERALD
(Cir. D. 9,805 S. 9,962)
March 13, 1964

Look Again

Look magazine, March 24, 1964, on page 88, gives us another one of those among us who have dared to disagree with the progress of socialists, communists, and the world government movement within our government.

The article, entitled, "MEMO from a Dallas Citizen," was written by [D.L. Singleton], a Dallas citizen. Mr. [Singleton] is Senior Vice President of the [Summit] Oil Company. His address is [   ], Dallas, Texas.

*   *   *   *   *

So Sorry!

When reading this *Look* magazine article by a Dallas citizen, [D.L. Singleton], it is hard to escape the impression that the author would have been a lot happier had the President, John F. Kennedy, been assassinated by someone among us who had dared to exercise the privilege as an American citizen, to disagree with the establishment, the communist-serving bureaucracy in Washington, D.C., instead of being killed, AS HE WAS, by an admitted communist.

Such hatred as reflected in this article graphically demonstrates why we, who are opposed to socialism, communism, and the loss of our national sovereignty to a world government, should thank God that the murderer of the President was immediately apprehended and as quickly identified as a member of the communist conspiracy.

Had he escaped, it is quite obvious that such unreasonable bitterness as revealed in this article could easily have resulted in either death or imprisonment for American patriots prominent in the conservative movement.

Without the guilty party in custody, it would have been much easier to have saddled the blame upon the conservatives or right-wing element among our citizens.

BUT THESE SMEAR WRITERS AND SPEAKERS NEVER QUIT TRYING!

*   *   *   *   *

Disappointed

Since November 22, when President John F. Kennedy was assassinated and Lee Harvey Oswald, who had applied for Russian citizenship, was apprehended as the accused slayer, the news media of this country has been flooded with articles and speeches designed to saddle part of the blame, if not all of the blame, for the assassination on our conservative people, termed rightists.

(Of course, we who oppose the establishment in Washington, D.C., are often described as members of the lunatic fringe.)

These writers and speakers actually seem disappointed that one of us, instead of a communist, HAD NOT killed our President.

reactions of suppliers, jobbers, and retailers. The two men knew that some criticisms had come from these sources, but they believed these had been substantially offset by favorable comments from the same sources.

The two men also thought about the reactions of the general public and the press. The range of such reactions is reflected in Exhibits 1–3. Although most of the letters received by Singleton himself had expressed support of his position, as indicated earlier, neither he nor Mangum could be certain about the volume of letters that might have been received elsewhere in the company.

The two had not agreed about the nature or strength of the reactions of members of the Citizens Council (referred to in the *Look* article), which is described in Exhibit 4. After Singleton's resignation became publicly known, Mangum talked to a number of prominent

---

EXHIBIT 2   The Individual and the Corporation

March ___, 1964

Dear Mr. [Singleton]:

I have just had an opportunity to read "MEMO from a Dallas Citizen" which was written by you and appeared in this month's *Look* magazine. The article was timely. It is excellent. It contains factual matter, most of which are matters of record. However, I am sure you realize that this article is going to call forth . . . your condemnation, with such statements that you are a socialist or communist. Some of them may even go so far as to apply to you the dirtiest word which these extreme rightists know; namely, a Democrat. I don't know what your politics are. I am still a Democrat regardless of the hard life one finds in Dallas.

You are well aware of the situation here. Like the members of your church not tolerating sermons that contradict their personal dogma, these [people] will not tolerate any idea that contradicts their personal ideas. For instance, the last sentence in your article implies that there is something "which ails Dallas." These citizens whom I am talking about will not admit that there is anything which ails Dallas. They are still teaching their children that our Federal Government is something to abhor and cuss, instead of pointing out to them the glories of our Government.

I am very hopeful that you own your own business . . . for you may be sure after the article they will do what they can to harm you in any way possible as their dogma and their philosophy cannot stand the light of day and you in this article are throwing a little light upon the ills of Dallas.

Congratulations again for this article, but I am afraid that it will not do Dallas much good because it will just go unheeded like the rest of the suggestions which have been made to cure the ills of Dallas. At least it is refreshing to know that men such as you live in Dallas and are willing to do whatever possible to try and make this city a better place in which to live even at the expense of having adverse criticism cast against you.

With kind regards, I am

Very sincerely,

(name deleted)

Dallas citizens, including several important members of the Citizens Council. All expressed regret at what happened to Singleton and emphasized that they had had nothing to do with the Singleton–Summit episode.

Singleton told the casewriter that he had been less certain than Mangum about the reactions of some of the other members of the

Citizens Council. He suspected that some of them had expressed dissatisfaction to Summit about his statements. He also knew that one member of the council, in making a speech in April, had said, "If Mr. Singleton would learn to know Dallas better, he would probably like it better. So much for the gratuitous defectors and journalistic buzzards that are still circling

---

EXHIBIT 3   The Individual and the Corporation

(The following is a reproduction of a letter that was sent to the president of Summit of Texas; a carbon of the letter was sent by its author to Mr. Singleton, and this reproduction comes from Mr. Singleton's carbon.)

April ___, 1964

Dear _____ :

I was delighted to read in the paper this morning of the resignation from your company of [Don Singleton]. If this is really a cover-up for your discharge of him or if it was due to pressure from you, I want to congratulate you. You will undoubtedly be charged with prejudice and hate by liberal eggheads of [Don Singleton's] persuasion; and, if so, I am sure it was not an easy decision from both your company and personal standpoint.

. . . I remain astounded that an executive of a sizeable public company such as yours would be so stupid as to make such an intemperate charge against his community as did [Singleton] in a national magazine. I am even more astounded by the conclusions drawn by him as expounded in the article, as he is close enough to the community to have felt the true nature of the feeling of this city. It indicates such a prejudice against conservative view as to indicate blindness towards the good things present in Dallas, or such a shallowness of observation as to render him useless for executive position.

Finally, . . . I have heard that [Singleton] did not consult the company management prior to the release of his article. This would be reason enough for the discharge of an executive of a public company, where the article in question could cause serious repercussions to the company. Such an act is simply rank insubordination.

Unfortunately, most news media are written by liberals, who have set the standard that liberals who disagree are merely forward-looking, while conservatives who disagree are vindictive haters. Please know that you have my wholehearted support.

Sincerely,

(name deleted)

cc: Mr. [D.L. Singleton]
     [Summit]

EXHIBIT 4   The Individual and the Corporation

The Dallas Citizens Council

The Dallas Citizens Council is a highly influential group of over 200 prominent businessmen. Membership is limited to company presidents or board chairmen, and the organization concerns itself with major problems or issues that involve the welfare of Dallas. In recent months, the Citizens Council has been the subject of much attention. For example:

> Every person interviewed stated without hesitation that Dallas leadership comes primarily from the business and financial sectors of the community. Throughout the interviews, no contradictory opinion was ever expressed (p. 31).

*   *   *   *   *

> In the initial interviews, . . . respondents stressed the role of a Dallas organization called the "Civic Committee" as having "moral control over what goes on here" than any other organization (p. 35). . . .

*   *   *   *   *

> The Committee as a body, they explained, meets officially only once a year, while the directors meet regularly. Whenever a serious problem arises in the city, the board may be convened quickly to decide what action should be taken.

The power of the organization was described by one of the respondents in this way:

> Why, the Board of Education would not think if proposing any bond issue, or doing anything without first clearing it with the Civic Committee. This body has the power to make or break any idea or proposal that certain groups may come up with. It is such a powerful group that nothing can succeed without its support (p. 37). . . .
>
> . . . recent decision to combine many charity campaigns into a United Fund drive. Other problems included the financial difficulties of the symphony orchestra and of the city-owned zoo, inadequate housing for Negroes, getting a "good slate" of nominees for school board elections, (and getting them elected), juvenile delinquency, school integration, and urban renewal. The range of problems in which the more influential leaders become involved seems unlimited (p. 59). . . .

*   *   *   *   *

> . . . The Civic Committee. . . functions as a mechanism for coordinating efforts of the various groups and interests within the community concerned with the particular problem at issue. . . . The leaders emphasized, however, that the board of the Civic Committee does not, itself, make decisions. Rather, it is the individual leaders who make the decisions. They use the organization as a tool for mobilizing verbal and financial support for their ideas (p. 61).*

*   *   *   *   *

* These quotations are taken from Carol Estes Thometz, *The Decision Makers, the Power Structure of Dallas,* (Dallas: Southern Methodist University Press, 1963) pp. 31, 35, 37, 59, and 61. Mrs. Thometz's book began as a master's thesis at Brandeis University and was later expanded and revised into book form. The Citizens Council to which Singleton's article refers is presumably the book's Civic Committee.

EXHIBIT 4 *(concluded)*

Fortune also commented on the Citizens Council in an article that discussed the general question of business's leadership role in Dallas:†

* * * * *

... this (Dallas) world would not have survived had it not had many positive qualities—the quality of action, of dynamism, the quality of community service and of high (if localized) morality. And it is this strange mix of the negative and positive that has come to characterize the business leaders of Dallas. Mostly self-made men, they nevertheless place public service above wealth as the supreme symbol of status; the people with the highest standing in Dallas are not necessarily the richest, but those who do the most for the community.

* * * * *

The nine most powerful men in Dallas, the inner circle of its business leadership, have many characteristics in common, including a high degree of individualism. All are directors of the unofficial but omnipotent Citizens Council, four having served as president. ... Of the eight who are college graduates, only three took degrees outside of Texas. Collectively, the power of these men is enormous; it reaches into every phase of life in Dallas, social, political, cultural, and economic.

* * * * *

Probably not one Dallasite out of five has any real idea of the power and purpose of this 27-year-old organization. Its membership of 250 maximum is by invitation only and perpetuates the original conception that none but the chief executive officers of the city's biggest corporations—men with the power to say "yes" or "no" to a project and have it binding on the enterprises they head—be invited.

* * * * *

In addition to the work of this organization, the influence of the business leadership is brought to bear on every aspect of community life through interlocking directorates or trusteeships.

† Richard A. Smith, "How Business Failed Dallas," *Fortune,* July 1964, p. 157.

our town. Don't waste your breath lashing back."[4] In any case, Singleton had no reason to suspect any organized activity on the part of the council.

As Singleton himself looked back on what had happened after the publication of his article, he said:[5]

---

[4] Reported in the *Dallas Morning News,* April 15, 1964.

[5] This quotation from Mr. Singleton has been taken from an article entitled "MEMO about a Dallas Citizen," *Look,* August 11, 1964, p. 64, copyright © 1964 by Cowles Magazines and Broadcasting, Inc.

When I resigned ... the impression got around that [Summit] asked for my resignation because it disagreed with what I wrote. This is not what happened and obscures the basic decision that most company men have to make, at one moment or, more likely, on the installment plan.

About a month after the article, and hours after the *Dallas Morning News* took me to its editorial-page woodshed a second time, I was suddenly confronted with a company demand: I must agree never to comment publicly without formally clearing each word in advance and in writing. The issue was not *what* I said, but whether I could say anything at all.

TOM REESE

Don't waste your time talking to the Accounting Department. That bunch of faggots doesn't do anything but count beans and play with each other all day.

Roy Mallick

Tom Reese, a consultant for Creative Insights Group (CIG), had endured comments like this from his client contact, Roy Mallick, throughout the first six weeks of his current assignment. Mallick was the production manager at Motor Technologies, CIG's most important new client. Since Mallick was Reese's primary contact within the client's organization, Reese had to spend as much as two hours a day with him.

While Tom Reese was accustomed to keeping his personal opinions to himself to facilitate client relationships, he had never before felt so frustrated and angry about staying silent. Tom explained:

> After holding it in for a month and a half, I really felt like the pressure was building up inside me. I didn't just want to say to him, "Look, that kind of comment really bothers me," I wanted to say, "Look, I'm *gay* and that kind of comment really bothers me." Imagine if you were Jewish and someone said something anti-Semitic in front of you because they assumed you weren't Jewish. You wouldn't just want to tell them you were offended—you'd want to tell them you're Jewish—and you're proud of it. You'd want to make a point to them so that maybe they'd think twice the next time.

Tom Reese

Tom Reese grew up in the Boston area, where he attended public high school and graduated

with top honors. He majored in psychology at Yale University, again attaining honors and distinguishing himself in varsity baseball and track. On graduation from Yale, he secured a job with a financial consulting firm. After working with this firm for two years in New York City, he attended the Harvard Business School and received his MBA in 1987. He then joined the Creative Insights Group, a strategic consulting firm, and began work in its Washington, D.C., office. Tom considered his years at CIG:

> For the most part it was a terrific experience. I really liked the work we were doing and I think I had a pretty good reputation in the firm. After working with a variety of managers in my first couple of years, I took pride in being one of the more sought-after consultants—and that was critical if you wanted to get promoted. I'd made a number of friends at CIG, but I really believed in keeping my private life to myself—I wasn't open with my co-workers about being gay.

Occasionally Tom felt the pressure of hiding his sexual orientation:

> I tried to walk a fine line by lying as little as possible about myself. I didn't talk about any of the men I dated, but I didn't make up stories about having girlfriends either. Usually this wasn't a problem. Most people just accepted the fact that I wasn't talkative about my private life—they didn't pressure me with questions. Whether this meant they *re*spected me or *sus*pected me I don't know. In any case, I got along with almost everyone in the office. The people who made me uncomfortable—the ones who were too nosy or made a lot of homophobic

Jay Steele prepared this case under the direction of Joseph Badaracco, Jr.

Harvard Business School case 391-145.

remarks—I just avoided to the extent I could. But they were a small minority.

Problems at Motor Technologies

Initially, Tom Reese was excited to be assigned as a project team leader on the Motor Technologies case, because he knew what an important opportunity it was for CIG. His boss, Anthony Ryland, made it clear that he was "expecting a lot" from Tom in handling Motor Technologies, so Tom felt more than the usual pressure to make the client happy. Tom's hopes for an enjoyable assignment dissolved as soon as he started spending time with his contact, Roy Mallick. Tom recalled:

> It was unbelievable. I never met anyone who made such incessant homophobic remarks. Roy Mallick's derogatory term for any man he disliked was "fag" or "faggot." He constantly brought up the subject, too—if he happened to spot two male co-workers walking down the hall together more than once in the course of a day, he'd say something like, "What are you two guys, faggots or something? You're always together. I'm going to stay away from you!"
>
> Unfortunately, there was no way around dealing with Roy. He was the key source for contacts and information in my case assignment. Nothing went on in manufacturing without his knowing it. And to make matters worse, he had a lot of influence with the division general man-

ager who had commissioned our consulting work. If I said the wrong thing to Roy, I knew it would find its way back up the ladder to the G.M.—then to my boss, then down to me.

Tom Reese thought at first that he would be able to simply "grin and bear it," but, after the first six weeks of what would likely be a four-month study, he realized that something had to be done.

> Some days I felt like I was going to explode. I started to hate my job—and myself.
>
> I felt like I really needed to make a statement—not sidestep the issue, but address it right in the face. The problem was that it was such a big unknown. And I had no way of knowing beforehand how my company would react. Once they found out I was gay, there was no reversing my steps. For God's sake, I'd worked hard to get where I was!
>
> A million things went through my mind as I tried to sort it all out. I remembered an incident with my boss that happened around the time of the Gay Pride March last year. Ironically, the CIG offices are in the Du Pont Circle area of Washington, which is home to a lot of gay people. My boss was looking out his window at a group of outrageously dressed men who were hanging out across the street. He said to me, "Geez, will you look at the faggots!"
>
> Was that the kind of reaction I would get? Or was he just not thinking?

PROTECH, INC.

It was late afternoon on February 8, 1986. Scott Clifford, vice president of the Control Systems

This case was prepared by Thomas R. Piper of the Harvard Business School.

Copyright © 1989 by the President and Fellows of Harvard College.

Harvard Business School case 289-054 (Revised 1993).

Division of ProTech, Inc., had returned to his office. His desk was a sea of pink telephone messages. Several were from Exxon's chemical plant in Beaumont, Texas. ProTech had submitted a bid to provide a highly sophisticated, computer-based process control system for the Beaumont plant. The competition was in its late stages and Exxon was nervous about

ProTech's commitment to its control system business. Clifford threw himself into his chair and began thinking about what to tell Exxon. A knock at the door interrupted his thoughts. It was Joanne Lembert, the plant manager for ProTech's control systems plant. Clifford sank further into his chair.

Lembert entered, "Scott, do you have a minute?" she asked. "I'm concerned about our handling of the control systems product line. With these inventory cutbacks you've imposed, it looks like we're trying to dump our product and move out of this line. Scott, we've worked together and been friends for a long time. I really need to know what's going on. What *is* our strategy for control systems. Are we dumping the business? Should I be looking for another job?"

Clifford knew that corporate was thinking seriously of eliminating the control systems line. The company was under heavy financial pressures, and management wasn't sure it could continue to fund the business until it reached breakeven in 1988. Efforts to find a strategic partner, while encouraging at times, had foundered.

Clifford still believed in the product line and its eventual success, but he had to keep Joanne and all his best managers on board to make the business work. He didn't know how to respond to all these inquiries. Should he tell Joanne the truth? Should he stall? What should he tell his customers and potential customers?

Process Control Equipment

Process control equipment (PCE) consisted of electronic and nonelectronic devices that observed, measured, and/or controlled a process so the process efficiently produced a product of desired quality and quantity. The PCE industry was divided into four major segments (1) measuring instruments, (2) actuators, (3) controllers, and (4) control systems.

Measuring instruments. These included built-in indicators that gave a direct measurement of temperature, pressure, flow, or level at the location of the sensor. In 1985, worldwide sales totalled $1.7 billion and accounted for 50 percent of total industry sales. ProTech was one of the leading producers of these instruments.

Actuators. These were devices that responded to an input signal from a controller or control system to move control valve closures in a process line. Most actuators—an overwhelming percentage—were pneumatic, but the trend was toward electronic actuators. Fisher Controls and Masoneilan dominated the market with a combined market share of 55 percent. The top 10 producers, including ProTech, made up 80 percent of the market.

Controllers. These instruments received input from measurement sensors and compared these signals to a standard. They then sent signals to valve actuators—or to other process devices—to control the process. Controller sales totalled $763 million and accounted for 22 percent of industry sales. Honeywell, Foxboro, EMC, ProTech, and Fisher Controls were the leading producers.

Control systems. These were custom-engineered, integrated combinations of instruments—often computer-based—for measuring and controlling complex processing units or an entire processing plant. Their sales totalled $511 million. Process control companies, including Honeywell, Foxboro, EMC, ProTech, and Fisher, represented 65 percent of systems sales. Computer companies, such as Hewlett-Packard, Digital, and Gould, produced the remaining 35 percent.

Total sales and PCE market share for the top 10 producers are shown in Table A.

Marketing Control Systems

Strong growth was forecast for the controller and systems segments of the process control

TABLE A PCE Sales and Market Share, 1985 ($ in millions)

Company	Total Sales	PCE Sales	PCE Market Share (%)
Honeywell	$5,490	$471	13.5%
Foxboro	603	412	11.8
Monsanto (Fisher)	6,325	325	9.3
ProTech, Inc.	317	317	9.1
Sybron (Taylor)	640	129	3.7
General Signal (L&N)	1,622	122	3.5
Fischer & Porter	182	115	3.3
Emerson	3,502	108	3.1
Masoneilan	2,260	80	2.3
Bailey	4,843	77	2.2

industry. Customers, facing rising materials, energy, and labor costs, sought improved productivity, efficiency, and quality from more sophisticated control systems. Shipments were expected to increase by 12 percent per year[1] over the next several years. Growth would be further accelerated by technological developments in computer process control and by the advent of integrated microprocessors.

The basis for a customer's buying decision had changed as the technological capabilities of the industry changed. Originally, customers were interested only in getting equipment that could take measurements accurately. The buying decision became increasingly complex as the industry began producing equipment that could constantly monitor and fine-tune a process. PCE purchasers preferred to deal with a manufacturer knowledgeable in the purchaser's specific industry and process control needs. PCE companies were beginning to customize systems. Manufacturers would learn about specific customer needs and design systems and the software around those needs.

However, as one industry executive emphasized, "There is still a competitive factor. You need to show you are the only company that can provide this solution—to cost, quality, or productivity problems—at this particular cost. You need to show a defensible position against the competition."

Service, too, was extremely important, both in the customer's buying decision and to the value of the equipment purchased. Some customers paid a premium for quality support and maintenance. Assurances that bridges could be built to connect existing systems with new state-of-the-art systems were an important selling point as well.

Achieving and maintaining product superiority in control systems required heavy research and development funding. Long lead times, rapid product turnover, and heavy capital investment were characteristic of this segment and required a substantial commitment to research and development.

Distribution of control systems was made via direct sales. Direct sales required a high degree of application and product knowledge on the part of the salesperson. Training the sales staff in products, markets, and applications was seen as the most important aspect of effective marketing, according to an industry survey.

---

[1] Assuming a 5 percent inflation rate, dollar-sales growth of the controller and control systems segments were forecast at 16 percent and 18 percent per year, respectively.

ProTech's Control Systems Division

From its inception in 1943, ProTech had focused its resources on the measuring instrument and actuator markets. With the rapid development of new technology, ProTech concluded that its success in these markets could not sustain it in the future. As one executive stated, "Microprocessors and computers were the future in PCE technology, and ProTech needed to develop a capability in this segment of the market. If you're not in controllers and control systems, you're not in PCE."

In 1979, Earl Parker, president and chief executive officer of ProTech, announced the company's entry into the control systems business at the annual shareholder's meeting:

> ProTech has always been a leader in PCE technology. We strive to achieve dominance in the world PCE market by providing our customers with state-of-the-art monitoring capability; and we follow that up with fast, efficient service.
>
> As our customers have become familiar with the power of the computer, they are demanding more sophisticated, reliable, computer-based control systems. We must provide for these changes to maintain our solid relationship and remain competitive.
>
> And so, it gives me great pleasure to announce our entry into the distributed controller systems market with our new PT1000. We are confident that this move to broaden our product line and develop a strong market for ProTech in the future will bring us great success.
>
> As in measuring instruments and actuator products, we are determined to become the internationally recognized leader in control systems and control systems technology.

Following three years of research and development, ProTech introduced its PT1000 distributed controller system in 1982. These systems were produced in a separate ProTech factory in Minneapolis, Minnesota. The division employed 263 workers, all of whom were members of the International Association of Machinists' Union.

Success was moderate in the first few years. Long lead times and start-up problems limited the number of systems produced and installed. In its first year of sales, the division took in $5 million. In 1983, sales jumped to $17 million. In 1984, sales reached $28 million on 102 units.

With a growing backlog of orders, the division planned to focus on operations to improve turnaround time and to assure the quality manufacture of up to 50 systems per quarter. The division expected to grow market share and felt that sales would grow substantially, although profits would grow at a slower rate, due to heavy investment to achieve market share. (The strategic projections made in 1983 for 1984 through 1987 can be found in Exhibit 1.)

By 1985, industry shipments of control systems totalled 2,060 units, at a value of $511 million (see Table B).

Changes in the Control Systems Market

Honeywell, a major player in the international PCE market, announced the development of its new TDC 3000 in late 1984. This machine was designed to focus on integrating computer, control, and communications technology. The system was more accurate than the current industry standard, and it eliminated the need for on-site recalibration of measuring instruments. The TDC 3000 was expected to be in full production by December 1986.

Foxboro, too, planned to increase its emphasis on systems development. At some time in the coming year, Foxboro was preparing to announce its EXACT control—a breakthrough in the use of computer technology to simulate human logic. EXACT stood for "expert adaptive controller tuning." It could continuously monitor a control loop's response to process disturbances and adapt the tuning parameters of the controller, thus assuring the best response to a load upset or control set-point change.

EXHIBIT 1   Strategic Projections for 1984–1987, Control Systems Division (in thousands)

	1984	1985	1986	1987
Statement of Operations				
Orders at list	$47,498	$69,568	$104,776	$122,242
Net sales	37,424	63,244	95,251	111,121
Cost of goods sold	25,377	31,623	42,863	46,674
Gross margin	12,047	31,621	52,388	64,455
New product development	6,482	8,430	10,620	11,113
Worldwide marketing	8,258	11,590	15,674	17,774
G&A expense	3,320	4,218	5,677	5,835
Other division income	(827)	(1,059)	0	0
Division income	$(6,840)	$ 6,324	$ 20,417	$ 29,733

Note: This strategic plan was prepared in 1983.

TABLE B   Industry Shipments of Control Systems

System	Producer	Total Units Installed	Year Developed	Share (%)	Price ($000)
TDC 2000	Honeywell	560	1976	27%	$228
Spectrum	Foxboro	327	1977	16	250
Emcon D/3	EMC	192	1982	9	320
PT1000	ProTech	149	1982	8	275
PROVOX	Fisher	115	1980	6	267
Other				35	

ProTech's Corporate Performance

ProTech's sales had expanded strongly from $128.3 million in 1978 to $317 million in 1984. Profits over this same period were erratic. In 1980, ProTech reported net profits of $12 million. In the following year, the figure was a net loss of $0.8 million. Net profit in 1983 was back up to $21.6 million. In 1984, it dropped again, to $14 million. The stock price fluctuated with earnings reports. In 1980, the price averaged $39 a share; in 1981, it fell to $11. As earnings recovered, so did the stock price, reaching a high of $55 in 1983.

The process control equipment industry fell victim to its cyclicality in 1985. Capital spending by many of the user-industries slowed. This caused PCE sales to decline unexpectedly. Companies were burdened with excess capacity and unwanted inventories. Price competition ensued.

ProTech's original predictions for 1985 set expected earnings at $27 million. By September 1985, that figure was revised down to $5 million. In late January 1986, management predicted a net loss of $12 million, not including reorganization charges of $13 million. The stock price fell from a high of $59 in 1984 to $15. (Balance sheets and income

EXHIBIT 2   Consolidated Balance Sheet (in thousands)

	1984	1985 (estimated)
Assets		
Current assets:		
Cash	$ 3,212	$ 2,076
Accounts receivable	103,086	73,245
Inventories	93,642	97,693
Other current assets	15,380	8,946
Total current assets	215,320	181,244
Property, plant, and equipment, net	102,404	123,528
Other assets	9,409	8,741
Total assets	$327,133	$313,513
Liabilities and Stockholders' Equity		
Current liabilities:		
Notes payable	$ 34,236	$ 45,587
Trade accounts payable	17,782	11,369
Accrued liabilities	20,632	21,214
Income taxes payable	1,336	1,557
Current portion of long-term debt and capital lease obligation	2,245	3,945
Total Current Liabilities	$ 76,231	$ 83,672
Long-term liabilities:		
Long-term debt and capital lease obligations*	$ 36,783	$ 38,823
Deferred income taxes	7,295	1,392
Accrued pensions	2,871	6,462
Total long-term liabilities	46,949	46,677
Stockholders' equity	203,951	183,164
Total liabilities and stockholders' equity	$327,131	$313,513

* Covenants on the long-term debt included the requirement that (1) the current ratio be at least 2.0; (2) stockholders' equity be at lest 200 percent of senior funded debt and at least 150 percent of funded debt; and (3) times interest earned average at least 2.5 times for the most recent three years.

statements for those years can be found in Exhibits 2 and 3.)

Reexamining the Control Systems Business

The systems business struggled along with the company. In 1984, revenues were $28 million and costs of goods sold were 88 percent of revenues. The division posted an operating loss of $12 million. The revised predictions for 1985 forecast sales of $55 million, costs of goods sold of $32 million, and a division income of $3 million. By February 1986, the group revised its figures to show revenues of $40.1 million,

EXHIBIT 3   Consolidated Statement of Operations ($ in thousands, except per share data)

	1983	1984	1985 (estimated)
Revenues	$281,109	$316,803	$277,246
Costs and expenses	132,070	149,153	151,626
SG&A	86,993	101,187	102,132
Research and development	29,461	39,623	41,414
	$248,524	$289,963	$295,172
Operating income (loss)	$ 32,580	$ 36,840	$(17,926)
Other income (expense):			
Interest income	1,109	1,962	256
Interest expense	(2,017)	(3,606)	(6,590)
Reorganization charges	—	—	(12,719)
Income (loss) before income taxes	31,672	25,196	(36,979)
Income taxes (benefit)	10,049	11,239	(18,192)
Net income (loss)	$ 21,623	$ 13,957	$(18,787)
	1983	1984	1985
Market price (per share):			
High	$ 55	$ 59	$ 27
Low	23	21	8
Average	39	40	14
Earnings per share	$ 1.50	$ 0.97	$ (1.31)*
Dividend per share	$ 0.10	$ 0.10	$ 0.10

* Estimated.

cost of goods sold at 68 percent, and an expected net loss of close to $11 million. (A comparison of actual results with the 1983 projections can be found in Exhibit 4.) Inventory levels ballooned to $32 million — about $15 million over the projected level — as sales fell far short of plan. Accounts receivable reached $13 million at year-end 1985.

The board of directors expressed a great deal of concern over the performance of ProTech's Control Systems Division. Manufacturing efficiency was proving more elusive than initially forecast, and the unexpected entry of new competitors was unnerving, to say the least.

The latest industry analysis predicted that the digital controller business was in a state of gross overcapacity, while demand remained weak. This was expected to lead to intense competition and price cutting.

Yet, the sales engineers were reporting a great deal of interest in the field. Important discussions were underway with several large potential customers. The management felt the market could take off.

At its quarterly meeting in January 1986, the board of directors expressed some doubts about continued investments in systems controllers. One director commented:

Frankly, I'm surprised by all the new developments in this market. Competition is much more intense than we expected. Our investment

EXHIBIT 4 Actual Results versus 1983 Strategic Projections, Control Systems Division ($ in millions)

	1984		1985	
	Projection	*Actual*	*Projection*	*Actual*
Net sales	$37	$ 28	$63	$ 40
Division income	$(7)	$(12)	$ 6	$(11)

EXHIBIT 5 Financial Forecosts, 1986–1988 ($ in millions)

	1986	*1987*	*1988*
I. Control Systems Division			
Sales	$ 60	$ 85	$126
Operating income	(3)	8	24
Accounts receivable	$ 20	$ 28	$ 42
Inventories	22	30	45
Net fixed assets	20	28	41
Accounts payable	3	4	6
Accrued liabilities	4	6	9
II. ProTech (including the Control Systems Division)			
Sales	$318	$367	$433
Operating income	38	48	60
Interest	5	8	12
Profits before tax	33	40	48
Tax	17	20	24
Profits after tax	$ 16	$ 20	$ 24

III. Consolidated Balance Sheet at December 30, 1988 (including the Control Systems Division)

Assets		Liabilities and Net Worth	
Cash	$ 5	Need for finance	$116
Accounts receivable	120	Accounts payable	21
Inventories	130	Accrued liabilities	30
Other	14	Current portion, dbt	4
Total current assets	269	Total current liabilities	171
Net fixed assets	161	Long-term debt	27
Other	11	Deferred taxes	4
Total	$441	Accrued pension	6
		Stockholders' equity	233
		Total	$441

in the business is already approaching the $85 million mark, and our technological position is still unclear.

Gary Shaw, ProTech's chief financial officer, reminded the group of the seriousness of the company's financial situation:

We must keep in mind that we are in the process of negotiating a refinancing of the company. Some of our banks are nervous about our losses and are threatening to pull our credit lines. We plan to float $40 million in convertible debentures in late April. That should reassure the banks sufficiently to avoid their canceling

our lines. However, we shouldn't plan on using them in the near future. The convertible issue is critical both as a source of refinancing now and as a base for financing future growth. We need somewhere between $75 million and $125 million over the next three years, assuming a resumption of industry growth. The rating agencies may give us a "Baa" rating, but subordinated debt is usually rated a grade down from the senior. We are already close to several of our debt covenants. Whatever action we take on control systems, we need to consider the consequences it will have on potential investors. [Shaw's financial forecasts are included in Exhibits 5 and 6.]

EXHIBIT 6 Financial Forecasts, Assuming the Liquidation of the Control Systems Division in Early 1986 ($ in millions)

	1985	1986	1987	1988
I. Operations				
Sales	$237	$258	$282	$307
Operating income		41	40	36
Interest		4	5	6
Profit before tax		37	35	30
Tax		19	18	15
Profit after tax		$ 18	$ 17	$ 15

II. Consolidated Balance Sheet at December 30, 1988*

Assets		Liabilities and Net Worth	
Cash	$ 3	Need for finance	$ 38
Accounts receivable	77	Accounts payable	12
Inventories	86	Accrued liabilities	25
Other	12	Current portion, debt	4
Total current assets	178	Total current liabilities	79
Net fixed assets	136	Long-term debt	27
Other	9	Deferred taxes	1
Total	$323	Accrued pension	7
		Stockholders' equity	$209
		Total	$323

* It is assumed that liquidation of the Control Systems Division would result in a realization of $22 million for the assets, or pretax loss of $39 million (aftertax loss of $20 million). For example, only $10 million would be realized for inventories with a book cost of $32 million.

After much debate, the board agreed to postpone any decision on the division until after the April financing. However, it did decide that, whatever the future of the division, inventory costs had to be cut. The current level of $32 million seemed far in excess of the level needed; it represented an important source of finance as well as an unacceptable exposure to high obsolescence risk.

Clifford's Dilemma

Scott Clifford began acting on the board's directive immediately. Yet, as the division's future became more and more uncertain in his mind, he became increasingly uncertain about how to handle questions from customers and associates. He'd been avoiding the issue for days. But here he was, in his office, with Joanne Lembert waiting for a reply. He still didn't know what he should tell her.

KATHRYN McNEIL (A)

Charles Foley, vice president of product control at Sayer MicroWorld, hung up his coat and sat down behind the desk he had left only eight hours earlier. Glancing at the clock, which read 7:15 A.M., he noticed a handwritten note atop the mound of unfinished paperwork that covered his desk. The note was from Lisa Walters, one of the department directors who reported to him. It was a complaint about Kathryn McNeil, one of Walters's employees—the third such complaint Walters had sent Foley in the past two weeks.

A 37-year-old single mother of a six-year-old boy, McNeil had been working at the company for four months as the product manager responsible for all IBM product lines. Claiming that McNeil's family responsibilities were preventing her from putting in the hours necessary for the job, Walters had repeatedly urged Foley to fire McNeil and replace her with someone able to work longer hours.

Jerry Useem prepared this case under the direction of Joseph Badaracco, Jr.

Harvard Business School case 394-111 (Revised 1994).

Heaving a deep sigh, Foley shut his office door, asked his secretary to hold his calls, and leaned back in his swivel chair to think. He felt that the troubles between Walters and McNeil had reached a head, and he was determined to resolve the issue before the end of the day.

Sayer MicroWorld

It was May 26, 1992, and Sayer MicroWorld was a brand-new business entity. A large personal computer reseller (or retailer) based in Framingham, Massachusetts, the company had been known previously as Sayer Information Technologies. It purchased computers directly from manufacturers and then resold them to customers, customizing individual orders by integrating various computer components. The company was a wholly owned subsidiary of Sayer Marks Systems, Inc. (SMS), a diversified, New Jersey-based corporation with $3.8 billion in annual revenues. On May 18, SMS had completed the acquisition of MicroWorld, the third-largest computer reseller chain in the United States, and merged it with Sayer Information Technologies to create Sayer Micro-World.

For years, SMS had stuck to its core businesses of environmental waste management and hydroelectric power system design. In only five years, however, SMS chairman James Vesterman had built the corporation into a titan in the personal computer business by buying up computer dealerships around the country and placing them under the umbrella of Sayer Information Technologies. MicroWorld, which SMS purchased for $44 million, was the corporation's sixth major acquisition in this area, and it nearly doubled the size of SMS's personal computer business. Corporate headquarters estimated that the MicroWorld deal would make computer retailing SMS's biggest business, producing $2.1 billion in annual revenues.

The acquisition, however, was a controversial one. Hit hard by the ongoing price wars among computer retailers, MicroWorld had lost money for five consecutive quarters, and its 1991 losses were more than $120 million. There were also reports that MicroWorld was rapidly losing its customer base and that its overhead costs were much higher than those of its competitors. These signs of trouble clearly had investors worried. Since the announcement of SMS's tender offer for MicroWorld on April 2, the SMS stock price had dropped by more than 25 percent. "I fear that Vesterman might be throwing good money after bad," said one investment analyst.

Vesterman countered by vowing to make Sayer MicroWorld profitable within 12 months, and he quickly implemented vigorous cost-cutting measures to achieve this goal. He closed the MicroWorld corporate headquarters in Santa Fe, New Mexico, to create a consolidated headquarters in Framingham and laid off 16 percent of the merged companies' 3,200 employees. Vesterman also announced he would close many of the MicroWorld retail stores and promised to produce $50 million in new cash flow by collecting on accounts receivable.

The task of integrating and making the newly merged company profitable fell to the managers at the Framingham headquarters. Vesterman's acquisition program had left SMS with a debt load of more than $300 million, and the challenge of digesting the numerous acquisitions had cut heavily into profits (the operating margins of SMS had declined from 6.9 percent to 3.8 percent in the last two years). Corporate headquarters, therefore, instructed the Framingham office to integrate MicroWorld as quickly as possible to improve margins.

Sayer MicroWorld president John Edmonds approached this task with great determination and singleness of purpose. The stern, 53-year-old Edmonds had been president of one of the firms that SMS had acquired early on, and Vesterman had kept him on to run SMS's entire computer business because Vesterman liked his no-nonsense, hands-on motivational style. Edmonds's subordinates considered him a "neck-breather" and jokingly referred to him as "Old Cattle Prod" behind his back. After the announcement of the merger, Foley received numerous memos and pep talks from Edmonds about the need to keep costs at a minimum and personal productivity at a maximum.

In general, computer retailing was a low-margin, highly competitive business, so even before the MicroWorld acquisition, the Framingham operation had little breathing room. Market observers predicted that the six or seven computer resellers currently in the market would be whittled down to two or three dealers within the next few years through economic Darwinism. Pressed to sell computers at rock-bottom prices, the 125 employees who worked in Framingham spent long hours in a crowded, ill-ventilated, nearly windowless converted warehouse. The announcement of the MicroWorld acquisition greatly intensified this hectic atmosphere. For Charles Foley, 14-hour days became common.

Charles Foley

A graduate of the University of Vermont, Foley had earned his MBA from Boston University in 1977 and subsequently went to work as a marketing director at a computer hardware manufacturer. The company folded in 1984, but Foley soon found employment with a computer reseller in Connecticut (one of MicroWorld's largest competitors) as a purchasing manager. After working his way up to vice president, he was lured away to Sayer Information Technologies in 1990 by the offer of a higher salary and the prospect of working for one of the fastest-growing firms in the business. As vice president of product control at Sayer, Foley supervised two department directors: Nolan Gminski, the director of purchasing, and Lisa Walters, the director of product management. (See Exhibit 1.) Walters in turn supervised six product managers, the most important of whom were the IBM and Apple product managers. Foley normally had the final say in all matters of hiring and firing within his business unit.

Forty-two years old, Foley lived in nearby Natick with his wife, Nancy, and their two daughters, ages 9 and 13. Like most people at Sayer, Foley put in long hours on the job, so he often felt that he did not have enough time to spend with his family. For example, because he frequently had to work on Saturdays, planning weekend trips with the family was always difficult. However, his wife worked only 20 hours a week as a part-time librarian in Natick, so child care was seldom a problem. Nancy was always home in the afternoon when the children returned from school, and she had been able to take a week off from work earlier in the year when their oldest daughter had pneumonia.

During his first year at Sayer, Foley had attempted on a few occasions to fit family obligations (such as going to see his daughter in her school play) into his workday schedule. This came to an end, however, when he started receiving subtle but clear signals of disapproval from above. Despite occasional pronouncements from Edmonds about the company's desire to be "family-friendly," Foley had long since come to accept the demands of the workplace as nonnegotiable. In general, the family issue had never presented a serious problem for senior management because most employees at the Framingham office were young and single with no children. Foley was the oldest of the three vice presidents, and the median age of the product managers was 26. With the exception of Kathryn McNeil, none of the product managers had children.

February 1992: McNeil Joins Sayer

Kathryn McNeil started working at Sayer Information Technologies in February 1992, two months before the bid for MicroWorld. Before McNeil joined the company, Lisa Walters had been the IBM product manager for more than two years. A single woman in her late 20s, Walters had performed very well in this position, consistently meeting deadlines and demonstrating initiative in promoting her product lines. Walters worked longer hours than most of her colleagues, never taking lunch breaks and only seldom leaving the office before 8 P.M. She also had an extremely serious, down-to-business personality. Her curt, almost military bearing alternately irritated and amused Foley; but, in general, he liked and respected Walters because he knew he could depend on her to come through, even in difficult circumstances. When the department director who supervised Walters resigned in January 1992, Foley promoted Walters to fill the post, where she continued to work as hard as ever.

Foley and Walters immediately began to interview applicants for the vacant IBM product manager job. The third candidate they interviewed was Kathryn McNeil. Foley had granted McNeil the interview because he had been impressed with certain aspects of her background. (See Exhibit 2.) McNeil had

EXHIBIT 1 Organizational Chart

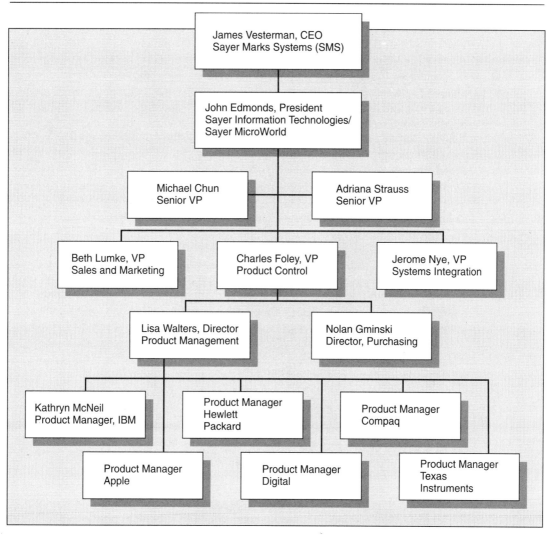

worked in marketing at IBM for eight years, rising through the ranks and performing many of the same functions that would be required of her at Sayer. Since the IBM product manager at Sayer spent a good deal of time in close contact with IBM marketing representatives, Foley figured that McNeil's familiarity with the inner workings of IBM marketing would give her an edge over other applicants.

In 1986, McNeil had left her job to take care of her newborn son and finish her education. After completing her bachelor of science degree at Framingham State College, she earned a master's degree in education from Boston

EXHIBIT 2   Résumé

Kathryn McNeil
360 Moore St.
Gloucester, Massachusetts 01930
(617) 555-3272

Professional Experience

1989–1991   **Owned and Managed a $300K Restaurant Business**
- Managed all financial and legal activities.
- Directed marketing and advertising.
- Negotiated and managed all vendor relationships.
- Hired and managed five employees; developed and implemented training programs.

1990–1991   **TEACHER/FACULTY SUBSTITUTE**
Framingham State College, Framingham, Massachusetts
- Taught fifth- and sixth-grade students at campus elementary school.
- Graduated early and was hired as substitute teacher on school's permanent teaching staff.

1986–1990   **Completed Education at Framingham State College and Boston University**

1982–1986   **MARKETING SPECIALIST**
International Business Machines, Somers, New York
- Marketing support to Japan, Australia, and Canada in personal computer sales.
- Researched, developed, and published monthly Product Manual.
- Provided home office technical support to subsidiaries, including daily product status.
- Coordinated with product managers in training, forecasting, and product introduction strategies.
- Traveled to subsidiaries as needed to ensure smooth operation.

1980–1982   **MARKETING SUPPORT SPECIALIST**
International Business Machines, Somers, New York
- Worked with marketing product managers and central order administration managers to provide continual and accurate information flow of products
- Implemented forecasting procedures.
- Performed well under pressure toward achieving budget goals and year-end deadlines.

1978–1980   **CORPORATE FLEET ADMINISTRATOR**
International Business Machines, Somers, New York
- Managed the Northeastern U.S. Fleet, providing sales and service representatives with 1,500 automobiles.
- Initiated and wrote the Corporate Fleet Policy Manual.
- Worked with field managers to supervise forecasting and budgeting of vehicles.

1977–1978   **SOFTWARE DISTRIBUTION CENTER COORDINATOR**
IBM Personal Systems, White Plains, New York
- Managed all secretarial, clerical, and data entry departmental requirements.

Education

Master of Education, Business concentration May 1990
Boston University, Boston, Massachusetts
Bachelor of Science in Education, Cum Laude January 1988
Framingham State College, Framingham, Massachusetts
Boston State College, Boston, Massachusetts
Liberal Arts, 1974–1977

University, with a concentration in business. She chose the education/business combination to give herself flexibility in her career path; that is, she thought she could either teach or return to the business world. McNeil financed her education by purchasing and operating a take-out seafood restaurant in Salem. When she applied for the job at Sayer, she had recently sold her restaurant and was working as a substitute teacher at an elementary school as part of a Framingham State College teaching program. Among the special skills and quali-fications McNeil listed on her job application was the ability to "manage stress very well" and to "assume large amounts of responsibility."

McNeil's first interview was with Lisa Walters. Walters began by giving McNeil an overview of SMS's growth as a computer re-tailer and by asking several questions about her education. While describing her investment in the restaurant, McNeil mentioned that she had been divorced five years earlier and was now the single parent of a young child. She ex-plained that she would have to make child care arrangements according to her work hours so she could pick up her son on the way home from work. McNeil also told Walters that she lived on the North Shore, in Gloucester, which was an hour-and-a-quarter drive from Framingham.

Walters explained that the business hours at Sayer were officially 9 A.M. to 5:30 P.M., Mon-day through Friday, but added that "the com-pany is not strictly a 9 to 5:30 operation." When McNeil asked Walters to clarify how many hours she would be expected to work, Walters replied that it depended partly on individual productivity and partly on the demands on the department. She added, however, that product managers normally worked overtime no more than two or three times a month—usually for evening department meetings.

At the end of the interview, Walters had a generally favorable impression of McNeil, and she escorted her down the hall to Charles Foley's office for her second interview. This interview covered many of the same subjects as the previous one. During the course of the conversation, McNeil mentioned once again that she was a single mother with a commute of more than an hour. On the subject of work hours, Foley told McNeil she would be ex-pected to work from 8:15 A.M. to 5:30 P.M., with no lunch break. "Lisa never took lunch breaks while she was IBM product manager, and we don't expect you to, either," he explained. McNeil indicated that this would not be a problem.

Foley was strongly impressed by McNeil's evident spirit of toughness; she had obviously overcome many obstacles on the path to her career. For example, he was impressed that, although McNeil had been forced to drop out of college after her junior year, when she ran out of funds, she had managed to complete her bachelor's degree 10 years later in the midst of a divorce, using her own savings. Foley decided he wanted to hire her. After consulting with Walters, who gave her approval, he of-fered the job to McNeil. She accepted, for a salary of $41,000 per year.

On February 3, 1992, McNeil arrived at the office at exactly 8:15 A.M. for her first day of work. Her tasks as IBM product manager were manifold. She managed the flow of inventory for all IBM personal computers nationwide, which averaged $40 million per month. To do this, she communicated with the IBM Corpo-rate Headquarters Team on a daily basis to place orders and make sure that every retail outlet had a six-week supply of computers on hand. The process included negotiating deliv-ery dates and ensuring that delivered products met customer specifications. When IBM an-nounced a new product, McNeil assessed the probable impact it would have on current products and determined the quantity of the new product that should be purchased. She also provided the Sayer management staff with daily, weekly, and monthly analyses of the productt lines in the form of reports and spreadsheets. Finally, McNeil stayed in close contact with the field representatives who sold the computers at the various Sayer-owned retail outlets throughout the country. She issued announcements to the field representatives when there was a change or a problem with a product, and her telephone was an open line for any representative who had a query or customer satisfaction issue that needed McNeil's attention. To fulfill these responsibilities, McNeil was given a support staff of two people: a purchasing assistant and a peripherals manager.

Performance and Problems

For the first couple months, as far as Charles Foley could tell, Kathryn McNeil performed her job well. Although Foley's personal contact with McNeil was limited, she was always working hard when he passed her desk or went to speak with her. Her small cubicle filled with reports and other paperwork, and her telephone constantly ringing with calls from troubled field representatives, McNeil appeared to juggle the constant demands of her job as gracefully as could be expected. She was never absent from work and was also apparently following Foley's advice not to take lunch breaks. Her reports were always on time and reasonably well written. She seemed, moreover, to have built a good working relationship with IBM; on several occasions, members of the IBM team remarked to Foley during telephone conversations that they enjoyed working with her. At this point, Foley privately congratulated himself for choosing the right candidate for the job.

Walters, too, seemed to be pleased with McNeil's performance, or at least she never complained to Foley about it. Not usually one to openly praise others for achievement, Walters nevertheless told McNeil that the IBM team was pleased with her and that she was "doing a good job." Because formal perfor-

mance reviews at Sayer were infrequent, this was the most significant feedback that McNeil received from her managers.

However, while McNeil's managers were happy that things were running smoothly, this period was full of unpleasant surprises for McNeil. Essentially, the job had turned out to be more demanding than she had expected, and she was having a hard time balancing her work and parental responsibilities. First of all, as Foley knew well, the volume of work with which McNeil had to contend was enormous—and perhaps overwhelming at times. Foley suspected that her previous work at IBM had not prepared her for this. After all, she had worked there in the high-job-security "good old days" of the early 1980s, and this was the super-competitive, belt-tightening 90s.

Walters, meanwhile, had been exerting a great deal of pressure on McNeil to hit the ground running during her first two months. Because Sayer did not provide a period of formal training, McNeil had enrolled in a Lotus training course in Gloucester, which met at 5 P.M. on Wednesdays. Walters, however, not wanting McNeil to leave the office early once a week, told her to quit the course and learn Lotus on her own. On another occasion, McNeil had reserved a conference room at the office for a meeting with the two people who worked for her, and Walters cancelled the reservation, informing McNeil that "we don't have time for that kind of thing here." She told McNeil to hold the meeting in her cubicle and to make it brief so they were not diverted from the work they had to do that day.

Most troublesome for McNeil, however, were the work hours at Sayer. She soon discovered that the other product managers remained in the office until 7 or 8 P.M. She also learned from other employees, to her dismay, that one reason Walters had been so successful as IBM product manager was that she had often worked 13- and 14-hour days.

Kathryn McNeil had full custody of her son, Scott, and received no child support payments from her ex-husband. McNeil had made child care arrangements for Scott based on the assumption that she would leave the office at 5:30. Scott attended a Catholic school in Middleton, and McNeil paid a woman in Middleton to take care of him after school five days a week. The drive between Framingham and Middleton took approximately one hour, so McNeil had arranged to pick up Scott at 6:30. From Middleton, it was another 30 minutes home to Gloucester.

However, unable to finish her work by 5:30, and reluctant to leave significantly earlier than the other product managers, McNeil usually worked until 6:30 or 7:00. On Fridays, the day her weekly report was due, she routinely left after 8 P.M. This meant she was almost always late picking up her son from the disgruntled baby-sitter. By the time McNeil and her son arrived home, it was often past Scott's 8 P.M. bedtime. In the mornings, McNeil had to wake up at 5:30 A.M. to leave the house at 6:30 so she could drop her son off at school and arrive at work on time. McNeil felt that this schedule was having an adverse impact on Scott. His first-grade teacher had told McNeil that he was overtired at school. Furthermore, McNeil felt that her relationship with her son was deteriorating because she had so little time to spend with him.

During this time, Kathryn McNeil did not tell her managers of her difficulties. She did, however, confide in Cesar Rodriguez, a technical services manager in another department who sympathized with her. McNeil told Rodriguez in detail of her predicament and wondered aloud to him how she was going to both hold on to her job and take care of her son. Rodriguez kept this to himself until late May, when he went to Foley to plead McNeil's case.

The Meeting

At about 3:45 on the afternoon of April 1, 1992, Kathryn McNeil walked into Lisa Walters's office to announce that she would have to leave work early because her son was sick. The baby-sitter had called a few minutes earlier to say that Scott had the flu and was running a 104-degree temperature. Walters, who had assigned McNeil a report on recent product changes earlier that day, said it would not be a problem for her to leave earlier than usual, but reminded McNeil that she still needed the report before the end of the day. McNeil said she would try to finish the report before leaving. She worked until 5:15, at which point she left a copy of the report, 80 percent complete, on Walters's desk and left the office.

The next morning, Walters, Foley, and the other managers at the Framingham office found memos on their desks announcing that John Edmonds, president of Sayer Information Technologies, was holding an urgent meeting at 11 A.M. Everyone from the product manager level on up was required to attend. At 8:30 A.M., Kathryn McNeil telephoned Walters from her home to say that her son's fever had not subsided. McNeil explained that after staying awake with Scott the entire night, she had called the doctor, who recommended that she bring Scott to his office right away. Scott had asthma, which caused the doctor to worry that complications could develop. McNeil told Walters that her efforts to find a friend or relative to take Scott to the doctor had failed, so she would have to take the day off from work to do it herself. Walters warned McNeil that she was expected to be present at the 11 A.M. meeting with the president, but McNeil apologetically stated that she could see no other alternative to missing the meeting, since she was seriously concerned about her child's health and nobody else was available to take care of him. "Well, if you're not going to make it, then I guess you're not going to make it," responded Walters. "We'll just have to deal with the consequences."

As soon as Charles Foley walked into the meeting at 11 A.M., he knew something strange was afoot. It was unusual for the president to preside over an assembly of so many people—there were more than 50 employees crammed into the conference room, many standing against the walls. It was also unusual that Foley had not been told what the meeting was about beforehand. Employees were asked to sit by department. At one end of the room, Lisa Walters sat with the five product managers who were present.

Edmonds cleared his throat and spoke: "Today, Sayer Marks Systems has made a tender offer to purchase the stock of MicroWorld, Incorporated, for the sum of $44 million. If the bid is successful, this office will no longer be the headquarters of Sayer Information Technologies, but of Sayer MicroWorld." The room broke into applause. The president then addressed the challenges and risks of the merger. First of all, layoffs would be necessary, although most of them would occur at the old Micro-World headquarters and retail stores. He continued:

> Our rivals will be watching, hoping that we're overextending ourselves by pursuing such a rapid growth strategy. I will not deny that there is some risk involved with this acquisition, but I have confidence that the people in this room will be able to rise to the occasion. This merger will generate a lot of paperwork, and we need every employee to pitch in and help tackle it over the next few months. Most important, we cannot lose sight of our number one goal, which is to make Sayer MicroWorld profitable in a short period of time. If we are to compete and rise to the top in this fierce market, we need to get the period of growing pain behind us and boost those margins.

Edmonds then turned the meeting to the details of how employees would help facilitate the merger. After asking questions of several employees who worked closely with Hewlett Packard, Edmonds turned to Walters and asked who the IBM product manager was. "Kathryn McNeil," Walters replied.

"Well, where is she?" the president asked.

Walters answered with hesitation. "Her son is sick, and she's out taking care of him."

There was a brief silence, and Edmonds looked surprised. "You mean to tell me that you've come to this meeting without one of your most important product managers?" he asked. When Walters, now red-faced from the sting of the rebuke, offered no response, the president continued: "This is the kind of thing that can really slow a company down. How can we pull together as a team to make this merger work if some of our key players have to run home every time their kid has a cold?" At the end of the meeting, Foley watched Walters hurriedly leave the room.

Probation

The day after the meeting, Lisa Walters walked into Charles Foley's office and sat down. "I think we should consider looking for someone to replace Kathryn McNeil," she said. "It's clear to me that this woman's outside responsibilities take precedence over her responsibilities to the company. I'm tired of her acting like she should be granted some sort of special status just because she's a mother. Missing that meeting was the last straw. And I don't see how my department will be able to function during the difficult time that's ahead if she can't give 100 percent."

Foley's first thought was that Walters was overreacting. Even though he agreed that Mc-Neil should have found some way to make the meeting, Walter's suggestion that they fire McNeil seemed out of place. After all, McNeil had proved to be competent at her job, and Foley had seen no evidence to suggest that the problem of her conflicting family responsibilities was as serious as Walters claimed. Also, the process of finding a replacement of equal caliber would take up valuable time in the busy weeks to come. Perhaps the fact that McNeil's absence from the meeting had personally embarrassed Walters was coloring her judgment,

Foley thought. He knew that Walters was inexperienced in managing people and was also sometimes prone to overstatement. She had done a superb job as a product manager, but her success in that position was the result of hard work and attention to detail, rather than to people skills.

On the other hand, Foley wanted to be careful that McNeil's conflicting responsibilities as a single parent did not develop into a serious problem over the long run. He could tolerate an employee missing one meeting; but, if this incident proved to be part of a larger pattern, then he might have to consider taking some sort of action. Foley's unit was under tremendous pressure to perform, and he could not afford to let McNeil impede performance for any reason. Foley thought, furthermore, that the other managers in the company would see things the same way; for example, he figured the president of the company would waste no time in firing someone who he thought was putting in a subpar effort due to family obligations.

Foley's solution was to tell Walters to "work something out" with McNeil. He advised her to tell McNeil that she would be expected to produce as much as the other product managers, regardless of her family responsibilities. Walters, though not entirely happy with this solution, agreed.

Foley heard nothing more of the issue for a week. Then, on the afternoon of April 10, Kathryn McNeil arrived in his office, obviously upset. "Could you tell me what I've done wrong?" McNeil asked. She handed him a single piece of paper, which Foley quickly glanced over. It was a formal letter addressed to McNeil from Lisa Walters, informing McNeil that she had been put on probation for an indefinite period. The letter cited several reasons for the measure: McNeil had been late with two reports, misdated a memo, and was "not a good fit with our working environment." Walters finished the letter with the warning:

"If performance is not improved, further disciplinary action or termination may result. Your performance will be evaluated on an ongoing basis." Walters had told Foley nothing about this letter. It was within Walters's authority as department director to place McNeil on probation, but Foley was nevertheless annoyed that she had not consulted him before taking this step.

"Have you had any problems with my work?" asked McNeil in a concerned voice. Foley did not know quite how to respond. He knew that McNeil was a good worker, yet he wanted to stand behind Walters in her effort to enforce performance standards. Foley began by saying that he had had nothing to do with putting her on probation. He went on to tell McNeil that, although he had found no serious problems with her work, he wanted to see her "contribute more effort." He reminded McNeil of the tough economic circumstances that the company was facing and said he needed her to give 100 percent. McNeil replied that, even though she felt she was already giving 105 percent, she would do her best to put in everything she could to her work. She asked Foley, "Please, if you're ever unhappy with my work, just tell me, and I'll be glad to work things out together." As she left the office, Foley tried to strike a positive note by telling her to "Go give 'em hell."

The Crisis

On May 13, five days before the MicroWorld acquisition was completed, Lisa Walters gathered the six product managers together for an announcement. Because of the impending merger, she said, senior management had determined that they would have to work extended hours. Walters said everyone should be prepared to stay until 9 or 10 every night, plus part of the day Saturday, with no extra pay. The extended hours would stay in effect for an indefinite period of time—probably several months. Walters explained that integrating MicroWorld with Sayer Information Technologies necessitated a myriad of tasks; for example, product inventories had to be combined and distribution networks had to be streamlined. Thus, it was the task of the product managers to carry out analyses and issue reports with their recommendations on how to go about implementing the various steps of the integration. The product managers would have to assume these responsibilities on top of their normal workloads.

When Walters was done speaking, she returned to her office, and Kathryn McNeil followed immediately on her heels. Inside the office, McNeil asked if they could talk for a moment, and Walters agreed. McNeil explained that as a single, commuting parent, she would find it absolutely impossible to stay until 9 or 10 every night. She said she was already hard-pressed to find child care, and constantly had to ask friends and relatives to cover for her by driving long distances to pick up her son when she worked late. McNeil said she knew of no baby-sitter who would be willing to take her son from early afternoon until 10 or 10:30 P.M. (not to mention all day on school holidays) and added that it would not be acceptable to her as a mother for her son to stay awake until 11 every night. "It also means I'll hardly see my child six days a week," said McNeil.

McNeil nevertheless offered to work late one or two nights a week and to take work home with her at night and on weekends. "I'll do whatever needs to be done, but I just can't do it on-site," she explained. Walters responded in a noncommittal voice, "Kathryn, we're aware of your situation," and promised to speak to her superiors about the issue.

After McNeil left the office, Walters wrote a note to Charles Foley, informing him of the situation. "I think this is definitely the last straw," she wrote. Foley, however, still decided to take no action. A week later, Walters followed up with another note. She reported that McNeil was leaving the office at 7 or 8 P.M. on most nights. Although McNeil had been doing some work at home, her contributions to the integration effort had been significantly less than those of the other product managers, Walters said. Part of the problem was that writing the integration reports required access to large bodies of information, such as company files and computer databases, which could be used only in the office; McNeil's productivity at home was therefore limited. Finally, the other product managers were unhappy because they perceived that McNeil was receiving special treatment as a mother. They all noticed that she left the office earlier than they, and two of them had already complained to Walters that they were "picking up the slack" for McNeil.

Before she left work on the evening of May 25, Lisa Walters left Charles Foley yet another note: "I really believe that we need to replace Kathryn now—this has gone on much too long."

Foley's Concerns

As Charles Foley pondered what to do on the morning of May 26, he weighed many factors. First of all, there were concerns in the legal realm. Two days earlier, he had passed the company's legal counsel in the hall and taken the opportunity to ask him for a brief report on the potential legal ramifications of firing Kathryn McNeil. The counsel's report stated that it would be simple to fire her because the employment contract McNeil had signed included a provision that read: "Employment with the company is at-will employment. This means that either you or the company is free to terminate the employment relationship at any time for any reason."

The counsel assured Foley that employment-at-will was a recognized legal principle that allowed an employer to fire an employee for any reason or for no reason at all, so long as the firing did not violate public policy. He explained that the public policy exception was the only loophole in the employee-at-will law and that the courts had narrowly tailored this loophole to protect only very specific and well-defined governmental interests, such as keeping employers from firing employees for fulfilling their legal obligations or for exercising their legal rights. (See Exhibit 3.) The courts' reluctance to widen the scope of the public policy exception had been underscored only one month earlier in the ruling of the Supreme Judicial Court of Massachusetts in *Wright* v. *Shriners Hospital for Crippled Children.* In any event, the counsel said he could not see how the public policy exception could apply to McNeil in any way.

Foley had spoken with McNeil's friend Cesar Rodriguez the day before. Rodriguez worked outside of Foley's business unit, but the two had become friendly because they lived on the same street in Natick. Rodriguez related McNeil's side of the story to Foley, describing the troubles she had faced since joining the company. He told Foley that McNeil had experienced a great deal of emotional distress since she had been placed on probation. In fact, she had come to him in tears several days earlier, frightened that she would have no way to support her child if she lost her job.

McNeil was very dedicated to her son, Rodriguez explained, and she currently spent almost every minute of her week working, commuting, and taking care of Scott. "She's putting in absolutely all she can," he said. "With all the work that has been placed on the product managers, she's juggling a million things at once, and I'm impressed that she's been able just to keep her head above water and not get dragged under by Lisa Walters's constant demands." Rodriguez asked Foley if he could find a way to make McNeil's job easier for her.

Yet Foley realized there were strong indications that McNeil's family obligations were already detrimentally affecting the performance of his unit. Several days earlier, John Edmonds had personally asked Foley for an inventory analysis that was supposed to have arrived on Foley's desk that morning. Looking through the paper trays on his desk, Foley found that the analysis had not yet arrived. When he checked the assignment chart to see who was responsible for performing the analysis, he found that it was Kathryn McNeil. Foley was forced to make excuses to Edmonds until McNeil arrived with the analysis that evening.

In addition, the fact that McNeil spent fewer hours in the office than her peers had hurt morale. Because everyone in the unit was working much harder than usual to handle the huge volume of work, a worker who could not carry her share of the load created incredible strain for everyone else. Foley could easily relate to the strain that the product managers were feeling, because he was under just as much pressure as they. Since the introduction of the extended hours, Foley, too, had spent nearly all his waking hours at work. He normally arrived home when his children were already asleep and left before they awoke. At night, he barely had enough energy to speak to his wife before he faded off to sleep, exhausted from a day of wading through stacks of reports.

Foley knew it was hard to measure the exact effect that McNeil's difficulties were having on the overall productivity of his business unit, but he also realized that perceptions could be as important as bottom-line numbers when it came to his own standing within the company. That is, if his fellow managers and the president saw that he was allowing one employee to work fewer hours than her colleagues, Foley could be perceived as a weak manager. McNeil's conspicuous absence from the April 2 meeting had already embarrassed his unit and alerted senior management to the fact that

EXHIBIT 3 Excerpts from Recent Judical Rulings Pertaining to Employment-at-Will

Judith M. Smith Pfeffer v. *Superintendent of the Walter E. Fernald State School,* Supreme Judicial Court of Massachusetts, 404 Mass. 145 (1989).

An employee-at-will at a public facility for the mentally retarded was fired without any stated reason. She sued the head of the facility, claiming that he fired her because she had criticized his administrative style. She asserted that because she was a dedicated, competent, public servant, her dismissal constituted a violation of public policy.

We have permitted redress for at-will employees based on public policy in some circumstances. Redress is available for employees who are terminated for asserting a legally guaranteed right (e.g., filing workers' compensation claim), for doing what the law requires (e.g., serving on a jury), or for refusing to do that which the law forbids (e.g., committing perjury). . . . In *Derose* v. *Putnam Management Co.,* 398 Mass. 205 (1986), we held that public policy protects an employee who is dismissed for refusing to heed his employer's instructions to give false testimony. In *Hobson* v. *McLean Hosp. Corp.,* 402 Mass. 413, 416 (1988), we held that an employee who alleged that she was discharged for enforcing safety laws as was her responsibility, stated a claim for discharge in violation of public policy. . . .

The plaintiff would extend the public policy exception to the at-will doctrine to cover discharges of employees without just cause if those employees are performing appropriate, socially desirable duties. She concludes from that principle that "her discharge without cause was for a reason that, as a matter of public policy, should be rejected as adequate ground for her discharge." *Phillips* v. *Youth Dev. Program, Inc.,* 390 Mass. 652, 657 (1983). Essentially, the plaintiff's argument would require us to convert the general rule that "an employment-at-will contract [can] be terminated at any time for any reason or for no reason at all," see *Gram* v. *Liberty Mut. Ins. Co.,* supra at 668 n.6, into a rule that requires just cause to terminate an at-will employee. The public policy exception to the at-will employment is not that broad. . . .

Judgment for the defendant.

Anita Wright v. *Shriners Hospital for Crippled Children & another,* Supreme Judicial Court of Massachusetts, 412 Mass. 469 (1992).

Hospital Administrator Salvatore Russo fired Anita Wright, a registered nurse who was an employee-at-will. Wright sued, claiming that Russo fired her because she had criticized the hospital during interviews with members of the Shriners national headquarters survey team.

We agree . . . that the provision of good medical care by hospitals is in the public interest. It does not follow, however, that all health care employees should be immune from the general at-will employment rule simply because they claim to be reporting on issues that they feel are detrimental to health care. . . .

Even if the evidence would have warranted a finding that Russo fired Wright in retaliation for her having complained to the survey team, a matter we are not deciding, that evidence alone would not have warranted a finding of improper motive, because, as we have held, the corporation had a right to discharge Wright for such a reason. As Wright's supervisor, Russo had a right to fire Wright unless he did so "malevolently, i.e., for a spiteful, malignant purpose, unrelated to the legitimate corporate interest." *Sereni* v. *Star Sportswear Mfg. Corp.,* 24 Mass. App. Ct. 428, 423–433 (1987). The record is devoid of evidence that Russo's purpose in discharging Wright was unrelated to a legitimate corporate interest. We conclude that the evidence was insufficient to warrant a verdict against the defendant Russo. . . .

so ordered.

there was a problem associated with McNeil's single-parent status. Foley also knew through casual conversations that Walters had been telling other managers about McNeil's inability to work longer hours.

Both the bottom-line results from his unit and his superiors' general assessment of his performance as a manager would affect Foley's compensation and career possibilities. In previous years, as much as one-third of his earnings had come from a year-end bonus, and Foley had come to depend on a sizable bonus to support his family. Although a more profitable year for his unit usually meant a bigger bonus, its size was also subject to the discretion of his superiors, who judged his personal performance.

But Foley's concern about his bonus paled in comparison with his biggest worry, which was holding on to his job. Although he had once aspired to climb higher in the company hierarchy, he now felt lucky just to have his job. Having seen SMS CEO James Vesterman slash Sayer MicroWorld's work-force by 16 percent, he realized how tenuous his position at the company was. In fact, in the days immediately following the announcement of the bid for MicroWorld, Foley had feared that his job might be in danger. Although this fear proved to be unfounded, Foley felt that if another round of downsizing became necessary, the ranks of middle management would be hit hard, and poorly performing or "weak" managers would be the first to go. If he lost his job, as he knew from speaking with several friends who had been laid off from other computer companies, finding a new job would not be as easy as it had been in 1984.

In light of all these factors, Foley was now seriously considering replacing Kathryn McNeil. He wondered, however, if he could fire an otherwise hard-working employee simply because she sometimes placed her responsibilities to her son ahead of her responsibilities to her employer.

MARTHA MCCASKEY

Martha McCaskey felt both elated and uneasy after her late Friday meeting with Tom Malone and Bud Hackert, two of the top managers in Praxis Associates' Industry Analysis Division (IAD). Malone, the division's de facto COO, had said that on successful completion of the Silicon 6 study, for which McCaskey was project leader, she would be promoted to group manager. The promotion would mean both a substantial increase in pay and a reprieve from the

This case was prepared by Bart J. van Dissel of the Harvard Business School.

tedious field work typical of Praxis's consulting projects. Completing the Silicon 6 project, however, meant a second session with Phil Devon, the one person who could provide her with the information required by Praxis's client. Now, McCaskey reflected, finishing the project would likely mean following the course of action proposed by Hackert and seconded by Malone: to pay Devon off.

Praxis's client, a semiconductor manufacturer based in California, was trying to identify the cost structure and manufacturing technologies of a new chip produced by one of its competitors. McCaskey and the others felt certain that Phil Devon, a semiconductor industry consultant who had worked in the competitor's West Coast operation some 12 years earlier, could provide the detailed information on manufacturing costs and processes required by their client (see Exhibit 1 for a summary of the required information). Her first interview with Devon had caused McCaskey to have serious doubts both about the propriety of asking for such information and about Devon's motivation in so eagerly offering to help her.

Malone suggested that she prepare an action plan over the weekend. Ty Richardson, head of the Industry Analysis Division, would be in town on Monday to meet with Malone and the two group managers, Bud Hackert and Bill Davies. McCaskey could present her plan for completing the Silicon 6 project at that meeting. Malone said all of them would be extremely interested in hearing her ideas. Silicon 6 was turning out to be a very important project. The client currently accounted for 15 to 20 percent of the division's revenues. In a meeting earlier that day, the marketing manager representing the client had offered to double the fee for the Silicon 6 project. He had also promised that there would be 10 more projects for the division to do that would be just as lucrative if they could come through on Silicon 6.

By Saturday afternoon, McCaskey had worked up several approaches to completing the Silicon 6 project. With the additional funds now available from the client, she could simply have Devon provide analyses of several alternatives for manufacturing state-of-the-art chips, including the one used at the competitor's Silicon 6 plant. The extra analyses would be expensive and time consuming, but Devon most likely would not suspect what she was after. Another option was to hand the project over to Chuck Kaufmann, another

---

EXHIBIT 1   Summary of Information Required by Praxis's Client

Project

Develop a competitive profile, in detail, of the Silicon 6 semiconductor manufacturing facility, obtaining:

1. Detailed cost information per 1,000 chips:
   - Utilities.
   - Scrap.
   - Depreciation.
   - Other materials.
2. Salaries for professionals.
3. Number of people in each category of hourly workers.
4. How overhead is split out between the different chips.
5. Equipment:
   - Description, including capacities.
   - Operating temperatures.
   - Actual production rates and expenses.
   - Do they use the same lines for different chips?
6. Raw materials:
   - Source.
   - Price.
   - Long-term contracts?
   - How to account for captive raw materials—transferred at cost or cost plus?
7. Marketing and service expenses.

senior associate. Chuck handled many of the division's projects that required getting information that a competitor, if asked, would consider proprietary.

McCaskey felt, however, that no matter which option she chose, completing the Silicon 6 project would compromise her values. Where do you draw the line on proprietary information, she wondered? Was she about to engage in what one of her friends at another consulting firm referred to as "gentleman's industrial espionage"? McCaskey reflected on how well things had gone since she joined the Industry Analysis Division. Until the Silicon 6 project, she felt that she had always been able to maintain a high degree of integrity in her work. Now, McCaskey wondered, would the next step to success mean playing the game the way everyone else did?

Praxis Associates

Praxis was a medium-sized consulting firm based in Chicago, with offices in New York, Los Angeles, and San Francisco. Founded in 1962 by three professors who taught accounting in Chicago-area universities, the firm had grown to nearly 350 employees by 1986. Over this period, Praxis had expanded its practice into four divisions: Management Control and Systems (which had been the original practice of the firm), Financial Services, General Management, and Industry Analysis. These expansions had taken place within a policy of conservative, controlled growth to ensure that the firm maintained a high-level quality of services and an informal, think-tank atmosphere. Throughout its history, Praxis had enjoyed a reputation for high technical and professional standards.

Industry Analysis was the newest and smallest of Praxis's four divisions. It had been created in 1982 in response to increasing demand for industry and competitive analysis by clients of the firm's Financial Services and

General Management Divisions. Industry and competitive analysis involved an examination of the competitive forces in industries and then identifying and developing ways in which firms could create and sustain competitive advantage through a distinctive competitive strategy.

Unlike the other three divisions, the Industry Analysis Division was a separate, autonomous unit operating exclusively out of San Francisco. The other divisions were headquartered in Chicago, with branch operations in New York and Los Angeles. The Industry Analysis Division had been located in San Francisco for two reasons: (1) much of Praxis's demand for competitive analysis came from clients based in California, and particularly in Silicon Valley, and (2) Ty Richardson, the person hired to start the division, was well-connected in northern California and had made staying in San Francisco part of his terms for accepting the job. Richardson reported directly to Praxis's executive committee. Richardson had also insisted on hiring all his own people. Unlike the rest of Praxis's divisions, which were staffed primarily by people who were developed internally, the Industry Analysis Division was staffed entirely with outsiders.

The Industry Analysis Division

By 1986, the Industry Analysis Division consisted of 15 professionals, 12 analysts (called associates), and 6 clerical staff. In addition to Richardson (who was a senior vice president), the division had one vice president (who served as Richardson's chief of operations) and two group managers. The remaining 11 professionals formed two groups of senior associates that reported to the two group managers. (See Exhibit 2 for a complete chart showing names and positions of members of both groups.)

The two groups of senior associates were distinctly different. The senior associates who reported to Bud Hackert were referred to as the "old guard." Several years earlier, they had all worked for Richardson when he had run

EXHIBIT 2   Praxis Associates — Staffing in the San Francisco Office

```
                          ┌─────────────────┐
                          │  Ty Richardson  │
                          │   Senior VP     │
                          └─────────────────┘
                                  │
                          ┌─────────────────┐
                          │   Tom Malone    │
                          │ Vice President  │
                          ├─────────────────┤
                          │ Group Managers  │
                          └─────────────────┘
              ┌───────────────────┼───────────────────┐
        ┌───────────┐      ┌─────────────┐      ┌─────────────┐
        │Bud Hackert│      │   Senior    │      │ Bill Davies │
        │           │      │ Associates  │      │             │
        └───────────┘      └─────────────┘      └─────────────┘
     ┌──────────────┐    ┌──────────────┐    ┌──────────────────┐
     │ Dan Rendall  │    │ 12 Associates│    │ Martha McCaskey  │
     │ Lee Rogoff   │    └──────────────┘    │ Rick Bartlett    │
     │ Chuck Kaufmann│                        │ Linda Shepherd   │
     │ Jeff McCollum│    ┌──────────────┐    │ Cory Williamson  │
     │ Mike Frisbee │    │  6 Clerical  │    │ Doug Forrest     │
     └──────────────┘    └──────────────┘    │ Bill Whiting     │
                                              └──────────────────┘
```

his own consulting firm in Los Angeles. In contrast to the old guard, the senior associates reporting to Bill Davies all had MBAs from well-known schools. Consequently, the "new guard" had significantly higher starting salaries. Another difference between the two groups was that members of the new guard tended to spend their time equally between individual and team projects. The old guard worked strictly on individual projects.

Senior associates and group managers received their project assignments from Tom Malone, Richardson's chief of operations. For the most part, however, roles and reporting relationships among the professional staff were loosely defined. Senior associates often discussed the status of their projects directly with Malone or Richardson, rather than with the group managers. Both group managers and

senior associates served as project leaders. On team projects, it was not unusual for the group manager to be part of a team on which a senior associate was project leader. The assignment of associates to projects, determined by a process of informal bargaining among associates and project leaders, served to further blur the distinction between senior associates and group managers.

Malone and the two group managers also had previously worked with Richardson. Hackert and Richardson met when Richardson, who had a PhD in business administration, left academia to join the Los Angeles branch of a well-known consulting firm. Richardson left shortly thereafter to start his own firm in Los Angeles, consulting to high-tech industries. Malone had managed Richardson's Los Angeles operation.

Clients and employees alike described Richardson as an exceptional salesperson. Very sharp in all his dealings, he had a folksy way with people that was both disarming and charismatic. Richardson was also a highly driven person who rarely slept more than four hours a night. He had taken major risks with personal finances, making and losing several fortunes by the time he was 35. Some of these ventures had involved Hackert, who had not made it in his previous employer's up-or-out system and had gone to work for a major Los Angeles real estate developer. By age 40, the demands both of being an entrepreneur and running his own consulting business had played havoc with Richardson's personal life. At his wife's insistence, Richardson switched careers and moved to San Francisco, where his wife started her own business and he accepted a high-level job with a major international consulting firm. Within the year, though, Richardson had grown restless. When Praxis agreed to let Richardson run his own show in San Francisco, he left the consulting firm, taking Bill Davies and several of the new guard with him.

Martha McCaskey

Martha McCaskey, 29 years old and single, had been with Praxis for 18 months. She joined the firm in 1985, shortly after completing her MBA at Harvard. Prior to the MBA, McCaskey had worked at a major consumer electronics firm for three years, after graduating from CalTech with a degree in electrical engineering. In the summer between her two MBA years, McCaskey worked as a consultant to a young biomedical firm in Massachusetts that specialized in self-administered diagnostic tests. While there, she developed product strategy and implementation plans for a supplement to one of the project lines and assisted in preparation of the firm's second equity offering. McCaskey thoroughly enjoyed the project orientation of the summer work experience and her role as

consultant. The firm indicated a strong interest in hiring her on completion of the MBA. McCaskey, however, had decided to pursue a career in consulting. In addition, she had grown up in the Bay area and wanted to return there if possible.

Praxis was one of several consulting firms with whom McCaskey interviewed. Her first interview at the San Francisco branch was with Tom Malone, the division's vice president. Malone told her that the Industry Analysis Division was a wonderful place to work, especially emphasizing the collegial, think-tank environment. He said that they were experiencing tremendous growth. He also said they were just beginning to get involved in some very exciting projects. The interview ended before McCaskey could push him on specifics, but she wasn't sure that such questions would have been appropriate. Malone had impressed her as very dynamic and engaging. Instead of interrogating her, as she expected, McCaskey commented later that he had made her feel "pretty darn good."

The rest of her interviews were similar. Although she grilled the other people she met, they all told her what a terrific place the IAD was. McCaskey was surprised that many of the senior associates—and even the two group managers—did not seem as sharp as she had expected. In one of the interviews, McCaskey was also surprised to see Jeff McCollum, a former classmate she had known slightly at CalTech.

On returning to Boston, McCaskey had a message from Ty Richardson, who had called to say he would be in town the following night and was wondering if she could meet him. Over dinner at one of Boston's most expensive restaurants, Richardson told her he was quite impressed with what he had heard about her. They were looking for people like her to help the business grow and to handle the exciting new projects they were getting. He also said that, for the right people, the Industry Analysis

Division offered rapid advancement—more so than she would likely find at the other firms with whom she was interviewing.

The next day Richardson called McCaskey with a generous offer. Later that afternoon she received a call from Jeff McCollum, who once again told her what a great place Praxis was to work, and how Richardson often would take everybody out for drinks Friday afternoon when he was around. In fact, Jeff laughed, there had been a golf outing the day before McCaskey's interview, and everyone had still been a little hung over when she arrived.

McCaskey called Richardson early the next week to accept the offer.

Working in the Industry Analysis Division

McCaskey's First Assignment

McCaskey's first day at work started with a visit from Malone. He explained that the division was experiencing a bit of a crunch just then, and they needed her help on a competitive analysis study. In fact, she would have to do the project by herself. It was unusual to give a new person his or her own project, Malone continued, but he had arranged for Bill Davies, her group manager, to provide backup support if she needed it. McCaskey reflected on her first project:

> It was relatively easy and I was lucky; it was a nice industry to interview in. Some industries are tough to interview because they tend to be very close-mouthed. Some industries are easier. The consumer electronics industry, for example, is pretty easy. Other industries, like the electronic chemicals areas, can be really tough. People making chips are very secretive.

Although it was her first assignment, McCaskey gave the client presentation and wrote a formal report detailing her analysis and recommendations. A few days later, Richardson dropped in on a working lunch among Davies's group to compliment McCaskey on her handling of the project. He went so far as to say that both he and Malone felt that her

analysis was the best they had yet seen by anyone in the division.

McCaskey's Second Assignment

Two weeks later, McCaskey was assigned to a major project involving a competitive analysis for a company that made printed circuit boards. As with her first assignment, she was to work alone on the study, consulting Davies if and when she needed help. It was during this period that Malone began suggesting that she talk with two members of the old guard, Dan Rendall and Chuck Kaufmann, about sources of information. The project involved gathering some fairly detailed information about a number of competitors, including one Japanese and two European firms. The old guard handled many of the projects that involved gathering sensitive information on target firms (i.e., the client's competitors). This was always information that was not publicly available—information that a target firm would consider proprietary. It appeared to McCaskey that Dan Rendall and Chuck Kaufman were the real producers in this group, often taking on projects when other members of the old guard had difficulty obtaining sensitive information.

Rendall was the recognized leader of the old guard. He could often be seen coming and going from Richardson's office on the infrequent occasions that Richardson was in town. Recently, Richardson had been spending about 80 percent of his time on the road. When McCaskey approached Rendall, however, she felt him to be difficult and uncooperative. McCaskey found subsequent attempts to talk with Rendall equally unproductive. Chuck Kaufmann was out of town on assignment for two weeks and thus was unable to meet with McCaskey.

Given her difficulty in following through on Malone's recommendation to work with the old guard, McCaskey developed her own approach to the printed circuit board project. The project turned out to be extremely difficult. Over a period of six months, McCaskey conducted nearly 300 telephone interviews, attended trade shows in the United States, Japan, and Europe, and personally interviewed consultants, distributors, and industry representatives in all three places. Toward the end, McCaskey remembered working seven days a week, 10 to 15 hours a day. Her European contacts finally came through with all the necessary information just three days before the client presentation. Despite the results that her efforts produced, McCaskey felt that Richardson and Malone disapproved of how she handled the project, that it could have been completed with less time and effort:

> The presentation went really well. Towards the end, I began to relax and feel really good. I was presenting to a bunch of guys who had been in the business for 30 years. There were a few minor follow-up questions, but mostly a lot of compliments. I was really looking forward to taking a break. I had been with the company at this point for nine months and never taken a day of vacation, and I was exhausted. And then, Richardson got up and promised the client a written report in two weeks.
>
> Davies was very good about it. We got in the car to go back to the airport, and he asked me wasn't I planning to take a vacation in the near future? But it went right by Richardson. Davies didn't press it, of course. Even though he had an MBA from Stanford, he was a really laid-back California type. That sometimes made for problems when you needed direction on projects or firm policy.
>
> The next day, I was a basket case. I should have called in sick, I really should have. I managed to dictate about one page. Richardson came by at the end of the day and said, "Well, what's the hold-up?" I was so mad, I got the report done in 10 days.

The rate at which McCaskey wrote the report was held up by Malone as a new standard for Industry Analysis projects.

McCaskey's handling of the written report on her next project led to an even tighter standard for the division's projects. Hoping to avoid a similar bind on the project, McCaskey planned to write the report before the client presentation. Malone had told her she would not have any other responsibilities while on the project because the deadline was so tight. Two weeks later, however, Richardson asked her to join a major project involving the rest of Davies's group.

> He kind of shuffled into my office and said something like, "Damn, you know, ah, gee Martha, we really admire you. I'd really like to have you on this team. We're a little behind schedule and we could really use your expertise. I've also asked Chuck Kaufmann to join the team and I'd like the two of you to work on a particularly challenging piece of the project."

Despite the dual assignment, McCaskey managed to complete the report on her original project before the client presentation. That also became a standard within the division.

The Environment at IAD

In mid-1986, several senior associates left the firm. Bill Whiting and Cory Williamson took jobs with competing firms. Doug Forrest was planning to take a job with one of Praxis's clients. Jeff McCollum left, complaining that he was burned out and that he planned to take several months off to travel before looking for work. Over the previous six months there also had been high turnover among the associates. It had become a running joke that Tuesday's edition of *The Wall Street Journal*, which carried the job advertisements, should be included in the set of industry journals that were circulated around the office.

While some of the turnover could be attributed to the increasing work load and performance expectations, a number of people had also been upset over the previous year's bonuses. Richardson and Malone had met with each senior associate prior to Christmas and explained that the division was going through a growth phase and wasn't the cash generator everybody seemed to think it was. They were all then given the same bonus and told how valuable they were to the firm, regardless of the length of time they had been with the firm or what they had accomplished. But, as McCaskey recalled, what really got to people was when Richardson and Malone showed up at the New Year's office party, each in a brand new Mercedes.

Chuck Kaufmann had gone to see Malone about the personnel situation. He warned Malone that, unless something was done to improve things, several more people would leave. Malone responded that he could put an ad in the paper and get 10 new people any time he wanted. Chuck was shocked. For McCaskey, however, Malone's response was not surprising. In the lighter moments of working on team projects, conversation among members of the new guard had naturally drifted to views on Richardson and Malone and on what made them so successful:

Malone was good-looking, married, with two kids. He usually drove a Ferrari instead of the Mercedes. He was very aggressive. You could hear this man all over the building when he was on the phone. We decided he was just really driven by money. That's all there was . . . he'd go whip someone and tell them to get work out by the end of the month so we could bill for it—and have no qualms about doing it—all right, 'cause he's counting his bucks. He was also a very smart man. If you spent a couple of hours with him in the car or on a plane explaining a business to him, he'd have it. The man had amazing retention.

Both he and Richardson were great salesmen. Malone could be an incredible bullshitter. At times, though, you wondered how much credibility you could put in these people. They kept saying they wanted you to be part of the management team. But then they'd turn around and wouldn't even tell us where or when they would go on a client call, so you really couldn't make a contribution.

Chuck's shock at Malone's response to the personnel question was also typical. McCaskey had worked with Chuck on a number of team

projects and found him to be different from most of the old guard. He was working on his MBA in the evening program at Berkeley and really seemed to enjoy being with the new guard. McCaskey knew that Chuck also had a reputation for working on what were referred to as the "sleaze" projects in the office: projects that involved questionable practices in contacting and interviewing people who could provide very detailed information about target companies. Even so, McCaskey felt that he did this work mainly out of a sense of loyalty to Richardson and Malone:

Chuck was always torn between doing the job and feeling, "These guys need me to help them run their business, because I'm going to be a group manager someday, and they really need me." He was torn between that and trying to be, not diplomatic, but objective about his situation, saying, "They're paying me less than anybody else, but look what these guys are asking me to do."

He wanted to do good in the eyes of people he looked up to, whether it's Richardson and Malone or peers like Dan or myself, because he has that personal attachment and can't step back and say, "They're screwing me to the wall." He just could not make that distinction.

Chuck had been fun to work with, though. McCaskey had observed that many of their team projects had required increasingly detailed information about a client's competitors. These projects had given rise to discussions among McCaskey and her colleagues about what constituted proprietary information and what, if anything, they should do if they found they had to obtain such information. While there was some discussion about the appropriateness of such projects, McCaskey recalled a particular conversation that characterized how the issue was typically handled:

We were on a quick coffee break and Linda Shepherd said she really needed to get psyched up for her next call. Linda was a member of the new guard whom I liked and respected. She had an MBA from Berkeley and had been there about a year longer than I had. We became good friends soon after I arrived and ended up working together a lot on team projects.

I said, "Yeah, I know what you mean. I tried to get some discounting information from a marketing manager this morning and all he would give me was list price. As usual, I started out with general questions, but as soon as I tried to get specific he was all over me. Like pulling teeth. Invariably, they slap it back at you. What information do you have? You know, and you don't want to give away the pot because then he'd know what you're doing."

Chuck's advice was pretty funny. He said that he was working on a project that was so slimy he had to take a shower every time he got off the phone, and maybe that's what we ought to do, too.

As was the norm on most of the division's projects, McCaskey usually identified herself as a representative of a newly formed trade journal for the particular industry in which she was interviewing. To McCaskey, that was not nearly as dishonest as visiting a target company on the pretense of interviewing for a job, as a friend of hers who worked for another consulting firm had done.

All in all, McCaskey felt that she had been given the freedom to do her work with integrity and quality. It was also clear that her performance was recognized by Richardson. Of the senior associates, Richardson spent the most time with Dan Rendall, McCaskey, or Chuck. While Dan often could be seen in Richardson's office, Richardson seemed to make a point of dropping in on Chuck and McCaskey. For McCaskey, these visits also seemed to be more social than work-related. Richardson's comments at a recent consumer electronics marketing research association convention were a typical example of how these meetings went. Martha described that evening:

We had gone to the dinner but decided not to hang around for the speeches. Instead, he asked me if I'd like to have a nightcap. I said

sure. So we went to a bar, and he spent the evening giving me all these warm fuzzies—about how he really enjoyed having me with the company, how I was an important member of the management team of the company, how everything was wonderful with me there, and that he hoped that I would be with them for a long time. And on and on.

At the end of 1986, McCaskey received a substantial increase in pay. She also received a $10,000 bonus. Most of the other senior associates had received much smaller bonuses—in many cases equivalent to what they had received the previous year.

The Silicon 6 Project

In January 1987, both Richardson and Malone met with McCaskey to talk about a new assignment. The project was for one of Praxis's oldest clients in the high-tech electronics field. Since its inception, the Industry Analysis Division had done a lot of work for this client. The project involved a new type of computer chip being produced by one of the client's prime competitors—a company that also had once been one of Praxis's major clients. The project had originally been assigned to Lee Rogoff, a senior associate who reported to Hackert. The client was interested in detailed information about manufacturing processes and costs for the new computer chip. Although Lee had made numerous calls to the target company's clients and distributors, he had been unable to obtain any of the required information.

Normally, Dan Rendall would have been asked to take over the project if it had previously been handled by a member of the old guard. Instead, Malone explained, he and Richardson had decided to approach McCaskey because of her background in electrical engineering. (McCaskey had in fact done some coursework on chip design at CalTech.) Malone also told her that they had been impressed with her creativity and success in obtaining difficult, detailed information on previous projects. Malone added that there was one constraint on the project. The client had insisted that Praxis not contact the target company, to avoid potential allegations of price fixing.

The project was code-named Silicon 6 after the plant at which the chip was produced—the sixth building of an industrial cluster in Silicon Valley. McCaskey began by contacting the Silicon 6 plant's equipment manufacturers. They were unusually close-mouthed. She was unable to get them even to say what equipment the plant had ordered, never mind its operating characteristics. McCaskey also contacted raw materials suppliers to semiconductor manufacturers. Again, she was unsuccessful in obtaining any information. She held meetings nearly every day with Malone (standard operating procedure for problem projects). For McCaskey, the meetings soon began to have a monotonous quality to them:

> How's it going? Well, OK. Let's retrench. Did you try this tack? Do you try that tack? Did you try this customer base? Did you try this group of calls?

Malone was especially interested in whether she was having any luck identifying ex-employees. On several of the projects McCaskey had worked on, particularly those requiring detailed data, the best source of information had been ex-employees of target companies. McCaskey had generally found these people quite willing to talk, sometimes out of vengeance, but also at times because there was a sympathetic, willing listener available. People love to talk about their "expertise," she often thought.

Industry consultants had been another good source of detailed information. It was not unusual for the Industry Analysis Division to hire consultants for $1,000 or $2,000 a day on specific projects. McCaskey felt that some of the senior associates had been rather creative in their use of this practice. Several months earlier, Chuck Kaufmann had confided to her that he had hired an ex-employee of a target company as a "consultant" to provide him with a list of software contracts for that target company. He said that this was something that Dan Rendall had done regularly on his projects. In one case, Dan had paid an ex-employee of a target company a "consulting" fee of $2,000 for a business plan and spreadsheets of the target company's upcoming new product information. Bud Hackert was there when Chuck had asked Dan if such information wasn't proprietary. Hackert had a reputation as a tough, no-nonsense manager who prided himself on running a tight shop and on his ability to get the job done, no matter what it took. Hackert said that if someone was willing to talk about it, then it wasn't proprietary.

McCaskey had mentioned this incident to Linda Shepherd. They both agreed that Dan's behavior, and Hackert's response, only confirmed what they had suspected all along about members of the old guard: they routinely paid ex-employees of target companies to obtain highly sensitive information for Praxis's clients. Linda ended the conversation with a comment that, given such behavior, the old guard wouldn't last long when the division really took off and headquarters became more interested in the San Francisco operation.

Many consulting firms had formal, written policies regarding the solicitation and performance of contracts. For example, some consulting firms required that their employees identify themselves as working for the firm before beginning an interview. The Industry Analysis Division did not have any written, formal policies as such. Richardson occasionally had given lunchtime talks concerning the division's policies, but, as McCaskey recalled, these tended to be quite vague and general. For example, for McCaskey, the bottom line in Richardson's "ethics" talk was, quite simply, we don't do anything unethical. Besides, McCaskey knew from her friends at highly reputable firms that people occasionally broke the rules even when formal, written policies existed.

After her discussion with Linda, McCaskey considered raising the old guard's use of ex-employees with Richardson, but he was out of the office for a couple of weeks. By the time he returned, she was in the middle of several large projects and had all but forgotten about it.

McCaskey's only lead on the Silicon 6 project occurred through a seemingly random set of events. Working through a list of academics involved in semiconductor research, she found a professor at a small East Coast engineering school who actively consulted with several European manufacturers of semiconductors. When she called him, McCaskey found that he could not provide her with any of the information on the list. Malone had suggested, however, that she fly out and interview him because he might have some gossip on the new chip. The interview served to clarify McCaskey's understanding of the manufacturing processes involved but, as she had suspected, did not provide her with any new information. He did suggest, however, that she get in touch with Phil Devon, a consultant in southern California. He did not know Devon personally but knew that Devon recently had been involved in the design and start-up of a plant for one of the European firms.

On returning to San Francisco, McCaskey called Devon to set up an interview. During the call she learned that he had been a vice president at the target company some 12 years earlier. When she told Malone about Devon, he was ecstatic. He congratulated her on once again coming through for the division, letting her know that both he and Richardson felt she was the one person they could always count on when the chips were down.

McCaskey Meets with Devon

McCaskey met with Devon the following Friday. He was in his mid-40s, very distinguished looking, and relaxed in his manner. McCaskey's first impression of Devon was that he was both professional and fatherly. Even before getting into the interview, she began to have qualms about asking for detailed information on the Silicon 6 plant. Feeling uneasy, McCaskey opened the interview by saying that she represented an international concern that was interested in building a semiconductor manufacturing plant in the United States. Devon responded by saying that he couldn't understand why anybody would want to build another plant, given the current global over-capacity for semiconductor production. He added, however, that he was willing to help her in whatever way he could.

McCaskey then suggested that they talk about the cost structure for a plant that would be employing state-of-the-art technology. Devon responded that he would need more information to work with if he was going to be of help to her. He explained that there were several new technologies available or under development, and it would make a difference which one they chose. It briefly crossed McCaskey's mind that this was an opportunity to talk about the Silicon 6 plant. Instead, she suggested that they might try to cover each of the options. Devon responded that it would involve an awful lot of work, and that it would be helpful if she could narrow things down. He then asked what kind of chips they intended to produce and whether there would be several products or just a single line. He added that, if he knew whom she was representing, it would help him to determine what type of facility they might be interested in.

McCaskey felt increasingly uncomfortable as the interview progressed. She felt that Devon was earnestly trying to help her. He seemed to have an excellent technical background and to know what he was doing. It was clear that Devon took pride in doing what he did and in doing it well. By mid-morning, McCaskey began to feel nauseated with herself and the prospect of asking Devon to give her proprietary information on the Silicon 6 plant. As she talked with him, she couldn't help thinking, "This is a guy who's trying to do good in the world. How can I be doing this? I have an EE degree from CalTech, an MBA from Harvard, and here I am trying to sleaze this guy."

At this point, McCaskey settled on a scheme to end the interview but keep open the option of a second interview with Devon. From the morning's discussion, she was convinced that he had access to the information she needed to complete the Silicon 6 project. Instead of probing for the information, she told Devon that her client had not supplied her with adequately detailed information to focus on a specific technology and plant cost structure. She added that his questions had helped her learn a lot about what she needed to find out from her client before she came back to him. She suggested, however, that if they could put together a representative plant cost structure, it would be useful in going back to her client. Once again, Devon said that he was willing to help her in whatever way he could. He said he had recently helped set up a state-of-the-art facility in Europe that might be similar to the type of plant her client was considering. At this point, McCaskey began to feel that perhaps Devon was being too helpful. She wondered if he might be leading her on to find out who she was working for.

As the morning progressed, Devon provided her with background on the European plant, including general information about its cost structure and other items on McCaskey's list. McCaskey was so uncomfortable about deceiving him about the purpose of her visit that she barely made it through lunch, even though she had contracted with him for the full day. After lunch, she paid Devon the full day's fee and thanked him. McCaskey said that she would get in touch with him after meeting with her client to see if they could focus on a particular plant design. Devon thanked her, said that he wished he could have been more helpful, and that he looked forward to seeing her again.

McCaskey Meets with Malone

A meeting on the Silicon 6 project was scheduled with the client for the following Friday. McCaskey worked over the weekend and through the early part of the next week putting together her slides and presentation. As she worked, she continued to reflect on her meeting with Devon. Devon had seemed so professional. She wasn't really sure how he would have responded to specific questions about the Silicon 6 plant. She felt sure he could have provided her with all the information they needed. On the other hand, although it sounded far-fetched, it seemed just possible that Devon was so straight he might have called the police had she asked him for the information. Or, given his prior employment at the target company, Devon might have called someone there about McCaskey's interest in the Silicon 6 plant.

On Wednesday, McCaskey met with Malone to provide him with an update on her meeting with Devon and to review her presentation. She told Malone that she was unable to get the information they needed. To her surprise, Malone did not press her to try to get more information from Devon. Instead, he asked McCaskey to go through her presentation. When she came to a slide titled "Representative Plant Cost Structure," Malone stopped her, saying that the title should read "Plant Cost Structure." When McCaskey asked him what he meant, Malone told her to cross out the word "Representative." They would conduct the presentation as if this was data they had gathered on the actual Silicon 6 plant. When McCaskey objected, Malone pointed out that the analysis was general enough that no one would know the difference.

McCaskey Meets with the Client's Plant Managers

Going into the presentation Friday morning, McCaskey had only 30 slides. On other projects she typically had used in excess of 100 slides.

To McCaskey's surprise, all of the client's senior plant managers were present for the presentation. She had been under the impression that the meeting was to be a dry run for a more formal presentation later on. The plant managers were courteous but stopped her 15 minutes into the presentation to say that she was not telling them anything new. If this was all she had, they said, it would be pointless to meet with senior management on the Silicon 6 project, although such a meeting was scheduled for the following month. They then asked her to identify all the sources she had contacted. McCaskey did not mention Devon, but the plant managers seemed satisfied with her efforts. Malone then explained that the lack of detailed information was due to the constraint of not being able to contact the target company.

The marketing manager in charge of the Silicon 6 project then asked his secretary to take McCaskey and Malone to his office while he held a brief meeting with the plant managers. On joining McCaskey and Malone, the marketing manager expressed his disappointment with Praxis's handling of the Silicon 6 project. Specifically, he said that his firm had never had any trouble getting such information before. Further, he pointed out how much business they provided for the Industry Analysis Division and that he had hoped the relationship could continue. Given the progress made by Praxis on the Silicon 6 project, however, he had doubts. Malone then brought up the possibility of still being able to successfully complete the project. Without mentioning Devon's name, he said that they had just made contact with an ex-employee who could provide them with the necessary information if provided with the proper incentives.

McCaskey was struck by how the marketing manager immediately brightened and told them that he didn't care how they got the information, as long as they got it. He then doubled the original fee that the Industry Analysis Division would be paid on completion of the project, adding that the additional funds should provide their source with an adequate incentive. He also told them that, if they could come through on Silicon 6, he had 10 more projects just like it for them that would also be just as lucrative.

As they climbed into Malone's Ferrari for the ride back to the office, McCaskey felt stunned by the turn of events. First, there had been the unexpected importance of the presentation; then, the marketing manager's proposition; and, now, Malone's enthusiasm for it. Malone could barely contain himself, delighting in how Richardson would react on hearing how things had worked out. McCaskey just looked at him, shook her head and said, "You're amazing!" Malone agreed with her, complimented McCaskey in return, and promised her she would be promoted to group manager as soon as she completed Silicon 6.

When they got back, Malone called Hackert into his office with McCaskey and briefed him on the meeting. Hackert's response was that it would be a "piece of cake." All they'd have to do is figure out how to handle Devon. Hackert then suggested that, given the importance of the project, Devon be offered a per diem consulting fee of $4,000 instead of the standard $2,000. Malone responded that he was unsure if that was how they should approach it, but he did agree that they should make it worthwhile to Devon to provide the necessary information. He then turned to McCaskey and suggested she think about how to proceed with Devon. He also told her not to overlook the option of having someone else, such as Chuck, meet with Devon. She could still manage the overall project. He grinned and said it would be good training for her upcoming promotion.

THE IBM–FUJITSU DISPUTE

In 1982, IBM, the largest computer company in the world, charged Fujitsu, its largest Japanese rival, with creating and selling computer programs that violated IBM's intellectual property rights. After eight months of negotiation, the companies reached a settlement, but it soon unraveled. Critics said the agreement had been poorly drafted.

In 1985, IBM filed a demand for arbitration with the American Arbitration Association (AAA), a private, nonprofit mediation group. Fujitsu agreed to the arrangement. Considering the complexity of the issues, the agreement providing for arbitration was quite short. An arbitrator later commented, "It didn't take long to write down what these two parties agreed on. . . . They have never agreed on anything, other than to agree that the only way to resolve this was to get us to solve it."

The companies disagreed sharply on two matters. One was whether Fujitsu had violated IBM's intellectual property rights in the past. Fujitsu vigorously denied IBM's charges. The other was whether Fujitsu could have access to certain IBM programming materials in future years.

To understand the decisions facing the arbitrators, it is important to understand the histories and strategies of the two companies, as well as the technical aspects of their dispute. Two background factors are also important: the differences between American and Japanese intellectual property laws and the controversy over whether Japanese companies unfairly copy technology from overseas.

Ilyse Barkan, J.D., prepared this case under the direction of Joseph Badaracco, Jr.

Copyright © 1990 by the President and Fellows of Harvard College.

Harvard Business School case 390-168 (Revised 1992).

The Two Companies

IBM

By the late 1980s, IBM had dominated the worldwide computer business for more than two decades. Mainframes had been the core of the computer industry, the third largest industry in the United States after automobiles and oil, and IBM dominated the mainframe business. Its success made IBM the most profitable company in history. During the 1980s, IBM earned 70–75 percent of world mainframe revenues, and these provided roughly two-thirds of IBM's profits. (See Exhibit 1 for IBM financial information.)

IBM's leadership was based in part on vast expenditures for manufacturing and R&D. Between 1986 and 1987, it spent more than $30 billion on R&D, and IBM held more than 10,000 patents. It invented the industry's first mass-produced electronic computing device, which it shipped in 1948. It took the lead in developing the floppy disc, one-transistor memory cells, the first all-semiconductor computer memory, and it was the first firm to mass produce several generations of memory chips. In two consecutive years, 1986 and 1987, IBM scientists won the Nobel Prize in physics.

IBM's dominant position had been built on the success of two lines of computers, the System 360 and the System 370. The 360, introduced in 1964, was a "bet-the-company" decision that replaced the company's entire product line. In some respects, the 360 was the first "family" of computers, ranging from small units to large ones, that all used the same programming instructions. In the early 1970s, IBM forged further ahead with its 370 series, which incorporated the then-new technology of integrated circuits.

IBM released its computer products in a multiwave attack. It would first introduce a new

EXHIBIT 1 IBM: 12-Year Comparison of Selected Financial Data*† ($ in millions)

	1988	1987	1986	1985	1984	1983	1982	1981	1980	1979	1978	1977	1976
For the year													
Revenue	$59,681	$55,256	$52,160	$50,718	$46,309	$40,180	$34,364	$29,070	$26,213	$22,863	$21,076	$18,133	$16,304
Net earnings	5,806	5,258	4,789	6,555	6,582	5,485	4,409	3,308	3,562	3,011	3,110	2,719	2,398
Return on stock-holders' equity	14.9%	14.5%	14.4%	22.4%	26.5%	25.4%	23.4%	21.1%	21.1%	21.2%	23.8%	21.2%	18.8%
At end of year													
Total assets	$73,037	$70,029	$63,020	$56,983	$44,989	$37,461	$32,591	$29,586	$26,703	$24,529	$20,771	$18,978	$17,723
Net investment in plant, rental machines, and other property	23,426	22,967	21,310	19,713	16,396	16,142	17,563	16,797	15,017	12,193	9,302	7,889	7,341
Long-term debt	8,518	7,108	6,923	6,368	4,232	2,674	2,851	2,669	2,099	1,589	285	256	275
Stockholders' equity	39,509	38,263	34,374	31,990	26,489	23,219	19,960	17,676	16,453	14,961	13,493	12,618	12,749

* IBM financial statement, Annual Report 1989, p. 43.
† Moody's Industrial Manual, 1989, p. 463.

255

mainframe series. Then, it would offer improved hardware or software, or both, enabling customers to run their computers faster or take advantage of new features. Finally, just as some competitors threatened to close the gap, IBM would introduce a whole new line of mainframes and start the cycle all over again. IBM's success with the System 370 drove rivals like GE and RCA out of the computer industry. IBM's approach was psychological as well. Its competitors had long complained that it played upon fear, uncertainty, and doubt—FUD, in industry jargon—to discourage customers from relying on other mainframe suppliers.

By the early 1970s, IBM's position in the U.S. computer market was so strong that its American competitors were sometimes called "the seven dwarfs." One of its rivals observed that "IBM is not the competition; it's the environment." IBM's sales force, larger than the entire workforce of most of its competitors, not only sold hardware but provided service and support after a computer was installed. For years, IBM's most daunting adversary was not a computer firm but the Antitrust Division of the U.S. Justice Department, which fought for 12 years to break up IBM, until the Reagan Administration dropped the suit in 1982.

IBM also defended its business in court. *Business Week* called it "one of the world's most ferocious legal combatants." In 1983, for example, after Hitachi pleaded guilty in federal court to criminal charges that it conspired to transport stolen IBM technical documents to Japan, IBM filed its own civil damages suit against Hitachi for stealing the technology. Hitachi settled the civil suit in 1983, agreed to pay IBM about $300 million, and allowed IBM to inspect future Hitachi products. IBM's case against Hitachi resulted from a complex "sting" operation devised by IBM and the Federal Bureau of Investigation. The climax of the effort was a payment of more than $500,000 made by a senior Hitachi engineer to a Silicon Valley consultant for IBM technology. The

consultant was actually working for IBM and the FBI. IBM's efforts led one observer to write that "the scale of the operation and the publicity it drew were more reminiscent of a high-security Soviet counterespionage program than a mere effort to protect trade secrets."[1]

During the mid-1980s, IBM's market had begun to change. The computer industry shifted from emphasis on single, large, central processing units, typically mainframes, to networks of computers. Mainframe sales slowed; some forecasts showed them growing only 3 percent a year between 1986 and 1996. Analysts also predicted that the personal computer market would soon surpass the mainframe market in sales volume. Moreover, hardware revenues were expected to grow at only slightly more than a third of the 20 percent annual rate of growth predicted for software revenues in the late 1980s and 1990s. IBM was moving into these new areas, but it faced much greater competition than in mainframes.

Fujitsu

In 1988, Fujitsu was Japan's largest computer maker and the third largest in the world. Fujitsu also sold telecommunications equipment, supercomputers, cellular telephones, and laptop computers. It was also one of the major Japanese semiconductor manufacturers, specializing in advanced logic chips and semiconductors made from advanced materials. *Fortune* described Fujitsu as "a technology driven company run by engineers."[2]

Like IBM, Fujitsu depended heavily on mainframe sales (which accounted for more than 60 percent of its profits and 70 percent of its sales), it built most of the parts it used, and its culture was said to be a Japanese

---

[1] Marie Anchordoguy, *Computers Incorporated* (Cambridge, Mass.: Council on East Asian Studies, Harvard University, 1989), p. 1.

[2] Brenton R. Schlender, "How Fujitsu Will Tackle the Giants," *Fortune,* July 1, 1991, p. 82.

version of IBM's stern, no-nonsense approach. Fujitsu distributed internationally but had limited influence outside Japan. Its overseas sales amounted to only 23 percent of total revenues (about half of IBM's comparable figures), and its profit margins were less than half of IBM's 9.7 percent. (See Exhibit 2 for Fujitsu financial information.)

Many factors—including management talent, manufacturing skills, a booming national economy—had contributed to Fujitsu's success. In the early years, government policy also played an important role. For example, during the 1960s, the government raised the tariff on computer imports from 15 percent to 20 percent. It also compelled the weaker overseas computer makers that wanted to do business in Japan to create technology licensing agreements with Japanese firms. Hitachi linked up with RCA, Mitsubishi with TRW, NEC with Honeywell, and Toshiba with General Electric. In the early 1960s, the Ministry of International Trade and Industry secured basic patents from IBM in exchange for the right to produce computers in Japan and pressured Japanese firms to buy domestic machines, despite bitter complaints about their quality.

The government itself, which accounted for about a quarter of domestic computer sales during the 1960s and 1970s, bought domestic machines almost exclusively. To expand the market for computers, MITI helped create the Japan Electronic Computer Company. Although JECC was jointly owned by the major Japanese computer makers, the government lent it approximately $2 billion between 1961 and 1981 so it could buy computers from its member firms and then lease them to customers at low rates.

During the 1960s and 1970s, the government provided low-interest loans, tax benefits, loan guarantees, and subsidies for high-risk joint R&D efforts. In the early 1970s, for example, MITI provided more than $200 million for the "New Series" project, a response to IBM's 370

series. It required the six firms receiving funding to work in three separate but coordinated groups, each concentrating on a different size of computer. Fujitsu and Hitachi were charged with entering the mainframe business. Fujitsu and Hitachi both chose a plug-compatibility strategy. This meant their customers could buy mainframes and then run IBM applications software—programs for payroll, data processing, and other functions—on these machines.

Fujitsu's efforts benefited from a strategic alliance with Amdahl Corporation, a California-based manufacturer of mainframes founded by Gene Amdahl. Even though Amdahl had designed the IBM 360 computer, he had difficulty raising capital in the United States for his new firm, so he accepted a $5 million investment from Fujitsu. By the mid-1970s, Amdahl had built mainframes that outperformed IBM's 370 series. While Fujitsu executives left the day-to-day operations of Amdahl to its American managers, they sent teams of engineers to work at Amdahl and eventually increased Fujitsu's stake in the company to 44 percent.

Government funds also flowed into computer research through Nippon Telephone & Telegraph, the government monopoly that controlled the telephone system. NTT used these funds to finance research and development at Fujitsu, NEC, Oki, and Hitachi, its principal suppliers. To help Japanese firms learn to make very large integrated circuits, MITI provided nearly $200 million in funding to two groups of laboratories, one at Mitsubishi, Fujitsu, and Hitachi and the other at Toshiba and NEC.

In 1981, MITI and the major Japanese computer firms announced their Fifth-Generation computer project. Japanese firms believed they had caught up with IBM, at least in technology, but wanted to set industry standards themselves, rather than play follow the leader. The Fifth-Generation project aimed to develop computer chips with the power of at least one million transistors, enabling computers to synthesize speech, recognize voices, process images, and

EXHIBIT 2 Fujitsu: 12-Year Comparison of Selected Financal Data* (in millions of U.S. dollars)

	1988	1987	1986	1985	1984	1983	1982	1981	1980	1979	1978	1977	1976
For the year													
Net sales	$16,374	$12,256	$9,399	$6,175	$5,401	$3,987	$2,353	$2,769	$2,004	$2,100	$1,761	$1,171	$1,029
Net income	337	148	216	352	298	201	129	88	63	51	37	33	22
Return on stockholders' equity	6.0%	3.6%	7.3%	16.2%	17.5%	15.1%	12.8%	13.1%	12.0%	10.3%	9.5%	10.5%	8.4%
At end of year													
Total assets	18,533	13,686	10,399	6,801	5,699	4,181	3,482	2,691	2,005	2,107	1,829	1,381	1,138
Net investment in plant, rental machines, and other property	4,735	3,741	3,078	1,996	1,467	1,039	815	646	443	450	398	288	439
Long-term debt	2,413	2,313	1,978	998	915	526	340	317	263	240	190	142	137
Common equity	6,616	4,660	3,535	2,405	1,935	1,465	1,140	825	514	541	442	339	287

* All financal data are from Fujitsu's annual reports for current year. The exchange rate used in converting from yen to dollars ranged from ¥125 = US$1 in 1988 to ¥253 = US$1 in 1985, ¥224 = US$1 in 1984, and ¥300 = US$1 is 1975.

even think—through artificial intelligence. These computers would be "knowledge processors," not mere data processors, and, like humans, they would learn, associate, and draw inferences from information.

By the early 1980s, Fujitsu was the center of an industrial group. The Fujitsu Group had nearly 200 subsidiaries and approximately 50 affiliated companies, which competed in the electronics industry, trading, chemicals, and several service industries. Fujitsu was also the principal electronics and communications firm in the large industrial group—or "keiretsu"—centered on the Dai-Ichi Kangyo Bank. DKB was one of the eight major industrial groups in Japan. Its member firms were part of a loose federation overseen by a presidential council, the "Sankin-Kai." This body consisted of the presidents of the leading companies in the DKB group. It met every month so members could exchange views on the general economic and financial situation, promising business opportunities, the maintenance of intra-group trademarks, and labor problems. The presidential council was not a policy-making body and Japanese observers said it was simply a forum to encourage friendship among presidents of group companies. Each company, they stressed, was independent and none was bound by the decisions or recommendations of the council.

By the mid-1980s, some Fujitsu mainframes outperformed comparable IBM products on a price-performance basis. By 1986, Fujitsu and NEC were the second- and third-largest mainframe makers in the world, and Hitachi ranked fifth. Amdahl was also prospering. In 1988, it had begun to sell new Fujitsu-made disc drives and controllers, along with new Fujitsu-supplied large-scale microprocessors that had almost a 50 percent performance edge over comparable IBM units and were cheaper, smaller, and lighter. Traditional IBM customers, such as Monsanto, General Electric, and General Motor's EDS subsidiary, had ordered the Amdahl machine.

Fujitsu was also expanding its overseas efforts through alliances with smaller companies. For example, in 1987 it bought Intellistor, a Colorado-based firm specializing in computer memories. While Intellistor had some impressive advanced technologies, its financial position was marginal. The Fujitsu acquisition brought it stability and the opportunity for engineers from both companies to share their expertise.

Fujitsu's success had taken a toll on IBM Japan. It held less than 30 percent of the Japanese computer market, by far the lowest market share of any IBM subsidiary around the world. In 1978, Fujitsu's domestic computer revenue had surpassed IBM's, as did NEC's in 1986. In response, IBM Japan had dramatically changed its way of doing business. It forged alliances with scores of other firms in Japan, ranging from giants like Nippon Steel and the Mitsubishi Bank to tiny software houses, all in an effort to turn itself into a version of a Japanese industrial group.

Despite its success, Fujitsu viewed itself, as did many outside observers, as an underdog in its contest with IBM. During the early 1980s, the sales of IBM's Japanese subsidiary alone were almost as large as Fujitsu's worldwide sales. In the minds of the Japanese, the IBM–Hitachi conflict "symbolized the ever-present threat of an IBM so powerful it could squash its competitors."[3]

While Fujitsu's domestic sales were growing very strongly, its foreign sales had suffered from IBM's allegations about Fujitsu's behavior and their protracted dispute. Fujitsu's European distributor, Siemens AG, stopped selling Fujitsu equipment in 1986 after IBM alleged copyright infringement. According to one press report, some Siemens' customers were embarrassed by surprise visits from auditors sent by IBM to determine the type of software they were using.

---

[3] Marie Anchordoguy, *Computers Incorporated*, p. 2.

The Central Dispute

The IBM–Fujitsu dispute was the most prominent in a long series of commercial and trade battles over technology. These controversies increasingly focused on protection of intellectual property rights, particularly for software and patents. The costs of developing new products and the increasing ease of copying, cloning, and improvement engineering exacerbated the problem. Disputes between nations were numerous, and many companies were involved in protracted litigation.

Trade negotiation bodies, such as the General Agreement on Tariffs and Trade (GATT), were trying to create minimum standards for protecting intellectual property and mechanisms for resolving disputes. Some countries had enacted new legislation. In 1988, for example, a new U.S. trade law made it easier to limit and penalize imports that infringed upon American patents.

While U.S. trade policy treated intellectual property rights as its most important trade issue — after farm products — not all countries endorsed stronger protection. Developing nations, such as Brazil, believed stronger protection kept them dependent on the technology and creativity of the industrialized world and stopped them from developing local capabilities to invent and create. Believing "knowledge was the heritage of all mankind," these countries viewed protection as "denying them the educational and instructional tools available from copyrighted works and the social and industrial contributions of patented products." Protection, they believed, made these tools and contributions too expensive for developing countries and available only under conditions that "violated the sovereignty of those countries."[4]

Operating system software stood at the center of the dispute between IBM and Fujitsu. IBM's principal charge was that Fujitsu had violated IBM's intellectual property rights in the operating system software it had developed. IBM had dominated the world market for operating systems software of mainframe computers. During the 1980s, the price of its software products grew at a compound annual rate of 28 percent.

An operating system is a collection of software that controls a computer's inner workings. Typically, it coordinates the flow of data between the computer's memory and peripheral devices like disk drives, keyboards, and printers, performs basic housekeeping functions for the computer system, and enables the computer to execute applications programs.

System software is like the phonograph stylus that turns the grooves on a record into music.[5] The better the operating system's design, the more efficiently applications software runs on it. Moreover, the operating system of a mainframe determines whether competitors' products, such as disk drives, personal computers, and other software, can be used with the mainframe. According to some computer experts, operating systems are the principal products of the industry and are critical to securing hardware orders.

This software was among the most complex programs in existence, with millions of lines of code, and IBM had thousands of programmers working continuously to develop it. Developing alternative products was extremely difficult: Amdahl, for example, spent six years and $10 million in such an effort and then gave up in 1988 because it concluded customers would not want to risk an alternative to IBM systems software, especially when they already had

---

[4] Helena Stalson, *Intellectual Property Rights and U.S. Competitiveness in Trade* (Washington, D.C.: National Planning Association, 1987), p. 48.

[5] Michael Miller, "Fujitsu Can Legally Clone IBM Software: The Question Now Will It Be Able to?" *The Wall Street Journal,* December 1, 1988, p. B1.

millions of dollars of customized software written for IBM mainframes and operating systems software.

Operating system software contains two kinds of information. One type tells what a computer does. Customers and others get this information so they can determine what peripheral equipment will be compatible with the computer or so they can write applications programs the computer can run. The second kind of information tells *how* the computer does what it does. Fujitsu had used the second, more sensitive information because it believed it was necessary for designing IBM-compatible mainframes, and IBM objected strongly to this.

In the 1970s, when Fujitsu developed its first IBM-compatible operating systems, its programmers made substantial use of IBM programming material.[6] Fujitsu's later operating systems, which it developed and introduced in the early 1980s, relied in part on its earlier systems and the IBM material included in them. IBM first sought U.S. copyrights for its operating system software in 1978. At the time, however, it was unclear whether Japanese or American copyright law protected operating system software. (This uncertainty was reduced in 1983 when a U.S. appeals court ruled that copyright protection did extend to operating systems, but the scope of protection for interface information remained unclear.)

Moreover, IBM had not clearly distinguished information about the internal design of its operating systems from interface information that outsiders could use. Interface information is like the specifications for plugs and holes in the back of a stereo amplifier, as opposed to information about the amplifier's internal design. IBM had revealed internal design information to customers, so they could develop their own applications software, and to independent software developers. Nevertheless, IBM and Fujitsu disagreed sharply about whether Fujitsu was right to use this information in developing its early operating systems.

Intellectual Property Laws in America and Japan

Legal protection for intellectual property differs between the United States and Japan. (In many respects, the Japanese approach is closer to that of continental Europe.) Copyright, patent, and trade secret laws in the countries differ between the United States and Japan, as do the legal theories justifying the protection. Under these laws, protection for computer software was ambiguous in both countries.

Copyrights

A copyright, in essence, protects the expression of an idea. Both the American and Japanese systems protect the particular form in which an idea is expressed, but not the underlying idea. Under both systems, the work had to be original and fall within the broad realms of literature, science, fine art, or music to be eligible for protection.

Until 1985, American and Japanese systems' copyright protection differed in duration. Generally, U.S. law gave works created on or after January 1, 1978, copyright protection for the life of the author, plus 50 years after the author's death. Japan formerly protected the work for only 20 years from the date of granting of the copyright; but in 1985 it adopted provisions like those in the United States.

Copyright infringement is the violation of any of the copyright owner's exclusive rights. Japan, however, permitted uses of copyrighted material that American law scrutinized more carefully. For example, under Japanese law the user of a copyrighted computer program could debug and upgrade it, and even modify it for

---

[6] This account of the dispute is based on *International Business Machines Corporation* v. *Fujitsu Limited,* American Arbitration Association, Commercial Arbitration Tribunal Opinion, case no. 13T-117-0636-85, November 29, 1988.

the purpose of replacement. Japanese copyright law also left ambiguous the distinction between upgrading and revising a computer program.

Patents

Patents, in essence, protect ownership rights in ways of doing things. American and Japanese patent law systems both required that patentable inventions be novel or contain an inventive step, and be nonobvious or useful. Both covered processes as well as products, and improvements to either.

Japan and most industrialized countries gave priority to the first of competing patent applicants to file an application for the patent on a technology. The United States granted the patent to the first to invent.

In general, a Japanese patent covered a single claim or novel advance. American patents, in contrast, often listed several independently valid claims. This compelled Japanese inventors to file more patents to cover a single technology. In 1983, for example, about 100,000 patent applications were filed in the United States, while more than 250,000 were filed in Japan.[7]

Japanese law, unlike U.S. law, permitted the government to grant other parties the right to use an invention if an inventor failed to do so or if working the patent would serve the public interest. This created incentives to make a patent as *narrow* as possible to maintain its exclusivity and, hence, its economic value. Multiple, narrow patents were each more likely to be worked sufficiently, and a narrow patent had more limited economic consequences than one encompassing a class of related inventions.

The application process in the two countries also differed. The U.S. system examined patent applications in the order in which applicants filed them. Japan examined applications only at the patent applicant's request and could defer examination for up to seven years. Confidentiality of the patent application was absolute in the United States; publication followed the grant of the patent, at which time the patentee could take legal action for copying and other infringement. Patent applications in Japan were published or "laid open" after 18 months, often before the patent was granted. Opponents of the grant of a patent could oppose it during the three months after examination was requested and before the patent was granted. In the United States, opponents had to wait until the patent was granted.

Some analysts believed that Japan's "laying open" of patent applications promoted a practice called "patent flooding": competitors would file multiple improvement patents to force the inventor to cross-license its technology, rather than defend the patent in litigation. Protection of rights in the technology also depended on the length of time between filing a patent application and the issuing of a patent on the technology. That period in Japan averaged six years, compared to a 20-month average in the United States.

Trade Secrets

Most U.S. states defined trade secrets as any "formula, pattern, device, or compilation of information used in one's business and which gives him an opportunity to obtain an advantage over competitors who do not know or use it."[8] Examples included chemical formulas, manufacturing processes, machine patterns, and customer lists. Japan did not identify any such trade secrets by statute, but it did protect trade secrets covered by contract.

---

[7] Krista McQuade and Professor Gomes-Casseres, "Fusion Systems Corporation," HBS case no. 390-021, 1990.

[8] Restatement of Torts §757, comment (b)(1939) as cited in Michael A. Epstein, *Modern Intellectual Property* (New York: Law & Business, Inc./Harcourt Brace Jovanovich, 1989 ed.), p. 3, n. 3.

U.S. law provided several ways of protecting trade secrets: trade secret and criminal statutes, such explicit contracts as postemployment noncompetition agreements and nondisclosure agreements, and implied contracts, created by special relationships such as licensor/licensee. Japan relied only on contracts.

In both countries, victims of infringement could seek damages and criminal sanctions. In the United States, however, it was easier to get a court injunction halting the infringement; and, unlike Japan, the United States had criminal sanctions covering infringement.

Imitation in Japanese Culture

The many and heated intellectual property disputes between American and Japanese companies led some observers to seek cultural perspectives on the issues. The most controversial of these, and perhaps the most common, was the view that Japanese culture sanctioned imitation to a greater degree than the American.

Proponents of this view emphasized that Japan has borrowed extensively from foreign cultures. Through contacts with China, for example, Japan imitated elements of Chinese culture, adopting a Chinese-style legal code as the basis for the criminal and administrative codes of its legal system. During the 19th century, Japan emulated European and American technology. Meiji Japan consciously imitated European and American organizational models in developing its postal and police systems and its newspapers. Japan selected its parliamentary system of government from among American and European models, and Germanic law informed Japan's civil law system, as did Anglo-American influences during the postwar occupation period.

Japanese artists have traditionally studied their crafts in apprenticeships and learned technique by copying that of the master. Between 1750 and 1850, Japanese artists, particularly Hokusai and Hiroshige, learned by imitating: their works and sketches originated in the drawings of seventh-century Buddhist figures. Masters generated schools of artists, whose followers produced works in particular style. Japanese artists did not begin to sign their works until the 16th century. The Zen tradition of repetition of a task or skill to yield mastery or perfection also greatly influenced and informed the arts, as well as other aspects of Japanese culture.

Scholars who have studied the history of Japanese fine arts have acknowledged a tendency toward imitation. One wrote, for example:

> It has been remarked that a pupil's training consists in copying and recopying his master's works and that there are model-books which show the proper method of painting various subjects. So much stress on tradition, at once a safeguard against radicalism and an obstacle to free development, naturally gave birth to pronounced school mannerisms and to restrictions which extend even to choice of subject and result in inevitable repetition. . . . It is probable, however, that the special references in the "Six Canons" [a classic guide to Japanese painting] to copying old masters was not intended to mean mere copying; rather, it should be interpreted as emphasizing the importance of preserving that part of tradition which ever lives as an eternal principle and of transmitting it to the next generation.[9]

Explanations of Japan's alleged tendency to emulation are diverse. Some suggest it is Japanese openness to other cultures. The Dutch journalist Karel Van Wolferen, a long-time resident of Japan, asserts that Japanese culture is based on "the notion that there is a perfect way of doing things . . . that mastery is reached by the removal of the obstacles between the

---

[9] Kojiro Tomita, "Art—Far Eastern Methods," in *Japanese Art: A Selection from the Encyclopaedia Britannica* (New York: Encyclopaedia Britannica, 1933), p. 34.

self and the perfect model, embodied by the teacher, a view which emphasizes great technical skill with a lack of personal expression, there is no room for the idiosyncratic individual."[10] In this view, imitation of aspects of Chinese, European, or American civilizations is part of Japan's "catching-up disposition," emulation deriving not merely from pursuit of perfection but also from a self-perception of "falling short."

In contrast, other writers attributed cultural emulation to Japanese self-assertion, viewing it as an effort to make Japan respected internationally. Still others argued that Japan was seeking to prevent any one nation from becoming indispensable to its modernization, while some believed Japan sought not to hold its own but to grow dominant.

The view of Japan as a peculiarly imitative nation was often criticized for bias. Some historical studies pointed to Japanese creativity. Its postal and police systems and its newspapers had been interpreted as examples of rapid, innovative adaptations of overseas models to Japanese circumstances. Other studies noted that numerous schools of artists existed in Japan, often at the same time, and new masters emerged, establishing new schools and traditions. Even Zen acts of repetition had been interpreted variously. Former Harvard professor and ambassador to Japan Edwin Reischauer saw them as triumphs of individualism and innovation—the application of one's whole being to a task, with a reliance on individual will, self-discovery, and self-discipline to master a practice or an idea.

Emulation was hardly unique to Japan, so the whole copying issue was a question of degree. Many other nations have looked to other nations' cultures and civilizations when

---

[10] Karel Van Wolferen, *The Enigma of Japanese Power: People and Politics in a Stateless Nation* (New York: Alfred A. Knopf, 1989), pp. 378–79.

developing their own. For example, British industrialists were horrified at the quality of the American guns on display at the Great Exhibition in London in 1851. They believed the Americans had unfairly appropriated British designs. In later decades, the British made similar complaints about German and American efforts in synthetic dyes, metals, armaments, penicillin, radar, and computerized tomography. Japan's defenders also pointed out that by 1986 Japan had a higher percentage of its population engaged in R&D than America, and by the mid-1980s it accounted for 20 percent of new ceramics patents, 26 percent in communication equipment, and 33 percent in office-computing and accounting machines.

Conclusion

The two arbitrators confronted a wide range of questions. Did Fujitsu violate IBM's intellectual property rights in the early 1970s, before IBM sought a U.S. copyright for its systems software? Did Fujitsu violate IBM's rights in subsequent years? What compensation, if any, was IBM owed? On what terms, if any, could Fujitsu inspect and use IBM programming material for systems software in the future? To what extent should the arbitrators consider the interests of computer customers in making their decision? What precedent would their decision create for other intellectual property disputes?

The arbitrators' challenge was compounded by the acrimony between the companies. One arbitrator commented: "These two parties have hardly been able to agree what color a stoplight is."

Sources

In addition to the documents cited in the footnotes, the data in this case were drawn from articles in the general business press and the more specialized publications covering the computer industry.

The discussion of Japanese culture and emulation draws, in part, on D. Eleanor Westney, *Imitation and Innovation: The Transfer of Western Organizational Patterns to Meiji Japan* (Cambridge, Mass.: Harvard University Press, 1987); William Watson, ed., *Artistic Personality and Decorative Style in Japanese Art* (London: University of London Colloquies on Art and Archeology in Asia, no. 6, 1976); and Henry P. Bowie, *On the Laws of Japanese Painting* (New York: Dover Publications, 1951).

The section on intellectual property laws in the United States and Japan is intended for background information only. It is not legal advice. This section drew on the following sources: Jay Dratler, Jr., "Trade Secrets in the United States and Japan: A Comparison and Prognosis, 14 *Yale Journal of International Law* 68 (1989); Michael A. Epstein, *Modern Intellectual Property* (New York: Law & Business, Inc./Harcourt Jovanovich, 1989, ed.); Tohru Nakajima, "Legal Protection of Computer Programs in Japan: The Conflict between Economic and Artistic Goals," *Columbia Journal of Transnational Law* 143 (1988), p. 27; Robert P. Benko, *Protecting Intellectual Property Rights: Issues and Controversies* (Washington, D.C.: American Enterprise Institute for Public Policy Research, 1987); Mary Ann Glendon, Michael Wallace Gordon, and Christopher Osakwe, *Comparative Legal Traditions: Text, Materials and Cases* (St. Paul, Minn.: West Publishing, 1985); Robert W. Russell, compiler, *Patents and Trademarks in Japan (A Handy Book)* (Tokyo, Japan, 1984); Fenwick, Stone, Davis & West, "Legal Protection of Computer Software in Japan," in Miles R. Gilburne, [symposium] chairman, *Intellectual Property Rights in High Technology Products and Sensitive Business Information* (New York: Law and Business, Inc./ Harcourt Brace Jovanovich, 1982); Earl W. Kitner and Jack Lahr, *An Intellectual Property Law Printer: A Survey of the Law of Patents, Trade Secrets, Trademarks, Franchises, Copyrights and Personality and Entertainment Rights* (New York: Clark Boardman Company, Ltd., 1982); and Tervo Doi, *The Intellectual Property Law of Japan* (Alphen aan den rijn; Germantown, Nd.: Sijthoff and Noordhoff, 1980).

PART IV

The Ethical Responsibilities of Organization Leaders

The cases and readings in this section spotlight another important sphere of management responsibility: the ethical obligations that managers have as leaders of organizations. These responsibilities do not replace the duties and commitments examined earlier in this book—their responsibilities as economic agents and their commitments and duties as human beings. Rather, the responsibilities of organization leaders are a crucial *additional* set of responsibilities that managers must meet.

From a historical perspective, the sphere of organizational responsibilities is "new"; that is, it has become important mainly during the last 100 years or so. While the responsibilities of political and military leaders have been carefully examined for centuries, the obligations of business managers as organization leaders did not begin to receive careful scrutiny until approximately 100 to 150 years ago. The reason is simple: large-scale or even medium-scale business organizations are themselves a recent historical phenomenon.

Most of the history of business organizations is essentially one of small and owner-managed entities. Putting aside a handful of exceptions, the vast majority of "businesses" were one-person operations in which a single individual was the owner and the sole employee. Blacksmiths and peddlers are examples. In the 600 pages of *The Wealth of Nations* (written in 1776, on the eve of the Industrial Revolution in England) Adam Smith mentions firms in only a few passing references to tiny operations like apothecaries, hatmakers, and farms.

A business entity the size of Toyota or IBM would have staggered the imaginations of Smith and the other classical economists. While many governments in their era and before had subsidized or even managed economic activities, there were simply no examples of large for-profit business organizations managed by a hierarchy of full-time business executives. In short, until the last century or so, the entrepreneurial capitalism of small-scale entities was the dominant form of business organization.

Managerial capitalism, the principal focus of this section, first appeared on the economic landscape in the United States during the mid-19th century. At first railroads, then steel firms, oil companies, food manufacturers, and other businesses grew into large, sometimes gigantic operations. These companies seized the opportunity to sell a high volume of goods to the vast, newly opened American market. As their scale of operations grew larger, the costs of manufacturing each unit of output fell. In turn, their profits grew, providing funds for research and development, for additional marketing, and for hiring more managers, all of which enabled these firms to expand their operations even more. In the industries that offered these economic opportunities, giant firms came to employ thousands or tens of thousands of people as workers and managers on a long-term basis. Some of these firms grew even larger than countries. In the mid-1960s, for example, General Motors' sales exceeded the gross national products of all but four countries; and, despite its recent woes, General Motors has now survived longer than the Soviet Union.

Power.   Managers' obligations as organization leaders originate, in large part, in the power they exercise over the lives, livelihoods, and welfare of the other people in their organizations. This power takes two forms.

One is the overt power to induce others to act in certain ways in exchange for clear rewards such as higher pay, bonuses, opportunities for advancement, and the like.

The other form of power—perhaps the more common and the more significant—is exercised in subtle, often unseen ways. Through their actions, decisions, and leadership style, executives shape the culture and ethical climate within their organizations. Political scientist James MacGregor Burns, who spent much of his career studying leadership, concluded that the most effective leaders were those who shared needs, aspirations, and values with their followers. These deeper connections among members of an organization define "what it is we really care about here," "how you get ahead in this company," and "how you get things done around here."

A company's ethical climate can encourage employees to speak honestly, to treat each other with respect, to obey both the letter and the spirit of the law, and to be responsible citizens of the communities in which the company operates. Conversely, as so many newspaper headlines indicate, the subtle but powerful influences of company culture can lead groups of otherwise decent and well-intentioned individuals into serious violations of the law and of commonly accepted ethical standards.

The Many Meanings of Work. Obviously, for the vast majority of people, work means a paycheck. Even if they do not live to work, they must work to live. But, taken by itself, this is far too simple a picture of the role that work plays in people's lives and of the responsibilities of organization leaders.

A Japanese scholar, Moriaki Tsuchiya, whose ideas are presented in this section, has described Japanese firms as "social capsules." By this he means that firms are often semiclosed societies; communal groups that enlist the loyalty and trust of employees and envelop much of their lives.[1] Indeed, the word *employee* is misleading in this context. People become *members* of these business organizations, they devote much of their life's energy to their work, and their lives and livelihoods are deeply bound up in company activities.

This phenomenon, of course, is hardly unique to Japan. Consider an episode at Levi Strauss, a leading apparel maker, just a few years ago. The company had made significant efforts to protect the rights of people with HIV, AIDS, and other chronic illnesses, and to help them continue working when they were ill. One Levi Strauss worker with AIDS, who benefited from this policy, said, "It was so important for me to come to work and get away from all the pain—the company was the environment that helped me keep my self-respect." Later, when this man died, one of his coworkers said: "I shed tears for him and for the great friend I had lost."

What does this vignette suggest? First, that work is a powerful source of meaning and value—in this case, self-respect—in individuals' lives. Many people realize some of their deepest aspirations—for security, for a sense of belonging, for a feeling of contribution or achievement—on the job. The coworker's comments are also a reminder of how workplaces can nurture deep loyalties, strong friendships, and abiding ties among individuals. Indeed, many people live much of their lives at work, rather than in neighborhoods, in religious and political groups, or even in their homes with their families.

Finally, this vignette is yet another example of the way in which business managers can influence and shape the ethical climate of their organizations. The power that they exercise, for well or ill, takes the form of subtle norms, practices, ideals, and ways of doing things that deeply influence the quality of the lives of other people in their organizations.

The "tools of management"—measurement and reward systems, culture, and the examples of peers and bosses—can exert enormous cumulative pressures on employees and managers. These can encourage people to

---

[1] Moriaki Tsuchiya, "The Japanese Business as a Capsule," in *Japanese Economic Studies,* Fall 1979, pp. 8–41.

cut corners and pursue a narrow self-interest, just as readily as they can affirm and encourage the idealistic aspirations many people have.

Organizations and Amorality.   Unfortunately, some of the basic facts of organizational life can lead companies and employees to behavior that is amoral or worse. Moreover, while some people give in to organizational pressure to act unethically, others stand on the sidelines and watch them do so. Responsibilities in organizations are often shared so that no one feels personally and directly accountable. People often say to themselves, "It's not part of my job," or "It's the CEO's call and he runs the place," or "I have to pick my battles and this isn't the right one."

The great 20th-century theologian Reinhold Niebuhr (some of whose ideas are presented later in this section) believed that individuals tend to behave less morally in groups than when they act as individuals. Niebuhr wrote: "In every human group, there is less reason to guide and check impulses, less capacity for self-transcendence, less ability to comprehend the needs of others and therefore more unrestrained egoism than the individuals who compose the group reveal in their personal relationships."[2]

Some thoughtful analysts have disagreed with Niebuhr's conclusion, but most individuals, after some reflection, can think of a number of examples of cases in which people whom they have known and trusted have fallen victim to the pressures and examples of peers and have done things that they later regretted; or they know of cases in which people simply stood by while others made serious mistakes. A powerful kernel of truth underlies such observations: The culture and climate of an organization can just as easily induce unethical as ethical behavior, and the ethical climate of the company can encourage commitment and responsibility or shirking and denial.

The Role of Leadership.   Business leaders have a dual role with respect to the ethical climate of their companies. As discussed above, they must exercise their leadership of "company communities" in ways that meet a basic threshold of decency and that show respect for the rights and dignity of employees and managers. Outstanding leaders will do this in ways that enlist the aspirations and commitments of the people in their firms.

But managers' responsibilities run even deeper and include what is, in effect, a responsibility to themselves. For the men and women who lead entire organizations, or for those who manage divisions, departments, and business units, work is often the setting in which they reveal and express many of their life's hopes and fears, in which they seek identity and purpose, and through which they gain a strong sense of achievement and

---

[2] Reinhold Niebuhr, *Moral Man and Immoral Society: A Study in Ethics and Politics* (New York, London: C. Scribner's Sons, 1932), pp. xi, xii.

self-worth for their lives. Business leaders shape not only their companies' cultures—they shape their own lives.

The ideals and aspirations of individual executives take many different forms, and they evolve and change over the course of a manager's life.

Nearly all of these values and aspirations, however, are variations on a core set of themes: Executives want to build companies that are independent, strong, growing, and vital; that attract and keep high caliber talent; that are challenging and rewarding places to work; that provide opportunities for employees to grow and develop; that will survive hostile, uncertain competitive environments, and will endure and prosper for decades. Some executives have even broader aspirations. Steve Job's mission for Apple Computer was "to make a contribution to this world by making tools for the mind that advance humankind." Merck, a pharmaceutical leader and one of the most-admired U.S. companies in recent years, describes its purpose as "preserving and improving human life." Executives pour a great deal of their lives and energy into their work. In doing so, they are influencing powerfully not only the lives of others but their own lives as well.

While companies must serve shareholder's interests, neither their executives nor their employees leap from bed in the morning eager to maximize the risk-adjusted present value of their company's future cash flows. The animating, creative forces of great human institutions originate elsewhere. And the men and women who build and guide enduring, productive, challenging human communities are engaged in efforts that are not simply financial and administrative but social, political, and moral.

The readings and cases in this part examine in detail the responsibilities that come with executives' power over corporate communities and the ways in which, for well or ill, managers shape the ethical climate of these human groups.

OVERVIEW OF READINGS AND CASES

The readings and cases that follow are arranged in a sequence that begins with issues faced by young managers and then moves to problems and challenges faced by mid-level and senior executives. This series of cases is preceded by two readings. One is a collection of excerpts from important works on management, entitled "The Moral Responsibilities of Organization Leaders." This collection serves two basic purposes. First, it describes and explains the origins of managerial capitalism and the basic features of the large firms that play such important roles in modern economies. Second, the readings introduce the varied complex ethical obligations confronted by the executives and managers of these organizations. The second reading, "A Company's Ethical Climate," is highly practical, focusing on the obstacles managers face in creating an ethical climate and the administrative tools they can bring to bear on these tasks.

The first four cases in this part examine the issue of managers' responsibilities for a company's ethical climate from the viewpoint of young men and women in the early stages of careers as business managers. A central fact about their situations is that they have little direct influence over the cultures of the organizations in which they work. They are young, typically new to their jobs, have few, if any, people working for them, and find themselves influenced by norms, values, and practices that have existed for many years. For the most part, they are not shapers of ethical climate; rather, they are shaped by the ethical climate and culture that they find. Sometimes, however, the ethical challenge facing a young would-be manager is clear. It is a question of whether to do something that seems sleazy or even unethical and illegal, or to say no and risk one's prospects and fragile status in a company. For example, this is precisely the problem in "Conflict on a Trading Floor." The protagonist of this case is unsure what the operating practices are in his organization. However, he has been asked to perform what he unambiguously regards as an act of deception, and his boss wants him to stop thinking about it and get on with the job.

With luck and hard work, some young people soon find that they do have responsibility over other members of an organization. Hence, early in their careers, they find themselves in positions to influence, albeit in limited ways, the norms and values of a team or department. At this point, they begin to face the central issue of this part: defining what responsibilities they have as a result of their power over other members of an organization and deciding how best to meet these responsibilities— especially in challenging, uncertain, high-pressure situations. The next two cases, "A Brush with AIDS" and "Where Is He?", focus directly on this type of problem.

The next two cases involve middle managers. Hence, several important factors distinguish their situations from those of entry-level people and complicate their ethical responsibilities. Typically, middle managers are pulled and pressured in a variety of directions. They must try to meet the demands and requirements of senior executives, to motivate and manage the people who are working for them, and to successfully navigate the complex politics of their organizations. Unlike their younger counterparts, middle managers often understand the ethical rules of the game in their organizations and can understand more clearly what is at stake in the decisions they make.

These stakes are typically much higher than for the younger people, since middle managers have more responsibilities and their actions are often more visible to others within a firm. Nevertheless, like many younger people in an organization, middle managers often find themselves in situations in which their options and behavior are shaped and constrained by corporate cultures that they cannot change. Two cases, "Laura Wollen and ARPCO, Inc.," and "Ann Hopkins," provide opportunities to analyze this complex set of issues.

The last three cases in this part focus on the fullest and most complex version of the problem of managers' organizational responsibilities. Each case deals with this issue from the viewpoint of a senior executive. This executive's perspective must, inevitably, take into account the firm's long-term strategy, its overall finances, its competitive position, and all of the social, administrative, and internal political factors that shape the organization. Moreover, when senior executives confront difficult ethical issues, many others in their organization are watching carefully. Hence, their decisions and actions, as well as the *way* in which they make their decisions, can set powerful precedents and, in turn, can modify the ethical climate of an organization. The saying "Watch what we do, not what we say" governs the consequences of senior executives' actions in these cases.

The first cases on senior executives responsibilities, "H. J. Heinz" and "Salomon and the Treasury Securities Auction," describe situations in which the behavior of a number of individuals and perhaps the ethical climate of an organization has led to what appear to be significant problems. The initial question for discussion in both cases is: How serious are these problems and what are their origins? Next, the discussion turns to the crucial question, What must the executives of these firms do to set matters right and begin to create an appropriate ethical climate? The final case, "James Burke: A Career in American Business," gives students an example of how a difficult set of ethical and managerial obligations is resolved. The case does not provide an "answer" to this question. As a consequence, the case places students in a situation very much like the one that the executives faced.

SUGGESTIONS FOR ADDITIONAL READING

Kenneth R. Andrews, "Can the Best Corporations Be Made Moral?," in Kenneth R. Andrews, ed., *Ethics in Practice* (Harvard Business School Press, 1989).

Ken Auletta, *The Art of Corporate Success* (New York: Penguin, 1983).

Joseph L. Badaracco, Jr., and Richard R. Ellsworth, *Leadership and the Quest for Integrity* (Boston: Harvard Business School Press, 1989).

Chester Barnard, *The Functions of the Executive* (Cambridge, Mass.: Harvard University Press, 1938).

Warren G. Bennis and Burt Nanus, *Leaders: The Strategies for Taking Charge* (New York: Harper & Row, 1985).

Alfred D. Chandler, Jr., *Strategy and Structure* (Cambridge, Mass.: MIT Press, 1962).

Abrahm T. Collier, "Business Leadership and a Creative Society," *Harvard Business Review,* January–February 1968, pp. 154–66.

Kenneth E. Goodpaster, "Note on the Corporation as a Moral Environment," in Andrews, *Ethics in Practice.*

Kenneth E. Goodpaster and John B. Matthews, Jr., "Can a Corporation Have a Conscience?" in Andrews, *Ethics in Practice.*

Robert Jackall, *"Moral Mazes: Bureaucracy and Managerial Work,"* in Andrews, *Ethics in Practice.*

Douglas McGregor, *The Human Side of Enterprise* (New York: McGraw-Hill, 1960).

Reinhold Niebuhr, *Moral Man and Immoral Society* (New York: C. Scribner's Sons, 1932).

Edgar H. Schein, *Organizational Culture and Leadership* (San Francisco: Jossey-Bass, 1985).

Abraham Zaleznik, "Managers and Leaders: Are They Different?" *Harvard Business Review,* May–June 1977, pp. 67–79.

THE MORAL RESPONSIBILITIES OF ORGANIZATION LEADERS

Like *The Moral Responsibilities of Economic Agents,* this note also addresses the basic question: Where do business executives' principal responsibilities lie?

These excerpts, however, focus not on entrepreneurial capitalism, but on managerial capitalism. This is an economic system in which many industries are dominated by a few oligopolistic firms. These firms are typically large, sometimes vast semipermanent economic, social, and political institutions. Companies like this simply did not exist when John Locke, Adam Smith, and John Stuart Mill developed their ideas about property rights, ownership, and marketplace competition.

Alfred D. Chandler, Jr.

Alfred D. Chandler is the Isidor Straus Professor of Business History, emeritus, at Harvard Business School. His studies of the evolution of the large corporation have won many awards, including the Pulitzer Prize for history. The first excerpt is from *Scale and Scope* and the second from *The Visible Hand.*

Of all the new forms of managerial enterprise, the modern industrial enterprise played the most fundamental role in the transformation of Western economies. They had been rural, agrarian, and commercial; they became industrial and urban. That transformation, in turn, brought the most rapid economic growth in the history of mankind. At the center of the transformation were the United States, Great Britain, and Germany, which accounted for just over two-thirds of the world's industrial output in 1870. Before the coming of the depression of the 1930s they still provided just under two-thirds. And the speed with which the output of the United States and Germany surpassed Great Britain, the world's first industrial nation, was striking. . . .

The first entrepreneurs to create such enterprises acquired powerful competitive advantages. Their industries quickly became oligopolistic; that is, dominated by a small number of first movers. These firms, along with the few chal-

Ilyse Barkan prepared this note under the direction of Joseph Badaracco, Jr.

Copyright © 1990 by the President and Fellows of Harvard College.

Harvard Business School note 391-052 (Revised 1991).

lengers that subsequently entered the industry, no longer competed primarily on the basis of price. Instead, they competed for market share and profits through functional and strategic effectiveness. They did so *functionally* by improving their product, their processes of production, their marketing, their purchasing, and their labor relations, and *strategically* by moving into growing markets more rapidly, and out of declining ones more quickly and effectively, than did their competitors. . . .[1]

The ability of the modern industrial enterprise to exploit fully the economies of scale, scope, and transaction costs was the dynamic that produced its three most significant historical attributes. First, such enterprises clustered from the start in industries having similar characteristics. Second, they appeared quite suddenly in the last quarter of the 19th century. Finally, all were born and then continued to grow in much the same manner.

The industries in which the new institution first appeared, and in which it continued to cluster throughout the 20th century, are indicated in Table 1.

The theme propounded here is that modern business enterprise took the place of market mechanisms in coordinating the activities of the economy and allocating its resources. In many sectors of the economy the visible hand of management replaced what Adam Smith referred to as the invisible hand of market forces. The market remained the generator of demand for goods and services, but modern business enterprise took over the functions of coordinating flows of goods through existing processes of production and distribution, and of allocating funds and personnel for future production and distribution. As modern business enterprise acquired functions hitherto carried out by the market, it became the most powerful institution in the American economy and its managers the most influential group of economic decision makers. The rise of modern business

enterprise in the United States, therefore, brought with it managerial capitalism.[2]

Adolf Berle and Gardiner Means

Adolf Berle, a legal scholar, and Gardiner Means, an economist, co-authored *The Modern Corporation and Private Property*, published in 1932. This book, from which the excerpts below are taken, has powerfully influenced many discussions and analyses of large corporations.

Why have stockholders? What contribution do they make, entitling them to heirship of half the profits of the industrial system, receivable partly in the form of dividends, and partly in the form of increased market values resulting from undistributed corporate gains? Stockholders toil not, neither do they spin, to earn that reward. They are beneficiaries by position only. Justification for their inheritance must be sought outside classic economic reasoning.

It can be founded only on social grounds. There is—and in American social economy, there always has been—a value attached to individual life, individual development, individual solution of personal problems, individual choice of consumption and activity. Wealth unquestionably does add to an individual's capacity and range in pursuit of happiness and self-development. There is certainly advantage to the community when men take care of themselves. But that justification turns on the distribution as well as the existence of wealth. Its force exists only in direct ratio to the number of individuals who hold such wealth. Justification for the stockholder's existence thus depends on increasing distribution within the American population. Ideally, the stockholder's position will be impregnable only when every American family has its fragment of that position and of the wealth by which the opportunity to develop individuality becomes fully actualized.

---

[1] Reprinted by permission of the publishers from *Scale and Scope: The Dynamics of Industrial Capitalism* by Alfred D. Chandler, Jr., Cambridge, Mass.: Belknap Press of Harvard University Press, Copyright © 1990 by Alfred D. Chandler, Jr.

[2] Reprinted by permission of the publishers from *The Visible Hand: The Managerial Revolution in American Business* by Alfred D. Chandler, Jr., Cambridge, Mass.: Belknap Press of Harvard University Press, Copyright © 1977 by Alfred D. Chandler, Jr.

TABLE 1   Distribution of the World's Largest Industrial Enterprises with More Than 20,000 Employees, by Industry and Country, 1973*

Group	Industry	United States	Outside United States	Great Britain	West Germany	Japan	France	Others	Total
20	Food	22	17	13	0	1	1	2	39
21	Tobacco	3	4	3	1	0	0	0	7
22	Textiles	7	6	3	0	2	1	0	13
23	Apparel	6	0	0	0	0	0	0	6
24	Lumber	4	2	0	0	0	0	2	6
25	Furniture	0	0	0	0	0	0	0	0
26	Paper	7	3	3	0	0	0	0	10
27	Printing and publishing	0	0	0	0	0	0	0	0
28	Chemicals	24	28	4	5	3	6	10	52
29	Petroleum	14	12	2	0	0	2	8	26
30	Rubber	5	5	1	1	1	1	1	10
31	Leather	2	0	0	0	0	0	0	2
32	Stone, clay, and glass	7	8	3	0	0	3	2	15
33	Primary metals	13	35	2	9	5	4	15	48
34	Fabricated metals	8	6	5	1	0	0	0	14
35	Machinery	22	12	2	3	2	0	5	34
36	Electrical machinery	20	25	4	5	7	2	7	45
37	Transportation equipment	22	23	3	3	7	4	6	45
38	Instruments†	4	1	0	0	0	0	0	5
39	Miscellaneous	2	0	0	0	0	0	0	2
–	Conglomerate	19	3	2	1	0	0	0	22
	Total	211	190	50	29	28	24	59	401

* The *Fortune* lists include enterprises of noncommunist countries only.
† Medical equipment and supplies, photographic equipment and supplies, and watches and clocks.

Sources: Compiled from "The Fortune Directory of the 500 Largest Industrial Corporations," *Fortune,* May 1974, pp. 230–57; "The Fortune Directory of the 300 Largest Industrial Corporations outside the U.S., *Fortune,* August 1974, pp. 174–81.

Privilege to have income and a fragment of wealth without a corresponding duty to work for it cannot be justified except on the ground that the community is better off—and not unless most members of the community share it. . . .

In its new aspect the corporation is a means whereby the wealth of innumerable individuals has been concentrated into huge aggregates and whereby control over this wealth has been surrendered to a unified direction. The power attendant on such concentration has brought forth princes of industry, whose position in the community is yet to be defined. The surrender of control over their wealth by investors has effectively broken the old property relationships and has raised the problem of defining these relationships anew. . . .

Corporations where this separation has become an important factor may be classed as quasi-public in character in contradiction to the private, or closely held, corporation in which no important separation of ownership and control has taken place. . . .

The separation of ownership from control produces a condition where the interests of owner and of ultimate manager may, and often do, diverge, and where many of the checks which formerly operated to limit the use of power disappear. Size alone tends to give these giant corporations a social significance not attached to the smaller units of private enterprise. By the use of the open market for securities, each of these corporations assumes obligations towards the investing public which transform it from a legal method clothing the rule of a few individuals into an institution at least normally serving investors who have embarked their funds in its enterprise. New responsibilities towards the owners, the workers, the consumers, and the State thus rest on the shoulders of those in control. In creating these new relationships, the quasi-public corporation may fairly be said to work a revolution. It has destroyed the unity that we commonly call property—has divided the ownership into nominal ownership and the power formerly joined to it. Thereby the corporation has changed the nature of profit-seeking enterprise.[3]

The Wall Street Journal

These two articles appeared in *The Wall Street Journal* in early 1990. The first, written by David Hilder, summarizes a decision by the Delaware Supreme Court in response to Para-

mount's bid to take over Time, Inc. The second, written by L. Gordon Crovitz, analyzes the decision.

Ruling by Court on Time, Inc.'s, Merger Affirms the Power of Corporate Boards

The Delaware Supreme Court, in a written opinion explaining its decision last July allowing Time, Inc., to escape a hostile takeover, broadly affirmed the power of corporate directors to reject hostile bids and pursue long-term business strategies.

In the 41-page opinion released yesterday, Delaware's highest court took the opportunity to explicitly reject the reasoning behind a series of lower court decisions in other cases that had encouraged hostile bidders.

The Delaware Supreme Court said, in effect, that companies can keep takeover defenses in place even when faced with an all-cash hostile bid that shareholders might want to accept.

The earlier lower court rulings said that, at the end of a long takeover battle, a corporate board must dismantle its defenses and allow shareholders to choose between keeping their shares or tendering them for cash. In several cases, including the battle for control of Pillsbury Company, such rulings have forced companies to put themselves up for sale.

The state supreme court said it rejected the lower court approach as a "narrow and rigid construction" of earlier Delaware Supreme Court decisions in takeover battles.

In yesterday's opinion, the Delaware court explained the legal reasoning behind its quick decision last July to allow Time to buy Warner Communications, Inc., for $14 billion in a friendly deal, thereby dooming a $200-a-share, or $12 billion, hostile bid for Time by Paramount Communications, Inc.

Lawyers who have advised companies to "just say no" to a hostile takeover bid cheered yesterday's written opinion. "The opinion in Time-Warner is a ringing endorsement of the 'Just Say No' response to a hostile tender offer," said Martin Lipton, a partner at the law firm of Wachtell, Lipton, Rosen & Katz, which represented Warner. The court, Mr. Lipton said in a

---

[3] Reprinted with permission of Macmillan Publishing Co. from *The Modern Corporation and Private Property,* Rev. ed., by Adolf A. Berle, Jr., and Gardiner C. Means. Copyright 1932 by Macmillan Publishing Co., renewed 1960 by Adolf A. Berle, Jr., and Gardiner C. Means. Revised edition copyright © 1968 by Macmillan Publishing Co.

brief memo to clients, "made it clear that a company can remain independent even in the face of an adequate all cash tender offer."[4]

*   *   *   *   *

Can Takeover Targets Just Say No to Stockholders?

Lawyer and antitakeover genius Martin Lipton had good reason to celebrate last week's Delaware court opinion explaining its decision in July to let Time fend off Paramount by merging with Warner. There was less cheering by the owners of Time, its stockholders. The new rule says stockholders don't get a chance to vote on a high bid for their shares if the board wants another merger and has a plan that might, maybe, someday nudge the share prices back up.

Paramount v. *Time* shows how far the law has moved from the notion that corporate boards exist to serve stockholders. Delaware corporate law risks losing touch with one reason corporations were created as a way of doing business in the first place. This is that people will offer their capital to strangers only if they know that their agents — corporate directors — are legally bound to maximize share prices.

Courts have a rule, the "business judgment rule," that they won't second-guess decisions by corporate boards such as mergers; stockholders select corporate directors, not judges, to make decisions for the corporation. But there is an exception. Judges are supposed to intervene when directors in some way violate their fiduciary duty to stockholders. The markets and common sense suggest that a failure to maximize share price is a pretty good indication that a board has let its stockholders down.

The law, naturally, is not so simple. The justices said Time's plan to merge with Warner didn't mean that Time had put itself up for sale, so it was free to reject bids, even Paramount's all-cash bid for all shares. "Absent a limited set of circumstances," they wrote, "a board of directors, while always required to act in an informed manner, is not under any *per se* duty to maximize shareholder value in the short term, even in the context of a takeover." It left unclear what duty directors owe to whom over what time period.

Instead, the justices noted that Time directors "expressed their concern that their stockholders would not comprehend the long-term benefits of the Warner merger" and that Paramount's "cash premium would be a tempting prospect." So tempting that Time changed the structure of its merger with Warner to avoid New York Stock Exchange rules that would have required stockholder approval.[5]

Jay Lorsch, with Elizabeth MacIver

Jay Lorsch is a professor at Harvard Business School and the author of many books on senior management and organizational behavior. Elizabeth MacIver is a former research associate at the school. The excerpt that follows is from *Pawns or Potentates,* their study of American boards of directors, published in 1990.

"Boardroom" — the word alone conjures up visions of power, wealth, and privilege in the minds of most Americans. Almost every publicly owned corporation in America has a boardroom, impressively designed and furnished in a fashion that does nothing to undermine the popular view. The boardroom's core, the symbol of its power, is a massive, highly polished table around which the directors are presumed to make decisions that govern the corporation and affect the wealth of its owners — the shareholders — and the livelihood of its employees.

This symbol of power seems as appropriate to the company's employees, including many of its managers, as it does to the general public who invest their savings, directly or indirectly, through mutual or pension funds in the shares

---

of the companies. This perception of the role and the power of the board of directors meshes, too, with the traditional legal view of corporate governance.

Directors, however, are less sanguine about their power and capacity to govern. While they don't see themselves as pawns of management, as did their predecessors of a decade ago, they acknowledge a number of constraints on their ability to govern in a timely and effective manner. Such constraints include their own available time and knowledge, a lack of consensus about their goals, and the superior power of management, particularly the CEO-chairman. . . .

The discussion above naturally raises the issue of how outside directors are selected for membership on a particular board. Legally, it is a multistep process, beginning when the incumbent directors search for potential nominees and ending when the shareholders elect those who are nominated by the directors or by the shareholders themselves. Traditionally, however, in most companies, selecting directors has been the exclusive responsibility of the CEO, who chose the candidates, then recommended them to the board for its approval. The sense of the CEO's ownership of the selection process was exemplified by how often one heard a CEO referring to "my board." Even today, many CEOs are a major influence in the selection of directors, and many still refer to the board as "my directors," but the trend is moving away from such CEO dominance, mainly because of the emergence of nominating committees. In our survey, 84 percent of the directors reported that the boards on which they served have such committees. Nevertheless, in many companies, these committees still have limited influence compared to that of the CEO. . . .

While few CEOs abuse their power, the norms of polite boardroom behavior discourage directors from openly questioning or challenging the CEO's performance or proposals, under normal conditions. Despite the fact that CEOs are expected to encourage director discussion and involvement, the reality falls far short of the ideal because of boardroom norms of conduct to which both CEOs and directors adhere.

When directors lack a forum, inside or outside the boardroom, to discuss tough issues together, to challenge management collectively, and to act quickly in crises, their numerical advantage over the CEO cannot easily translate into real strength.[6]

Gordon Donaldson and Jay Lorsch

Like Jay Lorsch, Gordon Donaldson is a professor at Harvard Business School. This excerpt is from their study of senior managers, *Decision Making at the Top,* published in 1983.[7]

. . . It is commonly believed that the primary goal of these corporate managers is the maximization of shareholder wealth. But we have found, in contrast, that their primary goal is the survival of the corporation in which they have invested so much of themselves psychologically and professionally. Therefore, they are committed, first and foremost, to the enhancement of *corporate* wealth, which includes not only the firm's financial assets reflected on the balance sheet but also its important human assets and its competitive position in the various markets in which it operates.

Those who argue that management strives to maximize shareholder wealth have also argued that management's strategic decisions are subject to the discipline of the capital market. From their perspective, management's choices are guided by the corporate rate of return on investment compared to the cost of that capital in the public market. But we have found that the top managers in these large, mature companies seek to minimize their dependence on the external capital market. They work to make

---

[6] Reprinted by permission of Harvard Business School Press from *Pawns or Potentates: The Reality of America's Corporate Boards* by Jay W. Lorsch with Elizabeth MacIver. Boston: 1989, pp. 1, 12, 26, 96. Copyright © 1989 by the President and Fellows of Harvard College.

[7] Reprinted by permission of BasicBooks, a division of HarperCollins Publishers, Inc. from *Decision Making at the Top* by Gordon Donaldson and Jay W. Lorsch. Copyright © 1983 by Basic Books, Inc.

their companies financially self-sustaining. Thus their goals reflect the characteristics of an internal capital market in which the demand for funds reflected in growth objectives must be balanced against the available supply provided primarily by retained earnings and secondarily by the borrowing available on a truly arm's-length basis.

Further, these corporate executives do not concern themselves solely with investor reactions and expectations, as the conventional wisdom would suggest. Instead, they reach choices that also assure that they will maintain or enhance their position in their product markets as well as meet the expectations of their fellow employees for stability and growth in career opportunities. . . .

. . . In particular, these experienced managers are loath to rely on the capital markets as the primary source of the funds essential to achieve vital corporate objectives. Such funds must be available at a time of management's choosing, on terms it considers acceptable, in the amount it requires. However, managers' experience has taught them that investors' judgments and expectations are often out of phase with their own judgments, expectations, and needs.

. . . These managers' preference for self-reliance was also evident in their debt policies. In every case they favored a conservative amount of debt; that is, that amount which normally provides a *wide* margin of safety to the lenders and which they are accustomed to lend on a truly *arm's-length* basis.

. . . Nevertheless, these corporate managers did give priority to their ability to survive on the firm's own resources, if necessary, and to emerge from a test of self-sufficiency with their essential capabilities intact. Their corporate strategies reflected that priority. They achieved balanced funds flows and financial self-sufficiency to avoid capital market constraints and interference. They diversified in varying degrees to free themselves from the competitive imperatives of any single product market. They adopted internal management practices designed to insulate the firm from the arbitrary consequences of a mobile and volatile market for personnel. . . .

To most managers, the key to organizational survival in an economic sense is the accumulation of corporate purchasing power or wealth by which they can command the goods and services essential to their mission. To "assure" survival, self-sufficiency, and success, these top managers strive continuously to conserve and augment corporate wealth. . . .

Peter Drucker

Peter Drucker is a professor of social sciences at the Claremont Graduate School and the author of many books on management. The excerpt below is from his classic study of General Motors, *The Concept of the Corporation,* published in 1946.

. . . the essence of the corporation is social, that is human, organization. This might appear like a redundant assertion. Actually for far too many people the essential in modern industrial production is not the social organization, but raw materials or tools. In our popular concept of industry we suffer from a rigid economic determinism—the legacy of the early 19th-century emphasis on natural resources as the determinant of the division of labor—and from a blind admiration for gadgets. As a result, most of us—including a good many people in industrial production itself—fail to understand that modern production, and especially modern mass production, is not based on raw materials or gadgets, but on principles of organization—organization not of machines, but of human beings, i.e., on social organization. . . .

Neither this sketch nor an organization chart can, of course, show the outsider how the organization actually functions. But it should give some impression of the administrative and organizational problems that have to be solved in order to make it run efficiently. There is the sheer size of the business—250,000 workers in peacetime, twice that number during the war. There is a problem of diversity: not only do the finished products—over 200 in peacetime—range from a diesel-electric locomotive costing $500,000 to a bolt costing a fraction of a cent; the production units required range from gigantic plants with 40,000 employees to machine shops. There is a problem in autonomy: the 500 men of ability, experience, and ambition who are needed in major executive jobs in order to turn out all these different finished products of General Motors could not possibly be organized and managed from the top. There is also a problem of unity: with the bulk of the company's products focused on one final utility, the automobile, and therefore directed toward the same market, the divisions could not be left to their own devices, but must be one in spirit and in policy. Divisional management must be both autonomous and directed; central management must at the same time give effective, unifying leadership and be confined to regulation and advice. . . . Hence, General Motors has become *an essay in federalism.*

That General Motors owes its strength precisely to that use of principles and concepts as guides for concrete, unplanned, and unforeseen action of which the "planner" knows nothing, is thus of general importance. The most successful attempt to provide a basis for the political organization of the future, the American Constitution, used the same method. The Constitution is not a "plan" of government, laying down what ought to be done. Neither is it "pragmatic." It establishes a few, simple organs of government with enormous powers of which only the limits are given. It establishes an objective yardstick in the law. It provides a few, very simple principles of decision in broad language; most of them, it is noteworthy, lay down how not to act, with the significant exception of the provisions for the revision of the Constitution which establish a positive procedure. But the actual organization and system of government were wisely left to concrete experience—a wisdom on which the success of the Constitution rests in large part. . . .

Above all, the General Motors policies successfully establish a functioning corporate government.

Moriaki Tsuchiya

Moriaki Tsuchiya is a member of the faculty of economics at the University of Tokyo. This excerpt is from his article, "The Japanese Business as a 'Capsule'," published in 1979.

Up to now, I have discussed the assimilation of employees by the firm in three parts. First, I explained the mechanism by which the seniority wage system in Japan brings about the dependence of the whole personality by producing on the part of employees the expectation of welfare benefits and the expectation of benevolence for the stabilization of livelihood in their old age. Next, it was pointed out that the firm is the place where employees can realize themselves through work as well as make a constructive contribution to society, and moreover, that the social significance of that enterprise can be repeatedly emphasized within the firm so that for the employee the firm comes to have an important meaning that affects even the justification of the existence of the self. Finally, I noted that when a common mode of contact takes root as company tradition through human contacts within a firm, the firm consciously and unconsciously pushes this onto its employees, and then discussed the process by which employees as a whole thus become a group with a common mental makeup or behavioral style.

Much as differences in degree do exist depending on the firm, these three mechanisms work synergistically within a Japanese firm; the employees' sense of unity with and loyalty toward the firm are strengthened; and the firm constitutes a communal group that subsumes the total personality of its employees. The people in this group are more privileged than the members of society at large, economically and in terms of social prestige and mental security. In addition, if all members as a group have a unanimous value orientation, it might even be said that a sort of wall exists between them and society as a whole.

In other words, the firm constitutes a kind of closed society that holds within it all of its employees. If we now agree to call this "business as a capsule," the inside of that capsule is so arranged that, even when the chilly wind rages outside, one can enjoy a comfortable life inside. The wilder the outside becomes, the more secure that capsule must become. The stronger the anticompany movement outside becomes, the more united the interior must become and lessen the direct effect from the outside on individual employees.

Thomas L. Beauchamp

Thomas L. Beauchamp is a professor of philosophy at Georgetown University. This excerpt is taken from his book *Philosophical Ethics: An Introduction to Moral Philosophy.*

As a simple example of some moral considerations that will be discussed in this chapter, let us look at a program of experimental research in social psychology conducted from 1960 to 1963 by Stanley Milgram at Yale University. The purpose of the experiment was to test ordinary citizens' obedience to authority. Subjects were solicited to participate in "a study of memory and learning" through an advertisement placed in a New Haven newspaper. Subjects of various occupations and levels of education between the ages of 20 and 50 were recruited. The announcement offered $4 (plus 50 cents carfare) for one hour of participation.

In the basic experimental design, two people were taken into the psychology laboratory to participate in what they were told was a "memory experiment." One person was a truly naive subject who had responded to the newspaper advertisement, while the other was really an accomplice in the experiment. The authority figure in the design of the research was a third person—the experimenter who greeted the subjects and instructed them about the study. The naive subject was designated as the "teacher" and the accomplice as the "learner." The experimenter explained that the study was concerned with the effects of punishment on the teaching and learning process.

The learning task conducted by the subject was a word-pair association. Punishment for the wrong answer came in the form of an electric shock from an apparently complicated machine. The learner receiving the shock was in an adjacent room, strapped into an "electric chair" apparatus. The teacher was placed before a shock generator ranging in voltage from 15 to

450 volts. The switches varied by increments of 15 volts and were labeled with verbal designators: "Slight Shock," "Moderate Shock," "Strong Shock," "Very Strong Shock," "Intense Shock," "Extreme Intensity Shock," "Danger: Severe Shock," and finally "XXX." The subject ("the teacher") was given a sample shock of 45 volts prior to the experiment.

The study began after the experimenter gave full instructions to the teacher. Whenever the learner failed to designate the correct answer, the teacher was required by the authority (the experimenter) to administer a shock of increasing intensity for each incorrect answer. The learner, or accomplice, did not actually experience shocks, but the teacher did not know this, and fake verbal protests objecting to the electrical shocks were repeatedly heard from the learner. At the 75-volt shock, he grunted; at 120 volts, he shouted that the shocks were becoming painful; at 150 volts and thereafter, he demanded to be released; and at 270 volts, he let out an agonizing scream. As the voltage increased, his protests became more vehement and emotional. At 300 volts, he no longer provided answers to the memory test and fell into dead silence.

The so-called teacher reacted differently to the learner's responses. When the latter first protested, the teacher frequently asked the experimenter whether to go on. The experimenter adamantly insisted that the experiment must proceed despite the wishes of the learner. The experimenter stressed that the shocks were painful but not dangerous. The teacher was then torn between following the orders of the authority figure, the experimenter, and refusing to continue to inflict pain on the learner. As the voltage was increased, the conflict became more acute.

Milgram's findings in this study show that approximately 60 percent of his subjects were obedient to authority. They punished the victim until they reached the most potent shock lever, labeled "XXX." This finding is far from what was expected prior to the experiment. Four groups of people were asked to predict the outcome of the experiment: psychiatrists, graduate students and faculty in behavioral sciences, college sophomores, and middle-class lay adults. They forecast that virtually all subjects would refuse to obey the experimenter. Only a small percentage (approximately one-tenth of 1 percent) was expected to proceed to the highest voltage lever.

Once the teacher either reached the highest voltage lever *or* refused to proceed, the experimental session ended. After the experiment, an interview was held with all subjects at which they were "debriefed." Some subjects were asked to fill out questionnaires that allowed them to express their feelings about the "memory experiment"; but all were then told that the learner in fact had not received any shocks. A reconciliation with the unharmed victim followed. When the experimental series was completed, subjects received a report of the details of the experimental procedures and results. They were also asked to complete a follow-up questionnaire regarding their participation in the research.

Milgram's experiment was later replicated in Munich, Germany, where it was shown that 85 percent of the subjects were "obedient to authority," in contrast with the 60 percent level of obedience found in New Haven.[8]

Reinhold Niebuhr

Reinhold Niebuhr, 1892–1971, was an important American theologian, known as a critic of capitalism and of optimistic views of social progress. Among the abiding themes of his many books was the persistence of evil in human life. This excerpt is from *Moral Man and Immoral Society,* published in 1932.

The thesis to be elaborated in these pages is that a sharp distinction must be drawn between the moral and social behavior of individuals and of social groups, national, racial, and economic. . . .

---

[8]Thomas L. Beauchamp, *Philosophical Ethics: An Introduction to Moral Philosophy,* Copyright 1982, pp. 107–8. Reproduced with permission of McGraw-Hill.

Individual men may be moral in the sense that they are able to consider interests other than their own in determining problems of conduct, and are capable, on occasion, of preferring the advantages of others to their own. They are endowed by nature with a measure of sympathy and consideration for their kind, the breadth of which may be extended by an astute social pedagogy. Their rational faculty prompts them to a sense of justice which educational discipline may refine and purge of egoistic elements until they are able to view a social situation, in which their own interests are involved, with a fair measure of objectivity. But all these achievements are more difficult, if not impossible, for human societies and social groups. In every human group there is less reason to guide and to check impulse, less capacity for self-transcendence, less ability to comprehend the needs of others and therefore more unrestrained egoism than the individuals, who compose the group, reveal in their personal relationships.

The inferiority of the morality of groups to that of individuals is due in part to the difficulty of establishing a rational social force which is powerful enough to cope with the natural impulses by which society achieves its cohesion; but in part it is merely the revelation of a collective egoism, compounded of the egoistic impulses of individuals, which achieve a more vivid expression and a more cumulative effect when they are united in a common impulse than when they express themselves separately and discretely. . . .

The larger the group the more certainly will it express itself selfishly in the total human community. It will be more powerful and therefore more able to defy any social restraints which might be devised. It will also be less subject to internal moral restraints. The larger the group the more difficult it is to achieve a common mind and purpose and the more inevitably will it be unified by momentary impulses and immediate and unreflective purposes. The increasing size of the group increases the difficulties of achieving a group self-consciousness, except as it comes in conflict with other groups and is unified by perils and passions of war. It is a rather pathetic aspect of human social life that conflict is a seemingly un-avoidable prerequisite of group solidarity.[9]

James MacGregor Burns

James MacGregor Burns is a political scientist and historian who teaches at Williams College. This excerpt is from his book *Leadership,* published in 1978.

I will deal with leadership as distinct from mere power-holding and as the opposite of brute power. I will identify two basic types of leadership: the *transactional* and the *transforming.* The relations of most leaders and followers are *transactional*—leaders approach followers with an eye to exchanging one thing for another: jobs for votes, or subsidies for campaign contributions. Such transactions compromise the bulk of the relationships among leaders and followers, especially in groups, legislatures, and parties. *Transforming* leadership, while more complex, is more potent. The transforming leader recognizes and exploits an existing need or demand of a potential follower. But, beyond that, the transforming leader looks for potential motives in followers, seeks to satisfy higher needs, and engages the full person of the follower. The result of transforming leadership is a relationship of mutual stimulation and elevation that converts followers into leaders and may convert leaders into moral agents.

This last concept, *moral leadership,* concerns me the most. By this term I mean, first, that leaders and led have a relationship not only of power but of mutual needs, aspirations, and values; second, that in responding to leaders, followers have adequate knowledge of alternative leaders and programs and the capacity to choose among those alternatives; and, third, that leaders take responsibility for their commitments—if they promise certain kinds of economic, social, and political change, they assume leadership in the bringing about of that change. Moral leadership is not mere preaching, or the uttering of pieties, or the insistence on social conformity. Moral leadership emerges from, and always returns to, the fundamental wants and needs, aspirations, and values of the followers. I mean the kind of leadership that can produce social change that will satisfy followers' authentic needs. I mean less the Ten Commandments than the Golden Rule. But even the Golden Rule is inadequate, for it measures the wants and needs of others simply by our own.

Bibliographic Notes

Alfred D. Chandler, Jr., with the assistance of Takashi Hikino, *Scale and Scope: The Dynamics of Industrial Capitalism* (Cambridge, Mass.; London, England: Belknap Press of Harvard University Press, 1990), pp. 3, 8, 18, 19.

Alfred D. Chandler, Jr., *The Visible Hand: The Managerial Revolution in American Business* (Cambridge, Mass.; London, England: Belknap Press of Harvard University Press, 1977), pp. 1, 3, 6, 7.

Adolf A. Berle and Gardiner C. Means, *The Modern Corporation and Private Property* (New York: Harcourt, Brace & World, 1968 rev. ed.), pp. 4, 6, 7, 64–65.

David B. Hilder, "Ruling by Court on Time Inc.'s Merger Affirms the Power of Corporate Boards," *The Wall Street Journal,* February 28, 1990, pp. A2(W), A3(2), col. 3.

L. Gordon Corvitz, "Can Takeover Targets Just Say No to Stockholders?" (Rule of Law Cohurin), *The Wall Street Journal,* March 7, 1990, p. A19.

Jay W. Lorsch with Elizabeth MacIver, *Pawns or Potentates: The Reality of America's Corporate Boards* (Boston: Harvard Business School Press, 1989), pp. 1, 7, 12, 20, 96.

Gordon Donaldson and Jay W. Lorsch, *Decision Making at the Top: The Shaping of Strategic Direction* (New York: Basic Books, 1983), pp. 7, 51, 53, 161–62.

Peter F. Drucker, *The Concept of the Corporation* (New York: New American Library, 1983), pp. 31, 49, 62–63, 70, 78.

[9]Reprinted with the permission of Charles Scribner's Sons, an imprint of Macmillan Publishing from *Moral Man and Immoral Society* by Reinhold Niebuhr. Copyright 1982 Charles Scribner's Sons; copyright renewed © 1960 Reinhold Niebuhr.

Moriaki Tsuchiya, "The Japanese Business as a Capsule," in *Japanese Economic Studies,* Fall 1979, pp. 8–41 [originally "Kigyo Kapuseru Ron," — thesis of *Business as a Capsule*]; Chapter 1 of Moriaki Tsuchiya (translated by Jun Uramatsu Smith), *Nihonteki Keiei no Shinwa* [The Myth of Japanese-Type Management] (Tokyo: Nihon Keizai Shimbun Sha, 1978), pp. 17–60, 31–32.

Thomas L. Beauchamp, *Philosophical Ethics: An Introduction to Moral Philosophy* (New York: McGraw-Hill, 1982), pp. 107-108.

Reinhold Niebuhr, *Moral Man and Immoral Society: A Study in Ethics and Politics* (New York; London: C. Scribner's Sons, 1932), pp. xi, xii, 4, 6, 7, 48.

James MacGregor Burns, *Leadership* (New York: Harper & Row, 1978), pp. 4, 20.

A COMPANY'S ETHICAL CLIMATE

Every organization—inevitably—has an ethical climate of some sort. This is true of political bodies, churches, academic institutions, labor unions, and companies. Through a variety of signals and incentives, overt and subtle, people learn "how we do things here," "what we really care about," and "how you get ahead."

It is important for managers to understand the full impact of their company's ethical climate. As individuals, they are subject to its influence. As leaders, they can sustain or change it. An organization's climate powerfully affects managers' sensitivity to ethical issues, their ability to make sound management judgments, and their willingness to take action based on those judgments.

The stakes can be very high. In 1986, the space shuttle Challenger exploded shortly after launch and seven people died. This tragedy resulted in part from the failure of a major contractor to tolerate honest disagreements within its ranks and its reluctance to disclose potential problems to its customer, the National Aeronautics and Space Administration.

A company's ethical climate can simply evolve, shaped by hiring and promotion decisions, prevailing industry and community norms, and the example set by the people in charge. Or, managers can make explicit efforts to create an atmosphere that encourages corporate members to meet high standards of respect and responsibility.

The task may be easy or difficult. When men and women join companies, they bring attitudes and values shaped by decades of life. Companies are only one of many influences on individuals, vying with families, friends, churches, political groups, the mass media, and other cultural forces. Much depends on the individual, a company's history and culture, and the ethical standards prevailing in an industry and in society.

Obstacles to Ethical Conduct

As managers work to create a positive ethical climate—one that respects the rights, duties, and interests of people inside and outside a firm—they need to be aware of the obstacles they will meet. The organizational factors that erode individuals' instincts to think and act ethically fall into four categories.

This note was prepared by the members of the Decision Making and Ethical Values teaching group at Harvard Business School.

Harvard Business School note 392-004 (Revised 1992).

Pressures for Conformity

"Don't rock the boat" is a familiar American aphorism. "The nail that sticks up gets hammered down" is its Japanese cousin. People in companies who raise irksome questions often meet strong resistance, and ethical issues are often regarded as troublesome intrusions in business decision making. Ethical issues can pose problems that are not generally easy to solve and involve many emotions and differing, often hard-to-articulate personal values; they can require time-consuming reflection and may require significant changes in course. Questioning others' ethical judgment can be perceived as questioning their integrity; the simple act of inquiry may be viewed as a breach of group loyalty.

Norms of conformity arise from the ways organizations usually integrate members. Individuals at the entry-level are often reluctant to question established policies and practices. With limited experience, they may be unsure of their own judgments: if no one else sees a problem, perhaps there is none. In time, a new member's silent tolerance of a dubious policy or practice can evolve into a rationalized acceptance. Sometimes people say to themselves, "I'll be more outspoken when I get higher up in the organization." However, by the time individuals reach positions of enough power and credibility to safely question a policy or practice, their hands may be dirtied by the practice. The long-standing questions may never get raised, even if they are still valid.

Evaluations and Rewards

In large part, evaluation and reward systems set the tone of an organization, reflecting the fact that "you get what you pay for." If managers find that they are not rewarded for attention to ethics, they may decide that ethical behavior is not worth the effort. Many evaluation systems intensify these problems because they focus on short-term, quantifiable results, while the positive effects of responsible conduct are subtle and pay their dividends over longer periods.

Fragmentation and Deference to Authority

The American writer Ambrose Bierce once defined a corporation as an ingenious device for obtaining individual profit without individual responsibility. Division of labor is one of the great virtues of organization. Unfortunately, it often has dangerous side effects, such as the fragmentation of authority and accountability. This encourages people to define their responsibilities narrowly and limits the information they have. Fragmentation also buffers people from the consequences of their actions. At worse, people feel little sense of personal responsibility or view themselves as cogs in a machine they cannot control.

A related danger is the willingness of many people to defer to the authority of those higher up in an organization. This can happen even in the face of grave, unambiguous moral wrong. The political scientist Hannah Arendt, who studied the German bureaucrats who unhesitatingly and unthinkingly implemented Hitler's "final solution," found that they acted out of a strong sense of obligation to obey superiors' orders.[1] The same tendency was also displayed graphically in some well-known experiments on obedience to authority. Subjects drawn from all walks of life showed a remarkable willingness to administer apparently severe electric shocks to other people as long as the experimenter insisted that the experiment required it.[2]

Job Pressures and Crises

Performance pressures, deadlines, and crises create another obstacle to ethical conduct. In these cases, people naturally focus on putting out fires. One study found, for example, that

---

[1] Hannah Arendt, *Eichmann in Jerusalem: A Report on the Banality of Evil* (New York: Viking Press, 1963).

[2] Stanley Milgram, *Obedience to Authority: An Experimental View* (New York: Harper & Row, 1974).

seminarians sent across campus to give a talk were unlikely to stop and aid an apparently ill person if they were running late.[3] Those who thought they had plenty of time were much more likely to stop. Ironically, it made no difference if the seminarians were giving a talk on the Good Samaritan or on career options for seminary students.

When the pressure is on in a company, additional complications—ethical or otherwise—are especially unwelcome, and crises exacerbate pressure for conformity. When a small group is operating in crisis mode, "groupthink" can take hold. The social scientist who coined this term and studied the phenomenon, concluded that it was responsible in part for several major disasters, including the U.S. Navy's failure to anticipate the attack on Pearl Harbor and the Bay of Pigs fiasco during the Kennedy administration.[4]

Considering these obstacles to ethical decision making, it is not surprising that researchers have found "moral muteness" to be a common characteristic of business organizations.[5] Many managers simply keep their ethical concerns to themselves. A positive ethical climate can counter this tendency, but creating and maintaining it is quite challenging.

Lenses and Levers

Unless managers work hard to meet these challenges, their company's values, attitudes, and norms will emerge willy nilly, perhaps in ways that weaken the firm and discourage honesty, respect, fairness, and a sense of responsibility within its ranks.

---

[3] John Darley and Daniel C. Batson, "From Jerusalem to Jericho," *Journal of Personality and Social Psychology* 27, no. 1, pp. 100–108.

[4] Irving Janis, *Victims of Groupthink* (Boston: Houghton Mifflin, 1972).

[5] Frederick Bird and James Waters, "The Moral Muteness of Managers," *California Management Review* 32, no. 1, pp. 73–88.

In concrete terms, a company's ethical climate depends on several basic factors. Each is both a lens and a lever. As lenses, each helps clarify what sort of ethical climate a company is encouraging. As levers, each can help managers reshape the climate of a company and counter the organizational obstacles described above.

1. **Goals and shared values:** What are the company's basic goals—strategic, organizational, and financial? How are they communicated? What common purposes do people in a company think they are serving? What do they think really matters? What basic values guide their behavior?

2. **Management example:** Judging from their actions, which speak louder than their words, what do the people in charge of a company believe is the right way to make decisions and communicate and implement them? To what values do they seem committed? Do they confront difficult issues head on or not? Do they tolerate or seem to tacitly accept sleazy behavior? On crucial, high-stakes decisions, what basic values have they revealed?

3. **Measures and rewards:** What performance does a company's systems measure? What behavior does its systems and formal incentives reward? Is getting the job done the only thing, or does it matter how it gets done?

4. **Recruiting and promotion:** Who gets hired and promoted? What mix of performance, attitude, and values advances a career? What mix of technical skill, character, and values?

While each of these factors is important in its own right, managers need careful judgment to decide the best way to bring about change. Some levers are more effective than others, depending on the particular circumstances. Sequence also matters. Measures and rewards might, for example, need to be changed to encourage a change in values.

At the same time, managers need to see the forest as well as the trees. To the extent that all four factors reinforce each other, the ethical climate of a company becomes stronger and clearer. "Fit," in a word, is crucial. The basic questions, hence, are these: How do all four of these elements fit together and reinforce each other? What sorts of behaviors, attitudes, and decisions do they cumulatively encourage?

Organizational Change

Like the company cultures with which they are interwoven, ethical climates resist change. Even change from the top can be slow, in part because executives are often products of a culture that needs change. These challenges are even greater for international companies, because they draw together people from many cultures and traditions.

Broadly speaking, two types of factor shape the attitudes and behavior of people in organizations. One type is commitments. The other consists of penalties and rewards. Over the long run, values and commitments are the most important and usually more effective, provided that the whole culture of an organization is supportive and its systems for measurement and reward reinforce these commitments. Unless many members of an organization become personally committed to certain values, the values are unlikely to endure. Changes pushed down from the top through compliance measures may undermine trust if they rely too heavily on oversight or monitoring systems, and they can be frustrated if management style, people, and pervasive values remain at odds with these changes. Typically, members of an organization must be involved in the process of change and feel ownership of the changes and commitment to the behavior and values they seek to promote.

Organizations seeking to change their values usually need an active process for surfacing information, self-examination, and encouraging dialogue. This helps managers understand what changes are needed and how they can best be carried out. Wide participation is important, especially for multinational firms. The views of senior executives are usually shaped by the political, economic, and social context of their early life and personal management experiences. This can skew their view of what a healthy ethical climate is and limit their understanding of the best ways to encourage change.

Some people think that a company's ethical climate can be modified overnight through a series of sweeping reforms. In reality, managing a company's ethical climate is an ongoing process requiring patience and persistence. Every action is both a result of and a contributor to the prevailing climate. Maintaining a strong and positive commitment to ethical values is a matter of continuing attention to the various factors that shape the climate.

CONFLICT ON A TRADING FLOOR (A)

And before a blind person you shall not put a stumbling block.

Leviticus, 19

Background

From March of 1986 through May of 1988, I worked on the FirstAmerica Bank's main trading floor in New York. I began as an assistant and eventually became a salesperson on the nondollar derivative products desk, where futures, options, and other items whose values are based on another security are traded in foreign currencies. I specialized in cross-currency interest rate swaps.

As an assistant, I had worked with three vice presidents, and particularly closely with a top salesperson named Linda. In fact, Linda had been instrumental in recruiting me to the bank in 1986. She had a reputation on the floor for her extremely volatile and hot-tempered nature, but was highly respected for her ability to close deals. She was very aggressive, both in pursuing new business and in ensuring that she received full credit for any profitable transactions.

After about six months on the job, in September 1986, I began to work with Linda on a new transaction for one of her largest accounts, Poseidon Cruise Lines. I had assisted her with a number of clients by that point and had become familiar with her working habits and idiosyncrasies. During the year and a half that Poseidon had been a client of First-America, Linda had developed a close rela-

---

Jerry Useem prepared this case under the direction of Joseph Badaracco, Jr.

Copyright © 1993 by the President and Fellows of Harvard College.

Harvard Business School case 394-060.

---

tionship with the treasurer and the chief financial officer of the cruise lines. Poseidon had transacted many small, simple deals through FirstAmerica—mostly short-term financing transactions that involved borrowing $20 million or $30 million from a credit line. The new Poseidon deal, however, was the largest transaction I had seen at the bank and it had a fairly complex structure. Essentially, Poseidon wanted to finance the construction of a new cruise ship to be built by a French shipyard. The ship would be one of the largest and most luxurious in the fleet. Construction was to be completed over a five-year period at a total cost of approximately $700 million.

Poseidon faced several challenges in this undertaking. First, the French shipyard had provided a schedule of the payment dates and amounts that comprised its bid for the project. Poseidon was obligated to make these payments in francs. As a U.S. corporation with most of its cashflow in dollars, these payments exposed Poseidon to significant currency risks. Second, the French government had agreed to subsidize the transaction by allowing Poseidon to borrow the francs it needed at a below market rate. The government did this with many major construction contracts. While Poseidon's executives felt that the ability to borrow francs cheaply definitely helped offset their risk, they were uncertain how to value this benefit. Third, while the treasurer and CFO of Poseidon were fairly active in the currency markets, neither of them had executed transactions of this size or complexity. They were uncertain about the French currency markets and about the possibility of hedging exchanges several years in the future. They were also unfamiliar with complex financial structures.

The Transaction

Over a period of approximately three months, Linda worked with the CFO to devise a structure that would result in the lowest possible all-in cost in dollars. They agreed that Poseidon should be completely hedged from all currency exposure. The structure Linda developed had three main components. First, Poseidon was obligated to make a 10 percent downpayment to the shipyard at the time the contract was signed. FirstAmerica, with the largest currency trading operation in the world at the time, would work to obtain the best possible spot price for this purchase of approximately $70 million of francs. Second, over the first three years of the transaction Poseidon was obligated to make a series of equal monthly interest payments to the shipyard on the outstanding balance of the purchase. FirstAmerica and Poseidon would enter into a "cross-currency interest rate swap," in which FirstAmerica would pay to Poseidon, on each payment date, the francs it needed to make its payments. In return, Poseidon would pay FirstAmerica an even stream of U.S. dollars, on the same dates, in predetermined amounts. This would effectively convert Poseidon's franc obligation into a dollar one. The third part of the structure involved the actual principal payments, which were to be made at the end of the years three, four, and five. These were large individual payments, which Linda proposed to hedge by having Poseidon purchase the francs from FirstAmerica in three "forward" contracts, effectively locking in the future exchange rates.

Although they had looked at a number of hedging alternatives, including buying foreign currency options, buying French government bonds or exclusively using forwards, Linda tried to convince the CFO that this combination

made the most sense. She told him that, by hedging through large, long-term contracts, Poseidon would save on transaction costs, because there would be fewer transactions to make. Linda also argued that Poseidon could save significantly by giving FirstAmerica sole responsibility for the financing. There was very little liquidity in the forward franc markets further than one year out, she explained, and the Poseidon deal was so large it could dramatically move the entire franc market. She argued that, if Poseidon "shopped" the deal, market participants would certainly try to profit from the knowledge and, by positioning themselves in front of the deal, they would dramatically increase Poseidon's costs. Impressed with her arguments, the CFO agreed to Linda's plan. From an objective standpoint, the plan was probably at least as good as the other hedging options. However, the crucial matter of how much Poseidon would pay for these transactions was still under discussion.

The Questions

As I assisted Linda throughout this process, I became aware of several issues that led me to question the way she conducted business. First, by dramatically exaggerating the need for secrecy in the transaction, she managed to convince Poseidon not to speak with other investment banks. This meant that Poseidon, because it lacked the sophistication and the market contacts to effectively price the structure itself, had to trust Linda on the fairness and accuracy of the pricing. While any salesperson would love to have a customer in this position, I wondered about the way Linda had achieved it. There was some truth to her argument that shopping the deal would disturb the market, but I learned from the franc traders that the cost of such "slippage" would probably not exceed 10 basis points ($\frac{1}{10}$ of 1 percent) on the transaction. Since Linda planned to use her exclusive relationship to charge Poseidon significantly more than that, I questioned the propriety of her argument.

The second issue that troubled me was the actual price that Linda quoted. Since forward points and swap rates are both determined by the interest rates in the relevant countries, the prices Linda quoted for the transaction can best be expressed in terms of interest rates. She told Poseidon that she could effect their transactions at a three-year franc rate of approximately 12.80 percent and a five-year rate of approximately 13.40 percent. While these rates represented significant premiums above current French government bond rates, Linda explained that the differential existed because of the credit risk of dealing with a corporate counterpart and because of market illiquidity. While there was a kernel of truth to these arguments, I knew that the rates Linda quoted were on average 80 basis points higher than the rates the traders needed for FirstAmerica to profitably hedge its positions. This profit margin, on the average size of the exchanges over their average lives, meant that Linda was charging Poseidon a fee of roughly $12.5 million to hedge its risk. The most profitable transaction I had ever heard of at the bank until that point had earned fees of $2.3 million, and there was no clear reason why the Poseidon deal should be worth that much more. Most disconcerting of all, however, was the fact that Linda explained to the CFO that FirstAmerica would net profits on the deal of approximately $1.2 million.

The Dilemma

As we prepared to execute the trades, we were in almost constant contact with the treasurer and CFO. I performed and sent numerous analyses illustrating the benefits of the transaction under a wide variety of possible economic scenarios. Ultimately, though, the two executives still had doubts about the structure and the fairness of the pricing. They told me

they would not execute the trade unless they could see for themselves that three to five-year French borrowing rates for a corporation with Poseidon's credit rating were actually hovering in the 12.50 to 13.50 percent range.

When I told Linda about this condition, she was visibly shaken. She told me to stay at my desk and watch the phones. Then she went to speak with one of the forward franc traders for about half an hour. When she returned, she still looked extremely nervous and agitated, but she seemed to have recovered some of her infectious confidence. She told me to pull up a particular Telerate page, print it out, and fax it to Poseidon. Telerate was a widely used computer information service that listed up-to-the-moment trading prices and interest rates from around the world. Linda said I should also call the CFO to let him know the information he wanted was on the way. When I commented that, with the transaction hanging in the balance, it might look better if she called herself, she became quite angry. She told me to just do it and stop asking questions.

I called up the page, which was in a part of the information system I had not used before. I noticed that the section was for nondollar bonds with trading restrictions. The French bonds in question, it appeared, were subject to a 10 percent government withholding tax if held by foreign investors. Although it was not mentioned on the page, the rates incorporated the return of the withholding tax, effectively increasing the yields by 100 to 120 basis points. This withholding tax would not apply to an off-balance-sheet transaction like a swap or a forward. I picked up the printout and returned to my desk. After thinking for a few seconds, I leaned over to Linda's desk and asked if she was aware of any withholding tax on the bonds. She told me to stop interrupting and send the fax immediately.

I opened my Rolodex to get the CFO's fax and phone numbers and then picked up the phone. As I started to place the call, I wondered if I could actually send the fax.

I was truly torn at that moment. My immediate reaction was to follow the instructions I had been given—for four reasons.

First, Linda was my direct supervisor at the bank and her instructions had been very clear. I strongly believe that it is important to respect the wishes and requests of people in positions of authority. (My background in team sports, my family, and my religious upbringing each reinforced this commitment.)

Second, despite the fact that I disliked many of Linda's habits and attitudes, I felt indebted to her for helping me get my job. She was the first FirstAmerica employee to interview me as a college senior and, ignoring my lack of experience or training, she recommended me for a position that is normally held by someone with an MBA. I felt that, since she had been willing to "bend the rules" to help me, I certainly owed her enough to return the favor.

Third, as an employee of the bank, I had a responsibility to help my desk make as much money as possible. A transaction like the Poseidon one would noticeably increase all of our bonuses; this deal alone could add $500,000 to $1 million to Linda's bonus, and I stood to make an extra $30,000 to $40,000, or as much as 70 percent of my base salary. The transaction would also help the bank show positive earnings at an extremely difficult time (the North American real estate market was deteriorating rapidly), and might even improve the bank's share price. In this sense, by helping to ensure that the transaction was completed, I would provide clear benefits to the employees, managers, and shareholders of the bank.

Finally, and perhaps the most pressing of all, I had just begun my new job and felt that I had a great deal of potential. It was extremely important for me to be seen as a dedicated professional who could be completely trusted. To challenge my boss directly and to risk losing an extremely large and profitable transaction would almost certainly end my career at FirstAmerica. In addition, if I could not help execute a large and profitable transaction because of nagging doubts, I had to wonder if I could ever hope to be successful in the industry.

On the other hand, there were four good reasons why I felt I could not send the fax or call the CFO.

First, I firmly believe that all people have an obligation to be honest. I am an observant Jew, as well as (I'd like to think) a generally decent human being. I feel that basic honesty in human interactions is a crucial building block for an enjoyable and happy world. Although I did not consciously formalize the dilemma into a religious question at the time, the religious beliefs that my family instilled in me did affect the way I looked at the problem. Having grown up in a small but tightly-knit Jewish community, I was raised in the modern orthodox tradition, which holds that people should obey the laws of the Torah while interacting with the modern world as much as possible. The experience that most strengthened my commitment to Jewish belief was the year I took off from college to go to Israel to work and study in a small settlement south of Jerusalem. There, I spent 10–12 hours a day at a Yeshiva, or Jewish seminary, studying Jewish law and tradition. I recalled from my studies that there are several specific commandments in the Jewish tradition that prohibit lying or intentionally misleading others. The one that seemed most directly applicable is "And before a blind person you shall not put a stumbling block" (Leviticus, 19). While Linda was not asking me to lie directly, the information I was asked to convey was certainly misleading enough to make me uncomfortable.

The second reason I felt I should not send the fax was my professional responsibility to the client. I felt that when I, as a person in a service industry, accepted a new job, I was committing myself to acting in that client's best interest.

In banking, there is always a tremendous tension because every dollar the banker earns ultimately comes out of the pockets of his clients. I knew that I would have to live with this conflict in every transaction I pursued, but the harm being done to Poseidon Cruise Lines seemed too large to ignore.

Third, while I knew that the transaction could have significant benefits for the bank's employees and shareholders in the short term, it was quite possible that gouging a major client could have a tremendous negative impact in the long run. In addition, if the amount of profit Linda had built into the trade ever became public knowledge, many of our other clients would almost certainly turn away. Linda evidently felt that the risk of a negative outcome was great enough that she did not want to call the CFO herself.

Last of all, it was possible that there might be professional benefits from staying completely honest and guarding the client's interest. Perhaps a senior person at FirstAmerica would be outraged by Linda's behavior and would reward me for not getting involved.

I reflected for a moment on the various senior people I might talk to. I had already spoken with the person most closely involved with the details of the transaction, the floor trader, Roger. Roger was a very bellicose individual who did not take kindly to interference from junior salespeople. Nonetheless, overcoming my reluctance to approach him, I asked him what he thought about the prices Linda was quoting. "Hey, whatever she wants to do, it's her deal," was his response. Roger was aware of Linda's tactics and was surprised that she would take such a risk, but his attitude was that, if she could get away with it, she should do it. Her methods worried him some-

what, but only from the standpoint that Poseidon might discover the profits we were making and back out of the deal.

Next up in the company hierarchy was the sales manager for derivatives, Peter. Unfortunately, Peter was a totally ineffective manager. He had been an undistinguished salesperson for 25 years and had been promoted to sales manager simply by virtue of the fact that he was the oldest person on the trading floor. Having built his career by executing the same simple transactions over and over again, Peter did not have a good feel for the more complicated derivative products that had appeared on the market in recent years, especially anything not based in U.S. dollars. As a result, he exercised very little control over salespeople like Linda. If he had wanted to investigate Linda's deal, he would have had to ask a trader to examine the numbers for him. Essentially, he would have been over his head, and I knew from his risk-averse disposition that he would not want to put himself in such a controversial situation. Thus, although it was Peter's job to prevent the people under him from committing improprieties, I felt that alerting him to Linda's intentions would not be an effective course of action.

Finally, if I had wanted to take the issue still higher up the management ladder, I could have gone to the senior vice president who managed FirstAmerica's entire 550-member trading floor team. I had seen this man only once, at a breakfast for new hires where he delivered a brief talk to 50 of us. For me, a junior salesperson, to approach him with the intention of "blowing the whistle" on my boss would have been incredibly intimidating. In fact, I could hardly contemplate it at the time.

A BRUSH WITH AIDS (A)

The Crisis

AIDS. These four letters together bring a chill to most people. This fear is felt strongly by the health care workers who provide care to AIDS victims. Health care workers, by their very profession, are committed to the welfare of people in need. But this commitment typically did not place the health care worker at risk. With the spread of AIDS, however, health care workers (such as physicians, nurses, i.v. therapists, orderlies) have become acutely aware of the disease's deadly and contagious nature. The primary challenge posed by AIDS is that physicians are unable to detect early-stage cases, in which the disease is no less deadly or contagious. Therefore, all patients must be handled as if they carried the HIV virus.

HIV is contracted by the exchange of bodily fluids, most commonly blood. Within the hospital environment, health care workers are most at risk when blood can be exchanged. This can happen during surgical procedures in which blood and surgical scalpels fly like ginsu knives, and general laboratory prework in which blood and other fluid samples are drawn from the patient. Both surgery and blood sampling are everyday occurrences in a hospital.

In 1987, the first case of a health care worker who contracted HIV through a needle prick was reported. This lone needle prick, also known as a needle stick, opened a gold mine of market opportunities for the makers of disposable, protective medical supplies. One

product in particular, sharps containers, a medical product developed and designed to accept used needles and syringes, benefitted enormously from the surge in demand.

Sharps containers had been in the hospital for a number of years. Before the AIDS crisis, however, they were not a high priority medical product. Traditionally, sharps containers were placed at the nursing station so that, after a nurse or i.v. therapist gave a patient a shot or withdrew blood for laboratory testing, he or she could walk to the nursing station and dispose of the needle. Often en route to the sharps container the nurse would prick herself with the needle tip. Given the hectic pace of a hospital, a nurse would occasionally leave a needle in a patient's room or at the nurse's station, leaving other health care workers at risk of accidentally being pricked or scraped by the used needle. In the past, a needle stick was an unfortunate bother for the hospital. Unless the needle stick was from a hepatitis patient, there was little cause for alarm.

After the 1987 needle stick incident, however, health care workers realized that every patient, and therefore every needle, represented the potential for HIV. Pandemonium took over. The Center for Disease Control and the Occupational Safety and Health Administration became involved and strongly recommended that sharps containers be placed in every hospital room, next to patients' beds, to allow for point-of-use disposal. Both organizations also recommended that the sharps containers be changed once a week.

The economics of these recommendations for medical product suppliers were phenomenal. There were roughly three million hospital rooms across the country, each requiring a sharps container that would be replaced once a week. At 70 percent occupancy, this repre-

Jerry Useem prepared this case under the direction of Joseph Badaracco, Jr.

Copyright © 1993 by the President and Fellows of Harvard College.

Harvard Business School case 394-058.

sented a market opportunity of 109 million sharps units, up 810 percent from a previous market of 12 million units.

Halsey Health Products

At this time, I was a senior market manager in the Nursing Services unit of Halsey Health Products, responsible for Halsey's line of sharps containers. Halsey is a leading health care company committed to providing the best products and services to health care customers around the world. Halsey distributes more than 60,000 products to U.S. hospitals, supplying some hospitals with up to 80 percent of their product needs.

I had gone to work at Halsey in 1986, straight out of college. I had graduated with a degree in public policy and spent three summers interning at IBM, assisting with marketing and support strategies. I had no prior interest in the health care products industry before I joined Halsey, but I wanted to work for a high-profile *Fortune* 500 company with a corporate atmosphere and opportunities for rapid career advancement, and Halsey offered that.

From the beginning, I was given a great deal of responsibility for someone my age. Starting out as a 21-year-old sales representative, I was in charge of selling products to 16 hospitals, which represented a yearly sales territory of $2.2 million. Halsey gave me access to the standard cost of production for each product, and I set the prices to maximize profit. The job was very demanding, and I had to work alone out of my home—factors that contributed to a high burn-out rate among sales representatives—but after a year and a half, I was promoted to market manager and transferred to company headquarters. As a market manager, I directed the development and maintenance of several product lines nationwide and assisted the sales force in marketing the products. At the beginning of 1989, I received another promotion to senior market manager.

Although my job responsibilities remained essentially the same, I was given more important product lines, the biggest of which was the sharps container.

Working at Halsey was a very positive experience for me. Most people who worked there were very ambitious, just as I was. The working environment was warm and friendly, I was making good money, and I could expect a promotion every 18–24 months if I did well. Most importantly, I found the health care industry extremely interesting and dynamic, and, by the time I became a senior market manager, I had decided that I wanted to stay in the industry as a career. In the short run, I was hoping that success in marketing could propel me into other parts of the company in which I was interested. For example, I wanted to become involved in InterLine, a computerized system that provided up-to-date information on product inventories.

In general, the organization hired highly professional individuals and was very committed to the customers it served. The corporation's mission, principles, and strategy reflected this commitment (see Exhibit 1). Like most companies, however, Halsey's mission contradicted the short-term performance measurements that were the basis for management evaluation. My goals as a senior market manager were exclusively gross profit dollar oriented. I was committed to making the profit plan that my managers gave me each year; they expected me to attain the profit target they set, and my own chances for personal advancement depended on it. Upholding quality measures and serving customer needs, although important, did not lead up the career ladder, even though there was a professionally framed mission statement proudly displayed in my office that stressed quality and commitment to the customer. As a result, a high-profit product got my attention.

However, in 1989, managing the profit objectives of the sharps product line became

---

EXHIBIT 1   Halsey International, Inc.

Mission: Our Primary Objective

We will be the leading health care company by providing the best product and services for our customers around the world, consistently emphasizing innovation, operational excellence, and the highest quality in everything we do.

Principles: What We Stand for

We are committed to:
- *Customers:* Aggressively meeting customer needs.
- *Employees:* Respecting employees as individuals and providing opportunities for their personal development.
- *Stockholders:* Achieving long-term growth and the best return for our investors. Through:
- *Teamwork:* Working strongly as a Halsey team.
- *Quality:* Reaching an objective understanding of customer requirements and using all our resources to satisfy those requirements.
- *Business excellence:* Acting ethically and continually striving for excellence in our performance.

Strategy: The Course We're Taking

We are unique in our product and service breadth and our technological depth. We will use these strengths to support three strategies:
- *Service:* Provide the undisputed best service to customers in both distribution and manufacturing.
- *Innovation technology:* Bring to market a stream of innovative new products in selected areas of medical technology, through internal development and external partnerships.
- *International expansion:* Increase global market penetration.

---

difficult as I became aware of the importance of my product to hospitals and of the potential risks to health care workers using it. For the first time, I was cognizant of serious potential conflicts.

The Product Failure

Following the 1987 surge in demand for sharps containers, a market that previously annualized at $9.6 million in sales was rapidly approaching $135 million. This once lazy and unattractive market rapidly began to heat up; and, by 1989, Halsey was aiming to snare 35 percent of the expanded market. As in the age-old children's tale, I watched an ugly duckling turn into a swan. With the AIDS frenzy in the hospitals and hospital management trying to appease its staff and employees, the sales force found the customer willing to pay almost any price. The profit margin on this product soared to an average of 45 percent, and I left the office with a smile every day as I reflected on the gross profit dollars that were pouring in. Although the competition intensified and medical product suppliers seemed to be introducing new lines of sharps containers monthly, there seemed to be enough demand to go around.

My 1989 sales targets were in the bag, and a promotion was surely forthcoming.

My smile soon turned into a frown, however, as the field sales force and customers began complaining about sharps product failures. It seemed that the sharps containers, made from plastic, were shattering in cold temperatures, and that used needles were able to penetrate the plastic casing. Given the dangerous and potentially lethal nature of a used needle, the malfunctioning of the sharps products represented a serious risk to all health care workers. This risk was especially pronounced with housecleaning personnel, who were responsible for disposing of the sharps containers in the patients' rooms.

Initially, the complaints trickled in, and the hospitals were easy to appease. Hospitals located in cold-weather climates were simply asked to place the sharps containers in room temperature storage to prevent the product from cracking. That seemed to solve the problem. However, solving the issue of protruding needles was more difficult.

The reason that the needles were penetrating the sharps wall was that the plastic was not thick enough. Solving the problem was really quite simple: increase the thickness of the plastic. However, in considering the decision to increase the plastic thickness, I recognized the implicit trade-offs. Improving the quality of the product for the customer risked eroding my product line's performance — and perhaps even missing my gross profit dollar target.

There were several other compelling justifications for inaction. First, the Halsey line of sharps containers already met CDC and OSHA recommendations on millimeter thickness. Additionally, there were no competing products that exceeded Halsey's millimeter thickness. Therefore, when a customer experienced a product failure, it was very easy for our sales force to respond with a standard "we meet the guidelines" argument and, even more compellingly, the customer could not purchase a more effective product. Third, after conferring with legal counsel, I concluded that Halsey was not at risk for product liability contingencies because the Halsey sharps product conformed to the CDC/OSHA guidelines. Fourth, we had built up a considerable inventory, roughly four months worth, and I was very concerned that if we developed a higher integrity product the sales force would not sell the old product and customers would quickly switch to the new product, thereby rendering the old stock obsolete. This would expose my performance plan to a $7,200,000 product write-off. Lastly, increasing the millimeter thickness of the product required retooling the product mold. In total we owned 16 different molds, and each would cost $25,000 for retooling. Although the charge would be depreciated on a straightline basis over five years, I knew retooling costs represented a $128,000 gross profit hit this year. Additionally, increasing the millimeter thickness added another 7 percent to the cost of raw materials. It would be up to the sales force to pass on the cost increase to the customer. Historically, it was difficult for product marketing to get Halsey's sales force to pass through product cost increases because the sales force was incented on revenue dollars.

Thinking through all of these issues, I found myself focusing not on how to solve the customer's problem but, instead, actively engaging in the risk management of my gross profit dollar plan. Sitting at my computer, I would simulate the profit losses that might affect my plan; and, because my plan rolled up to my director, his profit loss exposure, through each of the proposed actions. My appointed target for the year was to sell 38.2 million sharps containers for profits of $21.2 million, but I was on a pace to sell 53.1 million units for $29.4 million in profits, which meant I would surpass my target by $8.2 million, if we did not alter the product.

These numbers would have a direct impact on my compensation. Under the company's incentive plan, my yearly base bonus of $10,000 would increase by 1 percent for every 1 percent I surpassed my target, and I would not receive any bonus if I did not reach the target. I also considered the negative impact that retooling might have on my career prospects. I knew that if retooling became a financial disaster, it would be a severe setback to my chances for promotion. Also, if I missed my first profit plan as a senior market manager, I would be on thin ice at Halsey: nobody who missed a profit plan two years in a row remained on the fast track.

I kept coming back to my first reaction: do nothing. After all, none of our competitors were improving their products, and I had learned from conversations with CDC and OSHA officials that so much was on their plate that they were not planning on taking immediate action to change the recommended guidelines. Perhaps I could engage in damage control by providing excuses to the sales force and to customers, finish the year with a profit plan "blow-out" (our term for a sizeable overshoot of the profit target), get promoted, and leave the whole mess behind. After all, I was not under pressure from my director, Phil, to act since he also stood to gain from a plan blow-out.

Phil

Phil was a typical middle manager. He had been a successful performer at the company for 13 years and was very committed to the company and his career path there. Although he was higher up than I was in the company hierarchy, he still had his own profit plan to fulfill and felt the same immediate performance pressures from above. He had the same bonus incentive plan as I, except that he had a base of $25,000, of which he would lose 75 percent if he did not reach his target. Phil also hoped eventually to rise to the senior management level—he was pursuing his MBA at night to further this goal—and his prospects

for doing so rested primarily on his profit performance. Finally, although everyone at the company was very focused on dollar goals, Phil might have been even more concerned with profit performance, because he had three children and his wife did not work. While I felt that I could afford to go a year without my bonus, I knew that Phil's financial responsibilities made the end-of-year payoff more important to him.

Moreover, since the Nursing Services business unit that Phil oversaw was generally successful, senior management put particular pressure on Phil to show large profits. The company depended on him to compensate for the business units in the division that were doing less well. As one of four directors who reported to the department vice president, Phil was supposed to produce $300 million of the vice president's $900 million sales target.

In the same way that Phil's superiors expected him to make higher-than-average profits, Phil in turn counted on me to be a top performer within his business unit. Although I was one of five senior market managers who reported to Phil, I accounted for about one-third of his revenues. Because the sharps container was by far the most important product that I sold (approximately 65 percent of my sales), the sharps sales alone comprised about 22 percent of Phil's revenues. He saw the success of this product as a safety net that would ensure he met his profit plan even if the other product lines in his unit did poorly. As a result, he had a powerful incentive to push the sharps sales as far as possible over the target.

As a manager, Phil was very friendly and supportive, although he was people-sensitive to the point that he would try to appease everyone, instead of taking strong stands on issues. On one occasion, I had approached him with a promotional idea for ice pack sales, and Phil had opposed the idea on the grounds that the promotion would be too much work for too little payoff. However, after the vice president caught wind of my idea and expressed support for it, Phil suddenly changed his tune. "I'm really excited about this promotion," he told the vice president, exclaiming that I was always coming up with "these great, creative ideas." Although Phil and I had a pleasant working relationship, such incidents made me uncomfortable, because I knew that he sometimes concealed what he really felt to make people happy.

My conscience, meanwhile, was signaling that focusing exclusively on profit motives was intrinsically wrong, and I was also growing concerned about the impact of the sharps product failures on the sales force. I really started to think about these issues often. I found myself driving to and from the office thinking about what to do. Also, I found myself having to fake my enthusiasm as Phil and the department vice president would congratulate me on my outstanding monthly performance numbers. Comments like "keep up the good work" would leave me feeling very uncomfortable.

There was certainly no quality or commitment to the customer shown by the decision to delay a product improvement so Phil and I could surpass the targets in our profit plans and earn bonuses and recognition by upper management. There was also the risk of jeopardizing the reputation Halsey had with its customers. How could a customer trust that we were the right company to provide 80 percent of its medical supplies, when we knowingly were marketing a product that didn't meet customer requirements? I found it disconcerting that my economic responsibilities completely excluded those to the health care community. But no one, including Phil, seemed to be concerned that the product complaints were increasing with increased product usage.

When I discussed the problem with Phil, he stayed true to his traditional style of management. First of all, he focused entirely on how the product failure would affect our profit performance. This frustrated and disturbed me, because I saw that we were confronted for the first time with an issue that went beyond mere numbers. When I first suggested to Phil that we might have an obligation to improve the product, my words fell on deaf ears. It seemed that he could not see an ethical dimension to the problem. At the same time, Phil was typically diplomatic about the issue. He was careful not to start a conflict by actively opposing my suggestion; he just wanted to stick to the comfortable territory of working toward his profit plan as he always had.

Realizing that Phil could not see past the short-term economic issues, I considered discussing the situation with more senior managers. Since the sharps container profits formed a much smaller part of their picture, I figured that they would be more receptive to weighing ethical factors, or to at least looking at the problem in a broader context. After all, management had recently set up a task force to educate employees about the meaning of the company mission statement. Bypassing one's director, however, was never looked on very favorably at Halsey, and I felt that speaking directly to senior management would harm the comfortable working relationship I had built with Phil.

The Grey Area

Although this was the first product failure I had seen that had potentially serious health ramifications, other instances at Halsey had given me cause to reflect on how I should interpret the company mission statement. First was the matter of pricing. Halsey made huge profit margins on some products, at times as much as 60–80 percent. Although I knew that the price was legitimately determined by the law of supply and demand, I sometimes pondered the role we were playing in contributing to the high cost of health care, and I wondered if we were truly serving our customers' needs best by charging them up to five times what it cost us to make a product.

Secondly, there had been other minor product failures. Several weeks earlier, I had received reports from hospitals that some of the blood pressure cuffs in one of my product lines were leaking air when pumped up. These cuffs were disposable, and an average of only 1 cuff in 60 was defective, so it was not difficult for a doctor to exchange a leaky blood pressure cuff for one that worked. Still, I had to judge whether I should intervene to fix the defect. The problem was hardly life-threatening, so I was not going to recall the product; we had already built up several months of inventory, and more cuffs were in transit from an overseas factory, so such a write-off would have been unduly costly. My solution was to require the manufacturer to open the cases in which the cuffs were delivered and test every cuff before they were shipped out. Although I took this precautionary measure primarily for economic reasons—I was concerned that too many faulty cuffs would hurt our credibility and jeopardize our market share—I learned from this experience that there were grey areas where a

manager must determine the point at which he or she will take active steps to ensure the customer receives a quality product.

The sharps container issue was one of these grey areas, and I was fully responsible for deciding whether to improve the product. My managers had always made it clear that I would be held directly accountable for the success or failure of my product lines, and they gave me a great deal of autonomy to manage my products. I would eventually have to answer to management if they questioned one of my decisions; but, aside from a monthly meeting with Phil to discuss my results and future sales plans, I had no direct supervision. This is not to say that I did not solicit input from anyone else in making decisions. There was a well-developed network for advice within the company that included specialists in such areas as transportation, purchasing, and regulatory affairs and quality assurance (RAQA). I often consulted an RAQA specialist, who in this case helped me think about the various business options I had. Such consultation, however, did not relieve me of the ultimate responsibility for deciding what to do.

WHERE IS HE? (A)

A question echoes in my mind. A question whose answer I will probably never know or want to know. A question I will ask the rest of my life. Where is he?

Jerry Useem prepared this case under the direction of Joseph Badaracco, Jr.

Copyright © 1993 by the President and Fellows of Harvard College.

Harvard Business School case 394-054.

The Setting

I had recently reported aboard a nuclear submarine in my sparkling, shiny ensign's uniform. It was quite a day in my life. The ultimate goal towards which I had been working for the past two years had arrived, and I was filled with a sense of urgency and a sense of uncertainty. As I walked down the pier, my clean uniform—embodying my newly acquired "knowledge," ideals, and simplicity—stood out in sharp contrast to the dark, sleek, deadly submarine—

embodying that still to be known, practical reality. The serenity with which it lay at the pier belied what was in store for me on board.

My first year aboard was busy and full of new experiences. The submarine was at sea about 50 percent of the time, usually for 30-day stretches. I spent much of my time studying the workings and "guts" of the submarine. At first the task appeared daunting. After crawling around and observing and operating each system, though, they started to become a part of me. While engaged in these activities, I also became exposed to a more interesting and subtle system. This was the closely networked social organization of a submarine crew. The environment, which consisted of 110 men living together in a tube of metal the length of a football field, acted as a crucible in which one could observe many instances of human beings in conflict as well as in tight cooperation. This forged an atmosphere of teamwork and commitment. A by-product of this process was the development of a rugged, hardened personality in each crewmember. All subjects were open to discussion and jocularity. The best way to ensure you gained a nickname was to let others know the name bothered you. Like a pack of wolves, the crew would sense the soft underbelly and go in for the kill. The root of this culture sprang from the hard life experienced by submariners, the need to release steam and not let problems fester, the need for the crew to trust each man's character, because of the interdependencies on which survival depended, and, finally, the long heritage of life on the sea. As I spent more time on board, this culture, along with the caring, brotherly attitude among the crew, became slowly evident. With each day and crisis, I was able to learn more and more about human nature and human interaction.

After a year on board, I felt like an old "salt." I had quickly learned the physical as well as the cultural and linguistic characteristics of the submarine and was performing well. I ran the Mechanical (M) Division, which con-

sisted of 25 machinist's mates responsible for the maintenance, testing, and operation of the ship's nuclear mechanical systems, and the Chemistry and Radiological Controls (CRC) Division, made up of five engineering laboratory technicians (ELTs) responsible for the monitoring and maintenance of the ship's nuclear radiation and chemistry levels. These responsibilities had built both my interpersonal and technical skills. Having seen many crises, I felt as if I could handle most any problem.

Latt

It was in this context that Petty Officer Latt arrived. Latt was a shy, single, 18-year-old recruit who was making his debut on a submarine. Six-foot-three and skinny as a rail, he had an expressive face that was quick to smile. Having excelled in his initial naval nuclear training, he had gone on to complete more advanced training and become qualified as an ELT. With this background, he was assigned to our submarine and my CRC division.

As Latt's division officer, I was one of the first crewmembers to welcome him aboard. I went through the standard arrival interview and explained what he would be doing, what was required of him, and that my door was always open if he had any questions, gripes, or problems. I explained that life on board a submarine could be both hard and demanding, especially considering the long days away from home port, and that it was my duty to look out for his welfare. Occasionally, this lifestyle posed a problem for newly reporting sailors who were experiencing personal difficulties. I asked if there were any issues or problems that I should know about. He said he had had some family problems in the past but had received counseling and was "over it." This not being an uncommon response, I thought nothing of it and tucked it away in the back of my mind.

Latt was a welcome addition to the CRC division, which had been an undermanned and poorly performing division prior to his arrival. He quickly established himself as an excellent performer, completing all his duties on time and with a fine attention to detail. As his experience and knowledge grew, he started to exhibit many of the "self-starting" qualities managers love. He would search out problems without having been told to do so and solve them, if possible, using his own resources. Additionally, everybody on board liked Latt. He was a mild-mannered, affable, sincere individual who quickly gained the crew's trust. He even learned to hold his own in the good-natured heckling that went on among the men, taking it in stride when the other crewmembers gave him "the business." Latt rarely complained and had a determined and participative attitude toward getting a job done. With this start, Latt was well on his way toward becoming one of the finest petty officers on the submarine.

Latt played an important role in the functioning of the submarine. He and the other ELTs monitored the primary and secondary loops of the nuclear reactor, measuring the chemical makeup and radioactive content of the coolants. Besides ensuring that the reactor functioned properly, this monitoring was a safeguard against radiation leakage. The ELTs were also responsible for performing surveys of radiation levels around the vessel. For example, they would measure various surfaces in the submarine with radiacs (hand-held radiation detectors) to test for radioactive particulate matter. Finally, the ELTs made sure that crew members followed proper radiation control procedures. All of these tasks required scrupulous attention to detail. Every measurement had to be carefully recorded in logs that I and my superior officers reviewed with close scrutiny. This tedious and repetitive work could easily wear on the ELTs, but, because the safety of everyone on the sub depended on the close control of the reactor and the radiation it produced, careless monitoring or record-keeping did not go unnoticed for long.

For approximately a year on board, Latt's performance had been quite impressive. Recently, however, I noticed he had been faltering in some of his responsibilities. It was not a glaring change but rather subtle and gradual. Errors had started to creep into his reports. Information would be missing from the logs he kept, and on several occasions he neglected to carry out surveys altogether. There had been ELTs in the past who made some of the same mistakes, but never to such an alarming degree as Latt.

One incident in particular grabbed my attention. Everyone on board wore a thermoluminescent device (TLD) that measured the total radiation to which they were exposed, and the TLDs had to be measured every month by a TLD reader machine. Latt was responsible for calibrating the reader every six months, a task that was of paramount importance, because the TLD readings could not be trusted if the instrument went out of calibration. When the reader was due to be calibrated, Latt failed to arrange for the proper technicians to be on hand to do the job. As a result, the crew could not get reliable TLD readings for several days and the other ELTs were forced to make a special trip to another submarine to get the readings done. The captain and engineer learned of this incident, and I was forced to make excuses for Latt and my division.

As the problem progressed, I became increasingly aware of its magnitude and the impact it was having on the division's morale. The other ELTs in the division were starting to talk about having to cover for Latt. For instance, if Latt did not show up to take his shift standing watch, the other ELTs would have to fill in for him. They also spent much time correcting the mistakes in Latt's reports and performing his missed surveys.

I discussed the situation with Petty Officer Sturgis, the senior enlisted man in the division.

He related to me that his interactions with Latt had become tense. Latt seemed to be rather uncommunicative and distracted. He was not belligerent but would get defensive when questioned about his work and only offer vague reasons for his errors. I myself had noticed a striking change in Latt's attitude. Whereas before Latt would respond to a job assignment by diligently taking notes and delivering a quick "aye aye," he now frequently claimed that he did not have time for a certain task and generally made himself out to be the martyr. Often, I would find him listlessly staring into space. It was at this time that I decided to sit down with Latt.

When he arrived in my stateroom, Latt appeared relaxed. I let him know I was concerned with some recent problems I had found with his work. I asked him if he could offer any solutions. Quietly looking away, his shoulders slumped as if preparing to lift a massive weight, he slowly explained to me that his family troubles had reopened. I asked him if he would like to tell me about them, and he promptly said he would rather not. He assured me he could handle them himself, but that being a couple hundred miles away from home did not help matters. With some time off to address the problem, matters could be quickly resolved. I said it would be no problem to arrange for him to take a week of vacation and shortly thereafter sent him on his way. During the ensuing week, the division barely survived. There was much work scheduled and, with the division undermanned without Latt, 14-hour days were common. I reasoned that Latt's return would alleviate the division's problems, and that his renewed vigor would add more slack to the other's schedules.

On Latt's return, the picture started looking brighter. He said his problem had been taken care of and this was quickly evident in his attitude and performance. For the next week, I heaved a sigh of relief. But my sigh proved to be premature. Latt quickly fell back into his previous despondent mood; his performance declined even more rapidly. The ELTs' morale was swirling down the tubes. Realizing that I could not depend on Latt, I had to shift much of his workload to the other members of the division. I also heard complaints from outside the division, such as the gripes of crewmembers who spent the better part of an hour looking for Latt to perform a test when he was supposed to be on duty.

The ELTs did not vent their discontent directly at Latt. He had built up enough goodwill with them over the preceding months that they tried to remain on friendly terms with him, and everybody realized that he was struggling internally with some sort of problem. However, Latt interacted much less than he had before with the other members of the division—the normal banter between them had ceased—and privately many of the ELTs expressed their frustration to me, deriding Latt for all the problems he caused.

Additionally, the captain and the executive officer were increasingly concerned with the division's performance. Although I and the ELTs tried to correct Latt's errors and omissions as much as possible before my superiors saw them, it would have required gross forgery to cover the problems completely, and I was not willing to resort to this. It was therefore inevitable that the captain and engineer, who both reviewed the logs, would become aware of the division's problems.

Captain Howland's management style, which was very effective, was to delegate his authority extensively while keeping a close eye on everything that happened on board. He also maintained very high standards and expectations. In this way, he managed to combine a hands-off style with a firm grip on the submarine. I felt empowered to make important decisions on my own; but, if I made a decision that turned out to be wrong, Captain Howland would press me to examine why I had made the wrong decision by asking questions. Was there a problem I hadn't known about when I made the decision? Was there a flaw in my decision-making process? What was the root cause of the difficulty and how would I fix it? I spoke with Captain Howland on an informal and everyday basis, so he would voice his concerns about my division to me directly. Although he perceived that there was a pattern of trouble within my CRC division, he did not know that Latt was the cause. When the captain's concern reached a critical level, he sent the engineer to have a long talk with me to try to find out the root cause of the division's poor performance. I did my best to conceal the origin of the problem by responding to his inquiries in general terms, playing down Latt's role in the division's difficulties. I said that Latt was having a few problems, but left it at that. The credibility I had built up during my two years on the submarine was allowing me to cover for the division, but I did not know how long this would last. It was getting more and more difficult to handle the questions and the constant crises.

The pressure from above and below was so strong that I quickly convened a meeting with Latt to discuss the situation. Letting him know that I did not believe the time at home had solved the problem, I earnestly told him I would have no choice but to start taking disciplinary measures if the circumstances did not change. I could not afford to allow the status quo to continue. I asked him a final time what the problem was and how we could resolve it. With the realization that he had no other options, he looked me in the eye and launched into an explanation of his problem.

His inner tension and the control he needed to relive the story were quickly apparent. When he was a child, his mother remarried after his father's death. Latt's stepfather had subsequently proceeded to sexually molest him. This had gone on for many years and finally Latt had sought some counseling on his own and joined the Navy to escape. Emotionally dev-astated by his stepfather's actions, he had been able to mend the wound through counseling and by avoiding contact with his stepfather. This did not last long. His stepfather found out how to contact him and proceeded to harass him over the phone and threaten to molest Latt's younger sister, who was still at home, if Latt did not return from his assignment on the submarine. Apparently, Latt's mother was not aware of what was going on or had psychologically blocked it out of her mind.

At this point, Latt decided to head home, which was about 500 miles from port, and fix the situation. While at home, he confronted his stepfather and threatened to hurt him if he laid a hand on Latt's sister. Apparently his stepfather backed down and Latt was confident the situation had been resolved. But Latt's stepfather had not seen it the same way and, after Latt returned to the ship, resumed the threats and harassment over the phone and by mail. At this point in the conversation, Latt said that he was at the breaking point. After talking to his sister and mother, he had found out that his stepfather was not doing anything to his sister. But the horrific remembrances and psychological anguish his stepfather was resurrecting were becoming too much for him to bear. The wound had been ripped wide open. Latt had started seeing a psychologist on the base but had been unable to make his appointments regularly due to the workload on the submarine.

I was astounded at this point. Overwhelmed with what Latt had just told me, both morally and emotionally, I did not know what to do. A severe toll was being taken on the division, and I had to start doing something fast to turn things around. But Latt had a serious problem with which he was grappling, and he needed a safe harbor in which to heal and come to grips with what had happened. I knew that if I brought this to the captain's attention, Latt would be given a short period to improve but would be separated from the Navy if improvements were not made soon. A final point made the decision even more difficult. Latt loved the Navy and wanted to make it his life. To lose a man with this passion would hurt both Latt and the Navy. All my previous experiences paled in comparison to the dilemma that had encircled me. The solution would not come easily.

The Crucible

Petty Officer Latt's inability to perform his duties was having a grave impact in the short run. By allowing his errors to negatively effect the overall performance of the ship, I would undermine the goals and mission of the U.S. government, U.S. Navy and, ultimately, the American taxpayer. Moreover, the careers of the captain, executive officer, and engineer all depended upon the sub's performance. Latt's poor performance put them at risk. I also had to think about my duties as a naval officer. I had taken an oath to defend and support the Constitution of the United States. This required maintaining the submarine in peak readiness condition in the event we were called to action. I had an obligation to do my utmost to ensure this goal was achieved.

The CRC division was also feeling the effects of Latt's problem. With the division undermanned and the ship in the middle of a rigorous refueling overhaul, all of the ELTs' spare time was being consumed. Setting this within the context of the Navy, where the primary tool with which to motivate your men is the reward of time off, gravely amplified the consequences of this sacrifice of time. The division was unable to fulfill its duties and the morale of each and every ELT was crumbling. In the small confines of a submarine, this performance degradation is quickly noticed. With the senior officers on board seeing the myriad mistakes being made, their reaction was to blame me first, and then the rest of the division. If this were to persist, it would be reflected in our yearly performance evalua-

tions. Finally, while I was devoting a disproportionate share of my time to the CRC division, M division was contracting many of the same ills, namely low morale and work overload, and also lacked sufficient guidance.

Alongside my role as organizational leader, there were certain duties derived from my being part of the human race. As a child, I had been raised to believe in a common bond among individuals. This bond and commonality demanded that each individual be treated equally and with respect. With this background, I felt compelled to help Latt with his wrenching problem.

I also felt tremendously uncertain about what was practical and what was unrealistic. In training, I had been told that I would have to deal with the personal problems of my men at times. The Navy had given me some training on how to tell when problems were affecting work performance, but this advice was very general and focused primarily on drug and alcohol problems. There had been nothing specifically about sexual abuse cases. I had only a very vague notion, furthermore, of the counseling programs that were available for such cases. As I considered these uncertainties, I realized that I couldn't become all things to all people. Virtue was not the same as success and I would have to sacrifice somewhere.

By standing behind Latt, I was risking both the mission of the ship and my standing with the senior officers. Sometimes it seemed to me as if there was not much of an issue. Latt should be let go. But something within me seemed to say no. My personal values would have to figure prominently in my judgment. Would I be able to look myself in the mirror when the day was over? I had come to believe that the development of a person's philosophy came about in a questioning and iterative process. It was a continual refinement as one was exposed to more varied experiences and used those to select what one believed to be right. It was as if the ultimate goal was to seek out a few truths and then define, within those truths, how one wanted to live. This process had developed in me a fervent belief in the equality of every individual and the common bond of humanity. In my mind, the need to help one's fellow human being was paramount. This was reflected in how I interacted with individuals, the respect with which I approached both senior and junior crewmembers, and the time I contributed to several charity organizations on my off time.

Here was Petty Officer Latt, a victim of fate, who was in dire need of help and patience, and it should have been clear cut. But it wasn't. With all of the changes that had occurred in my life since leaving the sheltered walls of academia, I had hit a crossroads brought on by the development of my personal philosophy and management views. Coming out of college, I had not had responsibilities in which people's lives depended on my decisions. As a naval officer, that all changed. I had come into the role of a manager and was confronted with one of the basic dilemmas managers face.

LAURA WOLLEN AND ARPCO, INC.

Laura Wollen, group marketing director for ARPCO, Inc., a manufacturer of small electrical tools and appliances, telephoned London from her Columbus, Ohio, office. She was getting ready to recommend her best product manager, Charles Lewis, for a position in the London office, a job that would give Lewis the international exposure he would need to progress toward senior management. She and David Abbott, her counterpart in the United Kingdom, had had several conversations about Lewis's candidacy, and Abbott had seemed impressed. Wollen simply wanted to touch base with him before making her recommendation formal.

Only two candidates were serious contenders for the U.K. product manager job: Frank

This case was prepared by Senior Research Fellow Mary C. Gentile of the Harvard Business School. This case was adapted from an earlier version published in the *Harvard Business Review,* July–August 1991.

Copyright © 1992 by the President and Fellows of Harvard College.

Harvard Business School case 393-003.

Billings and Charles Lewis. Billings had joined ARPCO the previous year as a product manager for the housewares division. Before that, he had been a sales representative for one of ARPCO's main competitors. Wollen knew Billings fairly well because he had reported to her for several months on a special project. She found him to be intelligent and hardworking.

Yet she believed that Lewis, who had reported to her for three years, had the same innate talents but was better prepared for the job and possessed a creative spark that Billings did not. With a bachelor's degree in business administration and two years of experience selling financial services, Lewis had joined ARPCO as a sales rep in the Midwest. He immediately proved himself a winner. Marketing often recruited high fliers from the sales force, so Lewis was soon offered a job as product manager for power saws.

Within a year, Lewis had such command of his product management job that Wollen asked him to head the introduction of an electrical charging system for ARPCO's new line of cordless power tools. The assignment required more than the usual amount of interdependence and collaboration, but Lewis worked carefully and cautiously to develop the relationships that he needed. The product introduction was a smashing success.

Now in 1990 the company wanted to launch the charging system along with several cordless power tools in the United Kingdom. It was ARPCO's first entry into the British home workshop market. Its success was important because the last few years — the late 1980s — had brought high interest rates and inflation that slowed consumer spending in the housewares division. Entry into the do-it-yourself home maintenance market was seen as a way to benefit from a slowing economy as consumers turned toward household projects to save money. ARPCO hoped to expand its revenues and to maintain its visibility in the United Kingdom, while waiting for the economy to pick up and for the opportunities that Europe 1992 would bring.

Jobs outside the United States were highly prized at ARPCO, and only very strong performers made the cut. When an opening occurred, marketing directors reviewed their product managers and selected appropriate candidates. They then discussed the candidates informally with the director who was doing the hiring, and each could recommend one candidate to his or her divisional vice president. The vice presidents typically reviewed the recommendations and passed them on unchanged to the director in the host country. ARPCO encouraged managers to recommend their best people; it rewarded managers for the number of people they put on the fast track and for the performance of the fast trackers in their first six months on the job.

To Wollen's mind, Lewis was a natural for the job. Although she hated to lose him, she was glad he would have the opportunity to demonstrate his ability in such a visible position, and she was eager to play a role in his professional development. But her friendly conversation with Abbott suddenly took an

unexpected turn as she learned that Abbott no longer shared her enthusiasm for Lewis.

"You're the group marketing director, Laura, so I can't tell you who to recommend for the position, but I'll go on record as preferring Billings to Lewis." Abbott's British enunciation had an insistent edge.

"That really surprises me," she responded. "I know Billings is bright and motivated and all of that, but his experience is in housewares, just as yours is. Lewis, on the other hand, has three years in the home workshop division. His experience can get the launch off to a good start, and I know how important that is to you."

"You're right, I do have a lot riding on this launch, and it will require a lot of coordination. That's why I'm trying to pull together a team of professionals who can work together in the British environment. I need people who are comfortable with our sales force, our research and support staff, and our buyers. When Billings was here on temporary assignment last fall, he demonstrated that ability. I'm sure he can learn the product line."

"But let's face it," Wollen said. "That assignment was a three-month fill-in in housewares and didn't include any client contact. Besides, Billings has been on line as a product manager for only 11 months. Compared with Lewis, he's less mature, less creative —"

"If you insist on recommending Lewis, fine, I won't refuse the hire," Abbott said crossly. "But I need someone who will fit in, someone who can work comfortably and constructively with the team I've put together, not some individual contributor whose main concern is the next rung on the career ladder."

Wollen hesitated, then, trusting her instincts, said, "We're not really talking about the same thing here, are we David? This isn't about market knowledge or ego. It's about race. You're concerned because Lewis is black, aren't you?"

"You didn't even mention it in our earlier conversations! If one of my managers hadn't mentioned it, I wouldn't have known until he walked in the door for the interview two weeks from now."

"Does it matter? Is it relevant here?" Wollen asked.

"The only thing that matters is that my new product manager is able to work well with the other managers and that he—or she—is able to adjust to the culture. Other managers like Lewis have been uncomfortable here, and we can't afford to botch this introduction. It's the key to our presence in the whole market."

"Look, David," Wollen reasoned, "in the three years Lewis has worked for me, he's had to work with all kinds of co-workers and customers, and they all had their own concerns and assumptions about him. But he managed to build productive relationships despite all those things. If you think he's too sensitive or inflexible, I can point to—"

"Don't misunderstand me, Laura. Lewis looks very good on paper. I'm certain he's very talented and will go far with ARPCO. I just don't believe that he is the most appropriate candidate for this position at this time. And when a manager doesn't last, everyone suffers from the loss of continuity. It will set the product line back months. Our group can recover from that kind of setback, but what about you? A failed recommendation will become part of your record. And just think what it will do to Lewis's career."

Wollen winced. "What would have happened to my career if Ralph Jordan hadn't been willing to take a chance by putting a woman product manager in the home workshop division for the first time? That's all I'm asking of you, that you give Lewis the chance to show what he can do."

"Perhaps this one is a bit too close to home, Laura. Are you sure this isn't just a personal issue?"

Wollen regretted giving Abbott that opening and closed the conversation coolly: "I'll think about what you've said and submit my recommendation by the end of the day."

Wollen hung up the phone and rushed from her office up to the eighth floor conference room for a meeting with the rest of the home workshop marketing directors and Ralph Jordan, their divisional vice president. Much as she tried to shift gears, she kept thinking about Abbott's question, "Are you sure this isn't a personal issue?"

ARPCO

ARPCO was a $2.5 billion business, based in Columbus, Ohio, that produced small appliances for the home and workshop, as well as larger equipment for the yard and garden. With over 200 products, the company was organized into three divisions:

Housewares. This was ARPCO's original business, representing $1.25 billion in sales. It included three product families—food and beverage preparation, personal care, cleaning and garment care.

Home Workshop. This division represented $750 million in sales and included the Power Tools, Garden Aids, and Watering and Lighting product families.

Groundskeepers. This was the newest division, representing $500 million in sales. It included two product families—LawnCare and WinterCare.

Throughout the 1980s, as the Housewares market matured, ARPCO relied more heavily on growth from new product development, expansion into the two newer divisions, and international markets. By the close of the decade, operations in Europe, the United Kingdom, Latin America, and Canada represented 30 percent of ARPCO's revenues. Although recession and economic uncertainty were slowing consumer spending in many of its markets, ARPCO managed to maintain modest growth in both 1989 and 1990 through innovative product introductions and expansion into new global markets.

This emphasis underlay the company's strong, explicit commitment to the development of international managers. ARPCO had a tradition of careful career tracking and attention to performance management and mentoring. Its leadership was convinced that the key to continued competitiveness was in the company's people, so career management systems had been modified to include opportunities for international assignments.

In the marketing area, line management career tracks followed a fairly straightforward progression. Product manager positions were the entry point for candidates recruited from several pools, including new MBAs who were hired directly into these positions and BA degree holders who distinguished themselves over a five-year period in several positions, typically sales as well as other marketing-support areas, such as research, distribution, or support services.

Successful product managers were circulated through different product families, different divisions, and/or different regions. Over the past five or six years, international assignments had become clearly necessary for promotion to the next level—product group marketing director—and competition for these posts was intense.

Performance evaluations for product managers were based on product performance as well as on supervisors' review. Evaluations for product group marketing directors were based on product group performance as well as supervisors' (in this case, marketing vice president) review. Among the criteria evaluated by the vice presidents was a marketing director's effectiveness in developing new managerial talent. This evaluation was based on both the number of product managers placed on the circulating track as well as their performance during the first six months of their new assignments.

Wollen's Career

Wollen had been with ARPCO for nine years, and, although she knew the company had its problems, she was proud of it. It was known for making high-quality tools and appliances and for being a responsible employer. The company was full of bright, dedicated people, many of whom had been with ARPCO for more than 20 years. But by the time Wollen reached Jordan's office, she found herself thinking about the time five years earlier when she nearly left in disillusionment and defeat. It was Jordan who convinced her to stay.

Having joined the ARPCO fresh from her MBA program, Wollen came ready to make her mark on the organization. She was particularly interested in the relatively new home workshop division. Her father was a carpenter, and she had spent many evenings and weekends watching and helping him. She loved that time working quietly beside her father and was proud of the skills he had taught her. She saw the home workshop division as the perfect place for her to combine her talents and interests.

In interviews with the ARPCO recruiters, she had stated her interest in the home workshop division, but they urged her to take a position with housewares. They assured her that, if she did well, she could circulate into another area. That began a four-year stint with food processors, vacuum cleaners, and electric knives. Wollen improved the performance of every product she managed, and, whenever she learned of an opening in the home workshop division, she notified her supervisor of her interest. Nevertheless, she was consistently passed over. Finally, after being overlooked yet again, she was ready to leave. Before she did, she made a last-ditch effort by going over her director's head to Ralph Jordan, who was then the divisional vice president of housewares.

Jordan knew Wollen's record, and, after listening to her story, he looked into the situation. Six days later, he told her she had an interview for product manager of ARPCO's power drills if she wanted it. She still remembered much of what he had said to her that afternoon: "Laura, you have an outstanding record in housewares, and you deserve to be circulated among other divisions and regions. You have potential to do well here, both for yourself and for the company. And I'm committed to developing talent whenever I find it.

"But I want you to listen to what I say to you now. Home workshop has never had a woman product manager before, partly because of a lack of interest on the part of our women product managers and also because of a lack of imagination on the part of our marketing directors. At any rate, you'll be working with managers and customer reps who will find you an anomaly. You're taking a risk by leaving housewares. But if you succeed, you will be opening a whole new set of doors for yourself.

"I can't guarantee that you'll succeed. I can't even guarantee you a level playing field. That's just the nature of the market you've set your sights on.

"What you do—and the challenges you face—are not within my control. But I'll do what is within my control: I'll provide you with the support and the authority you merit—just as I would with any other talented manager—no more, no less."

Wollen interviewed for the position, and, when it was offered to her, she promptly accepted.

Wollen and Lewis

In a way, Wollen had a personal stake in Lewis's situation. She had embraced Jordan's philosophy of developing talent. When Lewis first went to work for her, Wollen had reflected on the fact that he was the only black manager in her group and one of very few in the division.

She was aware that he was not as well knit into the social fabric of the group as other managers hired around the same time. Although Lewis got along with his colleagues professionally, he didn't socialize with them and their families, except for formal ARPCO events. Wollen had felt stymied, uncertain as to how she could assist Lewis to work his way into the organization. She believed she couldn't change people's attitudes and so she looked for a structural solution to the problem. She was always more comfortable working with systems and frameworks than with efforts to persuade or negotiate.

When the opening arose for a product manager to introduce the charging system for ARPCO's new line of cordless power tools, Wollen had some concern that Lewis's outsider status would cause problems for the project if it meant that he couldn't work himself into the information loop with the other product managers. On the other hand, the social distance could give him a balanced perspective, free of personal loyalties that might complicate the task. Finally, she thought the charging system assignment might be just what Lewis needed to hook into the product managers' informal network.

The posting provided the opportunity for Lewis and Wollen to begin to develop a close mentoring relationship. Wollen was open and accessible to Lewis, and she made a point of checking in frequently with him during the first few months of his new assignment. This support was an important signal to Lewis and to the other product managers as well. They were made aware of how important the collaborative project was to the entire group. And, in fact, this cordless segment of the power tools market had been growing at a rate five times that of the rest of the group over the past two years.

At about the time Wollen had begun to look around for an international assignment for Lewis, she learned of ARPCO's plan to enter the British home workshop market with the cordless line. The timing and fit seemed perfect.

Although he had no prior international experience, Wollen felt that Lewis was by far her strongest candidate. When considering any manager for an overseas assignment, ARPCO encouraged its executives to conduct extensive conversations with candidates, detailing the benefits and the challenges of such posts: financial and career implications; cultural barriers; family implications; reentry considerations; and so forth. Wollen had called Lewis in several weeks earlier and had raised the topic with him. She had encouraged him to view the series of video training programs that ARPCO's HR team had developed to help managers anticipate the issues they might face overseas.

Back in her office after a difficult lunch discussing cuts in the research budget, Wollen tried to prepare for a 1:30 meeting with Charles Lewis. Lewis had requested the meeting hastily, which meant one thing: he wanted to get to Wollen before she submitted her recommendation. The two of them had discussed the position at great length when it first opened, and initially Lewis was excited but concerned — excited about the implications of such an assignment, concerned about the impact on his family. After many long conversations with his wife, who had just rejoined her law practice after a year-long maternity leave, Lewis had told Wollen that he was willing to make the one-and-a-half to two-year commitment.

As Lewis entered the office, Wollen could see that the concern was back.

"Thanks for seeing me on such short notice," Lewis started. "It's about the U.K. position, of course. I know you haven't promised me anything . . ."

"But I told you you're high on the list. Go on."

"It's just that I've heard rumors from some of the guys over in housewares, and I don't know how much credence to give them."

"What exactly did you hear?" Wollen asked.

"Vague comments, really. When they found out I was being considered for the London slot, they shook their heads and said things like 'I hear it's real conservative over there' and 'Don't expect a lot of warmth.' I thought they were jealous. But then they got more explicit. They told me about a product manager who was assigned there — a black manager. He found the environment very difficult."

"You know we can't promise that all your client contact will be smooth sailing," Wollen said. "You deal with that all the time, and you've always been able to establish your credibility firmly and quietly."

"But that's just it," Lewis replied. "With this other manager, the customers weren't the problem, or not the only one. It was the other managers and even the supervisor, David Abbott. I know I can deal with difficult clients, but I've always counted on my boss's — on your — support. I've got to know there's some authority behind me. I'll need David Abbott's support."

Wollen hoped Lewis couldn't read her face. She knew Lewis was right about needing Abbott's support, and she was undecided about how to handle Abbott's message from the morning's call. She was also concerned about putting ARPCO in legal jeopardy.[1]

Wollen didn't know how much candor she could afford, so she proceeded cautiously. "You know, Charles, when U.S. companies

---

[1] As of Novemember 21, 1991, the Civil Rights Act of 1991 extended protection from discrimination in employment to U.S. citizens working in foreign countries while employed by U.S. firms. This act extended the coverage of Title VII of the Civil Rights Act of 1964 and of the Americans with Disabilities Act to such employees. Before this, the applicability of Title VII to U.S. employees on foreign soil had been a contested area of the law. In March of 1991, the Supreme Court upheld an earlier decision in *Boureslan* v. *Arabian American Oil Co.* and ruled that Title VII did not apply outside U.S. territory. The new Civil Rights Act of 1991 addressed and changed that situation.

EXHIBIT 1 ARPCO, Inc. — Organization Chart

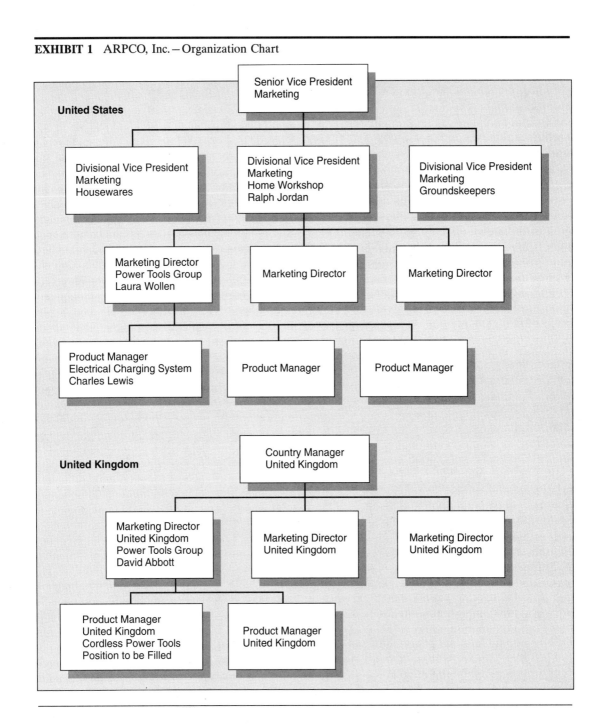

send expatriate managers overseas, there are bound to be obstacles. Sometimes people are outright hostile, if only because they think you're taking opportunities away from them. When you—"

"That's not what I'm talking about," Lewis interrupted. He sat silent for a long, uncomfortable moment, then said, "I've given this opportunity a great deal of thought. My wife and I have considered the pros and cons for both of our careers, for our marriage, and for our daughter. We don't expect it to be easy, but we're ready to face the challenge.

"I'm not asking for any guarantees of success," Lewis continued. "But I am asking you to consider whether or not you think I truly have a shot in this slot. Is this a suicide mission? If it is, then don't recommend me. I'll trust your judgment. Maybe I don't have the right to ask that of you, but you know more about the situation than I do, and I don't see that I have a choice."

Lewis and Wollen ended the meeting with a solemn handshake. Wollen's forced smile faded when Lewis closed the door.

Earlier in the day, Wollen thought nothing could dissuade her from recommending Lewis. Now she sat at her desk poring through the personnel files, looking for a reason to change her mind.

The company policies were clear: "promote the most qualified person, regardless of race,

gender, or ethnic background" and "capitalize on the considerable investment ARPCO makes in its people by applying their skills in ways that will maximize benefit to the company and the individual." In Wollen's opinion, Lewis was the most qualified, and making him product manager in Britain would leverage his training and experience in the United States. She also wondered how long he would remain at ARPCO if he didn't get this opportunity. Lewis knew international circulation was critical to his career there and he was very ambitious.

The criteria used to evaluate her performance were also clear. Her vice president would consider the number of product managers she placed on the circulation track and how those managers performed in the first six months of their new assignments. Lewis was her best—virtually her only—shot.

But policies and her own career aside, there were other considerations, such as the realities of the London office and Lewis himself. Could he succeed in the United Kingdom without Abbott's support? Could she—or the firm—provide support for Lewis once he was in Abbott's shop? And finally she wondered: Should she just make the recommendation and let Lewis decide for himself whether or not to accept it?

Wollen glanced back at the recommendation papers she held in her hands. It was 5 P.M. and Ralph Jordan was waiting for her.

ANN HOPKINS (A)

The general method of maintaining an informal executive organization is so to operate and to select and promote executives that a general condition of compatibility of personnel is maintained. Perhaps often and certainly occasionally men cannot be promoted or selected, or even must be relieved, because they cannot function, because they "do not fit," where there is no question of formal competence.

Chester I. Barnard, *The Functions of the Executive,* 1938, 1964

Many of the best companies really do view themselves as an extended family.

Thomas J. Peters and Robert H. Waterman, *In Search of Excellence,* 1982

Ann Hopkins was nominated for partnership at Price Waterhouse in August 1982. A senior manager in the firm's Office of Government Services (OGS) in Washington, D.C., Hopkins specialized in large-scale, computer-based systems designed for government agencies. Her 1982 partnership class included 87 other candidates; Hopkins was the only woman in the group. Price Waterhouse offered partnerships to 47 of them, rejected 21, and placed 20, including Hopkins, on hold.[1]

Soon afterward, Hopkins met with the firm's chairman to discuss the decision and the admissions committee's recommendations. It had

suggested that she be given more work with partners and undertake a quality control review to demonstrate her skills and allay concerns about her. In 1983, however, one of her original supporters at OGS said he opposed her renomination and a second OGS partner joined him. Shortly afterward, Hopkins was told it was unlikely that she would ever become a partner at Price Waterhouse.

Hopkins then had four options. She could leave the firm. She could join the international area "on the hope of slim chance" she would be proposed for partnership the next year. She could continue working with Price Waterhouse as a career manager, without any chance of partnership.[2] The final option, which she ultimately pursued, was to leave the firm and initiate a lawsuit charging Price Waterhouse with sex discrimination. She also asked the courts to order the firm to make her a partner.

Ann Hopkins

Ann Hopkins was born December 18, 1943. She described herself as "third generation, small town Texas" and as an Army "brat" who "learned from her childhood how to be an

---

Ilyse Barkan, J.D., prepared this case under the direction of Joseph Badaracco, Jr.

This case is based on approximately 6,500 pages of legal documents relating to the case of *Ann B. Hopkins* v. *Price Waterhouse,* 618 F. Suppl. 1109 (D.D.C. 1985), 263 U.S. App. D.C. 321, 825 F.2d 458 (1987), reversed and remanded in 490 U.S. 228 (1989), on remand, *Price Waterhouse* v. *Hopkins,* 737 F. Supp. 1202 (D.D.C. 1990), affirmed, *Hopkins* v. *Price Waterhouse,* (U.S. App. D.C.) 920 F.2d 967 (1990). The quotations in the case are taken from courtroom testimony and pretrial depositions in the public record.

Harvard Business School case 391-155 (Revised 1991).

[1] 825 F.2d 458 at 462.

---

[2] Plaintiff's testimony, Tr. 112.

outsider."[3] She said her mother taught her that "when you shake hands, you should always shake hands firmly, and when you walk into a room, you should walk in as if you owned it." Her father, she said, was an "army career officer who disapproved of army wives working." Hopkins's mother, however, worked as a nurse and believed her career was important. Press reports said Hopkins used such phrases as "hills to die on" and said setbacks were "opportunities to manage." "I think of myself," she said, "as tough-minded, which is different than tough. To be tough-minded is to challenge whatever the assertions are."[4]

Hopkins graduated from high school in 1961 at the age of 17. She majored in mathematics at Hollins College in Roanoke, Virginia, where she earned a BA in 1965. Two years later, she received a master's degree in mathematics from Indiana University. Hopkins then returned to Hollins College to teach mathematics.

After a year, Hopkins left her teaching position to join IBM. In her early months there, she worked as a mathematical physicist and managed a seven-person project for NASA's Goddard Space Flight Center.[5] In 1972, Hopkins joined Computer Sciences Corporation, where she continued to work on NASA accounts. About two years later, she moved on to Computer Usage Corporation. Although she continued to develop business at NASA, she began work in marketing and split her time between working for NASA and developing and installing computer systems for banks in New York and Chicago.[6]

In 1976, Hopkins joined Touche Ross, a major public accounting firm, as a systems management consultant. Her projects included the development of a system for payroll, personnel, and budgeting for the Federal Home Loan Bank Board. She also implemented a health claims processing system for the United Mine Workers. This project took more than two years, and Hopkins headed a team of as many as 20 Touche Ross consultants and UMW consultants and programmers. During this period, she married the man she called "the love of her life." Hopkins and her husband had three children.

In late 1977, when her husband came up for partnership at Touche Ross, she left the firm because it would not consider anyone for partnership whose spouse worked there. Hopkins joined American Management Systems (AMS) in 1978 and soon recognized that the move was a mistake. "I realized I basically preferred a multiproject environment and a broader focus," Hopkins said. Touche Ross referred her to Price Waterhouse.[7] In August 1978, Hopkins left AMS and began working at Price Waterhouse as a manager in the Management Advisory Services (MAS) department of OGS.[8]

Price Waterhouse was a professional partnership that specialized in auditing, tax, and management consulting services. Its principal clients were private corporations, including many *Fortune 500* companies. It also worked for government agencies. In the early 1980s, in its 90 offices across the United States, Price Waterhouse had 662 partners.[9] The partnership worldwide had approximately 2,600 partners.

[3] Tamar Lewin, "Winner of Sex Bias Suit Set to Enter Next Arena," *New York Times,* May 19, 1990 (National edition, p. 7).

[4] William Galberson, "Determined to be Heard: Four Americans and Their Journeys to the Supreme Court," *New York Times Magazine,* October 2, 1988 (Sunday), pp. 33–40 at p. 38.

[5] Plaintiff's testimony, Tr. 7.

[6] Plaintiff's testimony, Tr. p. 7–9.

[7] Plaintiff's testimony, Tr. 12–13; *see also,* Plaintiff's deposition, Vol. I, p. 25.

[8] Plaintiff's testimony, Tr. 13–14.

[9] 825 F.2d 458, citing 618 F. Supp. 1109, 1111 (D.D.C. 1985); *see also,* 109 S. Ct. 1775, 1781 (1989).

The firm was divided into three departments. Accounting and auditing represented 46 percent of the business; tax services, 20 percent; and management advisory services, the remaining 34 percent. Unlike auditors and accountants, who usually came to Price Waterhouse directly from college or the military, consultants typically had five or more years' experience and additional academic training.[10]

The Partnership Admission Process

The senior partner of Price Waterhouse and a policy board managed the firm and elected all new partners through a formal annual nomination and review process that culminated in a partnership-wide vote. There was no formal limit on how many partners could be elected in a year.[11]

Partnership was, in essence, a lifetime appointment. "One of the great risks of admitting partners to our firm," said Timothy Coffey, the partner in charge of MAS, "is that, one, they're less supervised, and, secondly, they are more tenured and, therefore, people that have a likelihood or potential of abusing authority can cause serious long-term problems for the firm."[12] In practice, if the management committee decided to drop a partner, they negotiated with the individual. If the person objected, a 75 percent vote of the entire partnership was required to force a partner out.[13] In the history of the firm, there had been two mandatory withdrawals.[14]

Partners had unlimited personal liability and were exposed to substantial legal and financial risks.[15] Information about partners' incomes was closely guarded. Estimates suggested that partners at Price Waterhouse earned on average about $125,000 a year in the early 1980s. As a senior manager, Hopkins earned approximately $65,000. At the trial, one expert estimated that she would have earned approximately $107,000 had she become a partner in 1983.

The partnership candidates in a particular year were called a "class," and the firm prepared a booklet for each class member. Its first page was the candidate's photograph. This was followed by an application for admission to partnership. Notes on counseling sessions, staff performance evaluations, partners' evaluations, statistical analyses of the quartile rankings for the candidate in each of the evaluation categories, and comparative rankings of the class candidates were typically included with the application.

Candidacy and review for partnership began when the partners in a local office proposed a candidate to the Admissions Committee.[16] The committee then invited every partner in the firm to submit written comments on each candidate.[17] Partners who had significant and recent contact with a candidate submitted a long form evaluation; those with more limited contact used a short form.[18] Occasionally, the committee interviewed partners who had submitted comments to learn more about the basis for their comments.[19]

The Admissions Committee met for three days in early December 1982 for its initial consideration of candidates.[20] The committee member who had visited each candidate's office summarized the results of the visit, the strength

[10] Connor's deposition of March 12, 1985, for Trial, p. 3, 8, 10.

[11] 825 F.2d 458, 461 (D.C. Cir., 1987); *see also,* 618 F. Supp. 1109, 1111 (D.D.C. 1985).

[12] Coffey's testimony in 1990 trial, Tr. 346.

[13] Coffey's testimony, Tr. 346.

[14] Connor's testimony for 1990 trial, Tr. 255.

[15] See, 1990 trial, Tr. 346–48.

[16] 109 S.Ct. 1775, 1781 (1989); Pet. App. 41a.

[17] 109 S.Ct. 1775, 1781 (1989).

[18] 825 F.2d 458 at 462; *see also,* Defendant's exhibits 21, 22, and 23.

[19] 825 F.2d 458 at 462; *see also,* Ziegler testimony and Defendant's brief, p. 5.

[20] Ziegler testimony, Tr. 257.

of the nominating office's support, and important material from the candidate's personnel file, and then described the candidate's strengths and weaknesses for the Admissions Committee.[21] Questions followed. The absolute number of positive and negative evaluations was not decisive, and negative votes were given more weight, often leading to "no" or "hold" decisions. The committee ultimately made recommendations on each candidate and forwarded these to the policy board.

The policy board reviewed the Admissions Committee's recommendations and then voted on whether to include each candidate on a firmwide partnership ballot, "hold" the candidate, or reject the candidate.[22] According to one partner, "the board could override the recommendations of the Admissions Committee and approve candidates on the basis of individual merit or the firm's business needs."

Some candidates had been held because of concerns about their interpersonal skills. According to testimony from Price Waterhouse partners, the firm had "consistently placed a high premium on a candidate's ability to deal with subordinates and peers on an interpersonal basis and to promote cordial relations within a firm which is necessarily dependent on team effort." Other testimony stated that "[t]he policy board takes evaluations or a negative reaction on this basis very seriously," even if the negative comments on short form evaluations were based on less contact with the candidate than glowing reports on long forms evaluations based on more extensive contact. The policy board had, however, recommended and elected two candidates "criticized for their interpersonal skills because they were perceived as being aggressive, overbearing, abrasive, or crude." The reason was that the firm had a specific need for their skills and feared

it would lose by putting them in the "hold" category.[23]

Approved candidates' names appeared on a ballot for partnership-wide election. For admission to partnership, two-thirds of the entire partnership had to approve a candidate.[24] Sixty percent of the female candidates and 68 percent of the male candidates who reached the final balloting had been elected to partnership.[25] Price Waterhouse had, however, only seven female partners.[26] It gave two explanations for this. One was the relatively recent entry of large numbers of women into accounting and related fields. The other was the success of clients and rival accounting firms in hiring away female potential partners.[27]

Hopkins's Candidacy

OGS nominated Hopkins for partnership in August 1982. According to Hopkins and the nominating proposal, OGS praised her "outstanding performance," said it was "virtually at partnership level,"[28] and underlined her "key role"[28] in connection with a large State Department project. No other 1982 candidate's record for securing major contracts was comparable.[29] Hopkins had also billed more hours (2,442 hours in 1982 and 2,507 in 1988) than any other candidate and generated more business than any other candidate considered for partnership in that year.[30] The proposal strongly urged her admission to the partnership."[31]

OGS had written several drafts of Hopkins's nomination proposal. Thomas Beyer,

---

[21] Ziegler testimony, Tr. 258.
[22] Price Waterhouse brief, p. 5.

[23] Testimony.
[24] Testimony of Ziegler or Coffey.
[25] 618 F. Supp. 1109 (D.D.C. 1985).
[26] See note 12.
[27] Ibid.; testimony of Partner.
[28] 109 S.Ct. 1775, at 1782.
[29] 109 S.Ct. at 1782, citing Plaintiff's exhibit 15.
[30] 825 F.2d 458 at 462; *see also,* 618 F.Supp. at 1112.
[31] 825 F.2d at 462; Plaintiff's exhibit 15 cited therein.

the partner in charge of consulting services at OGS, testified:

> The proposal is terribly important because it is the only document offered to the partners which demonstrates or shows what the individual has done and is the only place in time where we are allowed, [sic] the unstated rules of the firm to . . . politic . . . , to campaign for an individual. That's the only chance you have. In fact, it's well known and well understood in the firm that anybody trying any other method is clearly in violation of the unstated law and is terribly frowned upon. So we had to have this right. It had to be done just exactly right. Every word. Every nuance.[32]

Four partners were involved in the drafting and redrafting of Hopkins's proposal. Beyer did the final review himself.[33]

The Admissions Committee then circulated long and short forms to all Price Waterhouse partners. Thirty-two partners, all male, responded about Hopkins.[34] Of the 32 initial evaluations, 13 supported her for partnership, 3 recommended that her candidacy be put on hold, 8 stated that they were uninformed as to her suitability for partnership, and 8 opposed making her a partner. (See Exhibit 1.)

During the fall, Donald Ziegler, the head of the Admissions Committee, followed up the evaluations by interviewing respondents at the two offices where Hopkins had worked, OGS and the St. Louis office.[35] Another member of the committee, Roger Marcellin, also visited OGS.[36] He summarized the contents of Hopkins's file for the Admissions Committee, encapsulating her performance reports, brief letters about her accomplishments, and other miscellaneous materials in her file. (See Exhibit 2.)

The Admissions Committee also tabulated the results of the evaluations for all the candidates and prepared quartile rankings of the class.[37] (See Exhibit 3.) Hopkins received very few "yes" votes and more "no" votes than all but two of the 88 candidates that year. These no votes and negative comments, mostly from partners outside OGS, placed Hopkins near the bottom of the class.[38]

Hopkins's Record at Price Waterhouse

The day before Hopkins was to start work, the partner who hired her called and said that firm policy prohibited hiring anyone who was married to a partner or had a close relationship with a partner in a national accounting firm.[39] Hopkins was told that, nevertheless, Price Waterhouse would stand behind its offer[40] and she began work as planned. For the first few months, she was not assigned to any client work.[41]

Hopkins's initial project began in the fall of 1978. It was one of four major assignments during her Price Waterhouse career. The first was for the Department of Interior. It consisted of two contracts worth approximately $200,000 each, one of which she later managed. The second client was the Department of State. Hopkins was in charge of developing a proposal, in competition with 11 other contractors, that led ultimately to a State Department contract whose long-term value to Price Waterhouse was $35 million. The third project was for the Department of Agriculture, a proposal valued at $2.5 million[42] for work for the

---

[32] Beyer's testimony, Tr. 207.

[33] Beyer's testimony, Tr. 208.

[34] Trial testimony (Ziegler).

[35] Trial testimony (Ziegler).

[36] Defendant's exhibit 30; *see* Testimony or Deposition (Ziegler).

[37] See Trial Record, p. 002012ff, exhibits 17ff, which were not necessarily ready for the December meeting.

[38] 618 F. Supp. 1109 (D.D.C. 1985).

[39] Plaintiff's deposition, vol. I, p. 24.

[40] Plaintiff's testimony, Trial or First Deposition, Tr. 84–85; see also, Plaintiff's deposition, vol. I, p. 24–26.

[41] Plaintiff's testimony, Tr. 13–14; see also, Plaintiff's deposition, vol. I, p. 27.

[42] Plaintiff's brief on Remand, p. 3.

EXHIBIT 1 Summary of Short Form and Long Form Comments

A.B. HOPKINS
SHORT FORM
  #1
                                           MO12

No comments. (Yes)   *Kelly*

My only contact with Ann was on the FMHA proposal this   *Green*
past July/Aug.
    She tended to alienate the staff in that she was extremely
    overbearing. Ann needs improvement in her interpersonal
    skills. She also demonstrated an apparent lack of tech
    skills. (Insuff)

Ann's performance at the State Dept can only be described   *Laughlin*
as "fantastic." She knows how to deliver superior, distinctive
client services. (Yes)

Ann has the "will" to get things done. There is no question   *Lohneis*
as to who leads the projects she is responsible for. Ann has
very high strength of conviction. (Yes)

    I am bothered by the arrogance & self-centered attitude   *Haller*
    that Ann projects.
Also while she may be admired by some she appears to be
    simply tolerated by others. She may not be of value out-
    side current (OGS) environment. (Insuff)

Observation through office association. (Yes)   *Simonetti*

Ann is hardworking, determined & relentless.   *Hartz*
    She can also be abrasive in dealing with staff members.
    I have no question about her tech competence.
I believe the key question regarding her admission is, "Will
    her personality limit her ability to successfully market
    work, retain staff, & maintain satisfactory relations with
    her ptrs?" (Insuff)

I have known Ann for the last 2 yrs. Her office is next to   *MacVeagh*
mine. I have not worked with her, but have been an interested observer of her mgmt of the 1st State Dept project &
her rapid growth as a professional & as a person. She unquestionably has the scope, stamina, skills, & experience to
run successfully the very large projects that contributed so
much to our present & potential growth. As a person she
has matured from a tough-talking somewhat masculine
hard-nosed mgr to an authoritative, formidable, but much
more appealing lady ptr candidate. She should now become
a lady ptr. (Yes)

EXHIBIT 1 *(continued)*

A.B. HOPKINS   MO12
SHORT FORM
#2
_____

I was second on a large project for Bureau of Indian Af-   *JB Adams*
fairs. Ann was project mgr. (Yes)

> I believe Ann does *not* possess the leadership qualities we   Wheaton
> desire in our ptrs. Also, in my exposure to her, albeit
> about 3 yrs ago, I seriously questioned her tech knowl-
> edge of data processing. (No)

A.B. HOPKINS   MO12
SHORT FORM
#3
_____

Known through frequent in-office interaction & review of   *Jones*
proposals prepared by her. (Yes)

During the QCR Ann demonstrated a high degree of inde-   *PR Powell*
pendence & impartiality of mind & courage of her convictions in evaluating the jobs she was assigned.
> She is however somewhat lacking in the congeniality dept.
> (Yes)

I have observed Ann on a casual in-office basis for the pe-   *Gross*
riod 8/79–12/81. I have been impressed & would be pleased
to have her as a ptr. (Yes)

Strength—ability to "pull together" the details into the   *Kercher*
QCR report, take charge attitude.
> Weaknesses—not good communicator, seemed "rough."
> (Insuff)

I have no first-hand working relationship with Ann.   *Docter*
> All my input comes through 3–5 MAS sr mgrs who have
> worked with her extensively—it is uniformily *negative.* She
> is not tech respected & her interpersonal relationships
> are extremely poor. (Insuff)

Relationship—Has offered to teach numerous times & has   *Markstein*
taught some MAS seminars, which is my only relationship to
Ann. She appears to me to be articulate, tough minded,
supportive of PW as opposed to being self-serving. (Insuff)

While I have only *limited* exposure to Ann as a result of   *Everett*
work in the OGS office,
> I do not want her as my ptr.

EXHIBIT 1 *(continued)*

I cannot comment on her technical skills,
> however she is universally disliked by the staff and, in my
> judgment, does not possess the interpersonal skills or per-
> sonal attributes that are critical. (No)

Basis of evaluation – exposure to candidate at firm mtgs.   *Carroll*
(No)

I know Ann through: attending a CE course she instructed;   *Brugos*
attending a MMGS seminar with her; having several discussions with her relating to government pricing. (No)

Ann is a "tough cookie." She is no nonsense. (Yes)   *Hart*

A.B. HOPKINS   MO12
SHORT FORM
  #3 – Page 2

In 1980 I conducted an ASR (QCR) in OGS; which in-   *Fridley*
cluded reviewing a project for the Bureau of Indian Affairs
which Ann served as project mgr.
> During my review of the BIA engagement, I was informed
> by Ann that the project had been completed on sked &
> within budget. My subsequent review indicated a signifi-
> cant discrepancy of approx $35,000 betw the proposed
> fees, billed fees, & actuals in the WIPS. I discussed this
> matter with Ann, who attempted to try & explain away or
> play down the discrepancy. She insisted there had not
> been a discrepancy in the amount of underrealization.
> Unsatisfied with her responses, I continued to question
> the matter until she admitted there was a problem but I
> should discuss it with Krulwich. My subsequent discussion
> with Lew indicated that the discrepancy was a result of
> 500 additional hrs being charged to the job (at the re-
> quest of Bill Devaney . . . agreed to by Krulwich) after it
> was determined that Linda Pegues, a sr consultant from
> the Houston off working on the project, had been in-
> structed by Ann to work 12–14 hrs per day during the
> project but to only charge 8 hrs per day. The entire inci-
> dence left me questioning Ann's staff mgmt methods &
> the honesty of her responses to my questions.

> In July/Aug 82 Ann assisted the St. Louis MAS practice
> in preparing an extensive proposal to the Farmers Home
> Admin (the proposal inc 2,800 pgs for $3.1 mil in fees/
> expenses & 65,000 hrs of work). This proposal was com-
> pleted over a 4-w period with approx 2,000 plus staff/ptr
> hrs required based on my particpation in the proposal ef-
> fort & sub discussions with St. L. MAS staff involved.

EXHIBIT 1   *(continued)*

Ann's mgmt style of using "trial & error techniques" (ie, sending staff assigned off to prepare portions of the proposal with little or no guidance from her & then her subsequent rejection of the products developed) caused a complete alienation of the staff towards Ann & a fear that they would have to work with Ann if we won the project. In addition, Ann's manner of dealing with our staff & with the Houston sr consultant on the BIA project, raises questions in my mind about her ability to develop & motivate our staff as a ptr. (No)

A.B. HOPKINS   MO12
SHORT FORM
  #3 – Page 3

My contact is limited to a few conversations. She is very intelligent but appears to be weak in interpersonal skills. (Insuff)   *FR Johnson*

Ann participated in Houston QCR in 82. Prior to that she managed a job that I provided a staff consultant to work for her (the 79–80 Bureau of Indian Affairs) – where the staff worked 10 or more hrs/day & reported 8 hrs.   *Devaney*
   This classic OGS technique blew up in my face when, upon return, the staff said what do I do to get paid for the 500+ hrs worked & not reported? (No)

I worked with Ann in the early stages of the 1st State Dept proposal. I found her to be *(a)* singularly dedicated,   *Whelan*
   (b) rather unpleasant. I wonder whether her 4 yrs with us have really demonstrated ptr qualities or whether we have simply taken advantage of "work-aholic" tendencies. Note that she has held 6 jobs in the last 15 yrs, all with outstanding companies. I'm also troubled about her being (having been?) married to a ptr of a serious competitor. (Insuff – but favor hold, at a minimum)

Ann's exposure to me was on the Farmers Home Admin proposal. Despite many negative comments from other people involved I think she did a great job and turned out a first class proposal. Great intellectual capacity,   *Blythe*
   but very abrasive in her dealings with staff. A suggest we hold, counsel her and if she makes progress with her interpersonal skills, then admit next year. (Hold)

EXHIBIT 1 *(continued)*

A.B. HOPKINS
LONG FORM
VI.

MO12

Beyer

She can write, sell, perform, & collect systems assignments like I've ever known. This gal will bring in far more than she could ever hope to take out of the firm. (Yes)

Epelbaum

Ann has many superior qualities. She is innovative, highly intelligent, articulate, self-confident, & assertive. She has worked long & hard in a difficult environment & has gained the respect of the client. She has played *the* key role in our PD activities at the State Dept.

At times, however, she can be abrasive, unduly harsh, difficult to work with &, as a result, causes significant turmoil.

Nonetheless, she has made an almost unprecedented contribution to the firm & deserves to receive our serious consideration for admission. (Yes)

Krulwich

Outstanding MAS professional in fastest growing area of MAS (+OGS) practice—systems design & implementation. First rate in handling the *most* difficult client asignments (Dept of State) & is very creative & analytical in developing & conducting work. Excellent in training & assisting staff. I trust Ann's judgment on both tech & business matters & believe she can become the "big job" client service partner we need. With her husband & family, she is a fine person with a high sense of integrity. (Yes)

A.B. HOPKINS
LONG FORM
VII.

MO12

Statland

Hopkins is aggressive, bold, & mesmerizing of clients and ptrs.

Staff does not like working for her. Her judgment is not always good, i.e., she will bend to client demands too easily.

Writes & speaks well; commands authority—little substance—potentially dangerous. (No)

Coffey

Ann needs a chance to demonstrate people skills.
She has a lot going for her,

but she's just plain rough on people. Our staff did not enjoy working for her. There is a risk that she may abuse authority. (Hold)

Warder

While Hopkins has made a major contribution to the firm, she still has a few rough spots which need to be corrected. (Hold)

EXHIBIT 1   *(concluded)*

A.B. HOPKINS   MO12
LONG FORM
   VIII.

Hopkins is probably too bright; she probably drives too   *Beyer*
hard.
   On occasion, she'll forget herself & lose sensitivity for
   staff.
But . . . not one staff member ever suggested, throughout
State project over 2 yrs in duration, that Ann was not an
outstanding leader & should be replaced. Ann should be a
ptr. (Yes)

A.B. HOPKINS   MO12
SHORT FORM
   #3

Contacts with Ann are only casual—several mtgs at OGS   *CG Hoffman*
and MMGS sessions.
   However, she is consistently annoying and irritating—believes
   she knows more than anyone about anything, is not afraid
   to let the world know it. Suggest a course at charm school
   before she is considered for admission. I would be embarrassed to introduce her as a ptnr. (No)

Farmers Home Credit Administration.[43] The fourth was also for the Department of State and involved implementing a worldwide real property management system, valued at $6 million.

Department of the Interior

At the Interior Department, Hopkins worked on a computer conversion project for the Bureau of Indian Affairs (BIA). An OGS partner later called her performance on the project "outstanding." He added, "She had to manage the project at a remote site [Albuquerque], using staff from Denver and Houston and work with a difficult client. Her project management skills are excellent."[44]

There were, however, criticisms of her work. Some came from Robert Kaplan, a consultant who worked with Hopkins in Albuquerque, New Mexico, on the BIA project. He cited problems with Hopkins as the reason he left the firm a few years later. According to Thomas Beyer, Kaplan called Hopkins from Albuquerque to review the BIA job, and Hopkins got into a violent argument with him, screaming obscenities at him for about 45 minutes. Kaplan believed Hopkins prevented him from advancing in the firm.[45]

---

[43] Plaintiff's complaint; *see,* Coffey evaluation in Supreme Court lodging.

[44] Defendant's Exhibit 7, Krulwich's Annual Manager Personnel Report, April 4, 1980.

[45] Beyer's testimony in 1985 Trial, Tr. 193.

EXHIBIT 2   Review of File

OFFICE VISIT

Ann B. Hopkins	Dept: MAS
	Years of Service: 5
November 17, 1982	Age: 39
	Contract Year: 1978

REVIEW OF FILE   PRIVATE
ANN HOPKINS

10–25–82   Memorandum to the file. Effective October 1, 1982, Ann assumes responsibility for the 10 people in word processing. She will manage the department, evaluate performance, determine compensation, and obtain high quality productivity. Ann is delighted to be able to assume this responsibility, particularly as this will demonstrate her ability to manage subordinates effectively. Memorandum signed by Beyer.

10–12–82   Report by Beyer on Foreign Buildings Operation—State Department. 1's and 2's. Very good report. The only suggestion for improvement being she could delegate a little more.

9–14–82   Report by Epelbaum on US Department of State. Chiefly 1's and 2's. A 3 in utilization of reference material, involvement in community and professional activities, and inter-personal skills—associates. Overall assessment was exceptional. Comments: performance has been outstanding. She is bright, imaginative and assertive, and an asset to the firm. By focusing on being more sensitive to others, she will become an extremely productive partner.

9–28–82   Report by Beyer on State Department. 1's and 2's except for 3's in interest in promoting full service to clients and involvement in community and professional activities. Exceptional overall assessment. A comment that she does believe that staff should have same dedication as herself. This is not always possible and sometimes leads to problems.

9–15–82   Report by Coffey on Farmers Home Administration proposal. 1, 2's, and 3's, with a 4 in interpersonal skills–associates. Comments: she should devote more time to communicating what she expects at task assignment time and dealing effectively and motivationally with staff is Ann's primary apparent weakness. It may be that our staff in St. Louis are used to being coddled but I suspect this is the one area where Ann needs to show improvement to become a partner. Overall assessment was "higher than expected."

EXHIBIT 2 *(continued)*

Summary comment: The big question with Ann is people skill. The St. Louis staff did not enjoy their experience on this proposal but certainly sympathized with Ann's position (full responsibility while working with those with whom she had never worked). We need partners with her technical and intellectual capacity, but she must demonstrate people skills. I believe we should help her do so.

Tom Beyer has added a note to this report saying: "Not at the risk of sloppy work or missed deadlines. I disagree after reviewing situation with Tim and Ann."

6–16–82 Report by Kercher on Houston MAS quality control review. All 1's and 2's. No adverse comments.

6–22–82 Counseling session with Epelbaum. Ann agreed that she is sometimes overly assertive and needs to be more tolerant of others. Disagreed that she needs to place greater focus on staff development. Her feeling is she needs to work with staff that have a future.

1–15–82 Report by Statland on US Department of State. All 1's and 2's. Comments: Ann is excellent on her client relationships, ability to organize work materials, ability to utilize staff ability to grasp the complex issues. Ann is sometimes overly critical of people's work, has relatively light technical (EDP) and accounting systems knowledge, and often allows judgment to be clouded by casual statements. She is dynamic but needs to learn how to execute under more control. Also not everything is to be made to appear black or white.

9–20–81 Report by Beyer on State Department. All 1's and 2's. Ann is the consummate professional and obvious partner candidate for next year. Needs time to increase maturity. Needs to be patient with superiors who are slower than she is.

6–17–81 Counseling session by Fred Laughlin. Mentions cleaning up her office and keeping partners informed. Bulk of the session devoted to people technique. Needs to soften her image; careful with her language—not just avoiding profanity but also guarding against unprofessional language and expressions. Ann agreed she would attempt to be more observant about whether her personality was threatening to the individual.

EXHIBIT 2 *(continued)*

11–13–79   Report by Lewis Krulwich on Bureau of Indian Affairs. All 1's and 2's. No unfavorable comments.

                     Other material in the file indicates she has been with Price Waterhouse since 1978, with American Management Systems 1977–78, with Touch Ross from 1973–1977 and with several other positions data back to 1968 with IBM.

2–26–81   Memorandum by Tom Beyer indicates a midyear compensation increase was affected in order to stave off a threatened termination for purposes of higher compensation.

Ann B. Hopkins

DISCUSSION WITH PARTNERS

MacVeagh—Remarkable change in last year or two. Apparently she has been counseled and is taking it to heart. On State Department job, she knew she was over her head on the EDP side; she held herself out as a project manager. Beyer wanted to staff out of OGS. In final analysis we won.

Haller—Has broad gauged abilities. Questions personality. Brings kids into office. Sees no evidence of change but she is worth saving.

Krulwich—Has not worked on State Department engagement but knows fairly well. Large systems area is key to growth. She is one of the best. She beat the feathers off of other firm on State Department. Would trust Ann with financial assets. Ann has a clearly different personality—outspoken, diamond in the rough. Many male partners are worse than Ann (language and tough personality). Her husband is no longer a Touche partner. Velvet glove with clients. Tom wants in the worst way to admit Ann. Ann does not hold herself out as a DP specialist. Thinks O.T. issue is irrelevant. Krulwich says responsibility was his. Thinks subject was discussed in general with PG early on. Krulwich told Ann to pass the buck to him. Thinks he sees improvement.

Gross—Good worker. Is in the office early in the mornings. Critical comments regarding personal characteristics come as a complete surprise. Would guess above average. Have to be tough to get along with her boss.

Wheaton—Spent about 40 hours with her on metro proposal. Several times told Dick that she didn't think her technical capabilities were up to that job. Dick did not see that job as a very complex job. She and Pshyk did not get along. Dick has reservations.

Kelly—I didn't see anyone quitting during course of state job. She will not change. Five minutes into discussion, client probably forgets she's macho. If you get around the personality thing, she's at the top of the list or way above average.

Lohneis—One of the two strongest—writing ability, quickness on feet, ability to sort out masses of opinions. Personal comments: she will not change.

EXHIBIT 2 *(continued)*

Ann B. Hopkins

DISCUSSION WITH PARTNERS

Beyer — Conscious of problems. Ranks her #1. Very hard worker. Very bright. FPC specalist (not intended to be EDP specialist). Outstanding ability to sell a client on her ability, on firm ability. Brings home profits. She is the partner on the job in the client's mind. On second phase of State Department work client specified Ann Hopkins. Has done a marvellous job demonstrating to Tim Coffee that she is a great technician. Ann went through hell writing St. Louis proposal. She couldn't even get word processing help. Coffee will change his original comments. Beyer told Hopkins he would have trouble proposing her for partnership. She came back and said, "I quit." Beyer got back and said, "I didn't say you don't have a chance." Her husband a partner at Touche was a problem. Her husband was not enamored with Touche. Two weeks later came in and left Touche. Ann came back and withdrew her request to terminate. Subsequent to that asked partners to increase compensation for 2 people because of hours worked and because of success to date. Under government contract hours over 2.030 reduce rate per hour. As practical matter would collect rate increase. In three weeks Ann got results out of word processing that Fred Loughlin and Hunter Jones had not been able to achieve. No longer any backlog — no people have quit.

Flamson — One tough lady! Very competent. Needs to be tough to supervise the type of people that have been working on her project.

Hartz — Was previously with Touche and had put in a system at UMW which had its faults but I don't know if Ann was necessarily responsible for those faults.

Epelbaum — Impressions based on daily and even hourly contact in the April to June period. I believe I know her well. Her accomplishments are unprecedented. Her management style is one of perpetual crisis. If she can't convince you there is a crisis, she will go out and create one. Ann could be a great success or a great failure. She sold a $20 million job. Neither Steve Higgins nor I could have done it. She apparently can work well with Beyer; I'm certain she could not work with everyone. [Ann wants to win; I don't know where she would draw the line.] I don't enjoy working with her. I avoid her socially.

Another problem surfaced when Hopkins's BIA work was reviewed by a partner in 1980. His report said:

I was informed by Ann that the project had been completed on sked within budget. My subsequent review indicated a significant discrepancy of approximately $35,000 betw[een] the proposed fees, billed fees [and] actuals in the WIPS. I discussed this matter with Ann who attempted to try [and] explain away or play down the discrepancy. She insisted there had not been a discrepancy in the amount of the underrealization. Unsatisfied with her responses, I continued to question the matter until she admitted there was a problem but I should discuss it with Krulwich [a partner at OGS]. My subsequent discussion with Lew indicated that the discrepancy was a result of 500 additional hours being charged to

---

EXHIBIT 2   (concluded)

PRIVATE   No. MO 12

ANN B. HOPKINS

(OGS)

DISCUSSION WITH ST. LOUIS PARTNERS

Blythe — Observed her in FMAA proposal effort. Had heard negatives about her before she came to St. Louis for proposal effort. In final analysis, she got the job done. May have some minor holes in it, but was a massive effort. She is very capable and bright. Within the OGS environment she is probably exceptional. She left town with a favorable impression. Has a reputation of being tough on staff, but Tom didn't see it.

Coffey — Worked closely with Ann on proposal for Farmers Home Administration accounting system. Had two concerns: she tends to be tough on people (runs over people) and uses trial-and-error type management techniques. May have overcompensated for being a woman. St. Louis would not have had a chance on proposal without her help. Will be a 65,000 hour job if we get it and it looks good. She is one of the brightest people Tim has met. He now switches his "Hold" to a "Yes" and fully supports her.

Fridley — Fridley reviewed one of her jobs, Bureau of Indian Affairs, in 1980 when he performed a quality control review of OGS. Felt she wasn't honest with him with respect to a number of matters. Ann said she had no problems with respect to fees, billings, etc. but couldn't reconcile inconsistencies. There was $30,000 excess written off, then the planned underrealization. Despite this, she insisted everything was OK and had tried to mislead John for 15 minutes. Apparently, Ann had told female consultant from Houston to work 12 hours per day, but charge only 8. Some 500 hours were charged back by Bill Devaney when he found out about this. Her style seemed to be — work what it takes to get the job done, but charge only what the budget will allow. Overall reaction now is that she does have substance. She came to help on Home Farm Mutual proposal. Final product was massive, but not quality. In the process, she alienated almost everyone who worked on the project. She seemed to be unorganized and worked as if it were a Chinese fire drill. No one wants to work with her on project if we get it.

D. R. Ziegler

---

the job (at the request of Bill Devaney . . . agreed to by Krulwich) after it was determined that Linda Pegues, a senior consultant from the Houston off[ice] working on the project had been instructed by Ann to work 12–14 hrs per day during the project but only to charge 8 hours per day. The entire incident left me questioning Ann's staff management methods and the honesty of her responses to my questions.[46]

---

[46] Fridley, in Short Form Partner Evaluation, comments #3, p. 2, Trial Record, p. 002004. This is from one of the documents in the Supreme Court Lodging.

EXHIBIT 3 Statistical Summary

Candidate MO12

Conduct of work:		Top Quarter	Second Quarter	Third Quarter	Bottom Quarter
As an auditor	(1)	—	—	—	—
As an accountant	(2)	—	—	—	—
As a tax specialist	(3)	—	—	—	—
As a MAS specialist	(4)	2	2	1	1
As an industry specialist	(5)	—	—	—	—
As other specialty	(6)	—	—	—	—
Imagination – creativity	(7)	3	2	1	—
– analytical	(8)	3	3	—	—
Consultation with others	(9)	1	1	3	1
Communication skills – speaking	(10)	2	3	1	—
– writing	(11)	5	1	—	—
– listening	(12)	2	1	3	—
Total conduct of work		16	13	9	2
Management skills:					
Client related:					
Independence and impartiality	(13)	3	2	1	—
Business sense – underst. client's needs	(14)	4	1	1	—
– decision-making ability	(15)	4	1	1	—
– promotes full service	(16)	—	2	1	—
Leadership	(17)	2	2	—	1
Administration – planning	(18)	2	3	1	—
– delegating	(19)	2	1	2	1
– supervising	(20)	2	1	3	—
– training	(21)	2	—	2	2
Financial mgt. – billing	(22)	2	2	—	—
– collecting	(23)	2	2	—	—
Total client related		25	17	12	4
Firm related:					
Practice development	(24)	1	3	2	—
Sells services outside own specialty	(25)	—	3	1	—
Willingness to accept assignment	(26)	6	—	—	—
Accepts non-client resp. – recruiting	(27)	1	3	1	—
– counseling	(26)	1	2	2	—
– contin. ed.	(29)	1	2	2	—
Total firm related		10	13	8	—

Table header: *Long Form Summation* spanning Top Quarter, Second Quarter, Third Quarter, Bottom Quarter.

EXHIBIT 3 *(continued)*

Candidate MO12

		Long Form Summation			
		Top Quarter	Second Quarter	Third Quarter	Bottom Quarter
Profession related:					
Activity in professional organizations	(30)	—	—	2	1
Civic activities	(31)	—	—	2	1
Acceptance by – partners	(32)	2	2	1	—
– staff	(33)	—	3	1	1
– clients	(34)	3	1	—	—
Total		5	6	6	3
Personal attributes:					
Basic intelligence	(35)	4	2	—	—
Outside interests	(36)	—	3	1	1
Judgment	(37)	2	2	2	—
Integrity	(38)	2	2	2	—
Tolerance	(39)	1	1	2	2
Practicality	(40)	2	3	1	—
Authority	(41)	5	1	—	—
Maturity, poise	(42)	2	3	1	—
Sensitivity, tact	(43)	—	2	2	2
Adaptability	(44)	2	3	1	—
Stamina	(45)	5	1	—	—
Perseverance	(46)	6	—	—	—
Sense of Humor	(47)	2	2	2	—
Self-organization	(46)	2	2	2	—
Total personal attributes		35	27	16	5

		Short Form Summation			
		Top Quarter	Second Quarter	Third Quarter	Bottom Quarter
Conduct of work:					
Technical competence	(1)	3	6	2	—
Communication skills	(2)	5	10	3	1
Total conduct of work		8	16	5	1

EXHIBIT 3 *(continued)*

Candidate MO12

		Short Form Summation			
		Top Quarter	*Second Quarter*	*Third Quarter*	*Bottom Quarter*
Management skills:					
Independence and impartiality	(3)	7	5	1	1
Business sense	(4)	8	5	1	1
Leadership	(5)	6	6	3	3
Administrative ability	(6)	6	4	1	–
Practice Development	(7)	6	4	–	–
Dedication to the firm	(8)	9	4	–	–
Outside activities	(9)	–	1	1	4
Total management skills		42	29	7	9
Personal attributes:					
Intellectual capacity	(10)	8	9	1	–
Integrity and judgment	(11)	5	9	–	2
Poise, authority, maturity	(12)	5	10	4	1
Stamina	(13)	7	5	–	–
Congeniality	(14)	1	5	10	7
Total personal attributes		26	36	15	10

	Long Forms	*Short Forms*
Favor admission this year	3	10
Favors hold	2	1
Do not favor admission	1	7
Insufficient basis for opinion	–	8
Total	6	26

	Long Form Percentages			
	Top Quarter	*Second Quarter*	*Third Quarter*	*Bottom Quarter*
Conduct of work	43%	31%	21%	5%
Management skills:				
Client related	43%	29%	21%	7%
Firm related	32%	42%	26%	–
Profession related	25%	30%	30%	15%
Total	37%	33%	24%	6%
Personal attributes	42%	33%	19%	6%
Overall evaluation	33%	17%	50%	–

EXHIBIT 3 *(concluded)*

	Short Form Percentages			
	Top Quarter	Second Quarter	Third Quarter	Bottom Quarter
Conduct of work	27%	53%	17%	3%
Management skills	48%	33%	8%	10%
Personal attributes	29%	43%	17%	11%
Overall evaluation	16%	32%	26%	26%
	Long Form Summation			
	Top Quarter	Second Quarter	Third Quarter	Bottom Quarter
Conduct of work	18	13	9	2
Management skills:				
Client related	25	17	12	4
Firm related	10	13	3	—
Profession related	5	6	6	3
Total	40	36	26	7
Personal attributes	35	27	16	5
Overall evaluation	2	1	3	—
	Short Form Summation			
	Top Quarter	Second Quarter	Third Quarter	Bottom Quarter
Conduct of work	8	16	5	1

The State Department

At the end of the Interior Department project in late 1979, Hopkins volunteered to write a proposal for developing a financial management system for the State Department. The proposal was the first phase of a competition with other firms. The winners would be paid to write a second proposal describing how they would implement their plans. Many Price Waterhouse people worked on the first-round proposal. The multivolumed document, which included a technical proposal with appendices and a cost proposal, was submitted on time in February 1980. In May, Price Waterhouse learned it was one of two finalists.[47] The State Department held an award signing ceremony in May 1980, and its chairman, Joseph Connor, came down from New York to attend.

From May 1980 until February 1982, a Price Waterhouse team varying from 4 to 12 people and composed of consultants, managers, accountants, and computer specialists worked on the second proposal. An OGS partner was the

---

[47] Plaintiff's deposition, vol. I, p. 43.

partner-in-charge for the proposal; Hopkins worked as project manager. The work required fieldwork at 20 to 30 overseas posts.[48] Partners from Price Waterhouse's international firm and personnel from embassy staff were also involved. Hopkins traveled to Asia for five weeks and then to Europe. Team members often worked from eight in the morning until late at night and on weekends.[49] During the project, Hopkins received a raise and was promoted from manager to senior manager.[50]

In early 1982, when the proposal was nearly due, Hopkins summoned the team to decide together whether to make the deadline or to request an extension. Hopkins said she played a game called "chicken," telling the team that they had two choices; to ask for the extension or to make the date. She warned them that the second alternative was "not going to be pleasant." According to Hopkins, the team decided to make the deadline.[51]

Hopkins believed the project group developed a sense of team spirit. She noted, for example, that Steve Higgins, one of the Price Waterhouse consultants, had a drink with her after work or dinner every other week.[52] Higgins sometimes brought his children from New York to the dinners at Hopkins's house. She was also with him when one of his children was born during the project.[53]

Thomas Beyer later recalled personnel problems on the project.[54] During one meeting of the project team, a consultant, Patricia Bowman, attempted to present some ideas in her area. "Ann struck out at her," Beyer said, "inasmuch as to smother her commentary and say we don't need that now...." Bowman "struck right back and said something to the effect you can't treat me that way. Don't you dare treat me that way." Beyer said Hopkins accepted it and continued the meeting.[55]

Beyer also said that Karen Nold, one of the senior managers, "was quite depressed about things...." Beyer said she "just felt that Ann's overbearing style was smothering her attempts to... bring forth her ideas, her conclusions, her recommendations, and suggestions." Beyer recommended that Nold speak up because her contributions were important.[56] Nold, however, characterized her conversation with Beyer as him telling her to become assertive.[57] Despite this incident, Nold praised Hopkins for some things.[58] "Ann is very smart, very to the point, very directed at getting good results... she cares about the people who work with and for her...." Nold said that Hopkins taught her about self-confidence, how to apply her knowledge and skills without self-doubt, and how to support her presentations with facts and numbers. She found working with Hopkins "very stimulating." "Did I enjoy it?," she said, "Yes and no."[59]

Other positive reports came from some State Department personnel. Robert Lamb, later the State Department's assistant secretary of administration and security, was the counselor for administration in the American embassy in Bonn, Germany, when he first worked with Hopkins on the project. "I had a lot of respect for her," Lamb said. "I thought she was a very good project manager. In fact, I've subsequently tried to hire Ann for the State Department because I thought

---

[48] Tr. 34–35; deposition, p. 48. The number of sites given in Plaintiff's deposition is 23, but at trial the number of sites was reported as 20 to 30.

[49] Deposition, vol. I, p. 50. Hopkins estimated her billable time that year at approximately 20,000 to 24,000 hours, Tr. p. 34–35.

[50] See Partner Admission File, summary, November 28, 1982.

[51] Trial testimony, Tr. 46–47.

[52] Trial testimony, March 15, 1985, p. 56–57.

[53] Testimony at trial, p. 53, 56.

[54] Beyer's testimony, Tr. 192.

[55] Beyer's testimony, Tr. 196.

[56] Beyer's testimony, Tr. 194–196.

[57] Nold's testimony, Tr. 421.

[58] Tr. 417–419.

[59] Tr. 420.

she was so good. I thought she provided a good sense of direction, a good sense of leadership for the team." Lamb referred to Hopkins as decisive but not dictatorial, ". . . quite interested in competing points of view . . . somebody that would hear her staff out on a question. I never saw her cut anyone off. . . ."[60]

Beyer, however, recalled difficult moments during this period. In the summer of 1981, Hopkins, Beyer, and Krulwich had lunch at the Mayflower Hotel. "They were eating and just kind of passing time . . . and something happened to Ann," Beyer said. He continued:

> I wasn't quite sure what. But she began to criticize a number of people in the office at different levels. In different fashions. At first I passed it off thinking well, this is, this is Ann. She's probably tired. . . . But Ann kept up with it. Lew was silent and — not saying anything and Ann kept on talking. . . . And it got more vitriolic. More striking. [A]fter awhile I began to get quite angry. . . . At that point, Lew, kind of trying to settle the situation, said, look, let's quit and go back to work. They walked back to the office in silence.

Beyer was angry and Krulwich upset. When they spoke about the incident back at the office, Beyer reminded Krulwich that, despite her problems with people, Hopkins was an integral part of the office and they needed her skills.[61]

That summer, Hopkins had her first session with Fred Laughlin, the partner assigned to counsel Anne Hopkins. (One such partner was assigned to each staff member.) This was part of a mandatory annual counseling policy instituted in 1981. Laughlin, Hopkins recalled, counseled her "to be more careful with my language. . . . I think he probably meant tone of voice, profanity, to some extent what I said, also in other instance[s], how I said it." During the last stages of the State Department work,

Hopkins said she "renewed [her] efforts to be sensitive to the cares, concerns, and well-being of the people that she worked with." "I still use a measure of profanity . . . ," she said, "I made an attempt to not intimidate, if you will, or be overbearing with little people, people who are innocent bystanders or people with whom we had no contact and I took that to heart."[62]

Near the end of the work, Beyer told Hopkins that he expected Price Waterhouse to win the proposal competition. He told her to write the proposal for implementing the firm's recommendations. Although she would not be the project manager, he said, she should write herself in "in an administrative, transitional kind of position."[63] Price Waterhouse won the contract, and Connor attended another award ceremony.

Despite their work on the proposal, neither Hopkins nor the partner-in-charge was involved in the rest of the project. The State Department's director of financial systems, who was principally in charge of conducting the work, had asked Price Waterhouse to remove the partner. The reason, according to Roger Feldman, then comptroller of the State Department, "had to do with his performance, attitude, his presentation, and the lack of constructive contribution on his part to that point. . . ."[64] In contrast, Feldman said Hopkins's replacement had nothing to do with her performance or her personal skills. "[T]he committee and team that determined the selection," he said, "were very favorably impressed with her performance during the orals and were also very favorably disposed to the written proposals that came from Price Waterhouse."[65] Feldman described her as "extremely competent, intelligent, a very capable person. Strong and forthright, very productive,

---

[60] Testimony of Robert Lamb, trial or deposition.
[61] Tr. 197–197A.

[62] Tr. 52–53.
[63] Tr. 136–137.
[64] Tr. 149.
[65] Tr. 146–152.

energetic, and creative" with a sense of humor.[66] He and his staff worked extensively with Hopkins and Feldman stated he had not seen Hopkins behave in any abusive, dictatorial, or unfair ways with her staff.[67]

Nevertheless, the department thought the project manager should be a partner because this would lend greater prestige to the project. According to Feldman, the department's director of financial systems also thought "the project was going to reach a dimension that was very large in anybody's terms of organization and structure . . . there would be a need to require top flight talent to be brought forth on throughout the firm and that a partner would be presumably well positioned to be able to tap on the different resources of the firm."[68]

In mid-1982, Beyer told Hopkins over lunch at the International Club that he would propose her as a partner in the admissions cycle about to begin.[69] Beyer then had the first of a series of conversations with Hopkins about how she could improve her chances for partnership, and gave her advice about her hair, makeup, clothing, and jewelry. Hopkins said she found these conversations offensive. When Beyer suggested that she style her hair, Hopkins explained to him that she already got up at five or six in the morning, had a lot to do, and didn't have the time. Beyer answered that Sandy Kinsey, another woman in OGS, managed to find the time.

By the summer of 1982, Hopkins was focusing her time on projects other than the State Department work. She participated, along with several partners, in an MAS quality control review in the Houston office.[70] Hopkins later complained to one of them about his writing

obscene anatomical references, such as "This is where our balls are on the line," in the margins of his work papers.[71] According to Hopkins, another confrontation with this partner occurred during a meeting in his office. The partner sat at his desk, repeatedly raising a stilletto letter opener and stabbing his desk with it. When Hopkins asked him to stop, he said, "Why, is it making you nervous?" Hopkins said, "Yes." "Well, if you think that makes you nervous," the partner responded, turning to pull a gun from a credenza behind his desk and turning back around to face her, "what do you think about this?" He pointed the gun into the air. When she later described this incident, Hopkins insisted that she had not been threatened with the gun.[72]

Farmers Home Credit Association

Beyer next assigned Hopkins to manage the St. Louis office's proposal for the design of an automated accounting system for recording and tracking loans to farmers. The client was Farmers Home Credit Association, a U.S. Department of Agriculture agency with major data processing operations in St. Louis. Arthur Anderson had done extensive work for the agency, and Beyer believed it was getting ready to work on the loan accounting project.[73]

From July through August 1982, Hopkins helped the St. Louis MAS department prepare a 2,000-page proposal for the work.[74] At stake were $3.1 million in fees and expenses[75] in a contract for 65,000 hours of work. Price Waterhouse partners and staff worked over 2,000

---

[66] Tr. 149–152.

[67] Tr. 146–149.

[68] Tr. 149.

[69] Plaintiff's deposition, vol. I, pp. 53, 57.

[70] See, Short Form evaluation notes in the Partnership Admission File.

[71] Plaintiff's deposition, vol. II, p. 24.

[72] Plaintiff's deposition and trial testimony.

[73] Letter of December 2, 1982, from Beyer to Connor, Plaintiff's exhibit 14.

[74] Fridley's Short Form Evaluation, repeated in Lodging, Short Form 3, p. 2. The project was also known as the Home Farm Mutual proposal and the FMH Association proposal; Fridley in Ziegler's Notes in Partnership Admission File.

[75] See, Ziegler's notes 1982.

hours during the four weeks it took to complete the proposal.[76] Hopkins spent 260 hours on the project.[77]

Along the way, she experienced two major problems. The first was getting the St. Louis office to prepare the proposal in the way she preferred. The local staff was accustomed to working on fixed price contracts, while this was a cost-plus contract.[78] Hopkins had to convince the staff that they should abandon their familiar way of preparing a proposal and that her way was correct, then show them how to do it and get the work completed on time. The problem had deeper roots, mainly the office's inexperience with this type of client. As Beyer later explained, "In OGS we had developed a streamlined fashion for efficiently dealing with proposal developments for generating deliverable on jobs. It became a way of life. It had to. It was the only way we could survive. The St. Louis office was not used to this. They had dealt more in the private sector and in state government work."[79]

Several members of the St. Louis office staff later complained about Hopkins. One consultant she said was "direct, abrupt, sometimes insensitive. And demeaning at times."[80] He recalled an exchange between Hopkins and the office's graphics contractor. "Ann wasn't pleased at all and expressed herself fairly directly . . . ," the consultant said. Afterward, feeling that he had done the work badly and that he was going to lose the Price Waterhouse account, the man called back. The consultant said that he assured him this was not the case.[81] The consultant also complained that "[T]he development of a fairly detailed work plan and

assignment of responsibilities really didn't occur." Hopkins prepared an outline "as to what she envisioned the document to look like," which he thought inadequate. He also said she was unable to direct staff members on improving their work. This lack of direction resulted in chaos,[82] and he said his co-workers expressed similar feelings to him.[83]

Hopkins and the staff ultimately produced a four-volume proposal and then helped two St. Louis partners prepare for oral reviews.[84] One of those partners, Timothy Coffey, said that the "[f]inal project was massive but not quality." He added that Hopkins "alienated almost everyone who worked on the project. She seemed to be unorganized and worked as if it were a Chinese fire drill. No one wants to work with her on the project if we get it."[85] He also said, "Ann needs a chance to demonstrate people skills. She has a lot going for her but she's just plain rough on people. Our staff did not enjoy working for her. There is a risk that she may abuse authority."[86] Coffey also suggested that Hopkins "[m]ay have overcompensated for being a woman." But he also said that "St. Louis would not have had a chance on [the] proposal without her help" and that she was "one of the brightest people he had met."[87]

In December 1982, the association awarded the contract to Price Waterhouse. Beyer sent

---

[76] Fridley, ibid.

[77] Coffey's Evaluation, Performance of MAS contract staff.

[78] Coffey's testimony at trial, Tr. 342–343.

[79] Beyer's testimony at trial, Tr. 171.

[80] Tr. 363.

[81] Boehm's testimony, Tr. 367–368.

[82] Tr. 363.

[83] Boehm's testimony, Tr. 364–365.

[84] Letter, Beyer to Connor, December 2, 1982; Plaintiff's exhibit 14.

[85] Ziegler's summary of discussion with St. Louis Partners, Defendant's exhibit 31, p. 003845.

[86] Ziegler, Long Form summary, 20006; Coffey later qualified himself: he said, "I would be highly surprised if I said she abuse[s] authority. I probably said she had the potential of abusing authority which is a concern that I [have]." Tr. 346.

[87] Ziegler's summary discussion with St. Louis Partner, Defendant's exhibit 31. See Ziegler's Notes on Discussions with St. Louis partners in Review of File, Long Form summaries, p. 002206, November 17, 1982.

Connor a letter telling him about how successful Hopkins had been.[88] Later, without OGS assistance, the St. Louis office wrote a successful federal government proposal worth several million dollars.[89]

Department of State

In October 1982, Hopkins got two new assignments.[90] One was managing the OGS word processing center. The other was developing a proposal for managing the real estate administered by the State Department abroad. When the State Department's comptroller contacted Beyer seeking Price Waterhouse's help in developing a system to manage its overseas service post properties, Beyer assigned the work to Hopkins. As for the word processing assignment, Beyer reported in Hopkins partnership admissions file that "Ann is delighted to be able to assume this responsibility particularly as this will demonstrate her ability to manage subordinates effectively."[91]

The 10-person word processing staff that Hopkins took over had been very troubled under its prior manager, with staff members complaining about inadequate compensation adjustments and a lack of consideration in relating staff skills to workloads and priorities.[92] Hopkins "went right to the core of those problems," Beyer said. "She cleaned up the backlog in the unit. Nobody quit. She addressed the personnel problems of people on the staff." Also, "I give Ann a lot of credit for keeping the department on a fairly even keel," Beyer said. "[I]t was one of the first times you had seen someone at that level of partner or manager get involved with the people themselves."[93]

The Partnership Decision

In March 1983, the admissions committee recommended that Hopkins be held "at least a year to afford time to demonstrate that she has the personal and leadership qualities required of a partner."[94] The policy board adopted the Admissions Committee's recommendation and suggested that Hopkins participate in a quality control review.

Hopkins learned from Lew Krulwich that she had not been promoted. The reason, he said, reporting what Connor had told Beyer, was that she had irritated some senior partners.[95] Hopkins said neither she nor Krulwich knew what that meant. Another partner suggested that she should probably not come to the office on the day the partnership list was posted. Hopkins believed he was concerned that she might lose control emotionally. According to her, the partner added that some of the names posted were "not competent to lick her boots."[96] The other two candidates OGS had nominated became partners. One had worked for Price Waterhouse for less time than Hopkins.

Hopkins went to New York to meet with Joseph Connor, the firm's chairman, and discuss the decision. She asked him how to overcome the "hold" and make it an "admit." Connor told her that she had to undergo a quality control review and come out of it with no negative comments. He also told her that OGS had to continue to be profitable. When Hopkins asked what her prospects were, Connor replied, "Fifty-fifty."[97] Connor also

---

[88] Beyer to Connor, December 2, 1982, Plaintiff's exhibit 14.

[89] Tr. 371.

[90] Plaintiff's Remand brief, p. 4.

[91] Ziegler in 1983 partnership admissions file, citing memorandum of October 26, 1982 signed by Beyer, Ziegler, p. 003841, Private and Protected.

[92] Beyer's testimony at trial, Tr. 210.

[93] Trial testimony.

[94] Pet. App. 43a quoting Plaintiff's exhibit 10; Tr. 267–268.

[95] Plaintiff's deposition, vol. I, p. 59.

[96] Plaintiff's deposition, vol. I, p. 70.

[97] Plaintiff's deposition, vol. I, p. 64–65.

advised her to relax and "to take charge" less often.[98]

Beyer also advised Hopkins.[99] According to Hopkins, he suggested she "soften her image in the manner in which she walked, talked, dressed...." He later said that "when she comes into the office or starts walking down the hall, it is with a lot of authority and forcefulness. I admire that quality. I respond to it. It does not always appear in the same view or in the same manner to other people." She also said he advised her to use less profanity and to alter her voice tone, to "look more toward appearing more feminine," to wear more jewelry and make-up, to style her hair, and to dress less in 'power blues.'"[100] He also suggested that she stop smoking, not drink beer at lunch, ... not carry a briefcase."[101] Hopkins said she explained that carrying a briefcase was easier for her than managing a handbag, a suitcase, and a briefcase simultaneously. She later said she did not wear makeup because she was allergic to it. Even if she weren't she said, "applying makeup would be difficult because she can't see without her trifocals."[102]

Soon after this, two of the OGS partners who had nominated Hopkins withdrew their support for her. The reason one of them gave was the difficulty he had with her as a senior manager and his concern that problems would grow worse if she acquired the power and authority of a partner. He complained that she routinely barged into his office, got her business done, and barged out again. The incident that

changed his mind, he said, occurred at a time when he was understaffed and Hopkins offered him one of her staff members, only to withdraw the offer the next day. According to the partner, she had insisted on making the offer without qualification, refused his suggestion that he think it over for a day, then told him the next day that he could not use the staff member she had offered.[103]

During the next few months, according to Hopkins, the firm failed to give her opportunities to demonstrate her abilities and gain more exposure. Four months after the policy board's recommendations, with two OGS's strong support, it was felt that her candidacy could not possibly be successful. Hopkins was advised that it was very unlikely that she would be admitted to partnership.

Reviews of her work on the State Department real estate management project were, on balance, favorable. An initial review by the partner who had been removed from the large State Department project was negative, but the subsequent quality control review conducted on the State Department work, including REMS, was a "strong positive."[104] It also suggested some changes, which Hopkins and the rest of the REMS team later made.

Hopkins later wrote that she was "the *only* candidate who was not admitted to Price Waterhouse – initially or after being put on hold – who was criticized solely for deficiencies in interpersonal skills."[105] Similarly situated men, she says, were admitted.[106] Hopkins was at the bottom of overall quartile rankings and only 13 of 32 partners favored her admission, but the firm had admitted one candidate who

---

[98] Plaintiff's deposition, vol. I, p. 65.

[99] Plaintiff's trial brief, p. 12; see also, Plaintiff's deposition, vol. I, p. 67.

[100] Plaintiff's trial brief, pp. 12–13. For a definition of the term *power blues,* and Hopkins's attorneys' comment, "Sometimes you just can't win," see Plaintiff's trial brief, p. 13, n.5.

[101] Plaintiff's deposition, vol. I, p. 68.

[102] Jaclyn Fierman, "Why Women Still Don't Hit the Top," *Fortune,* July 30, 1990, p. 40–62, at p. 50.

[103] Epelbaum's deposition or trial testimony in 1985.

[104] Plaintiff's Answer to Interrogatories, Interrogatory 10; *see also,* Protected Document, exhibit 12 in Beyer deposition, March 7, 1985, pp. 2–3.

[105] Plaintiff's remand brief, p. 20, n. 2 citing Defendant's exhibit 64.

[106] Plaintiff's remand brief, p. 20, no. 2.

had support from 14 of 30 partners and another who ranked 39th of 42 in overall quartile rankings.[107]

In December 1983, she learned she would not be reproposed for partnership. Hopkins tendered her resignation and left Price

Waterhouse in January.[108] In 1984, she started her own management consulting firm. She also filed suit against Price Waterhouse, claiming that she had been denied a partnership because of sex discrimination. She sought an award of backpay for lost wages and reinstatement at Price Waterhouse as a partner.

---

[107] Plaintiff's remand brief, p. 20, n. 3 citing Defendant's exhibit 73 at 1102 and Defendant's exhibit 36 at 3859, No. A 228 is Puschaver.

[108] 618 F. Supp. 1109 (D.D.C. 1985).

H. J. HEINZ COMPANY: THE ADMINISTRATION OF POLICY (A)

April is the cruelest month.

T. S. Eliot

In April 1979, James Cunningham, H. J. Heinz Company's president and chief operating officer, learned that since 1972 certain Heinz divisions had allegedly engaged in improper income transferal practices. Payments had been made to certain vendors in a particular fiscal year, then repaid or exchanged for services in the succeeding fiscal year.[1]

These allegations came out during the investigation of an unrelated antitrust matter. Apparent improprieties were discovered in the records of the Heinz USA division's relationship with one of its advertising agencies. Joseph Stangerson—senior vice president, secretary, and general counsel for Heinz—asked the advertising agency about the alleged practices. Not only had the agency personnel confirmed the allegation about Heinz USA, it indicated

that similar practices had been used by Star-Kist Foods, another Heinz division. The divisions allegedly solicited improper invoices from the advertising agency in fiscal year (FY) 1974 so they could transfer income to FY 1975. While the invoices were paid in FY 1974, the services described on the invoices were not rendered until some time during FY 1975. Rather than capitalizing the amount as a prepaid expense, the amount was charged as an expense in FY 1974. The result was an understatement of FY 1974 income and an equivalent overstatement of FY 1975 income.

Stangerson reported the problem to John Bailey, vice chairman and chief executive officer; to Robert Kelly, senior vice president–finance and treasurer; and to Cunningham. Bailey, CEO since 1966, had presided over 13 uninterrupted years of earnings growth. He was scheduled to retire as vice chairman and CEO on July 1 and would remain as a member of the board of directors. James Cunningham, who had been president and chief operating officer since 1972, was to become chief executive officer on July 1, 1979.

This case was prepared by Richard J. Post under the direction of Kenneth E. Goodpaster.

Copyright © 1981 by the President and Fellows of Harvard College.

Harvard Business School case 382-034.

[1] H. J. Heinz Company, form 8-K, April 27, 1979, p. 2.

Subsequent reports indicate that neither the scope of the practice nor the amounts involved were known. There was no apparent reason to believe that the amounts involved would have had a material effect on Heinz's reported earnings during the time period, including earnings for FY 1979 ending May 2. (Heinz reported financial results on the basis of a 52–53 week fiscal year ending on the Wednesday closest to April 30.) Stangerson was not prepared to say whether the alleged practices were legal or illegal. "This thing could be something terrible or it could be merely a department head using conservative accounting practices; we don't know,"[2] one Heinz senior official stated to the press.

Background

Henry J. Heinz, on founding the company in 1869 in Pittsburgh, Pennsylvania, said: "This is my goal — to bring home-cooking standards into canned foods, making them so altogether wholesome and delicious and at the same time so reasonable that people everywhere will enjoy them in abundance."[3] The company's involvement in food products never changed, and in 1979 Heinz operated some 30 companies with products reaching 150 countries. Heinz reported sales of over $2.2 billion and net income of $99.1 million in FY 1978.

After a sluggish period in the early 1960s, a reorganization was undertaken to position Heinz for growth. Under the guidance of John Bailey and James Cunningham, Heinz prospered through a major recession, government price controls, and major currency fluctuations. The 1978 annual report reflected management's pride in Heinz's remarkably consistent growth:

---

[2] "Heinz to Probe Prepayments to Suppliers by Using Outside Lawyers, Accountants," *Wall Street Journal,* April 30, 1979, p. 5.

[3] H. J. Heinz Company, annual report, 1976.

Fiscal 1978 went into the books as the fifteenth consecutive year of record results for Heinz. Earnings rose to another new high. Sales reached more than $2 billion only six years after we had passed the $1 billion mark for the first time in our century-long history. We are determined to maintain the financial integrity of our enterprise and support its future growth toward ever-higher levels. [Exhibit 1 presents a financial summary of fiscal years 1972–78.]

Although Heinz was a multinational firm, domestic operations accounted for 62 percent of sales and 67 percent of earnings in FY 1978. Five major divisions operated in the United States in 1979.

Throughout the 1970s, Heinz's major objective was consistent growth in earnings. While Heinz management did not consider acquisitions to be crucial to continuing growth, it looked favorably on purchase opportunities in areas where Heinz had demonstrated capabilities. Bailey and Cunningham stressed profit increases through the elimination of marginally profitable products. Increased advertising of successful traditional products and new product development efforts also contributed to Heinz's growth. Heinz's commitment to decentralized authority as an organizational principle aided the management of internal growth as well as acquisitions.

Organization

In 1979, Heinz was organized on two primary levels. The corporate world headquarters, located in Pittsburgh, consisted of the principal corporate officers and historically small staffs (management described the world headquarters as lean). World headquarters had the responsibility for "the decentralized coordination and control needed to set overall standards and ensure performance in accordance with them."[4] Some Heinz operating divisions

---

[4] H. J. Heinz Company, form 8-K, May 7, 1980, p. 7.

EXHIBIT 1 Financial Summary, Fiscal Years 1972–1978 ($ in thousands except per share data)

	1978	1977	1976	1975	1974	1973	1974
Summary of Operations							
Sales	$2,150,027	$1,868,820	$1,749,691	$1,564,930	$1,349,091	$1,116,551	$1,020,958
Cost of products sold	1,439,249	1,262,260	1,228,229	1,097,093	939,565	772,525	700,530
Interest expense	18,859	16,332	22,909	31,027	21,077	13,813	11,463
Provision for income taxes	69,561	71,119	53,675	49,958	36,730	30,913	30,702
Income from continuing operations	99,171	83,816	73,960	66,567	55,520	50,082	44,679
Loss from discontinued and expropriated operations	–	–	–	–	–	3,530	2,392
Income before extraordinary items	99,171	83,816	73,960	66,567	55,520	46,552	42,287
Extraordinary items	–	–	–	–	8,800	(25,000)	–
New income	$ 99,171	$ 83,816	$ 73,960	$ 66,567	$ 64,320	$ 21,552	$ 42,287
Per Common Share Amounts							
Income from continuing operations	4.25	3.55	3.21	2.93	2.45	2.21	1.98
Loss from discontinued and expropriated operations	–	–	–	–	–	0.16	0.11
Income before extraordinary items	4.25	3.55	3.21	2.93	2.45	2.05	1.87
Extraordinary items	–	–	–	–	0.39	(1.10)	–
Net income	4.25	3.55	3.21	2.93	2.84	0.95	1.87

EXHIBIT 1 *(concluded)*

	1978	1977	1976	1975	1974	1973	1974
Other Data							
Dividends paid:							
Common, per share	1.42	1.06⅔	0.86⅔	0.77⅓	0.72⅔	0.70	0.67⅓
Common, total	32,143	24,260	19,671	17,502	16,427	15,814	15,718
Preferred, total	3,147	3,166	1,024	139	146	165	184
Capital expenditures	95,408	53,679	34,682	57,219	44,096	48,322	28,067
Depreciation	31,564	29,697	27,900	25,090	22,535	20,950	20,143
Shareholders' equity	702,736	655,480	598,613	502,796	447,434	399,607	394,519
Total debt	228,002	220,779	219,387	295,051	266,617	249,161	196,309
Average number of common shares outstanding	22,609,613	22,743,233	22,696,484	22,633,115	22,604,720	22,591,287	22,538,309
Book value per common share	28.96	26.27	23.79	22.04	19.61	17.50	17.26
Price range of common stock:							
High	40	34⅛	38	34⅜	34⅞	30⅞	31½
Low	28¾	26½	28⅞	18	24⅞	25⅜	25⅞
Sales (%):							
Domestic	62	62	59	58	59	58	57
Foreign	38	38	41	42	41	42	43
Income (%):							
Domestic	67	78	66	71	57	53	54
Foreign	33	22	34	29	43	47	46

Source: Company records.

reported directly to the president; others reported through senior vice presidents who were designated area directors (see Exhibit 2). World headquarters officers worked with division senior managers in such areas as planning, product and market development, and capital programs.

Heinz's divisions were largely autonomous operating companies. Division managers were directly responsible for the division's products and services, and they operated their own research and development, manufacturing, and marketing facilities. Division staff reported directly to division managers and had neither formal reporting nor dotted-line relationships with corporate staff.

World headquarters officers monitored division performance through conventional business budgets and financial reports. If reported performance was in line with corporate financial goals, little inquiry into the details of division operation was made. On the other

EXHIBIT 2 Organization Chart, April 1979

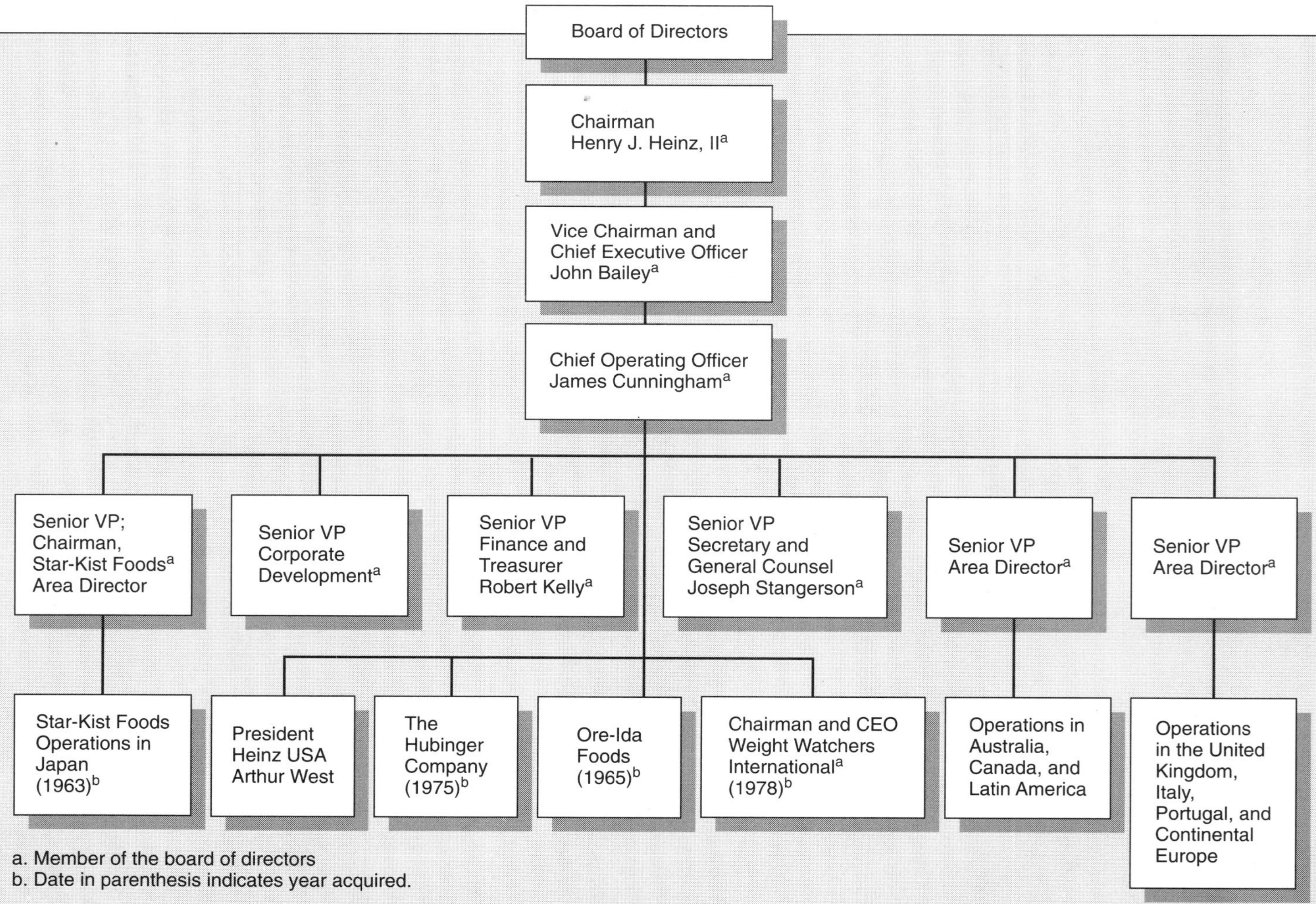

```
                          Board of Directors
                                 │
                          Chairman
                          Henry J. Heinz, II[a]
                                 │
                          Vice Chairman and
                          Chief Executive Officer
                          John Bailey[a]
                                 │
                          Chief Operating Officer
                          James Cunningham[a]
                                 │
    ┌──────────────┬────────────┼─────────────┬──────────────┬──────────────┐
    │              │            │             │              │              │
Senior VP;     Senior VP    Senior VP     Senior VP      Senior VP      Senior VP
Chairman,      Corporate    Finance and   Secretary and  Area          Area
Star-Kist      Development[a] Treasurer    General        Director[a]    Director[a]
Foods[a]                    Robert Kelly[a] Counsel
Area Director                             Joseph
                                          Stangerson[a]
    │              │            │             │              │              │
Star-Kist      President    Ore-Ida       Chairman and   Operations in  Operations
Foods          Heinz USA    Foods         CEO            Australia,     in the United
Operations in  Arthur West  (1965)[b]     Weight         Canada, and    Kingdom,
Japan          The Hubinger               Watchers       Latin America  Italy,
(1963)[b]      Company                    International[a]                Portugal, and
               (1975)[b]                  (1978)[b]                      Continental
                                                                         Europe
```

a. Member of the board of directors
b. Date in parenthesis indicates year acquired.

hand, variations from planned performance drew a great deal of attention from world headquarters; then, divisions were pressured to improve results. A review was held near the end of the third fiscal quarter to discuss expected year-end results. If shortfalls were apparent, other divisions were often encouraged to improve their performance. The aim was to meet projected consolidated earnings and goals. Predictability was a watchword and surprises were to be avoided.[5] A consistent growth in earnings attended this management philosophy.

Management Incentive Plan

Designed by a prominent management consulting firm, the management incentive plan (MIP) was regarded as a prime management tool used to achieve corporate goals.[6] MIP comprised roughly 225 employees, including corporate officers, senior world headquarters personnel, and senior personnel of most divisions. Incentive compensation was awarded on the basis of an earned number of MIP points and in some cases reached 40 percent of total compensation.

MIP points could be earned through the achievement of personal goals. These goals were established at the beginning of each fiscal year in consultation with the participant's immediate supervisor. Points were awarded by the supervisor at the end of the year, based on goal achievement. In practice, personal goal point awards fell out on a curve, with few individuals receiving very high or very low awards.

MIP points were also awarded based on net profit after tax (NPAT) goals. (On occasion, other goals, such as increased inventory turnover or improved cash flow, were included in

MIP goals.) Corporate NPAT goals were set at the beginning of the fiscal year by the management development and compensation committee (MDC) of the board of directors. The chief executive officer, the chief operating officer, the senior vice president–finance, and the senior vice president–corporate development then set MIP goals for each division, with the aggregate of division goals usually exceeding the corporate goal. Two goals were set — a fair goal, which was consistently higher than the preceding year's NPAT, and a higher outstanding goal. The full number of MIP points was earned by achieving the outstanding goal.

Senior corporate managers were responsible for executing the system. While divisional input was not uncommon, division NPAT goals were set unilaterally and did not necessarily reflect a division's budgeted profits. Once set, goals were seldom changed during the year. The officers who set the goals awarded MIP points at the end of the fiscal year. No points were awarded to personnel in a division that failed to achieve its fair goal, and points were weighted to favor results at or near the outstanding goal. One or more bonus points might be awarded if the outstanding goal was exceeded. Corporate officers also had the authority to make adjustments or award arbitrary points in special circumstances. The basis for these adjustments was not discussed with division personnel.

MIP points for consolidated corporate performance were awarded by the MDC committee of the board. Corporate points were credited to all MIP participants except those in a division that did not achieve its fair goal. The MDC committee could also award company bonus points.

Heinz also had a long-term incentive plan based on a revolving three-year cycle. Participation was limited to senior corporate management and division presidents or managing directors for a total of 19 persons.

---

[5] Ibid., p. 8.
[6] Ibid., pp. 10–12.

Corporate Ethical Policy

Heinz had an explicit corporate ethical policy that was adopted in May 1976.[7] Among other things, it stated that no division should:

1. Have any form of unrecorded assets or false entries on its books or records.
2. Make or approve any payment with the intention or understanding that any part of such payment was to be used for any purpose other than that described by the documents supporting the payment.
3. Make political contributions.
4. Make payments or gifts to public officials or customers.
5. Accept gifts or payments of more than a nominal amount.

Each year the president or managing director and the chief financial officer of each division were required to sign a representation letter which, among other things, confirmed compliance with the corporate Code of Ethics.

[7] Ibid., p. 12.

April 1979

Heinz itself had originated the antitrust proceedings that led to the discovery of the alleged practices. In 1976, Heinz filed a private antitrust suit against the Campbell Soup Company, accusing Campbell of monopolistic practices in the canned soup market. Campbell promptly countersued, charging that Heinz monopolized the ketchup market.[8] Campbell attorneys, preparing for court action, subpoenaed Heinz documents reflecting its financial relationships with one of its advertising agencies. In April 1979, while taking a deposition from Arthur West, president of the Heinz USA division, Campbell attorneys asked about flows of funds, "certain items which can be called off-book accounts." West refused to answer, claiming Fifth Amendment protection from self-incrimination.[9] Stangerson then spoke with the advertising agency and received confirmation of the invoicing practices.

[8] "Heinz slow growth behind juggling tactic?" *Advertising Age,* March 24, 1980, p. 88.
[9] "Results in Probe of Heinz Income Juggling Expected to be Announced by Early April," *The Wall Street Journal,* March 18, 1980, p. 7.

H. J. HEINZ COMPANY: THE ADMINISTRATION OF POLICY (B)

In April 1979, Heinz's senior management learned of improper practices concerning the transfer of an undetermined amount of reported income from one fiscal year to the next.

This case was prepared by Richard J. Post under the direction of Kenneth E. Goodpaster.

Copyright © 1981 by the President and Fellows of Harvard College.

Harvard Business School case 382-035.

At two of the Heinz operating divisions, payments had been made to vendors in one fiscal year, then repaid or exchanged for services in the succeeding fiscal year. The scope of the practice and the amounts involved were not then known.

Aware that the practice might have affected the company's reported income over the past seven fiscal years, management consulted an outside legal firm for an opinion on the seriousness of the problem. Based on that opinion,

---

EXHIBIT 1 Form 8-K Excerpt, April 27, 1979

Item 5: Other Materially Important Events

On April 27, 1979, the registrant announced that it had become aware that since 1972 in certain of its divisions or subsidiaries payments have been made to certain of its vendors in a particular fiscal year, which were repaid or exchanged for services by such vendors in the succeeding fiscal year.

The registrant stated that at this stage it was not possible to determine the scope of the practice or the total amounts involved, but that there was no reason to believe there would be any material effect on the registrant's reported earnings for any fiscal year including the fiscal year ending May 2, 1979.

The Audit Committee of the registrant's board of directors has retained the law firm of Cravath, Swaine & Moore, independent outside counsel, to conduct a full inquiry of the practice. Cravath, Swaine & Moore will retain independent public accountants to assist in the investigation.

The registrant has heretofore advised the Securities and Exchange Commission and the Internal Revenue Service of the foregoing. At this time the registrant is unable to estimate the extent of any adjustments which may be necessary for tax purposes.

John Bailey, Heinz's chief executive officer, notified the Audit Committee of the board of directors. Composed entirely of outside directors, this committee was responsible for working with internal auditors and financial officers and with the firm's outside auditors, thus preserving the integrity of financial information published by Heinz.

The Audit Committee held a special meeting on April 26, 1979. After hearing from outside counsel and from Joseph Stangerson (Heinz's general counsel) about the practices, the committee adopted a resolution retaining an outside law firm and independent public accountants to assist in a full investigation of the matter.[1]

An attorney from Cravath, Swaine & Moore, the outside law firm, accompanied Stangerson to Washington to advise the Securities and Exchange Commission of the information avail-able and of the investigation then under way. (An excerpt from form 8-K filed with the SEC is attached as Exhibit 1.) The two also informed the IRS of possible tax consequences of the practice.

On April 27, 1979, Heinz publicly announced its investigation. "At this stage," the formal statement said, "it isn't possible to determine the scope of the practice or the total amounts involved." It also stated there "isn't any reason to believe there will be any material effect on the company's reported earnings for any fiscal year including the current fiscal year." While the investigation would cover the period from 1972 to 1979, Heinz would not identify the divisions or vendors involved. Stangerson stated: "We aren't prepared to say whether [the practices] were legal or illegal." He added that the company had informed the SEC and the IRS.[2]

---

[1] "Report of the Audit Committee to the Board of Directors: Income Transferal and Other Practices," H. J. Heinz Company, form 8-K, May 7, 1980.

[2] "Results in Probe of Heinz Income Juggling Expected to be Announced by Early April," *The Wall Street Journal*, March 18, 1980, p. 7.

The Investigation

The Audit Committee supervised the conduct of the investigation. Teams composed of lawyers and accountants from the two outside firms interviewed present and former company and vendor personnel about possible improprieties. The investigators focused on the following areas:

1. Practices that affected the accuracy of company accounts or the security of company assets.
2. Practices in violation of the company's Code of Ethics.
3. Illegal political contributions.
4. Illegal, improper, or otherwise questionable payments.
5. Factors contributing to the existence, continuance, or nondisclosure of any of the above.

The investigating teams interviewed over 325 Heinz employees, many of them more than once. The teams also interviewed personnel employed by many of Heinz's vendors, including advertising agencies. Accounting records, correspondence, and other files were examined. The board of directors at its regular May meeting asked for the cooperation of all officers and employees.[3]

On May 10, 1979, Heinz announced that a settlement had been reached in its private antitrust suit against the Campbell Soup Company. The settlement resulted in the dismissal of Heinz's action against Campbell, which had been brought in 1976, and of Campbell's counterclaim against Heinz. The court ordered the record of the suit sealed and kept secret.[4]

On June 29, 1979, Heinz disclosed a preliminary figure of $5.5 million of aftertax income associated with the income transferal practices. Stressing that this was a "very soft number," the company indicated that it was delaying release of audited results for FY 1979 (ended May 2, 1979) and that its annual meeting, scheduled for September 12, would be postponed until the investigation (which could continue well into the fall) was completed. The preliminary unaudited figures released by Heinz showed net income of $113.4 million ($4.95 per share) on sales of $2.4 billion, after the $5.5 million deduction. Press reports indicated the investigation was being broadened to include Heinz's foreign units.[5]

On September 13, 1979, it was reported that the preliminary figure had grown to $8.5 million. Heinz's statement, filed with its first quarter FY 1980 earnings report, also stated FY 1979 income as $110.4 million or $4.80 per share. Most of the $3 million growth was attributed to the discovery of improper treatment of sales in addition to the improper treatment of prepaid expenses discovered earlier.[6]

Heinz's 1979 annual report contained audited financial statements for FY 1979 and restated financial statements for FY 1978. The report contained an unqualified opinion from Peat, Marwick, Mitchell & Company, Heinz's auditors, dated November 14, 1979. In Note 2 to the 1979 financial statements, the report also contained a restatement and reconciliation of sales, net income, and earnings per share for the previous eight fiscal years. (The 1979 results are shown in Exhibit 2. The restatement of FY 1971–FY 1978 are shown in Exhibit 3.) This information was filed with the Securities

---

[3] Audit Committee report, form 8-K, May 7, 1980, p. 4.

[4] H. J. Heinz Company, form 8-K, May 10, 1979, p. 2; *The Wall Street Journal*, March 18, 1980, p. 7.

[5] "Initial Study of Some Heinz Units Finds $5.5 Million in Profit Juggling Practices," *The Wall Street Journal*, July 2, 1979, p. 8.

[6] "Heinz Discloses Profit Switching at Units Was Much Broader than First Realized," *The Wall Street Journal*, September 13, 1979, p. 15.

EXHIBIT 2   Financial Summary, 1979 ($ 000s except per share data)

	1979	1978*	Change
Sales	$2,470,883	$2,159,436	14.4%
Operating income	214,735	187,062	14.8
Net income	110,430	99,946	10.5
Per common share amounts:			
Net income	$ 4.80	$ 4.28	12.1%
Net income (fully diluted)	4.64	4.17	11.3
Dividends	1.85	1.42	30.3
Book value	32.29	29.33	10.1
Capital expenditures	$ 118,156	95,408	23.8%
Depreciation expense	38,317	31,564	21.4
Net property	481,688	412,334	16.8
Cash and short-term investments	$ 122,281	$ 84,044	45.5%
Working capital	401,169	453,517	(11.5)
Total debt	342,918	228,002	50.4
Shareholders' equity	778,397	711,126	9.5
Average number of common shares outstanding	22,330	22,610	
Current ratio	1.70	2.14	
Debt/invested capital	30.9%	24.7%	
Pretax return on average invested capital	20.7%	20.7%	
Return on average shareholders' equity	14.8%	14.5%	

* As restated.

Source: 1979 annual report.

and Exchange Commission on November 20, 1979.[7]

In February 1980 Heinz reorganized its top management structure (see Exhibit 4). Arthur West, formerly president of Heinz USA, was promoted to world headquarters as area director. He assumed responsibility for the Hubinger Company and Weight Watchers International, both of which had previously reported directly to James Cunningham, Heinz's president and new CEO. West was also to be responsible for Heinz's Canadian subsidiary. Heinz USA would now report through Kevin Voight, senior vice president, rather than directly to Cunningham. Unlike other area directors, West would be neither a senior vice president nor a member of the board of directors.[8]

In April 1980, Doyle Dane Bernbach, the only publicly held firm among the advertising

---

[7] Audit Committee report, form 8-K, May 7, 1980, p. 2.

[8] "H. J. Heinz Realigns its Senior Management in Consolidation Move," *The Wall Street Journal,* February 19, 1980.

EXHIBIT 3 Restated Financial Data, 1971–1978

Change in Sales, Net Income, and Earnings per Share (in thousands except for per share amounts)

	1971	1972	1973	1974	1975	1976	1977	1978
Sales as previously reported	$876,451	$1,020,958	$1,116,551	$1,349,091	$1,564,930	$1,749,691	$1,868,820	$2,150,027
Net increase (decrease) resulting from restatement to current improper treatment of sales	—	—	14,821	(1,777)	(4,747)	4,725	8,480	9,409
Sales as restated	$876,451	$1,020,958	$1,131,372	$1,347,314	$1,560,183	$1,754,416	$1,877,300	$2,159,436
Net income as previously reported	$ 37,668*	$ 42,287*	$ 21,552*	$ 64,320*	$ 66,567	$ 73,960	$ 83,816	$ 99,171
Net increase (decrease) in income before income taxes resulting from restatement:								
Correct improper treatment of sales, net of related costs	—	—	1,968	309	(1,527)	1,815	1,294	2,872
Correct improper recognition of income/expense	1,290	512	1,813	5,615	(1,861)	(684)	3,822	(1,417)
Income tax effect	(671)	(263)	(1,566)	(2,698)	1,254	(604)	(2,203)	(680)
Net adjustments	619	249	2,215	3,226	(2,134)	527	2,913	775
Net income as restated	$ 38,287	$ 42,536	$ 23,767	$ 67,546	$ 64,433	$ 74,487	$ 86,729	$ 99,946

* Net income as previously reported above includes losses from discontinued and expropriated operations and extraordinary items as shown.

EXHIBIT 3 *(continued)*

Change in Sales, Net Income, and Earnings per Share (in thousands except for per share amounts)

	1971	1972	1973	1974	1975	1976	1977	1978
Income per common share amounts:								
Income from continuing operations as previously reported	$1.71	$1.98	$2.21	$2.45	$2.93	$3.21	$3.55	$4.25
Net increase (decrease) from restatement	0.02	0.01	0.09	0.14	(0.09)	0.03	0.12	0.03
Income from continuing operations as restated	1.73	1.99	2.30	2.59	2.84	3.24	3.67	4.28
Loss from discontinued and expropriated operations	0.02	0.11	0.16	—	—	—	—	—
Income before extraordinary items	1.71	1.88	2.14	2.59	2.84	3.24	3.67	4.28
Extraordinary items	—	—	(1.10)	0.39	—	—	—	—
Net income	$1.71	$1.88	$1.04	$.298	$2.84	$3.24	$3.67	$4.28

In Thousands

	Income from Continuing Operations	Loss from Discontinued and Expropriated Operations	Extraordinary Items	Net Income as Previously Reported
1971	$38,171	$ (503)	—	$37,668
1972	44,679	(2,392)	—	42,287
1973	50,082	(3,530)	$(25,000)	21,552
1974	55,520	—	8,800	64,320

EXHIBIT 3 *(concluded)*

The following table (in thousands except per share amounts) presents the as-reported and as-restated interim results, which are unaudited, for 1978 and 1979.

	Sales		Gross Profit		Net Income		Earnings Per Share	
	As Reported	As Restated	As Reported	As Restated	As Reported	As Restated	As Reported	As Restated
1978								
First quarter	$ 491,469	$ 472,955	$156,538	$152,639	$19,645	$ 17,621	$0.83	$0.74
Second quarter	520,051	525,440	169,476	170,348	23,613	22,676	1.00	0.96
Third quarter	523,640	517,738	170,621	169,001	19,901	20,208	0.85	0.86
Fourth quarter	614,867	643,303	214,143	221,992	36,012	39,441	1.57	1.72
Total	$2,150,027	$2,159,436	$710,778	$713,980	$99,171	$ 99,946	$4.25	$4.28
1979								
First quarter	$ 555,558	$ 536,301	$178,250	$171,330	$21,161	$ 16,783	$0.91	$0.72
Second quarter	620,230	619,627	203,708	203,964	28,204	26,026	1.23	1.13
Third quarter	575,410	566,747	202,171	199,497	23,301	21,192	1.01	0.91
Fourth quarter	—	748,208*	—	267,584*	—	46,429*	—	2.04*
Total	$ —	$2,470,883*	$ —	$842,375*	—	$110,430*	$ —	$4.80*

* Not previously reported.

Source: 1979 annual report.

EXHIBIT 4 Organization Chart, February 1980

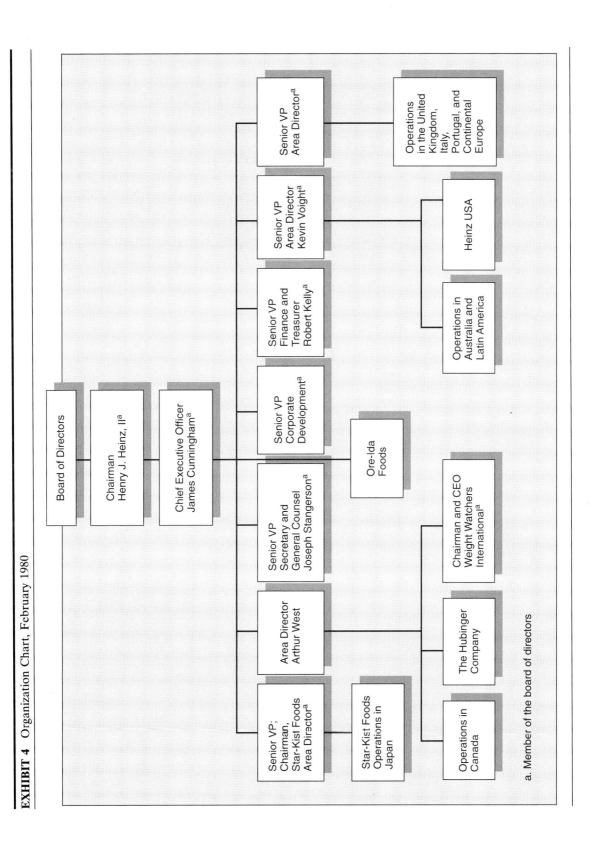

a. Member of the board of directors

and consulting firms included in the Audit Committee's investigation, admitted in an SEC filing that it had participated in the income-juggling practices by prebilling and issuing bills that did not accurately describe the services provided.[9]

On May 7, 1980, the Audit Committee presented its report to the Heinz board of directors. The 80-page report was filed on form 8-K with the SEC on May 9, 1980. (The remainder of this case is derived substantially from the Audit Committee's report.)

The Findings

The Audit Committee reported widespread use of improper billing, accounting, and reporting procedures at Heinz's divisions, including Heinz USA, Ore-Ida, and Star-Kist, and a number of Heinz's foreign operations. The two major areas of impropriety were:

1. *Improper recognition of expenses:* These were most often advertising and market research expenses, improperly recorded in the current fiscal period when in fact the services were performed or goods delivered in a later fiscal period. This treatment resulted in an overstatement of expenses (and understatement of income) in one period and a comparable understatement of expenses (and overstatement of income) in a later fiscal period.
2. *Improper recognition of sales:* Sales were recorded in a fiscal period other than that in which those sales should have been recorded under generally accepted accounting principles.

Table A indicates the amounts involved. The accumulated effects of such practices on shareholders' equity and working capital did not exceed 2 percent.

---

[9] "DDB admits Heinz role," *Advertising Age,* April 28, 1980, pp. 1, 88.

The Audit Committee indicated that these income transferal practices were designed to adjust the income reported by divisions to corporate headquarters and were motivated primarily by a desire to meet the constantly increasing profit objectives set by world headquarters. While division management supported the publicly announced goal of steadily increasing profits, the committee reported that the management incentive program (MIP), under which the goals were administered, created significant pressures. Aside from obvious personal financial considerations, many division-level personnel reportedly viewed the achievement of MIP goals as the key to advancement at Heinz. One manager told the committee that failure to achieve these goals constituted a "mortal sin."

The Heinz principle of decentralized authority extended to financial reporting and internal control procedures. Division financial officers were not responsible to corporate headquarters but to their division president or managing director. The MIP goal pressures provided the incentive, and autonomous control the opportunity, for adopting the improper practices being reported.

One reason for using such reporting techniques was explained to the committee:

If this fiscal year's goal is, say, $20 million net profit after tax (NPAT), it can be anticipated that next year's goal will be, say, 15 percent higher, or $23 million NPAT. This year seems to be a good one and it is anticipated that earnings will be $24 million NPAT. But, if that figure is reported to world headquarters, it is likely that next year's goal will be about 15 percent higher than the $24 million NPAT, or approximately $27 million NPAT. Of course, there is no assurance that there will not be some unforeseen disaster next year. Thus, if it is possible to mislead world headquarters as to the true state of the earnings of the [division] and report only the $20 million NPAT, which is the current fiscal year's goal, and have the additional $4

TABLE A   Increase (Decrease) of Consolidated Income before Tax, Net of Recoveries ($ in thousands)

	Improper Recognition			Net Income before Tax		
FY	Expenses	Sales	Other Practices	Increase (Decrease)	Total after Restatement	% Effects of Restatement
1972	$ (513)	—	—	$ (513)	$ 75,894	(.7)
1973	(1,814)	$(1,968)	—	(3,782)	84,777	(4.5)
1974	(4,250)	(309)	$(1,364)	(5,923)	98,173	(6.0)
1975	2,476	1,527	(615)	3,388	113,137	3.0
1976	(111)	(1,815)	877	(1,049)	128,682	(.8)
1977	(4,139)	(1,294)	268	(5,165)	160,101	(3.2)
1978	734	(2,872)	671	(1,467)	170,198	(.9)
1979	8,888	7,085	396	16,369	183,178	8.9
1980	76	(354)	(233)	(511)	—	—

million NPAT carried forward into next year, the [division] will have a good start toward achieving its expected $23 million NPAT goal next year and will not have to reach $27 million NPAT.

Explanations for accepting these practices at lower levels included job security and the desire to impress superiors.

The committee's report stated: "There is no evidence that any employee of the company sought or obtained any direct personal gain in connection with any of the transactions or practices described in this report. Nor did the investigation find any evidence that any officer or personnel at world headquarters participated in any of the income transferal practices described in this report." The report went on to describe activities at each division in greater detail.

Division Income Transfer Practices

Heinz USA

Income transfer at Heinz USA started late in FY 1974 when world headquarters realized that Heinz USA might report profits in excess of those allowed by the wage and price controls in effect at the time. World headquarters sought to have Heinz USA report lower profits, although no evidence indicates that any world headquarters personnel intended GAAP to be violated. After some commodity transactions lowered expected profits, there was a reluctance in Heinz USA to reduce its expected profits further. Nevertheless, to accomplish the further reduction, $2 million in invoices for services that would not be performed were obtained from an advertising agency and recorded as an expense in FY 1974.

Heinz USA reported FY 1974 NPAT of $4,614,000. NPAT goals for the year were $4.9 million (fair) and $5.5 million (outstanding). In calculating NPAT for MIP purposes, world headquarters allowed an adjustment of $2 million ($1 million after tax) for advertising. This adjustment resulted in Heinz USA achieving its outstanding goal for FY 1974. The division also received a bonus point. The use of improper invoices to manage reported income continued after FY 1974 at Heinz USA, although there was no evidence that world headquarters personnel knew about these transactions.

Beginning in FY 1977, additional income transfer methods were developed. Distribution centers were instructed to stop shipments for the last few days of the fiscal year to allow the recording of sales in the subsequent year. These instructions presented practical difficulties and some of the shipments were not held up. Without the authorization of division senior management, paperwork was apparently altered or misdated to record the sales as desired.

Vendors' credits were often deferred and processed in the subsequent fiscal year to assist the income management program. Detailed schedules were privately maintained that served as the basis for discussions on income management. One employee had the job of maintaining private records to insure the recovery (in subsequent fiscal years) of amounts paid to vendors on improper invoices.

The use of improper invoices spread to the departmental level as well. Individual department managers used either prepaid billing or delayed billing, as required, to insure complete use of their departmental budget without overspending. This practice provided protection against future budget cuts during those periods when the full budget would not otherwise have been spent. Division management actively discouraged these transactions.

Vendor cooperation was not difficult to obtain. One Heinz manager described it as "the price of doing business with us." During the period in question, 10 vendors participated in improper invoicing at Heinz USA, and 8 participated at the department level. Most vendors' fiscal years did not coincide with Heinz's.

In FY 1975, a sugar inventory write-down was used to transfer income. Sugar inventory, valued at an average cost of 37 cents per pound, was written down to 25 cents per pound. This adjustment, which amounted to an increase in FY 1975 expense of $1,390,360, was justified on the basis of an expected decline in price early in the next fiscal year. This would result in lower selling prices in FY 1976 for some division products. The lower NPAT figure that

resulted was used for establishing FY 1976 goals; but when FY 1975 performance was evaluated, world headquarters adjusted Heinz USA's income up by the amount of the sugar write-down. The anticipated price decline did not occur.

At other times, inflated accruals, inventory adjustments, commodity transactions, and at least one customer rebate were used to report income other than that required by GAAP.

Ore-Ida

Improper invoices to transfer income were also used at Ore-Ida during that period, and the issue of obtaining these invoices was discussed at meetings of Ore-Ida's management board. Even though the invoices contained descriptions of services that were generic or had no correlation to the actual services to be rendered, members of the management board believed the practice was appropriate because comparable services would have been purchased at some point. During two fiscal years Ore-Ida received interest payments from an advertising agency in connection with the payment of these invoices.

Ore-Ida's management believed that members of world headquarters' management were aware of the income transfer practices, but raised no objections to them. Documents submitted to world headquarters by Ore-Ida contained references to special media billing, prebills, year-end media billing, special billing adjustments, and advertising and promotion prebilling. Some documents indicated that these items actually applied to the fiscal year following that of expense recognition. The amount of these expenses was indicated each year to world headquarters' management (in one year, the amount was understated). In FY 1974, corporate management increased Ore-Ida's income before tax by the amount of the prebilled advertising expense for MIP award purposes. Ore-Ida's management did not know if world headquarters' management appreciated the fact that this practice did not conform to GAAP.

Star-Kist

Both improper expense recognition and improper sales recognition were used to adjust reported income at Star-Kist. Improper invoices were solicited from vendors to accumulate an advertising savings account. Sales during the last month of a fiscal year were recorded during the first month of the next fiscal year by preventing selected documents from entering the sales accounting system. These practices were apparently present only in Star-Kist's marketing department.

Similar practices were also discovered at some of Heinz's foreign subsidiaries.

Other Improper Practices

Although it focused primarily on income transferal practices, the investigation uncovered a number of other practices. Again, the committee stated that no member of world headquarters' management appeared to have any knowledge of these practices, and no employee sought or obtained any personal financial gain. All of these transactions took place outside the United States. None of the countries in which the transactions took place were identified by the committee.

In one country, six questionable payments totaling $80,000 were made during FY 1978 and FY 1979. Two were made to lower-level government employees in connection with alleged violations of import regulations. One was made to a lower-level government employee in connection with the settlement of a labor dispute. Municipal employees received one payment in connection with real estate assessments. Labor union officials received the remaining two payments. In January 1979, three of these payments were reported by division management to world headquarters. A brief investigation ensued and the board of

directors reprimanded certain officers of the division.

Star-Kist was involved in several transactions listed in the following section of the report:

1. In one country the payment of interest to nonresidents was prohibited. Star-Kist collected interest on its loans to fishing fleets through the falsification of invoices indicating the purchase by Star-Kist of supplies for the fleets.
2. In another country Star-Kist acted as a conduit through which funds flowed to facilitate a fish purchase involving two other companies. Letters of credit requiring the approval of the exchange authorities were used.
3. In a third country Star-Kist received checks from a fish supplier and endorsed those checks to a wholly owned U.S. subsidiary of the supplier. These transactions were not recorded in Star-Kist's accounts.

The Heinz operating company in yet another country made payments for goods to individual or designated bank accounts rather than to the supplier involved. These payments were not made through the normal cash disbursement procedure; rather, the division was acting at the supplier's request.

Contributing Factors

The Audit Committee reported that only a small part of the failure to detect these practices could be attributed to weakness in Heinz's internal controls. In most cases, those controls were circumvented by or with the concurrence of division management. With the autonomy enjoyed by division management, it would have been difficult for world headquarters personnel to detect these practices.

The committee attributed part of the problem to a lack of control consciousness throughout the corporation. *Control consciousness* referred to the atmosphere in which accounting controls existed and it reflected senior management attitudes about the importance of such controls. Clearly, control consciousness was not then present in most Heinz divisions. The committee blamed world headquarters' senior management for creating an environment that was seen as endorsing poor control consciousness:

> If world headquarters' senior management had established a satisfactory control consciousness, internal accounting controls that were cost/benefit justified should have been able to survive reasonable pressures to meet or exceed the defined economic goals. In establishing this atmosphere, world headquarters' senior management apparently did not consider the effect on individuals in the [divisions] of the pressures to which they were subjected.

Other factors cited by the committee included:

- Corporate internal auditing personnel report to their respective division managers and not to the director–corporate audit.
- The lack of an effective Code of Ethics compliance procedure.
- The lack of standardized accounting and reporting procedures for all Heinz divisions.
- The lack of an effective budget review and monitoring process.
- The lack of enough competent financial personnel at world headquarters and at the divisions.
- The lack of a world headquarters electronic data processing manager responsible for the control procedures of the divisions' EDP departments.

Conclusions of the Audit Committee

1. The amounts involved in the income transferal practices were not material to the consolidated net income or shareholders' equity of the company in the aggregate during the investigatory period (FY 1972–FY 1978).

2. The income transferal practices were achieved primarily through circumvention of existing internal controls by division personnel who should have exercised responsibility in the enforcement of such controls. Such practices were also assisted by certain inadequacies in the internal control systems of the divisions.

3. Although world headquarters' personnel did not authorize or participate in the income transferal practices, their continuance was facilitated by the company's philosophy of decentralized management and the role played by world headquarters' financial personnel in reviewing the financial reports from divisions.

4. No individual employee obtained any direct financial benefit from the practices uncovered in the investigation.

5. Perceived or de facto pressures for achievement of MIP goals contributed to the divisions' desirability of providing a cushion against future business uncertainties.

6. The income transferal practices did not serve any valid corporate need.

7. The income transferal practices and other questionable practices described in this report [of the Audit Committee] indicate the lack of sufficient control consciousness within the corporate structure; that is, an understanding throughout the company and the divisions that responsible and ethical practices are required in connection with all transactions.

8. The entrepreneurial spirit of the divisions fostered by the philosophy of decentralized autonomy should be continued for the good of the company and its shareholders.

9. World headquarters did not have the number of competent financial personnel needed to fulfill its role.

10. The continuance of the income transferal practices was aided by the independence of division financial personnel from world headquarters.

11. The continuance of the income transferral practices was aided by the reporting relationships of the internal audit staffs within the company.

12. The administration of the MIP and the

goal-setting process thereunder did not result in adequate dialogue between senior world headquarters management and managements of the divisions.

13. The board of directors and management of the company have the duty to take all steps practicable to ensure safeguarding the assets of the company and that all transactions are properly recorded on the books, records, and accounts of the company.

SALOMON AND THE TREASURY SECURITIES AUCTION

In early June 1991, Salomon vice chairman John Meriwether had a problem. The U.S. Treasury was inquiring about the possibility that Salomon had engineered a "squeeze" in the market for $12 billion in new Treasury notes auctioned on May 22, 1991. Ordinarily, the Treasury's concern over the possibility of a squeeze was not particularly problematic. Squeezes—that is, an unpredicted shortness of supply or high demand for a security—were not uncommon and developed for a variety of reasons. Unfortunately, Meriwether had reason to believe that one of Salomon's bond traders had recently violated the Treasury's auction rules. Paul Mozer, the managing director under Meriwether overseeing Salomon's trading in U.S. Treasury securities, had disclosed to Meriwether in late April that he had broken the Treasury's limit on the size of a dealer's bid in Treasury auctions. Mozer had admitted that he submitted a bid in a February auction using the name of a customer without authorization and had managed to buy more bonds than the Treasury guidelines allowed.

The problem struck close to the heart of Salomon's business. Although Salomon was among the leaders in the traditional investment banking activity of debt and equity underwriting—acting as the intermediary between issuers of new securities (corporations and governments) and the investors who bought them—its trading in securities markets drove the firm's profitability and was a key part of its heritage. Profits from "principal transactions," largely the buying and selling of securities for Salomon's own account, generally provided 20 percent of Salomon's revenues, considerably more than the 10 to 12 percent found at most investment banks (Exhibit 1). In addition, Salomon's corporate culture revolved around trading. The CEO's desk was located on the firm's trading floor and seven of Salomon Brother's nine vice chairmen had come up through the trading side of the business. John Gutfreund (pronounced *good*friend), Salomon's chairman and CEO, had also worked his way up to the top of the firm as a successful trader.

Salomon and the Investment Banking Community

The primacy of bond trading at Salomon Brothers dated to the firm's founding in 1910, when the social dynamics of investment banking limited the firm's opportunities. At the time of Salomon's founding, an aristocracy of such established firms as Morgan Stanley, Kidder Peabody, and Kuhn Loeb controlled the traditional investment banking activity of

This case was prepared by Professor Dwight D. Crane of the Harvard Business School.

Copyright © 1992 by the President and Fellows of Harvard College.

Harvard Business School case 292-114.

EXHIBIT 1 Selected Financials, Salomon, Inc., 1986 to 1990 (all figures in millions)

	Year Ending December 31				
	1986	*1987*	*1988*	*1989*	*1990*
Revenues:					
Interest and dividends	$ 4,932	$ 4,161	$ 3,360	$ 5,758	$ 5,920
Principal transactions	1,064	1,154	1,711	2,513	2,389
Investment banking	577	403	564	470	416
Commissions	208	266	206	226	207
Other	8	19	35	32	14
Total	6,789	6,003	6,146	8,999	8,946
Interest expense	(4,484)	(3,973)	(3,541)	(6,093)	(5,959)
Noninterest expense	(1,512)	(1,805)	(1,852)	(2,166)	(2,481)
Income before taxes	793	225	753	740	506
Net income	$ 516	$ 142	$ 280	$ 470	$ 303
Total assets	$78,164	$74,747	$85,256	$118,250	$109,877
Stockholders' equity	3,545	3,481	3,459	3,565	3,523

Source: Annual reports, Salomon, Inc.

securities underwriting. As underwriters, these banks worked closely with the finance departments of large corporations to help them raise capital by selling new equity securities (stocks) and debt instruments (notes and bonds) through each bank's sales force. In exchange for a guarantee to buy any new securities that outside investors were unwilling to buy, the investment banks received an underwriting fee. At the time of Salomon's founding, only the reigning investment banks had the connections and reputations necessary to approach potential investors and assure them of the quality of the new securities. With this distribution capability, the established investment banks could assure their corporate customers that they would be able to find enough investors for the new securities.

In contrast, the original three Salomon brothers, Arthur, Percy, and Herbert, were recent entrants to both the country and the investment banking industry and had little access to the wealthy investors who controlled much of the country's capital before the Second World War. As a result, Salomon was less able to approach the large corporations as an underwriter because it lacked adequate placement power (the ability to find investors for new securities). Instead, the firm focused on U.S. government debt where the Treasury selected underwriters on the basis of competitive bids[1] and Salomon could place the new securities with insurance and trust companies, rather than individuals.[2] Unlike corporations that hired underwriters for new securities, the U.S. government did not pay underwriting fees. Instead, Salomon and other government debt underwriters made their money by buying the securities in a government-run auction, then

---

[1] Robert Sobel, *Salomon Brothers 1910–1985: Advancing to Leadership* (New York: Salomon Brothers, © 1986), p. 17.

[2] *Ibid.,* pp. 33, 66.

reselling them to investors at a slightly higher price.

To carve a place for itself in U.S. government debt underwriting, Salomon worked hard to build its reputation for customer service. A key element of this service was the firm's commitment to trading and making a market in the securities it sold. When it placed new U.S. government securities with a customer, the firm stood ready to buy them back at the prevailing market price if the customer needed to sell the bonds. If another customer for the bonds could not be found immediately, Salomon carried the bonds in its inventory.[3] This willingness to trade earned Salomon the loyalty of many of its customers.

Carrying bonds in inventory entailed considerable risk, but the trading skills, which this risk forced Salomon to develop, ultimately proved quite lucrative. While the bonds were held in inventory, a fall in prices could cost the firm dearly. As a result, Salomon had to hone its trading skills so it did not get caught by changing market conditions. Conversely, an upward movement in the price of bonds held in inventory could generate substantial profits. As Salomon's knowledge of the bond markets grew, the firm expanded its trading activities beyond what was necessary to meet the needs of its customers and began seeking trading opportunities that generated profits for the firm.

In contrast to Salomon's emphasis on trading, the more traditional firms continued to focus on corporate securities underwriting. Although these banks had to engage in some trading as a service to their customers, these activities were secondary to the underwriting and advisory services they provided to their corporate customers. The bulk of their income resulted from the fees they received for underwriting new securities. Several of these banks extended their traditional underwriting relationships with large corporations into the area of investment advice on mergers and acquisitions. For a fee, these firms would help their clients evaluate potential acquisitions or respond to merger proposals. (In the merger boom of the 1980s, this line of business proved exceptionally lucrative.)

Salomon eventually built a successful corporate underwriting business, ranking fourth among its United States-based competitors in 1990. However, its core competence remained in the buying and selling of securities for its own account. The firm's $52 billion inventory of securities dwarfed that of Merrill Lynch, the leading corporate underwriter on Wall Street, due largely to the enormous trading positions that Salomon was willing to take. Consistent with this large inventory, Salomon had a $3.5 billion capital base that was easily the largest among investment banks.

Salomon's trading orientation and culture made it possible for "star" performers to shine. Successful traders were highly compensated and favored with managerial responsibilities. For example, Lewis Ranieri rose from the trading desk to vice chairman of Salomon because of his success in developing mortgage-backed securities.[4] Beginning in 1979, Ranieri created the market for these newly developed securities, and then built a team of traders, analysts, and salespeople who dominated the product into the mid-1980s. In its heyday, the mortgage-backed securities trading desk reportedly accounted for 50 percent of Salomon's net earnings, generating an estimated $225 million in 1985.[5]

In the late 1980s, the bond arbitrage group and its traders rose to prominence within the firm. In its simplest form, arbitrage involved

---

[3] *Ibid.,* pp. 23–24.

[4] A mortgage-backed security was an interest-paying ownership share in a pool of mortgages.

[5] John F. Berry, "Under Siege," *Business Month,* June 1988, p. 67.

buying securities at a low price in one market then selling them in another market at a slightly higher price, or trading to take advantage of price discrepancies between two securities. Although price discrepancies were often small and transient, firms that were willing to commit large amounts of capital could generate substantial returns from these small opportunities.

Salomon's John Meriwether, who headed the firm's arbitrage unit until the late 1980s, when he was picked to head all of Salomon's fixed income securities activities,[6] was one of the first people on Wall Street to spot the opportunities presented by sophisticated arbitrage trading. Under his direction, the arbitrage unit became an acknowledged star in the Salomon organization. In 1990, the group produced an estimated $400 million in profits for Salomon, roughly 80 percent of the firm's pretax earnings.[7]

In spite of its contribution to Salomon's bottom line, the bond arbitrage unit had raised a considerable amount of rancor within the firm in 1990, because of a controversial compensation system it negotiated with chairman John Gutfreund and Salomon president Thomas Strauss. Under the compensation arrangement, the 12 members of the arbitrage unit shared a bonus pool equal to 15 percent of the profits that the unit earned. In 1990, the group's bonus pool was reported to total $60 million. The five most senior managers of the unit shared 90 percent of the bonus pool, with Lawrence Hillibrand, the unit's head, receiving an estimated $23 million bonus.[8] The size of the bonuses angered many managers within other areas of Salomon, whose compensation continued to be based on more subjective evaluations of how their units performed and the overall performance

of the firm. Notwithstanding these managers' complaints, total compensation at the firm had risen by 22 percent since 1988, while Salomon's profits had fallen by 19 percent. By 1990, 106 people earned more than $1 million per year.[9]

Salomon's Government Bond Trading

Among participants in the market for U.S. government securities, Salomon had the reputation as the biggest and most active trader. Approximately $20 billion in Treasury bills, notes, and bonds (short-, medium-, and long-term securities) moved through its trading operation each day.[10] The firm bid aggressively for new securities in the Treasury auctions and held large inventories of those securities it believed would rise in value. In addition, Salomon often acted as the buyer of last resort when its customers needed to sell securities in weak markets. Customers might not like the price Salomon offered, but they knew the firm would submit a bid.

Salomon's large share of the government bond trading activity allowed the firm to make money on trades where other dealers could not. Unlike equity securities, Treasury securities were not traded on an exchange where all participants in the market could easily see the going price for a given security. Government securities were traded over the telephone and, often, only the two parties involved in the trade knew the price and volume of the transaction. Therefore, the largest firms that handled the most transactions had the best information about which investors were seeking to buy or sell U.S. government securities.[11] This

---

[6] Fixed income securities consist of debt securities issued by governments and corporations.

[7] *The Wall Street Journal,* January 7, 1991, p. C1.

[8] Ibid.

[9] *The New York Times,* October 29, 1991, p. D14.

[10] Bernice Kanner, "Saving Salomon," *New York,* December 9, 1991, p. 43.

[11] Lynn Feldman and Jack Stephenson, "Stay Small or Get Huge—Lessons from Securities Trading," *Harvard Business Review* (May–June 1988) pp. 117–18.

knowledge of "who holds the bonds" allowed Salomon to see and act on opportunities before its competitors.

For example, two days before the May 22, 1991, auction for $12 billion in two-year notes, Steinhardt Partners, a large New York money manager, approached Salomon with a request to finance a $6 billion position in the forthcoming notes. Essentially, Steinhardt had committed to buy $6 billion worth of notes and needed to borrow the money to pay for them when it took delivery after the auction (a common practice on Wall Street). This request signaled to Salomon that demand for the notes in the auction would be brisk. As a result, Salomon bid aggressively in the auction on the assumption that the notes would rise in value, because the high demand would lead to an escalation in the price of the securities.[12]

Since 1988, Paul Mozer had directed Salomon's Treasury bond trading activities with the assistance of another managing director, Thomas Murphy. The two oversaw six traders arranged in a cluster of desks on the bond trading floor and assigned to securities of varying maturities. The close physical proximity of the bond group meant that each trader could overhear the activities of the other members of the group and, therefore, incorporate the changes in securities of one maturity quickly into trading decisions for another. Both Mr. Mozer and Mr. Murphy reported to John Meriwether, whose desk on the trading floor allowed him to observe, hear, and manage the sea of fixed income securities traders spread out over the entire 41st floor of Seven World Trade Center in lower Manhattan. Mr. Meriwether, in turn, reported to both Thomas Strauss and John Gutfreund.

Mr. Mozer had joined Salomon Brothers as a corporate bond salesman in 1979 after completing a master's degree in management at Northwestern University and a bachelor's degree in economics from Whitman College in Walla Walla, Washington. After switching to U.S. Treasury securities in 1980, Paul Mozer steadily worked his way up the Salomon hierarchy until he was named a managing director in 1985, working for John Meriwether's bond arbitrage group. After only a year and one-half as a managing director, senior managers asked Mozer to head Salomon's Treasury securities trading activities.[13]

As the head of U.S. Government bond trading activities, Paul Mozer's energy, intelligence, and fairness earned him the respect of his colleagues at Salomon. Confident yet soft-spoken and composed under pressure, Mozer was a hardworking trader who kept in constant touch with the bond markets. He also maintained close relationships with Salomon's clients. Mozer often talked to the firm's largest customers and took their orders directly, rather than communicating via Salomon's bond sales force.[14] His trading instinct, hard work, and close relationships with the firm's customers made him an unqualified success at Salomon and earned him a reported $10 million in bonuses between 1988 and 1990.[15]

The Treasury Securities Market

At $2.4 trillion, the public market for U.S. government debt was the largest securities market in the world. On average, $110 billion in securities traded hands every day, making the Treasury securities market the most liquid as well. This liquidity — the ability to immediately find a buyer or seller for virtually any volume of securities — made Treasury securities particularly attractive to many investors and reduced the government's borrowing costs. Each

---

[12] *The Wall Street Journal,* September 17, 1991, p. C21.

[13] *The New York Times,* August 25, 1991, sec. 3, pp. 1 and 10.

[14] Ibid.

[15] *The New York Times,* September 11, 1991, p. D1.

week the U.S. Treasury sold approximately $30 billion in new Treasury securities of selected maturities, ranging from 90 days to 30 years. In a typical year, the Treasury conducted over 150 separate auctions. The new securities sold in these auctions replaced maturing government debt and funded the ongoing deficits of the U.S. government. Once issued, Treasury securities quickly changed hands and moved throughout the globe in an active "secondary" market. In this market, the investors, brokers, and dealers holding U.S. government debt could sell the securities to others seeking investments that were free of credit risk.

The Market for Government Securities

There were vast numbers of investors, brokers, and dealers in the market for U.S. government securities. Investors typically bought the securities and held them to maturity or until they found more profitable investments in which to invest. The brokers generally acted as intermediaries between investors, buying from one and quickly reselling to another. Brokers invested very little of their own money in Treasury securities and held only enough securities in inventory to serve the needs of customers who wished to buy U.S. government debt. Their earnings were based on the narrow spread that they maintained between the price at which they purchased the securities (the bid price) and the price at which they sold them (the asked price). The dealers, in contrast, actively invested their own capital in principal transactions and attempted to make money from the changes in the price of securities over time.

The large number of players in the U.S. government bond market forced profits down to an absolute minimum. Therefore, successful bond trading required a willingness to exploit any opportunity that presented itself. Since information was key to the market, traders ruthlessly turned any confusion or misjudgment on the part of their fellow traders into a profit for their firm's account. In the words of

Salomon chairman and erstwhile trader John Gutfreund: "It's a harsh world, where mistakes are not charitably dealt with."[16]

In the January 1990 auction of 40-year bonds, for example, several dealers were duped into buying the new issue when one of the large dealers started a rumor that a major pension fund would place a substantial bid for the bonds. At the time, many dealers were uncertain about the demand for an issue with a maturity considerably longer than the Treasury's benchmark 30-year bonds. The rumor that a major investor would bid on the bonds eased the concerns of many dealers and encouraged them to bid aggressively at the auction. After the auction, bond prices fell when the rumor proved to be false and customer demand for the bonds failed to materialize. Dealers who sat out the auction then earned hefty profits by buying the notes cheaply from dealers who had believed the rumor and gotten stuck with the notes.[17]

Primary Dealers

Salomon Brothers was the largest and most active of a group of Treasury market participants designated as primary dealers by the Federal Reserve Bank. The term *primary dealer* referred to the fact that the Federal Reserve Bank bought and sold securities only from these dealers when it implemented money supply policy through its open market committee.[18] The Fed also permitted primary dealers to submit bids on behalf of other investors in the Treasury's weekly auctions of new securities.[19] As of August 1990, the Fed

---

[16] *The New York Times,* August 17, 1991, p. 44.

[17] *The Wall Street Journal,* August 19, 1991, p. A1.

[18] The Fed open market committee bought securities from primary dealers when it wished to increase the money supply and sold securities to primary dealers when it wished to decrease the money supply.

[19] The Fed also permitted commercial banks and other depository institutions to submit bids on behalf of other customers.

had 39 primary dealers with which it maintained this special relationship. In exchange for the special treatment provided to primary dealers, the Fed required these dealers to bid at every Treasury auction and to actively make a market in Treasury securities of all maturities.

From a securities dealer's perspective, the primary dealer designation provided several benefits but not necessarily higher profits. First, the title provided a measure of self-assurance, because it was limited to only those firms that the Fed recognized as leaders in the U.S. government securities market. Second, the Fed allowed primary dealers to submit bids without a deposit. Most other bidders had to deposit the full amount of their bid at the Fed or present a guarantee from a commercial bank or primary dealer. Third, the ability to bid for other buyers provided primary dealers with additional market information with which to improve the accuracy of their bidding efforts. Finally, the information about market conditions gathered in the Treasury auctions could be leveraged in the markets for many other securities that were either linked or strongly influenced by the market for U.S. government debt. Unfortunately, these benefits did not translate into consistently higher profits from Treasury securities. As recently as 1989, primary dealers as a group lost $10 million on their U.S. government securities business. As a result a number of securities firms had withdrawn as primary dealers since the group peaked at 46 in 1988.

The Treasury Securities Auctions

At regularly scheduled weekly intervals, the Federal Reserve Bank, acting as the Treasury's fiscal agent, conducted the Treasury securities auctions by accepting competitive bids from interested bond buyers. In the auction, potential buyers submitted bids to the Fed that stated the amount of securities they were willing to purchase and the yield that they

required on the securities. For example, a dealer might submit a bid for $100 million in two-year notes at a yield of 6.51 percent.[20] The yield a bidder requested was the effective interest rate at which the buyer was willing to loan money to the U.S. government.

After receiving tenders from all interested buyers, the Fed awarded the securities to the bidders in order of lowest yield to highest. That is, the Fed first filled the bid of the buyer requesting the lowest interest rate. Next, it filled the bid of the buyer requesting the next lowest interest rate, and so forth until the entire issue had been awarded. In virtually every auction, the Fed reached a point where the bids at a given yield exceeded the number of securities still to be awarded. At this point, known as the stop-out yield," the Fed allocated the remaining securities among all the bidders who submitted bids at the stop-out yield. These bidders received a prorated share of the remainder based on the size of their bid relative to all bids received at the stop-out yield. For example, in the February 21, 1991, auction of five-year notes, the notes available at the stop-out yield amounted to only 54 percent of the amount desired at that yield. Therefore, bidders at the stop-out yield received only 54 percent of their bids (Exhibit 2). Because of the efficiency of this market, the interest rate spread between the lowest bidder and the highest bidder receiving securities generally ranged from 0.02 to 0.03 percentage points (2 to 3 basis points).

In spite of its size and importance, the Treasury auction was probably the least automated securities market in the United States. Bond dealers bought and sold huge volumes of securities through verbal agreements made

---

[20] The yield quoted was the total yield to maturity and represented the internal rate of return generated by the future interest payments (coupons) and repayment of principal at maturity.

EXHIBIT 2   Example of Treasury Auction Bids and Awards

February 21, 1991, Auction of 5-Year Notes ($ in millions)

Notes available	$ 9,040
Bids at 7.50% (lowest yield)	3,914
Bids at 7.51% (stop-out yield)	9,492
Bids above 7.51%	15,780
Notes available	9,040
Less notes awarded at lowest yield (7.50%)	−3,914
Notes available at stop-out yield (7.51%)	5,126
Bid proration at stop-out yield:	
Notes available at stop-out yield	5,126
Bids at stop-out yield	+9,492
Proration percentage	54%

Source: Casewriter's estimates.

over the telephone. These transactions were largely governed by the unwritten code of ethics among traders, "my word is my bond," a code so strong it was given the weight of a legal contract. The legality of these verbal agreements was clearly illustrated by a court case involving a savings and loan that reneged on a telephone commitment to buy mortgage-backed securities from Salomon Brothers. In its case, the thrift argued that the transaction was a real estate deal and in real estate, an oral agreement was not binding. In the end, the court ruled in Salomon's favor, deciding that the deal was a bond transaction and, therefore, that oral commitments were binding.[21]

In bidding at Treasury auctions, the dealers frantically took orders from their customers over the telephone as the auction approached. Just before the 1:00 P.M. deadline for bids, the dealers called their runners in the lobby of the Federal Reserve Bank of New York with instructions for bidding. The runners filled out

---

[21] Michael Lewis, *Liar's Poker* (New York: Norton, 1989), p. 101.

paper copies of the dealers' orders and literally stuffed them into a box at the Fed. Two hours later the Fed announced the winners of the auction.

The bidding among dealers in the auction was extremely competitive and very sophisticated. Bidders in the Treasury securities auctions always tried to bid a yield just low enough to get their orders filled. If they bid a yield too high, dealers ran the risk of not receiving any securities or only a portion of their bids; in which case, they might not have enough securities in inventory to sell to their customers. Conversely, if they bid a yield too low, the dealers would fill their orders but at a yield that might be below the average interest rate and leave them with bonds that would have to be sold at a loss. In the days and hours leading up to the auction, dealers and investors discussed their likely orders in an elaborate ritual of bluffing and betting. Each player tried to sway the others' perception of the market in a manner that would create a profitable opportunity in the auction or later secondary market. David Mullins, vice chairman of the Federal Reserve Bank, once quipped that the U.S. government securities market was full of "dealers who'd turn in their grandmothers for a quarter of a point."[22]

Given the often conflicting information prior to an auction, market share was critical to successful bidding. Those firms with the largest share in U.S. government securities markets had the best feel for the likely yield on a new issue. This superior information, in turn, attracted more customers and extended the firm's reach into the market, enhancing further its information and position. Therefore, the major dealers sought to capture a significant share of each auction at the highest yield to maintain their position.

The competition for market share between the major dealers in the securities market spilled over into the markets for securities issued by quasi-government agencies like Fannie Mae and Freddie Mac.[23] In the auctions for the securities issued by these agencies, dealers routinely bluffed each other and the agencies by overstating their customers' interest in the new issues. As Fannie Mae chairman James Johnson once conceded, dealers' orders always contained "a certain amount of puffery, hype, and uncertainty."[24]

Regulation[25]

The Treasury securities auction and secondary market were governed principally by the actions of the Department of the Treasury. These actions were both informal and evolutionary, driven by the Treasury's perception of the changing dynamics of the market. In general, the Treasury would reject any bid it deemed disruptive to the auction. On August 27, 1962, for example, the Treasury rejected a bid that would have given a dealer an exceptionally high portion of an auction for three-month Treasury bills. The next day, the Treasury announced that it would limit auction winners to a maximum award of not more than 25 percent of any new issue of three- or six-month Treasury bills. No limits were placed on the size of bids, but a bid in excess of 25 percent of the auction would not be filled above the 25 percent award limit. Subsequently, it became generally understood that the 25 percent rule applied to Treasury securities of all maturities, although the Treasury never announced formally any additional rule changes. After some minor modifications in the intervening years, the Treasury announced via a press release in 1981 that it would raise the award limit to 35 percent.[26]

The market for Treasury securities was also governed to a limited extent by the Securities and Exchange Commission (SEC), which implemented regulations set forth in the Securities Exchange Act of 1934 (often referred to as the Exchange Act). Section 10 of the Exchange Act gave the SEC the authority to protect investors from "any manipulative or deceptive device" in the sale of securities (Exhibit 3). Under Section 10, the SEC could issue rules banning specific activities as *per se* manipulative. In addition, the SEC could bring a court action against brokers and dealers that had acted in a way that the SEC believed violated Section 10, even if the dealer or broker

---

[22] Mike McNamee, "David Mullins' Brisk Stride at the Fed," *Business Week,* December 16, 1991, p. 86.

[23] Fannie Mae, the Federal National Mortgage Association, was created in the 1960s to insure home mortgages. It was subsequently sold to the public in the 1970s. Freddie Mac, the Federal Home Loan Mortgage Corporation, was created by the Federal Home Loan Bank (the central bank for the savings and loan system) to insure mortgages issued by S&Ls. These agencies buy mortgages, package them into securities and then resell them via securities dealers.

[24] *The Wall Street Journal,* October 2, 1991, p. C1.

[25] Research associate Michael A. Santoro assisted in the preparation of this section under the supervision of Professor Lynn Sharp Paine.

[26] Statement of the Honorable Jerome H. Powell, assistant secretary of the Treasury for domestic finance, before the Subcommittee on Telecommunications and Finance, United States House of Representatives, September 4, 1991, p. 8.

EXHIBIT 3 Selected Sections of the Exchange Act and SEC Rules

---

Sec. 10(b) [It shall be unlawful] to use or employ, in connection with the purchase or sale of any security . . . any manipulative or deceptive device of contrivance in contravention of such rules and regulations as the [SEC] may prescribe.

Sec. 17 Every . . . broker or dealer who transacts business in securities . . . shall make and keep for prescribed periods such records . . . as the [SEC] prescribes.

S.E.C. Reg. §240.17a-3. (a) . . . every broker or dealer registered pursuant to Section 15 of the Securities Exchange Act of 1934, as amended, shall make and keep current the following books and records relating to his business:

(1) Blotter (or other records of original entry) containing an itemized daily record of all purchases and sales of securities, all receipts and deliveries of securities, all receipts and disbursements of cash, and all other debits and credits.

(3) Ledger acounts itemizing separately as to each cash and margin account of every customer and of such member, broker, or dealer and partners thereof, all purchases, sales receipts, and deliveries of securities and commodities for such account.

(6) A memorandum of each brokerage order, and of any other instruction, given or received for the purchase or sale of securities, whether executed or unexecuted.

(7) A memorandum of each purchase and sale for the account of such member, broker, or dealer showing the price and, to the extent feasible, the time of execution; and, in addition, where such purchase or sale is with a customer other than a broker or dealer, a memorandum of each order received, showing the time of receipt, the terms and conditions of the order, and the account in which it was entered.

(8) Copies of confirmations of all purchases and sales of securities including all repurchase and reverse repurchase agreements, and copies of notices of all other debits and credits for securities, cash and other items for the account of customers and partners of such member, broker, or dealer.

Sec. 20(a) Every person who, directly or indirectly, controls any persons liable under any provision of this title or any rule or regulation thereunder shall also be liable jointly and severally with and to the same extent as such controlled person . . . unless the controlling person acted in good faith and did not directly or indirectly induce the act or acts constituting the violation.

Source: Commerce Clearing House, *Federal Securities Law Reports.*

---

had not broken a specific rule. The Exchange Act also gave the SEC authority to issue rules governing record keeping (Section 17) and officer liability (Section 20). However, the SEC believed that its authority in the government securities markets was extremely limited and had historically deferred to the Treasury with respect to the regulation of Treasury securities.[27] Thus, there were no

---

[27] Testimony of Richard C. Breeden, chairman of the Securities and Exchange Commission before the House Subcommittee on Telecommunications and Finance, September 4, 1991.

specific SEC rules explicitly governing the auction and sale of Treasury securities.

Although Congress modified the Exchange Act in 1986 to give the Treasury (but not the SEC) formal rule-making authority over the market for government debt, the Treasury chose not to issue formal, codified rules in the belief that new rules would create unnecessary costs, reduce the efficiency of the government debt market, and ultimately increase the borrowing costs of the United States government. Instead, the Treasury continued to rely on informal rule announcements via press releases. These rule changes were based in part on feedback the Treasury received during quarterly meetings with representatives of several large U.S. government securities dealers. At these informal meetings, the Treasury suggested possible changes and asked the representatives of the dealers to comment.

The New Bidding Regulations

The Treasury's 35 percent limit on awards remained the only significant limit on the auction until the summer of 1990, when the regulators began to worry about the inflation in bids at the stop-out yield by the large bidders. Because the Fed awarded a prorated share of the issue to all bidders at the stop-out yield, Salomon and other large bidders used a bidding strategy that entailed submitting very large orders at the estimated stop-out yield to increase their prorated share. Salomon also used a similar approach in submitting bids for its customers. The strategy generally resulted in Salomon and its customers receiving the largest shares, often up to the 35 percent maximum, among all bidders at the stop-out yield. In 30 out of the 230 auctions of notes and bonds held between 1986 and 1990, Salomon and its customers acquired in aggregate over 50 percent of the securities in the auction.[28] (Neither Salomon nor any of its customers received more than the 35 percent maximum award in any of these auctions.)

Salomon's aggressive strategy raised concerns among Treasury officials who worried that the firm's bidding might undermine the integrity of the auctions. On June 27, 1990, Salomon submitted a bid that exceeded the total value of the issue. Michael Basham, the deputy assistant secretary of the Treasury for federal finance, promptly warned Salomon about submitting excessively large bids. The conflict came to a head two weeks later when Salomon submitted a massive bid of $30 billion for $10 billion in 30-year notes.[29] The size of the bid, three times the total size of the auction, embarrassed the Treasury and prompted an immediate response from Michael Basham. He announced that, henceforth, the Treasury would not accept any bid, either for a dealer's own account or on behalf of its customers, in excess of 35 percent of the total auction. At the time, Michael Basham commented: "We want to maintain the competitive nature of the auction process for the taxpayers as well as the investment community."[30]

In response, Paul Mozer blasted the Treasury for its attempts to curtail Salomon's bidding activities: "The Treasury made a rash decision without consulting the dealer community about this change.... Potentially, this ties the hands of the larger dealers, who, time in and time out, buy the bulk of the debt."[31] He went on to note that curbing the big dealers' ability to take large positions in the auction could undermine their ability to provide the liquidity that was an essential component of the Treasury securities markets. Mozer's outburst rankled Basham and led to chilly relations between Mozer and the Treasury (the new rule became known on Wall Street as the Mozer/Basham rule). As a result of the bitterness,

---

[28] *The New York Times,* September 22, 1991, sec 6, p. 1.

[29] *The New York Times,* August 25, 1991, Sec 3, p. 10.
[30] *The Wall Street Journal,* July 13, 1990, p. C1.
[31] Ibid., p. C23.

Mozer's assistant, Thomas Murphy, took over the responsibility of interacting with the Treasury.

The conflict between Salomon and the Treasury highlighted an inherent ambiguity in the Treasury's role. On the one hand, the Treasury needed to find a market for the $30 billion in new government debt that was auctioned each week. To this end, the Treasury wanted to ensure that bidders in the auction made enough profit to compensate them for assuming the risk inherent in underwriting new government debt. Since the large dealers like Salomon took the bulk of each auction, the Treasury had an undeniable interest in seeing that Salomon and the other large dealers earned a profit on their government debt underwriting activities. On the other hand, the Treasury had responsibility for regulating the auctions and ensuring their fairness. If the market perceived that Salomon and other large dealers had too large an advantage in the auction, smaller dealers might choose not to participate, thus reducing competition and ultimately raising the government's borrowing costs.

Mozer's Treasury Auction Activities[32]

When Paul Mozer came to John Meriwether on April 27, 1991, he disclosed that he had used a customer's name without authorization. Mozer admitted that on February 21, 1991, he submitted an unauthorized bid for 35 percent of the $9 billion five-year note auction in the name of Warburg, a Salomon customer, in addition to a bid for 35 percent in Salomon's name. Salomon's two bids turned out to be at the stop-out yield and the Fed awarded $1.7

billion in notes each to Salomon and Warburg. After the auction, Mozer instructed the trading desk to transfer the notes awarded to Warburg to Salomon's account and to suppress the written customer confirmation of the activity. In the end, Salomon ended up with 38 percent of the auction, only slightly more than the 35 percent limit, because the unauthorized Warburg bid crowded out Salomon's own bid and lowered the proration percentage to 54 percent.

What brought Mozer to Meriwether's desk was the fact that the Federal Reserve had noticed that Warburg had submitted two different bids in the auction, one for its own account of $100 million and another via Salomon Brothers for $1.7 billion. When the Fed contacted Salomon to ask about the Warburg bid, Mozer instructed Thomas Murphy to tell the Fed that the bid should have been in the name of Mercury Asset Management, an operationally separate affiliate of S. G. Warburg, another primary dealer.

When the Fed forwarded the correction received from Salomon to the Treasury, the Treasury decided that the relationship between S. G. Warburg and Mercury Asset Management was close enough to limit the combined bids of both entities to 35 percent of the auction. In a letter dated April 17, 1991, sent to the head of Mercury, the Treasury reviewed the two bids by Warburg and noted that the legal relationship between the two required that they limit their combined bids to 35 percent of an auction. The Treasury sent a copy of the letter to Paul Mozer, S. G. Warburg, and S. G. Warburg, plc, the parent of Mercury and S. G. Warburg.

In an effort to stem any further investigation by the Treasury, Paul Mozer contacted Mercury and requested that the firm not respond to the Treasury's letter.[33] Mozer

---

[32] This section draws heavily on the written statement of Salomon, Inc., submitted in conjunction with the testimony of Warren Buffett before the House Subcommittee on Telecommunications and Finance on September 3, 1991.

[33] The letter did not request a response.

explained the problem as a mistake and asked that Mercury not embarrass Salomon by volunteering information about the mistake to the Treasury. Thomas Murphy also tried unsuccessfully to set up a meeting between Paul Mozer and an acquaintance of his at S. G. Warburg, who happened to be the managing director who had received the Treasury's letter. When Murphy failed to arrange a meeting, Mozer notified Meriwether on April 27, 1991, of the Treasury's letter. In the meeting, Meriwether warned Mozer "that the matter was very serious and represented career-threatening conduct."[34] When Meriwether pressed Mozer on the extent of his unauthorized use of customers' names, Mozer had assured him that there had been only one such incident.

Over Mozer's objections, Meriwether immediately notified Tom Strauss and informed him of Mozer's disclosures. The following morning, April 28, 1991, Meriwether, Strauss, and Donald Feuerstein, Salomon's chief legal counsel, met to discuss Mozer's admissions. All three agreed that John Gutfreund, who was traveling on business at the time, needed to be informed of the violations. When the group informed Gutfreund the next day, April 29, 1991, all four agreed that they had to report Mozer's offense to the regulators supervising the sale of Treasury securities. The group discussed how best to report the matter, but did not reach a decision on how to approach the government with the disclosures. Mozer remained the head of the Treasury securities trading activities.

The May Squeeze

Meriwether's attention was drawn again to Mozer's Treasury securities trading activities shortly after the May 22, 1991, auction of $12 billion in two-year notes. In that auction,

Paul Mozer submitted a $4.2 billion bid in Salomon's name (34 percent of the auction), a $2 billion bid for Tiger Investments (17 percent of the auction), and a $4.3 billion bid for Quantum Fund (35 percent of the auction). All three bids were at the aggressive yield of 6.81 percent, 2 basis points below most dealers' expectations for the auction. As a result, Salomon's and its customers' bids offered the government the best rate in the auction and the Treasury awarded Salomon, Tiger, and Quantum the full amount of their bids without proration.

Salomon and its customers now controlled $10.6 billion of the new notes awarded to bidders at the May 22 auction. One week after the auction, Tiger sold its entire position to Salomon, which in turn sold $600 million in notes to Quantum. These two transactions occurred at market prices that were higher than the auction price and generated a profit for Tiger. Salomon and Quantum continued to control the majority of the notes issued in the auction.

After the auction, the two-year notes rose in price as dealers scrambled to buy notes with which to meet their commitments to provide new notes to their customers and other dealers. Because so few notes were available for sale after the auction, many dealers had to borrow them from Salomon and Quantum under "repurchase agreements," a standard arrangement under which the notes would go back to Salomon after a specific time. Because of the short supply, Salomon and Quantum were able to charge a higher than normal interest rate for the temporary use of the new notes.

For example, Michael Irelan, a trader for St. Louis-based Boatmen's Bank, had made pre-auction commitments to deliver $120 million in notes to other dealers after the auction. In making these commitments, Irelan had ignored the advice of his friend, Thomas Murphy, at

---

[34] *The New York Times,* September 5, 1991, p. D23.

Salomon, who had suggested that demand for the notes would be high after the auction and that they would be hard to find. After the auction, no notes were available and Irelan was forced to borrow them from Salomon, costing Boatmen's Bank a net loss of $8,000 per day.[35]

Irelan was not alone in getting caught in the May squeeze. Many speculators had expected lackluster demand for the notes and declining prices after the auction. Together with Irelan, they complained bitterly to the Fed about Salomon's position. In response to these complaints, the Fed contacted Salomon and asked that it sell or loan its two-year notes to alleviate the squeeze. Paul Mozer told the Fed that he would do what he could to make sure that the notes were available to short sellers at a rate that allowed them to meet their commitments.

Tight markets like the May squeeze were not uncommon in Treasury trading. Just one month prior, Salomon itself had been caught short of two-year notes in a squeeze that developed when two large investors, Caxton Corp and Steinhardt Partners, each bought $8 billion of April two-year notes. The squeeze developed when the two investors sold the securities to foreign banks that would not lend them to dealers on Wall Street. As late as June, many of the biggest dealers continued to lose money in the squeeze.[36]

Although the Treasury was upset about Salomon's possible involvement in the May squeeze, the U.S. government and American taxpayers probably benefitted from Salomon's aggressiveness. Salomon's bid of 6.81 percent saved the government almost $5 million in interest. Furthermore, most of the large and small investors in the U.S. government securities market were not hurt. The state governments, pension funds, and government bond mutual funds that held most of the government debt did not make pre-auction commitments like the ones arranged by Michael Irelan. If these investors bought the notes at the May auction, they benefitted from the tight conditions that developed.

Meriwether's Concerns

By early June 1991, Salomon had still not disclosed Mozer's unauthorized bid in the February auction and the Treasury was now upset about the firm's possible role in the May squeeze. As the vice chairman with responsibility for U.S. Treasury securities trading activities, Meriwether was ultimately responsible for the actions of Mozer and the other traders in his department.

---

[35] *The Wall Street Journal,* October 31, 1991, p. A1.

[36] *The Wall Street Journal,* October 7, 1991, p. A1.

JAMES BURKE: A CAREER IN AMERICAN BUSINESS (A)

In 1989, James Burke's tenure as chief executive officer of Johnson & Johnson was drawing to a close. Burke's career at the company began when he became brand manager for Band-Aids in 1953. At first he doubted whether Johnson & Johnson was the place for him. Soon, however, he committed himself wholeheartedly to the company, and he was quickly promoted to important positions within it. In 1976, he became chairman and chief executive officer. With Burke at the helm, the company grew smartly in terms of both sales and earnings (see Exhibit 2).

One reason for this growth was an increase both in the number and the variety of products that the company marketed, as well as in the vigor with which they were managed. Tylenol, for example, was still a specialty product in 1976—little known outside the hospital setting. By 1981, it had become the leading analgesic in the country by a wide margin (see Exhibit 8).

Not all the company's products fared so well, however. Some, such as CAT scanners, met with failure.

James Burke's Early Life

James Edward Burke was born on February 28, 1925, in Rutland, Vermont. He spent his formative years in Slingerlands, New York, a small town near Albany. His father had served as an Army officer before becoming an insurance and bond salesman. "My father had a wonderful view of the world," Burke said.

> He was an optimist from the word go. He knew exactly what he believed in, and I never had any doubts to speak of about right and wrong because my father had no doubts. And I had no doubt that if I didn't behave in the way he saw the world, I'd learn of his displeasure, which was something I didn't want to learn about. My mother loved intellectual ferment. She taught us to challenge everything. Our dinner table was constant arguing over anything and everything. My father didn't enjoy the arguing so much—he sometimes would get up and excuse himself—but my mother did, and all of us children enjoyed it.

Burke attended Bethlehem Central High School through the ninth grade. Bethlehem Central was testing new educational methods while Burke was there. "It drove my mother and father crazy," he said, "but I loved it." When Burke's father realized that his son was doing very little work and getting As, he decided to send him to the Vincentian Institute, a strict, Catholic high school. "It turned out to be the greatest favor my family ever did for me," Burke recalled. "Many of my friends from Bethlehem Central didn't make it into college, and the state eventually threw out the whole experiment."

The United States had been at war with Japan and Germany for nine months when Burke entered the College of the Holy Cross in Worcester, Massachusetts, in September 1942. Holy Cross participated in the Navy's V-12 program, which required almost all its students to enlist in that service. After completing the school's NROTC program, Burke was commissioned as an ensign and spent a year in the South Pacific on a landing craft. "We were kind of spectators in the war," Burke

Note: A profile of all individuals in both this (A) case and the (B) case is provided in Exhibit 1.

This case was prepared by Professor Richard S. Tedlow of the Harvard Business School.

EXHIBIT 1 Guide to the Individuals in the Case

Daniel B. Burke.   Brother of James Burke; was working for Capital Cities Broadcasting Corporation in New York when Datril began its comparison advertisements against Tylenol in the mid-1970s. Daniel Burke first alerted his brother to the development.

Joseph R. Chiesa.   Presidebt of McNeil Consumer Products at the time of the 1982 and 1986 Tylenol poisonings; member of the Tylenol Strategy Committee in 1986.

David R. Clare.   President of Johnson & Johnson, 1976–1989; member of the Tylenol Strategy Committee in 1982 and 1986.

David E. Collins.   CEO of McNeil Consumer Products at the time of the 1982 and 1986 Tylenol poisonings; member of the Tylenol Strategy Committee in 1982 and 1986.

Lawrence G. Foster.   Johnson & Johnson's corporate vice president of public relations, 1973–1989; helped create Johnson & Johnson's first public relations department in the late 1950s; member of the Tylenol Strategy Committee in 1982 and 1986.

George Frazza.   Johnson & Johnson's associate general counsel in 1975 at the time Datril was challenging Tylenol for the acetaminophen market; general counsel at the time of the 1982 and 1986 Tylenol poisonings; member of the Tylenol Strategy Committee in 1982 and 1986.

Dr. Thomas N. Gates.   Medical director of McNeil Consumer Products at the time of the 1982 Tylenol poisonings; appeared in the first post-poisoning television commercial for Tylenol.

Richard L. Gelb.   President and CEO of Bristol-Myers, the company which marketed Datril.

Edward Gerbic.   Vice president of advertising and merchandising of the Operating Company* in 1953 when Burke first joined Johnson & Johnson. Gerbic convinced Burke to return to Johnson & Johnson after Burke quit in 1954.

Arthur Hayes.   Director of the Food and Drug Administration at the time of the first Tylenol poisoning.

Philip B. Hofmann.   Chairman and CEO of Johnson & Johnson, 1963–1973.

Robert W. Johnson II, (d. 1968).   Usually referred to as the General; chairman and CEO of Johnson & Johnson, 1932–1963; chairman of the Finance Committee 1963–68.

Robert W. "Bobby" Johnson III, (d. 1970)   The General's son; president of Johnson & Johnson, 1961–65; and member of the Executive Committee from 1955 (the year it was formed) to 1965.

Gustav O. Lienhard.   Burke's mentor; president of Johnson & Johnson, 1963–70; and member of the Executive Committee, 1955–70.

John McLaughlin.   Burke's direct boss when Burke first joined Johnson & Johnson in 1953; Burke was unknowingly caught in a political battle between McLaughlin and Edward Gerbic.

Wayne K. Nelson.   First president of McNeil Consumer Products, which was created in 1976; company group chairman with corporate responsibility for McNeil at the time of the 1982 Tylenol poisoning; member of the Tylenol Strategy Committee formed in October 1982.

Arthur M. Quilty.   Member of Johnson & Johnson's Executive Committee, 1972– ; member of the Tylenol Strategy Committee in 1982.

Richard B. Sellars.   President of Johnson & Johnson, 1970–73; chairman and CEO, 1973–76.

George Smith.   President of the Operating Company in 1957 when Burke was named acting director of advertising and merchandising of the Operating Company; made the decision to move the company into pharmaceuticals in 1958; this resulted in the acquisiton of McNeil Pharmaceutical—which created Tylenol—in 1959.

William Webster.   Director of the Federal Bureau of Investigation during the first Tylenol poisoning.

* The Operating Company was the division of Johnson & Johnson that manufactured and sold products with the Johnson's name on them—mainly Band-Aids and baby products.

EXHIBIT 2 Johnson & Johnson's Sales and Earnings, 1976–1981 ($ in millions)

Year	Sales	Aftertax Earnings
1976	$2,522.5	$205.4
1977	2,914.1	247.3
1978	3,497.3	299.1
1979	4,211.6	352.1
1980	4,837.4	400.7
1981	5,399.0	467.6

recalled. "We used to bring material and manpower from ship to shore because the harbor at Naha [on Okinawa] had been bombed to pieces. The only way you could get things in was through landing-craft tanks like ours. Sometimes our craft were mistaken for aircraft carriers — they had the same lines, but were much smaller — but we weren't worth anyone's ammunition."

When the war ended, Burke returned to Holy Cross, and in 1947 he graduated with a BS in economics. Burke was uncertain what direction to take on graduation, but his brother-in-law convinced him that the Harvard Business School would be invaluable to his future career. "I was not even sure I wanted to be in business," Burke recalled. "I got in with relatively modest marks. I probably couldn't get in now. In those days you had three interviews, and you were accepted on the basis of those. In any case, I got in; and it was the most liberating experience I can think of."

The Harvard MBA Program in the Postwar Years

The Harvard Business School was undergoing many changes in the late 1940s. During the war, it became a virtual military academy. In June 1943, the school suspended all regular civilian instruction. From 1942 to 1945, eight officer training programs were set up for the Army, Navy, and Air Force. The programs, which varied in length from five weeks to one year, were (1) the Army Air Forces Statistical School, (2) the Army Supply Officers Training School, (3) the Navy Supply School, (4) the Army Air Forces War Adjustment course, (5) the Midshipmen Officers School, (6) two Navy Industrial Accounting courses, and (7) a Navy War Adjustment course. With the exception of the Navy Supply School, instruction for the wartime courses was provided at least in part by members of the business school faculty, who used the case method of instruction.[1]

The business school resumed civilian instruction in February 1946. To accommodate the three-year backlog of applicants who had been serving in the armed forces, the school began operating on a three-term basis, with continuous programs and no vacations. New first-year classes were admitted in June 1946 and February 1947, as well as in the fall of each of those years. In September 1948, the regular two-term prewar program was resumed, with admission of a first-year class each autumn.

The wartime suspension of civilian instruction provided an unusual opportunity to reexamine the MBA program. A committee on educational policy was appointed to prepare recommendations for revision of the curriculum. As a first step, a subcommittee on objectives composed a statement concerning "the

---

[1] Melvin T. Copeland, *And Mark an Era: The Story of the Harvard Business School* (Boston: Little, Brown, 1958), pp. 119–20.

abilities and understandings which the educational program of the School should be designed to help the students develop." These included:

- Ability to analyze business situations, recognize problems and determine issues, seek pertinent facts, develop alternatives, and reach reasoned decisions.
- Ability to organize.
- Ability to use oral and written communications.
- Ability to deal with people.
- Ability to train subordinates.
- Ability to use figures effectively for administrative purposes.
- Ability to establish standards and to control and judge performance.
- Ability to execute selected operating tasks, including those involving severe time pressures.
- Acquaintance with sources of business information.
- Understanding of the useful generalizations of political economy, and ability to develop at least the beginnings of an integrated social and economic philosophy.
- Understanding of ethical considerations as an integral part of business administration, and ability to develop a unified set of ethical concepts for personal guidance in administration.
- A spirit of vigorous and courageous enterprise.[2]

The committee also proposed a new program of instruction for all first-year students. Previously, first-year students were required to take several common courses, but had a choice among certain electives. In the new program, just one course — Elements of Administration (E.A.) — was required of all MBA candidates. Elements of Administration was divided into six "subjects": Production, Marketing, Finance, Control, Administrative Practices, and Public Relationships and Responsibilities. In addition, "E.A. General" was required for instruction in report writing.[3] The more noteworthy innovations in the first-year program came about through Administrative Practices — which focused on the problems of executives in promoting teamwork and effective action in business organizations; Control — which combined accounting principles and business statistics for the first time; and Public Relations and Responsibilities — which dealt with the relationship of business administrators to government and public institutions.

James Burke at the Harvard Business School

James Burke entered the Harvard Business School with the class of 1949, which was later to become famous for generating so many leading figures in the business world.[4] For example, Burke's roommate at Harvard, Peter McColough, eventually became the chairman of Xerox. Other well-known classmates included Sumner L. Feldberg, chairman of Zayre; Vincent L. Gregory, Jr., chairman of Rohm and Haas; Thomas Murphy, chairman of Capital Cities/ABC, Inc.; and John Shad, former head of the Securities and Exchange Commission.

"We were a bunch of exuberant and ambitious young veterans," Burke recalled, "trying like everyone else after the war to catch up with life in all respects. We were older than most when we went to the Harvard Business School, and we had seen more of the world than most of the students of today."

Burke enjoyed his years at the business school for a number of reasons:

First of all, everyone I met I liked. Secondly, it was intellectually a real turn-on. I never worked

---

[2] Copeland, *Era*, pp. 124–25.

[3] Copeland, *Era*, p. 126.

[4] Marilyn Wellemeyer, "The Class the Dollars Fell On," *Fortune*, May 1974, pp. 224–29, 340–52, passim.

so hard in my life and enjoyed every minute of it. And finally, the thing that amazed me, and was totally unexpected, is that in everything we did, we were reminded of the moral values — the importance of the moral values in our decision making. We all spent a lot of time talking about it, and many had the same doubts. It was not just me. I guess partly because of the way I was brought up, I had a set of values that I knew I was going to have difficulty compromising ever. And whether we like it or not, in our educational system, even at a place like Holy Cross, there is an underlying doubt about the enterprise system. I got the feeling from what I read in the papers and saw in the media that there was something a little bit corrupt about business. But the business school was a remarkable experience for me and I was convinced, or almost convinced, when I got out that what I believed in was going to work.

Procter & Gamble

After graduation from the Harvard Business School, Burke went to work for Procter & Gamble as a sales representative. After a year on the road, he became an assistant brand manager for a new product called Lilt home permanent, which had been introduced in 1949. The president of Procter & Gamble was Neil McElroy. McElroy had made a name for himself by proposing the basic principles of brand management that came to be widely used in marketing packaged products.

P&G's introduction of Camay soap in the 1920s first suggested to McElroy that marketing responsibility for each P&G brand should rest in the hands of a specific executive, who would concentrate on that brand exclusively and manage it as a separate business. Camay's early performance had been disappointing. It did not become the great challenger to Ivory that company officials had anticipated. McElroy believed that it was being held back by "too much Ivory thinking." Camay was being handled by the same advertising agency as Ivory, and McElroy saw

that Camay's advertising was being weakened so as to avoid negative reflections on Ivory.[5]

It was in May of 1931 that McElroy wrote his historic memorandum to P&G's president. The memorandum clearly defined McElroy's vision of the duties and responsibilities of a brand manager, as well as those of the team of assistants and field "checkup people." He predicted that brand managers would eventually take over a large part of the sales manager's ancillary work, leaving the sales team free to sell.[6] He was so persuasive that P&G's president agreed to implement a system that would dismantle a hundred-year-old way of doing business.

The concept of brand management was new at the time. No American company had ever encouraged such competition among its own brands. This concept necessarily changed the definition of job responsibilities within P&G. Brands such as Ivory, Camay, Crisco, Duz, and Oxydol became profit centers with their own budgets. Many outside the company believed P&G would be shattered by the new system. Many insiders saw their chances for advancement threatened as the traditional avenue for promotion was supplanted by the new organization.[7]

When Burke joined P&G in 1949, brand management was a decade and a half old and was being adopted by every major marketing company in the country; but P&G was still the leader in the field. Many other top business executives spent their formative years at Procter & Gamble, including Robert Beeby, president and CEO of PepsiCo International; James McManus, founder/president-CEO of Marketing Corporation of America; William E. Phillips, chairman-CEO of the Ogilvy Group;

---

[5] Oscar Schisgall, *Eyes on Tomorrow: The Evolution of Procter & Gamble* (Chicago: J. G. Ferguson Publishing, 1981), pp. 159–61.

[6] Schisgall, *Tomorrow,* p. 161.

[7] Schisgall, *Tomorrow,* p. 162.

and James Schadt, president-CEO of Cadbury Schweppes North America.[8]

Burke stayed at P&G for three and a half years but eventually decided he wanted freedom to pursue some of his own ideas for marketing consumer products. "When I left Procter & Gamble, I left with considerable restlessness," he recalled, "but without a very clear idea of what I was going to do with my life. I decided to leave without a job, because I had several things I wanted to do on my own. I went into three separate ventures after I left, and I was still hanging on to two of those in my spare time even after I joined Johnson & Johnson in 1953." None of these products proved successful.

Burke's Early Career at Johnson & Johnson

Burke was offered a position at Johnson & Johnson in 1953 as product director for Band-Aids. A friend had warned against joining "a family company," however, so, before accepting the job, Burke looked into several positions at advertising agencies. The advertising jobs were exciting from a financial point of view—Burke's salary would double if he accepted one of the offers. They also seemed to allow him more authority over his own destiny. However, he felt there was something wrong with all of them:

> I remember coming out to New Brunswick on the train with a lot of confusion in my mind. Johnson & Johnson offered me $10,000 a year to start, which was less than any of the advertising agencies offered, and I wasn't very excited about going there. Finally, I decided to screw up my courage and tell them I'd come to work there if they gave me $12,000. They did, and so I did. I did it in part because I felt it was the right thing for me to do, rather than with any great enthusiasm; but I can't say I did it with any great logic, or even common sense.

Johnson & Johnson's Early History

Johnson & Johnson was founded in New Brunswick, New Jersey, in 1886 as a medical products company by two brothers, James and Edward Mead Johnson. Later, a third brother, Robert Wood Johnson, joined the company and provided not only necessary capital but the kind of strong leadership the young company needed. Robert Johnson had been impressed by the theories of Joseph Lister, the English surgeon who founded modern antiseptic surgery. Antiseptic surgical dressings were among Johnson & Johnson's first products. Another early specialty of the company was the medicinal plaster, precursor of one of Johnson & Johnson's most famous products, the Band-Aid, which was first marketed in 1920.[9]

During his first year at Johnson & Johnson, Robert Johnson met Fred Kilmer, a pharmacist at a New Brunswick drug store. The two men shared an interest in Lister's ideas. In 1888, Kilmer compiled a booklet, which Robert Johnson published, entitled *Modern Methods of Antiseptic Wound Treatment*. "In many respects, it was a 'how to' manual, and soon it was being proclaimed as the most authoritative treatise ever presented on the subject. [W]ithin months, 85,000 copies were in distribution, . . . and in time over four million copies were in distribution all over the world."[10] That same year, Kilmer joined Johnson & Johnson as the director of scientific affairs.

Johnson & Johnson quickly gained a reputation as a major health products company. It was constantly searching for new products and over the years introduced sutures and ligatures, insect fumigators, dental specialties, and maternity and obstetric kits. In 1890, Johnson's Baby Powder was introduced. This was used

---

[8] Editors of *Advertising Age, The House That Ivory Built* (Lincolnwood, Ill.: NTC Business Books, 1988), pp. 91–99.

[9] Lawrence G. Foster, *A Company That Cares: One Hundred Year Illustrated History of Johnson & Johnson* (New Brunswick, N.J.: Johnson & Johnson, 1986), pp. 9–15.
[10] Foster, *Cares,* p. 21.

originally to soothe skin irritation resulting from medicated plaster. The company expanded internationally shortly thereafter, signing on agents in Canada, England, Australia, and New Zealand.

Kilmer pursued his interest in surgical and first-aid products and techniques, making several scholarly contributions to medical literature, while Robert Johnson focused his attention on advertising. Shortly after the company was formed, Johnson retained the services of a young advertising man by the name of J. Walter Thompson. Every advertisement had to be approved by Johnson personally; and although he had a keen instinct for what would sell, his meddling was often trying on his agency staff.[11]

Johnson involved himself in every aspect of the business. He began each day by presiding over the opening of the company's mail and often responded personally to customer complaints. He worked long hours and expected the same of others. Despite his sometimes dogmatic ways, he was well respected by his employees, and his enthusiasm was widely admired.[12]

Robert Johnson's sudden death in 1910 left a void in the company. Many of its 2,500 employees feared that it could not continue to be successful without his leadership. Johnson's younger brother, James, became the new president, but it was with Robert Johnson's eldest son — Robert II — that the future of the company lay.

Robert Johnson II was just 16 when his father died, but he had already shown interest in the business. On graduation from high school, the young Johnson joined the company full time. He started in the factory power plant and moved from department to department, staying just long enough to learn each one's function. Johnson eventually specialized in sales and marketing, areas for which he, like his father, had a natural affinity.

Following the First World War, Johnson exerted increasing influence on the company's policies. He staunchly supported the development of international manufacturing operations. It took several years of persuasion, but eventually he won the company over to his point of view. The first international plant was opened in 1924 in England, just outside London.[13]

Johnson became vice president and general manager of Johnson & Johnson in 1930 and president in 1932. He soon gained national prominence as a creative industrialist. In 1926, Johnson built the "world's most modern textile mill," a showplace of technical excellence and beauty at a time when most textile mills were bleak and dingy places with oppressive and unsafe working conditions. In 1933, Johnson wrote a letter to President-elect Franklin Delano Roosevelt calling for a federal law increasing wages as well as reducing the work week.[14]

In the 1940s, Johnson criticized the National Association of Manufacturers for advocating a labor management philosophy that, he felt, entailed "a return to the hands-off economics of the 1880s, which would reduce labor to a commodity that can be sold, bought, and scrapped like so much machinery."[15] During the Second World War, he served as a brigadier general, in charge of the New York Ordinance District. Thenceforth he was often referred to within the corporation as "the General."

As president, Johnson emphasized the advertising and marketing of consumer products as well as the research and development of new products. During his 25-year tenure as head of

---

[11] Foster, *Cares*, p. 32.
[12] Foster, *Cares*, pp. 34–35.

[13] Foster, *Cares*, pp. 84–85.
[14] Foster, *Cares*, pp. 90, 97.
[15] *The New York Times*, July 10, 1947, p. 14.

Johnson & Johnson, he became well known for such creative advertisements as "Modess... because" and a series of children's paintings commissioned from noted artist Gladys Rockmore Davis for use in a first-aid products advertising campaign.[16]

In the 1940s, the General developed a Credo for the company, which represented a formalization of his views on corporate public and social responsibility. He was a strong believer in decentralization. Decentralization demands trust, which was a fundamental tenet of the Credo. Just as top executives must be trusted to balance the interests of the company's constituencies, top executives must in turn trust middle management to make the right decisions from both a business and an ethical point of view.[17]

The far-flung "family" of Johnson & Johnson companies grew out of this management philosophy. Decentralization came about in several ways, and there was no set formula for accomplishing it. Companies in the family were managed as separate entities, each with its own president and board of directors and each having its own research, marketing, and production departments.

By way of example, Ethicon, Inc., resulted from an acquisition in 1918, and eventually it was made an affiliate company because of the General's strong belief that managers would become more successful if they were given full responsibility and credit for all decisions concerning their company. Ortho Pharmaceutical Corporation grew out of research in Johnson & Johnson's own laboratories in the field of family planning. It, too, became an affiliate when strong management had been established.[18]

Many of Johnson & Johnson's top executives received their early training rising through the ranks of one of the corporation's numerous affiliated units. Philip B. Hofmann, who became chairman of the corporation in 1963,[19] got his start as a salesperson for Ortho. Hofmann was responsible for building Ortho during the 1930s and 1940s, selling contraceptive jellies at a time when many people considered such a business improper.[20]

The General was also concerned with balance — between manufacturing and marketing, between financial and operating people, and especially between consumer and professional products. As a result, no single product during his tenure accounted for as much as 5 percent of total sales.[21]

The Credo brought together Johnson's belief in fair employee treatment, decentralization, and product quality; and it underscored what he viewed as his company's responsibilities to its customers, to its employees, to the communities in which it operated, and finally to its stockholders. In time, the principles embodied in the Credo, and particularly the strong emphasis on decentralization, came to represent major factors that shaped the Johnson & Johnson way of doing business. In the words of one consultant who has studied Johnson & Johnson's Credo:

> The Credo is an extremely powerful document... [because it] is at all times tied in to the regular concerns of business management: product choice, delivery times, costs, employee compensation, corporate taxes, maintenance

---

[16] Foster, *Cares,* pp. 112–13.

[17] Laura Nash, "Johnson & Johnson's Credo," in *Corporate Ethics: A Prime Business Asset* (New York: Business Roundtable, 1988), p. 80.

[18] Foster, *Cares,* p. 101.

---

[19] During Robert Johnson's tenure, the division of Johnson & Johnson that manufactured and sold products with the name *Johnson's* on them (mainly baby products and Band-Aids) was known as the "Operating Company." Johnson & Johnson as a whole was referred to as the "Corporation."

[20] Lee Smith, "J&J Comes a Long Way from Baby," *Fortune,* June 1, 1981, p. 60.

[21] "Prescription for Growth," *Forbes,* June 26, 1978, p. 97.

EXHIBIT 3 Johnson & Johnson's Credo (as originally written
by Robert W. Johnson)

We believe that our first responsibility is to the doctors, nurses, hospitals, mothers,
and all others who use our products.
Our products must always be of the highest quality.
We must constantly strive to reduce the cost of these products.
Our orders must be promptly and accurately filled.
Our dealers must make a fair profit.

Our second responsibility is to those who work with us — the men and women in our
plants and offices.
They must have a sense of security in their jobs.
Wages must be fair and adequate, management just, hours reasonable, and working
conditions clean and orderly.
Employees should have an organized system for suggestions and complaints.
Supervisors and department heads must be qualified and fair minded.
There must be an opportunity for advancement — for those qualified — and each
person must be considered an individual standing on his own dignity and merit.

Our third responsibility is to management.
Our executives must be persons of talent, education, experience, and ability.
They must be persons of common sense and full understanding.

Our fourth responsibility is to the communities in which we live.
We must be a good citizen — support good works and charity, and bear our fair
share of taxes.
We must maintain in good order the property we are privileged to use.
We must participate in promotion of civic improvement, health, education, and
good government, and acquaint the community with our activities.

Our fifth and last responsibility is to our stockholders.
Business must make a sound profit.
Reserves must be created, research must be carried on, adventurous programs de-
veloped, and mistakes paid for.
Adverse times must be provided for, adequate taxes paid, new machines purchased,
new plants built, new products launched, and new sales plans developed.
We must experiment with new ideas.
When these things have been done, the stockholder should receive a fair return.
We are determined, with the help of God's grace, to fulfill these obligations to the
best of our ability.

---

of company property, research and innovation, new equipment, and financial reserves.
Equally important, profit is not a dirty word.
The Credo puts forth a world view in which
profit is obtainable through just and ethical
behavior.[22] [See Exhibit 3.]

---

[22] Nash, *Ethics,* p. 83.

A Rising Star

In James Burke's view, his first year at Johnson
& Johnson was not very productive, in part
because he was still working nights and weekends trying to salvage his own new products,
which were in the process of failing. In addition, he was discouraged because no one paid
much attention to the consumer brands with

which he was involved. "Nobody would show up for the Nielsen meetings," he said, "and we were losing share in 92 percent of our product categories. It was really a very small consumer business—and I didn't think it was going anywhere. I also wanted to start a New Products Division, but I couldn't get anyone interested. I was bored. Finally, after a year of frustration, I quit."

A few days after he left, Burke got a call from Ed Gerbic, his boss's boss. Gerbic offered Burke a chance to set up a New Products Division, along with a 50 percent raise in salary. Despite his resolution to leave the company, Burke could not turn down this opportunity. He realized only later that he had been caught in a political battle between his immediate boss, John McLaughlin, and Ed Gerbic. Gerbic had offered Burke the position because he wanted to prove to management that he could hold good people and that McLaughlin could not. (A few years later, both McLaughlin and Gerbic had left the company, and Burke was promoted to Gerbic's job.)

Burke returned to Johnson & Johnson and went to work establishing a new products development plan. He quickly discovered that very few models existed in other companies. Burke recalled:

> I did find HBS classmates of mine [Sam Johnson at S.C. Johnson, and Conrad Jones at Booz, Allen] who were interested in doing exactly what I was doing. So we had a lot of fun getting together and comparing ideas. There was also an advertising agency—now out of business—that had done a study on the life span of new products, and I did some research on my own to add to it. The study did a lot to remind people that there weren't too many new-product successes—you had to take a lot of shots before you had any successes. That was important to me and important to this company because most people believed if a person tries twice and fails twice with a new product, they're a failure as a manager. Now people are more sophisticated and realize that only about 1 out of 10 of these efforts ever work, but it was

helpful in the beginning to give courage to the organization to take the chances that I sensed needed to be taken.

One of Burke's notable successes from this time was a line of athlete's-foot remedies, which eventually sparked the work in R&D that created the product now marketed under the name *Micatin*. Also during this period, Burke began to upgrade the line of baby products to encourage more adult use. One product line in that category failed for an unexpected reason. As Burke explained:

> A friend of mine, an entrepreneur, had come out with a liquid product for children. It was a substitute for aspirin, but in a liquid form. I thought the concept was good, so I bought the product—for $15,000, think of it!—and called it Liquiprin. To go along with this product, we designed the first-ever safety container. There was a stainless steel spring inside the bottle, with a plastic plug on top. The mother could put the dropper in and push the plug aside and take out the dose for the child; but if the child pulled the dropper out, the plug filled the bottle and the child couldn't drink it. That product was fairly successful and it gave us the idea to design a line of children's medications which would be safer and easier to use. We added a nose drop, a cough medicine, and a chest rub, and marketed the entire line under the *Arrestin* trademark.
>
> All three new products failed, and in essence the entire concept was lousy, but it took me a long time to understand why. Basically, even with children, while safety is important, and "easier to use" is important, what the consumer is really looking for is results. And under the name *Johnson's,* no matter how good the product performed, mentally the consumer is making the decision, "This probably isn't as strong as what I'm used to using." So if the child is coughing, and nobody can get any sleep, the consumer is more inclined to rationalize and say "I'm sure Vick's is safe, and I know it's stronger because it doesn't have the name *Johnson's* on it."

As a result of this experiment, Burke also had his first real encounter with the General.

Burke had come into the office at 9:15 one morning to find a message that the General had called him half an hour earlier. Burke knew right away that the meeting would be about the failed product line. He went over to the General's office, convinced he was about to be fired.

Much to Burke's surprise, the General congratulated him on his attempt to create the new-product line. He said, "What business is all about is making decisions, and you don't make decisions without making mistakes. Now, don't ever make that mistake again, but please make sure you make other mistakes."

"That incident was extremely important to me," Burke related, "and the General became important to me—first of all because he was tougher than hell; he was egocentric, but he was very creative. He loved to argue, almost as much as I do. On anything. I don't know that he was a mentor of mine, but he loved young people and he was very close to what was going on in the company."

During his tenure as director of new products, Burke was supervised by Robert "Bobby" Johnson III—the General's son—and the two young men became friends. Burke's enthusiasm, his ability to attract bright, young marketing people, and his knack for conceptualizing successful consumer products impressed Johnson. After two years, Bobby recommended Burke for the job of vice president of product management of the Operating Company. George Smith, then president of the Operating Company, had reservations about Burke and expressed them forcefully to both Bobby Johnson and to Burke himself. Burke was too young, he believed, and not prepared to assume the responsibilities that the job entailed.

Smith decided to give Burke a one-year trial in which to prove himself. Burke was named acting director of advertising and merchandising, and Smith suggested that Burke see him whenever he had any questions or difficulties. "He was always available," Burke recalled, "and that year with him I learned as much as I think I've learned from most people."

A short time after this new arrangement was agreed on, Burke found himself in personal financial difficulties as a result of his previous personal marketing ventures. "In those days," Burke remarked, "you weren't allowed to sell Johnson & Johnson stock. So I went to Bobby Johnson and I laid it all out. I told him I hadn't been paying attention to my finances, I couldn't pay the interest charges on loans I had taken out, and I was in real trouble. Bobby went to Gus Lienhard, who was chairman of the executive committee, argued my case, and asked him to help me out."

Lienhard not only helped Burke reorganize his financial affairs, he arranged for Burke to sell his stock and to take out a $30,000 loan from the corporation. He also made it clear that if Burke ever got into that kind of trouble again, he would be fired. "First of all, it was remarkable that the company would do this," Burke said, "but secondly, it taught me a lesson I never forgot as to the importance of managing your own personal affairs. And I subsequently became quite close to Gus Lienhard. He was very good for me because he was very oriented to the bottom line. He was an auditor by background, and he later became president of the corporation. He was a tremendous president. In 1965, I became the youngest member of the executive committee he chaired, so I used to see him then almost every night. He spent a great many hours of his life trying to help develop me."

At the end of a successful year working under George Smith, Burke was promoted to vice president of product management for the Operating Company. At this time, Smith was thinking about moving the corporation into the pharmaceutical business. He wanted to market a broad range of pharmaceuticals—branded generics, in effect, under the name *Johnson & Johnson*. Burke felt that this was a flawed idea for two reasons. First, the company would be selling products with no improved end benefit, and Burke was concerned that this might injure the Johnson & Johnson name. Second, Burke's experience with children's medications had taught him that the Johnson's name suggested gentleness, rather than potency, and that the name would be more hindrance than help.

Bobby Johnson agreed with Burke's reservations. After two years of indifferent performance in pharmaceuticals, the corporation came around to their point of view, which was also shared by others in the company. Johnson & Johnson decided to purchase a pharmaceutical company in the United States and a research laboratory in Europe. The regulatory process in Europe allowed drugs to gain approval more quickly than in the United States, and a research laboratory in Europe would provide the corporation with an income stream. An established U.S. pharmaceutical company would provide a marketing channel once a compound had been approved by the Food and Drug Administration.

Johnson & Johnson acquired McNeil Pharmaceutical in the United States and the Janssen Company in Belgium. McNeil had a good reputation. It was a family company, run by two brothers who joined the board of directors at Johnson & Johnson. Janssen proved to be a boon for Johnson & Johnson. Through 1988, it had created more successful new compounds than any other comparable company in the world. Pharmaceuticals were among the many products that became independent of the Operating Company in the 1950s and 1960s.

Burke advocated separating the marketing function of the Operating Company into Baby Products and First Aid Products. The two would still share manufacturing, but Burke believed that the companies would grow faster if the marketing and research functions were independent of one another. In 1962, Burke was named president of the Baby and Proprietary Products Company.

Shortly after this reorganization took place, the General let it be known that he thought results were so weak that he was considering putting this business back into the Operating Company and removing the managers in charge, including Burke. Burke felt that his team had been doing a superb job and that the General did not understand the investments that the company was making in advertising and new products.

"I was furious," Burke recalled. "I went to Gus Lienhard and told him I wanted the opportunity for my people to show the General what we had been doing. The General agreed, and we took about two months to prepare for that presentation. I was really convinced that the story we had to tell would put him away. I was super-confident." The presentation was for the General and the entire executive committee. It started at 9:00 A.M. and was to last throughout the morning. At 10:15 A.M. the General got up and walked out. "I almost followed him, I was so mad," Burke recalled. But he finished the presentation, and it was well received. Once the executive committee fully understood the nature of the investments, the numbers spoke for themselves.

Burke was too angry to speak with the General, so he went to see Gus Lienhard. Lienhard had already questioned the General on his sudden departure from the meeting. "It was perfectly obvious that the business is in complete control and very well managed," the General responded. "Why waste any more time on it? You know," the General continued, with a twinkle in his eye, "I don't think it really hurt Burke, do you?"

"That made me start thinking," Burke related. "Not only didn't it hurt us, the business was much better managed as a result of the General's challenge. We got rid of things we were doing as we started studying the business. We re-did our advertising and we changed prices. We did a whole series of things that never would have happened if the General hadn't challenged us, and I never forgot it."

In 1964, Burke was promoted to executive vice president for consumer products, with both the divisions reporting to him; and in 1965, he was selected to run the Domestic Operating Company, a position formerly held by George Smith. He also became a member of the executive committee. One particularly memorable occurrence during these years was the attempted introduction of a new product called Baby Liquid Cream—a skin lotion that was to be marketed for both baby and adult use. Burke remembered it as "a beautiful product, beautifully packaged."

This became a special project for Bobby Johnson. He was its manager and its champion. He wanted to introduce it nationally without test-marketing it because of his confidence in it. Shortly before it was to be shipped, the company received the results of clinical tests from a nearby women's college. The tests revealed a slight level of irritation in about 5 percent of the subjects.

The clinicals suggested, however, that unless the lotion was used on a very intensive basis by women with pre-existing skin problems, the irritation did not occur. There were arguments within the company about what to do with the product. Some members of the executive committee rationalized that the problems were not severe; but Burke remembered Bobby Johnson saying, "We're not going to go ahead. Dump it in the Raritan River if you have to."

"What he meant," Burke explained, "was get rid of it. And he did. He made the decision like that, and it cost the corporation a lot of money. I thought at the time that this was the kind of thing that made Johnson & Johnson different, and that thought returned many times over the years."

The Credo Challenge Meetings

In 1975, Burke caused a stir when he decided to "challenge" the Credo. At the time, he was

president of the corporation and had already been named as the successor to chairman and CEO Richard B. Sellars. Burke had worked closely with the General over the years and had inherited his strong belief in the Credo. But the document was now over 30 years old, and Burke wondered if it was still a meaningful statement of responsibility for all of Johnson & Johnson's managers, as the General had intended it to be. It bothered Burke to think that the document might lose visibility and significance at Johnson & Johnson over time. If the Credo were no longer meaningful, Burke felt it would be better to "tear it off the walls" than to have it stand for nothing. He decided to hold a series of discussion meetings with top management to get their opinions on the usefulness of the Credo in their own decision-making processes.

Public relations vice president Lawrence G. Foster wanted to film the first of these Credo challenge meetings, but Burke felt that cameras would ruin the atmosphere and discourage managers from revealing their true feelings. Foster prevailed by promising to turn the cameras off after half an hour if they were impeding the discussion. As Burke recalled, however, 15 minutes into the meeting the cameras were forgotten as the focus turned toward challenging the fundamental beliefs of the corporation as well as those of the individual executives.

When Richard Sellars heard about the meeting, however, he "went bananas." It was the only time Burke could recall Sellars losing his temper. Sellars said, "You're not about to challenge the Credo as long as I'm here. I'm chairman, and no one has the right to challenge that document." However, after he saw the tape, and as he began to think about what was happening, he gradually became a supporter of the challenge idea—particularly since what came out of the meeting was a rewording and a reaffirmation of the Credo by management (see Exhibit 4). Burke and Sellars then made a tape together and launched further meetings

---

EXHIBIT 4 Johnson & Johnson's Credo (revised version)

We believe our first responsibility is to the doctors, nurses, and patients, to mothers and all others who use our products and services.

In meeting their need, everything we do must be of high quality.

We must constantly strive to reduce our costs in order to maintain reasonable prices.

Customers' orders must be serviced promptly and accurately.

Our suppliers and distributors must have an opportunity to make a fair profit.

We are responsible to our employees, the men and women who work with us throughout the world.

Everyone must be considered as an individual.

We must respect their sense of dignity and recognize their merit.

They must have a sense of security in their jobs.

Compensation must be fair and adequate, and working conditions clean, orderly, and safe.

Employees must feel free to make suggestions and complaints.

There must be equal opportunity for employment, development, and advancement for those qualified.

We must provide competent management, and their actions must be just and ethical.

We are responsible to the communities in which we live and work and to the world community as well.

We must be good citizens—support good works and charities and bear our fair share of taxes.

We must encourage civic improvements and better health and education.

We must maintain in good order the property we are privileged to use, protecting the environment and natural resources.

Our final responsibility is to our stockholder.

Business must make a sound profit.

We must experiment with new ideas.

Research must be carried on, innovative programs developed, and mistakes paid for.

New equipment must be purchased, new facilities provided, and new products launched.

Reserves must be created to provide for adverse times.

When we operate according to these principles, the stockholders should realize a fair return.

---

throughout 1979, and all employees of the company took part.

The Chief Executive Officer

When Burke became CEO in November of 1976, his vision of Johnson & Johnson's future called for strengthening the company's commitment to science and technology and broadening its base in the health care field. Eventually the company would market products or services in all 23 disciplines of medicine, ranging from anesthesiology to urology.

One of the early challenges that Burke faced was the moving of Tylenol from a prescription analgesic to an over-the-counter pain medication. To accomplish this, the company engaged in a head-to-head clash with Bristol-Myers and its Datril product, and came out the victor.

Burke pushed Johnson & Johnson's disposable diapers to sales of over $100 million in 1977.[23] Stiff competition from Procter & Gamble's Luvs and Kimberly-Clark's Huggies—both of which adopted stretch diapers more quickly than did Johnson & Johnson—eventually drove Johnson & Johnson out of the U.S. market; but the company continued to sell diapers overseas. In 1977, largely as a result of Burke's earlier efforts with the product, Johnson & Johnson's baby shampoo became the best-selling shampoo in the country.

Nineteen eighty saw the introduction of a new painkiller called ZOMAX, thought to be as effective as injected morphine, but nonaddictive. It was an early success, but McNeil, which marketed the product, found that some patients suffered allergic reactions, some of them fatal, and in 1983 ZOMAX was removed from the market.

Burke also planned to lead the company into some high-technology health care fields, which he viewed as the wave of the future. In 1978, Johnson & Johnson acquired a manufacturer of kidney dialysis machines for $35 million, and a heart valve laboratory for $26 million. In 1979, the company acquired Technicare, a failing manufacturer of computerized axial tomography (CAT) machines and ultrasound scanners, for $75 million in stock, and assumed its $50 million in debt.[24] The technology allowed the creation of "a three-dimensional image of an object by taking multiple X-ray measurements of the object from different angles, then using a computer to reconstruct a picture from the data contained in hundreds of overlapping and in-

tersecting X-ray slices."[25] The image could be used by a physician to make a diagnosis without the need for exploratory surgery. But Technicare never reached its full potential, and Johnson & Johnson had difficulty managing it. In 1986, Johnson & Johnson withdrew from the business and sold what assets there were to General Electric.

In 1981, Johnson & Johnson ranked 74 among the 500 largest U.S. industrials. It was made up of 150 subsidiaries manufacturing such disparate products as dental floss, blood analyzers, drugs to control parasites in cattle, and $800,000 CAT scanners. Nearly half the company's sales and more than half its aftertax earnings were derived from its overseas markets.[26] The corporation owned some of the best-known brands in the world and was regarded as a blue-chip growth stock on Wall Street. In the words of a former colleague at Johnson & Johnson, "Burke evolved from being a packaged-goods salesman to a man with a mission in health care."[27] (See Exhibit 5.)

The Tylenol Poisonings

On the morning of Wednesday, September 29, 1982, Mary Kellerman, a 12-year-old girl, and Adam Janus, a 27-year-old postal worker, both living in neighboring suburbs of Chicago, died of mysterious causes. Later the same day, Janus's brother died from the same mysterious cause, and his brother's wife fell into a coma from which she never recovered. Medical authorities were considering quarantining the entire area, when two paramedics noticed a strange coincidence. In all cases, the victims had recently taken Extra-Strength Tylenol. A spot check quickly confirmed authorities' worst fears. Cyanide, one of the most rapidly acting

---

[23] *Forbes,* June 26, 1978, p. 97.
[24] *Fortune,* June 1, 1981, p. 66.

[25] Christopher A. Bartlett, "EMI and the CT Scanner (A)," HBS no. 9-383-194.
[26] *Fortune,* June 1, 1981, p. 58.
[27] *Fortune,* June 1, 1981, p. 61.

EXHIBIT 5   A Snapshot of the Business: Johnson & Johnson in 1976 and in 1981

Sales to Customers in 1976	*$ in millions*	*Sales to Customers in 1981*	*$ in millions*
Consumer Segment[a]		Consumer Segment[a]	
Domestic	$ 448	Domestic	$1,238
International	414	International	1,125
Total consumer	862	Total consumer	2,363
Professional Segment[b]		Professional Segment[b]	
Domestic	491	Domestic	1,128
International	284	International	607
Total professional	775	Total professional	1,735
Pharmaceutical Segment[c]		Pharmaceutical Segment[c]	
Domestic	366	Domestic	511
International	257	International	497
Total pharmaceutical	623	Total pharmaceutical	1,008
Industrial Segment[d]		Industrial Segment[d]	
Domestic	188	Domestic	149
International	75	International	145
Total industrial	263	Total industrial	294
Worldwide total sales	$2,523	Worldwide total sales	$5,400
Aftertax earnings on income	$ 205	Aftertax earnings on income	$ 468

a. Toiletries and hygienic products, including baby care items.	a. Toiletries and hygienic products, including baby care items, first aid products, and non-prescription drugs.
b. Prescription and nonprescription drugs, diagnostics, therapeutics, contraceptives, and veterinary products.	b. Prescription drugs, including contraceptives and therapeutics, and veterinary products.
c. Surgical dressings, ligatures and sutures, surgical instruments, surgical specialties, and related items.	c. Ligatures and sutures, medical wound closure products, diagnostic products, dental products, medical equipment and devices, surgical dressings, surgical apparel and accessories, surgical instruments, and related items.
d. Industrial tapes and adhesives, textiles, paper products, and other related items.	d. Textile products, collagen sausage casings, and fine chemicals.

Source: Johnson & Johnson annual report, 1976.   Source: Johnson & Johnson annual report, 1981.

and deadly of poisons, had been placed into capsules of Extra-Strength Tylenol, and people were dying from taking the product.

History of the Product

Tylenol's rise was one of the headiest marketing success stories of the 1970s, and James Burke was regarded as the man most responsible for it. The product was developed by McNeil Laboratories, a pharmaceutical company that had been acquired by Johnson & Johnson in 1959. Until 1960, Tylenol was sold exclusively as a prescription drug. Its only active ingredient, acetaminophen, was a compound any drug company could make.

Throughout the 1960s and early 1970s, Tylenol was advertised only through medical trade journals and directly to doctors and pharmacists as a gentler-to-the-stomach alternative to aspirin. It was not until the mid-1970s, however, that the drug really began to take off.

Although Tylenol fell outside of Burke's purview as general manager of the Domestic Operating Company, he closely followed the brand's growth during the 1960s.[28] By 1970, he was convinced that Tylenol could present the company with a superb marketing opportunity if McNeil would lower its price and advertise to the public.

"What we really wanted to do," Burke recalled, "was take that professional heritage and use it to build the business with the consumer. The pharmaceutical people told me they were doing very well on their own, and they were. Tylenol was growing 20 to 30 percent a year; and it was forecast to be a $60 million business by 1974 or 1975, which was very substantial for a pharmaceutical specialty which in effect was a generic compound."

In the early 1970s, a series of highly publicized studies questioned consumers' uncritical dependence on aspirin. Tylenol was ideally positioned to take advantage of this turn of events. Sales of acetaminophen increased from 5 percent of a $550 million over-the-counter painkiller market in 1972 to 13 percent of a $680 million market in 1974. Tylenol accounted for approximately 90 percent of those sales.[29]

"Hospitals trust Tylenol" became a major selling point for the brand. By 1975, two-thirds of Tylenol consumers had been referred to the drug by their doctors, and 25 percent of those consumers had been advised by their doctors to switch from an aspirin brand because of possible side effects, such as upset stomach, stomach and intestinal bleeding, or irritated ulcers. These symptoms were especially problematic in arthritis sufferers and others who took large daily doses of aspirin.[30] Another reason for Tylenol's popularity with the medical profession was McNeil's hospital distribution policy. McNeil made sure that hospitals consistently obtained their product more cheaply than that of the competition. The combination of these two factors led McNeil to advertise Tylenol as the drug most used (and, by implication, most trusted) by doctors.[31]

Meanwhile, Bristol-Myers, hoping to capture a share of the lucrative acetaminophen market, quietly went into test market for its own acetaminophen brand, Datril, in Albany, New York, and Peoria, Illinois. Part of this test was a television advertisement claiming that Datril was just as effective as Tylenol, while costing one dollar less. At the time Datril began this campaign, Tylenol held 10.6 percent of a total over-the-counter analgesics market worth close to $700 million at retail prices. Tylenol had just edged ahead of Bristol-Myers' Excedrin (8.5 percent), but still trailed American Home Products' Anacin (15.3 percent), Sterling's Bayer (12.3 percent), and Bristol-Myers' Bufferin (12.3 percent). (See Exhibit 6.)

Burke first learned of the Datril test market not from McNeil but from his brother Dan, who was then manager of the Albany station of Capital Cities Broadcasting Corporation.

---

[28] Tylenol was controlled by the pharmaceutical arm of the corporation, at McNeil. The Domestic Operating Company controlled all U.S. products with the Johnson's name on them. Although Burke did not have line responsibility for Tylenol, he did have information concerning its progress, due to his position on the executive committee.

[29] "A Painful Headache for Bristol-Myers?" *Business Week,* October 6, 1975, p. 78.

[30] Dennis Kneale, "Remedy Ruckus: Tylenol, the Painkiller, Gives Rivals Headache in Store and in Court," *The Wall Street Journal,* September 2, 1982, p. 12.

[31] William Power, "A Judge Prescribes a Dose of Truth to Ease the Pain of Analgesic Ads," *The Wall Street Journal,* May 13, 1987, p. 33.

EXHIBIT 6   Brand Share and Advertising Expenditure for Five Major Analgesic Brands, 1975 ($000)

		In a $680 Million Retail Market	
Company	*Brand*	*Market Share (%)*	*Advertising Expenditure*
American Home Products	Anacin	15.3%	$27,685
Sterling	Bayer	12.3	17,291
Bristol-Myers	Bufferin	12.3	14,659
Johnson & Johnson	Tylenol	10.6	142
Bristol-Myers	Excedrin	8.5	15,576
Other	Other	41.0	na

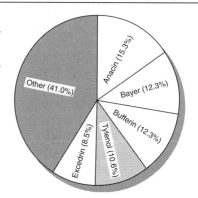

Source: "A Pained Bayer Cries 'Foul,'" *Business Week,* July 25, 1977, p. 142; and "Top 200 Advertised Brands Directory," *Marketing & Media Decisions,* July 1979.

Burke raced to Albany as soon as he heard the news, but by that time Datril was well into its test and had already cut Tylenol sales in the Albany area by more than a third.

Burke returned convinced that the company had to move aggressively. He told CEO Richard Sellars that Tylenol simply had to be managed as though it were a consumer business, starting right away, and the price had to be cut by one-third. That would mean a $20 million reduction in profit—a lot for any corporation to swallow.

To Burke's surprise, Sellars agreed instantly. Even before the Datril advertisements broke nationwide, Johnson & Johnson organized "Operation Teamwork" to blunt their effect on Tylenol. Although a small group of McNeil sales specialists were already working with supermarkets on expanded distribution, the product was quickly taken on by Johnson & Johnson's Health Care Division, which marketed Band-Aid bandages, Micrin mouthwash, and Shower-to-Shower body powder, among other products. At McNeil, Wayne Nelson was selected to establish a new Consumer Products Division to handle future sales of an expanded Tylenol line.

Within weeks of the time Burke first learned of the Datril challenge, Tylenol had 90 percent distribution in food stores to go along with its 98 percent distribution in drug outlets. Datril, as a new item, had considerably less. In addition, a video presentation on Tylenol's new price policy was shown simultaneously to 700 sales managers and territorial salespeople in 16 cities. They were instructed to contact their customers immediately about the price change and offer them a rebate on their inventory.[32] The price to the trade for a 100-tablet bottle dropped from $1.69 to $1.19. If the trade took advantage of deals, the price would go as low as 69¢, compared with Datril's promotional price of 70¢.[33]

The fact that every Datril advertisement gave almost equal exposure to Tylenol, coupled with the medical profession's familiarity with the Tylenol brand, indicated to Burke that Johnson & Johnson would not have to outspend Bristol-Myers in advertising. Nevertheless, it was

---

[32] *Business Week,* October 6, 1975, p. 80.
[33] Nancy Giges, "J&J Readies Effort to Protect Tylenol: New Datril Spot Airs," *Advertising Age,* July 28, 1975, p. 61.

apparent that the Datril advertisement could do a great deal of harm to Tylenol's market share if allowed to continue running.

On June 3, 1975, shortly before the Datril advertisement was scheduled to run nationwide, Burke telephoned Richard L. Gelb, president and CEO of Bristol-Myers, to notify him that Tylenol's price to the trade had been reduced 30 percent, effective immediately, and that therefore any advertisement claiming that Datril was cheaper would be misleading.[34] "He thanked me for the call," Burke related, "hung up, and increased the advertising budget for Datril. The commercial aired the following day."

Burke faced weeks of difficulty trying to convince the major networks to discontinue the Datril price-comparison advertisement since, in the opinion of Johnson & Johnson, it was no longer true. Bristol-Myers took the position that while Johnson & Johnson may have made a decision to cut the price of Tylenol, the decision had not yet been implemented. As long as this was true, Bristol-Myers felt the advertisement's claims were justified.

Johnson & Johnson submitted price-comparison surveys to the National Advertising Division (NAD) of the Council of Better Business Bureaus, showing that in stores where both Datril and Tylenol were sold, pricing patterns were erratic. Neither Datril nor Tylenol was consistently cheaper. Bristol-Myers, on the other hand, found in mid-July 1975 that the nationwide average price of Datril was $1.57 while Tylenol's nationwide average price was $2.23.[35]

In an official complaint to the NAD, Johnson & Johnson's associate general counsel George S. Frazza wrote:

> When Bristol-Myers conceived its advertising scheme, it obviously concluded that Johnson & Johnson would not match its prices. It is undeniable that Johnson & Johnson has done so, but Bristol-Myers refuses to abandon its preconceived marketing plan of "cost less" advertising. It is indisputable that this campaign does not square with the realities of the marketplace, misleads the consumer, and causes irreparable damage to our business.[36]

CBS ultimately decided to discontinue the Datril advertisement entirely, while the editors at NBC and ABC forced revisions that resulted in the weaker claim that "Datril can cost less, depending on where you shop."[37]

One year after Bristol-Myers began its campaign to enter the acetaminophen field, and after an estimated expenditure of $20 million, Datril had a 1 percent market share, while Tylenol's had increased to 11.5 percent. Bufferin and Bayer both showed slight declines.[38]

When Burke became chairman and CEO of Johnson & Johnson in 1976, Tylenol took the offensive. Over $4 million was spent that year to advertise it as a safer alternative to aspirin. The following year the figure tripled to over $12 million. (Tylenol had an advertising budget of $142,000 in 1975 prior to the Datril offensive.)[39]

Tylenol sales did not drop from $60 million to $40 million with its price cut, as the McNeil people had feared. Burke explained:

> The wonder and beauty of all this is that it's just another description of how the free-enterprise system works. Our business just took off, and our units made up for all the loss in dollars. Now we weren't making any money. We were spending a great deal of money. But it was obvious during all those early days that we had a winner and it was going to remain a winner.

[34] *Business Week,* October 6, 1975, p. 80.

[35] "J&J Slashes Tylenol's Price, Objects to Datril Ad Approach," *Advertising Age,* July 14, 1975, p. 1.

[36] *Advertising Age,* July 28, 1975, p. 61.

[37] *Business Week,* October 6, 1975, p. 80.

[38] "A Pained Bayer Cries 'Foul,' " *Business Week,* July 25, 1977, p. 142.

[39] "Advertising Expenditures of the Top 200 American Brands," *Marketing & Media Decisions,* July 1979, p. 116.

Johnson & Johnson introduced Extra-Strength Tylenol after the results of a 1976 survey showed that consumers did not believe Tylenol to be as efficacious as other brands because it had no side effects. Extra-Strength Tylenol was the first over-the-counter analgesic to contain 500 milligrams of painkiller per tablet. (Regular dosage for analgesics was 325 milligrams of painkiller per tablet, while "extra-strength" was defined as 400 milligrams of painkiller per tablet.)[40] Johnson & Johnson had to file a new drug application with the Food and Drug Administration to increase the "extra-strength" dosage for Extra-Strength Tylenol.

Extra-Strength Tylenol was heavily advertised as "the most potent pain reliever you can buy without a prescription," and sales surged. Year-end audits in 1976 by A. C. Nielsen put the Tylenol brand[41] in the number one position, with 18.2 percent market share. Regular-Strength Tylenol just edged out Bufferin for the number one spot in the $300 million regular-strength segment of the analgesics market, while Extra-Strength Tylenol lagged only Anacin and Excedrin in the $150 million extra-strength segment.[42]

By 1979, the Tylenol brand had captured 25 percent of the over-the-counter analgesics market, with the Extra-Strength version accounting for 70 percent of all Tylenol sales. As the success of Extra-Strength Tylenol became apparent to its competitors, several tried to copy the product. American Home Products and Bristol-Myers introduced their own "extra-strength" versions of Anacin and Excedrin with little success, while Sterling's attempt to introduce a nonaspirin (read,

acetaminophen) version of Bayer flopped.[43]

To Burke and the rest of the top executives at Johnson & Johnson in early 1982, Tylenol seemed unstoppable. Johnson & Johnson had spent over $155 million since 1976 to advertise the brand and, in the words of a *Wall Street Journal* article in September 1982, had "resorted to knuckle-buster lawsuits to beat down competitors' attempts to catch up." From 1976 through 1981, Johnson & Johnson had won four lawsuits against American Home Products' Anacin, preventing the company from advertising what it asserted were Anacin's benefits over Tylenol. Johnson & Johnson also sued Sterling Drug in 1981 to prevent it from advertising that its regular-strength Bayer aspirin was as effective as Extra-Strength Tylenol.[44]

Johnson & Johnson's tactics were not unique. Analgesic companies often sued each other, and most analgesic companies advertised heavily. The major analgesic companies' advertising expenditures averaged 20 percent of sales and went as high as 66 percent of sales when a new brand was introduced.[45]

Tylenol's performance was nonetheless remarkable. McNeil succeeded where other companies failed, and spent less advertising money to do so (see Exhibit 7). In 1981, Tylenol held a 35 percent share of market—as much as the next three brands combined (see Exhibit 8). Johnson & Johnson's sales revenue from all varieties of Tylenol in 1981 was estimated at over $400 million and was expected to reach $500 million by 1983. Tylenol was named one of 1981's top 15 marketing successes by *Marketing & Media Decisions*. In the words of a media planner for a competing aspirin product:

> You walk into a supermarket and go to the shelves with the over-the-counter pharmaceuti-

---

[40] *The Wall Street Journal,* September 2, 1982, p. 12.

[41] Includes all forms of over-the-counter medication bearing the "Tylenol" name.

[42] Nancy Giges, "Long-Awaited Tylenol Ad Drive Highlights Extra-Strength Tablet," *Advertising Age,* May 17, 1976, p. 2.

---

[43] *The Wall Street Journal,* September 2, 1982, p. 12.

[44] *The Wall Street Journal,* September 2, 1982, p. 1.

[45] Ibid.

EXHIBIT 7   Advertising Expenditures for Five Major Analgesic Brands, 1976–1981 ($000)

| | *AHP's Anacin* | *Sterling's Bayer* | *Bristol-Myers'* | | *J&J's Tylenol*[a] |
			Bufferin	*Excedrin*	
1976	$29,889	$15,581	$14,233	$15,841	$4,204
1977	33,981	17,995	12,922	16,252	12,721
1978	34,290	22,510	14,183	16,196	16,988
1979	39,671	25,072	14,818	15,959	23,670
1980	43,513	23,519	14,430	17,297	26,495
1981	44,641	24,650	20,321	19,603	36,766
Total	$225,985	$129,327	$90,907	$101,148	$120,844

[a] Includes all products bearing the Tylenol name.

Source: "Top 200 Advertised Brands Directory," *Marketing & Media Decisions,* July 1979, July 1982.

EXHIBIT 8   Brand Share and Advertising Expenditure for Five Major Analgesic Brands, 1981 ($000)

| | | *In a $1.2 Billion Retail Market* | |
Company	*Brand*	*Market Share*	*Advertising Expenditure*
Johnson & Johnson	Tylenol[a]	35%	$36,766
American Home Products	Anacin[b]	14	44,641
Sterling	Bayer	11	24,650
Bristol-Myers	Bufferin	10	20,321
Bristol-Myers	Excedrin	9	19,603
Other	Other	21	na

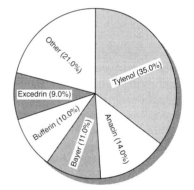

[a] Includes all products bearing the Tylenol name.
[b] Includes Anacin-3.

Source: "The Race to Grab Up Tylenol's Market," *Chemical Week,* November 3, 1982, p. 30; and "Top 200 Advertised Brands Directory," *Marketing & Media Decisions,* July 1982.

cals and you come across what appears to be a million brands. Each brand claims to alleviate the same pain faster than the product next to it, which is made from virtually the same chemical substance as the first one.

On top of this crowd of products, you've got to add the no-name brands that are gaining a foothold, especially in the supermarket chains.

In that kind of cluttered, competitive field, Tylenol has somehow managed to establish itself as the generic term for a non-aspirin pain reliever.[46]

---

[46] Craig Reiss, "How Tylenol Outslugs a Fierce Field," *Marketing & Media Decisions,* Spring 1982 Special, p. 167.

J&J's Response to the Poisonings

The news of the poisonings reached James Burke on Thursday morning, September 30, 1982. That such a tragedy could occur was unthinkable. Nothing of the sort had ever happened in the industry. Burke realized immediately that the company was facing a very serious public health problem. His greatest fear was that the contamination had somehow occurred in one of McNeil's plants.

Thursday, September 30: Crisis and Confusion

Reports out of Chicago were sketchy at best. The Cook County medical officials refused to release any data until they had finished performing autopsies on all of the victims.

At 11:30 A.M., the news arrived that Mary Reiner, a 27-year-old housewife and mother of four, had died earlier that morning. Her purse contained six capsules of Extra-Strength Tylenol, four of which tested positive for cyanide.

Burke decided to take charge of the management of the crisis at the corporate level.[47] Wayne Nelson, a company group chairman with corporate responsibility for McNeil, was in Australia at the time of the poisonings. "One of my first reactions," Burke recalled, "was to get him on the phone and try to find out what could have happened. I remember him saying that he would bet his bonus and a year's salary that the contamination did not occur in the plant because of the controls they had there. That made me somewhat relieved, but I was

still very concerned because we did not know at that point in time that the poisonings were isolated to the Chicago area."

At noon, the Cook County officials held a press conference at which they confirmed that cyanide poisoning was the cause of death in all of the victims. They noted that cyanide had been detected only in random capsules in the bottles of Extra-Strength Tylenol found near the victims. All bottles found had been coded with the batch number MC 2880. The batch originated at a McNeil plant in Fort Washington, Pennsylvania, and was made up of 93,000 bottles containing 4.7 million capsules.

David Collins, the 48-year-old chairman of McNeil Consumer Products, was on a helicopter heading for Fort Washington less than half an hour after learning of the crisis. On his arrival, he found managers were racing between banks of phones and the office of McNeil's president Joseph Chiesa. Collins's first mission at McNeil was to ascertain whether cyanide was used on the premises. Top executives assured him there was no cyanide anywhere in the plant, and he relayed this information to the corporate office. Later, however, Collins learned to his dismay that small amounts of cyanide were present as part of a quality assurance process, required by the FDA, which tested the purity of raw materials used in the manufacture of Tylenol. The Johnson & Johnson public relations office later had to clarify this with the media because of the earlier contention that there was no cyanide in use at the manufacturing site.[48]

---

[47] Thomas Moore, "The Fight to Save Tylenol: The Inside Story of Johnson & Johnson's Struggle to Revive Its Most Important Product," *Fortune*, November 29, 1982.

[48] *Fortune*, November 29, 1982.

PART V

Ethical Responsibilities in Cooperative Capitalism

If this book had been written 25 to 30 years ago, this last section might not have been included. Or it may have taken the form of a brief afterword, because of the widespread belief at the time that companies were, in the words of one economist, "islands of managerial coordination in a sea of market relationships."[1]

This view of economic reality implied that executives' responsibilities stopped at the boundaries of their firms. In other words, executives had authority over what happened "inside" their firms, and within this sphere they had the obligations discussed in the last section. In contrast, "outside" their companies, the managers' relationships with other organizations in society were governed by market competition and by the laws of the society in which they did business.

In the past quarter century, however, it has become increasingly difficult for business executives to think or act as if their responsibilities stopped at their firms' boundaries. It has also become quite difficult to discern just where those boundaries lie. Hence, executives like John Welch, the chairman of the General Electric Corporation, now speak of the "boundaryless" firm.

To understand this dramatic shift in perspective and its consequences for managers' responsibilities, it is important to understand, first, the traditional view of the firm and, second, the powerful forces that have been reshaping it.

---

[1] G. B. Richardson, "The Organization of Industry," *Economic Journal*, October 1972, p. 883.

THE TRADITIONAL VIEW OF FIRMS' BOUNDARIES

The classical view of a firm describes it as, more or less, a medieval castle, the economic equivalent of a large structure built of heavy stone and protected by moats and turreted walls.[2] At the center of the fortress were executives and managers who decided when and how they would react to changes "outside" the firm, such as moves by competitors, changes in government regulation, macroeconomic trends, and so forth. The sphere of authority was defined by four different sets of organizational arrangements. Each was a way of defining what was inside and outside the firm.

Financial Boundaries.   During the decades immediately following World War II, most American companies defined their boundaries in financial terms. They sought to own all of the assets—plants, equipment, intellectual property, like patents and copyright, and so forth—that were crucial to their businesses. They also relied heavily on internal cash flow for financing their operations, which reduced their dependence on such outside sources of capital as banks and the stock market. By reducing their dependence on external capital, the executives of these companies increased their autonomy and enhanced their ability to make independent decisions about how to react to the opportunities and challenges in their companies' environments.

Administrative Boundaries.   The financial boundaries of the traditional firm were reinforced by complementary administrative arrangements. These typically appeared on a company's organization chart. It displayed the formal hierarchical structure of authority within the firm. In essence, a firm's administrative boundaries defined the sphere within which managers exercised hierarchical control over employees; on the other side of this boundary, market forces (decisions by suppliers, customers, and competitors) rather than managerial decision making, determined the allocation of resources.

Social Boundaries.   The third organizational arrangement that separated companies from markets and other organizations was social. This is because companies can be viewed not simply as bundles of wholly owned assets or as administrative hierarchies but as social groups or communities. This perspective on firms was described in detail in the introduction to Part IV.

As members of "corporate communities," employees are bound together in varying degrees by shared values, social norms, and a sense of common

---

[2] This account of the traditional view of firms' boundaries draws heavily on Joseph L. Badaracco, Jr., *The Knowledge Link* (Boston: Harvard Business School Press, 1991), pp. 1–5.

purpose. In some organizations, of course, these social boundaries are weak and loose: Employees feel tenuously connected to each other and their firm. In other cases, epitomized by start-up firms led by a small team of highly dedicated individuals, the sense of membership, belonging, and teamwork is intense. In these cases, it is quite clear who "really belongs" to a company and who does not. In such circumstances, the social boundaries of membership reinforce a company's financial and administrative boundaries.[3]

Contractual Boundaries. The final way of defining and protecting a sphere of managerial power is through what some economists have called "classical contracting." This means the creation of precise, formal, legal arrangements—typically specified in long and detailed contracts—that demarcate the rights and obligations of a firm and the rights and obligations of the parties outside it. In essence, two or more separate parties, each acting in its own self-interest, agree on a particular set of rights that each will retain and on the obligations that each will assume. In the United States, companies have traditionally relied on clear, formal, arm's-length, legally punctilious contracts to define relationships with suppliers, dealers, franchisees, labor unions, and other parties.[4] Within the limits of these obligations, managers can exercise power and make decisions.

None of these four boundaries was ever impermeable. Employees and managers changed jobs; assets were bought and sold; contracts included provisions requiring or encouraging separate parties to collaborate on particular activities; and, despite patents and copyrights, information often flowed freely among different organizations. Nevertheless, many executives worked hard to define and defend their company's boundaries and to maintain a sphere in which they could make independent decisions.

This view of companies as separate entities was, in the minds of many, a powerful normative view. That is, these ideas were not simply a description of the world; they also indicated how companies, economies,

---

[3] The idea that a firm is a social organization originated with the writings of sociologist Ferdinand Tonnies. He distinguished between two different kinds of social organizations. One was a *Gesellschaft*. This is a group that is formed to achieve a particular objective, and its value depends on how well it accomplishes this aim. The other kind of group, which Tonnies called a *Gemeinschaft*, arises, often unintentionally from habit, mutual sympathy, or common beliefs. And it is valued as an end in itself, rather than simply as a means to certain objectives. Tonnies used neighborhoods, towns, and religious bodies as examples of *Gemeinschaft*. See Ferdinand Tonnies, *Community in Society* (East Lansing: Michigan State University Press, 1957), pp. 16–28. A modern version of Tonnies' idea appeared in the readings for Part IV in the excerpt from James MacGregor Burns, in which he distinguished "transformational" leadership from "transactional" leadership.

[4] This account of classical contracting is based on Ian R. MacNeil, "Contracts: Adjustment of Long-Term Economic Relations under Classical, Neo-classical, and Relational Contract Law," *Northwestern University Law Review,* June 1978, pp. 854–905.

and markets *should* be organized. Ever since Adam Smith wrote *The Wealth of Nations* in 1776, basic economic theory has argued that economic efficiency was best achieved through free markets in which independent, atomistic businesses competed against each other. In this system, the owners and managers of each competing firm had direct stakes in the performance of their company, and they also had the power to make major and minor decisions. Hence, responsibility, authority, and accountability all coincided. Competition among these businesses provided discipline: Those that best served consumers' desires prospered; others fell by the wayside.

In theory, in a world of atomistic business units, managers can be held accountable, the rights of property owners are preserved, resources flow to their most productive uses, and society is protected against the economic and political abuses that arise when firms, especially large ones, collude with each other. The twin ideas that firms have fairly well-defined boundaries and that these should be kept sharp are fundamental assumptions in much of our ordinary thinking about businesses and markets. In many cases, however, these ideas are outdated.

DRIVING FORCES

Several powerful forces had been reshaping company boundaries, particularly in the United States, during the past quarter century. As a result, many longstanding, familiar ideas about the roles and responsibilities of managers, about firms and markets, and about business organization have come under attack, and important new ways of thinking about managers, firms, and markets are now emerging.

SOCIAL RESPONSIBILITY AND CORPORATE STAKEHOLDERS

A long-standing, powerful force blurring company boundaries and creating complex links between firms and other organizations falls under the broad heading of "corporate social responsibility."

The basic idea that companies have responsibilities to the communities in which they operate and, in particular, to their stakeholders. A company's stakeholders are, in essence, the groups that may be affected by a company's decisions and those that can influence these decisions. They typically include a company's shareholders, employees, customers, suppliers, and the communities in which the company operates; but other groups may be among the stakeholders as well.

Corporate social responsibility has a long history that may be traced back for many decades. However, beginning in the 1960s, a series of social and political changes led many American managers to reflect more carefully and explicitly on their stakeholders and their responsibilities to groups outside their traditional boundaries. Both the civil rights movement and the environmental movement of the 1960s prompted politicians, civic leaders, members of the clergy, legislators, and others to demand that companies take more active roles in changing the practices and values that they believed to be harmful to groups "outside" the companies.

In addition, during the 1960s, the federal government created the several new regulatory agencies—the Environmental Protection Agency, the Occupational Safety and Health Administration, the Equal Employment Opportunity Commission, and the Consumer Safety Product Commission. These agencies began aggressively issuing regulations affecting activities that many managers had long believed to be their own internal company matters. Though many companies vigorously resisted the early efforts of these agencies, others sought to change their relationships with the outside regulators, seeking to find ways of working cooperatively with government officials to find compromises on disputed issues.

NEW STAKEHOLDERS

After the first oil shock in 1973, a second factor—slower economic growth—brought even more attention to the issue of corporate social responsibility and led, in turn, to a further blurring of companies' traditional boundaries. The oil shock slowed productivity growth in the United States and, except for a few brief periods, it never returned to the levels of the 1960s. In addition, the slower growth was accompanied by intensified competition from overseas—first from the Japanese in crucial industrial sectors like steel, automobiles, and electronics, and then from other competitors in Asia, particularly the "Four Dragons": South Korea, Taiwan, Hong Kong, and Singapore.

As a result of these competitive pressures, companies began to pay more attention to their relationships with important stakeholder groups— particularly workers, labor unions, and local governments. Often, companies sought to shift from adversarial to cooperative relationships with these groups. Employees, labor unions, and local communities became increasingly concerned about job security, particularly when companies began closing plants or moving them to lower-cost sites overseas. As a result, workers and some labor unions began collaborating more closely with managers to find ways to raise productivity and halt the erosion of jobs. At the same time, state and local governments began competing more aggressively for new corporate investments, trying to create "company-friendly" local economic environments that would attract investment, boost local jobs, and raise local tax revenues.

General Motors's Saturn subsidiary is perhaps the most famous example of these developments. Saturn's managers collaborate closely with representatives of the United Auto Workers union on virtually every facet of the plant's operations, and both the state and local governments in Tennessee competed vigorously to have GM locate the Saturn production facility in Tennessee, and they had worked closely with GM executives to help make the plant more competitive.

JAPAN AND AMERICA

One of the most powerful forces behind the rethinking of firms' boundaries has been the rise of Japan as an economic power, with the relative decline of the U.S. economy in comparison to the Japanese. (Note that this decline is described as "relative," not absolute. The question of whether or to what degree the U.S. economy is declining absolutely has, at times, been a matter of intense controversy among economists, political figures, and others.) After World War II, Japan began a 25-year period of "miracle growth." Its gross national product—the total output of a nation's goods and services—grew at a rate of 8 percent per year over this entire period, an economic achievement unprecedented in world history.

Inevitably, many people sought to understand the origins of this extraordinary economic transformation. Many theories have evolved (the bibliography for this section suggests additional readings on this topic), and there is as yet no generally accepted account of what mix of managerial ingenuity, government intervention, marketplace competition, and geopolitical opportunity brought about Japan's success.

Nevertheless, nearly every analyst of the Japanese miracle has called attention to a distinctive feature of Japanese companies: their blurred boundaries. Japanese companies are typically linked with their suppliers, customers, and even competitors, with government agencies, and with labor unions through complex webs of long-term relationships. During the 1950s and 1960s, such government agencies as the Ministry of International Trade and Industry worked closely with the managers of companies in strategic sectors of the economy—such as steel, autos, and electronics—to shape the companies' strategies, their financial plans, and the government policies affecting tariffs, imports, technology transfer, and other factors that shape the competitive environment of Japanese firms. Japanese labor unions were and are organized on a company-by-company basis; their members often include managers of the unionized company; and unions and management have traditionally collaborated closely on many aspects of the management of Japanese firms. Unlike American banks, Japanese banks not only lend funds but also own shares in Japanese companies, thereby forming close and long-term links between the sources of capital and industrial firms.

Studies of Japanese industrial organization also describe an extraordinary form of intercompany collaboration typically known as *enterprise groups* or *keiretsu*. In contemporary Japan, there are two sorts of *keiretsu*.

One is a successor to the *zaibatsu,* which were huge conglomerates that dominated industrial life in Japan for the first half of this century. Although the U.S. Occupation broke up the *zaibatsu* after World War II, many of the original groups later reemerged, though with looser links among the members. The presidents of member companies met regularly, the board of directors of member firms shared common members, and the firms owned small fractions of each others' shares. Through these various links, member firms coordinated important economic decisions.

The second type of *keiretsu* is represented by large manufacturing firms like Toyota. These companies control large networks of suppliers—by holding minority equity positions in suppliers, choosing some of the members of their suppliers' boards of directors, providing financial aid in the form of trade credit, loans, and credit guarantees, and by occasionally providing personnel or technical guidance to aid the managers of the supplier firm.

Many analysts who have studied these complex arrangements for interfirm cooperation in Japan have concluded that they have made important contributions to Japan's economic success.[5] These arrangements helped companies share important information, reduce the risks of large-scale investments, create and operate just-in-time production systems, avoid duplicating each others' research projects, and helped companies to plan and invest with a long-term perspective. As American managers learned more about the many forms of cooperation within the Japanese economy, and as they witnessed the extraordinary success of many Japanese companies, they began to experiment with various kinds of strategic alliances. The result has been a blurring of the traditional boundaries of many American firms.

THE KNOWLEDGE EXPLOSION

Another force leading firms to collaborate with each other and with other organizations is commonly referred to as the "knowledge explosion." In basic terms, this means that the pool of potentially commercializable knowledge throughout the world has been expanding rapidly and is likely to continue to do so in the future. According to some estimates, 90 percent of all the scientists and engineers who have ever lived are living and working at the present time; moreover, their number is likely to double within the next 10 to 15 years. These scientists and engineers are working and competing with each other, not only in the United States and in

---

[5] This brief account of Japanese industrial organization is based on Joseph L. Badaracco, Jr., "The Boundaries of the Firm," in Amitai Etzioni and Paul R. Lawrence, *Socio-Economics: Towards a New Synthesis* (Armonk, N.Y.: M.M.E. Sharpe, 1991), pp. 293–329.

developed countries but in almost every nation. As a result, the pool of knowledge, skills, technology, and know-how that companies can turn into products and services is expanding rapidly.

For firms and managers, the consequences of the knowledge explosion are dramatic. Even the largest and most prosperous firms are finding that they can no longer "go it alone" to develop technology and skills for their future products and services. As a result, the 1980s witnessed an explosion of so-called strategic alliances among American corporations. These alliances take many different forms: joint ventures, minority equity ownership (in which one firm buys a small fraction of another firm's shares), R&D consortia, and various informal linkages between companies, or sometimes between companies and university research labs, hospitals, or government agencies.

These alliances enable companies and other organizations to share the costs and risks of developing new knowledge and technology, as well as to bring together complementary skills and capabilities. Taken together, this explosion of strategic alliances has further blurred the boundaries of the vast majority of American companies, because the partners in these alliances usually share the management authority and financing of their joint activities.[6]

An Historical Perspective.   It is important to place the blurring of firms' boundaries in a longer-term perspective. Against the broad sweep of the history of commerce and business organization, the concept of a company as a clearly defined zone of ownership and control, surrounded by market relationships, is an unusual way of describing economic reality.

The history of business, until the Industrial Revolution, is basically a story of indefinite, shifting, flexible boundaries around business activities. "Businesses" were usually enmeshed in relationships with families, which for centuries were basic economic units; with villages and manors, the organizing units of agriculture; with guilds, which regulated the relationship of apprentices, journeymen, and masters; and with towns and local communities. Only in Great Britain, about 200 years ago, did a self-regulating market of separate economic units appear, and the United States subsequently adopted this pattern of economic behavior. However, as Britain's economic might grew, the nations of continental Europe responded by creating even closer links among and between companies, government agencies, labor unions, and other elements of society. Similarly, when Japan was threatened with the prospect of foreign invasion 130 years ago, it responded by creating its own distinctive pattern of collaboration

---

[6] For an extended analysis of the relationship between the creation of a rapidly growing global knowledge pool and the increasing reliance on strategic alliances, see Joseph L. Badaracco, Jr., *The Knowledge Link* (Boston: Harvard Business School Press, 1991).

throughout society. Hence, as firms today create boundary-blurring arrangements, they are not creating new forms of corporate organization but, rather, recreating modern versions of long-established ways of doing business.

NEW RESPONSIBILITIES FOR MANAGERS

Extensive cooperative relationships among companies and other organizations create a new set of responsibilities for business managers. Unfortunately, however, responsibilities of executives in the system of cooperative capitalism are far from well-defined. As noted earlier, the ethical responsibilities of individuals have been a topic of reflection and analysis for millennia; and managers' responsibilities as economic agents and organization leaders have been studied carefully for many decades. However, this fourth sphere of responsibilities is for the most part uncharted territory, and the five basic issues described below, as well as the readings and cases in this section, provide an introductory map for a newly emerging, rapidly evolving, and particularly complex sphere of responsibilities. The basic issues may be described in terms of five questions.

WHERE DOES THE BUCK STOP?

The new forms of cooperation raise the question of how far managers' responsibilities extend. Clearly, when managers' authority extends beyond their firms, their accountability does so as well. But how far?

In the traditional "Adam Smith world" of separate firms, each run by a manager responsible to shareholders, accountability was quite clear. The market provided a series of economic hurdles, and shareholders decided how well or how poorly managers had met the rigors of the marketplace. However, this classic model of social responsibility assumed that firms had sharp boundaries and that a single group of managers had authority over an organization. But where, in President Harry Truman's phrase, does the buck stop when a company and another organization share ownership and control of some activity and when do the contractual arrangements between the parties encourage cooperation, instead of precisely defining rights and obligations?

WHO HAS LEGITIMATE POWER?

The traditional idea of firms with sharp boundaries meshed well with fundamental ideas about political legitimacy. In theory, in a democratic state, the will of the people is transformed by the political system into legitimate laws, and everyone—including companies and their executives—is obligated to obey these laws. The American way of translating this principle into political reality was strongly influenced by deep suspicion of concentrated political or economic power. This is reflected in the United States Constitution, which divides the federal government into three competing branches and which reserves important powers for state governments. The fear of concentrated economic power also appears in the long American tradition of antitrust law and regulation.

But what happens if large companies, surrounded by networks of smaller firms that supply the giant firm or buy its products, come together in close and collaborative relationships with each other and with important government agencies? This creates the possibility of large-scale concentrations of both economic and political power. It also raises the risk that government decisions will reflect less the will of citizens and more the interests of the firms collaborating with government agencies. The phrase "Japan Inc." is a shorthand way of underlining the enormous power that a handful of Japanese government agencies and a small number of huge firms wielded over the entire Japanese economy in the decades immediately following World War II.

As a result, when companies blur their boundaries through extensive collaboration with suppliers, customers, government agencies, local communities, and other stakeholders, their executives must decide how to use their *political* power, as well as their economic power, in responsible ways.

WHERE DO A MANAGER'S BASIC LOYALTIES LIE?

Because the markets for capital, knowledge, goods, and to some extent labor have become global, some business executives now confront a serious question about their basic loyalties. In short form, the question is this: As firms expand their international operations and become involved in more boundary-blurring relationships in other countries, should their executives think of themselves as "global managers," or do they owe some basic loyalty to the nation of which they are citizens? In other words, should an American executive simply search worldwide for the best deal for her company? Or should she take into account the interests of the fellow Americans who make up these companies' workforces, managerial ranks, suppliers, and so forth?

An important reason to take local and national interests into account is that many companies have depended heavily on the resources and contributions of their home countries. Hence, it is plausible to argue that they have incurred obligations that must be repaid. This would mean that American companies cannot simply take technology developed in the United States and make it available in places where it will be commercialized and used in ways that harm the interests of American workers and communities.

This set of questions becomes even more complex in a world in which many countries practice different forms of industrial policy. The term *industrial policy* refers to government policies which, directly or indirectly, aim to support and build a country's position in important industries. After World War II, for example, the Japanese government used a program of tariffs, subsidies, government guidance, exemptions from antitrust policy, and other policies to help companies in steel, autos, electronics, and other industries achieve international competitiveness. Following the Japanese model, many other countries now practice similar policies. In essence, if other countries are directly pursuing their own national interests by supporting domestic firms and trying to build them into "national champions," then the executives of firms in other countries may have a responsibility to defend and support their own nations' interests.

These questions have become even more complex in recent years with the rise of economic regionalism. Many analysts believe the global economy is evolving into three significant blocks. One is the European Community, another is the North American free trade zone, and the third is an East Asian block, which is now led by Japan and may ultimately be dominated by China. The ties within these regions originate not only in trade patterns but also in common cultural, religious, and historical heritages. For example, some believe that the early years of the 21st century will be dominated by the Confucian-based Pacific economies whose economic dynamism will overcome the waning Judeo-Christian Atlantic community of nations. Again, the same question arises: Should an executive simply seek the best deal for his or her firm on a global basis, or should companies give weight to loyalties, common histories, national and regional interests, and common ties that distinguish regions or nations from each other?

SHOULD ONE DO AS THE ROMANS DO?

As companies expand their international operations, their executives face a classic business ethics issue. This is the question of which ethical standards should govern their decisions: Those of the home country of a business executive or those of the host country? Or some international or universal set of ethical principles? And if companies from two or more different traditions form a strategic alliance, whose standards and values should govern their decisions?

The old saying "When in Rome, do as the Romans do" is one answer to these questions, and it often leads to pragmatic ways of resolving difficult issues. By following the Roman approach, a manager can avoid ruffling feathers or creating animosity. But what if the local practice involves bribery, discrimination, or violations of antitrust and other laws that executives are obligated to obey at home? Executives in these circumstances can then face difficult moral and practical dilemmas.

Unfortunately, a common bias in thinking about issues of cultural relativism is to assume that Western or Anglo-American standards are morally superior and that countries following different norms are somehow backward or morally deficient. This assumption often blinds people to the fact that other nations and cultures, while they may view particular practices in a different ethical light, do so because of laws, traditions, and principles, and these often have histories and ethical claims that merit the same respect as the Anglo-American approach or may even be superior to it. Put differently, many issues of cultural relativism are issues of "right versus right," not right versus wrong.

HOW SHOULD A MANAGER BALANCE RESPONSIBILITIES TO COMPETING STAKEHOLDERS?

In the traditional model of firms and markets, managers had responsibilities to a single set of external stakeholders—the shareholders of their company. In the contemporary world of blurred boundaries, strategic alliances, industrial policy, and corporate social responsibility, the situation is significantly different. Now, managers must find ways to balance their responsibilities to a wide range of stakeholder groups. Some remain "outside" a firm that they are not connected to through a strategic alliance or some other form of collaboration; others may be collaborating actively with the company and its managers. In both cases, however, the decisions of a company's managers affect the stakeholders, and the stakeholders often have the power to affect the firm.

Because the issue of managers' responsibilities within cooperative capitalism is a relatively new one, there are no clearly defined rules or guidelines that managers can use when they are engaged in the inevitable balancing act created by competing responsibilities to different stakeholders. In some cases, the issue is not a difficult one. Hard work, open communication, and imagination can often lead to "win-win" solutions from which all stakeholders benefit. The more difficult cases arise, however, when a win-win solution is not in the cards and an executive must make hard choices among a range of competing and legitimate obligations to different stakeholders.

Since there are few if any widely accepted guidelines for such dilemmas, a sound way for managers to approach these situations is to rely on the fundamental principles presented in the first section of this book. These concepts, which were introduced as different elements in the framework of individual decision making, can also serve as valuable guides to balancing responsibilities to different stakeholder groups:

1. The ethics of *consequences,* for example, asks managers to carefully assess the benefits, harms, and risks for all the parties who will be affected by a decision. Thus, the utilitarian perspective encourages them to find ways to resolve an issue that maximizes benefits and minimizes harms.

2. The ethics of *rights and duties* suggests another crucial idea, one that balances some of the deficiencies of a purely utilitarian approach. It reminds managers that they have a duty to respect the rights of various stakeholder groups. It tells them, in effect, that they cannot run roughshod over these rights—whether out of narrow self-interest or in a rush to do the greatest good for the greatest number.

3. The ethics of *character and virtue* asks managers to assess their obligations to different stakeholder groups in terms of organizational and personal values. In particular, this way of thinking asks them to assess which of various alternatives, each with different consequences for stakeholders and each with a different effect on stakeholders' rights, the managers can live with. It also asks them to consider which alternative harmonizes best with the values and commitments that distinguish their company.

4. The pragmatic *Machiavellian* approach is a reminder that, whatever alternative is chosen for balancing stakeholder responsibilities, it must work in the world as it is. Taken in concert with the three other perspectives, this view can help to guide managers in selecting an alternative that has a higher risk of being implemented successfully.

The drawback of relying solely on these four perspectives is that they are all quite abstract. Hence, a final important step for managers is to examine the terms of their relationships with various stakeholders and strategic allies. Often, these involve explicit agreements about how each party will behave. These explicit understandings or agreements can provide guidance for managers seeking responsible, practical ways of resolving an ethical issue involving a company's stakeholders. In other cases, in which there is no explicit agreement, managers may find commitments and expectations *implicit* in the way they and other parties have dealt with each other in the past that can guide them toward a sound resolution—in both ethical and practical terms—of the problem they face.

OVERVIEW OF READINGS AND CASES

Like the other three sections, this one begins with a collection of extended excerpts from important classical thinkers, such as Niccolo Machiavelli, as well as the works of several contemporary historians, economists, and political scientists. The readings all address a single central question: What responsibilities do executives have when their companies are engaged in complex forms of collaboration with other organizations?

While some of the excerpts describe the forces leading companies to cooperation and others describe the various forms that cooperation can take, two of the excerpts—one written by Machiavelli and another by Robert Axelrod—suggest fundamentally different approaches for managers who must make decisions in the emerging world of cooperative capitalism. Each of the two readings presents what is, in effect, a basic paradigm for effective and responsible decision making.

For Machiavelli, the optimal strategy in a world of uncertain boundaries and complicated alliances is the sophisticated pursuit of an organization's self-interest. Machiavelli's ideas were forged during the tumultuous years of the 15th century in Italy, a period of extraordinary political turmoil, as well as of artistic and technological ferment. J. H. Plumb, an expert on the Italian Renaissance, has written:

> Diplomacy as we know it arose in the Italy of the Renaissance. It grew strong in the 15th century through the equilibrium of power created by the three great northern states of Italy—Milan, Venice, and Florence. It appealed to the leaders of these mercantile societies. They enjoyed and believed in the efficacy of hard bargaining and were not unaware of the merits of partnership for the destruction of rivals (and partners needed supervision as well as persuasion). The collection of intelligence, the assessment of personalities and contingencies, was, early on, the stock-in-trade of bankers. The application of these commercial techniques to the service of the State was effortlessly made.[7]

Machiavelli's ideas, though developed as political advice for the leaders of Florence, can be used—by analogy—as guidance for business executives whose companies must make their way in an uncertain world of competitors, partners, and stakeholders. In the minds of many, of course, Machiavelli's approach to these issues is purely pragmatic and essentially amoral; for others, it is a hyperrealistic approach to ethics, because it starts with an unvarnished view of the harsh environment in which countries and, by extension, firms often find themselves. It places survival—whether of city states or companies, their employees, and the communities and other stakeholders that depend on them—at the center of leaders' responsibilities.

The alternative perspective provided by Robert Axelrod, a professor of political science and public policy, offers a more optimistic perspective. His analysis of contemporary game theory, as well as the application of this theory to many spheres of life, suggests that a philosophy very different from Machiavelli's is more likely to succeed in the long run.

Axelrod's approach is sometimes called "Tit for Tat." It seeks to avoid unnecessary conflict by *(a)* initially offering cooperation with other parties, *(b)* retaliating when other parties act unfairly, *(c)* quickly forgiving others for failure to cooperate, and *(d)* not deviating from *(a)*, *(b)*, and *(c)*, so other parties can understand that a person or a company is following this approach and can make their plans accordingly.

---

[7] J. H. Plumb, *The Italian Renaissance* (Boston: American Heritage/Houghton Mifflin Company, 1985), pp. 18–19. Reprinted by permission of *American Heritage* magazine, a division of Forbes, Inc., © Forbes Inc., 1985.

The cases that follow the readings provide an opportunity to apply and test these ideas in circumstances in which managers and their companies are involved in alliances with other organizations. At the same time, the cases provide an opportunity to examine the specific issues of responsibility described earlier in this introduction: the questions of where the buck stops, of legitimate political power, of loyalty to nations or regions, of cultural relativism, and of balancing stakeholder commitments.

For example, the first case in this section — "AT&T Consumer Products" — raises the issue of whether a large American company, whose past prosperity has depended heavily on the support and contributions of governments, individuals, and other groups in the United States, has a responsibility to try to keep jobs in the United States when it considers the possibility of international expansion. Then, the case raises specific questions of implementation that companies face when they expand their operations internationally. In particular, do they follow local practice, home country practice, or some sort of "global best practice" when they make decisions about wages, environmental controls, gender-based hiring, bribery, and government relations.

Other cases in this section focus on some of the particular issues described above. "McDonnell Douglas and Taiwan Aerospace" concentrates on the question of whether companies that are considering the export of technology have a duty to consider the interests of their home country as they make these decisions. In addition, this case deals with the issues of honesty and fair negotiations in creating a strategic alliance.

Several of the cases concentrate on important contemporary issues of corporate social responsibility. "Burroughs Wellcome & AZT" examines the issues of fair pricing of products that have significant effects on the health and lives of the people who use them. "BayBank Boston" considers the problems many banks face when developing the lending policies that treat different communities fairly and the company's efforts to create alliances with important stakeholders in the Boston community. "Australian Paper Manufacturing" places stakeholder issues in the context of major strategic commitments and environmental pollution. And "Lotus MarketPlace:Households" poses the question of what constitutes socially responsible behavior when new technology raises issues of privacy and risks a backlash against a company and its products.

The last two cases in this section place all of these issues in an international context. "Bribery and Extortion in International Business" asks students to analyze a series of episodes and decide which of them involve appropriate relations between a company and other groups in society and which violate some important ethical guidelines.

Finally, "RU 486" serves as a summary case, since it raises virtually every one of the issues that managers face when new relationships blur their corporate boundaries. The protagonists in the case, the executives of Roussel UCLAF, a French pharmaceutical firm, must decide whether to commercialize a new product, RU 486. This drug, when taken by a woman in her pregnancy, causes a miscarriage approximately 95 percent of the time. Hence, it has been dubbed "the French abortion pill." The executives of Roussel had to decide whether and how to commercialize this product in France, the United States, and China. Their company was involved in strategic alliances with the French government, with important French research laboratories, with the World Health Organization, and with the German chemical giant, Hoechst. Each of these relationships introduced a particular set of responsibilities for Roussel's managers. The social consequences of the widespread use of RU 486 were likely to be very significant. Standards and practices on the abortion issue varied among the different countries in which Roussel could market its product, thereby raising the question of which country's standard should be followed. The company needed an appropriate political strategy to accompany its ethical and managerial decisions, because of the intense and complex politics surrounding the abortion issue. It was also far from clear where the responsibility of Roussel's executives ended and those of other organizations began. And finally, Machiavellian policies were one set of options open to Roussel's managers.

"RU 486" is, in fact, a summary case for this entire book. It raises issues of individual values and commitments for Roussel's executives; it asks how strong their responsibilities to the company's shareholders were; and it asks students to examine the issues of stewardship that these executives faced as they considered the effects of different courses of action on the other managers and employees of Roussel. And, as noted above, the case raises virtually every issue that arises from the blurring of firms' boundaries.

SUGGESTIONS FOR ADDITIONAL READING

Joseph L. Badaracco, Jr., *The Knowledge Link,* (Boston: Harvard Business School, 1991).

Richard T. DeGeorge, *Business Ethics* (New York: MacMillian Publishing, 1992), chapters 14, 15, and 16.

Thomas Donaldson, *The Ethics of International Business,* (New York: Oxford University Press, 1989).

William M. Evan and Edward R. Freeman, "A Stakeholder Theory of the Modern Corporation: Kantian Capitalism," in Thomas L. Beauchamp and Norman E. Bowie, eds., *Ethical Theory and Business* (Englewood Cliffs, N.J.: Prentice Hall, 1988), pp. 89–99.

Amitai Etzioni, *The Moral Dimension: Toward a New Economics* (New York: Free Press, 1988), chapters 11–14.

R. Edward Freeman and Daniel R. Gilbert, Jr., *Corporate Strategy and the Search for Ethics* (Englewood Cliffs, N.J.: Prentice Hall, 1988).

John R. Meyer and James N. Gustafson, eds., *The U.S. Business Corporation: An Institution in Transition* (Cambridge, Mass.: Ballinger, 1988), chapters 6, 7, and 11.

N. Craig Smith, *Morality and the Marketplace* (London: Rutledge, 1990).

MORAL RESPONSIBILITIES IN COOPERATIVE CAPITALISM

The excerpts in this note address one question: What responsibilities do business executives have when their companies are involved in complex relationships with other organizations—relationships that blur the traditional boundaries of the firm?

The excerpts are all taken from contemporary works, with the exception of a passage from *The Prince* by Niccolo Machiavelli. The reason for the contemporary focus is that in recent years many companies, particularly in the United States, have been creating novel cooperative relationships. These now link many firms with their suppliers, customers, investors, labor unions, governments, and even their competitors. This development has prompted scholars in many fields to seek new paradigms for understanding the work and responsibilities of business executives.

There is, as yet, no "Adam Smith" of cooperative capitalism, but these excerpts cast light on its driving forces, basic characteristics, and wide-ranging implications.

Chalmers Johnson

Chalmers Johnson is a professor at the University of California, San Diego, and a long-term student of Japan. These excerpts come from his book *MITI and the Japanese Miracle.*[1]

The Japanese case differs from the Western market economies, the communist dictatorships of development, or the new states of the postwar world. The most significant difference is that in Japan the state's role in the economy is shared with the private sector, and both the public and private sectors have perfected means to make the market work for developmental goals.

The broad pattern of development since the late 1920s has been from self-coordination to its opposite, state control, and then to a synthesis of the two, cooperation. The chief advantage of this form is that it leaves ownership and management in private hands, thereby achieving higher levels of competition than under state control, while it affords the state much greater degrees of social goal-setting and influence over private decisions than under self-control. Its principal disadvantage is that it is very hard to achieve.

This form of the government–business relationship is not peculiarly or uniquely Japanese; the Japanese have merely worked harder at perfecting it and have employed it in more sectors than other capitalist nations. The so-called military-industrial complex in the United States, to the extent that it identifies an economic relationship and is not merely a political epithet, refers to the same thing. If one were to

---

[1] Reprinted from *MITI and the Japanese Miracle* by Chalmers Johnson with the permission of the publishers, Stanford University Press. © 1982 by the Board of Trustees of the Leland Stanford Junior University.

Ilyse Barkan prepared this note under the direction of Joseph L. Badaracco, Jr.
Reprinted with permission.

extend the kinds of relationships that exist between the U.S. Department of Defense and such corporations as Boeing, Lockheed, North American Rockwell, and General Dynamics to other sectors of industry, and if one were also to give the government the power to choose the strategic sectors and to decide when they were to be phased out, then one would have a close American approximation of the postwar Japanese system.

As noted earlier, the cooperative government–business relationship in the capitalist developmental state is very difficult to achieve and maintain. Even with such deeply entrenched social supports for cooperation as a shared outlook among government and industrial leaders because of common education (for instance, at Todai Law) and an extensive cross-penetration of elites because of early retirement from government service and reemployment in big business, the Japanese have difficulty in keeping public–private cooperation on the tracks. Industry is quite willing to receive governmental assistance, but it does not like government orders (as the steel and automobile industries illustrate).

In addition, the Japanese have fostered social supports for cooperations. We have already mentioned two of them—the essentially bureaucratic education of both public and private managers and the extensive "old boy" networks.

Some other social supports for government–business cooperation include the virtual impotence of corporate stockholders because of the industrial financing system; a workforce fragmented among labor aristocrats enjoying semi-lifetime employment, temporaries, small-scale subcontractors and enterprise unions; a system of collecting private savings through the postal system, concentrating it in government accounts, and investing it in accordance with a separate, bureaucratically controlled budget (FILP); some 115 government corporations covering such high-risk areas as petroleum exploration, atomic power development, the phasing out of the mining industry, and computer software development (these corporations are the successors to the national policy companies of the 1930s, the *eidan* of the wartime era, and the *kodan* of

the occupation); and a distribution system that serves not only to retail goods but also to keep the unemployed, the elderly, and the infirm working, thereby weakening demands for a welfare state in Japan.

Perhaps the most important market-conforming method of intervention is administrative guidance. This power, which amounts to an allocation of discretionary and unsupervised authority to the bureaucracy, is obviously open to abuse, and may, if used improperly, result in damage to the market. But it is an essential power of the capitalist developmental state for one critical reason: It is necessary to avoid overly detailed laws that, by their very nature; are never detailed enough to cover all contingencies and yet, because of their detail, put a straitjacket on creative administration. One of the great strengths of Japanese industrial policy is its ability to deal with discrete complex situations without first having to find or enact a law that covers the situation. Highly detailed statutes serve the interests primarily of lawyers, not of development. The Japanese political economy is strikingly free of lawyers; many of the functions performed by lawyers in other societies are performed in Japan by bureaucrats using administrative guidance.

The Japanese of course rely on law, but on short and highly generalized laws. They then give concrete meaning to these laws through bureaucratically originated cabinet orders, ordinances, rules, and administrative guidance.

Alfred D. Chandler, Jr.

Alfred D. Chandler is the Isidor Straus Professor of Business History, emeritus, at Harvard Business School. His studies of the evolution of the large corporation have won many awards, including the Pulitzer Prize for history. This excerpt is from *Scale and Scope.*[2]

---

[2] Reprinted by permission of the publishers from *Scale and Scope: The Dynamics of Industrial Capitalism* by Alfred D. Chandler, Jr., Cambridge, Mass.: Belknap Press of Harvard University Press, Copyright © 1990 by Alfred D. Chandler, Jr.

German entrepreneurs made the investments and created the organizational capabilities needed to form a number of major industries. But the new large enterprises in Germany concentrated on the production of industrial goods, whereas those in the United States produced and distributed consumer goods as well. The basic difference between the two countries was, however, that industrial leaders in the United States continued to compete functionally and strategically for market share, while in Germany they often preferred to negotiate with one another to maintain market share at home and in some cases abroad. In the United States managerial capitalism was more competitive; in Germany it became more cooperative. This brand of modern industrial capitalism — *cooperative managerial capitalism* — was one aspect of the arrival in Germany of what scholars have termed organized capitalism.

Economic differences — those of markets, sources of supply, and methods of finance — played a part in the differentiating process. So did cultural differences, as reflected in "rules of the game" (legal or otherwise) and in educational systems. The most striking legal difference — the ability to enforce cartels and other agreements between competitors in courts of law — meant that German industrials had much less incentive to merge into industrywide holding companies. Instead, agreements as to price, output, and marketing territories were enforced through looser and more temporary federations — conventions, syndicates, and communities of interest — legal devices that were rarely used in Britain or the United States.

In the economic realm the most important difference came in the financing of enterprise. Differences in markets were important, too (differences in sources of supply were less important in the long run), but the German financial arrangements were especially distinctive. Self-financing remained the major source of growth; in Germany, however, unlike Britain and the United States, large multipurpose banks played a major role in providing funds for the initial investment in the new, capital-intensive industries — investment that was essential to achieve the economies of scale and scope. Such a role

meant that the representatives of banks sat on the boards of many enterprises and so participated in top-level decisions more than was the case in either Britain or the United States.

The Economist

These excerpts are taken from a survey entitled "Capitalism: In Triumph, In Flux" that appeared in *The Economist* in May 1990.[3]

It used to be so simple. Between roughly 1850 and 1880 the capitalist system developed some clear categories of people and the things they did. There were workers, managers, shareholders, creditors, customers, entrepreneurs. Shareholders, creditors, and workers provided the vital inputs of capital and labor. Shareholders employed managers to organize these inputs to produce outputs, the goods and services that they sold to their customers. The entrepreneurs buzzed around, full of ideas for new companies or new products. Then, as now, it was hard to define an entrepreneur, but you knew one when you saw one.

These simple certainties have long since given way to all sorts of complexities. Now workers want a say in management, and a slice of the profits. Managers want to own shares. Many people want their own companies, in which they are manager, shareholder, and worker all in one. None of these demands is unnatural; they all reflect a world in which people are richer, better educated, more confident, and praise be for all that.

Yet, there is another side to them. It has little to do with the drawbacks that are usually attributed to stock markets — their periodic volatility, their indifference to "real values" (whatever those may be), their gullibility. These alleged defects are, at most, symptoms of a much deeper malaise, which began with the introduction of publicly traded shares and has grown ever since: the change in the meaning of ownership.

To hold equity in a company is to own part of it: that is a legal axiom, which has changed

---

[3] Copyright © 1990 The Economist Newspaper Group, Inc. Reprinted with permission.

hardly at all in more than 100 years. Behind the legal front, however, the functional reality of equity has been transformed. To shareholders in a typical public company in America or Britain — call it Anglo-Saxon, Inc. — a share is now little more than a betting slip.

There are three questions worth putting to professional money managers in America and Britain. When they buy a slice of Anglo-Saxon, Inc., do they think of themselves as a part owner? Or are they placing a bet on tomorrow's race? Or, which is increasingly the case, have they bought the shares only because the company is a constituent of a particular stock market index which they are tracking?

The answers are usually revealing. Few think of themselves as owners, and they tend to be older than the rest. If the trend continues, every one of the next generation of British and American money managers will be punter-capitalists. Yet they usually have good, rational reasons for becoming punters. They are there to maximize the returns on the savings entrusted to them.

Buy-outs are the most visible sign of the revolt against punter-capitalism. That does not mean they are its only alternative. The Anglo-Saxon version of stock market ownership and institutionalized savings never caught on in some countries; and even in America and Britain there are conspicuous exceptions to the rule. All belong to an older tradition — that of proprietor-capitalism.

Michael E. Porter

Michael Porter is a professor at Harvard Business School. These are excerpts from *The Competitive Advantage of Nations,* published in 1990.[4]

The competitive industries in a nation will not be evenly distributed across the economy, as

---

[4] Reprinted with the permission of The Free Press, an imprint of Simon & Schuster from *The Competitive Advantage of Nations* by Michael E. Porter. Copyright © 1990 by Michael E. Porter.

emerges clearly from the analysis of individual nations in Part III. A nation's successful industries are usually linked through vertical (buyer/supplier) or horizontal (common customers, technology, channels, etc.) relationships.

A particularly striking example is in Denmark. Figure 4–5, which includes a number of the industries in which Denmark is internationally competitive, illustrates how these industries are all connected. Within Denmark there are also clusters of competitive industries related to the home (household products and furnishings) and to health (pharmaceuticals, vitamins, medical equipment, and the like). The health cluster is linked to the agricultural cluster by technology and raw material requirements.

Once a cluster forms, the whole group of industries becomes mutually supporting. Benefits flow forward, backward, and horizontally. Aggressive rivalry in one industry tends to spread to others in the cluster, through the exercise of bargaining power, spin-offs, and related diversification by established firms. Entry from other industries within the cluster spurs upgrading by stimulating diversity in R&D approaches and providing a means for introducing new strategies and skills. Information flows freely and innovations diffuse rapidly through the conduits of suppliers or customers who have contact with multiple competitors. Interconnections within the cluster, often unanticipated, lead to the perception of new ways of competing and entirely new opportunities. People and ideas combine in new ways. Silicon Valley provides a good example.

The cluster becomes a vehicle for maintaining diversity and overcoming the inward focus, inertia, inflexibility, and accommodation among rivals that slows or blocks competitive upgrading and new entry. The presence of the cluster helps increase information flow, the likelihood of new approaches, and new entry from spin-offs, downstream, upstream, and related industries. It plays, in a sense, the role of creating "outsiders" from within the nation that will compete in new ways. National industries are thus more able to sustain advantage instead of losing it to other nations who innovate.

Joseph L. Badaracco

Joseph L. Badaracco, Jr., is a lecturer at the Harvard Business School. These excerpts are from an article entitled "Changing Forms of the Corporation."

The form, or forms, of American companies may be undergoing a sea change with potentially dramatic effects. The transformation could make U.S. companies more competitive or less so. It could reshape our thinking about the workings of markets, the tasks of business managers and public officials, and the political role of firms. The new forms could even alter basic concepts of the corporation.

The nature and extent of this transformation are difficult to determine. The new forms rearrange familiar organizational building blocks, such as joint ventures, in protean, sometimes bewildering patterns. Changes are taking place on the boundaries of firms, rather than at their core, where analysts and observers have, for decades, sought and found them.

Much thinking about firms presupposes that boundaries of some sort separate them from their markets or, more broadly, their environments. Arm's-length, explicitly contractual, market-based relations with other organizations define a firm's boundaries, within which managers exercise authority and deploy assets that the firm owns or controls. But recently, in myriad ways, managers have been blurring these boundaries with networks of cooperative arrangements with other companies, labor unions, universities, and government bodies.

Sharp boundaries around firms are temporal exceptions and not the eternal rule; yet, blurred boundaries are new for certain large, powerful American firms with vast resources and long traditions of independence. . . .

IBM's preference for independent action was epitomized during the early 1960s by its internal development of the 360 series computers. Despite the colossal financial and technological risks involved in this project, IBM did not seek partners. IBM's later decision to create relationships with Intel, MCI, Rolm, and others was a startling departure from its postwar strategy: In the previous 30 years, it had made only a few minor acquisitions and engaged in only a handful of joint projects.[5] The same pattern appears in IBM's overseas activities. Like many other multinationals, IBM was often compelled to use local partners because of government requirements and unfamiliarity with local markets in its early years. But IBM resisted pressure to collaborate. It chose to withdraw from India, rather than sell a minority interest in its Indian concern to local partners. Only the coercive powers of the Japanese state compelled IBM, during the late 1960s and 1970s, to share some of its technology—which proved to be patents on the verge of obsolescence—with Japanese firms. It was not until the 1980s that IBM abandoned its policy of avoiding joint projects with other companies.[6]

Cooperative arrangements are also new in a second sense: During the early 1980s they became much more common in certain service and manufacturing industries. Several recent studies have revealed this pattern. One, for example, documenting a rise in the number of domestic U.S. joint ventures, showed the greatest increases occurring in service industries, such as advertising, financial services, communications systems and services, and database development and management. The next largest cluster of expanding cooperation appeared among manufacturers of electrical equipment, consumer electronics, computer peripherals, software, robots, electrical components, and aerospace technology. In some of these sectors, more domestic joint ventures were announced in a single year of the early 1980s than in the previous 15 or 20 years.[7] In Europe, cooperative agreements may have increased nearly tenfold between 1980 and 1985. International joint ventures involving U.S. firms and overseas partners have nearly doubled since 1978.[8]

---

[5] Robert Sobel, *IBM vs. Japan* (New York: Stein and Day, 1986), p. 191.

[6] Ibid., pp. 155–56.

[7] Kathryn Rudie Harrigan, *Strategies for Joint Ventures* (Lexington, Mass.: D.C. Heath, 1985), pp. 7–12.

[8] Karen J. Hladik, "International Joint Ventures" (PhD dissertation, Harvard Business School, 1984), p. 56.

Finally, cooperative relationships proliferated in functional areas where they had not been common. Most of the industries mentioned above are R&D dependent or even R&D intensive. Technical cooperation and joint research and development were the fastest growing subcategories of cooperative arrangements among European firms between 1980 and 1985, and a similar trend appears in international joint ventures involving U.S. firms.[9] This last is notable because, during the 1960s and 1970s, U.S. firms that relied heavily on R&D tended to form wholly owned subsidiaries for their overseas business, rather than use joint ventures.[10] The extensive cooperation among universities, their faculties, and private companies in biotechnology has recently been dubbed "the university-industrial complex."[11]

Charles H. Ferguson

Charles H. Ferguson is a research associate at the Center for Technology, Policy, and Industrial Development at M.I.T. These are excerpts from his article. "From the People Who Brought You Voodoo Economics," which appeared in the *Harvard Business Review* in 1988.[12]

In the wake of voodoo economics, U.S. corporate executives must now defend themselves against an equally dangerous successor—voodoo competitive doctrine. In fact, this country faces serious problems that cannot be solved by the unaided efforts of individual entrepreneurs, however ingenious. Nor does the decline of vital U.S. industries—financial services, automobiles, steel, advanced electronics—reflect the immanent advantages of small companies over large companies.

Japanese, Korean, and even German competitors seem not to share America's passion for fragmentation and entrepreneurial zeal. U.S. industry falls victim not to nimble, small companies but to huge, industrial complexes embedded in stable, strategically coordinated alliances often supported by protectionist governments—exactly by the kind of political and economic structures that, according to the free-market entrepreneurship argument, give rise to stagnant cartels.

The Japanese semiconductor industry is—like Japanese steel—a stable, concentrated, government-protected, vertically integrated oligopoly that built its success not on new companies and novel ideas but on imported U.S. technology and high-quality mass manufacturing. The United States prototyped and patented innovative technologies. Japanese companies then licensed, imitated, or sometimes stole them, ultimately overpowering smaller U.S. companies in maturing world markets.

Six companies—Hitachi, Fujitsu, NEC, Toshiba, Mitsubishi, and Matsushita—have consistently controlled 80 percent of Japanese semiconductor production. (They also account for 60 percent of Japanese semiconductor consumption.) Not counting unconsolidated affiliates, of which each company has many, the smallest of these companies now has annual revenues exceeding $15 billion. These same companies also control 80 percent of Japanese computer production, 80 percent of telecommunications equipment production, and about half of Japanese consumer electronics production. All have close linkages, including equity cross-ownership, with suppliers and affiliated industrial groups, banks, insurance companies, and trading houses. They have a long history of cooperation with MITI, Nippon Telephone & Telegraph (NTT), and each other.

Linkages unthinkable in the United States are routinely found in the Japanese industry. In 1986, for example, Sumitomo Bank and Sumitomo Life Insurance together held not only 12.1

---

[9] Ibid., p. 64.

[10] John M. Stopford and Louis T. Wells, Jr., *Managing the Multinational Enterprise* (New York: Basic Books, 1972), p. 108.

[11] Martin Kenney, *Biotechnology: The University-Industrial Complex* (New Haven, Conn.: Yale University Press, 1987).

[12] Reprinted by permission of *Harvard Business Review.* An excerpt from "From the People Who Brought You Voodoo Economics," by Charles H. Ferguson, May–June 1988. Copyright © 1988 by the President and Fellows of Harvard College; all rights reserved.

percent of NEC (the major semiconductor producer in the Sumitomo group) but also 3.7 percent of Sharp and 9.2 percent of Matsushita. (Matsushita, Japan's fifth largest semiconductor producer, is a diversified electronics firm with revenues of more than $35 billion.) In 1986, another financial institution, Dai-Ichi Mutual Life, held 2.9 percent of NEC, 2.8 percent of Hitachi, 4.9 percent of Toshiba, 2 percent of Mitsubishi, and 6 percent of Oki.

If this is entrepreneurship, then the Soviet Union is a democracy. Yet this combination of oligopoly, strategic coordination, and national protectionism did not impede Japanese industry. On the contrary, stability, long time horizons, and low investment costs permitted Japanese producers to make long-term investments and to overpower and outmaneuver U.S. industry in strategic confrontations—whether in technology licensing, price competition, or Japanese market access.

Faith in the market must give way to a more sophisticated view of strategic of the incentive effects of government action, and of relationships among technology, management, and industry performance.

Michael C. Jensen

Michael Jensen is a professor at Harvard Business School. These are excerpts from his article "Eclipse of the Public Corporation," which appeared in the *Harvard Business Review* in 1989.[13]

The publicly held corporation, the main engine of economic progress in the United States for a century, has outlived its usefulness in many sectors of the economy and is being eclipsed.

New organizations are emerging in its place—organizations that are corporate in form but have no public shareholders and are not listed or traded on organized exchanges. These organizations use public and private debt, rather than public equity, as their major source of capital. Their primary owners are not households but large institutions and entrepreneurs that designate agents to manage and monitor on their behalf and bind those agents with large equity interests and contracts governing the use and distribution of cash.

Takeovers, corporate breakups, divisional spinoffs, leveraged buyouts, and going-private transactions are the most visible manifestations of a massive organizational change in the economy.

Three major forces are said to control management in the public corporation: the product markets, internal control systems led by the board of directors, and the capital markets. But product markets often have not played a disciplining role. For most of the last 60 years, a large and vibrant domestic market created for U.S. companies economies of scale and significant cost advantages over foreign rivals. Recent reversals at the hands of the Japanese and others have not been severe enough to sap most companies of their financial independence. The idea that outside directors with little or no equity stake in the company could effectively monitor and discipline the managers who selected them has proven hollow at best. In practice, only the capital markets have played much of a control function—and for a long time they were hampered by legal constraints.

The widespread waste and inefficiency of the public corporation and its inability to adapt to changing economic circumstances have generated a wave of organizational innovation over the last 15 years—innovation driven by the rebirth of "active investors." By active investors I mean investors who hold large equity or debt positions, sit on boards of directors, monitor and sometimes dismiss management, are involved with the long-term strategic direction of the companies they invest in, and sometimes manage the companies themselves. . . .

Active investors are creating a new model of general management. These investors include LBO partnerships, such as Kohlberg Kravis Roberts and Clayton & Dubilier; entrepreneurs,

[13] Reprinted by permission of *Harvard Business Review*. An excerpt from "Eclipse of the Public Corporation" by Michael C. Jensen, September–October 1989. Copyright © 1989 by the President and Fellows of Harvard College; all rights reserved.

such as Carl Icahn, Ronald Perelman, Laurence Tisch, Robert Bass, William Simon, Irwin Jacobs, and Warren Buffett; the merchant banking arms of Wall Street houses, such as Morgan Stanley, Lazard Frères, and Merrill Lynch; and family funds, such as those controled by the Pritzkers and the Bronfmans. Their model is built around highly leveraged financial structures, pay-for-performance compensation systems, substantial equity ownership by managers and directors, and contracts with owners and creditors that limit both cross-subsidization among business units and the waste of free cash flow. Consistent with modern finance theory, these organizations are not managed to maximize earnings per share but, rather, to maximize *value,* with a strong emphasis on cash flow.

Active investors are creating new models of general management, the most widespread of which I call the "LBO Association." A typical LBO Association consists of three main constituencies: an LBO partnership that sponsors going-private transactions and counsels and monitors management in an ongoing cooperative relationship; company managers who hold substantial equity stakes in an LBO division and stay on after the buyout; and institutional investors (insurance companies, pension funds, and money management firms) that fund the limited partnerships that purchase equity and lend money (along with banks) to finance the transactions.

M. C. Jensen and W. H. Meckling

William H. Meckling is a professor and former dean of the Graduate School of Management at the University of Rochester. These excerpts are from a paper by Jensen and Meckling, "Theory of the Firm, Managerial Behavior, Agency Costs, and Ownership Structure," published in the *Journal of Financial Economics* in 1976.[14]

[14] Excerpt reprinted from the paper by M. C. Jensen and W. H. Meckling, "Theory of the Firm: Managerial Behavior, Agency Costs, and Ownership Structure" published in *Journal of Financial Economics* 3, 1976, pp. 310–11.

Ronald Coase in his seminal paper on "The Nature of the Firm" pointed out that economics had no positive theory to determine the bounds of the firm. He characterized the bounds of the firm as that range of exchanges over which the market system was suppressed and resource allocation was accomplished instead by authority and direction. He focused on the cost of using markets to effect contracts and exchanges and argued that activities would be included within the firm whenever the costs of using markets were greater than the costs of using direct authority. Alchain and Demsetz object to the notion that activities within the firm are governed by authority, and correctly emphasize the role of contracts as a vehicle for voluntary exchange. They emphasize the role of monitoring in situations in which there is joint input or team production. We sympathize with the importance they attach to monitoring, but we believe the emphasis which Alchian-Demsetz place on joint input production is too narrow and therefore misleading. Contractual relations are the essence of the firm, not only with employees but with suppliers, customers, creditors, etc.

It is important to recognize that most organizations are simply *legal fictions which serve as a nexus for a set of contracting relationships among individuals.* This includes firms' nonprofit institutions, such as universities, hospitals, and foundations; mutual organizations, such as mutual savings banks and insurance companies and cooperatives; some private clubs; and even governmental bodies, such as cities, states, and the federal government; government enterprises, such as TVA, the post office, transit systems, and so on.

The private corporation or firm is simply one form of *legal fiction which serves as a nexus for contracting relationships and which is also characterized by the existence of divisible residual claims on the assets and cash flows of the organization which can generally be sold without permission of the other contracting individuals.* While this definition of the firm has little substantive content, emphasizing the essential contractual nature of firms and other organizations focuses attention on a crucial set of questions— why particular sets of contractual relations arise for various types of organizations, what the consequences of these contractual relations are, and how they are affected by changes exogenous to the organization. Viewed this way, it makes little or no sense to try to distinguish those things which are "inside" the firm (or any other organization) from those things that are "outside" of it. There is in a very real sense only a multitude of complex relationships (i.e., contracts) between the legal fiction (the firm) and the owners of labor, material, and capital inputs and the consumers of output.

Robert Axelrod

Robert Axelrod is a professor of political science and public policy at the University of Michigan. These excerpts come from his book *The Evolution of Cooperation.*[15]

This project began with a simple question: When should a person cooperate, and when should a person be selfish, in an ongoing interaction with another person? Should a friend keep providing favors to another friend who never reciprocates?

There is a simple way to represent the type of situation that gives rise to these problems. This is to use a particular kind of game called the iterated Prisoner's Dilemma. The game allows the players to achieve mutual gains from cooperation, but it also allows for the possibility that one player will exploit the other, or the possibility that neither will cooperate. As in most realistic situations, the players do not have strictly opposing interests. To find a good strategy to use in such situations, I invited experts in game theory to submit programs for a Computer Prisoner's Dilemma Tournament.

The Prisoner's Dilemma is simply an abstract formulation of some very common and very interesting situations in which what is best for each person individually leads to mutual

defection, whereas everyone would have been better off with mutual cooperation.

Professional game theorists were invited to submit their favorite strategy, and each of these decision rules was paired off with each of the others to see which would do best overall. Amazingly enough, the winner was the simplest of all strategies submitted. This was TIT FOR TAT, the strategy which cooperates on the first move and then does whatever the other player did on the previous move. A second round of the tournament was conducted, in which many more entries were submitted by amateurs and professionals alike, all of whom were aware of the results of the first round. The result was another victory for TIT FOR TAT! The analysis of the data from these tournaments reveals four properties which tend to make a decision rule successful: avoidance of unnecessary conflict by cooperating as long as the other player does, provocability in the face of an uncalled for defection by the other, forgiveness after responding to a provocation, and clarity of behavior so that the other player can adapt to your pattern of action.

The winner was the simplest of all the programs submitted, TIT FOR TAT. TIT FOR TAT is merely the strategy of starting with cooperation, and thereafter doing what the other player did on the previous move.

What makes it possible for cooperation to emerge is the fact that the players might meet again. This possibility means that the choices made today not only determine the outcome of this move but can also influence the later choices of the players. The future can therefore cast a shadow back upon the present and thereby affect the current strategic situation.

But the future is less important than the present—for two reasons. The first is that players tend to value payoffs less as the time of their obtainment recedes into the future. The second is that there is always some chance that the players will not meet again.

Based on the tournament results and the formal propositions, four simple suggestions are offered for individual choice: do not be envious of the other player's success; do not be the first to defect; reciprocate both cooperation and defection; and do not be too clever.

---

[15] Excerpt reprinted by permission of BasicBooks, a division of HarperCollins Publishers, Inc. Robert Axelrod, *The Evolution of Cooperation*, pp. vii, viii, 9, 12, 20, 22–23. Copyright © 1984 by Robert Axelrod.

J. H. Plumb

J. H. Plumb is a professor of history at Cambridge University. This excerpt is from his book *The Italian Renaissance.*

It is a sobering thought that the great Italian achievements in almost every sphere of intellectual and artistic activity took place in a world of violence and war. Cities were torn by feud and vendetta: Milan warred against Venice, Florence against Pisa, Rome against Florence, Naples against Milan. Alliances were forged only to be broken, the countryside was constantly scarred by pillage, rapine, and battle, and in this maelstrom the old bonds of society were broken and new ones forged.

Yet this violence worked like yeast in the thought of men, and profoundly influenced the way they were to regard problems of power and government for hundreds of years. They ceased to look for answers to the fate of man in the dogmas of the Church. They searched the histories of antiquity for precedents that might guide them to the truth, but they also sought to explain, as Machiavelli did, the world in which they lived by what they knew to be the nature of man. Indeed, it was during the Renaissance in Italy that many men came to feel that truth was elusive, a mood afterward strengthened by the discovery of the world beyond Europe.

Diplomacy as we know it arose in Italy of the Renaissance. It grew strong in the 15th century through the equilibrium of power created by the three great northern states of Italy—Milan, Venice, and Florence. It appealed to the leaders of these mercantile societies. They enjoyed and believed in the efficacy of hard bargaining and were not unaware of the merits of partnership for the destruction of rivals (and partners need supervision as well as persuasion). The collection of intelligence, the assessment of personalities and contingencies, was, early on, the stock-in-trade of bankers. The application of these commercial techniques to the service of the state was effortlessly made.

The princes and the republics of the Renaissance lived in a dangerous, excitable, and exciting world of power. Morality was not involved, only success. But, of course, only a few princes, nobles, and merchants were concerned in any state. The mass of the people eschewed office, and the disasters of government troubled them only in military defeat.

Niccolo Machiavelli

Machiavelli, who lived from 1469 until 1527, was an Italian political thinker and politician. This passage is taken from his most famous work, *The Prince,* which he dedicated to Lorenzo de Medici, the ruler of Florence in the early 16th century.

It remains now to see what ought to be the rules of conduct for a prince towards subjects and friends. How one lives is so far distant from how one ought to live, that he who neglects what is done for what ought to be done, sooner effects his ruin than his preservation; for a man who wishes to act entirely up to his professions of virtue soon meets with what destroys him among so much that is evil.

Hence, it is necessary for a prince wishing to hold his own to know how to do wrong, and to make use of it or not according to necessity.

Those princes who have done great things have held good faith of little account, and have known how to circumvent the intellect of men by craft, and in the end have overcome those who have relied on their word. You must know there are two ways of contesting, the one by the law, the other by force; the first method is proper to men, the second to beasts; but because the first is frequently not sufficient, it is necessary to have recourse to the second. Therefore, it is necessary for a prince to understand how to avail himself of the beast and the man.

A prince, therefore, being compelled knowingly to adopt the beast, ought to choose the fox and the lion; because the lion cannot defend himself against snares and the fox cannot defend himself against wolves. Therefore, it is necessary to be a fox to discover the snares and a lion to terrify the wolves. Those who rely simply on the lion do not understand what they are about. Therefore a wise lord cannot, nor ought he to, keep faith when such observance may be turned against him, and when the reasons that caused him to pledge it exist no longer. He who has known best how to employ the fox has succeeded best.

But it is necessary to know well how to disguise this characteristic, and to be a great pretender and dissembler; and men are so simple, and so subject to present necessities, that he who seeks to deceive will always find someone who will allow himself to be deceived.

Bibliographic Note

Chalmers Johnson, *MITI and the Japanese Miracle: The Growth of Industrial Policy, 1925–1975* (Stanford, Calif.: Stanford University Press, 1982), pp. viii, 311, 312, 313, 318, 319.

Alfred D. Chandler, Jr. (with Takashi Hikino), *Scale and Scope: The Dynamics of Industrial Capitalism* (Cambridge, Mass.: Belknap Press of Harvard University, 1990), pp. 12, 397–98, 423, 424.

"Capitalism: In Triumph, In Flux," *The Economist,* May 5, 1990, pp. 7, 8, 9, 15, 19.

Michael E. Porter, *The Competitive Advantage of Nations* (New York: Free Press, 1990).

Joseph L. Badaracco, Jr., "Changing Forms of the Corporation," in John R. Meyer and James M. Gustafson, eds., *The U.S. Business Corporation* (Cambridge, Mass.: Ballinger, 1988), pp. 1, 74–75.

Charles H. Ferguson, "The People Who Brought You Voodoo Economics," *Harvard Business Review,* May–June 1988, pp. 55, 57, 59, 60, 61, 62. Reprint no. 88304.

Michael C. Jensen, "Eclipse of the Public Corporation," *Harvard Business Review,* September–October 1989, pp. 61, 64, 65, 68.

Michael C. Jensen and William H. Meckling, "Theory of the Firm: Managerial Behavior, Agency Costs and Ownership Structure," *Journal of Financial Economics* 3 (1976), 305–60, at pp. 310–11.

Robert Axelrod, *The Evolution of Corporation* (New York: Basic Books, 1984), pp. vii, viii, 9, 12, 20, 22, 23.

J. H. Plumb, *The Italian Renaissance* (Boston: American Heritage/Houghton Mifflin, 1985), pp. 18–19, 25–26.

Niccolo Machiavelli, *The Prince,* translated by W. K. Mariott, introduction by Herbert Butterfield (London: Dent, Everyman's Library, David Campbell Publishers; New York: Dutton, 1974 edition), pp. 83, 84, 85, 92, 93, 97, 98.

AT&T CONSUMER PRODUCTS

In the fall of 1988, Nick Stevens, the vice president of manufacturing at AT&T Consumer Products, had to select a site for a new answering systems manufacturing facility. He was inclined to choose Mexico, but he had not ruled out Malaysia or the United States.

As Stevens pondered the many factors that would affect his decision, he could not help but reflect on the profound changes that had occurred at AT&T in recent years. AT&T in 1988 was vastly different from the company he had joined 22 years earlier. Some changes were clearly reflected on the organizational chart, others involved new policies, but the most challenging ones related to AT&T's role in

Wilda White prepared this case under the direction of Joseph Badaracco, Jr.

Harvard Business School case 392-108 (Revised 1993).

society, and Stevens had to consider all these factors in making his decision.

History

Like Singer with its sewing machines and Gillette with its razors, American Telegraph and Telephone was an American icon. Long known as Ma Bell, AT&T had been the world's largest corporation. In the early 1980s, it had more than $150 billion in assets and its annual revenues of $70 billion represented almost 2 percent of the U.S. gross national product. Until January 1984, AT&T employed one million people and had over three million shareholders. (See Exhibit 1.)

Alexander Graham Bell, who patented the telephone in 1876, founded the Bell Telephone Company in 1877. While Bell was credited with inventing the telephone, it was Theodore Vail who created the Bell System. Vail, one of the first managers hired by the founders of what would become AT&T, stated as early as 1879 that AT&T's goal was "one system, one policy, universal service."[1] Since Vail's time and until the 1984 divestiture, AT&T's annual reports consistently reiterated a commitment to furnishing "the best possible service at the lowest possible cost."[2]

Vail devised an organizational structure that lasted for a century without fundamental change. Local telephone companies, known as Bell Operating Companies, were organized as nominally independent subsidiaries. They provided local telephone service and access to the long-distance network. (See Exhibit 2.) They also billed customers for long-distance and international service provided by the AT&T Long Lines Department.

---

[1] Robert W. Garnet, *The Telephone Enterprise: The Evolution of the Bell System's Horizontal Structure, 1878–1909* (Baltimore: Johns Hopkins University Press, 1985), p. 173.
[2] Ibid.

Western Electric Manufacturing Company was founded in Cleveland in 1869 as an electric-equipment shop. In the 1870s, it became a mecca for inventors. In 1881, Bell Telephone bought an interest in Western Electric, and the following year it formally became the manufacturer of Bell telephones and equipment.

In addition to producing or procuring practically all Bell System telephone equipment, Western Electric developed the high vacuum electronic amplifying tube that made possible coast to coast telephone calls and cleared the way for radio broadcasting, sound motion pictures, and television; it produced the first air-to-ground radio telephones; made and installed one of the pioneer commercial radio broadcasting systems, WEAF in New York; developed the first motion-picture sound system; built all of the radar used by the U.S. armed forces in World War II; and, in the space age, built the Nike missile systems, the DEW line radar defense system, the Sentinel and Safeguard antiballistic missile systems, and much of the communications and control equipment for the U.S. space program.

Western Electric was the largest component of the Bell System. Had it not been wholly owned by AT&T, Western Electric would have been the 12th largest industrial company in the United States. At its height, Western Electric operated 23 major plants scattered around the United States from Atlanta, Georgia, to Phoenix, Arizona, to North Andover, Massachusetts.

Bell Telephone Laboratories was formed out of the Western Electric engineering research department in 1925. It was equally owned by Western Electric and AT&T. Bell Labs developed and designed the equipment that Western Electric manufactured and the Bell System used. Originally a small organization, Bell Labs grew into a giant as a result of World War II military hardware requirements. Before divestiture, it had 25,000 employees, an annual budget of $2 billion, and employed 20,000

EXHIBIT 1 Seven-year Summary of Selected AT&T Financial Data ($ in millions, except per share amounts)

	1982	1983	1/1/84	1984	1985	1986*	1987	1988*
Results of Operations								
Total revenues	$ 70,022	$ 72,357		$33,187	$34,496	$34,213	$33,773	$35,218
Total costs and expenses	50,678	57,338		30,892	31,476	33,847	30,252	38,276
Net income (loss)	7,279	249		1,370	1,557	139	2,044	(1,669)
Dividends on preferred shares	142	127		112	110	86	23	1
Income (loss) applicable to common shares	7,137	122		1,258	1,447	53	2,021	(1,670)
Earnings (loss) per common share	$ 8.06	$ 6.00		$1.25	$1.37	$0.05	$1.88	($1.55)
Dividends declared per common share	$ 5.81	$6.10		$1.20	$1.20	$1.20	$1.20	$1.20
Assets and Capital								
Property, plant and equipment—net			$20,569	$21,343	$22,262	$21,101	$20,808	$15,280
Total assets	$150,004	$140,229	35,545	39,773	40,688	39,534	39,473	35,152
Long-term debt including capital leases			9,137	8,718	7,794	7,660	7,919	8,128
Common shareowners' equity			12,368	13,763	14,633	13,550	14,455	11,465
Other information (data at year end except 1/84)								
Market price per share	$ 62.86	$ 63.02	$ 17.88	$ 19.50	$ 25.00	$ 25.00	$ 27.00	$ 28.75
Employees	1,000,000		373,000	365,200	337,600	316,900	303,000	304,700

* 1988 data were significantly affected by a charge for accelerated digitization program costs. 1986 data were significantly affected by major charges for business restructuring, an accounting change, and other charges.

EXHIBIT 2   Predivestiture AT&T

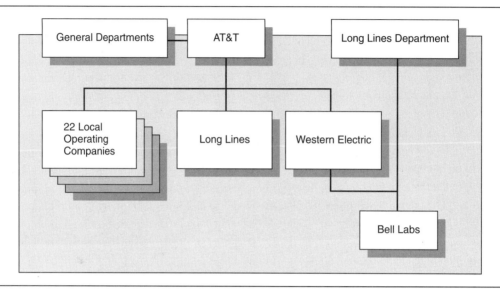

PhDs. It maintained 17 locations in nine states. Its inventions included the electrical digital computer (1937), transistors (1947), lasers (1958), the communications satellite, Telstar (1962), radar, semiconductors, fiber optics, and electronic switching equipment.

Regulatory History

In 1934, the United States Congress created the Federal Communications Commission (FCC) to regulate the telephone industry. Its mission was "to make available, so far as possible, to all the people of the United States a rapid, efficient, nationwide and worldwide wire and radio communications service with adequate facilities at reasonable charges." Under FCC regulation, each Bell Operating Company was guaranteed an area of operation without competition and assured a certain maximum profit margin. Local operating companies were required to serve anyone within their operating area who requested telephone service. Charges for local telephone service were subject to state or local government approval.

As of the late 1960s, all telephone sets, private branch exchanges, and other standard equipment used in residences or by businesses were owned by the telephone company and leased to users. Nearly all telephone equipment (referred to as customer premises equipment (CPE) by the telephone industry) was manufactured by Western Electric and sold to the operating companies.

Carterfone

In 1968, the FCC issued its *Carterfone* decision. This case arose when AT&T refused to permit the *Carterfone,* a non-Bell device that linked mobile car radios with the national telephone network, to be connected to the Bell System. AT&T threatened service termination to anyone connecting the device to the network, arguing that non-Bell equipment could harm the system. When Tom Carter appealed to the FCC, the commission ruled in his favor and ordered AT&T to allow customers to connect their own telephone equipment to the Bell System. However, customers were required to lease a protective device from AT&T to link the non-Bell device and the Bell System telephone line.

Many consumers and competitive telephone equipment manufacturers complained that the protective devices constituted a barrier to competition, intended to protect AT&T's monopoly. In 1972, the FCC reexamined its *Carterfone* ruling and held that any equipment could be connected to the network without a protective device, if it had been certified as safe for use on the network. This decision became effective in 1980.

1982 Modified Final Judgment Decree

In January 1982, AT&T and the U.S. Department of Justice announced that they had reached a settlement of the government's long-standing antitrust case against the company. The 1974 lawsuit had charged AT&T with monopolizing the market for telephone equipment and long-distance service. The government maintained that, as long as AT&T controlled the local circuits that provided the only access to most consumers, competition could not exist in long-distance service, data services, private branch exchanges, key telephone systems, large telephone switching machines, or other telephone equipment and services.

The settlement, which became known as the Modified Final Judgment, called for the divestiture of the Bell Operating Companies by AT&T on January 1, 1984. The 22 BOCs would be regrouped under 7 separate and independent Regional Bell Operating Companies and would be restricted to providing local telephone service. They could not offer long-distance services and would be barred from manufacturing telephone equipment. They could, however, sell telephone equipment manufactured by others.

Under the terms of the settlement, AT&T would retain part of Bell Labs, all of Western Electric, and its long-distance and customer premises equipment operations. The settlement forbade AT&T's use of the "Bell" name, except for Bell Laboratories. It permitted AT&T to enter other electronics businesses, including computers. Many observers expected the settlement to initiate a great commercial contest between IBM and AT&T in the telecommunications and computing fields.

The New AT&T

Organizational Structure

In anticipation of divestiture, AT&T's vertically integrated, functional organizational structure was replaced by an organizational structure built around the lines of business in which the company would now be engaged. Each line of business would be responsible for its own profitability and its contribution to AT&T's revenues.

Two sectors were created and given responsibility for the overall management of resources to support the lines of business. AT&T Communications would handle the long-distance service, and AT&T Technologies encompassed the unregulated parts of the business and included AT&T Consumer Products. (See Exhibit 3.)

Regulation

After 1984, only telephone equipment was fully deregulated. All telephone services remained under federal and state regulation. For example, AT&T's prices for long-distance services still had to be approved by the FCC.

Labor

Before divestiture, three unions represented over two-thirds of the Bell System's one million workers. The Communications Workers of America (CWA) represented 675,000 AT&T

EXHIBIT 3 Postdivestiture AT&T

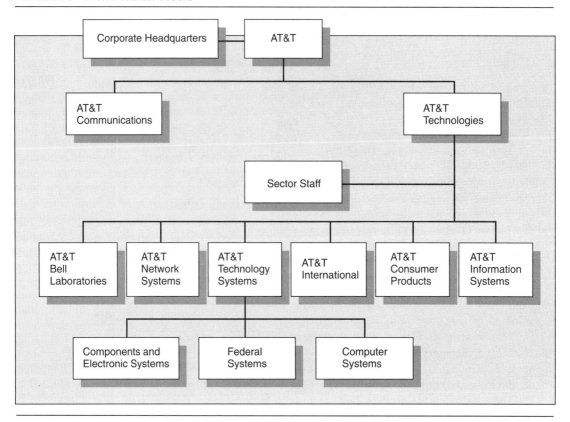

workers, the International Brotherhood of Electrical Workers (IBEW) represented 100,000 AT&T workers, and the Telecommunications International Union (TIU) represented 50,000 AT&T workers.

On August 7, 1983, after the antitrust settlement was announced but before it became effective, a nationwide strike against the Bell System began after the unions representing Bell System employees rejected the Bell Systems' wage package. The strike was the first since a six-day walkout in 1971. Beyond the wage dispute, the pending January 1984 divestiture of AT&T's 22 operating companies had cast a shadow across the bargaining table. The unions pushed for an "employment security" package that would provide training and retraining for members and that would protect jobs after divestiture. AT&T, faced with nonunion competition in a deregulated environment, was trying to control costs and maintain maximum flexibility in the way it utilized its workforce.

After 22 days, AT&T and the unions reached an accord. In addition to wage increases for each of the three years of the contract, AT&T agreed to increases in retirement pay, better pension protection for workers transferred to lower-paying jobs, and additional training, transfer rights, and retraining for laid-off workers.

After divestiture, the unionized workers were spread throughout AT&T and the divested Bell Operating Companies. Of AT&T's 375,000 workers remaining after divestiture, 63.6 percent were members of a union.

Range of Businesses

After divestiture, AT&T described its primary business as "moving and managing information." It provided consumers with basic long-distance service, special calling plans, and other miscellaneous services. AT&T also sold and leased telephones and answering systems to consumers. To businesses, the company offered communications and networked computer systems and telemarketing services. It also provided communications services and products and computer systems to all levels of government in the United States and abroad.

Dealings with the U.S. Government

AT&T's largest customer was the U.S. government. It sold its full range of customized and standard products to such agencies as the U.S. Army, Navy, and Air Force, and to the Federal Aviation Administration. AT&T also managed Sandia National Laboratories as a service to the U.S. government on a nonprofit, no-fee basis. Sandia was one of the government's largest research and development engineering facilities, with projects in such areas as the safety, security, and control of weapons systems, and the development of new energy sources.

International Activities, Joint Ventures, and Alliances

AT&T did business in more than 40 countries and had approximately 21,000 employees outside the United States. It was involved in numerous joint ventures and alliances, both in the United States and abroad. For example, it had agreements and alliances with British Telecom, France Telecom, and Kokusai Denshin Denwa of Japan. It also had an agreement to share technology with Mitsubishi and to make and market worldwide a static random access

memory chip. AT&T was also cooperating with NEC in Japan on a wide range of semiconductor products and technologies. AT&T also had an agreement with Zenith to co-develop an all-digital, high-definition television system using AT&T's microchips and video compression research and Zenith's television technology.

AT&T Consumer Products

Although consumers were permitted as early as 1980 to connect non-Bell telephone equipment to the Bell System, the market for residential telephones did not take off until 1983, when leasing charges were listed separately from service charges on consumers' bills. The unbundling of leasing charges alerted consumers to the economic benefits of owning their own telephones. In 1983, retail telephone sales jumped 230 percent to about $1.1 billion.[3] In the first nine months of 1983, imports of telephones from Taiwan, Hong Kong, Japan, and Korea increased 568 percent over the same period in 1982 to 25.7 million telephones.[4]

The imported telephones were unlike the old U.S.-manufactured electromechanical telephones, which were built to operate over a 30-year depreciation period. Some were one-piece models selling for as little as $20. Japanese companies, led by Matsushita under the Panasonic label, introduced feature-laden electronic telephones with integrated chips that made possible the inclusion of a variety of features at a reasonable cost.

The onslaught of new competition spelled trouble for AT&T Consumer Products (CP). This unit, formed after the telephone equipment market was deregulated, had never sold as much as a telephone cord before 1983. Moreover, AT&T's telephones were never

---

[3] "The Big and Bruising Business of Selling Telephones," *Business Week*, March 12, 1984, p. 103.

[4] Ibid.

designed to be marketable. In many ways, AT&T's attitudes toward its customers had been "we make it, you take it." Its telephones had cost $20 to make, while a repair call cost $60, so AT&T's goal had been to make highly reliable telephones, even if they were somewhat overengineered. As Jim Bercaw, a 35-year AT&T veteran described it: "We would bring pellets and metal in the back door, and send telephones out of the front door. We even made our own screws."

In the face of daunting competition, declining revenues, and unacceptable profit levels, CP consolidated its residential telephone production in AT&T's Shreveport, Louisiana, facility and spent tens of millions of dollars to upgrade and automate the facility. After the expense of integrating new technology and methods, CP discovered that its labor costs were still too high. A McKinsey & Company competitive analog study revealed that CP was out of line with its competitors on all points and scores, including such critical areas as cost of goods sold and SG&A. In fact, the cost of goods sold was 90 percent of revenues, and CP executives reasoned that it had to be at 65 percent to be competitive. In late 1984, AT&T corporate told CP management to "fix the business or exit the business."

CP soon began making changes. In recalling their impact on its people, Ken Bertaccini, a 25-year veteran of AT&T and president of CP since 1985, said:

> On January 1, 1984, our people went from a world of guaranteed customers, guaranteed profits, and guaranteed jobs—to the much less certain world of a fiercely competitive consumer electronics world—with the only guarantee of success coming from excellent and sustained performance.

Employee surveys revealed massive trauma within the workforce; morale was low and employees were angry and frustrated.

CP's Competitors

In the mid-1980s, three types of competitors were in the telephone equipment market: (1) telephone companies; (2) consumer electronic companies; and (3) housewares companies. The telephone companies included AT&T, other traditional providers of service and equipment, such as GTE and ITT, and some of the divested Bell Operating Companies. As providers of telephone services, these companies had a strategic interest in the telephone equipment market. But like AT&T, these companies were, for the most part, unfamiliar with the world of competitive consumer marketing.

The consumer electronic companies ranged from sophisticated Japanese manufacturers like Matsushita and Sony, which offered full lines of consumer products, to smaller, specialized companies like Code-A-Phone, Unisonic, and PhoneMate. The consumer electronic companies were market-driven competitors with well-developed distribution networks and considerable expertise in designing products for the consumer market.

Consumer electronics companies' interest in the market was based on long-term possibilities and not just short-term profit and loss. As homes became more and more automated, telephones seemed likely to take on more the role of a home computer terminal. Therefore, the consumer electronics companies wanted the telephone terminal business as a platform for new generations of higher value-added products.

The housewares companies were primarily represented in the telephone equipment market by General Electric. It had a good reputation for reliability and quality and significant experience designing, marketing, and distributing consumer products.

Matsushita, a $40 billion Japanese company, which manufactured under the Panasonic label, was CP's most formidable competitor. Panasonic was the predominant residential telephone vendor in Japan. Its strategy had been to offer products that competed with the market leader, but offered marginally more functions for the price. Matsushita manufactured its telephone products entirely in Japan. It used a highly automated manufacturing process and did not subcontract any of its production. Because of the volume of business it did and the wide range of associated products it manufactured, Matsushita was able to operate its manufacturing operations at full capacity year round.

CP's Survival Period: 1985–1986

Establishing a Foundation and Culture for CP

CP's management realized that it had to be transformed from a regulated monopoly to a highly flexible organization that not only accepted change but embraced it. "Business Passion" and "Shared Values" were established as the new foundation of CP. They were

created to provide the basis and guidelines for all CP decisions and actions. Said Nick Stevens, CP's vice president of manufacturing: "The passion is truly part of the decision process and there is seldom a decision not made in its frame of reference."

"Business Passion," depicted in Exhibit 4, signified CP's commitment to "Be the Best" for its owners, customers, and people. CP referred to its workers as "people." Executives strongly discouraged the use of the term *employees,* and they incurred a fine for using what they called the "E-word." Management believed that to achieve long-term success it had to weigh equally the effect of each business decision on all three stakeholder groups. The pyramid in the background of the "Business Passion" graphically represents the relationship between the "Business Passion" and "Shared Values."

CP's "Shared Values" described what the business was and aspired to be. On an individual level, the business wanted to create an

---

EXHIBIT 4 AT&T Consumer Product Business Foundation: Business Passion and Shared Values

Business Passion   Shares Values

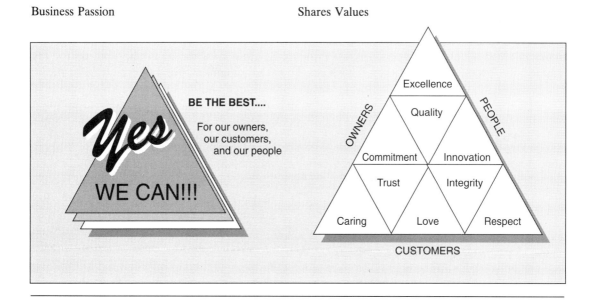

environment of caring, trust, love,[5] integrity, and respect. On a business level, CP wanted to create an environment that valued commitment, quality, and innovations, and achieved excellence in everything it did. CP managers placed a significant part of their compensation "at risk," making it dependent on the unit's performance.

CP also made what its executives called a "huge" investment in its people. It developed education programs as well as honor and recognition programs. Everyone had the opportunity for two weeks of business education each year. There were also several recognition events each year. Spouses or guests were invited to an annual event honoring CP's top performers.

Creating an Organizational Structure

CP's organizational structure was redesigned to promote flexibility and market focus. The nine product lines were formed into strategic business units (SBUs).[6] Product managers and representatives from all relevant functional areas (e.g., sales, finance, etc.) formed a SBU. These SBUs operated as profit centers.

Between 1985 and 1988, the number of executive-level managers was reduced from 40 to 16. The workforce was reduced by almost half. In 1985, CP had as many as six layers of supervision between its operational levels and its president. In 1988, CP had as few as three.

---

[5] "Love" had not always been a part of CP's "Shared Values." After extensive discussion, it was included in 1989 to deepen, in the words of one manager, "CP's commitment to live up to its personal values of caring, trust, and respect." This decision was reinforced by the outpouring of support for a CP executive who successfully battled cancer during the mid-1980s.

[6] CP's product lines were: (1) leased telephones; (2) corded telephones; (3) cordless telephones; (4) answering systems; (5) special needs systems (communications products for people with hearing, speech, motion, and vision impairments); (6) telephone accessories; (7) home security systems; and (8) public pay telephones.

A comprehensive measurement system was also developed and implemented. The system focused on assessing owner, customer, and people satisfaction on a regular basis by looking at profits, needs, and attitudes, respectively.

Developing a Business Strategy

In late 1984, Jim Bercaw, who was vice president of manufacturing at the time, was told to develop a "global manufacturing plan." To that end, he traveled to the Far East. His trip revealed that all of CP's competitors were manufacturing in Asia. He later said: "I have a second-fastest-gun-in-the-West philosophy. If you can't be the fastest gun in the West, it is better to travel in crowds."

With all its competitors in Asia, CP decided that it also had to move its manufacturing operation there. At the same time, it also decided to contract out the remainder of its manufacturing requirements to Asian original equipment manufacturers (OEMs). After 1986, CP no longer had any U.S. production of residential telephone equipment: (See Exhibit 5.)

The Decision to Move Offshore

Choosing a Location

CP chose Singapore as the site of its first offshore manufacturing operation. The facility would first manufacture corded and then cordless telephones. Singapore, an island nation in southeast Asia, was founded as an *entrepôt* because of its strategic position and excellent natural harbor. In 1988, however, manufacturing employed almost a third of the labor force, and the Singaporean government played a major role in managing the economy.

CP management chose Singapore in part because it was an English-speaking country and its Economic Development Board provided a kind of one-stop shopping for foreign companies that wanted to do business there. Corruption was not a problem: "The place was

EXHIBIT 5 U.S. Manufacturers' Shipments, Exports, and Imports of Telephone Sets, Selected Years, 1978–1988 (millions of dollars)

	1978	*1982*	*1988*
Shipments	$824	$1,065	$ 359
Exports	10	24	56
Imports	42	149	1,400
Apparent consumption	856	1,190	1,703

Source: United States Bureau of Census, "Selected Electronic and Associated Products, 1979, 1983," series MA36N, and "Communications Equipment, 1988," series MA36P.

squeaky clean," recalled a CP manager. In addition, an existing building was available immediately for lease. According to Jim Bercaw, Singapore was not the lowest-cost option, but it was considerably cheaper than the United States. Jim Bercaw described the decision this way:

> It was a jiffy quick decision. In January 1985, we began to negotiate; in March 1985, we received budgetary and financial approval. In May 1985, we buttonholed a lease in an existing factory. By January 1986, we shipped our first product.
>
> Logically, the decision to go to Singapore and sacrifice 500 jobs to save 10,000 jobs was a "no-brainer." However, culturally the decision created a struggle around taking jobs from our own facility out of America.[7]
>
> We also had to decide what kind of facility we wanted Singapore to be. We knew we wanted to attract the right kind of people there. We wanted to treat our people well. The labor rate was not crucial because the gap was so large. We wanted the facility to be world-class. And, we had a notion, that at some point, we wanted the factory to be solely operated by Singaporeans. We did not want to create an American factory in Singapore.

---

[7] Approximately 10,000 people worked throughout CP. According to CP management, these jobs were at risk if CP did not make competitively priced telephones.

The move to Singapore reduced CP's labor costs 90 percent and its overhead costs 40 percent. Overall, CP saved 30 percent of its manufacturing costs by moving to Singapore, even after accounting for tariffs and transportation costs.

Impact on Labor

In 1985, the Shreveport Western Electric plant employed between 6,000 and 7,000 workers and was the largest employer in northwestern Louisiana. Some 750 workers at the plant were involved in the production of telephones. These workers were represented by the International Brotherhood of Electrical Workers (IBEW).

In July 1985, AT&T laid off 875 workers at the plant, 100 of whom made residential telephones. The remaining 650 residential telephone workers were phased out through later layoffs, transfers, or attrition. At the time of the July 1985 layoffs, AT&T announced that it was shifting the manufacture of residential telephones from the Shreveport facility to a new leased building in Singapore to cut costs and remain competitive.

The Singapore announcement came in the second year of the union's three-year contract. Under the union contract, union workers were not permitted to strike while the contract was in force. The local union officials in Shreveport characterized the union as extremely vocal and unified in its opposition to the move to

Singapore. According to the union local, AT&T did not attempt to discuss or negotiate alternatives to moving offshore with the union.

In recalling this period, Ken Bertaccini said:

> The decision to downsize was very difficult but clear. It cost American jobs and sacrificed the livelihoods of people who were part of the AT&T family. It meant moving jobs to parts of the world without any associations or relationships with AT&T. Patriotic emotions were involved, as well as the pain of looking great people in the eye and telling them that they would no longer have jobs.

Laid-off workers received trade readjustment payments, as well as the benefits outlined in the union contract. These included severance pay based on years of service as well as extended medical benefits.

During the 1986 contract talks, the union negotiated retraining programs for its membership to help prepare them for life after AT&T. An Enhanced Training Opportunity Program was adopted, which provided educational opportunities for workers, including computer training and classes at community colleges.

Excellence Period — 1987–1988

When Nick Stevens joined CP in November 1987, he noticed that the Singapore facility had strayed from its original manufacturing strategy. Stevens decided CP needed another manufacturing location. The new facility would focus exclusively on manufacturing corded telephones.

According to Nick Stevens, the new location had to be able to sustain a world-class facility. Geographic proximity to Singapore, the cost and availability of labor, government incentive packages, and infrastructure were all among the criteria considered by Stevens. Ultimately, he decided on Bangkok, Thailand.

Thailand, known early as Siam, was one of the world's largest producers of rubber. Thai was spoken by approximately 97 percent of the population and was the official language, although English was used in government and commerce. Manufacturing accounted for about one-fifth of the country's gross national product and employed about 11 percent of the workforce. In the late 1980s, the country had one of the highest rates of economic growth in the world.

In February 1988, Stevens presented his Bangkok proposal to the AT&T board and received approval. By June 1988, the facility was announced in Bangkok.

Answering System Market

In 1987, CP adopted a five-year plan to make CP's answering systems the market share leader by 1992. As early as 1985, industry experts predicted a robust market for telephone answering systems. Unit sales in 1986 exceeded four million. (See Exhibit 6.)

The answering systems market had two segments: adjuncts and integrated. Adjunct

EXHIBIT 6   Growth of U.S. Telephone Equipment Markets, 1984–1988 (millions of current dollars; 1990)

Type of Market	1984	1985	1986	1987	1988
Telephone sets — corded	$1,200	$1,585	$1,685	$1,750	$1,825
Telephone sets — cordless	410	305	410	438	474
Answering systems	298	371	535	557	634

Source: North American Telecommunications Association, *Telecommunications Market Review and Forecast,* 1990 ed., pp. 12, 144, 154, 162, and 178.

answering systems did not include a telephone, while integrated systems did. In both segments, the strongest competitors were Panasonic, PhoneMate, and GE/Thompson. The market set the price for answering systems and there were no real differences in the margins between the segments. In both segments, however, low-end products (those with less features) commanded smaller margins. In general, the market for answering systems was in affluent countries. In 1987, the largest market by far was the United States. Europe, especially Germany, was expected to develop in future years.

CP's goal for answering systems required it to look for another site for an answering systems manufacturing facility. Stevens's goal for 1988 was to explore the opportunities in Mexico and Europe. In June 1988, he saw an item in *The Wall Street Journal* advertising a seminar in Tucson, Arizona, on Mexican *maquiladoras*.[8] The seminar included a side trip into Nogales and Hermisillo, Mexico, to tour various *maquiladora* operations. (See Exhibit 7.)

Mexico

Mexico was the third largest country in Latin America, after Brazil and Argentina. In 1988, approximately 83,528,000 people lived in Mexico, making it the 11th most populous country in the world. Officially known as the United States of Mexico, it was organized into 31 states and a *distrito federal*. It shared a 2,000-mile border with the United States of America.

Although Mexico secured its independence from Spain in 1821, it was the Mexican revolution in 1910 that initiated a period of dra-

matic social change. A new constitution was adopted in 1917, which restricted foreign economic control and gave workers new protections. In 1929, the *Partido Revolucionario Institucional* (PRI) was formed. Since its founding, it never lost an election. Rapid industrial growth after 1940 improved living standards for much of Mexico. Import substitution, which entailed manufacturing locally what had been previously imported, and aggressive promotion of Mexican products for Mexican consumption were adopted as the country's strategy for development.

Unrest in the late 1960s spurred increased government investment in the infrastructure as well as increased spending on social programs. Despite these aggressive policies, the six-year term (1970–76) of president Luis Echeverría Alvarez was marked by 30 percent annual inflation, budget deficits, and political unrest.

In the late 1970s, major new oil fields were discovered in Mexico, which gave it easy access to foreign credit at low interest rates. Public debt nearly doubled between 1979 and 1981 from US$40 billion to US$78 billion. Despite the growth in government expenditures, by the end of the 1970s about 50 percent of all Mexican households lacked running water and sewage services, 25 percent lacked electricity, and 22 percent had neither running water, sewer services, nor electricity. Twenty percent of the population suffered from malnutrition and 45 percent of the population did not receive adequate health care.[9]

The decline of world oil prices in the early 1980s, as well as a sharp rise in world interest rates, plunged Mexico into economic crisis. In August 1982, Mexico announced that it could not meet the interest payments on its foreign debt of US$88 billion. In September, banks were nationalized and new currency controls were put in place.

---

[8] A *maquiladora* is a plant that assembles components that are usually imported into the home country of the *maquiladora* duty free. The assembled components are then re-exported. On re-export, a duty is paid only on the value of the labor that assembled the components and the value of any other home country inputs.

[9] Helen Shapiro, "Mexico: Escaping from the Debt Crisis?" (Cambridge, Mass.: President and Fellows of Harvard College, 1991), p. 6.

EXHIBIT 7 Map of Mexico

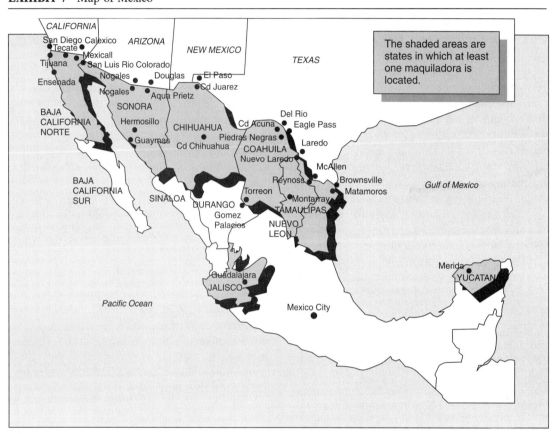

The shaded areas are states in which at least one maquiladora is located.

	Population Estimates
Mexico City	14,000,000 to 18,000,000
Guadalajara	3,000,000 to 5,000,000
Monterrey	2,700,000
Ciudad Jaurez	1,120,000
Puebla de Zaragoza	1,100,000
Leon	1,000,000
Tijuana	600,000
Acapulco	500,000
Chihuahua	400,000
Mexicali	350,000

In December 1982, foreign debt exceeded US$91 billion. Mexico turned to the International Monetary Fund (IMF) for assistance. The government budget was slashed, food subsidies were eliminated, and the peso was sharply devalued. The combination of inflation and the peso devaluation substantially reduced the real wages of workers. (See Exhibit 8.) In

EXHIBIT 8 Hourly Compensation of Production Workers in Manufacturing

Country	*Wages (US$ per hour worked)*								
	1980	1981	1982	1983	1984	1985	1986	1987	1988
United States	$9.84	$10.84	$11.64	$12.10	$12.51	$12.96	$13.21	$13.40	$13.85
Japan	5.61	6.18	5.70	6.13	6.34	6.43	9.31	10.83	12.80
Singapore	1.49	1.79	1.96	2.21	2.46	2.47	2.23	2.31	2.67
Hong Kong	1.51	1.55	1.67	1.52	1.58	1.73	1.88	2.09	2.40
Taiwan	1.00	1.18	1.22	1.27	1.42	1.50	1.73	2.26	2.82
Thailand	NA	NA	NA	NA	NA	NA	NA	NA	1.40
Brazil	1.38	1.64	1.86	1.26	1.07	1.12	1.47	1.38	1.46
Mexico	NA	3.71	2.54	1.85	2.04	1.60	1.09	1.06	1.32
Malaysia	NA	NA	NA	NA	NA	NA	NA	NA	1.60

Note: Hourly compensation is defined as (1) all payments made directly to the worker-pay for time not worked, pay for time not worked, all bonuses and other special payments, and the costs of payments in kind, and (2) employer contributions to legally required insurance programs and contractual and private benefit plans.
NA means not available.

Source: Except Malaysia and Thailand, 1980, 1984–1988, United States Department of Labor, Bureau of Labor Statistics, May 1991, Report 803; 1981–1983, unpublished data from United States Department of Labor Bureau of Labor Statistics, Office of Productivity and Technology. Malaysia and Thailand, 1988, Bank of Swiss.

1986, in exchange for new foreign loan agreements with the IMF, the World Bank, and its commercial bank creditors, Mexico agreed to major reforms of its economic policies, including liberalization of foreign investment, reductions in public spending, tax reform, and divestiture of state-owned enterprises.

In July 1988, Carlos Salinas de Gortari, the PRI's candidate, won the presidency with 50.4 percent of the vote,[10] amid widespread charges of irregularities in the polling. Cuauhtémoc Cárdenas, the son of the Mexican president who had nationalized the oil companies in 1938, had mounted a strong campaign against the PRI. Cárdenas was critical of the PRI for abandoning Mexico's history of national self-determination. According to the PRI, Cárdenas won 31.1 percent of the vote in the election, including four states and the *distrito federal.* However, many Mexicans believe that Cárdenas actually won the election. As president, Salinas renegotiated the foreign debt, continued the austerity plan, and continued privatizing government-owned businesses.

Maquiladoras

In 1965, the government of Mexico initiated the Border Industrialization Program. The program permitted foreign corporations to establish wholly-owned subsidiary operations in Mexico. Under the program, the subsidiary could import into Mexico duty free, machinery, raw materials, and component parts to be used in processing or assembling goods in Mexico.[11]

So long as the end product was exported, Mexican duties were not levied on the imported components. Under the laws of the United States and most industrialized countries, when the imported components are exported back to their country of origin in the form of finished products, only the value added in Mexico — labor, overhead, raw materials — and not the value of the imported raw materials or components — was subject to duty.[12] Operations established under this program were commonly known as *maquiladoras, maquilas,* or in-bond assembly operations.[13]

Maquiladora or *maquila* is derived from the Spanish verb *"maquilar,"* which means to measure or take payment for grinding corn. In colonial times, the *maquila* was the portion of flour that the miller kept as payment for grinding the corn. In the 1980s, *maquiladora* or *maquila* referred to the system under which foreign companies provide the corn (e.g., electronic components), Mexico keeps its portion for assembling or processing (e.g., foreign currency changed into pesos for wages and production costs), and the assembled goods return to their country of origin with a duty paid only on the value added in Mexico.

Twin plant is another term often associated with *maquilas.* Originally, the Border Industrialization Program envisioned the establishment of complementary plants across the

---

[10] In comparison, de la Madrid received 71.6 percent of the vote in 1982 and López Portillo received 95 percent of the vote in 1976. M. Delal Baer, "Electoral Trends," in *Prospects for Mexico,* ed. George W. Grayson (Washington, D. C.: Center for the Study of Foreign Affairs, Foreign Service Institute, Department of State, 1988), p. 43.

[11] Without the provisions of the Border Industrialization Program, products could not be imported into Mexico without an import license. After Mexico joined the General Agreement on Tariffs and Trade (GATT) in 1986, tariffs at an initial level of 50 percent were substituted for import

---

licenses. At the end of 1987, the tariff ceiling for most items was lowered to 20 percent. Import licenses are still required for electronic and computer equipment and automotive imports. Sidney Weintraub, *Transforming the Mexico Economy: The Salinas Sexenio* (Washington, D. C.: National Planning Association, 1990), p. 5.

[12] In the United States, tariff items 806.30 and 807.00 permit the portion of the product made of U. S. components to reenter the United States duty free.

[13] All maquiladora facilities that export the assembled products are part of the "In-Bond Industry." The in-bond feature of the BIP requires that an importing maquiladora plant guarantee the payment of duties on imported materials that would otherwise be due. The guarantee usually consists of a surety bond. After processing, if the assembled products are exported, the bond is canceled.

border from one another. The Mexican twin was intended to provide labor-intensive assembly of components fabricated in the United States. The assembled components would then be shipped to the twin in the United States where they would be finished, inspected, distributed, and sold. However, in most cases, the complementary U.S. plant was not located along the border but elsewhere within the United States at preexisting facilities. In 1987, fewer than 10 percent of all Mexican maquilas had a U.S. twin.[14]

The Border Industrialization Program was adopted to provide permanent employment for Mexico's rapidly growing population along the U.S.–Mexico border. The program sought to create jobs by attracting foreign manufacturing facilities that would not compete directly with domestic Mexican producers. The program also attempted to absorb migrant agricultural workers displaced by the expiration of the U.S. Bracero Program.[15] To address the problems resulting from the end of the Bracero Program, the law initially required that all foreign-owned assembly operations be located within a 20-kilometer strip along the U.S.–Mexican border. New regulations were adopted in 1977 that permitted maquilas to locate in the economically depressed interior regions of Mexico. In 1983, the Mexican government extended the program to all regions of Mexico. However, by

1986, over 88 percent of all maquila operations were still concentrated along the border. Maquiladoras located near the border accounted for approximately 87 percent of the total maquiladora workforce.[16]

The number of maquiladoras grew from 12 in 1965 to over 1,450 in 1988.[17] Over the same period, the number of maquiladora workers grew from 3,000 to over 361,800. (See Exhibit 9.) The type of maquila production had also changed. In 1965 and 1966, the vast majority of maquiladoras were textile firms. In 1988, maquiladora production included automobiles and auto parts, electronics, telecommunications equipment, and scientific instruments.

Beginning in the early 1980s, a substantial number of major U.S. multinationals, including many Fortune 500 companies, established maquiladoras. Several European and Japanese firms also established maquiladoras or employed subcontractors to perform their assembly in Mexico. In 1987, there were 20 Japanese maquiladoras in Mexico. The most prominent Japanese manufacturers operating maquiladora facilities were Sanyo, Sony, Toshiba, Hitachi, Matsushita, and TDK.[18]

Maquiladoras for Mexico

Impact on the Economy

Mexico earned foreign exchange on the value added to products assembled or processed in Mexico and then exported. (See Exhibits 9 and 10.) In less than 25 years, the maquiladora industry had become Mexico's second largest

---

[14] U. S. International Tariff Commission (USTIC), *The Use and Economic Impact of TSUS Items 806.30 and 807,* Publication No. 2053 (Washington, D. C.: U. S. International Trade Commission, January 1988), p. 8–2.

[15] The Bracero, or Mexican Labor Program, allowed migrant Mexican workers to enter the United States on a temporary (seasonal) basis from 1942 through 1964. It was initiated to alleviate labor shortages in the U.S. agricultural and railroad industries during World War II. The Bracero Program attracted to the border unemployed workers from the Mexican interior who were seeking the guaranteed U. S. minimum wage. The railroad portion of the program ended in 1946. The agricultural program expired in 1964. A large segment of the border population became dependent on income earned by braceros in the United States.

[16] U. S. International Tariff Commission (USTIC), *The Use and Economic Impact of TSUS Items 806.30 and 807,* Publication no. 2053 (Washington, D. C.: U. S. International Trade Commission, January 1988), p. 8–4.

[17] Khosrow Fatemi, ed., *The Maquiladora Industry: Economic Solution or Problem?* (New York: Praeger Publishers, 1990), pp. 4 and 28.

[18] U. S. International Tariff Commission (USTIC), *The Use and Economic Impact of TSUS Items 806.30 and 807,* Publication no. 2053 (Washington, D. C.: U. S. International Trade Commission, January 1988), p. 8–12.

EXHIBIT 9 Selected Data on the *Maquiladoras*

	1980	1981	1982	1983	1984	1985	1986	1987	1988
Number of firms	620	605	585	600	672	760	891	1,125	1,450
Average annual employment (000)	119.5	131	127	151	200	212	250	305	362
Imported materials (million US$)	$1,750	$2,227	$1,979	$2,823	$3,749	$3,825	$4,351	$5,507	$ 7,808
Exported material (million US$)	2,523	3,202	2,830	3,641	4,904	5,092	5,646	7,105	10,146
Value added (million US$)	773	975	851	818	1,155	1,267	1,295	1,598	2,337
Wages, salaries, loans	458	596	463	385	595	660	586	739	1,141
Domestic raw materials and packaging	30	29	26	37	51	36	54	86	132
Utilities and other expenses	129	153	174	183	206	238	295	314	388
Miscellaneous expenses	155	197	189	213	303	334	360	458	676

Note: Figures may not add to rounding.

Source: Banco de Mexico, "La Industria Maquiladora de Exportación, 1980–1986," mimeo. Mexico, 1987; 1987 and 1988, INEGI, "Advances de Informacion Economica – Industria Maquiladora de Exportación," November 1988 and November 1989.

EXHIBIT 10 Selected Data on Mexico's Balance of Payments

	1980	1981	1982	1983	1984	1985	1986	1987	1988
Merchandise exports	16,070	19,940	21,230	22,312	24,196	21,663	16,031	20,655	20,566
Merchandise imports	(18,900)	(24,040)	(14,435)	(8,550)	(11,255)	(13,212)	(11,432)	(12,222)	(18,898)
Trade balance	(2,830)	(4,100)	6,795	13,762	12,941	8,451	4,599	8,433	1,668
Foreign direct investment	2,090	2,540	1,655	461	390	491	1,160	1,796	635
Current account balance	(8,160)	(1,390)	(6,307)	5,403	4,194	1,130	(1,673)	3,968	(2,443)

Trade Balance, also known as Balance of Trade, is a country's exports of goods minus its imports of goods.
Foreign Direct Investment is the acquisition of physical assets outside the home country with substantial management control (usually defined as 10% or more of the ownership of a company) held by the parent corporation or the home country.
Current Account Balance is the net of the country's imports, exports, services, and government unilateral transfers (sums sent outside the home country by the government for foreign aid, emergency relief, etc.).
Balance of Payments is the record of the goods and services an economy has received from and provided to the rest of the world and of the changes in the economy's claims on and liabilities to the rest of the world. Michael G. Rukstad (ed.), *Macroeconomic Decision Making in the World Economy: Text and Cases* (Florida: Holt, Rinehart, & Winston, 1989), p. 485.

Source: *Balance of Payment Statistics*, vol. 41 Yearbook, part 1 (IMF: 1990).

industry after oil and oil-related production. In 1987, the maquiladora industry accounted for approximately 44 percent of Mexican exports to the United States. That year, maquiladoras contributed approximately US$1.6 billion in foreign exchange earnings. Between 1982 and 1987, the industry created 178,000 new jobs out of a total of 408,000 jobs created over this period.[19]

Impact on Environment

It was estimated that maquiladoras generated over 20 million tons of hazardous waste annually. Such wastes include corrosive acids and bases, sludge from electroplating processes, cyanide solutions, paint sludge and thinners, and such heavy metals as cadmium, chromium, lead, mercury and silver.[20] Under the Mexican law, which had regulated maquiladoras since 1983, hazardous wastes had to be returned to their country of origin.[21] American-owned maquiladoras had to comply with both Mexican and U.S. laws regulating hazardous waste disposal. U.S. law required would-be generators of hazardous waste to obtain an EPA identification number. In addition, maquiladoras that planned to transport hazardous waste for off-site treatment, storage, or disposal within the United States had to prepare a manifest. Each time the waste changed hands, the manifest had to be signed. Biennial reports were required to be submitted to the EPA by all companies shipping hazardous waste to the United States.

EPA records showed that, in 1987, only 20 out of more than 1,000 U.S. maquiladoras returned their hazardous waste to the United States.[22] A study by the Texas Center for Policy Studies found that in a two and one-half year period only 33 of the approximately 600 maquiladoras in the Texas–Mexico border area had filed the required notices for return of their hazardous wastes to the United States.[23] A November 1990 study by the Secretaria de Desarrollo Urbano y Ecología (the Ministry of Urban Development and Ecology, or SEDUE), the Mexican government's equivalent of the U.S. Environmental Protection Agency revealed that only 19 percent of the plants using toxic materials could show that they had disposed of wastes properly.[24] Other studies had revealed that primary sources of drinking water in the border area have been contaminated with industrial solvents and other chemicals.[25]

Historically, Mexico had less stringent environmental standards than the United States and lax enforcement of its standards.[26] In a 1988 survey of maquiladoras in Mexicali, a Mexican state near the California border, by El Colegio de la Frontera Norte, 10 percent of the 100 maquiladoras surveyed freely admitted that "environmental legislation" in Mexico was one of the main factors in their decision to leave the United States and relocate in Mexico. Seventeen percent of those surveyed considered it a factor of importance.[27]

In 1988, Mexico enacted the General Law on Ecological Balance and Environmental Protection. The administrator of the

---

[19] Instituto Nacional de Estadística, Geografía e Informática (INEGI), National Income and Product Accounts, 1988.

[20] Douglas Alexander and L. Roberto Fernandez, "Environmental Regulation of Business in Mexico," *Doing Business in Mexico* (New York: Matthew Bender, 1990), pp. 79–29 and 79–30.

[21] 1982 Decree for Promotion of the Maquiladora Industry (Diario Oficial, August 15, 1983), art. 26.

[22] "Transfrontier Health and Environmental Risks," *Natural Resources Journal,* Winter 1990, p. 177.

[23] Remarks of Mary E. Kelly, executive director, Texas Center for Policy Studies, before the Senate Finance Committee, February 20, 1991, p. 3.

[24] "Border Industry's Nasty Byproduct Imperils Trade," *The New York Times,* March 31, 1991, p. 16, col. 3.

[25] Ibid, p. 4.

[26] "The Texas Border: Whose Dirt?", *The Economist,* August 18, 1990, pp. 24–25.

[27] "Transfrontier Health and Environmental Risks," *Natural Resources Journal,* Winter 1990, p. 177.

U.S. Environmental Protection Agency said about the law:

> what we know about Mexico's 1988 comprehensive environmental law indicates that it may be sufficiently stringent to rebut the "pollution haven" argument. Properly enforced, the law should result in greatly improved environmental protection.[28]

SEDUE was the federal Mexican agency charged with enforcing the 1988 environmental law. Its annual budget for pollution control was approximately US$3.1 million. In contrast, in the same year, Texas's annual budget for pollution control was US$50 million. In Ciudad Juarez, a Mexican state near El Paso, Texas, there was one Mexican federal inspector for over 300 maquiladora plants and all Mexican domestic industry.[29]

Most of the maquiladoras were clustered around Tijuana–San Diego in California and Ciudad Juarez–El Paso in Texas. The resulting population growth in these cities severely strained the water supply and infrastructure. A 1981 University of Mexico study on border resources found that the aquifer under El Paso–Ciudad Juarez was being depleted faster than it was being replenished. In the lower Rio Grande Valley, closer to the Gulf of Mexico, municipal and industrial needs were expected to reduce drastically the water available for crop irrigation by the year 2000.[30]

Wages and Working Conditions

The Mexican constitution and federal Mexican labor law set forth the minimum rights and benefits to which Mexican workers were entitled. The law regulated such employment conditions as work schedules, overtime, vacation periods, legal holidays, payment of salaries, employment of women and minors, occupational risks, and minimum wages. Article Three of Mexico's federal labor law provided:

> Work is a social right and social obligation. It is not an article of commerce; it requires respect for the freedom and dignity of the person performing it and it shall be carried out under conditions protecting the life, the health, and a decent standard of living for the worker and his family.[31]

Mexican workers also had the right to unionize. In major Mexican cities, nearly all workers were members of a union. Under Mexican law, the union had the right to approve or disapprove an employer's hiring decisions.

A survey conducted by the International Trade Commission found that U.S. companies viewed the Mexican minimum wage as the major attraction of foreign investment in Mexico.[32] (See Exhibit 11.) Minimum wages in Mexico were set by commissions comprised of members of the government, organized labor, and private industry. The commissions set minimum wages for 86 different unskilled and skilled occupational classifications in 11 different economic zones in Mexico. The highest minimum wages had traditionally been along the northern border.[33]

Base maquiladora wages averaged about $3.50 to $4.00 per day for production workers.[34]

---

[28] "William K. Reilly, "Mexico's Environment Will Improve with Free Trade," *The Wall Street Journal,* April 19, 1991, p. A15, col. 2.

[29] Remarks of Mary E. Kelly, executive director, Texas Center for Policy Studies before the Senate Finance Committee, February 20, 1991, pp. 6–7.

[30] "The Texas Border: Whose Dirt?", *The Economist,* August 18, 1990, pp. 24–25.

[31] Commercial, Business and Trade Laws, Mexico, F. Labor Law, (Title first to ninth) (United States of America: Oceana Publications, Inc., 1983), p. 3.

[32] U. S. International Tariff Commission (USTC), *The Use and Economic Impact of TSUS Items 806.30 and 807,* Publication no. 2053 (Washington, D. C.: U. S. International Trade Commission, January 1988), p. xxx.

[33] Barbara Chrispin, "Manpower Development in the Maquiladora Industry: Reaching Maturity," in Khosrow Fatemi, ed., *The Maquiladora Industry: Economic Solution or Problem?* (New York: Praeger Publishers, 1990), p. 75.

[34] Ibid., p. 76.

EXHIBIT 11   Average Hourly Compensation
Cost for *Maquiladora* Workers

Year	Compensation
1980	$1.42
1981	1.67
1982	1.23
1983	0.91
1984	1.06
1985	1.07
1986	0.80
1987	0.75
1988	0.80

Source: 1980–1986, U.S. International Tariff Commission
(USTIC), *The Use and Economic Impact of TSUS Items 806.30
and 807,* Publication No. 2053 (Washington, D.C.: USTIC, January 1988), p. 8–9; 1987 and 1988, Leslie Sklair, *Assembling for
Development* (Boston: Unwin Hyman, 1989), p. 72.

(See Exhibit 11). According to the American
Friends Service Committee, comparable Mexican manufacturers in major cities paid two to
three times maquiladora wages.[35] Common
fringe benefits, such as attendance bonuses and
transportation subsidies, could raise the wage
to $7 to $9 per day. Attendance bonuses were
in response to a 10 to 35 percent turnover rate
that came to characterize maquiladoras. The
average hourly wages paid to maquiladora
workers placed strict limits on their purchasing
power. In the town of Mantamoros, for example, the average worker had to work an hour
and a half to buy a half-gallon of milk, three
hours to buy a box of cereal, five and a half
hours to buy two pounds of beef, and 17 hours
to buy a toddler-size dress.[36]

Limited studies of maquiladora working conditions indicated that employees had experienced many work-related health and safety
problems. Eye disease and the weakening of
the optic nerve were prevalent among electronics workers. Among textile workers, inadequate seating had been associated with the
development of lumbago.[37]

In a Tijuana, Mexico, maquiladora of one of
CP's Asian competitors, the casewriter observed an assembly line of workers, 98 percent
of whom were women, hunched over a moving
conveyor belt that carried printed circuit
boards (PCBs) in various stages of completion.
The plant made cable boxes and tuners. The
women workers sat on nonergonomic stools
while placing capacitors or other minute components on PCBs. Some workers used mag-
nifying glasses to place components on the
printed circuit boards. Some women soldered
or tested PCBs. Testing was done by manually
manipulating a component on a PCB or by
staring at a computer screen as the PCB was
tested by a machine.

The maquiladora employed a handful of
male workers. These workers attended the
automated processes in the plant, though there
seemed to be little for them to do. No women
were assigned to the machines. All employees
worked a nine and one-half hour day, from 8:00
A.M. to 6:00 P.M., with a half-hour break for
lunch. A trailer outside the plant indicated that
it was for the storage of hazardous waste.

Half of Mexico's population was below the
age of 18. Although it was illegal in Mexico
to hire children under 14, the Mexico City
Assembly estimated that between 5 to 10
million children were employed illegally, often
in hazardous jobs.[38] *The Wall Street Journal*

---

[35] *Background and Perspectives on the U. S.–Mexico–
Canada Free Trade Talks* (Pennsylvania: American Friends
Service Committee, April 10, 1991), p. 6.

[36] Simon Billenness and Kate Simpson, "Franklin's
Insight," September 1992, Boston, p. 8.

---

[37] Judith Ann Warner, "The Sociological Impact of the
Maquiladoras," in Khosrow Fatemi, ed., *The Maquiladora
Industry: Economic Solution or Problem?* (New York: Praeger Publishers, 1990), p. 193. Lumbago is pain in the lower
back (lumbar region) often caused by muscle strain.

[38] Matt Moffett, "Working Children: Underage Laborers Fill Mexican Factories, Stir U. S. Trade Debate," *The
Wall Street Journal,* April 8, 1991, p. 1, col. 1.

EXHIBIT 12 Distribution of Men and Women in the Maquila Workforce in 1986

Various Manufacturing Activities	*Men*	*Women*
Electrical and electronic machinery and equipment	9,610	29,001
Furniture and fixtures	5,803	1,910
Nonelectrical equipment and parts	1,857	897
Footwear and leather products	1,776	2,052
Transportation equipment and accessories	17,850	23,144
Total industry	64,812	139,076

Source: USTC, Publication no. 2053, January 1988, pp. 8–11.

profiled Vincente Guerrero, a 12-year-old Mexican boy who had been compelled to leave the sixth grade to work in a shoe factory.[39]

> Vincente spends most of his time . . . smearing glue onto the soles of shoes with his hands. The glue he dips his fingers into is marked "toxic substances . . . prolonged or repeated inhalation causes grave health damage; do not leave in the reach of minors." All [the boys who work in the factory] ignore the warning.
>
> Impossible to ignore is the sharp, sickening odor of the glue. The only ventilation in the factory is from slits in the wall where bricks were removed from a window near Vincente that opens only halfway. Just a matter of weeks after he started working, Vincente was home in bed with a cough, burning eyes, and nausea.
>
> When a teacher came by the factory to chide school dropouts [the plant superintendent's 13-year-old son] rebuked her. "I'm earning 180,000 pesos a week," he said. "What do you make?" The teacher, whose weekly salary is 120,000, could say nothing.[40]

Estimates placed the savings, compared to average maquiladora wages, from hiring younger (ages 14–18) and less skilled workers at 30 to 40 percent.

Some critics charged that maquiladoras had disrupted the social and family structure of Mexican society by discriminating against Mexican males, the traditional breadwinners, and hiring predominately women. The critics also contended that women were preferred over men because they were more docile, politically unaware, inexperienced, and less demanding. In the 1970s, women comprised 23 percent of the Mexican labor force overall but 72.3 percent of the maquila industry.[41] (See Exhibit 12.)

Living Conditions

In the Mexican border towns, many maquiladora workers lived in dwellings fashioned from cardboard and scraps of wood taken from maquiladora trash bins. Some of the cardboard had once contained polyvinyl chloride; written on the cardboard walls were warnings that the former contents could release hazardous fumes. The workers' water supply was stored in 55-gallon drums also found in maquiladora trash bins. The drums contained labels indicating that their former contents were fluorocarbon solvents whose vapors were harmful if inhaled.

---

[39] Ibid.
[40] Ibid., p. A14, col. 1.

---

[41] Leslie Sklair, *Assembling for Development: The Maquila Industry in Mexico and the United States,* (Boston: Unwin Hyman, 1989), pp. 165–66.

Maquiladoras and the United States

Impact on the Economy

Advocates argued that maquiladoras help keep U.S. manufacturing internationally competitive, saving jobs that would otherwise be lost if U.S. manufacturers went to the Far East, since maquiladoras primarily use components made in the United States. According to a U.S. Department of Commerce report, nearly 75,000 U.S. workers were employed during 1986 to produce and ship $2.9 billion of components and raw materials used annually by maquiladoras.[42]

Organized labor in the United States contended that maquiladoras take jobs out of the United States—some of which could be held by the estimated 27 million workers and unemployed people in the United States who were functional illiterates. The Communications Workers of America (CWA) estimated that had there been no increase in foreign production by U.S. companies, over 20,000 of the 120,000 jobs lost in the telecommunications industry since 1981 would have been saved.[43] In 1988, the jobless rate in the U.S. electronics industry was 86 percent higher than it was in 1979. In the five years between January 1979 and January 1984, employment for production workers manufacturing telephone and telegraph equipment declined in the United States by 23.4. percent.[44]

Maquiladora workers tended to shop in U.S. border towns that returned a portion of their maquila wages to the United States. Studies have suggested that maquila workers spent more than half of their wages in the United States, mainly in the stores and shopping malls of the U.S. border towns.[45]

Impact on the Environment

The maquiladoras brought rapid development on the U.S. side of the border. The pace of development outstripped the ability of the region to absorb it. Mexican officials have complained that growing development on the U.S. side of the border threatened surface-water supplies promised to Mexico under a 1944 treaty. A legal advisor to the Mexican Foreign Ministry believed that by the mid-1990s the United States would be unable to deliver the volume of water promised Mexico.[46] The primary source of drinking water on the Texas border was the Rio Grande, which was consistently drunk dry.[47]

Not only was there a shortage of water, but the water that was available was frequently contaminated. Most Mexican border towns did not have sewage treatment plants. Ciudad Juarez dumped all of its raw sewage into a canal that paralleled the Rio Grande. A study in San Elizario, Texas, showed that everyone there had been exposed to hepatitis at least once by the time he or she was 20 years old.[48] More than 20 million gallons of untreated sewage and chemicals ran into the Tijuana River each day. Some ended up on the Imperial Beach on the California coast, which has been closed for ten years.[49] Recreational use of the

[42] U. S. International Tariff Commission (USTIC), *The Use and Economic Impact of TSUS Items 806.30 and 807,* Publication no. 2053 (Washington, D. C.: U. S. International Trade Commission, January 1988), pp. 8–15.

[43] John Cavanagh, Lance Compa, et al., *Trade's Hidden Costs: Worker Rights in a Changing World Economy,* (Washington, D. C.: International Labor Rights Education & Research Fund, 1988), p. 21.

[44] Full Employment Action Council, "Economic Dislocation and Structural Unemployment: The Plight of America's Basic Industries," September 6, 1985.

[45] Leslie Sklair, "Mexico's Maquiladora Programme," in George Philip, ed., *The Mexican Economy,* (London: Routledge, 1988), p. 299.

[46] "The Natural Limits to Growth," *The Economist,* April 20, 1991, p. 24.

[47] Ibid.

[48] "Border Industry's Nasty Byproduct Imperils Trade," *The New York Times,* March 31, 1991, p. 16, col. 3.

[49] "The Texas Border: Whose Dirt?" *The Economist,* August 18, 1990, p. 24.

Rio Grande below Laredo, Texas, has long been considered unsafe because its sister city in Mexico, Nuevo Laredo, dumps about 25 million gallons of untreated sewage into the river every day.[50]

The air quality along the border had also been affected. On the Mexican side of the border across from El Paso, Texas, firewood was the chief cooking and heating fuel for most of the 1.2 million residents of Ciudad Juarez, Mexico. Rubber tires were burned in kilns that made decorative tiles. Along with pollution from motor vehicles and industry, the smoke from these fires produced an acrid cloud over both cities under certain weather conditions.[51]

Considerations on Plant Location

In late 1988, Stevens enrolled in the seminar advertised in *The Wall Street Journal* and toured the maquiladora operations situated around the U.S.–Mexico border. Stevens described his reactions to the tour:

---

[50] "Border Industry's Nasty Byproduct Imperils Trade," *The New York Times,* March 31, 1991, p. 16, col. 3.
[51] Ibid.

I did not like what I saw. I saw exploitation in the form of sweat shops, I saw wage inflation, horrible environmental conditions, and huge workforce turnover.

CP management had also heard that bribery and corruption were a way of life in Mexico.

Stevens was considering other sites in Mexico, including Monterrey, Hermisillo, Chihuahua, and Guadalajara. He was also considering locations outside Mexico: Malaysia, a U.S. greenfield operation in Texas, and a U.S.–AT&T "factory-within-a-factory" operation. A plant outside the United States would employ approximately 1,800 people at full capacity of 3.5 million units per year. The work week would average 45 hours.

Projections indicated that a maquiladora plant in the border region was the lowest cost option. (See Exhibit 13.) Wages elsewhere in Mexico were likely to be higher—by 15 to 20 percent, for example, in Guadalajara. Expenditures on pollution controls were another cost issue. Complying with U.S. "good citizen" standards with on-site facilities would add $2 to $3 million to the estimates in Exhibit 13 during the first few years. However, a number of companies avoided those expenditures by paying local firms relatively small amounts to

---

EXHIBIT 13 Initial Estimates of Average Cost per Unit at Alternative Sites (labor costed at average maquiladora rates)

	Greenfield	Existing AT&T Factory		Malaysia	Mexico
		Full	*Incremental*		
Landed cost*	$47.33	$52.33	$51.89	$ 41.48	$39.94
Additional cost†	0.72	0.66	0.65	3.40	2.96
Total cost	$48.04	$52.99	$52.54	$ 44.89	$42.89
Incremental carrying costs				0.49	
				$ 45.37	

Note: Data have been disguised. The essential relationships have, however, been preserved.
* Landed cost includes material, labor, and overhead.
† Additional cost includes transportation fees, duties, asset tax, and a charge for AT&T's internal hurdle rate.

dispose of waste—though some of these disposal firms did not actually comply with Mexican laws and regulations.

Malaysia offered several advantages. AT&T had significant experience in Asia, as well as infrastructure and support systems in the area, and the Malaysian Industrial Development Authority offered, like Singapore, a central one-stop shopping opportunity for foreign companies. On the negative side, Stevens was concerned about putting too many eggs in one basket in Asia and feared that Malaysian wages and salaries would rise as more companies moved there.

At the time Stevens was considering where to locate CP's new manufacturing facility, AT&T's senior management was reviewing its capital budgeting process. It seemed it would be more difficult to get approval for the current project than for the Singapore and Thailand operations.

Wherever the plant was located, the plant would be devoted to manufacturing answering systems. Electronic components, printed circuit boards, power adapters, pellets, and cardboard boxes would be brought into the plant. The plant would make the body of the answering systems in-house using plastic injection molding. Completed answering systems would leave the plant boxed and ready to ship.

Even if the project were approved, Stevens and CP management still had to reach decisions on wages and benefits, sourcing of components, the profile of its workforce in terms of gender, age, and educational background, as well as a host of other issues.

McDONNELL DOUGLAS AND TAIWAN AEROSPACE

> *... globalization is a euphemism for American decline and even for colonialization.*

Clyde Prestowitz, *Economic Strategy Institute*

Dozens of gleaming white aircraft perched on the grounds of McDonnell Douglas's Long Beach, California, assembly facility in October 1991. Some roared down nearby runways and into the air during the final stages of flight testing that preceded delivery. Others, bearing insignia of the airlines to whom they had been sold, were about to enter active duty. It seemed a day like any other for McDonnell Douglas, the world's third largest producer of commercial aircraft, and its 120,000 employees.

But a thousand miles away, in McDonnell Douglas's St. Louis corporate headquarters, John F. McDonnell, chairman and CEO, faced a momentous decision. He and vice president Gareth Chang had been working for months on a deal to sell a substantial portion of the company's commercial division to an Asian buyer. Today Chang had told McDonnell that a Taiwanese consortium was prepared to offer $2 billion for a 40 percent stake in the company's commercial airliner division. The chairman had been under heavy criticism for a variety of reasons since he ascended to the top

Allen P. Webb prepared this case under the direction of Joseph L. Badaracco, Jr. for class discussion rather than to illustrate either effective or ineffective handling of an administrative situation.

Harvard Business School case 392-092.

of the company in 1988. Now questions were racing through his head. Could McDonnell Douglas count on the Taiwanese to do high-quality work under strict deadlines? Was this the best offer his company could get? Were there options for raising cash in the U.S. capital markets? Finally, would a deal of this sort be stalled or halted by political opposition? McDonnell wasn't sure.

The Taiwan Aerospace Deal

Executives within McDonnell Douglas had been curious when McDonnell began targeting Taiwan as a potential equity partner as part of his "DG" (Douglas Global) strategy. After all, the country had never produced parts for a commercial jet. Nonetheless, Taiwan was attractive in several ways. The country had a huge stash of foreign currency reserves, more than $76 billion in late 1991.[1] Private and public leaders hoped to use these funds, largely earned by exporting inexpensive imitations of Western and Japanese products, to move into more technologically advanced industries and become more innovative.

Taiwan's government aided these efforts, funneling resources into research and development and encouraging manufacturers to automate production. But the swashbuckling nature of Taiwanese capitalism also played a significant role. Even the nation's star performers in such fields as computers and electronics were far smaller than their counterparts in South Korea and Japan. Tatung Company, for instance, Taiwan's biggest electronics firm, had total sales of $1 billion in 1990, while Samsung, its South Korean rival, sold goods worth $6.37 billion.[2] Success in Taiwan had frequently come to small, flexible, entrepreneurial firms.[3]

On the negative side, Taiwan had been accused of operating a "casino" economy. Its principal stock market index climbed from 800 in 1986 to 12,495 in early 1990 before plummeting nearly 80 percent to the 2500 level between February and October of that year. 1991 had brought broad banking, equity, and bond market reforms, but some Americans who did business with Taiwan still believed its corporate leaders were more interested in earning short-term profits than developing a high-tech economy. An executive in an electronics firm claimed: "These guys would just as soon be selling shoes if there were as much money in it."[4]

The nation had been producing military aircraft for nearly two decades. In 1973, Taiwan entered an agreement with the United States to coproduce F-5E fighters in a massive Taichung facility. Another plane, the XA-3 single-seat attack fighter, entered production in 1980.[5] And Taiwan also produced the AT-3 jet trainer. By 1991, around 300 companies produced aircraft components.

However, many of these firms manufactured only low-tech parts. Moreover, the Taiwanese military was a less-demanding customer, especially with regard to delivery promptness, than a commercial company like McDonnell Douglas would be. Yang Shih-chien, the government official responsible for the development of Taiwan's aerospace industry, had said: "The local industry has a long way to go. That's

---

[1] "A McDonnell Deal in Asia Would Jolt the Airliner Industry," *The Wall Street Journal*, November 15, 1991.

[2] "An Ambitious Taiwan Beckons U.S. Electronics Partners," *Electronic Business*, December 9, 1991, p. 34.

[3] "Unlikely Leader: Taiwan, Long Noted for Cheap Imitations, Becomes an Innovator," *The Wall Street Journal*, June 1, 1990.

[4] "An Ambitious Taiwan Beckons U.S. Electronics Partners," *Electronic Business*, December 9, 1991, p. 35.

[5] Janne E. Nolan, *Military Industry in Taiwan and South Korea* (New York: St. Martin's Press, 1986), pp. 53–54.

why we are encouraging foreign companies to come in."[6]

Taiwan Aerospace, led by president Denny Ko, was the vehicle for this encouragement. In October 1991, the company had fewer than 30 employees and an empty factory in Taichung. The government had put up 29 percent of Taiwan Aerospace's initial $250 million in capital, with the rest coming from such firms as Tatung Group, an electronics and heavy machinery manufacturer, and Formosa Plastics Group, the nation's largest industrial conglomerate. Many companies, believing Taiwan Aerospace might not be profitable for years, were wary of investing. But the government seemed committed to providing whatever financial support was necessary to make the $2 billion deal a reality.

Aircraft Manufacturing

Aircraft makers were engaged in a never-ending battle to win sales and increase production. Their business was labor intensive and nonroutine; the more planes they made, the more efficiently their workers could turn out the next one. American manufacturers discovered during World War II that every time they doubled their output, the number of labor hours (and hence labor costs) required per unit fell by approximately 20 percent.

This learning curve, which plane makers needed to move rapidly down through high-volume production, played a dominant role in industrywide competition. Manufacturers set prices based on the projected cost for the three or four hundredth plane and—inevitably—they lost money on the initial units they sold. Failure to sell sufficient numbers of a plane marked it as a failure and might force its producer to exit the industry. Success could yield a "cash cow," whose high rate of profitability subsidized new and less-successful aircraft.[7]

The plane makers were in this unenviable position because of their relationship with the airline industry. Carriers around the world knew how desperately their suppliers wanted to move down the learning curve and edge closer to profitability on a particular project. They therefore played manufacturers off against one another remorselessly to gain the lowest price. Competition could take strange twists. Boeing once grabbed a TWA order from Airbus, its European competitor, when Tex Boullioun, head of the company's commercial operations at the time, bet TWA's board of directors that Boeing's 767 would use less fuel than Airbus' A-310.[8] And all manufacturers helped their customers finance the planes they purchased. Price-cutting and financing concessions were a way of life. John McDonnell, when he was president of McDonnell Douglas in the early 1980s, summed up the cut-throat process: "You are driven by each deal to make the sacrificial price. You can rationalize each additional cut in the price, because with each additional airplane sold you are that much further down the learning curve. Whichever manufacturer is the most desperate will get the next order."[9]

Just as the airlines squeezed the companies that supplied them with planes, so the aircraft producers could pressure the "subtier" firms that provided them with components for final assembly. In the United States, individual subcontractors might produce similar parts for Boeing, McDonnell Douglas, General Dynamics, and Lockheed. The role of suppliers was nearly as important as that of the aircraft manufacturers themselves. Subcontractors

---

[6] "Taiwan's Aerospace Sector Gets a Lift with McDonnell Deal to Build Jetliner," *The Wall Street Journal*, November 21, 1991.

[7] John Newhouse, *The Sporty Game* (New York: Alfred A. Knopf, 1982). See pp. 19–20 for information on start-up costs and the learning curve.

[8] Newhouse, p. 212.

[9] Newhouse, p. 21.

produced equipment as important as engines, and as mundane as lavatory parts. In 1989, when 113,000 people were directly involved in the production of finished commercial transport jets, suppliers employed 322,500. That same year, the value of complete commercial aircraft exported was $13.45 billion, while that of nonmilitary components exported was $11.97 billion. Over half ($5.71 billion) of the latter figure was comprised of aircraft engines and parts, which were produced by General Electric and Pratt and Whitney. A British company, Rolls Royce, also competed in this market, but was a poor third. Even Airbus, the European aircraft producer, purchased nearly all of its engines from the American giants.

Developing new aircraft was wildly expensive and risky. Boeing's late-1970s investment in two new airliners, the 757 and 767, exceeded the company's net worth. The primary expenses were divided between design, development, and engineering (around 40 percent); retooling and modifying manufacturing sites (around 20 percent); and certifying, administering, and carrying overhead during the launch of the plane.[10] The entire process typically lasted five years.

Aircraft makers did not launch a new product without a commitment for a substantial purchase from at least one major airline. Competition for "launch customers" was naturally intense. But even when manufacturers secured initial orders from several major carriers, they

---

[10] Harvard Business School case study 9-386-193, p. 3. "The Technology Web" and "New Aircraft Launch" were created by the casewriter exclusively to illustrate "McDonnell Douglas and Taiwan Aerospace." Like the rest of the case, they may not be reproduced without permission of Harvard Business School.

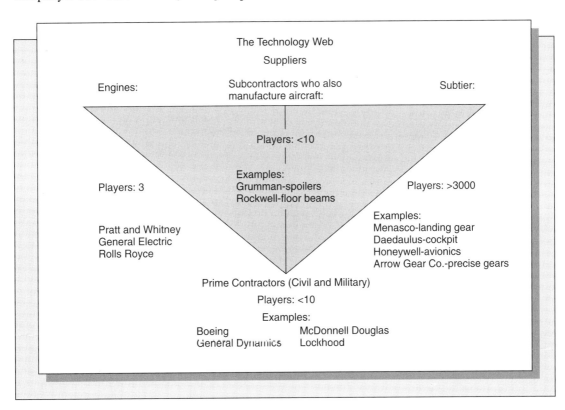

The Technology Web

Suppliers

Engines:

Subcontractors who also manufacture aircraft:

Subtier:

Players: <10

Players: 3

Examples:
Grumman-spoilers
Rockwell-floor beams

Players: >3000

Pratt and Whitney
General Electric
Rolls Royce

Examples:
Menasco-landing gear
Daedaulus-cockpit
Honeywell-avionics
Arrow Gear Co.-precise gears

Prime Contractors (Civil and Military)

Players: <10

Examples:

Boeing   McDonnell Douglas
General Dynamics   Lockhood

still had commitments for far fewer aircraft than the 350 or 400 they needed to break even; these could take more than a decade to secure. High start-up costs interacted with the learning curve and complex competitive dynamics to produce an industry that was considered by its leaders to be "sporty." "In this business," noted Boeing executive John Sutter, "you have to put the company on the line every three or four years."[11]

Aircraft manufacturing was not only risky but also highly complex. A Boeing 747 contained six million parts and 175 miles of wiring.[12] Moreover, commercial jets embodied cutting edge technology in such diverse areas as

computers, advanced specialty fabricating materials, electronics, and aerodynamic design.

The most important technology in 1991 was in the realm of design. Computer aided design (CAD) systems, which permitted extensive analysis of aerodynamics and system integration without the use of models or test flights, played an increasing role in new aircraft development. Designers employed CAD on one-third of Boeing's 767 components, and planned to do so on nearly all of the 777s. Though many countries were able to assemble or produce significant subsections of finished aircraft, only Boeing, McDonnell Douglas, and Airbus could carry out the design process fully.

Another critical area was aerodynamics, especially wing design. The wing, on which the rest of the plane hung during flight, encompassed more high technology than any other section. Once engineers settled on an

[11] Newhouse, p. 7.

[12] Boeing Co. Is Girding for Dogfight over Market Share," *The Wall Street Journal,* January 14, 1992.

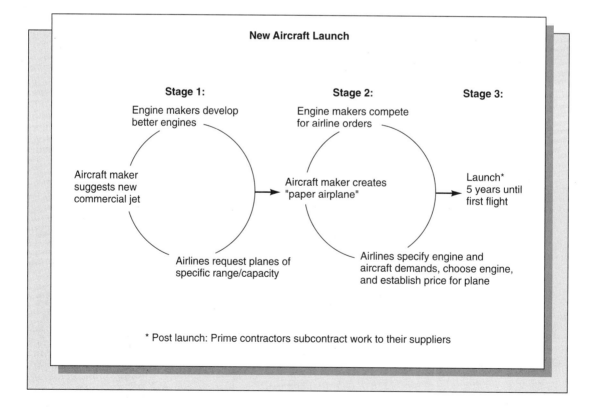

New Aircraft Launch

Stage 1:

Engine makers develop better engines

Aircraft maker suggests new commercial jet

Airlines request planes of specific range/capacity

Stage 2:

Engine makers compete for airline orders

Aircraft maker creates "paper airplane"

Airlines specify engine and aircraft demands, choose engine, and establish price for plane

Stage 3:

Launch*
5 years until first flight

* Post launch: Prime contractors subcontract work to their suppliers

appropriate shape and size, they had to design wing flap assemblies, the hydraulic and electronic components that would operate them, and backup systems to safeguard the aircraft in the event of a malfunction in any of these parts. A particularly tricky problem was developing the nacelle *(na-Sell)*, a pod that housed the engine and created the aerodynamic interface between engine and wing.[13] Flight control systems, advanced structures, propulsion integration, and avionics were other important technological components.

The United States and Europe had roughly equivalent capabilities in all of these areas by the mid-1980s. Japan was behind in most, though its expertise in electronics made it the most advanced source for color CRT hardware used in piloting systems. However, MITI had announced its intention in 1980 to be a technological peer of the United States and Europe in aerospace by 2010.

U.S. Government Policy

The U.S. government became an active participant in the country's aircraft industry soon after Wilbur and Orville Wright flew their first, primitive biplane in 1904. Congress established the National Advisory Committee for Aeronautics (NACA) in 1915 to fund generic aerospace research that would have both civil and military applications. NACA pioneered early propeller technology and contributed to the creation of the Douglas Corporation's DC-3, one of the first successful pre-World War II commercial aircraft.[14]

NACA became the National Aeronautic and Space Administration (NASA) in 1958, as the United States sought to match Soviet advances in space following the launch of Sputnik. The boundary between private and public research

efforts was blurry. NASA carried out the early phases of basic and applied research but did not present airplane makers with prepackaged technology ready for application. Boeing and McDonnell Douglas both had their own research departments, which perfected useful NASA developments while pioneering others of their own.[15] NASA was a less-active participant in aeronautic research than NACA had been. NACA employed between 4,000 and 6,000 scientists during the years after World War II until its conversion to NASA in the late 1950s. NASA employed between 2,000 and 4,000 scientists on nonspace projects from the early 1960s through the mid 1980s.[16] In 1991, NASA engineers were coordinating industry efforts to develop a new generation of airliner that could fly from Washington to Tokyo in under three hours.[17]

Even more important than NACA and NASA during the early postwar years was the Department of Defense. Its orders for jet bombers and the KC-135 transport plane helped Boeing defray the costs of developing its first commercial jet, the 707. By 1991, the technology flow had been reversed in many cases. Commercial advances in fuel efficiency, aluminum alloys, flight management systems, and composite structures were employed in new military planes during the 1970s and 1980s. Yet government research funding through various channels, both civilian and military, continued. In 1990, government research spending was estimated to comprise 71.66 percent of total R&D in the aerospace

---

[13] Newhouse, 1982, pp. 193–4.

[14] Theodore H. Moran and David C. Mowery, "Aerospace," *Daedalus,* Fall 1991, p. 136.

[15] *The Competitive Status of the U.S. Civil Aviation Manufacturing Industry,* 1985, pp. 135–39. The U.S. Civil Aviation Manufacturing Industry Panel suggested that NASA should place more emphasis on the later phases of R&D.

[16] *The Competitive Status of the U.S. Civil Aviation Manufacturing Industry,* 1985, p. 135.

[17] Joint Economic Committee Hearing on the McDonnell Douglas–Taiwan Aerospace Agreement, testimony by Clyde Prestowitz, December 3, 1991.

EXHIBIT 1   Research and Development Funds as a Percentage of Net Sales, 1978–1988

	Aerospace		All Manufacturing	
Year	Total	Company Funds	Total	Company Funds
1978	13.3%	3.2%	2.9%	2.0%
1979	12.9	3.5	2.6	1.9
1980	13.7	3.8	3.0	2.1
1981	16.0	4.6	3.1	2.2
1982	17.1	5.1	3.8	2.6
1983	15.2	4.1	3.9	2.6
1984	15.4	4.0	3.9	2.6
1985	14.9	3.9	4.4	3.0
1986	13.4	4.0	4.7	3.2
1987	14.7	3.6	4.6	3.1
1988	15.4	3.5	4.8	3.2

Source: *Aerospace Facts and Figures 90–91,* Washington: Aerospace Industry Association of America, Inc., 1990, p. 107.

industry.[18] This infusion of government funds helped the aerospace industry's spending on research and development to dwarf that of other industries (see Exhibit 1).

The Players: Past and Present

Boeing

Although Boeing had developed more highly profitable aircraft (the 707, 727, 737, and 747) than any other firm, the Seattle firm was not always on top. Prior to the mid-1950s, the Douglas Aircraft Company sold more propeller-driven passenger planes than any other company. Boeing began wrestling dominance from Douglas in 1956, when its 707 beat the DC-8 to the market and became the first successful long-range commercial jet airliner. Boeing followed the 707 with the shorter-range 727 in 1960, which served as the backbone for domestic airline routes for more than two decades. Then in December of 1965, Boeing signed a letter of

intent with Pan American World Airways to produce the 747, a twin-aisle, wide-body, four-engine plane. Boeing again beat the competition to the market with a new generation of aircraft.

Manufacturing the 747 nearly drove Boeing out of business. No airlines ordered the plane between 1969 and 1972, as start-up costs mounted. Strapped with debt, the company reduced its workforce from 101,000 to 37,000 between mid-1968 and mid-1971. This trial by fire caused Boeing to reexamine and reorganize its manufacturing practices, leading to much greater productivity. Pan American flew its first 747 to London in 1970, the plane gradually entered widespread use for long distance flights, and Boeing emerged from the crisis a leaner and more efficient company.

By 1990, Boeing's average production costs were estimated to be 5–7 percent lower than those of McDonnell Douglas. Moreover, the firm's aggressive development of new planes allowed it to offer a complete "family" of aircraft that covered most ranges and capacities (see Exhibit 2). These strengths brought Boe-

---

[18] *Aerospace Facts and Figures, 1990–91,* p. 106.

EXHIBIT 2 Competing Jet Airliners, 1991

Aircraft	No. Engines/ Aisles	Seating Capacity	Range	Delivered through 1990	Year Introduced
Short-range, low capacity:					
Boeing 737 (-200/-300/-400)	2/1	120–159	2,500 nmiles	2,003	1968
Boeing 757	2/1	186–200	4,500	332	1982
MD-80 (formerly DC-9)	2/1	130–155	2,500	1,857	1982
Airbus A-320	2/1	150	3,500	117	1988
Mid-range, mid-sized:					
Boeing 767	2/2	174–290	6,650	343	1982
Airbus A-300/310	2/2	210–260	4,900	468	1974
Long-range, high capacity:					
Boeing 777	2/2	298–400	7,800	0	1995
MD-11 (formerly DC-10)	3/2	320–405	7,000	386	1990
Airbus A-330	2/2	330–440	5,200	0	1993
Airbus A-340	4/2	262–440	7,800	0	1992
Long-range, jumbo:					
Boeing 747	4/2	452–509	8,400	867	1971
MD-12	3/2	375–520	9,000 ?	0	1997

Notes: MD-80 and MD-11 sales include previous deliveries of DC-9 and DC-10.
Nmiles represent nautical miles.
Seating capacities depend on seating configuration purchased by airline.

Source: Annual reports: Aerospatiale; Boeing; British Aerospace; Messerschmitt-Bolkow-Blohm; McDonnell Douglas. *Interavia Aerospace Review,* December 1990, pp. 1064–68. *Aviation Week and Space Technology,* November 4, 1991, pp. 36–43. Harvard Business School case studies 9-588-014, 9-386-193, N9-390-141. *Aerospace Facts and Figures 90–91,* p. 35.

ing superiority in many regional markets, particularly in Asia. Dominance in this expanding market, projected to equal that of the United States in size by 2010, augered well for Boeing's future. Its diverse product line also contributed to the company's enormous financial success. By late 1991, it had a commercial order backlog worth $91 billion that would require nearly 5 years to fill.[19] Boeing was highly profitable (see Exhibit 3), though some analysts worried that the firm was overly dependent upon its 747, which provided over 70 percent of all profits.[20]

---

[19] "How Boeing Does It," *Business Week,* July 9, 1990.
[20] "Boeing Co. Is Girding for Dogfight over Market Share," *The Wall Street Journal,* January 14, 1992.

Nonetheless, Wall Street had looked favorably on Boeing's burgeoning order books in the late-1980s (see Exhibit 4).

McDonnell Douglas
At the time Boeing launched the 747, the Douglas Aircraft Company, in spite of offering two fine planes, the DC-9, which competed with the 727, and the DC-8, aimed at the 707, was near collapse. Its attempt to simultaneously build three new, larger versions of the DC-8 and several variations on the DC-9 while keeping up with brisk demand for the DC-9 had stretched Douglas beyond its resource base. And poor management had remained ignorant of the company's mounting problems until too late.

EXHIBIT 3 Boeing Company—Selected Financial Highlights, 1970–1990

Year	Aircraft Sales			Earnings			Capital Expenditure		
	Commercial	Military†	Total‡	Commercial	Military	Total	Commercial†	Military	Total*
1970	2,921	339	3,677	NA	NA	22	NA	NA	21
1975	2,238	767	3,719	NA	NA	76	NA	NA	71
1980	7,665	923	9,426	678	78	600	463	91	668
1982	5,135	2,372	9,035	16	269	292	204	77	331
1984	5,457	3,103	10,442	17	346	390	112	144	337
1986	9,820	4,852	16,444	411	367	665	332	356	795
1987	9,827	3,979	15,505	352	60	480	286	316	738
1988	11,369	3,668	17,340	585	(95)	614	326	241	690
1989	14,305	3,962	20,623	1,165	(559)	973	612	506	1,362
1990	21,230	4,123	28,043	2,189	(299)	1,385	1,001	407	1,586

* Total sales, earnings, and capital expenditure figures include nonaircraft divisions.
† Represents operating earnings before taxes.
‡ Represents total earnings after taxes.

Source: Boeing annual reports. Harvard Business School case study N9-390-141.

EXHIBIT 4 Stock Data—Boeing and McDonnell Douglas, 1987–1990

| | McDonnell Douglas | | | Boeing | | |
| | Stock Price | | Outstanding Shares (000) | Stock Price | | Outstanding Shares (000) |
	High	Low		High	Low	
1990	63⅝	34	38,300	61⅞	37¾	343,573
1989	94½	59⅝	38,300	41¼	25¾	230,556
1988	79⅝	59	38,200	30	16½	153,233
1987	87½	54½	38,716	24	15	152,280

Source: *Standard & Poor's N.Y.S.E. Stock Reports,* December 30, 1991, p. 340; February 20, 1992, p. 1448, *Moody's Industrial Manual,* 1988–91.

The McDonnell Corporation rescued the firm in 1967 by merging with it to form the McDonnell Douglas Corporation. McDonnell was a large manufacturer of military aircraft but had no experience in the commercial business. Its St. Louis headquarters was far from Douglas's Long Beach operations. Like Douglas, McDonnell was a family firm. Its founder, James S. McDonnell, was a strong-willed leader who brought greater managerial discipline to Douglas's commercial operations. Unfortunately, his experience in the military aerospace sector had not prepared him well for the complex dynamics of long, uncertain production runs and nail-biting negotiations with airlines.

McDonnell immediately sought to compete with Boeing in the wide-body "jumbo" market. His firm's offering, the DC-10, was a three-engine, double-aisled aircraft with a smaller capacity than the 747 that was more appropriate for domestic transcontinental flights. Unfortunately for McDonnell Douglas, the Lockheed Aircraft Corporation, another military contractor, had also set its sights on this rich market. The DC-10 and the Lockheed L-1011 "Tri-Star" were nearly identical in length, width, wing span, seating capacity, operating cost, range, and speed. The L-1011 boasted a more advanced electronics and navigation system and a superior cockpit and flight

controls; it was also easier to maintain and could be more easily landed in poor weather. The DC-10 had the advantage of being produced by a long-time industry player. Some airlines preferred dealing with McDonnell Douglas to buying from a company that had never before produced a commercial jet.

After ferociously competitive and topsy-turvy negotiations, the L-1011 and DC-10 split the market, virtually ensuring that neither would make much money.[21] The "Tri-Star" proved to be Lockheed's last commercial offering. The Nixon administration had to grant loan guarantees of $250 million in 1971 to save the company from bankruptcy during the L-1011's launch. In 1982, after selling around 300 of a plane that was "more admired within the industry than any other," Lockheed exited commercial aircraft manufacturing, having lost an estimated $2.5 billion on the Tri-Star.[22]

Although the DC-10 did not force McDonnell Douglas out of business, it still cost the company dearly. In March of 1974, a Turkish Airlines DC-10 dropped from the sky near Paris, killing 346 passengers. DC-10s operated by American airline companies were involved

---

[21] American and United purchased the DC-10, while TWA, Eastern, and Delta bought the L-1011.

[22] Newhouse, p. 4.

EXHIBIT 5 DC-10 Orders, 1968–1982

Year	Firm Orders	Year	Firm Orders
1968–75	230	1979	34
1976	16	1980	12
1977	29	1981	3
1978	43	1982	0

Source: McDonnell Douglas annual reports.

in four accidents in which a loss of life occurred. The most serious occurred at Chicago's O'Hare Airport in 1979, when a failed take-off killed all 273 passengers and crew members aboard. The FAA withdrew the DC-10's airworthiness certificate while it investigated this tragedy. Though the plane was allowed to return to the skies, its reputation had been seriously damaged. Sales slowed to a trickle (see Exhibit 5). The poor sales and unfavorable publicity generated by the DC-10 left a bitter taste in James McDonnell's mouth. He refused to commit his company's resources to a new commercial airliner throughout his tenure as chairman, which ended with his death in 1980.

The heavy burdens imposed by their wide-body programs meant Boeing, McDonnell Douglas, and Lockheed were ill-prepared to launch new aircraft or fend off foreign challenges in the early 1970s. It was precisely at this time that a European consortium named Airbus Industrie launched a new plane that was to permanently alter the industry.

Airbus

Airbus Industrie was a last ditch effort by the governments of France, West Germany, and Great Britain to produce commercial jets. Europe's previous offerings had been dismal failures. Britain's Comet was structurally unsound and broke apart in mid-flight. France's Caravelle stayed together in the air but sold poorly. The two nations began cooperating in the 1960s on the supersonic Concorde project and

ultimately turned out a technologically advanced but commercially unsuccessful plane. Finally, in the late 1960s the governments of all three countries agreed to combine forces and produce a commercial airliner for the global market. Britain dropped out of the program in 1969 when France and West Germany voted in favor of using an American General Electric engine for the new plane, rather than one produced by Britain's Rolls–Royce. So it was left for the remaining two countries to form a Groupement d'Intéret Economique called Airbus Industrie.

Airbus's structure was unique. The company's top leadership made all design, production, and marketing decisions and negotiated with customers, helping Airbus to avoid the squabbling that had plagued the Concorde project. However, Airbus itself paid no taxes, earned no profits, and bore no financial risks. These responsibilities were undertaken by the companies that actually produced the plane: France's Aerospatiale and West Germany's Deutsche Airbus, whose principal member was the giant Messerschmitt-Bolkow-Blohm. These firms were liable for all of Airbus' commitments.

The governments of France and the F.R.G. could strongly support the consortium through preferential loans and other forms of financing to the constituent firms without meddling in Airbus' decision making. Government loans defrayed start-up costs on new planes. And national export-promoting agencies helped

Airbus to finance the generous terms of credit it gave foreign airlines. Airbus's leaders countered American claims that European governments had pumped $12 billion into the program by 1990, giving it an unfair advantage over private firms, with charges that the U.S. government, operating through the Department of Defense, NASA, and tax incentives, paid $22 billion in indirect subsidies to McDonnell Douglas and Boeing between 1976 and 1990.[23]

Airbus's complex structure would have been of no use if it did not build an airplane that airlines wanted. Fortunately for the Europeans, their A-300 filled an empty market niche. The plane was a short to medium-range wide-body with only two engines. The DC-10 and L-1011 were larger, not as fuel efficient, and less suitable for short-haul traffic. Nonetheless, Airbus's plane was not an immediate commercial success. Air France flew the first A-300 in 1974, but by 1977 only 38 A-300s had been sold. The second oil shock brought rising energy costs that made the A-300's fuel efficiency a major competitive advantage; by the end of 1979 firm orders and potential commitments approached 300.[24]

Airbus followed up the successful A300 with a stretched version, the A310, and a new short-range, twin-engine, single-aisle plane called the A320. In 1979 , British Aerospace climbed back aboard the Airbus express, joining Spain, which had become a 4 percent member of the consortium, and Belgium and the Netherlands, who had earlier entered as junior subcontracting partners.

The arrival of Airbus intensified the crucible of competition for Boeing, McDonnell Douglas, and Lockheed (see Exhibits 6 and 7). Lockheed's cancellation of the L-1011 was hastened by the European presence. James

McDonnell, wary of the commercial business, avoided new investments. Boeing, however, launched two new planes in the mid-to-late 1970s to meet the Europeans head-on. The 767, like the A-300 and A-310, was a mid-range, wide-body twin jet. The 757, which replaced the 727, competed with the A-320. Airbus launched a new long-range, wide-body jet, the A-330/340, in the mid-1980s. Boeing countered with the 777 in 1990 (see Exhibit 2).

Global Manufacturing

Although McDonnell Douglas's efforts in Asia were in part a reaction to intensified international competition, cooperative production ventures were nothing new. Since the 1950s, the United States had coproduced military jets with Japan and Europe. And in the late 1960s, McDonnell Douglas shared its design for the DC-10's engine nacelle with Airbus in return for a financial contribution to the development process. McDonnell Douglas and Airbus had each decided to use a General Electric engine for their new planes, the DC-10 and A-300. Consequently, the same engine nacelle was appropriate for both. Airbus managed to save time and money by piggy-backing on McDonnell Douglas's design efforts.[25] It was not until the mid-1970s, however, that U.S. manufacturers, seeking to lower their production costs and pave the way for sales to foreign airlines, began buying components from suppliers abroad.

Boeing led the way with its 767. Italy's Aeritalia built the trailing edge of the wing and some of the tail section. Japan's Civil Transport Development Corporation, a consortium made up of Mitsubishi Heavy Industries, Kawasaki Heavy Industries, and Fuji Heavy Industries produced about 15 percent of the plane, including most of its rear exterior body (fuselage)

---

[23] "EC Report Claims U.S. Plane Makers Receive Subsidies," *The Wall Street Journal,* December 5, 1991.

[24] Newhouse, p. 28.

[25] Newhouse, p. 194.

EXHIBIT 6   Market Share as Determined by Aircraft Delivered

Year	McDonnell Douglas Deliveries	Share (%)	Boeing Deliveries	Share (%)	Airbus Deliveries	Share (%)
1950s–1977	1,757	34.2%	3,322	64.7%	53	1.6%
1978	40	16	201	78	16	6
1979	75	19	286	74	25	6
1980	63	16	299	75	37	9
1981	97	25	257	66	37	9
1982	49	18	176	65	46	17
1983	54	18	204	69	38	13
1984	54	22	146	59	48	19
1985	82	25	203	62	42	13
1986	103	27	242	65	30	8
1987	105	26	270	67	31	8
1988	131	27	290	61	57	12
1989	119	24	284	58	83	17
1990	142	23	385	62	95	15
Total, 1978–1990	1,114	22.5%	3,243	65.6%	585	11.8%

Note: Market share calculated as a proportion of total aircraft, rather than total passenger seats delivered, exaggerates McDonnell Douglas's position and underestimates that of Airbus, because Airbus sells more wide-body aircraft than McDonnell Douglas.

Source: Annual reports: Aerospatiale; Boeing; British Aerospace; Messerschmitt-Bolkow-Blohm; McDonnell Douglas. Harvard Business School case study 9-588-014.

panels and advanced drag reducing forms, placed on the wing tips, called fairings. Japanese engineers spent a year in Seattle and built manufacturing facilities in Japan that were quite similar to Boeing's. McDonnell Douglas followed Boeing's lead with its MD-80 and MD-11. Around 16 percent of the former, and 20 percent of the latter, were foreign-produced. Mitsubishi supplied the MD-11's tail cone, and a small section of the MD-80's wing. The Japanese firm began producing the Boeing 747's wing flap in 1987.[26]

In 1990, Boeing expanded its relationship with Japan's Civil Transport Development Corporation. Boeing and the consortium's members discussed and decided against an equity deal, in which the Japanese firms would put up 25 percent of the new 777's development costs, or around $1 billion. However, they ultimately agreed that Mitsubishi, Kawasaki, and Fuji would be "super-subcontractors" for the new plane. The three firms would play a larger role than was typical for individual suppliers; their share in the project's work would increase from the 15 percent undertaken on the 767 to approximately 20 percent. "It's a step up from what they're doing on the 767," said Lawrence Clarkson, Boeing's senior vice president for government and international affairs, "but not a big step."[27] Nonetheless, the Japanese companies would be allowed to send 250 or 300 engineers to Boeing during the

[26] Mitsubishi Heavy Industries, Ltd., publication: "Nagoya Aerospace Systems Works," pp. 11–12.

[27] "Japanese Get Only Small Role on Boeing Plane," *The Wall Street Journal,* April 16, 1990.

EXHIBIT 7 Market Share as Determined by Firm Orders

Year	McDonnell Douglas Orders	Share (%)	Boeing Orders	Share (%)	Airbus Orders	Share (%)
1985	117	19.5%	390	65.1%	92	15.4%
1986	112	21.0	341	64.0	80	15.0
1987	134	18.9	366	51.6	209	29.5
1988	246	23.5	636	60.6	167	15.9
1989	233	16.1	887	61.2	329	22.7
Total, 1985–89	842	19.4	2,620	60.4	877	20.2
Sept. 31, 1991 Total firm backlog	450	14.4%	1,695	54.2%	985	31.5%

Note: Marketshare calculated as a proportion of total aircraft, rather than total passenger seats ordered, exaggerates McDonnell Douglas's position and underestimates that of Airbus because Airbus sells more wide-body aircraft than McDonnell Douglas.

Source: Annual Reports: Aerospatiale; Boeing; British Aerospace; Messerschmitt-Bolkow-Blohm; McDonnell Douglas. *Aviation Week and Space Technology,* December 9, 1991, p. 24 (estimates prepared by Paine Webber).

design and development phase of the project. They would manufacture the plane's fuselage panels, its landing gear doors, and aerodynamic fairings.

Though Boeing was capable of producing these items, the company had planned from the outset to subcontract them. Working with the Japanese consortium would reduce the work done by American suppliers, but not by Boeing itself. Furthermore, the Japanese were not permitted to look at Boeing's books during the program; nor could they attend Boeing's internal marketing meetings or negotiations with the airlines. Finally, Boeing would not share process technology necessary for final assembly and component integration.

Boeing's decision not to make the Civil Transport Development Corporation an equity partner in the 777 may have stemmed in part from the outcry that arose when General Dynamics entered a relationship with Mitsubishi and the Japanese Defense Agency. In 1986, the government of Japan announced that it would build 130 jet fighters, to be called the FS-X, rather than buy them from American manufacturers. American officials, fearing an

increase in the country's trade imbalance, objected. Bowing to pressure, the Japanese agreed in October of 1987 to use the F-16 as the basis for their new fighter, and to develop it in conjunction with General Dynamics.

It was not until January of 1989 that General Dynamics and Mitsubishi reached a preliminary agreement, which called for a "free exchange" of advanced technology. General Dynamics hoped to learn about the advanced construction materials Mitsubishi planned to use in the plane's single-piece composite wings; the Japanese stood to gain design and computer expertise from General Dynamics. The following month, U.S. Commerce Secretary Robert A. Mosbacher persuaded President Bush and the National Security Council to delay their decision on the FS-X until its technological implications for both the commercial and military aircraft industries were more closely examined.

At this point, politics muddled the debate. Jesse Helms of North Carolina, disregarding development costs, the learning curve, and economies of scale in aircraft manufacturing, suggested the Japanese should purchase 50 or

60 F-16s before beginning FS-X codevelopment with General Dynamics. Proponents of the alliance argued that the F-16 technology that General Dynamics would be sharing was 20 years old, and hardly likely to give Japan a significant advantage in its own commercial program.[28] Critics were opposed to General Dynamics sharing its software "source codes," which enabled the F-16 to fly and engage in combat.

Ultimately, the two governments arrived at a compromise in which General Dynamics agreed to restrict certain sensitive software packages from Mitsubishi. The Japanese also agreed that American subcontractors would be alloted 40 percent of production work on the FS-X. With these assurances, the U.S. Senate approved the alliance by a 52–47 vote in mid-May of 1989. Mitsubishi and General Dynamics had a number of smaller squabbles even after government approval. The Japanese Defense Agency removed a key stumbling block when it agreed to compensate Japanese companies for technology shared by them with General Dynamics. Finally, in February of 1990, the project was set to get underway.

The Roots of the Deal: McDonnell Douglas in the 1980s

McDonnell Douglas entered the 1980s with new leadership. James McDonnell died in August 1980 and was succeeded as chairman and CEO by his nephew Sanford. The founder's son John became president, and industry insiders believed he would provide the most significant day-to-day leadership. Described as "unassuming," "affable, articulate, and low key," John McDonnell had risen through the corporation's finance depart-

ment.[29] He and Sanford assumed control of a company with $6 billion in sales, split fairly evenly between the combat and commercial aircraft divisions. McDonnell Douglas's third, smaller division produced space systems and missiles (see Exhibit 8).

The new chairman and president did not share James McDonnell's aversion to the commercial division and recognized that they would have to develop new products if it was to continue operation in the long run. Nonetheless, their headquarters was still in St. Louis, site of the combat aircraft unit. If this weren't enough to tilt their attention toward the military division, the early 1980s provided fantastic opportunities for that side of the business.

The defense build-up of the early Reagan years was a gold mine for McDonnell Douglas. The firm's military aircraft earnings more than doubled between 1980 and 1985, skyrocketing from $197.8 million to $521.2 billion. In an attempt to expand its profitable defense sales, the company acquired Hughes Helicopters, Inc., in January 1984 for $472.3 million. Though this transaction forced McDonnell Douglas to take on more debt than it had carried for a number of years, the stream of payments from Hughes' advanced Apache AH-64 attack helicopter promised to more than compensate for interest payments. The U.S. Army had already pledged to purchase 675 of the firm's new helicopters, and was expected to ultimately buy over 1,200. It was morning in America, and McDonnell Douglas's combat aircraft division was clearly on the right side of the bed.

The commercial division, on the other hand, suffered from a bad hangover early in the decade, operating in the red until 1984. Sanford

---

[28] *Aviation Week and Space Technology,* "Japan's FS-X Puzzle," February 27, 1989, p. 9.

[29] "McDonnell Douglas Chairman Pins Hopes on Success of His Taiwan Deal," *The Wall Street Journal,* Wednesday, November 20, 1991. Newhouse, 1982, p. 22.

EXHIBIT 8 McDonnell Douglas Corporation—Selected Financial Highlights, 1970–1990

Year	Aircraft Sales			Earnings			Capital Expenditure		
	Commercial	Military†	Total‡	Commercial	Military	Total	Commercial†	Military	Total*
1970	617	853	2,088	NA	NA	93	NA	NA	73
1975	1,313	1,406	3,256	NA	NA	86	NA	NA	33
1980	2,220	2,694	6,066	(144)	198	145	45	73	266
1982	1,810	3,708	7,331	(69)	304	215	33	82	248
1984	2,041	5,341	9,663	57	483	325	42	176	438
1986	3,554	5,988	12,505	121	389	277	168	341	680
1987	3,682	6,190	13,080	108	337	313	253	223	672
1988	4,637	6,288	14,435	110	418	350	219	202	619
1989	4,511	6,124	14,581	(167)	207	219	213	189	582
1990	5,812	5,830	16,246	(177)	46	306	146	92	406

* Total sales, earnings, and capital expenditure figures include nonaircraft divisions.
† Represents operating earnings before taxes.
‡ Represents total earnings after taxes.

Source: McDonnell Douglas annual reports. Harvard Business School case study N9-390-141.

461

and John McDonnell led a division whose first task was not selling the DC-10, but rather reclaiming its reputation after the 1979 Chicago crash. In July of 1980, the company launched a public relations campaign seeking to do just that. The campaign did not succeed. Practically all the firm's commercial sales were of the revamped DC-9 Super 80, renamed the MD-80 in 1982. This plane faced ferocious competition from Boeing's new 757, which began service in 1982, and the older 737, along with Airbus's A320 model. It was little wonder that Sanford and John McDonnell wrote in their 1983 report to shareholders that the commercial division appeared "unpromising."

But the McDonnells were not ready to give up on their transport aircraft division. They could only succeed with a larger plane to replace the DC-10 and complement the MD-80. In 1986, the company launched the MD-11, an improved version of the DC-10, which the company believed was cheaper to operate over long distances than Boeing's 747. After a stony initial reception from the airlines, the MD-11 achieved 45 firm orders in 1987, 43 in 1988, 38 in 1989, and 52 in 1990. Simultaneously, a revival in airline demand and aggressive pricing helped sales of the MD-80 to zoom skyward. McDonnell Douglas had taken only 43 firm orders for the plane in 1983. This figure leaped to 103 in 1984, 114 in 1985, 109 in 1986, 126 in 1987, 203 in 1988, and 195 in 1989. American Airlines, alone, had 200 MD-80s in its fleet by September of 1990.[30] At decade's end, the prospects of McDonnell Douglas's commercial division seemed radically improved from the early 1980s, at which time, according to the firm's annual report, it was "close to extinction."

However, the company paid handsomely for its full order books. It had enticed the airlines with prices far below those of Boeing: The MD-80 cost $25 million, while the competing 737 went for $31 million; and the MD-11, at $100 million, cost $20 million less than the 747.[31] These discounts were not offset by lower per-unit production costs. In fact, McDonnell Douglas and its suppliers were unprepared for the surge in MD-80 orders that began in the mid-1980s. Employment in the transport aircraft division more than doubled, from 17,000 in 1984 to 44,000 in 1988. By the latter date, more than half of its plant-level employees had been with the firm for under two years, a condition that slowed production and increased incremental costs. Furthermore, McDonnell Douglas' suppliers and its own factories were unable to meet the challenge of providing enough parts for all phases of production. Output slowed, until by 1989 MD-80 customers faced a four year wait for delivery.[32]

John McDonnell became chairman and CEO in 1988 and sought to overcome bottlenecks and high costs through a radical reorganization of both production workers and management. The "Total Quality Management System" emphasized precise manufacturing, cooperation among employees in the plant and between labor and management, and above all, as John McDonnell wrote in his 1989 report to shareholders, "trust and support."

Unfortunately, the uprooting and shifting of employees at all levels and redefinition of work roles proved, in McDonnell's words, "disruptive," and highly costly during their initial phases. Critics charged that the company's reorganization had cost far more money than it saved. It certainly had antagonized the firm's managerial staff of 5,000, all of whose jobs were eliminated. They were eligible to apply for 2,800 new positions in a much leaner corporate hierarchy.[33] The

---

[30] McDonnell Douglas Corporation annual reports.

[31] Harvard Business School case study N9-390-141, p. 9.

[32] Harvard Business School case study N9-390-141, p. 9.

[33] Harvard Business School case study N9-390-141, p. 13.

combination of low prices and high costs led the commercial aircraft division to incur heavy losses during 1989 and 1990, totalling nearly $350 million.

As McDonnell Douglas was trying to control its production costs, large expenses in both the commercial and defense segments further clouded the company's financial picture. The firm spent nearly $2 billion on the MD-11 between its launch in 1986 and first delivery at the end of 1990. Furthermore, the overthrow of Communist regimes in Eastern Europe and economic collapse in the Soviet Union caused the U.S. government to rethink its defense needs. McDonnell Douglas, which had spent nearly $1.5 billion on defense-related research, development, and plant construction between 1986 and 1990, suddenly faced diminished demand for its products. The government reduced its contribution to three long-term projects during 1990, requiring McDonnell Douglas to invest an additional $800 million in those programs. In January 1991, the U.S. Navy canceled one of these products, the A-12 Avenger, causing McDonnell Douglas to project a further $350 million in losses.

The Hughes Helicopter Apache AH-64 program proved a further disappointment. Having invested $328 million in new facilities in Mesa, Arizona, in 1985, the company was disturbed to learn in 1986 that the administration planned to terminate the program after fiscal 1988, which meant fewer than 600 Apaches would be delivered. McDonnell Douglas wrote off $137 million in losses on its helicopter operations in 1989. The Department of Defense's budget for 1990 granted the Apache a slight reprieve, but still ended all funding for the program after fiscal 1991, which was far sooner than the company had initially anticipated.

McDonnell Douglas hoped sales to European and Middle Eastern countries might allow production to continue through the mid-1990s. Israel and Egypt did indeed order 42 AH-64s in 1990, but by this date the company admitted the helicopter was "moving toward the end of production." The diminished profitability of the Apache program meant that the Hughes acquisition had been a costly one. In short, McDonnell Douglas reaped bitter fruit from the end of the cold war. By 1990, the military aircraft division's earnings had plummeted to $46 million.

The cumulative impact of these disturbances caused the company's debt level, which had been below $100 million from 1977 to 1984, to skyrocket. It had increased to $603 million by 1985, following the Hughes acquisition, and spiraled out of control during the following five years, as the MD-11's development costs and declining military business combined to squeeze McDonnell Douglas. By 1990, its aerospace division was $2.97 billion in debt (see Exhibit 9). In that year, its credit rating was downgraded twice, which combined with a national credit crunch to destroy the firm's capacity to raise funds in public debt markets. The company's bankers continued lending to it, and by early 1991 its level of indebtedness had reached $3.3 billion. At this point the Pentagon publicly suggested McDonnell Douglas should raise cash.

In 1990, John McDonnell's reorganization began to pay off, as MD-80 assembly productivity increased by 30 percent. Yet delays continued to plague the project and caused customers to look elsewhere for their aircraft. During the first three quarters of 1991, the number of cancellations exceeded the numbers of new firm orders by 21.[34] In spite of the fact that the airlines liked the MD-80 and MD-11, McDonnell Douglas was having trouble making any money on them.

---

[34] *The Wall Street Journal,* "McDonnell Douglas Chairman Pins Hopes on Success of His Taiwan Deal," November 20, 1991, B6.

EXHIBIT 9   McDonnell Douglas—Long-term Debt, 1971–1990 ($ in millions)

Year	Aerospace Debt	Equity	Debt/Equity	Interest Paid
1979	87	1,378	0.06	11
1980	76	1,513	0.05	12
1981	71	1,654	0.04	70
1982	70	1,820	0.04	27
1983	60	2,068	0.03	10
1984	41	2,344	0.02	62
1985	603	2,635	0.23	95
1986	992	2,845	0.35	207
1987	1,613	2,970	0.54	242
1988	1,856	3,186	0.58	339
1989	2,597	3,287	0.79	564
1990	2,970	3,514	0.85	613

Source: McDonnell Douglas annual reports.

John McDonnell's Decision

In these circumstances, John McDonnell began to search for a foreign partner that would assist in the launch of the MD-12. This wide-body tri-jet was to be the first commercial airliner with a capacity and range that was equal to or greater than Boeing's 747. McDonnell Douglas's engineers believed it would be cheaper for the airlines to operate on extended routes, particularly those from North America to Asia. Income generated by the MD-80 and MD-11 might have been sufficient to finance the MD-12 if it were not consumed by interest payments. Taiwan Aerospace's $2 billion would be used to pay down McDonnell Douglas' debt, making launch of the MD-12 possible within a year. Moreover, the lower wage rates paid by Taiwanese subcontractors, who would do more than 60 percent of the work on the MD-12, would help McDonnell Douglas price the new plane extremely competitively.

As McDonnell pondered the Taiwanese offer, he looked more than a decade into the future toward a final goal: development of two new mid-sized planes, the MD-95 and MD-XX. These aircraft would round out McDonnell Douglas's product line and allow it to compete with Boeing in all segments of the market. McDonnell thought back to the glory days of the Douglas Aircraft Company, when its DC-3, DC-4, DC-5, and DC-6 dominated the global market for propeller-driven commercial aircraft. Boeing's ascent to dominance had occurred in only 10 years. He wondered if the Taiwan Aerospace deal might be a means of similarly up-ending the international aerospace order.

McDonnell also considered the opposition that announcement of the deal would unleash. United Aerospace Workers Local #148 represented nearly 20,000 McDonnell Douglas workers in Long Beach. They would emphasize, correctly, that aircraft assembly was almost entirely a manual process. The only automated task was precision drilling. In the back of his mind, he could hear Richard Rios, the local's president, telling reporters and government officials that his members were the most highly skilled workers in the United States, and that they were at the core of aircraft manufacturing.

McDonnell Douglas's subcontractors would object to creating a supply capability in Taiwan. Those who also made parts for military aircraft manufacturers could argue that the loss of

EXHIBIT 10 Aircraft Manufacturing in the U.S. Economy (export figures in $ million)

	1987	1988	1989	1990	1991
Exports, civilian aircraft	7,518	10,294	14,257	19,519	24,694
Exports, engines, and parts	4,396	5,420	6,629	6,710	7,910
Other components	6,497	7,228	8,198	9,421	10,363
Total civilian exports	18,411	22,942	29,084	35,650	42,967
Proportion of total U.S. exports	7.24%	7.12%	7.99%	9.05%	NA
Employment	678,200	683,800	712,400	710,800	NA

Notes Engine and component sales include some parts used in military aircraft.
Government employment figures do not differentiate between civilian and military workers.

Source: *Aerospace Facts and Figures 90–91*, pp. 126–27. U.S. Bureau of the Census, *Statistical Abstract of the United States: 1991*, Washington, D.C., 1991, p. 633. U.S. Department of Commerce, *U.S. Foreign Trade Highlights 1990*, Washington, D.C., 1991, p. 9. U.S. Department of Labor, *Employment, Hours, and Earnings, United States, 1909–90, vol. I*, Washington, D.C., 1991, p. 342.

work, which McDonnell Douglas's deal was sure to entail, would lead to fewer subcontractors and leave America vulnerable if demand for military parts increased during war.

With recession hanging over incumbents in congress like a dark cloud, McDonnell also expected an outcry in Washington. Though the company could argue that its MD-12 assembly facility, still to be built, would create thousands of engineering and support jobs, he knew the loss of employment, particularly in Long Beach, might be high. Moreover, economic nationalists in congress would probably raise fears over how much control McDonnell Douglas could retain in the relationship.

Proponents of the deal within the company had some answers. They hoped to diffuse concern over military technology transfer by formally dividing its Transport Aircraft Division into a commercial and military segment. More important, they could point out to doubters that McDonnell Douglas would maintain control over most highly skilled phases of the MD-12 project, including design, systems integration, final assembly, and flight testing. Taiwan Aerospace would carry out basic manufacturing, fabrication, and subassembly but would not be poised to turn out its own commercial jets.

Still, John McDonnell had some nagging doubts. He tried to imagine what his father and Donald Douglas, founder of the Douglas Aircraft Company, would have done under similar circumstances. He did not think either would want to preside over a company whose real work was done in Taiwan by Taiwanese with diminishing American guidance. McDonnell also looked beyond his firm. He wondered if the alliance with Taiwan Aerospace, even if it were the best choice for McDonnell Douglas, might not be best for the country that had given birth to the firm.

BURROUGHS WELLCOME AND AZT (A)

Extreme diseases demand extreme cures.

Hippocrates.

On the morning of Thursday, September 14, 1989, seven men from the activist group ACT UP (The AIDS Coalition to Unleash Power) entered the New York Stock Exchange dressed in business suits and wearing forged name tags of the investment bank Bear Stearns. A minute before trading was to start, five of the men chained themselves to the railings of the balcony above the trading floor, activated an electronic foghorn smuggled into the building, and unfurled a large banner that read: "Sell Wellcome." The other two men photographed the protest action, including the ensuing pandemonium on the trading floor, and immediately rushed the images to the international media. Although police quickly removed the intruders from the NYSE, hundreds of protesters marched in sympathy on the streets outside the building. Concerted demonstrations were held that day as well in San Francisco and London.[1]

Wellcome PLC, the target of the protests, was the British pharmaceutical company whose American subsidiary, Burroughs Wellcome Company, had brought to market the only drug approved in the United States for use in the treatment of AIDS (acquired immune deficiency syndrome). ACT UP and other advocacy groups for people with AIDS decried the continuing high price of the drug, AZT, which retailed for approximately $8,000 per person per year at the time. "Wellcome is involved with shameless profiteering," declared a hospital administrator in a front page article appearing in *The Wall Street Journal* the day after the protest. Executives at Burroughs Wellcome's North Carolina headquarters disagreed fundamentally with the assertions of its critics. "There's a myth out there that we're robber barons, ripping people off," contended David Barry, MD, the firm's vice president of research. "It would be theoretically possible for us to give away all our drug. Everyone would get it for a while, and then we'd go bankrupt."[2] Nevertheless, Barry and other Burroughs Wellcome executives were perplexed about the demonstrations and wondered what response would be most appropriate.

Wellcome PLC

Wellcome PLC (public limited corporation) was one of the world's oldest multinational pharmaceutical firms. The firm was founded in 1880 by two American druggists in London, Silas Burroughs and Henry Wellcome, and over the decades its scientists had won half of the eight Nobel prizes for medicine awarded to industry. From 1936 to 1985, the company was registered as a charitable trust, using the income

---

[1] Bruce Nussbaum's *Good Intentions* (New York: Atlantic Monthly Press, 1990) served as a particularly useful reference for this and other sections of the case.

This case was written by Professor Willis Emmons of the Harvard Business School.

Copyright © 1991 by the President and Fellows of Harvard College.

Harvard Business School case 792-004 (Revised 1993).

[2] Marilyn Chase, "Burroughs Wellcome Reaps Profits, Outrage from Its AIDS Drug," *The Wall Street Journal*, September 15, 1989, p. 1.

EXHIBIT 1 Wellcome PLC: Five-Year Financial Summary, 1985–1989
(million £, except where otherwise indicated)

	Fiscal Years Ending August 31				
	1985	*1986*	*1987*	*1988*	*1989*
Income Statement					
Revenues					
Human healthcare	826.5	825.4	940.4	1058.3	1253.8
Discontinued Ops[a]	177.1	180.0	192.0	192.2	154.6
Total revenues	1003.6	1005.4	1132.4	1250.5	1408.4
Cost of sales	b	(341.1)	(368.5)	(397.8)	(413.7)
Other op costs	b	(421.0)	(461.8)	(477.2)	(529.9)
R&D (human health)	(110.2)	(118.0)	(133.0)	(154.3)	(182.0)
Income before taxes	121.7	125.3	169.1	221.2	282.8
Taxes	(66.0)	(64.0)	(71.4)	(89.4)	(110.5)
Net income	55.7	61.3	97.7	131.8	172.3
Balance sheet (year end)					
Current assets	534.6	594.6	678.9	733.7	826.4
Fixed assets	356.8	392.0	446.9	522.3	592.2
Total assets	891.4	986.6	1125.8	1256.0	1418.6
L.T. debt	164.6	164.1	186.4	181.3	168.5
Equity capital	438.6	513.6	559.0	652.6	821.2
Total capitalization	603.2	677.7	745.4	833.9	989.7
Ratios and Share Data					
Gross margin	b	66.1%	67.5%	68.2%	70.6%
Return on sales	5.6%	6.1%	8.6%	10.5%	12.2%
Return on equity	13.6%	12.4%	16.8%	19.5%	20.2%
Dividends/earnings	28.0%	27.2%	25.2%	23.9%	23.6%
Shares outstanding (m)	800	824	843	844	845
Share price: High	c	£2.34	£5.14	£5.70	£7.56
Low	c	£1.56	£1.78	£2.92	£4.00
Avg. £/$ exchange rate	1.23	1.46	1.55	1.76	1.68

[a] Coopers Animal Health—nine months results included for 1989.
[b] Not available.
[c] Shares were not issued to the public until 1986.

distributed by the business to promote research in medical and allied sciences. In 1986, 25 percent of the company's shares were floated on the London International Stock Exchange, while the remaining shares were retained by The Wellcome Trust, Britain's largest charitable organization. By 1989, Wellcome's annual revenues reached £1.4 billion,[3] almost half of

---

[3] Based on an average exchange rate of $1.68 = £1 for 1989, revenues were approximately equal to $2.37 billion.

EXHIBIT 2   Wellcome PLC: Revenues by Product Group, 1985–1989

| | *Fiscal Years Ending August 31* | | | | | | | | | |
	1985	1986	1987	1988	1989	85	86	87	88	89
	(million £)					*(percentages)*				
Antivirals:										
Zovirax	58	105	160	216	293	7	13	16	20	23
Retrovir	0	0	16	90	134	0	0	2	9	11
Total antivirals	58	105	176	306	427	7	13	18	29	34
Cough/cold medic	140	135	127	126	148	17	16	13	12	12
Other pharmaceutical	512	484	503	494	525	62	57	53	46	42
Nonpharmaceutical	116	119	152	132	154	14	14	16	13	12
All categories	826	843	958	1058	1254	100	100	100	100	100

which originated from its American Burroughs Wellcome subsidiary (see Exhibit 1 for data on Wellcome's financial performance). The company employed almost 18,000 people worldwide, 19 percent of whom were engaged in research and development. Wellcome's best-selling drugs included medications for herpes (Zovirax), AIDS (Retrovir[4]), and allergies/colds (Actifed and Sudafed). Exhibit 2 presents data on Wellcome's revenue by product group.

From its earliest years, Wellcome was regarded as an innovator, pioneering the tablet as an alternative to medical powders and establishing the practice of direct sales calls to physicians ("detailing"). The firm's early emphasis on research, particularly charitable research, led it to emphasize less-profitable areas, such as tropical or obscure diseases. Wellcome's research on antiviral drugs, dating back to the 1940s, was one of the first and most extensive efforts in the industry. By the mid-1980s, the firm had the fourth largest drug research staff in the world, despite ranking 24th

in prescription drug sales. Because of the firm's strong research orientation, it was sometimes referred to by its employees and outside analysts as "Wellcome University," highlighting both its academic prestige as well as its historic emphasis on science over profits.

Acquired Immune Deficiency Syndrome (AIDS)

Mysterious Appearance of AIDS
In the late 1970s, the medical community began to take notice of an unusual rise in the incidence of several rare diseases, including pneumocystis carinii, an uncommon form of pneumonia, and Kaposi's sarcoma, a rare form of skin cancer characterized by bruise-like purple spots on the body. By themselves, these illnesses were not incurable. However, those afflicted suffered from unexplainable immune deficiencies that, in combination with these diseases, appeared to always lead to death. Many of the victims also experienced depression, severe weight loss, and memory loss similar to that of senility before succumbing to the disease.

At this time the patients were almost always urban males from San Francisco, Los Angeles,

---

[4] Retrovir was Wellcome's trademarked brand name for zidovudine, which was itself the generic name of the chemical compound azidothymidine (AZT).

EXHIBIT 3 Reported U.S. Cases of AIDS and Deaths Attributed to AIDS: 1981–1989

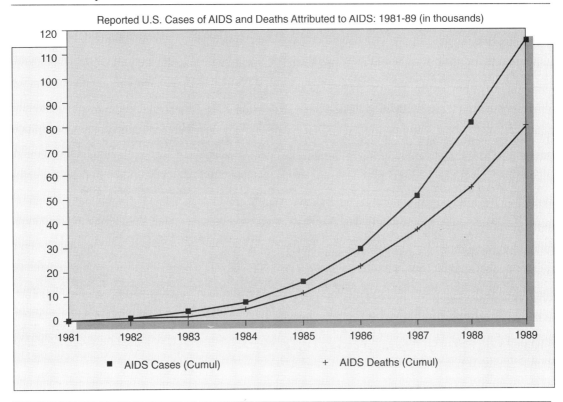

Reported U.S. Cases of AIDS and Deaths Attributed to AIDS: 1981-89 (in thousands)

■ AIDS Cases (Cumul)   + AIDS Deaths (Cumul)

Source: *Statistical Abstract of the United States: 1990*, pp. 83, 166; Centers for Disease Control, *HIV/AIDS Surveillance Report*, various editions.

or New York. A distinguishing feature shared by these men was their homosexuality, thus leading some physicians to refer initially to the condition as gay-related immune deficiency syndrome (GRIDS). By 1982, after it was apparent that certain members of other groups, including drug addicts and hemophiliacs, were also suffering from the condition, the medical community settled upon the more neutral descriptor: "Acquired Immune Deficiency Syndrome" (AIDS). In April 1983, the Center for Disease Control in Atlanta reported roughly 3,000 cases of AIDS, including 1,000 fatalities (see Appendix 1 for an overview of key U.S.

government agencies involved with AIDS, and Exhibit 3 for data on reported cases of AIDS and deaths attributed to AIDS in the 1980s).

In spite of the growing number of deaths from AIDS, little attention was devoted to the syndrome in the popular press until reports emerged of heterosexuals contracting AIDS via blood transfusions. Even so, the general public remained largely unaware of AIDS or simply regarded it as an affliction of certain marginal groups in society. Some religious fundamentalists interpreted AIDS as a plague sent by God to punish homosexuals. Although the National Institutes of Health devoted some research funds to studying AIDS, its spending levels appeared low in comparison with funding for such illnesses as toxic shock syndrome and legionnaires' disease.[5] One person with AIDS (PWA) commented about the limited governmental response: "I wonder if it had been 1,500 Boy Scouts, what they would have done."[6]

Discovery of the Human Immunodeficiency Virus (HIV)

By 1983, scientists had concluded that AIDS was linked to some blood-borne agent, although the precise cause of the syndrome was still unknown. A year later, scientists in France, followed shortly thereafter by researchers at the U.S. National Cancer Institute, linked AIDS to a virus that was eventually termed the human immunodeficiency virus or HIV. Researchers believed that, after HIV entered a person's bloodstream, it gradually destroyed a key part of the body's immune system (white blood cells), leaving the affected individual vulnerable to a variety of infections and diseases, including the pneumocystis carinii pneumonia (PCP) and Kaposi's sarcoma observed in many AIDS patients. However, the time elapsed between infection with HIV and the onset of AIDS itself (i.e., the emergence of so-called opportunistic infections) could differ widely from person to person. In fact, a person harboring HIV could be ignorant of the fact for months or years yet spread the virus to others.

In spite of its devastating potential, scientists established over time that HIV was an extremely fragile virus that could not be spread through casual contact in the manner of such viruses as the common cold. Instead, HIV could be passed only through direct contact between a body fluid of one person and that of another.[7] Even when such direct exposure to HIV took place, the virus would not necessarily take hold in the body of the previously uninfected person. However, at that time, scientists were at a loss to explain why direct exposure to HIV did not always result in infection or why the speed of progression from HIV to AIDS differed so dramatically from person to person. More disturbingly, medical researchers had little to offer in terms of AIDS treatments, much less a cure or vaccine.

Search for AIDS Treatments

Scientific Challenges

When infected with a virus, the human body generally produces proteins known as antibodies that are designed to attack and destroy the invading virus. However, these antibodies are not powerful or plentiful enough to eliminate certain viruses, including HIV. Therefore, scientists attempt to devise alternative means of attacking such viruses, either by creating vaccines that will help the body produce more effective antibodies prior to infection, or by designing drugs that will destroy the virus once it has entered the body. Antiviral treatments are particularly difficult to develop, however, because viruses, like guerilla fighters, can often hide very effectively in the complex landscape of the body. In contrast to other infectious organisms, viruses can multiply only inside living cells. Thus, any drug designed to destroy the virus might instead do more damage to the body's healthy cells while the virus continues to spread. HIV was an unusual type of virus,

---

[5] According to a Congressional Research Service report, in 1982 the National Institutes of Health had spent $36,100 per person dead from toxic shock syndrome; $34,841 per person dead from legionnaires' disease; but only $8,991 per AIDS death. Figures cited in Randy Shilts, *And the Band Played On* (New York: St. Martin's Press, 1987), pp. 157, 186.

[6] Ibid., p. 335.

[7] Unprotected anal or vaginal intercourse and the sharing of hypodermic needles appeared to be two particularly risky behaviors in terms of the likelihood of HIV transmission if the virus were present.

a so-called retrovirus,[8] that had previously been found to exist only in animals. Furthermore, HIV appeared to mutate, creating variations of the virus in addition to lying dormant for years like a Trojan horse inside the body.

Because of the complete absence of any drugs approved for use against HIV, people with AIDS in the early 1980s searched desperately for any compound that could conceivably halt, if not reverse, the deterioration of their immune systems or that could help the body recover from the various opportunistic diseases associated with AIDS. In some cases, PWAs traveled to Mexico, where local pharmacies provided access to various unregulated anticancer and other compounds. In the United States, a network of informal lay researchers, often linked by newsletters, began conducting underground trials of their own on drugs from outside the country or from kitchen laboratories. In general, PWAs were frustrated with the apparent inability of the medical community to find a treatment and with the unwillingness of the U.S. government to sanction the use of experimental medications.

Drug Development Process

By the 1980s, most new drugs were discovered through an expensive trial and error process comparable conceptually to oil exploration, where typically many "dry holes" were drilled before any petroleum was actually located. This type of effort required massive allocations of time and financial resources to cover the costs of pursuing false leads and for taking promising new compounds through the regulatory approval process (see Appendix 2 for an overview of the discovery and approval process for new drugs). In the United States, the federal

government sometimes participated as well in the development process, either indirectly, through funding basic research at university laboratories and at the National Institutes of Health or, more directly, in cases requiring urgent attention, through collaborations with pharmaceutical firms.

For pharmaceutical companies, a primary incentive for developing new drugs was the prospect of obtaining patent protection and, hence, exclusive rights to their discoveries over a 17-year period. Patent rights were particularly valuable in the U.S. market, where firms were typically allowed to set product prices themselves, as opposed to through negotiations with the government, as was common abroad.[9] The Orphan Drug Act of 1983 provided additional incentives in the United States for the development of new drugs for rare diseases by awarding tax incentives, grants, and guaranteed seven-year marketing exclusivity[10] to firms for products applicable to patient groups numbering up to 200,000. Besides financial incentives, pharmaceutical firms and individual scientists could anticipate international recognition and prestige for major life-saving or life-improving discoveries.

Despite these broad incentives, pharmaceutical companies in the mid-1980s were somewhat skeptical about pouring significant sums of money into the development of drugs for the AIDS market. Prior experience with retroviruses was limited and the prospect of working with the deadly AIDS virus, even in a laboratory setting, was viewed as dangerous. In addition, the market for AIDS drugs appeared very small at that time, compared with markets for the treatment of cancer or diseases

---

[8] Retroviruses are composed of the genetic material RNA. In the early 1980s, scientists had only limited research experience with retroviruses, which transcribe (transform) their RNA into DNA before attacking the body's cells.

[9] In some cases, these "negotiations" represented little more than a perfunctory approval by the appropriate government agency of the manufacturer's proposed price. At other times, the negotiations were more contentious.

[10] This period of exclusivity would be valid even if the substance was not patentable or if its patent had expired.

affecting the cardiovascular or central nervous system. Nevertheless, one major pharmaceutical firm, Wellcome, was anxious to bring its historic expertise in antiviral research to bear on finding a treatment, if not a cure, for AIDS.

Burroughs Wellcome and Compound S

In the mid-1970s Wellcome's American subsidiary, Burroughs Wellcome, was heavily involved in antiviral research that ultimately led to the commercialization of the anti-herpes drugs trifluridine (trademarked "Viroptic") and acyclovir (trademarked "Zovirax"). At that time, the subsidiary began studying retroviruses as well, although it was then unclear what role these viruses played in human diseases. In 1977, Burroughs Wellcome augmented its viral research capabilities through the hiring of Dr. David Barry, a physician employed at the FDA's Division of Virology, who was particularly well-versed in both clinical and regulatory matters.

In the summer of 1984, Dr. Barry, inspired partly by a visit to Burroughs Wellcome by one of the French codiscoverers of HIV, decided to press ahead with an ambitious new goal: to find an antiviral that would be effective against the AIDS virus. Barry, by that time vice president of research for Burroughs Wellcome, contacted Dr. Dani Bolognesi, a retrovirus expert at Duke University, to assist in the development effort. Bolognesi had previously helped test Wellcome drugs and possessed the laboratory facilities necessary to work with the dangerous AIDS virus.

During the next few months, Burroughs Wellcome scientists began the tedious, time-consuming process of screening compounds for further testing against live HIV. According to Phillip Furman, head of viral research: "We looked at all our known antivirals on the off chance that one would work against retroviruses."[11] There were plenty of compounds to

choose from, given that the company routinely created over 1,500 novel compounds a year. However, Barry decided to restrict the search to those drugs that had already undergone testing in animals or in humans because these would be quicker to develop for commercialization. Most of the compounds screened were rejected since they either killed too many cells or too few viruses. However, several dozen promising substances were sent both to Bolognesi and to FDA laboratories in late 1984 for testing against HIV.[12]

Bolognesi informed Barry in the meantime that a close friend, Dr. Samuel Broder of the National Cancer Institute (a branch of the National Institutes of Health), had become chairman of the Public Health Service Committee on AIDS Therapeutics. In this capacity, Broder had begun traveling across the nation, exhorting pharmaceutical companies to conduct more research on HIV and AIDS and encouraging these firms to send samples of promising drugs to his lab for testing. In October 1984, at the invitation of Burroughs Wellcome, Broder traveled to the firm's headquarters in Research Triangle Park, North Carolina, to discuss his own efforts in searching for a treatment for AIDS and to offer testing services. Barry subsequently forwarded to Broder many of the compounds that were also under evaluation by Bolognesi and the FDA. In each case, compounds were given code names to preserve Burroughs Wellcome's proprietary position as well as to preclude testing biases.

On November 28, 1984, Barry sent "Compound S" to the FDA for testing. The chemical compound was, in fact, azidothymidine (AZT), a substance first synthesized by Dr. Jerome Horwitz of the Detroit Institute for Cancer

---

[11] Brian O'Reilly, "The Inside Story of the AIDS Drug" *Fortune*, November 5, 1990, p. 116.

[12] Given the relative newness of the testing processes and their unknown degree of accuracy, Barry felt that it was important to have the compounds evaluated at multiple sites.

Research in 1964. After the drug proved to be ineffective against cancer at that time, it remained unpatented in the public domain. In 1974, West German scientists discovered that AZT was effective against certain retroviruses in mice. However, this work was virtually ignored because retroviruses had not yet been found to affect humans. In the early 1980s, Burroughs Wellcome chemist Janet Rideout resynthesized and studied the compound as an antibacterial. Although these initial investigations proved fruitless, company scientists determined in 1984 that AZT might be effective at interfering with HIV replication, thereby slowing down, if not arresting, the breakdown of the body's immune system and the subsequent appearance of AIDS.[13]

After testing Compound S, the FDA reported that it, like other compounds submitted by Burroughs Wellcome, did not appear to offer promise in the fight against AIDS. Barry, frustrated with the disappointing news, sent Compound S to Bolognesi's laboratory in December to be tested through an alternative process. Much to Barry's delight, Bolognesi concluded that the compound appeared to be effective against HIV in the test tube. As a "tiebreaker," Barry shipped Compound S to Broder's NIH laboratory in February 1985, indicating that he wished to proceed with human testing if the results were positive. Within two weeks, Broder reported back excitedly that "S" was by far the most effective anti-HIV compound tested by the NIH to date. Soon thereafter, Broder flew down to Burroughs Wellcome headquarters to encourage the firm to initiate the costly clinical trial process that would be required before the drug could even be considered for regulatory approval. Barry had already obtained the nec-

essary commitment from his superiors in the United States and from Wellcome's top management in London and had begun preparations for the first testing of AZT in humans. Meanwhile, Wellcome filed for a British patent for the use of AZT against the retrovirus HIV.

To conduct U.S. clinical trials on AZT, Burroughs Wellcome was required to apply to the FDA for "Investigational New Drug" (IND) status for the drug. In preparing the application, the company compiled archival data from Burroughs Wellcome's earlier tests with AZT in laboratory animals and more recent data from tests in Broder's laboratories and its own. Throughout this period, Barry maintained regular contact with Dr. Ellen Cooper, the head of the FDA's antiviral section, whom he knew from his former years of interaction concerning acyclovir. In June 1985, Cooper granted approval for IND status in a record-breaking five working days after receiving the application. In July, Burroughs Wellcome gained Orphan Drug status for AZT and shortly thereafter, the firm applied for a U.S. patent for the drug. Although the patent was originally rejected due to insufficient data, it was subsequently approved when the test data from several laboratories, including Broder's, was added to the application.

AZT Clinical Trials

Safety Trials (Phase I)

Phase I clinical trials typically utilized healthy volunteers to determine the range of tolerable dosages of a drug and any side effects that might occur as a result of taking the drug. However, to accelerate the discovery process of the impact of AZT on AIDS sufferers, the FDA permitted Burroughs Wellcome to conduct its Phase I AZT trials with seriously ill PWA volunteers. These trials were planned at two sites: at the NIH hospital under Broder's supervision and at Duke, where Bolognesi and an associate would head up the study team.

---

[13] AZT seemed to mimic molecules that HIV required for reproducing itself. By repeatedly "fooling" the virus to attempt replication with AZT molecules, it was hoped that the virus would be prevented from expanding its damaging presence in the body.

On July 3, 1985, Broder and an associate injected AZT for the first time into a human patient, J.R., a furniture salesman from Boston. Initially, J.R.'s temperature rose dangerously; his condition stabilized, however, and the trial continued. After several days, his immune system displayed signs of improvement and his weight showed a moderate increase. Trials were subsequently initiated with 12 more PWAs at the NIH and 7 at Duke.

In late July, the American public was shocked at movie star Rock Hudson's announcement from Paris that he was suffering from AIDS. The fact that Hudson had traveled to France to gain access to an experimental AIDS drug unavailable in the United States was an embarrassment of sorts to the American health establishment.[14] The tremendous publicity surrounding the event, combined with Hudson's widespread popularity, helped to begin breaking the taboo on mainstream discussion of AIDS and created a new sense of urgency toward finding a treatment or cure for the syndrome. Celebrities such as Elizabeth Taylor lent their support to raise funds for AIDS research, while the U.S. Congress appropriated $234 million to the cause for fiscal year 1986, more than doubling its funding level from the preceding year.

As the Phase I trials of AZT continued in the fall of 1985, Burroughs Wellcome realized that it would soon face a relative shortage of thymidine, a key component in the production of AZT. Broder helped in the short term by tracking down over 200 pounds of leftover thymidine from within the NIH, which provided it to the company in exchange for an equivalent amount of AZT. In the meantime, Burroughs Wellcome located a small German chemical firm that had produced the substance in the past and negotiated an arrangement to purchase thymidine from the firm by the ton. The trials continued on course through early 1986, with only two of the original volunteers dropping out. Virtually all of the PWAs remaining in the trials gained weight and experienced some improvement in their immune systems, in spite of certain side effects, such as anemia, resulting from the inherent toxicity of the drug.

Efficacy Trials (Phase II)

The apparently strong performance of AZT in the Phase I trials ironically created several dilemmas in the design of the Phase II trials. On the one hand, the standard testing practice of randomly administering the new drug to half of the trial participants, while providing the other half (the control group) with placebos, would deny an apparently beneficial, if not life-saving, drug to every person who fell into the latter group. On a broader level, any PWA denied the opportunity to participate at all in the trials might die before the necessary regulatory approval had been secured for general sale of AZT.

Scientists traditionally argued that, to measure accurately the impact of a new drug, it was critical to perform trials on a fairly homogeneous group of patients, all of whom would be given what appeared to be medication, but only half of whom would actually receive the new drug.[15] By measuring the differences in health indicators of the two groups during the trials, scientists would presumably be able to isolate the effects of the drug itself. An alternative to this "placebo

---

[14] However, the drug HPA-23 was ultimately shown to be completely ineffective as a treatment for HIV and AIDS.

[15] These trials were typically conducted in a "double blind" fashion, whereby neither the patient nor the administering physician knew whether the actual drug or a placebo was being taken. Only the independent board of physicians and other experts in clinical trials charged with evaluating the clinical data was informed as to the category to which each participant had been assigned.

trial" methodology was the use of "historical trials," in which the new drug would be given to all participants in the study. In this case, scientists would compare such indicators as survival rates of trial participants with historical data on persons suffering from the disease. Some researchers, however, argued that historical trials might not yield very useful data in a study of AZT, given changes over time in the speed of diagnosis and improvements in treatments available for various opportunistic infections affecting AIDS patients. Scientists also warned of the impact of the placebo effect in historical trials, whereby patients might show temporary improvement due solely to the psychological effect of taking a drug believed to have life-enhancing powers.

The issue of the number of participants was a controversial one as well. Phase II trials were typically conducted at a limited number of locations and with no more than a few hundred relatively homogeneous patients to keep tight control over the process and to limit the scope of the data-gathering effort. Yet thousands of people were living with AIDS at this time and many thousands more were infected with HIV. For most of these people, AZT appeared to be the only real hope for improvement, at least in the short term.

Burroughs Wellcome eventually decided to employ (double-blind) placebo trials in the Phase II clinical trials of AZT and to restrict participation to about 300 seriously ill PWAs who had suffered a recent episode of the opportunistic disease, PCP. According to Barry, who was responsible for the design of all of Burroughs Wellcome's clinical tests, the choice of placebo over historical trials "was one of the most difficult decisions I ever made."[16] The company was subsequently criticized for this decision at a congressional hearing conducted by Representative Ted Weiss in July 1986.

Nevertheless, Barry was convinced that his decision would result in the most timely and accurate evaluation of AZT.

The Phase II trials began in early February 1986 and were scheduled to continue through December 1986. Although Burroughs Wellcome had hoped to obtain some funding support and participation from the NIH for the trials, the firm ultimately covered all of the Phase II costs itself. Over the course of the trials, a supervisory board of physicians and other clinical trial experts monitored the entire clinical testing process to ensure objectivity. Although many of the participants required blood transfusions as a result of AZT-induced anemia, the trials continued through the summer. In mid-September, the supervisory board asked that the trials be halted, revealing what they felt to be overwhelming evidence in support of AZT's effectiveness: of the 137 participants receiving placebos, 19 had died, whereas only one of the PWAs receiving AZT had died. The statistical significance of the results surprised even Burroughs Wellcome, whose president, Theodore Haigler, remarked: "All of us realized, for the first time, all of a sudden, that we've got a significant product we will have to manage."[17] Nevertheless, virtually all observers agreed that AZT was not the ultimate treatment for AIDS since the drug merely slowed, but did not reverse, the replication of HIV in the body. In addition, the severe toxicity of the drug remained a continuing concern, particularly in patients with advanced HIV infection.

In January 1987, after an accelerated review of the Phase II trials data, the FDA advisory committee recommended market approval of AZT for use by persons with AIDS;[18] the FDA

---

[16] O'Reilly, "The Inside Story," p. 120.

[17] O'Reilly, "The Inside Story," p. 124.

[18] The advisory committee also recommended and the FDA also approved the use of AZT by persons in an advanced stage of HIV infection referred to at that time as ARC (AIDS Related Complex).

consented in March 1987.[19] This feat of gaining market approval without Phase III trials and within a total time frame of under two years was dubbed by *Fortune* magazine as "the pharmaceutical equivalent of an under-two-minute-mile."[20] NIH's Broder, who had continued his enthusiastic promotion of AZT throughout the clinical trials process, declared: "I think that this shows what can happen when government and the private sector collaborate."[21] Shortly thereafter, a second series of clinical trials was initiated to study the effects of AZT on people infected with HIV but not yet showing symptoms of AIDS.

Bringing AZT to Market

In moving from the clinical trials to the commercialization phase of AZT, Wellcome faced challenges with respect to both manufacturing and pricing. Over 20 manufacturing steps were required in taking AZT from the raw materials stage to final capsule form. Given the potentially explosive nature of some of the processes as well as the high degree of precision required in various stages of the process, manufacturing facilities would have to be designed carefully. Because of these requirements, Wellcome informed the public that supplies of the drug were likely to be tight in the short term and that priority would be given initially to persons with the most advanced cases of AIDS. However, since thousands of PWAs were desperately seeking the drug, the capacity for manufacturing AZT on a large scale would need to be developed as soon as possible.

The decision about how to price AZT also proved challenging. Beyond the costs associated with production, Wellcome felt it was important to consider the fact that the firm had poured over $700 million into R&D in the early 1980s in its search for new drugs before striking success with AZT.[22] On the demand side, analysts estimated that the initial market for the drug would be only 15,000 to 20,000 people; future demand was difficult to forecast given uncertainty regarding both the spread of AIDS and the development of alternative treatments. On February 13, 1987, Wellcome announced in a London press release that it would initially set a U.S. wholesale price of $1.88 per 100 mg. capsule of Retrovir, its trademarked version of AZT.[23] Since patients were to take two capsules every four hours, every day of the year, the annual wholesale price per person for AZT would exceed $8,200. With an estimated $0.30 per capsule retail markup, the final price to the consumer would exceed $9,500 per year, making AZT the most expensive prescription drug on the market. Although Wall Street analysts had projected a relatively high price for the drug, their annual wholesale price estimates had been in the range of $5,000 to $7,000 per year.[24]

The surprise of analysts, however, was overshadowed by the outrage of many PWAs and their advocates. Since most health insurance plans in the United States did not reimburse expenditures on prescription drugs, PWAs would incur sizable out-of-pocket costs to purchase AZT at the same time that many of these

---

[19] During the period October 1986 to March 1987, Burroughs Wellcome provided AZT free of charge to over 4,800 PWAs through a program in which doctors could request the drug for patients with documented cases of PCP. Interview with Dr. David Barry, October 30, 1991.

[20] O'Reilly, "The Inside Story," p. 113.

[21] Irvin Molotsky, "U.S. Approves Drug to Prolong Lives of AIDS Patients." *The New York Times,* March 21, 1987, p. 32.

[22] Dr. Barry estimated that the firm had spent more than $80 million to develop and test AZT itself. Marilyn Chase, "Wellcome Unit's AZT Is Recommended as First Prescription Drug to Treat AIDS," *The Wall Street Journal,* February 17, 1987, p. 11.

[23] For the remainder of the case, "AZT" always refers to Wellcome's trademarked drug, Retrovir.

[24] Marilyn Chase, "Wellcome Unit's AZT Is Recommended as First Prescription Drug to Treat AIDS," *The Wall Street Journal,* February 17, 1987, p. 11.

individuals faced the loss of employment due to illness or discrimination.[25] Although the most indigent PWAs could rely on Medicaid to pay for AZT, this option would not be available to other AIDS patients unless and until they became sufficiently impoverished. Therefore, PWAs and numerous support groups appealed to congress for intervention.

Congressional Hearings

In response to charges of price gouging and pleas to congress for financial assistance for PWAs, the House Subcommittee on Health and the Environment held hearings on "Cost and Availability of AZT" on March 10, 1987. Subcommittee chairman Representative Waxman, along with several other representatives, questioned Burroughs Wellcome's president Haigler and vice president of research Barry extensively during the hearings, excerpts of which appear below.[26]

Rep. Waxman

As I look at the timetable, Burroughs Wellcome has done about a year of screening for drugs and seven months of clinical trials involving only a few hundred people, as opposed to the thousands that are usually required. You've also received orphan drug status for AZT, which should contribute as much as a 72 percent tax subsidy of your clinical costs. And in addition to that, you get a 25 percent tax credit for increased research and development. After taxes, how much do you estimate that it cost to get AZT to the point of manufacture?

[25] Prior to the passage of the Americans with Disabilities Act in 1990, PWAs held no legal protection against discrimination in private sector employment and accommodations.

[26] The three excerpts were taken respectively from p. 12, pp. 12–14, and pp. 20–21 of *Hearings before the Subcommittee on Health and the Environment*.

Mr. Haigler

You have asked a lot of questions there, Mr. Chairman, and I think first, if I might, in arriving at our price for Retrovir, we looked at all of the usual factors that go into—that influence drug-pricing decisions. These certainly include, as you said, the cost of research, . . . the cost of development of the drug, the cost of production of the drug, which includes certainly material costs, which in those cases are a fairly high cost, labor, overhead, yields that come about out of the process itself, waste management, capital expenditure cost, cost of distribution, medical information cost . . . the uncertainties of the market, the uncertainties about the full usefulness of Retrovir, the possible advent of new therapy . . , all of these factors are usual factors in arriving at a drug-pricing decision. . . . We also, I think, carefully considered two factors that are specific to Retrovir, and that is the high cost of producing this particular drug, and the needs of those patients for whom this drug was developed.

*　*　*　*　*

Rep. Waxman

You did have a quick time frame for getting this drug to [the] FDA, for which you are to be commended. It's essential that we get this drug out there as fast as possible. On the other hand, the shorter period of time and the fewer number of patients involved meant there was less cost to you. . . . Do you have a figure that you could give us after you take the tax credits as to how much it cost to do research and development to get to the point of manufacture of the drug? . . .

Dr. Barry

I really honestly don't have that cost figure, because it's difficult to differentiate from our entire research and development program, particularly in the antiviral area. But I did want to emphasize that, although the number of patients were relatively small compared to the thousands of patients that are often examined in clinical trials, the expense in the relative term was not significantly less from other studies . . .

Rep. Waxman

. . . what you want to do, and you are entitled to, is to recoup your investment. And you say that the pricing structure includes revenues to cover your development costs. If just the 4,500 patients that are now getting AZT continue, your income this year, when you are approved, would be $45 million. By the end of this year, there will probably be 25,000 living AIDS patients in the United States. If all of them take AZT, your income next year would be about $250 million . . . it looks like you have the potential to recover [your investment, the development cost of this drug] many fold. One pharmaceutical newsletter suggested that your markup of AZT is 100 percent, that half the price is going to be profit. Do you agree with that statement?

Mr. Haigler

I'm sorry, I can't respond to that, Mr. Chairman. I think, to go back to what I said earlier, the potentials of this drug may be there, but it's on the market, what those sales will be, we have no way of really knowing. We certainly don't know what's going to happen in the next year or two as far as new therapies are concerned. Whether this drug will continue to be the drug of choice and really used, we don't know. So I don't think we can speculate on what sales we will have or what profits we might see.

*   *   *   *   *

Rep. Wyden

Did you assume that AIDS patients are going to come up with the money? Or did you assume that the government was going to come up with the money?

Mr. Haigler

I guess we assumed that the drug . . . would be paid for in some manner by the patient himself

out of his own pocket or by third-party payers. We really didn't get into a lot of calculations along those lines.

Rep. Wyden

I know overseas things are very different. Some [nations] have national systems and can tell a company such as Burroughs Wellcome exactly what they are going to pay. I gather that the United States price doesn't take that into account.

Mr. Haigler

The American pricing structure is a free pricing structure, yes.

After the hearings, congress appropriated $30 million to subsidize AZT costs for low-income PWAs. For its part, Burroughs Wellcome extended free access to AZT for up to three months on a case-by-case basis to give PWAs additional time to secure third-party funding for the drug. Over the next few years, a significant portion of the money spent on purchases of AZT in the United States was to come from government funds in the form of Medicaid and other subsidies.

The Rise of AIDS Activism

Over the course of 1987 and 1988, Wellcome continued to expand its AZT manufacturing capacity, while maintaining a fairly low profile in terms of public relations. However, this period witnessed a surge in visibility on the part of AIDS activists, exemplified most dramatically by the actions of the group ACT UP.

Emergence of ACT UP

In spite of the regulatory approval of AZT, most people with HIV and AIDS remained extremely frustrated in early 1987. Six years and over 20,000 deaths after the first reported case of AIDS, the long-term prognosis for those contracting the disease still appeared bleak.

Although AZT offered the hope of slowing the replication of HIV and the onslaught of opportunistic infections, it was not a cure for AIDS, and furthermore, the side effects of its toxicity were worrisome. These facts were particularly troubling since (1) progress on other anti-HIV drugs and treatments for AIDS-related opportunistic diseases was minimal and (2) the prospects for a vaccine seemed remote. Many PWAs and their advocates continued to accuse the Reagan administration of largely ignoring the disease as a result of the association of AIDS with homosexuals and, increasingly, drug addicts. In addition, the FDA was accused of relying on cumbersome procedures that delayed or denied PWAs access to compounds believed by activists to be at least marginally effective against HIV and AIDS.

Wellcome's announced pricing policy for AZT and the subsequent congressional hearings served as a catalyst for the formation of the AIDS Coalition to Unleash Power (ACT UP), under the leadership of New York playwright and long-time gay activist, Larry Kramer. The group, made up of PWAs and supporters, was "united in anger to end the AIDS crisis" by channeling their frustration into "highly focussed, disciplined, and directed" actions, including acts of civil disobedience.[27] ACT UP's first protest action was a demonstration on Wall Street on March 24, 1987, involving 250 protesters who blocked rush hour traffic, distributed flyers condemning Burroughs Wellcome's AZT pricing policy, and hung an effigy of FDA commissioner Frank Young. However, the action garnered little media attention and no response from Burroughs Wellcome. Nevertheless, the protest inspired acts of civil disobedience by other AIDS advocacy groups in Washington,

D.C., and San Francisco and led eventually to the formation of ACT UP chapters in Los Angeles, Boston, and Philadelphia by the end of 1987. ACT UP eventually adopted as its logo the phrase "Silence = Death" suspended on a black background under a pink triangle.[28]

Price Cut for AZT

In December 1987, Burroughs Wellcome announced a 20 percent reduction in the price of AZT—from $1.88 to $1.50 per capsule—citing manufacturing efficiency improvements at Wellcome's production facilities in Greenville, North Carolina, and Dartford, England. In the news release, Burroughs Wellcome president and CEO Haigler stated: "We are delighted that the efforts of our production people and our suppliers have brought us to this point before we thought it would be possible."[29]

AIDS activists, however, were unimpressed with the price cut. In March 1988, ACT UP again staged a protest on Wall Street, resulting in the arrest of over 100 activists. Meanwhile, PWAs continued their love/hate relationship with AZT. Although providing dramatic health improvements for some AIDS patients, the 1,200 mg. daily dosage destroyed so many red blood cells that many PWAs were forced to undergo blood transfusions several times a month or simply discontinue use of the drug. A small number of physicians reacted by prescribing lower dosages of AZT for certain patients. At the same time, many PWAs continued to experiment with unapproved drugs available through underground "buyer clubs."

---

[27] ACT UP/NY. *ACT UP: The AIDS Coalition to Unleash Power* (informational brochure), 1991.

[28] The pink triangle was a symbol used by Nazis to identify homosexuals in concentration camps during the 1930s and 1940s. By adopting this stark logo, ACT UP hoped to "force people to confront their own inaction towards [AIDS] and their own feelings toward gays." Nussbaum, *Good Intentions,* p. 206.

[29] Quoted in Nussbaum, *Good Intentions,* p. 189.

ACT UP and the FDA

In an attempt to pressure the FDA to approve some 60 experimental drugs for use by PWAs, ACT UP joined with a number of other AIDS activists to stage a massive demonstration at the FDA administration building outside of Washington, D.C., on October 11, 1988. Describing their protest as a "die-in," activists carried placards in the form of tombstones and traced outlines of bodies on the surrounding sidewalks, writing in the names of people who had died from AIDS. The over 1,000 protesters succeeded at shutting down the FDA and garnered substantial media attention. On October 20, the FDA published an interim rule designed to accelerate the approval process for drugs intended for previously untreatable, life-threatening diseases by eliminating the requirement of Phase III clinical trials for these drugs as it had already done with AZT. Later that year, FDA commissioner Young announced in a speech to AIDS activists that the FDA would not interfere with mail-order importation from overseas of any unapproved drugs for individual use.

Burroughs Wellcome Reaches Out

In late 1988, Burroughs Wellcome began to take a more active approach with respect to government affairs and public relations — activities still somewhat foreign to a firm that historically viewed itself as a research institution whose primary external constituency was the scientific and medical community. Burroughs Wellcome's low-visibility approach to AZT in particular could also be attributed to its parent company's decision to designate AZT as a special "chairman's project," which left all key decisions involving the drug in the hands of the London-based board of directors. Given the uneventful nature of AZT's approval and public reception in the U.K. market, there was no real counterpart in London to the controversy surrounding the drug in the U.S.

market.[30] Nevertheless, in December 1988, the company established a presence in Washington, D.C., hiring Richard Teske, former deputy assistant secretary of the U.S. Department of Health and Human Services, to represent Burroughs Wellcome to government officials and monitor political developments relevant to the firm.

In January 1989, Burroughs Wellcome agreed to meet with representatives of ACT UP at the company's headquarters to discuss the pricing of AZT.[31] Although the activists were able to air their grievances in face-to-face meetings with vice president Barry and members of the public relations department, they were unable to extract any price concessions from the company. Burroughs Wellcome, on its part, emphasized the complex array of cost factors underlying its pricing policy and noted that, as soon as AZT had been approved, the company had created a program to provide AZT free of charge to indigent PWAs who had nowhere to turn for financial assistance. Although the program had indeed benefitted several hundred people, ACT UP complained that it was completely unpublicized and arbitrarily administered.

In mid-April, ACT UP returned to Burroughs Wellcome headquarters, although this time uninvited. In an action designed to attract media attention, four activists dressed in business suits sneaked past Burroughs Wellcome security and sealed themselves in a third floor office with a high-powered drill. The activists then used a cellular telephone to conduct an interview with the Associated Press until police removed them from the

[30] Barry interview (see footnote 19); O'Reilly, "The Inside Story," p. 128.

[31] Key information for this section was obtained in an interview with ACT UP/NY member Peter Staley, conducted on April 3, 1991.

building. Burroughs Wellcome, which felt that it had made a good faith effort to reach out to AIDS activists, was irritated by ACT UP's stunt, regarding it as childish and unproductive. In addition, as the only pharmaceutical firm having developed an approved treatment for AIDS, the company found it particularly ironic that it should serve as a "punching bag" for activists' ire.

Meanwhile ACT UP, in conjunction with other AIDS activist groups, sought new ways of exerting pressure on Burroughs Wellcome. One strategy involved an attempt to organize a consumer boycott of Wellcome's leading over-the-counter drugs, Sudafed and Actifed. A second approach entailed renewed lobbying of congress, particularly of Representative Waxman and other members regarded as sympathetic to the concerns of PWAs. Finally, the activist groups began studying possible strategies for challenging Burroughs Wellcome's patent on AZT and its corresponding monopoly on the production and distribution of the drug. Although none of these strategies appeared to be particularly effective in the short term, activists hoped that, with persistence, they would eventually begin to realize results.

Regulatory and Scientific Developments

In June 1989, AIDS activists claimed credit for two major regulatory developments. At the Fifth International Conference on AIDS in Montreal, Dr. Anthony Fauci, by then the key administrator of AIDS research programs at the NIH, endorsed the adoption of a "parallel track" testing procedure that would allow any PWA access to "investigational new drugs" during the clinical trial process without having to enroll as an official participant in the trials. With Fauci's support, activists were confident that the FDA would sanction the principle of the parallel track within months, specifically in conjunction with the Phase II clinical trials

for Bristol-Myers's antiviral AIDS drug, DDI.[32]

In a second development later in June, the FDA granted marketing approval for the aerosolized delivery of the drug pentamidine for use in preventing the pneumonia PCP, the leading cause of death of people with AIDS. Of particular significance was the fact that research on pentamidine, a drug originally developed to treat sleeping sickness, had been conducted not by a large pharmaceutical company or government institutes but by a network of community-based physicians. This marked the first time that an AIDS drug had been approved without placebo trials and the only instance in which a drug's safety and effectiveness had been determined solely on the evidence provided by grass-roots clinical data. In spite of its effectiveness, aerosolized pentamidine posed no competitive threat to Burroughs Wellcome's AZT. In fact, this second AIDS drug would presumably boost demand for AZT by prolonging the lives of PWAs who otherwise would have succumbed to PCP.

In August 1989, a development with even more significance to Burroughs Wellcome took place: Dr. Fauci announced to the national press that clinical trials[33] measuring the effectiveness of AZT on HIV-infected persons with only mild symptoms or no symptoms of AIDS indicated that the drug appeared to delay the progression from HIV infection to AIDS in patients whose T4 cell count (a key indicator of immune system strength) had fallen below half the normal level.[34] At the

---

[32] Even if DDI were to prove successful in Phase II trials, it was not clear whether the drug would become a complement to or a substitute for AZT. Hoffman LaRoche was also developing an antiviral AIDS drug, DDC, which was scheduled to enter Phase II clinical trials during the summer of 1989.

[33] These trials were conducted by the NIH with the assistance of Burroughs Wellcome.

[34] Such persons accounted for approximately 50 percent of the total HIV-positive but AIDS-asymptomatic, population. Barry interview (footnote 19).

same time, Fauci revealed that the trials, which had also tested the impact of variations in drug dosage, showed that AZT was as effective and elicited fewer toxic reactions when administered at 500 mg. per day as opposed to 1,200 mg. per day. At the reduced dosage, the percent of AZT users suffering from severe anemia declined from 30–40 percent to just 1 percent.

Although the recommended dosage for AZT was likely to fall almost 60 percent from its original level, Wellcome's stock price on the London exchange jumped 32 percent to £6.73 on the day following Fauci's announcement (see Exhibit 4). This response on the part of investors could be easily explained, however, by the tremendous increase in total demand for AZT expected as a result of the expansion of the potential market to include asymptomatic persons infected with HIV. Prior to Fauci's announcement, the number of AZT users in the United States totaled approximately 25,000 — or about half of all PWAs (most of the others could not tolerate AZT). However, an estimated 1.5 million people were believed to be infected with HIV in the United States and millions more in other parts of the world.[35] Given the rapid spread of HIV, these numbers were expected to rise dramatically in the 1990s. Yet it was unclear how many of these individuals were aware of their HIV status and

_____

[35] Nussbaum, *Good Intentions,* p. 316.

EXHIBIT 4   Monthly Closing Price of Wellcome Stock on the London Stock Exchange: September 1986–August 1989

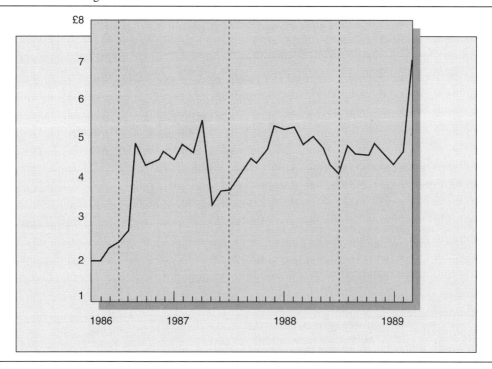

Source: Marilyn Chase, "Burroughs Wellcome Reaps Profit, Outrage from Its AIDS Drug," *New York Times,* September 15, 1989, p. A5.

both willing and financially able to take AZT.[36] Nevertheless, some industry analysts projected that sales of AZT could reach $1 billion per year by 1992.[37]

Pressures Mount on Burroughs Wellcome

Although the FDA did not immediately sanction the use of AZT for all individuals infected with HIV nor lower the recommended dosage, it was expected that the agency would do so in the fall of 1989 as a result of the new clinical data. Meanwhile, AIDS activists and government officials watched to see how Burroughs Wellcome would react to the recent developments. Although the anticipated dosage reduction would, in effect, lower the annual retail cost per person of AZT to about $3,300, ACT UP and others argued that Burroughs Wellcome should be willing to lower its unit price significantly, given the presumed explosion in demand for the drug. The company, however, remained silent and on September 5, representatives of 15 leading AIDS activist groups traveled to Burroughs Wellcome headquarters to demand price cuts. Although Burroughs Wellcome personnel met with activists for some two and a half hours, no pricing concessions were offered. Before leaving, members of ACT UP warned that, if Burroughs Wellcome did not give in to their demands, major demonstrations would be held against the company on Wall Street and elsewhere on September 14.[38] The activists also threatened to organize a nationwide boycott of Wellcome products.

Meanwhile, additional pressure was brought to bear on Burroughs Wellcome. Representative Waxman wrote to Haigler, stating his belief that the high price of AZT was unwarranted, given the level of government support received by the company in the development of the drug. Waxman also warned that he might reopen congressional hearings on AZT pricing. In a similar vein, NIH researcher Sam Broder, in interviews with the national media, alleged that Burroughs Wellcome had not given sufficient credit to government scientists in the process that ultimately led to the company's receipt of an exclusive patent for AZT. Finally, it was rumored that government lawyers were investigating the legality of a variety of punitive measures, ranging from price controls, to government manufacture of AZT, to the application of an obscure 1910 law that permitted the government to revoke patents where monopoly producer threatened strategic supplies.

As the target date of September 14 approached, ACT UP continued to develop its plan to infiltrate the New York Stock Exchange and intimidate, if not embarrass, Burroughs Wellcome into lowering its price for AZT. The effort was led by Peter Staley, a PWA and former Wall Street bond trader who been taking reduced dosages of AZT long before Fauci's announcement, owing to the severe anemia he had suffered at the full recommended dose. The activists carefully studied the NYSE through zoom lenses, obtained false trader badges through a Greenwich Village pawnshop and, on September 11, carried out a "dress rehearsal" of the event at the exchange itself. On September 14, ACT UP's "direct action" was executed according to plan. Staley and his associates were pleased with the extensive media coverage of the event, including a front page *Wall Street Journal* story on September 15 under the headline: "Burroughs Wellcome Reaps Profits, Outrage from Its AIDS Drug: Mounting Protests over the Cost

---

[36] Since 1985, tests had been available for determining whether a person was infected with HIV. However, it was estimated that at most, only 20 percent of Americans with HIV had been tested as of late 1989. Barry interview (footnote 19).

[37] Philip Hilts, "Wave of Protests Developing on Profits from AIDS Drug," *The New York Times,* September 16, 1989, p. A1.

[38] Staley interview (footnote 31).

of AZT Tarnish the Firm and Intensify Regulation." The price of Wellcome common stock, which had fallen steadily after reaching £7.47 per share in early September, closed at £6.74 on the London Stock Exchange on the day following the protests.

Formulating a Response

Burroughs Wellcome had weathered protests in the past and was extremely reluctant to set a precedent of making "knee-jerk" concessions to activists. Furthermore, the company felt strongly that it had fairly earned its AZT patent and pricing rights, in spite of the assistance it received during the development period from governmental entities, which frequently provided services to other pharmaceutical companies as well. Nevertheless, Wellcome PLC's chairman Sir Alfred Shepperd would expect to receive a clear recommendation within the next 24 hours from Burroughs Wellcome's executive committee with respect to what strategy to adopt in response to the latest round of demonstrations.

Appendix 1

Overview of Key U.S. Government Agencies Involved with AIDS

Most of the key scientific and regulatory agencies involved with AIDS in the United States were administered by an arm of the Department of Health and Human Services: the U.S. Public Health Services, chartered in 1912. Primary among these agencies were the National Institutes of Health (NIH), the Food and Drug Administration (FDA), and the Centers for Disease Control (CDC).

National Institutes of Health (NIH). Founded after World War II, the NIH, which was headquartered in Bethesda, Maryland, was a powerful directional force for U.S. medical research. The NIH not only disbursed government grants to universities — $4.6 billion in 1987 out of the NIH's total budget of $6.1 billion — but also maintained 11 separate world-class research institutes of its own, each specializing in a distinct disease class. Although the NIH's spending on biomedical research was dwarfed by that of pharmaceutical firms, it was nevertheless regarded by the international medical research community as the "flagship" U.S. health research institution. Because of the complex manifestations of HIV and AIDS, two of the NIH's institutes became involved in AIDS research: the National Cancer Institute (NCI) and the National Institute of Allergy and Infectious Diseases (NIAID). The NCI originally initiated AIDS research under Dr. Samuel Broder in response to the appearance of Kaposi's sarcoma skin cancer in some AIDS patients in the early 1980s. The infectious nature of HIV itself elicited the eventual involvement of the NIAID under the leadership of Dr. Anthony Fauci. Although both of these institutes were part of the same agency, the issue of jurisdiction between the two over AIDS research was a delicate one, given the considerable sums of government research money earmarked for AIDS. By the late 1980s, it was clear that the NIAID had become the major site for AIDS research within the NIH.

Food and Drug Administration (FDA). The Food and Drug Administration, located in Rockville, Maryland, was the key agency charged with regulating the drug approval process in the United States. The FDA and its predecessor agencies derived their authority from the Pure Food and Drug Act of 1906 and subsequent amendments to the act adopted in 1938 and 1962. Over time, the FDA's mandate with respect to drug regulation had expanded from insuring proper labelling to verifying both the safety and efficacy of each new drug prior to approval for sale to the public. In the 1980s, the FDA was regarded as the most stringent drug marketing approval agency in the world. The typical 10–12 year drug development and regulatory approval process (see Appendix 2) raised fears during the AIDS crisis that the FDA's policies might actually cost lives by preventing promising drugs from reaching people with HIV/AIDS in time. These concerns were magnified by the apparent constraint on the FDA's resources during the years of the Reagan administration: from 1981 to 1989 the agency's budget rose a mere $49 million to $324 million in constant 1979 dollars, while its personnel declined from 7,900 to 7,350 over the same period.

Centers for Disease Control (CDC). The CDC, located in Atlanta, Georgia, was a center of epidemiological study that tracked the spread of new and existing diseases. The agency, formally established in 1980 from a predecessor organization dating back to World War II, helped establish the linkage between the mysterious opportunistic infections that accompanied AIDS as part of a single disease syndrome. All health care entities throughout the United States were required to report to the CDC new cases of AIDS and deaths from AIDS on a regular basis.

Appendix 2

Overview of the Discovery and Approval Process for New Drugs in the United States
The search for a single commercializable drug in the 1980s typically started with the trial and error screening of some 10,000 compounds before testing the most promising of the substances in animals and humans. A significant portion of the total investment—one that consumed tens of millions of dollars and generated thousands of pages of supporting documentation—consisted of taking the drug through the U.S. Food and Drug Administration's exacting regulatory process. It was estimated that the average cost of developing a new drug (in current dollars) rose from $1.3 million in 1960 to $50 million in 1979 and topped $230 million by the end

of the 1980s. A brief outline of the process appears below.

Initial Screening (1–2 years). During the initial screening stage, the thousands of compounds regarded as potential candidates for treating a specific medical condition were reduced to approximately 20 through chemical and structural analysis.

Preclinical Testing (2–3 years). Preclinical trials involved the testing of compounds in the laboratory and in animals to assess safety and to analyze the biological effects of each of the drug candidates. Approximately five of the compounds would subsequently be accepted as investigational new drugs (INDs) by the FDA for clinical testing in humans with respect to a specific indication (disease or other medical condition).

Clinical Testing (6 years). Clinical trials involved the testing of INDs in human volunteers. This stage of the process was divided into three separate phases:

- *Phase I Trials (1 year).* The Phase I safety trials in humans were designed to determine the safety and pharmacological properties of a chemical compound. Each drug was typically tested in 20 or more healthy volunteers. On average, 70 percent of all INDs moved on to the Phase II human trials.
- *Phase II Trials (2 years).* The Phase II efficacy trials were designed to evaluate the effectiveness of the drug and to isolate side effects. Tests were typically conducted with several hundred (volunteer) patients, half of whom received the IND and half of whom received a placebo. Only about one-third of all INDs survived both the first and second phases of clinical testing.
- *Phase III Trials (3 years).* The Phase III efficacy trials measured the effect of the IND on thousands of patients over several years. These trials helped ascertain long-term side-effects and provided additional information

on the effectiveness of a range of doses administered to a rich mix of patients. Approximately 27 percent of all INDs moved on to the FDA review stage.

FDA Review (2–3 years).   On the completion of the Phase III clinical trials, firms were required to file a new drug application (NDA) with the FDA and submit documen- tation of all relevant data for review. The FDA created a special advisory committee for each NDA, typically approving the final recommendation of the committee on whether the drug should be released for commercial sale. Postmarketing safety moni- toring continued even after approval. Only 20 percent of all INDs ultimately made it through the full testing and approval stages.

NOTE ON PHARMACEUTICAL INDUSTRY REGULATION

For much of history, the fruits of mankind's quest for effective medicinal treatments of a wide range of health-related ailments were fairly limited. In the 1940s and 1950s, however, a *therapeutic revolution*[1] transformed both the practice of medicine and the structure of the pharmaceutical industry.[2] Before this revolu- tion, the industry consisted largely of bulk chemical producers supplying pharmacists and physicians with active ingredients, which they, in turn, fashioned into finished products. Yet technology and public policy together reshaped these producers over time into the large, in- tegrated firms that dominated the industry in the early 1990s. Although these firms still relied on wholesalers to distribute their goods, they had by that time developed extensive R&D and promotion functions. This note examines the evolution of U.S. federal drug policy and its effects on the development of the prescription (as opposed to the over-the-counter) drug industry.[3]

The Origins of Federal Drug Policy

I firmly believe that if the whole materia medica, as now used, could be sunk to the bottom of the sea, it would be better for mankind and all the worse for the fishes.

Oliver Wendell Holmes, M.D.,
address before the Massachusetts Society, 1860

Jeremiah O'Regan and Monica Brand prepared this note under the direction of Willis Emmons.

Copyright © 1991 by the President and Fellows of Harvard College.

Harvard Business School note 792-002 (Revised 1993).

[3] In addition to Temin's book cited above, this note draws on a variety of historical references, including Henry Grabowski and John Vernon, *The Regulation of Phar- maceuticals: Balancing the Benefits and Risks* (Washing- ton: AEI, 1983); William Grigg, "1938–1988: The Making of a Milestone in Consumer Protection," *FDA Consumer* (1988, various issues); Walter Measday, "The Pharma- ceutical Industry," *The Structure of American Industry* (New York: Macmillan, 1986); Milton Silverman and Philip Lee, *Pills, Profits, and Politics* (Berkeley: University of California Press, 1974); and William Wardell and Louis Lasagna, *Regulation and Drug Development* (Washington: AEI, 1975).

---

[1] Peter Temin, in *Taking Your Medicine: Drug Regulation in the United States* (Cambridge: Harvard University Press, 1980), documents the discovery of sulfanilamide and peni- cillin (nontoxic, antibacterial drugs) as initiating a "thera- peutic revolution" in the production, distribution, and efficacy of medical drugs (see pp. 58–87).

[2] The terms *pharmaceutical* and *drug* will be used interchangeably in this note even though "drugs" also encompass illicit substances, such as narcotics.

The Pharmaceutical Industry before World War I
Through the end of the 19th century, most drugs were crude botanical products containing varying amounts of useless and often unsafe active ingredients. Thousands of drug products including arsenic, hemlock, rabbit testicles, and even powdered human skull had been used at one time or another for medicinal purposes. Over the century, the introduction of synthetic drugs (those that were chemically extracted from a crude product), such as nitrous oxide (1844), ether (1846), and nitroglycerine (1869), increased the reliability and potency of medical treatment. Yet, in spite of these important discoveries, there were few effective drugs and still fewer ways of identifying them.

By the end of the 19th century, there were two distinct classes of drug products on the market: *patent* or *proprietary* drugs and *ethical* or *formulary* drugs. *Patent* drugs were not "patented" per se, but rather secret in composition and process of production.[4] Their ingredients unrevealed, these drugs were sold in liquid form under trademarked names by physicians and pharmacists alike. These elixirs were composed largely of such ingredients as water and alcohol. Although manufacturers often made insupportable and outrageous claims about their products, proprietary drugs often managed to relieve such symptoms as pain at a time when few ethical drugs could do more.

The *ethical* drug industry developed in response to practitioners' need for standardized drugs, as medicine itself became more scientific. Unlike patent medications, ethical[5] drugs were of known, fixed chemical constitution. The typical ethical drug manufacturer in the 19th and early 20th centuries bought the basic chemicals to make active drug ingredients from "fine" chemical firms, such as Merck, Pfizer, or Mallinckrodt. These chemicals were typically sold through wholesalers to pharmacists and physicians who followed chemical "recipes" to make finished medicines from these bulk powders and crystals.[6] Because ethical drugs could be purchased with or without a prescription, manufacturers did not assiduously cultivate relationships with the medical community nor did they heavily promote their products.[7] Furthermore, manufacturers at this time rarely engaged in large-scale research since they believed drug technology to be relatively fixed. Accordingly, the range and number of ethical drugs available on the market remained fairly stable.

***Drug Regulation:* Caveat Emptor**
At the end of the 19th century, the sale and distribution of drugs were not heavily regulated. Prescriptions did not restrict access to drugs: little more than a means of communication between the physician and pharmacist, a single prescription could be used by different people on different occasions. Concern over the quality of drugs in this environment was exercised at the local level and was dominated largely by voluntary self-regulation. As part of the movement to create standards within the industry, numerous professional organizations and two national formularies, the *United States Pharmacopoeia* (*USP,* 1820) and the *National Formulary* (*NF,* 1888), had been established.[8]

---

[4] Although Congress established the patent system in 1790, patents did not come into widespread use in the pharmaceutical industry until the therapeutic revolution.

[5] The term *ethical* was applied to drugs promoted only to physicians after the 1847 code of ethics of the American Medical Association (AMA) excluded advertising to the public. This term's meaning has changed over time. Today, ethical drugs refer to those sold by prescription in contrast to those sold over the counter (proprietary drugs).

---

[6] At the time, physicians often supplemented their income by dispensing their own drug preparations.

[7] Patent drugs, which were more popular at this time, were heavily advertised.

[8] Contained within these *formularies,* as the name suggests, was a listing of all ethical drugs, described by their chemical makeup and technique of manufacture.

Compulsory regulatory measures, on the other hand, were limited to legislation by a few states governing licensing and drug adulteration. Hence, patent drug manufacturers were not dissuaded from making bogus claims about their products. Arousing the ire of medical practitioners and progressive reformers, the patent drug industry, as a result, came under increasingly sharp attack around the turn of the century.

Push for Legislation. Toward the end of the 19th century, progressive reformers seeking to preserve community values called for greater government regulation of a variety of businesses as part of a reaction against industrial capitalism and the new managerial class. Given the marginal medical importance of drugs at the time, appeals for tighter controls over the sale and distribution of drugs took place within the context of concern over food adulteration. Within the government, Harvey W. Wiley, chief of the division of chemistry in the Department of Agriculture, established the "Poison Squad" in 1902 to uncover harmful side effects caused by food additives. Although the information struck a cord with the public, political pressure from food and agriculture interests managed to defeat nearly 200 pure food bills introduced in Congress between 1871 and 1905. But in 1906 came the shocking publication of Upton Sinclair's *The Jungle,* a dramatic account of the "spoiled-meat industry" that created a public furor and an overwhelming demand for legislative redress.[9] Accordingly, several months after the novel's publication, Congress passed

the Pure Food and Drug Act of 1906, commonly referred to as the Wiley Act.[10]

The Pure Food and Drug Act of 1906. The Wiley Act prohibited the adulteration or misbranding of drugs with "any statement . . . which shall be false or misleading in any particular" and directed the Bureau of Chemistry to seize such products and prosecute their manufacturers. Specifically, the Wiley Act deemed a drug adulterated or mislabeled if *(i)* the manufacturer labeled the drug with a particular name listed in either the *USP* or the *NF* but failed to abide by the standards set in those formularies; *(ii)* the drug was sold under a false name or in the package of another drug; or *(iii)* if the label failed to specify the identity and quantity of certain addictive substances, such as alcohol, morphine, opium, cocaine, and heroin. While the law did not force patent drug manufacturers to disclose the nonnarcotic contents of their products, it did empower the government to monitor the accuracy of any claims made on the label.

Federal drug policy, however, had little effect on the supply of drugs before the New Deal. First of all, Wiley and his progressive allies were most concerned with food adulteration: only 135 of the first 1,000 judgments under the new law dealt with drugs. Furthermore, the Wiley Act's scope was limited to claims of drug content, not therapeutic effect: any drug, no matter how dangerous or worthless, could be marketed freely, provided that it was not mislabeled.[11] Although the law curbed misrepresentation, it did little to restrict consumers' access to drugs, as the legislation was not intended to hamper "self-medication." In

---

[9] Despite opposition from the powerful meat-packing industry and the Proprietary Association, which represented the patent drug manufacturers, the business community was divided over the question of federal regulation. Some companies wanted to dispel the anxiety aroused by Sinclair's exposé, which included such graphic depictions as diseased cattle covered with boils and sausages tainted with rat dung, sawdust, and borax.

---

[10] Pure Food Act, 34 Stat. 768 (1906).

[11] The law was successful, however, in lowering the narcotic content of patent medicines, although some of the credit for this accomplishment belongs to the Harrison Anti-Narcotics Law of 1914.

general, federal drug policy was dictated by the hands-off maxim: *caveat emptor* ("let the buyer beware").

The Proprietary Association quickly found that it could live with the Wiley Act. Any manufacturer could introduce a new, nonnarcotic drug and avoid scrutiny altogether by packaging it under a novel name and making no manifestly false claims about it. While the Wiley Act eliminated some marginal producers from the market, the larger patent manufacturers remained unscathed.[12] The new law seemed to confer on these companies newfound respectability.

Drug Companies and Drug Regulation between the Wars

> *There is no issue . . . [in] the enforcement of the Food and Drug Act about self-medication. This bill does not contemplate its prevention at all . . . what is desired is to make self-medication safe.*

> W. G. Campbell, FDA chief,
> *Testimony before Congress*
> *on FFD&C Act, 1938*

The Pharmaceutical Industry in the Early 20th Century

Although American pharmaceutical companies did not take on their present form in the opening decades of the 20th century, some of the groundwork for their rapid transformation in the 1940s and 1950s was laid during this period. German companies and products dominated the industry until World War I, when American physicians and pharmacists were cut off from their traditional supplies and American companies were forced to step in to meet

rising wartime demand. Although a number of companies had extensive production capabilities by the 1920s, research activities were still limited.

Going against this trend were a few firms, such as Eli Lilly, which created a department of experimental medicine in 1919. In 1923, Lilly entered into a joint development effort with two faculty scientists at the University of Toronto to bring to market significant quantities of insulin, discovered by the scientists a year earlier. As a result of the company's success with insulin, Lilly hired additional research scientists and began a program of sponsoring research fellowships at major universities. In the 1930s, Abbott, Merck, and Squibb, in addition to Lilly, built extensive new research facilities. Nonetheless, relatively few new products emerged from these laboratories and the overall supply of drugs remained largely inefficacious.

Drug Regulation in the 1930s

Establishment of the FDA. By 1931, the Bureau of Chemistry had grown considerably in scope and size and was renamed the Food and Drug Administration (FDA). However, the Wiley Act did not give the FDA free rein to administer the law, but, instead, required it to work through the secretary of agriculture and the Department of Justice for prosecutions.

Impetus for New Regulation. As a reflection of the New Deal ethos supporting an increased role of government in the national economy, several congressmen proposed legislation in 1933 requiring pharmaceutical companies to establish both the safety and efficacy of their products prior to marketing them. Although the business community closely associated the bill with the socialist Rexford G. Tugwell, the newly appointed assistant secretary of agriculture, the bill failed to gain the immediate support of the Roosevelt administration or

---

[12] The production of the Proprietary Association's member firms grew 60 percent between 1902 and 1912, and, by 1929, patent medicines still accounted for over half of all retail drug sales.

Congress. In fact, the bill lay dormant until 1938, when a public health tragedy widely covered in the press led to enormous public pressure on Congress for action.

In the mid-1930s, the Massengill Company of Bristol, Tennessee, a well-respected drug manufacturer, wanted to market a liquid form of sulfanilamide, an antibacterial drug. Company scientists could not dissolve the drug in the usual biological solvents and, therefore, decided to employ diethylene glycol, apparently without testing for toxicity. In late 1937, the American Medical Association (AMA) received reports of six deaths resulting from Massengill's Elixir Sulfanilamide. Although the FDA acted quickly to seize all shipments of the drug, 107 people ultimately died from the effects of the elixir. Without the authority to prosecute the manufacturer for selling an unsafe drug, the FDA was forced to settle for a fine of $26,000, the maximum penalty for misbranding (an *elixir* is an alcohol solution, not a diethylene glycol solution). On a wave of popular support, a bill banning interstate commerce in harmful substances was introduced in Congress and quickly inserted into the Tugwell bill. Signed into law in 1938, the Federal Food, Drug, and Cosmetic Act (FFD&C Act) contained a provision to insure the safety of future new drugs, but carried with it a good deal of tangentially related provisions.[13]

The Federal Food, Drug, and Cosmetic Act of 1938. The FFD&C Act *(i)* called for more drug label information, including the disclosure of all contents and the provision of clear instructions for usage with appropriate warnings; *(ii)* established the category of *new drugs,* which would require premarket approval by the FDA; and *(iii)* exempted drugs dispensed on the written prescription of a licensed physician from certain labeling requirements. The producers of new drugs were required by the FFD&C to file a new drug application (NDA) that provided evidence obtained through animal tests and clinical (human) investigations of the drug's safety for use under the recommended conditions. Additional material, including a detailed description of the drug's contents, manufacturing methods and facilities, and proposed labeling information was also required as part of the NDA filing. However, the application would be approved automatically unless, within 60 days of the filing, the secretary of agriculture found that the drug did not meet the specifications of the new law.

Although the FFD&C Act's prescription provision did not specify which drugs would be sold by prescription and did not explicitly prohibit the sale of certain drugs without one, the FDA issued regulations six months after the law's passage that essentially left this decision to the manufacturer.[14] By affixing the label, "Caution: To be used only by or on the prescription of a physician," the manufacturer could create a class of drugs that could not legally be sold without a physician's approval. Federal drug policy thus placed a whole category of drugs beyond the immediate reach of consumers, thereby restricting self-medication.

Despite the safeguards contained in the FFD&C Act, critics complained of what they perceived to be worrisome limitations of federal drug policy. Since the FDA's jurisdiction did not begin until just before the drug

---

[13] Federal Food, Drug, and Cosmetic Act, 52 Stat. 1040 (1938).

---

[14] The right of manufacturers to classify drugs as either prescription or over-the-counter was not formally clarified in the FFD&C Act until the passage of the Humphrey-Durham Amendment in 1952. Under the amendment, the FDA retained the right to sue a manufacturer for misbranding if it disagreed with the company's labeling designation. Although the designation of a substance as a prescription drug limited the access of consumers to the product, this disadvantage was often outweighed by the higher testing, labeling, and marketing costs associated with OTC drugs.

marketing stage, unsafe drugs could be distributed to investigators for clinical study. Even at the NDA stage, the FDA was not required to give its stamp of approval prior to marketing but could simply allow the clock to run out, thus allowing manufacturers to sell a drug without a thorough review. Although the FFD&C Act provided the first statutory basis for factory inspections, enforcement required a lengthy criminal prosecution and, therefore, was seldom employed. Finally, advocates of more stringent regulations argued that the drug supply remained replete with innocuous drugs offering little therapeutic value, a situation only exacerbated by the fact that drug advertising remained unregulated.

The Postwar Expansion of Federal Drug Policy

> *The doubling of the United States population in the past 50 years is largely attributable to the biomedical advances made during this period.*
>
> Dr. Walsh McDermott, professor of Public Health, Cornell, *senate testimony, 1968*

The Therapeutic Revolution: Genesis of the Modern Drug Industry

In 1935, Gerhard Domagk, a pharmacologist at I.G. Farbenindustrie, discovered a drug with remarkable antibacterial properties: Prontosil, whose active ingredient was sulfanilamide. Yet the discovery of sulfanilamide, the first sulfa drug,[15] failed to have an immediate effect on the pharmaceutical industry in the midst of the Great Depression. However, the clinical application of penicillin (the first antibiotic) during World War II provided something of a catalyst. Although neither penicillin nor sulfanilamide were patentable,[16] pharmaceutical companies moved swiftly to develop and manufacture them to meet wartime needs. For its part, the government spent $3 million subsidizing antibacterial research and sold its penicillin plants at half their cost after the war. Drug research mushroomed thereafter, spurring the therapeutic revolution and transforming the pharmaceutical industry.

New Discoveries. Innovative technologies introduced new opportunities for pharmaceutical companies, altering the way they did business. For example, after the war, Selman Waksman of Rutgers University developed a technique to screen soil samples for antibiotics. Using this method, Waksman discovered streptomycin, which Merck introduced commercially in 1946 and patented in 1948.[17] Subsequently, other drug companies successfully applied the screening technique to find new antibiotics, which they then patented. The manufacturers of the broad-spectrum antibiotics (the tetracyclines), however, broke sharply with the tradition of nonexclusive licensing and retained exclusive production rights.[18] By the end of the 1950s, the pattern of restricted licensing had become widespread.

---

[15] Sulfa drugs were revolutionary because, like antibiotics, this broad class of antibacterial drugs could discriminate between bacteria and healthy cells, attacking and destroying the former without harming the latter.

[16] At that time pharmaceuticals were eligible for patents only in the case of *chemical, composition,* and/or *process* innovations. Penicillin and sulfanilamide had been identified by scientists long before their antibacterial properties in humans had been established and, hence, were not patentable.

[17] The Patent Office ruled at that time that the chemical modifications made to streptomycin created both a product and a process that were patentable. In 1952 the office issued a general ruling that new uses of existing chemical substances were eligible for patent protection.

[18] Fearing criticism for using public facilities for private gain, Waksman convinced Merck to license streptomycin production on an unrestricted basis. Consequently, streptomycin, like penicillin, was sold under its generic name by many firms and its price dropped continuously.

Research and Development. Retaining exclusive production rights on new discoveries provided the potential for a temporary monopoly, especially if the drug was awarded patent protection. Given this incentive, many pharmaceutical companies added or expanded existing R&D activities. Yet some of these expenditures were directed toward the search for "me-too" versions of existing drugs as opposed to new chemical entities. These molecular modifications of competitors' drugs already on the market frequently offered no substantial benefit over existing drugs but provided companies with a convenient way around patents. Nonetheless, many new drugs were introduced in this period, and the supply of powerful and effective pharmaceuticals multiplied. These new drugs included a variety of sulfa derivatives (some with diuretic or antidiabetic properties) as well as myriad antibiotics, tranquilizers, steroids, and birth control pills.

Promotion. Pharmaceutical companies altered the intensity and direction of their promotional activities in the postwar period. To differentiate their products, many companies intensified their advertising and sent out "detail men" to market new and existing drugs to physicians. These efforts helped drug firms develop strong company identities and brand names. During this period of aggressive product development and promotion, drug prices remained relatively stable (see Exhibit 1). In the quarter century after 1940, the share held

EXHIBIT 1   Selected U.S. Price Indexes: 1947–1980 (1947 = 100)

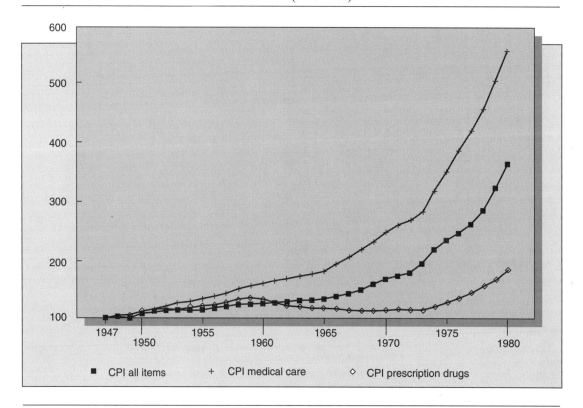

Source: U.S. Department of Labor, Bureau of Labor Statistics.

by prescription pharmaceuticals in total drug sales rose from 12 to 40 percent.[19]

Integration. Increased R&D and promotional activity transformed the structure of the pharmaceutical industry. Many drug companies integrated vertically, allowing them to develop, manufacture, package, and sell a wide variety of drugs directly to hospitals and pharmacies. In particular, the early producers of the broad-spectrum antibiotics (in sharp contrast to the penicillin producers) integrated forward to protect market share. Accordingly, large firms over time came to dominate the pharmaceutical industry, although smaller producers were not driven from the market. The fact that any company with sufficient resources could screen samples for pharmacological substances or modify the molecular structure of existing drugs prevented any one firm from achieving complete

dominance. Competing patents, furthermore, restricted the market power of all players. Finally, the potential for high returns elicited by the highly *inelastic* demand for many drugs provided a strong incentive for entry into the industry.[20]

Profits. Financial returns in the pharmaceutical industry in the postwar period consistently surpassed the average ratios reported for most other manufacturing companies.[21] (For comparative profit data, see Exhibit 2.) Profits after

---

[19] Temin, p. 85.

[20] Consumer demand for pharmaceuticals was rather *inelastic* (unresponsive to price), given the actual and perceived benefits of these products as life-improving, if not life-saving substances.

[21] Representatives of the pharmaceutical companies maintained that their reported returns were exaggerated as a result of misleading accounting procedures. Specifically, they claimed that because U.S. accounting policies required firms to expense R&D outlays, rather than capitalizing them as long-term investments, the capital base on which profit ratios were calculated was understated.

EXHIBIT 2 Comparative ROE: Pharmaceutical Industry vs. All Manufacturing (1958–1990)

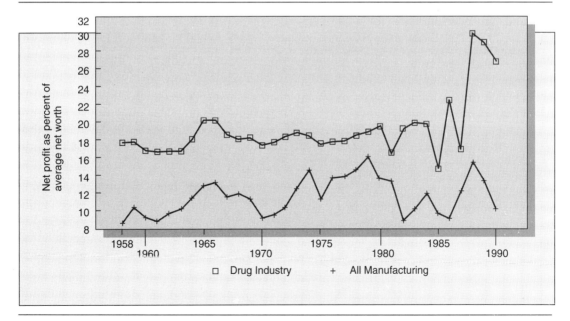

Source: U.S. Federal Trade Commission, *Quarterly Financial Report* (various).

taxes averaged 19 percent of net worth in the quarter century after 1960, with the larger firms usually earning well above industry average. Given that investment in R&D was a speculative venture with high fixed costs, drug companies argued that strong profits were necessary to compensate for the above-average risks associated with these investments. However, these margins also increased the industry's visibility in the public eye.

Expansion of Regulation

New Concerns. In 1959, Senator Estes Kefauver (D–Tennessee) opened hearings on competition within the pharmaceutical industry in the wake of a Federal Trade Commission study revealing high rates of profitability in the industry and in response to a series of reports published by the science editor of the *Saturday Review* alleging false and misleading advertising practices on the part of drug companies. Producing spectacular headlines, the Kefauver hearings uncovered evidence of enormous disparities in drug pricing, not only between generics and brand names but geographically, between different regions of the country and even within the same community.

The findings were particularly sensational, as public awareness of the pharmaceutical industry had been quite limited up to that time. Patients were usually more concerned with their health than with the cost of treatment. Moreover, consumer demand was not only affected by the nature of the product but also by the structure of the market. Added to the typical buyer–seller relationship was an intermediary, the physician, who often operated on the principle that the cost of treatment was of secondary importance. Senator Kefauver noted in the hearings, "He who orders does not buy; he who buys does not order."

In 1961, Kefauver proposed the Drug Industry Antitrust Act to amend the Sherman Antitrust Act. The amendment would have outlawed private patent settlements like the one created for tetracycline and would have mandated compulsory licensing to foster competition. More importantly, the proposed legislation would have also amended the FFD&C Act by requiring drug companies to provide evidence of efficacy as well as safety. The strict regulatory bill faced certain death by adamant industry interests; yet, like its predecessors, the legislation was saved by scandal.

The William S. Merrell Company had applied in September 1960 for premarket approval of thalidomide, a new tranquilizer already in use around the world. The FDA examiner, Dr. Frances Kelsey, kept returning the application to the company on the grounds of insufficient information despite the fact that tests on laboratory animals revealed no danger. In late 1961, thalidomide was found to be the cause of an outbreak of phocomelia (a condition in which children are born with seal-like flippers in place of hands or feet) across Europe, especially in Germany. Although the NDA was withdrawn by Merrell in March 1962, clinical testing of the drug, over which the FDA had no control under the 1938 law, had already taken its toll. The company had distributed some 2.5 million tablets to 1,200 physicians, resulting in a relatively small but well-publicized phocomelia outbreak. Dr. Kelsey was hailed by the press as a heroine, and a groundswell of public support forced Congress to reconsider the pending legislation. Although the provisions designed to lower the price of brand-name drugs were dropped, the Kefauver-Harris Amendments were signed into law on October 10, 1962.[22]

The Kefauver-Harris Amendments. The Kefauver-Harris Amendments *(i)* established a more stringent process for the premarket approval of new drugs introduced after 1962; *(ii)* increased FDA surveillance over the manufac-

---

[22] Drug Amendments of 1962, 76 Stat. 780 (1962).

ture and marketing of all drugs; and *(iii)* granted the FDA sweeping new powers to remove from the market drugs previously granted approval.

Approval procedures. The Kefauver-Harris Amendments required the manufacturer of a new drug to submit an investigational new drug (IND) plan describing the chemical and pharmacological properties of the drug and the process by which the drug would be tested. Under the amendments, a manufacturer could proceed with clinical testing to obtain "substantial evidence" of both the drug's safety and effectiveness for the new drug application if the FDA did not object to the IND plan.[23] The amendments lengthened the FDA's time limit for acting on an NDA and furthermore, required the agency's explicit affirmation of approval before marketing could begin.

More muscle. The Kefauver-Harris Amendments empowered the FDA to establish regulations defining "good manufacturing practices" for production and quality-control procedures. They also authorized the FDA to remove from the market any approved drug for a variety of reasons, including new proof of harmful side-effects, material misstatements in the NDA, or lack of evidence of effectiveness.[24] Faced with roughly 16,000 therapeutic claims, involving more than 4,000 drugs introduced between 1938 and 1962, the FDA in 1966 contracted the National Research Council of

the National Academy of Sciences to perform the Drug Efficacy Study (DES). By the early 1970s, the DES had found roughly 66 percent of these claims to be without scientific support.[25] As a result, the FDA banned hundreds of products from the market and forced countless label changes.

Drug Advertising. In the wake of the Kefauver-Harris Amendments, the FDA also expanded its regulation of drug advertising.[26] In 1948, the FDA had proposed a new regulation placing all written, printed, and graphic material used in the promotion of a drug in the category of drug labeling. Yet the agency rarely challenged a drug company's advertising and then, always on the ground that it contained scientifically unsupported claims of safety. However, in 1966 the FDA issued regulations that limited the promotional claims of drug advertisements to those contained in the FDA-approved package insert. These regulations required advertisements to include a summary of the effectiveness for the conditions for which the drug was approved, along with side-effects, contraindications, precautions, and warnings.

Criticisms of Public Policy. Although the regulatory reforms of the 1960s granted pharmaceutical consumers increased protection, objections soon surfaced. The numerous safeguards imposed by the FDA at every step of the premarket approval process imposed a costly and time-consuming barrier through which few new drugs could pass. Many pharmaceutical companies argued that the work

---

[23] Although the amendments were passed in 1962, it was not until eight years later that the FDA outlined specifically what constituted "substantial evidence" of safety and efficacy. While in the interim it enforced the law on a case-by-case basis, the FDA issued a ruling in May 1970 that established a rigorous format of "adequate and well controlled investigations" for new drugs, to be conducted in three distinct phases (see **Exhibit 3** for an overview of the process).

[24] Although it tentatively deemed all drugs approved before 1938 effective under a kind of "grandfather clause," the FDA gave the producers of drugs approved between 1938 and 1962 two years to provide "substantial evidence" of effectiveness.

[25] Because medical science had not accumulated vast amounts of scientific data on the effectiveness of drugs, the DES's 30 panels drew heavily on their own clinical experience to determine the meaning of "substantial evidence."

[26] The 1962 amendments required that all drug advertisements, labels, and package inserts include generic names.

EXHIBIT 3 Drug Development and Approval Process

	Preclinical Testing	FILE IND	Phase I	Phase II	Phase III	FILE NDA	FDA	Approval
Years	3.5		1	2	3		2.5	Total = 12
Test Population	Laboratory and animal studies		20 to 80 healthy volunteers	100 to 300 patient volunteers	1,000 to 3,000 patient volunteers			Post-marketing safety monitoring
PURPOSE	Assess safety and biological activity		Determine safety and dosage	Evaluate effectiveness. Look for side effects.	Verify effectiveness, monitor adverse reactions from long-term use.		Review process	Large-scale manufacturing / Distribution / Education
Percent of all new drugs that pass			70% of INDs	33% of INDs	27% of INDs		20% of INDs	

Expedited Review: Phases II and III combined to shorten approval process on new medicines for serious and life-threatening diseases.

Source: Vance C. Gordon and Dale E. Wierenga, "The Drug Development and Approval Process," *New Drug Approvals in 1990*, January 1991. © 1991 by the Pharmaceutical Manufacturers Association. Reprinted by permission.

involved in getting a new drug approved would make the costs of innovation prohibitively high. Criticized for overlegislating in the efficacy realm, federal drug policy was also attacked from the opposing side for not doing enough in terms of price regulation. The objections voiced by Senator Kefauver concerning price levels and variations were not addressed in the 1962 legislation. However, the price differential between generic and brand-name drugs left an opening in the public arena for future debate.

Reaction and Refinement

> *Friend and foe alike of the industry point with all sorts of degrees of alarm, shame, disgust, distrust, and perplexity at what is certainly a situation at best hard to justify, and at worst completely unreasonable, chaotic as well as shortsighted and stupid.*

> George Squibb, *U.S. Senate testimony, 1967*

The Pharmaceutical Industry after 1962
Structural Hierarchy. As the pharmaceutical industry emerged from the therapeutic revolution, its structure was rather polarized. Despite the plethora of companies, a handful of large, integrated firms managed to dominate each therapeutic class, promoting their brand names and the fruits of their R&D directly to physicians. While this kind of competition was at times fierce, the brand-name companies, unlike the hundreds of smaller generic manufacturers that occupied the industry's lower tier were able to maintain high prices on new drugs.[27]

In addition to the intense price competition at the industry's lower tier, the aggressive promotional activity of brand-name firms hindered generic development in the 1970s.

Brand-name companies, via their representative detail men, distributed glossy brochures and free samples of their products, encouraging physicians to dispense them. Advertisements in medical journals further reinforced doctors' recognition of brand labels, which were shorter and easier to recall than cumbersome generic names.[28] These firms also underwrote medical education seminars and held conferences—often in vacation locations—where the line between clinical information and product promotion was sometimes fuzzy. Finally, by sponsoring advertisements that questioned the safety and efficacy of competing products, brand-name firms played on lingering fears of physicians and pharmacists that they would be liable for any injury caused by a generic equivalent they substituted. Accordingly, although numerous congressional studies conducted in the late 1960s provided a measure of confidence in the quality of generic drugs, brand-name pharmaceuticals continued to dominate the industry.[29]

Adverse Industry Trends. Shortly after the Kefauver-Harris Amendments were passed, the therapeutic revolution seemed to lose momentum. Although roughly half of the world's drug production took place in the United States at the time of passage, the country's share fell during the 1960s due to the internationalization of the industry. In addition, patent terms began to erode in the subsequent decade, as the average life of a drug patent dropped from 13.8 years in 1966 to 9.5 years in 1979 as lags in the

---

[27] This dual hierarchy began to blur in the 1980s as some brand-name companies aggressively pursued generic drug business and as some generic firms achieved the critical mass necessary to launch new drug development programs.

[28] Physicians had to go to great lengths to prescribe the lowest-priced drugs, since comparative pricing data was difficult to obtain. Many physicians relied on the *Physician's Desk Reference,* a commercial advertising compendium that the major drug companies distributed without charge—and without generic price listings.

[29] For example, in 1967 a task force formed by Health Education and Welfare secretary John Gardner concluded that brand-name manufacturers' claims of generics' biological and clinical (therapeutic) nonequivalency had been exaggerated.

EXHIBIT 4   Number of New Drugs* Approved by the FDA: 1950–1990

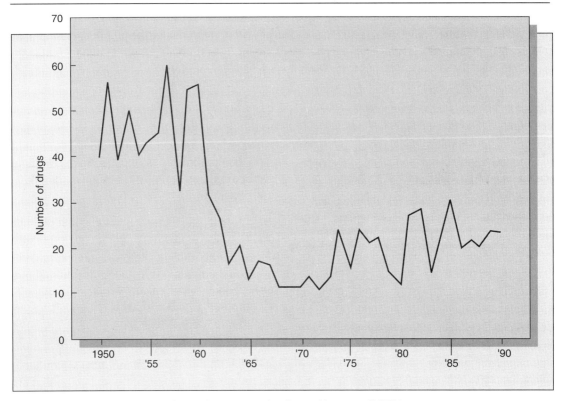

* In this exhibit, "New Drugs" refers only to new molecular entities, not all NDAs.

Source: FDA, Bureau of Drugs, *New Drug Evaluation Project Briefing Book* (various).

regulatory process mounted.[30] Yet the most notable and disturbing trend was the precipitous decline in the number of new drugs introduced in the United States (see Exhibit 4).

Numerous studies conducted in the late 1960s and 1970s attributed the industry's deteriorating rate of innovation to the new drug approval process under the recently passed federal amendments. One study estimated the uncapitalized development costs (not including discovery costs) for a single new chemical entity (NCE) at $16 million in the early 1970s, a far cry from the $1 million to $2 million required a decade earlier.[31] Other investigations focussed more directly on the agency itself (rather than its legislation), blaming the FDA's overzealousness for the industry's declining innovation. These studies found that the attrition rate for drugs undergoing clinical trials had increased from roughly 66 percent before 1962 to 90 percent some years later and that the actual time required by the FDA to examine NDAs rose throughout the 1960s, more than doubling to 44 months in 1969. Noting

---

[30] Grabowski and Vernon, p. 50.

[31] Ibid., p. 30.

that in the 1960s nearly four times as many new drugs were introduced in Britain as in the United States, Dr. William Wardell suggested that this *drug lag* — the delay in introducing new drugs in one country as compared to other technically advanced countries — was detrimental to American public health.[32]

Yet several other explanations of the drug industry's declining innovation rate surfaced. In terms of bureaucratic accountability, the drop in new drug introductions actually preceded the change in the FDA's approval process, which *effectively* became more stringent in 1970, rather than in 1962.[33] Moreover, according to the "research depletion hypothesis," the opportunities for additional NCEs opened up by the discovery of the sulfa drugs and antibiotics in the 1930s and 1940s were exhausted by the time the Kefauver-Harris Amendments were passed (i.e., the therapeutic revolution was nearly over by 1962). For its part, the FDA argued that the pharmaceutical industry, in face of increasingly complex drug technology, had returned to its prewar pattern of marketing existing drugs and introducing me-too products, rather than discovering new ones. Furthermore, the FDA saw its role as protecting the public from therapeutically innocuous drugs as well as dangerous ones: hence, some beneficial drugs would be slower in coming to market to keep the ineffectual ones out altogether. Finally, the FDA believed that it had received a mandate from the American public to err on the side of caution. According to Jerome Halperin, deputy director of the FDA's Bureau of Drugs, "Our critics seem to feel there is a public health gain in having all new drugs first. But . . . this [streamlining] is a bit on the risk-taking side for us, and I think the societal climate now says 'Don't take risks.'"[34]

Yet the theory behind the policy was slowly coming under question.

Legislative Reform

Attributing adverse industry trends to federal regulation, industry spokesman and economists lashed out at the FDA. The agency did make efforts to streamline the drug approval process, including its decision in 1975 to accept data from foreign drug studies. Although the drug lag diminished towards the end of the 1970s, a barrage of legislative proposals nonetheless ensued.

The Orphan Drug Act. In March 1982, a report commissioned by Representative Waxman's House Subcommittee on Health and Environment identified some 134 "orphan drugs" for rare diseases, only 47 of which were approved for use in the United States.[35] The small number of people with any given rare disease, in addition to the side-effects these drugs often caused, not only made clinical trials difficult to conduct but also typically made such pharmaceutical investments unprofitable. The Pharmaceutical Manufacturers Association complained that the FDA had made the drug approval process extremely cumbersome and argued that, to encourage further orphan drug development, a more streamlined approval process, not further legislation, was needed. Despite opposition from the Reagan administration because of the additional domestic spending entailed in the proposal legislation, a bill emerged quickly from Waxman's committee. The Orphan Drug Act was signed into law on January 1983.[36]

The Orphan Drug Act *(i)* provided the developer of drugs for rare diseases (defined by congress in 1984 as those with a population

---

[32] For background information on these studies, see Temin, pp. 143–51.

[33] See note 23.

[34] Kelly, "Bridging America's Drug Gap," p. 101.

[35] In 1990, there were some 5,000 known "rare diseases" in the United States that afflicted fewer than 200,000 people each.

[36] Orphan Drug Act, 96 Stat. 2049 (1983).

of not more than 200,000) with seven years of market exclusivity and a 50 percent tax credit for certain clinical research expenses; and *(ii)* established a grant program to fund clinical research by independent investigators acting without corporate support. The act encouraged drug companies to sit down with FDA early in the development process to plan the most efficient route to approval. The FDA abbreviated clinical investigations involving orphan drugs, due to the extreme nature of the circumstances: "Drugs that are dramatically effective do not need large patient populations to demonstrate the point. Similarly, benefit-risk appraisal is usually not difficult when a drug is highly beneficial to a small group of patients whose alternatives are limited."[37] Sensing a shift in policy priorities toward innovation, the large pharmaceutical companies took advantage of the harmonious environment to push for additional legislative support.

Patents and Pioneer Drugs.   Perceiving a decline in the return to R&D investments, research-intensive drug firms appealed to congress in the early 1980s to extend the lives of pioneer drug patents beyond the statutory 17 years to provide revenue streams needed to fund increasing expenditures for pioneer drug research. Spokesmen for brand-name pharmaceutical companies pointed out that innovative drugs often replaced more costly, invasive medical procedures and, hence, were particularly attractive investments from a social cost-benefit perspective.

Generic drug manufacturers and consumer groups rejected patent-term extension legislation and its goal of increasing the revenues of companies whose profits remained robust. Contesting industry's claims of patent-term erosion, these groups argued that pioneer drug manufacturers had in some instances delayed generic

competition by "evergreening" (i.e., filing applications to extend the original patent beyond 17 years to reward incremental product or process improvements).[38] Hoffman-La Roche, for example, achieved 22 years of de facto patent protection for its blockbuster tranquilizer, Valium, using this approach. Critics also pointed to other incentives to develop new drugs, such as R&D tax credits, which pioneer drug companies continued to enjoy. Furthermore, no legislation could guarantee that the additional revenues would be reinvested in R&D (versus promotional) activities or that they would be directed toward the development of innovative (versus me-too) drugs. Finally, generic drug manufacturers cautioned that patent-term extension would further retard their entry into the market and, thus, hinder price competition.

Generic Substitution.   Patent expirations in the 1960s and 1970s increased price competition within the pharmaceutical industry very slowly; in fact, generics had captured only about 10 percent of pharmaceutical sales by the mid 1970s.[39] In addition to nonpatent barriers, such as concerns about the quality of generic drugs and the aggressive promotional activities of brand-name firms, federal drug policy continued to impede competition by generics within the pharmaceutical industry.

The FDA had developed an abbreviated NDA (ANDA) process for the generic versions of pioneer drugs approved before 1962 ("pre-1962" drugs). The ANDA did not require safety and efficacy data for these drugs, only proof that they were chemically and biologically equivalent to the pioneer drug. In 1980, the FDA authorized "paper NDAs" for generic versions of post-1962 drugs, which allowed

---

[37] Committee on Energy and Commerce, *Orphan Drug Act,* 97th Cong., 2nd sess., 1981, H. Rept. 97-840, Part I.

[38] There was no statutory limit on the number of times a patent application could be refiled (a *continuation* application) to obtain a reconsideration.

[39] Temin, p. 243.

generic manufacturers to submit the published results of studies supported and conducted by others. Yet the limited number of published studies on post-1962 pioneer drugs restricted the utility of the paper NDA approach. Moreover, these applications still had to contain all the animal and human safety and effectiveness data required for the general NDA. The policy trade-off between safety and speed still favored the former.

Yet as third-party payers expanded their coverage of U.S. health care expenditures, the high prices of brand-name drugs began to eclipse concerns over the quality of generics. Both Medicare (the federally funded health insurance program for the elderly) and Medicaid (the health insurance program for low-income individuals funded jointly by the federal and state governments) substantially increased the demand for prescription drugs. Consequently, the government became increasingly critical of the industry's pricing practices. However, industry spokespersons claimed that high prices merely reflected the high and escalating costs of R&D. Moreover, they noted that, in the 1960s, average prescription drug prices remained stable, even though the overall health care component of the consumer price index (CPI) was rising dramatically at that time (see Exhibit 1 and Exhibit 6). Nonetheless, generic drugs were often considerably cheaper than their pioneer counterparts, as the former shared neither the latter's development and promotion costs nor its monopoly position. Hence, federal and state governments took an active interest in promoting generic substitution.

In 1977, the federal government launched the Maximum Allowable Cost (MAC) program, which specified the highest amount the government would reimburse a pharmacy under Medicare and Medicaid for a given drug. Similarly, numerous states mandated the use of generic drugs in Medicaid programs, and some private insurance companies notified their policyholders that only generic versions would receive full reimbursement. Moreover, many hospitals and health maintenance organizations established formularies to insure that low-cost generics would be dispensed. By 1984, all 50 states had passed laws allowing pharmacists to substitute a generic version for a brand-name prescription unless expressly forbidden by the physician.[40] U.S. generic drug sales tripled to over $3 billion between 1978 and 1983 to capture 20 percent of the domestic prescription drug market. (Exhibits 7a and 7b). Nonetheless, given the substantial informational requirements involved in completing a "paper NDA," only 12 new generic drugs had been approved by June 1983.

The Great Compromise. In the early 1980s, the FDA projected that greater generic substitution would save consumers as much as $1 billion over 12 years, given the many important pioneer drugs about to come off patent.[41] Although certain congressional representatives advocated an easing of the approval process for generic drugs, Representative Waxman in particular felt that such legislation would not succeed without the inclusion of a "sweetener" for the larger brand-name pharmaceutical companies. Such a compromise was in fact achieved, resulting in the Drug Price Competition and Patent-Term Restoration Act (Waxman-Hatch Act) of 1984.[42]

The Waxman-Hatch Act *(i)* enhanced the ability of generic manufacturers to gain approval for ANDAs; *(ii)* provided new statutory protection for pioneer drugs; and *(iii)* extended

---

[40] State legislatures, concerned about potential public health threats posed by black-market products, had passed *antisubstitution laws* in the 1950s that required pharmacists to dispense specific brands prescribed by physicians.

[41] Charles Alexander, "Prescription for Cheap Drugs," *Time,* September 17, 1984, p. 64.

[42] Drug Price Competition and Patent Term Restoration Act of 1984, 98 Stat. 1585 (1984).

EXHIBIT 5   R&D Expenditures as Percentage of Pharmaceutical Industry Sales*: 1965–1988

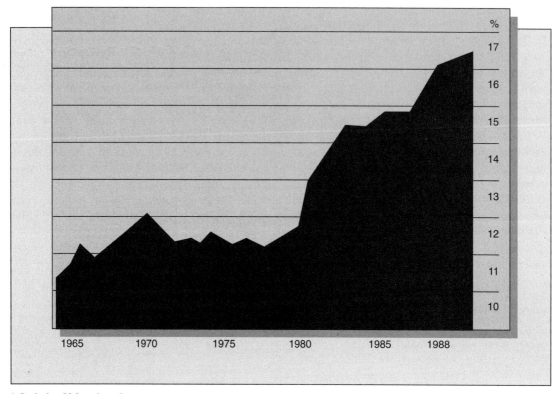

* Includes U.S. sales plus exports.

Source: Pharmaceutical Manufacturers Association, *Annual Report* (1989).

patent-terms for pioneer drugs under certain circumstances. The legislation stipulated that generics' ANDAs need only provide evidence of bioequivalence to the relevant pioneer drug to obtain approval. In return, Waxman-Hatch provided safeguards for company trade secrets used in assessing ANDAs and guaranteed specified periods of market exclusivity during which time no ANDA could become effective. The statute also granted innovator firms patent-term restoration for up to five years. The length of the extension awarded would be proportional to the amount of regulatory delay incurred with respect to the drug in question.

Recent Developments

Changes in Industry Structure and Performance
Generic drug companies performed extremely well in the immediate aftermath of the Waxman-Hatch Act, bringing to market equivalent versions of 40 percent of all prescriptions drugs and boosting sales to $6 billion a year by 1989.[43] In face of this new competitive force,

---

[43] James N. Baker and Mary Hager, "Not What the Doctor Ordered: Was the FDA Careless about Generic Drugs," *Newsweek,* August 28, 1989, p. 32; and Michael deCourcy Hinds, "The Battle over Generic Drugs Heats Up," *The New York Times,* March 4, 1989, p. 35.

EXHIBIT 6 Drug Sales as Percentage of U.S. Health Care Expenditures: 1965–1987

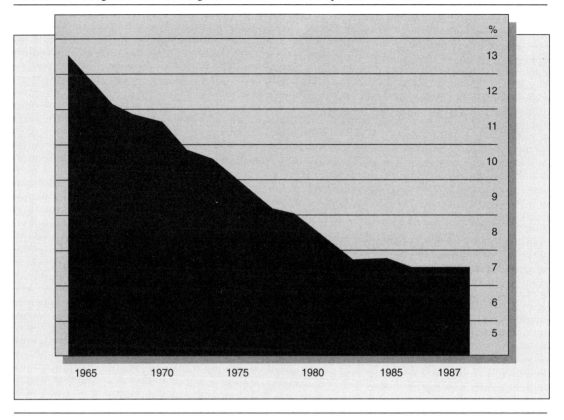

Source: Pharmaceutical Manufacturers Association, *Annual Report* (1989).

which was compounded by the growing presence of strong international drug manufacturers, some brand-name companies diversified their product line into the generic business while at the same time continuing to invest aggressively in R&D.

In response to increasingly complex technology and to development costs that exceeded $200 million per successful new drug, on average,[44] a growing number of pharmaceutical companies expanded globally through subsidiarics, cooperative agreements, and acquisitions to spread the costs of R&D, clinical trials, and production over larger markets. Such globalization strategies also helped these firms reduce dependence on any one "blockbuster" drug, while establishing international linkages and greater contact with research scientists and physicians. The industry also appeared to be shifting away from developing me-too drugs to more innovative research. The chairman and CEO of Johnson & Johnson explained that "only distinctly different medicines whose benefits can justify premium prices can generate the profits to underwrite big-time research."[45]

---

[44] A 1990 Tufts University study derived a figure of $231 million per new drug, although other studies presented somewhat lower estimates.

[45] Michael Waldholz, "Drug Industry Still Has Room to Merge," *The Wall Street Journal*, June 25, 1991, p. A2.

EXHIBIT 7a   U.S. Prescription Drug Sales by Type: 1978–1989

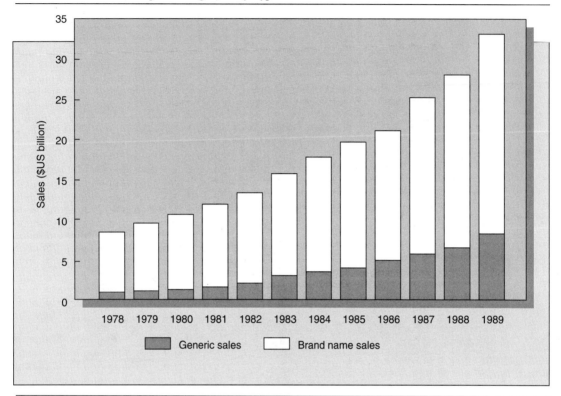

Firms expanded technologically as well as geographically. In the 1980s, researchers began to employ "rational drug design," which used computers and molecular biology to tailor drugs for specific conditions far more efficiently than the tedious screening method. The promise of rational drug design and the close association between the pharmaceutical and burgeoning biotechnology[46] industries, exemplified by Hoffman-LaRoche's acquisition of Genentech and Lilly's acquisition of Hybritech, convinced some analysts that the pharmaceutical industry was on the verge of another therapeutic revolution. These analysts pointed to a number of drugs on the market and in the development stage that were designed to treat the chronic illnesses of the elderly and thereby provide the industry with a strong basis for future growth as the baby-boom generation aged.[47] Exhibit 8 presents performance indicators of leading U.S. pharmaceutical firms in the 1980s.

FDA Setbacks and Crises

In the context of burgeoning federal deficits and a philosophical commitment to deregulation, the Reagan administration worked to

---

[46] Biotechnology, unlike traditional chemical pharmacology, involved the replication and manipulation of the natural products of the body.

[47] Jane H. Cutaia, "A Healthy Payoff from Nonstop Research," *Business Week,* January 11, 1988.

EXHIBIT 7b Generics Share of Total U.S. Prescription Drug Sales: 1978–1989

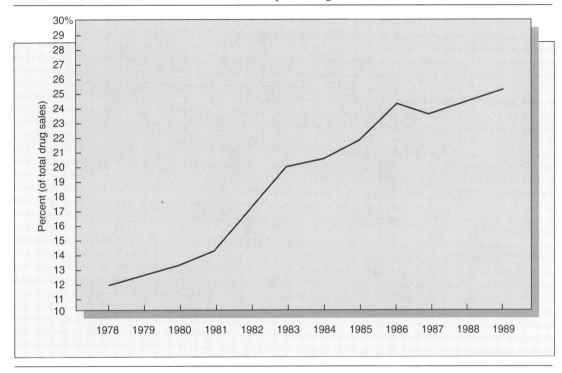

Source: Adapted from Alice Naude, "Generics Furor Leaves Bright-Looking Future," *Chemical Marketing Reporter,* March 19, 1990, p. SR14; and Pamela Hollie, "Generic Drugs in Bigger Role," *The New York Times,* July 23, 1984, p. IV,1.

reduce financial support of the FDA in the early 1980s (see Exhibit 9 for historical data on FDA appropriations and personnel). At the same time, however, the agency received additional administrative responsibilities (e.g., in the orphan drug area) and was further confronted with a number of public health crises, including product tamperings, the AIDS epidemic, a blood-bank emergency, and panic over cyanide-laced grapes from Chile. Understaffed and resource-constrained, the agency was further demoralized by corruption in its dealings with generic drug manufacturers.

Generic Drug Scandal. In 1988, complaints from Mylan Laboratories, Inc., prompted an investigation of the generic drug industry and the FDA by the House Energy and Commerce Committee. The congressional inquiry uncovered favoritism within the FDA's ranks, as some generic drug companies had received speedy approval on their applications in exchange for payoffs to reviewers. Among the beneficiaries were the generic firms Par Pharmaceutical, Inc., and its subsidiary, Quad Pharmaceuticals, Inc., which together received 77 drug approvals in 1986, almost twice as many as any other company. Although no damage to the public health resulted, the scandal produced numerous criminal convictions and the recall or withdrawal of over 100 adulterated, contaminated, or mislabeled generic drug products. Operating on an arbitrary, case-by-case basis, the FDA was overwhelmed by the deluge of applications prompted by the Waxman-Hatch Act. When the scandal was brought to

EXHIBIT 8   Financial Statistics of Major U.S. Pharmaceutical Firms

	Bristol Myers Squibb	*Eli Lilly & Co.*	*Merck & Co.*	*Pfizer Inc.*	*Schering-Plough*	*Upjohn Co.*
Operating revenues						
1990 (millions)	$10,300.0	$5,191.6	$7,671.5	$6,406.0	$3,322.9	$3,032.7
Compound growth (%):						
1–year	12.1%	24.3%	17.1%	13.0%	5.2%	4.0%
5–year	18.3	9.7	16.7	9.1	11.5	8.5
10–year	12.5	7.3	10.9	7.8	6.7	5.5
Net income						
1990 (millions)	$ 1,748.0	$1,127.3	$1,781.2	$ 801.2	$ 565.1	$ 458.1
Compund growth (%):						
1–year	134.0%	20.0%	19.1%	17.6%	19.9%	47.3%
5–year	26.9	16.8	27.0	6.7	24.0	17.7
10–year	20.5	12.7	15.7	12.1	9.0	10.4
Financial ratios (range: 1986–90):						
Gross margin	69%–72%	63%–70%	68%–77%	61%–65%	69%–76%	69%–73%
ROS	8%–17%	11%–23%	16%–23%	12%–15%	11%–17%	11%–15%
ROA	11%–20%	8%–17%	14%–24%	9%–14%	9%–15%	10%–13%
ROE	17%–33%	14%–31%	26%–49%	16%–21%	18%–28%	18%–28%
Debt/TC	4%–6%	6%–12%	3%–5%	3%–7%	8%–16%	11%–21%
P/E (hi–lo)	41–11	38–13	33–14	19–10	21–11	33–13
Market/book (hi–lo)	6.8–2.7	8.1–3.0	15.4–3.9	3.8–1.8	5.9–2.5	6.0–2.5

Source: Adapted from Standard & Poor's "S&P Industry Surveys/August 22, 1991: Healthcare."

light, the FDA reorganized its generics division, instituting a program of expanded inspections and administrative reform.

The AIDS Crisis. The onset of the AIDS crisis helped frame the debate over the future of federal drug policy. AIDS, or acquired immune deficiency syndrome, was caused by the human immunodeficiency virus (HIV), which severely weakened the body's immune system, leaving a person with AIDS vulnerable to a range of opportunistic infections and, ultimately, death. Between 1981 and mid 1991, more than 132,000 persons had been diagnosed with AIDS in the United States. Furthermore, epidemiologists estimated that approximately 1–2 million people in the United States were infected with HIV in the early 1990s.[48] With the exponential spread of the virus came calls for a more streamlined drug approval process and innovative approaches to treatment.

Fast track. Early in the AIDS crisis, FDA commissioner Frank E. Young granted AIDS treatments special "1-AA" status, a top review priority, requiring FDA action within 180 days of submission. In May 1987, the FDA issued "treatment" or "compassionate" IND regulations, which allowed doctors to dispense

---

[48] "Institute Opposes Policy to Ban Travelers Infected with HIV," *Harvard Gazette*, May 24, 1991, p. 24.

EXHIBIT 9 FDA Appropriations and Personnel: 1931–1991

Fiscal Year	Appropriations (million current $)	Appropriations (million 1986 $)	Personnel (FTE's)
1931	$ 1.7	$ 20.8	541
1936	1.9	24.7	518
1941	2.6	27.5	875
1946	2.8	26.4	948
1951	6.0	37.7	1,815
1956	6.1	32.1	1,065
1961	20.5	92.2	2,112
1966	58.7	225.4	4,994
1971	87.5	244.4	4,615
1976	207.8	386.9	6,362
1981	326.9	400.7	7,777
1986	402.2	402.2	6,757
1991	656.5	542.4	8,259

Source: U.S. Office of Management and Budget, *The Budget of the U.S. Government, and Appendix* (various years).

experimental medicines to patients with life-threatening illnesses. Responding in October 1988 to pressure from AIDS activists and drug companies alike to shorten the drug approval process, the FDA established regulations eliminating the need for Phase III clinical trials for drugs designed to treat certain life-threatening diseases (see Exhibit 3 for an overview of the drug approval process).[49] While the "fast-track" approach consumed considerable resources, it greatly shortened the time required to approve new AIDS therapies, which, by 1989, required an average of 4.2 years to develop compared with 7.8 years for other drugs.[50] The FDA insisted that its fast-track process had facilitated the distribution of AIDS therapies to those who needed them without sacrificing its mandate to protect those inflicted. Yet as commissioner Young explained, "The more desperate a disease, the more willing we are to trade on safety and efficacy."[51]

New testing approaches. The AIDS crisis also brought about a revolution in clinical drug testing. According to Dr. Mathilde Krim of the American Foundation for AIDS Research, "There's a rebellion against doctors playing God by preventing you from having access to something you believe is good." In August 1988, the FDA allowed AIDS patients to import unapproved drugs sold in other countries for personal use to curb a growing underground network. Further relaxing regulations in 1989, the agency allowed patients outside clinical studies access to promising experimental medicines at extremely early stages of drug development. The enormous reception to this "parallel-track" program reflected the disillusionment with the traditional

[49] A precedent for suspending Phase III trials had been set in late 1986 with the FDA's accelerated approval of Wellcome's AIDS drug, AZT.

[50] Bruce Ingersoll and Gregory Stricharchuk, "Generic Drug Scandal at the FDA Is Linked to Deregulation Drive," *The Wall Street Journal,* September 13, 1989, p. A14.

[51] Sharon Begley, Mary Hager, and Larry Wilson, "Desperation Drugs," *Newsweek,* August 7, 1989, p. 48.

placebo trial approach to clinical testing among AIDS patients.[52] An even further departure from standard procedures, community-based clinical trials (CBCTs) became a popular alternative to traditional, university testing. In contrast to the latter process, CBCTs, typically run by independent physicians or local clinics, allowed patients more input into the process and often did not use placebo trials. Proponents argued that the more personal CBCTs engendered a higher degree of trust than traditional clinical trials and did a much better job of recruiting minorities and the poor. Critics, however, believed that CBCTs sacrificed science on the altar of compassion by dabbling in a host of remedies, thus complicating the search for the best medication. As William Vodra, the FDA's chief counsel from 1974–79, posited: "If we really change the system, will we end up with cures or quackery?"[53]

The Orphans Mature. By 1990, the discoveries facilitated by the Orphan Drug Act were impressive. From 1983 to 1990, federal grants for orphan drug development increased from $500,000 to $7.5 million.[54] During these years, more than 40 orphan drugs, some of them developed by small start-up firms, were approved by the FDA, and at least 150 more were being actively developed. In some cases, the markets for these drugs proved to be quite significant. For example, Genentech and Eli Lilly were granted exclusive licenses to market alternative versions of human growth hormone (hGH) and thereby split an estimated demand of $175 million per year for the product.[55] Wellcome's sales of its orphan AIDS drug, AZT, exceeded $250 million per year by 1990.

Some AIDS activists and congressmen concerned with the epidemic's growing costs called for changes in the Orphan Drug Act's provisions to promote competition. Accordingly, in April 1990, Representative Waxman proposed a bill to eliminate the seven-year exclusive marketing period granted for developers of orphan drugs. Orphan drug status (and the corresponding entry barriers) would be repealed if a competitor developed the drug within six months of the first firm's designation or if the patient population grew beyond 200,000. Waxman argued that "The Orphan Drug Act was not intended to be a way for drug companies to get a large monopoly for a drug that had potential to create large profits." However, companies that were marketing these drugs viewed the amendments as a breach of contract. Amgen CEO, Gordon M. Binder, argued that developing orphan drugs was a high-risk proposition that required the prospect of commensurate profits: "The expectation of orphan drug exclusivity was critical to our ability to attract the kind of investment needed to pursue this breakthrough therapy, and our investors should be allowed to receive a reasonable return."[56] The Waxman amendments passed both houses of congress but were pocket-vetoed by President Bush at the end of the 1990 session.

On the Horizon

Costs and Payment.   Between 1984 and 1989, Medicaid payments for prescription drugs increased 85 percent from roughly $2 billion to

---

[52] Under traditional clinical testing procedures, half of the trial participants received the actual drug while the other half (unknowingly) received a placebo. Although these controlled trials permitted careful analysis of a drug's effects, they also prevented half of the volunteer patients from receiving a potentially life-saving drug.

[53] Gina Kolata, "The Philosophy of the 'New F.D.A.' Is Mostly a Matter of Packaging," *The New York Times,* May 19, 1991, p. E4.

[54] Robert A. Hamilton, "Rare Disease Treatments: 'Orphans' Saving Lives," *FDA Consumer,* November 1990, p. 10.

---

[55] John Carey and J. Hamilton, "These 'Orphans' Don't Need Any Nurturing," *Business Week,* July 2, 1990, p. 38.

[56] "Orphan Drug Act Needs Discipline," *The Wall Street Journal,* May 23, 1990, p. A21.

$3.7 billion. In terms of total Medicaid expenditures, the proportion devoted to prescription drug costs rose from 5.8 to 6.7 percent in this same period, making it the fastest-growing category of Medicaid spending.[57] To contain drug prices, congress passed the Medicaid rebate law in late 1990, opting for "prudent purchasing" in lieu of formularies. Under this *open-formulary* plan, a pharmaceutical manufacturer had to provide a rebate to Medicaid based on the difference between the average manufacturer's price and the best price offered to preferred customers. In response, however, some manufacturers considered eliminating virtually all discounts as a way of neutralizing the impact of the expensive rebate requirement.

U.S. health care costs, which by 1990 represented over 12 percent of GNP, continued to

grow as the population aged and as medical technology became more complex (see Exhibit 10). Moreover, during the 1980s, prescription drug prices on average rose faster than the overall rate of inflation (see Exhibit 11).[58] Since in 1990, 44 percent of drug sales—$15.1 billion—resulted from personal, out-of-pocket expenditures,[59] some observers feared that individuals would have increasing difficulty supporting the financial burden imposed by these increasing drug costs and might be forced to forego treatment. Public policy makers searching for stricter cost-containment measures looked abroad for alternative models, such as national health insurance. Chronic budget deficits and a general resistance to federal inter-

---

[57] Medicaid was the pharmaceutical industry's largest U.S. customer, paying for roughly 10 percent of all drug purchases.

[58] Michael Waldholz, "During 1980s, Prescription Drug Prices Rose Almost 3 Times the Inflation Rate," *The Wall Street Journal,* September 25, 1991, p. B3.

[59] Milt Freudenheim, "Drug Makers Face Pressure to Restrain Price Increases," *The New York Times,* May 11, 1991, p. A1.

EXHIBIT 10 U.S. Health Care Expenditures: 1965–1990

Year	Nominal Expend (billion $)	Percent of GNP	Real Expend* (billion 1990 $)
1965	41.6	5.9%	276.0
1970	74.4	7.3%	359.7
1975	132.9	8.3%	457.0
1980	249.1	9.1%	543.1
1981	288.6	9.4%	559.3
1982	323.8	10.2%	565.4
1983	356.1	10.5%	584.4
1984	387.0	10.3%	598.5
1985	420.1	10.5%	608.6
1986	452.3	10.6%	608.3
1987	492.5	10.8%	626.1
1988	544.0	11.1%	646.8
1989	601.1	11.5%	662.0
1990	675.7	12.4%	675.7

* Calculated using the consumer price index for "Medical Care."

Source: U.S. Department of Commerce, *U.S. Industrial Outlook 1991,* p. 44.

EXHIBIT 11 Selected U.S. Price Indexes: 1980–1990

Year	CPI All Items	CPI Medical Care	CPI Prescrip Drugs
1980	100.0	100.0	100.0
1981	108.9	112.5	112.6
1982	113.1	124.9	126.2
1983	117.4	132.9	138.4
1984	122.0	141.0	152.1
1985	126.7	150.5	164.6
1986	128.0	162.1	179.4
1987	133.7	171.5	193.7
1988	139.6	183.4	208.9
1989	146.1	199.0	228.7
1990	155.0	218.0	251.3

Source: U.S. Department of Labor, Bureau of Labor Statistics.

vention in the market, however, had impeded serious consideration of such a radical overhaul in healthcare policy. Yet drug manufacturers became embroiled in the debate as a result of drug prices in the United States that exceed those charged in some foreign countries by a factor of two or three (see Exhibit 12). Pharmaceutical companies had defended themselves in the debate thus far by arguing that, since many foreign governments set strict price controls on drugs, manufacturers were forced to charge higher prices in noncontroled markets to recover the huge fixed costs incurred in the drug development process.

EXHIBIT 12 Index of Average Drug Prices in Selected Countries: 1991

Country	Index
Netherlands	299
United States	279
Germany	269
Denmark	230
England	217
Italy	131
France	127
Spain	106
Greece	100

Source: Gina Kolata, "Why Drugs Cost More in U.S.," *The New York Times,* May 26, 1991, p. D1.

FDA: Responsibility and Role. In spite of fast-track reforms in the 1980s, the U.S. drug approval process remained in 1991 one of the most lengthy and costly in the world. However, regulators had begun to broaden their philosophy, supplementing "safety and efficacy" considerations with "benefit/risk" analysis, incorporating such factors as the severity of the patient's condition when determining the appropriate thoroughness standard for drug tests. The FDA had also, on occasion, employed the policy of "conditional approval," whereby a drug whose efficacy was not yet established could nonetheless be licensed provisionally and later withdrawn if proven to be ineffective. Finally, in revisiting the concept of "efficacy," the FDA was beginning to wrestle with the possibility of approving drugs based on their ability to improve the quality of life, rather than their capacity to prolong it.

In 1991, David A. Kessler, M.D., the newly appointed commissioner of the FDA, brought with him a determination to revitalize the dispirited agency. Kessler, a Harvard-trained pediatrician and University of Chicago law graduate asserted, "What I care about most is restoring the credibility and the integrity of the Food and Drug Administration." Shifting the regulatory impetus of the agency from responsive to aggressive, Kessler initiated a vigorous, highly publicized crackdown on food-labeling practices, forcing a number of firms to modify or delete claims regarding the freshness, fat content, and cholesterol content of their products. He also proposed a major overhaul of food-labeling regulations to increase both the amount of information required and the number of products covered. With respect to pharmaceuticals, Kessler declared, "Traditionally, the medical officer reviewing a new drug application saw himself as a guardian standing between the manufacturer and the patient, but that attitude is slowly being modified. Today the goal is not only to keep unsafe drugs off the market but to get safe drugs onto the market."[60] In addition, Kessler planned an attack on alleged promotional abuses in the pharmaceutical industry, such as encouraging physicians to prescribe existing drugs for unapproved uses. However, the industry, strongly objecting to what it saw as unjustified or exaggerated charges, was ready to fight back. As the FDA's resources remained overextended, it remained unclear what effect Kessler's efforts would have on the long-embattled regulatory agency, the pharmaceutical industry, and, ultimately, the health of the American populace.

---

[60] Herbert Burkholz, "A Shot in the Arm for the FDA," *The New York Times Magazine,* June 30, 1991, pp. 15, 31.

BAYBANK BOSTON

As Richard Pollard, chairman of BayBank Boston, got off the phone with Richard Syron, president of the Boston Federal Reserve Bank (the Fed), he could not help but feel a mixture of concern and satisfaction about the results of the Fed's new study of mortgage lending. A bomb was dropped on the Boston banking industry in 1989 when a Fed study of neighborhood lending patterns provided evidence of discrimination. A 1990 analysis of home mortgage lending data seemed to confirm the earlier study. Local bankers had been quick to point out that neither of these studies reflected all the variables that go into a lending decision. The bankers argued that the patterns discovered by the Fed could simply reflect differences in the quality of loan applications, rather than racial discrimination.

The 1992 study was designed to meet this objection, thanks in large part to the participation of Boston bankers, who voluntarily opened their mortgage files to the Fed researchers. As Syron explained it, the researchers confirmed Pollard's belief that the banks were not turning down qualified black applicants. Rather, the study detected a more subtle

---

This case was written by Professor Gregory J. Dees of the Harvard Business School.

Copyright © 1993 by the President and Fellows of Harvard College.

Harvard Business School case 393-095.

source of bias in the mortgage lending process. (See Exhibit 1 for BayBank's mortgage loan process.) According to the new study, applicants who met the credit criteria on the first cut were given loans without regard to race. However, a large number of applicants

---

EXHIBIT 1   BayBank Mortgage Loan Approval Process

STEP 1: Preliminaries
  (*a*) A potential applicant identified a property to purchase and negotiated a price.
  (*b*) The applicant decided to approach BayBank for a mortgage.

STEP 2: The Applicant Inquired at Branch Office
  (*a*) A mortgage specialist conducted the preliminary interview, focusing on the applicants ability to service the debt, based on gross income.
  (*b*) If the applicant was interested in applying for one of the mortgage products offered, he or she was given a BayBank Mortgage Application Package.

STEP 3: Branch Review of Completed Application
  (*a*) After the mortgage specialist received the application, an appointment was made to review the application process with the applicant.
  (*b*) At the appointment, the application was reviewed for completeness and for any obvious obstacles to making the loan. If there were any missing forms or problems, the applicant may be asked to supply additional information.
  (*c*) The applicant paid an application fee and one point (1% of the loan).

STEP 4: Bank Underwriting Process at BayBank Mortgage Corporation
  (*a*) An underwriter and loan processor reviewed the application using secondary market criteria. Credit reports were ordered, income and bank accounts were verified, and the property was assessed.
  (*b*) A senior underwriter reviewed the work of the underwriter and loan processor. The file was passed through a quality control process. The senior underwriter finalized the decision and sometimes recommended an alternative method for making the loan.
  (*c*) If the underwriter recommended the loan be denied, the senior underwriter must review the loan to assure that all possibilities for approving the loan have been exhausted. If the senior underwriter agreed with the recommendation, the loan was given to the CRA manager for review. If the CRA manager did not find an alternative program to grant the loan, the loan was reviewed by senior staff at BayBank Mortgage Corporation. If senior staff agreed with the decision, a denial letter was written that explained the reasons for denial.
  (*d*) The bank's closing department prepared instruction and closing documents for the bank's attorney. The attorney made an appointment with the applicant for the closing.

(80 percent) initially failed to meet standard credit criteria. In most of these cases, the problems were eventually overcome and a mortgage was approved. It was in this discretionary process of working the application that racial differences were found, even after all credit factors were considered. Black and Hispanic applicants were more likely to be denied a mortgage. The racial disparity found in this study was much lower than that implied by the previous studies, but it was significant nonetheless. (See Exhibit 2 for excerpts from the 1992 study.)

During the last three years, Pollard had spent a tremendous amount of time and energy both as the chairman of BayBank Boston and of the Massachusetts Bankers Association (MBA) dealing with the issues raised by the earlier studies. The new study forced Pollard to ask himself: Would existing programs adequately address the problem? If not, what else needed to be done to provide equal access to banking services and resources? Was BayBank Boston doing enough?

The Evolution of BayBanks, Inc.[1]

Once called Baystate Corporation, BayBanks had always had a strong regional presence in the suburbs around Boston. Until the mid-1970s, Baystate was made up of 11 banks, each with its own name, identity, and customer base. Baystate was a substantial player in the state, holding 11 percent of Massachusetts' deposit base throughout the late 1970s. By 1976, its eight banks in the Boston suburbs had 144 branches. Its hallmark was a commitment to customer service and an appeal to local bank loyalty.

William Crozier's Plan. In the mid-1970s, Baystate began to reevaluate its decentralized structure and local marketing strategy. William Crozier, then newly appointed chief executive officer and chairman, proposed a common corporate identity, to improve marketing and advertising impact, and to increase operating efficiency by centralizing data processing. With the approval of the Baystate shareholders in the spring of 1976, Crozier's proposal became a reality and BayBanks, Inc., was born. The local banks took on the new BayBank name and retained their regional identity as a surname. For instance, Harvard Trust in Cambridge became BayBank/Harvard Trust.

Crozier also made a decision to strengthen the corporate side of the business. A presence in Boston's financial district was essential to corporate banking in Massachusetts. Richard Pollard, a commercial banker from the Chase Manhattan Bank, was hired and a new bank, BayBank Boston, was created to house the corporate banking function. The bank eventually became a base for retail expansion in Boston, with subsequent expansion into the so-called streetcar suburbs of Boston.

Electronic Banking. In a preemptive strike, Crozier bet early and heavily on technology, particularly automatic teller machines (ATMs) and electronic funds transfer capabilities. Crozier's bet turned out to be a good one.

> As the growth of the 1980s erupted on all fronts, BayBanks met market needs by launching an expansion program unparalleled in the company's history. The stars of that expansion were the BayBank Card and the X-Press 24[SM] network, one of the most successful electronic banking programs ever executed in the United States.[2]

By the middle of 1989, BayBank ATMs had 39 percent of Suffolk county's ATM market

---

[1] Unless otherwise noted, facts and figures from this section were drawn from Professor Walter J. Salmon's "Baystate Corporation" cases (HBS cases (A) No. 579–117, (B) No. 579–118, and (C) No. 579–119).

[2] BayBanks, Inc., annual report, April 1990, p. 6.

EXHIBIT 2 Excerpts from "Mortgage Lending in Boston: Interpreting HMDA Data" (1992)

The Home Mortgage Disclosure Act (HMDA) data for 1990, which were released in October 1991, showed substantially higher denial rates for black and Hispanic applicants. These minorities were two to three times as likely to be denied mortgage loans as white applicants were. In fact, high-income minorities in Boston were more likely to be turned down than low-income whites. The 1991 HMDA data, which are being released currently, show a similar pattern.

This pattern has triggered a resurgence of the debate on whether discrimination exists in home mortgage lending. Some people believe that the disparities in denial rates are evidence of discrimination on the part of banks and other lending institutions. Others, including lenders, argue that such conclusions are unwarranted, because the HMDA data do not include information on credit histories, loan-to-value ratios, and other factors considered in making mortgage decisions. These missing pieces of information, they argue, explain the high denial rates for minorities.

The results of this study indicate that minority applicants, on average, have greater debt burdens, higher loan-to-value ratios, and weaker credit histories and are less likely to buy single-family homes than white applicants, and that those disadvantages do account for a large portion of the difference in denial rates. Including additional information on applicant and property characteristics reduces the disparity between minority and white denials from the originally reported ratio of 2.7 to 1 to roughly 1.6 to 1. But these factors do not wholly eliminate the disparity, since the adjusted ratio implies that, even after controlling for financial, employment, and neighborhood characteristics, black and Hispanic mortgage applicants in the Boston metropolitan area are roughly 60 percent more likely to be turned down than whites. This discrepancy means that minority applicants with the same economic and property characteristics as white applicants would experience a denial rate of 17 percent, rather than the actual white denial rate of 11 percent. Thus, in the end, a statistically significant gap remains, which is associated with race.

Estimating an equation that includes an explicit measure for race is not the only way to test whether race is an important factor in the mortgage lending decision. An equally good alternative is to estimate an equation for white applicants and then plug in the obligation ratios, loan-to-value ratio, credit history, and other values for each black/Hispanic applicant to calculate that applicant's probability of denial. The resulting discrepancy between the actual minority denial rate and the estimated minority denial rate based on the white equation can be interpreted as the effect of race on the mortgage lending decision.

Probability of Black/Hispanic Denials Based on White Experience

Characteristics and Experience	Denial Rates (%)
Actual denial rate for blacks/Hispanics in sample	28.1%
Denial rate for blacks/Hispanics with black/Hispanic characteristics but white experience	20.2
Denial rate for blacks/Hispanics with white characteristics but black/Hispanic experience	18.2
Actual denial rate for whites in sample	10.3

EXHIBIT 2   *(concluded)*

If blacks/Hispanics had their own characteristics — that is, high obligation ratios, weaker credit histories, higher loan-to-value ratios, and less likely to buy a single-family home, but were treated by lenders like whites — their average denial rate would be 20.2 percent, rather than the actual 28.1 percent experienced by minority applicants. In other words, economic, property, and neighborhood characteristics explain much of the higher minority denial rate, but 7.9 percentage points remain unexplained.

If the 7.9 percentage point discrepancy is attributed to the effect of race on the lending decision, this amount can be added to the white denial rate to estimate the racial impact starting from the white base — that is, the third line (in the above table) shows what the denial rate would have been for black and Hispanic applicants, if they had white obligation ratios, loan-to-value ratio, credit histories, and other characteristics but were treated by lenders like minorities. Thus, even if minorities had all the economic and property characteristics of whites, they would have experienced a denial rate of 18.2 percent, 7.9 percentage points more than the actual white denial rate of 10.3.

This study has examined one avenue through which differential treatment could affect minorities' access to credit and opportunities for homeownership. It found that black and Hispanic mortgage applicants in the Boston area were more likely to be turned down than white applicants with similar characteristics.

It is important to clarify the limited focus of this analysis; it abstracts from discrimination that may occur elsewhere in the economy. For example, if minorities are subject to discrimination in education or labor markets, they will have lower incomes and their applications may reflect higher obligation ratios, greater loan-to-value ratios, or poorer credit histories. Similarly, if blacks and Hispanics are discouraged from moving into predominantly white areas they will limit their search to neighborhoods sanctioned for minorities. They tend to be older central cities with high-density housing, such as two- to four-family homes. Denial of a mortgage loan application on the basis of either these economic or property characteristics would not be considered discriminatory for the purpose of this study.

Even within the specific focus of conventional lenders, the reported measure of the hurdles faced by minorities should be placed in perspective; differential treatment can occur at many stages in the lending process. For example, minorities may be discouraged from even applying for a mortgage loan as a result of a prescreening process. Similarly, if white applicants are more likely than minority applicants to be "coached" when filling out the application, they will have stronger applications than similarly situated minorities. In this case, the ratios and other financial information in the *final* applications, which were the focus of this analysis, may themselves be the product of differential treatment. This study does not explore the extent to which coaching occurs, but rather focuses on the impact of race on lenders' decisions regarding the final applications received from potential borrowers.

Source: Alicia H. Munnell, Lynn E. Browne, James McEneaney, and Geoffrey M.B. Tootell, "Mortgage Lending in Boston," Federal Reserve Bank of Boston, Working Paper no. 92–7, October 1992.

share. BayBanks, Inc., profited financially, due to a boost in individual accounts and service charges. By the end of the 1980s, BayBanks, Inc., was approaching $10 billion in total assets.

Adjusting to Life in the City.   Over the course of a decade, BayBanks, Inc., had created an organization that incorporated the strengths of the suburban community banks, aggressive corporate marketing, an extended ATM network, and a growing corporate business. As the rapid growth of the 1980s subsided, BayBanks management decided to expand the Boston branch network beyond the downtown business district and the airport into some of the residential neighborhoods.

> The prospect of slower economic growth requires a modification of the rapid expansion strategies that worked to our great advantage during the 1980s. . . . To be sure, growth opportunities continue to present themselves. For example, we are now engaged in a major program of service to residential communities of the City of Boston where we have not had a presence.[3]

BayBank Boston planned to capitalize on the retail banking skills developed by its parent. However, just as this expansion strategy was being developed in 1988, events began to unfold that made it all too clear that doing business in the city was quite different from serving the suburbs. Not only were the economics and competitive dynamics of city banking different, but city banks had to deal with a much more complex set of social and political issues.

The Challenges of Inner-city Banking

Over several decades, the living conditions in U.S. urban centers had steadily deteriorated. "Crime rates were soaring, riots were erupting in black neighborhoods, city treasuries were empty, city streets were clogged with traffic, and signs of continued decline were pervasive."[4] According to many community activists, banks had facilitated the decline through "redlining" and "disinvestment." Redlining referred to "a practice by which local lenders draw a red line around sections of a city, literally or figuratively, to delineate areas within which they will not lend."[5] Disinvestment was defined as taking deposits from an inner-city community and using them to make loans elsewhere. Critics argued that restricted access to bank credit had several negative effects on inner-city neighborhoods: constraining opportunities for home ownership, discouraging rehabilitation and maintenance of residential and commercial property, and undermining local business development efforts. The credit gap had been filled in part by higher-priced, less carefully regulated sources: rent-to-own programs, consumer credit companies, second-mortgage companies, even loan sharking.

The bankers' response stated simply was: If fewer loans have been made in inner cities, it has largely been because inner cities present fewer prudent and profitable loan opportunities. Banks had an obligation to their depositors (including inner-city depositors) and to their shareholders to allocate loan funds to their most profitable use within the constraints of prudent lending practices. Because banks operated on rather thin margins, it took only a small increase in loan default rates to eliminate the profit on a large loan portfolio. Concerns about prudence were enforced by banking regulators and by secondary markets.

---

[3] Ibid., p. 7.

[4] Jon C. Teaford, *The Rough Road to Renaissance: Urban Revitalization in America, 1940–1985* (Baltimore, Md.: Johns Hopkins University Press, 1990), p. 168.

[5] Katharine L. Bradbury, Karl E. Case, and Constance R. Dunham, "Geographic Patterns of Mortgage Lending in Boston, 1982–1987," *New England Economic Review,* September/October 1989, p. 3.

By the 1980s, it had become common practice for banks to sell the mortgages they originate to organizations (such as Federal National Mortgage Association) that package them as mortgage backed securities. These organizations have criteria for the kinds of mortgage loans they will purchase. Banks that did not comply limited their capacity to originate new loans. Accordingly, bankers argued that the lack of bank credit should be seen more as a symptom, rather than a cause, of urban decline.

Trying to Be Part of the Solution.   In the early 1960s, in response to public criticism, a number of Boston savings banks formed the Boston Banks Urban Renewal Group (B-BURG).[6] Working with Mayor Collins, the group committed $2.5 million to rehabilitate affordable housing and to provide home ownership loans insured by the Federal Housing Administration (FHA). By 1968, with inner-city tensions at new heights, newly elected Mayor Kevin White attempted to reinvigorate and to expand B-BURG by arranging a $29 million low-income, minority loan pool funded by large financial institutions and insured by the FHA. The results of this expanded effort were tragic.

> In the early 1970s, more than 70 percent of B-BURG-assisted homeowners were unable to keep up their mortgage payments. . . . The banks foreclosed on more than a thousand single-family homes and multiunit dwellings in the area. The local HUD [Housing and Urban Development] office took over these houses after paying the banks full compensation for their lost loan moneys. . . . The solution for beleaguered bureaucrats became condemnation.[7]

Shoddy underwriting practices and drive-by inspections contributed to the extraordinary default rate. "It was simple human nature. With the government assuming the risk, screening standards always seemed to diminish."[8] Because the target area for B-BURG loans was limited to the Jewish communities of Dorchester and Mattapan, B-BURG has also been criticized for indirectly destroying those communities. With B-BURG money readily available to black applicants, "opportunistic real estate brokers fueled white flight by engaging in unscrupulous blockbusting practices, resorting to threats and even break-ins and arson to encourage Jews to sell their homes at below market prices."[9]

Increasing Federal Regulations.   Lobbying by community groups generated enough political awareness that inner-city residents were starting to demand legal recourse for lending injustices. In response to the public outcry, the Home Mortgage Disclosure Act of 1974 (HMDA) required that banks submit information on mortgage application denial and acceptance percentages to the federal regulators. The idea was that this data could identify patterns of discrimination.

Three years later, Senator William Proxmire (D–Wisconsin) introduced the Community Reinvestment Act (CRA) to reinforce the idea that "a bank charter carries with it an obligation to serve the credit needs of the area the bank is chartered to service, consistent with prudent lending practices."[10] A supporter of the CRA, Ralph Nader, urged that the CRA "would, in effect interject the community service factor into the market calculations of depository institutions."[11] Bankers rejected the need for regulation and claimed that if good business were present, the bankers would find it, as A.A.

---

[6] See *The Death of an American Jewish Community* (Free Press, 1990), for details about B-BURG.
[7] Ibid., p. 332.

[8] Ibid., p. 175.
[9] Ibid.
[10] Congressional Record S. 406, January 24, 1977, p. 1.
[11] Ibid., p. 20.

Milligan of the American Bankers Association articulated:

> We do not deny that there is a problem . . . we believe that competitive pressures will in the future, as they have in the past, force [any offending] banks to change their policies. Their competitors within their communities will take advantage of these local loan opportunities and will advertise the fact that they are concerned about community development, whereas the other institutions are not.[12]

Nader pushed the Senate Committee to put some "teeth" in the CRA, while others like Senator Jake Garn (R–Utah) objected:

> The answer isn't more rules and regulations. Piecemeal, we are heading for credit allocation and government bureaucrats back here interfering with the private sector. I'm sick and tired of the antibusiness attitude of this committee . . . the Ralph Nader's have their asses kissed every day and are told how wonderful their testimony is over and over again, while we are building up a regulatory burden that is going to destroy the housing industry in this country.[13]

Despite Garn's objections, the CRA was passed in 1977. (See Exhibit 3.) It would be enforced by the banking regulators, such as the Federal Reserve Board and the Comptroller of the Currency. Banks reported on their community activities and were given a rating by their federal supervisory agency. Furthermore, bank regulators considered CRA compliance in approving or denying bank requests for branch expansion, merger, or acquisition. It was in this process that community groups had their leverage.

The Boston Banking Controversies, 1989–92

For a decade, the passage of the CRA appeared to many community groups as merely a symbolic victory. As Nader feared, the CRA seemed to lack "teeth." Bank credit was still perceived as a major problem in inner-city communities. CRA reports seemed superficial and few banks got unsatisfactory ratings. By 1988, "of more than 50,000 applications for merger or expansion by banks made since the act took effect, only 8 have been denied on grounds that banks were not complying."[14]

Leak of the Fed Study

In 1988, a group of researchers at the Boston Federal Reserve Bank began working with 1982–87 real estate transaction data to explore "how the Community Reinvestment Act (CRA) could be used more effectively to promote the creation of affordable housing."[15] Just as Bay-Bank Boston began to establish a presence in city neighborhoods, news began to leak about the Boston Fed's research. January 11, 1989, was a day that would change the next three years for Pollard, BayBanks, and the Boston banking industry, because of the following headline:

**Inequities are cited in Hub mortgages
Preliminary Fed finding is "racial bias"[16]**

The Boston newspapers had received a copy of a preliminary draft of the study. The article stated that the study:

> concludes from statistical analysis that if banks and thrifts competed with equal aggressiveness in white and minority neighborhoods, they would have made "far fewer loans in predominantly white neighborhoods . . . and would have more than doubled their actual number of

---

[12] Ibid., p. 315.
[13] Ibid., p. 324.

[14] Teresa M. Hanafin, "Lending law is faulted as largely ineffective," *Boston Globe,* January 11, 1989, p. 13.
[15] James T. Campen, "The Struggle for Community Investment in Boston, 1989–1991," in Gregory D. Squires, ed., *From Redlining to Reinvestment: Community Responses to Urban Disinvestment* (Philadelphia: Temple University Press, 1992), p. 38.
[16] Steven Marantz, "Inequities Are Cited in Hub Mortgages," *The Boston Globe,* January 11, 1989, p. 1.

EXHIBIT 3   Excerpts from the Community Reinvestment Act of 1977

Findings and Purpose

SECTION 2.   (a) The Congress finds that —

(1)   regulated financial institutions are required by law to demonstrate that their deposit facilities serve the convenience and needs of the communities in which they are chartered to do business;

(2)   the convenience and needs of the communities include the need for credit services as well as deposit services; and

(3)   regulated financial institutions have continuing and affirmative obligation to help meet the credit needs of the local communities in which they are chartered.

(b)   It is the purpose of this Act to require each approrpriate Federal financial supervisory agency to use its authority when chartering, examining, supervising, and regulating financial institutions, to encourage such institutions to help meet the credit needs of the local communities in which they are chartered consistent with the safe and sound operation of such institutions.

Community Reinvestment Programs and Procedures

SECTION 4.   Each appropriate Federal financial supervisory agency shall develop programs and procedures for carrying out the purposes of this Act. Such programs and procedures shall include —

(1)   requring that in connection with an application for a deposit facility, the applicant

(A)   delineate the primary savings service area for the deposit facility;

(B)   analyze the deposit and credit needs of such area and how the applicant proposes to meet those needs;

(C)   indicate the proportion of consumer deposits obtained from individuals residing in the primary savings service area by the deposit facility that wil be reinvested in that area; and

(D)   demonstrate how that applicant is meeting the credit needs of the primary savings service areas in which it or its subsidiaries have already been chartered to do business;

(2)   using, as factors to be considered in approving applications for deposit facilities, the applicant's record in meeting the credit needs of the primary savings service areas in which it or its subsidiaries have already been chartered to do business, and its proposal for meeting the credit needs of the primary savings service area associated with the pending application;

(3)   permitting and encouraging community, consumer, or similar organizations to present testimony at hearings on applications for deposit facilities on how the applicant has met or is proposing to meet the credit needs of the communities served by or to be served by the applicant or its subsidiaries; and

(4)   requiring periodic reports from regulated financial institutions concerning the amount of credit extended in the institutions' primary savings service areas and making such reports available to the public.

Annual Report

SECTION 5.   Each appropriate Federal financial supervisory agency shall include in its annual report to the Congress a section outlining the actions it has taken to carry out its responsibilities under this Act.

mortgage loans in the predominantly black areas of Mattapan/Franklin Park and Roxbury." . . . "Long after the passage of the CRA, banks and thrifts continue to compete more aggressively in white neighborhoods and leave minority neighborhoods to mortgage companies," the study says. "Boston has become a city with significant unmet credit needs for affordable housing and continues as a city with significant racial lending bias."[17]

This story started an avalanche of media attention. One banking expert claimed that, in the 90 days after January 11, the Boston media did not miss a single day of coverage. Racial bias, redlining, disinvestment—none of these charges were new; so, how could this headline capture the attention of journalists, readers, viewers, and bankers? James Campen, a professor at the University of Massachusetts, suggested that:

> What mattered even more than the study's findings . . . was its sponsorship. This was the first study ever by any of the four federal bank regulatory agencies that had contained such conclusions. The fact that the study was done at the Fed gave it and its findings a respectability and credibility that no study sponsored by community advocates or the media could hope to achieve.[18]

Richard Syron, the week-old president of the Boston Fed, called the conclusions of the study "premature" and stated that his staff "had a responsibility to pursue them and make some determination whether the Boston-area banks were discriminating."[19] More research into lending practices was planned.

The Banking Industry Response. Bankers were convinced that they were being falsely accused. Pollard remembered his own reaction:

> Banks wanted to make mortgages. In the late 1980s, the competition was fierce. The banks were booming and mortgage companies were stealing our business. We wanted all the mortgages we could get—black or white—it did not matter. If anything, we were willing to stretch to make a mortgage to a minority applicant just because we needed the volume. It was inconceivable to us that we could be discriminating.

Other industry executives echoed this response. The Massachusetts Bankers Association's (MBA) president, Robert Sheridan, encouraged further study, stating that "I think the record of the industry is impeccable, and we would welcome any intensive scrutiny. . . . A thorough, complete analysis will show no bias."[20]

Falsely accused or not, Pollard suspected that this issue would dominate his professional life for a while. Not only was he chairman of a Boston bank, but he was to become chairman of the MBA in June. The MBA represented more than 200 financial institutions. Edward P. Shea,[21] a vice president of the MBA, recalled "our pitch was that we, as the trade association, could represent their combined interests, or they [the banks] could take a chance on their own." As the media, the politicians, and the community groups probed into the allegations of the leaked study, the banks opted for a collaborative effort. Though it put pressure on Pollard as in-coming MBA chairman, collaboration was welcomed by BayBank Boston. As

[17] Ibid.

[18] James T. Campen, "The Struggle for Community Investment in Boston," in Gregory D. Squires, ed., *From Redlining to Reinvestment: Community Responses to Urban Disinvestment* (Philadelphia: Temple University Press, 1992), p. 41.

[19] Peter G. Gosselin, "Boston Fed Chief Promises Further Study," *Boston Globe,* January 11, 1989, p. 13.

[20] Steven Marantz and Teresa Hanafin, "Report of Lending Bias Draws Mix of Reactions," *Boston Globe,* January 12, 1989, p. 1.

[21] The author would like to thank Ed Shea for his time and council in preparing this case. Special thanks also goes to the staff of the MBA for sharing information on this subject.

the newcomer to city banking, BayBank Boston did not have much experience to draw on and its record of lending in inner-city neighborhoods was nearly nonexistent. There was strength in numbers.

Given its expansion plans, BayBanks, Inc., was vulnerable to attentive CRA scrutiny. BayBank/Harvard Trust had made a formal request to open a new branch in Allston, a working-class neighborhood on the west end of Boston. Community groups were aware of BayBank's request and used the opportunity to express their concerns. They picketed an existing branch to fuel opposition to the Allston request. Community activists felt that BayBank should not be allowed to expand until it addressed CRA issues. Pollard remembered that day well, "because once they finished picketing at the branch, the community activists walked a few blocks to my house, where they demonstrated and left messages in my mailbox."

Fortunately, Crozier, chairman of BayBanks, Inc., had anticipated the need for expertise in community relations. After a lengthy "courtship," Crozier hired Thomas Kennedy. Kennedy was well versed in the issues of inner-city life. While studying at the Episcopal Theological School, Kennedy had volunteered for an internship program in New York City, working as a retail salesman and living in East Harlem. Kennedy reflected on his experience as "formative and pivotal, exposing me to urban living and poverty." On returning to Boston and being ordained as an Episcopal priest, Kennedy spent a number of years in church-sponsored outreach activities that he referred to as "street ministry," including a period as dean of the Cathedral Church of St. Paul. He first met Crozier serving on a private school board in 1971. Kennedy remembered a conversation they had in 1987:

Crozier was talking stream of consciousness, saying that his bank needed to reach out to

the community and understand its needs. As he described the role of an individual helping the bank in that capacity, I looked at him and said, "Are you talking about having a clergyman come to your bank?" This was the craziest idea I had ever heard. However, he was persistent. By May of 1989, I was community affairs officer at BayBanks, reporting directly to Pollard and indirectly to Crozier.

Kennedy worked with Pollard, tackling the sensitive issues of discrimination and inner-city lending.

As BayBanks dealt with the Allston branch challenge, members of the MBA met weekly for breakfast to discuss the scope of the problem, possible explanations, and an industry response. Pollard analyzed the discussions:

The key was to break the issue into its elements. We decided that the mortgage lending issue was the tail wagging the dog. It was the symptom of the disease—not the disease. The inability of a minority applicant to get a mortgage is caused by disinvestment in that community, lack of economic growth, poor income level—all of which needed to be dealt with differently.

This realization led to the identification of four problem areas: mortgage lending, affordable housing, access to bank services, and small-business loans. Each problem was addressed by the MBA by setting up task forces chaired by bankers. Clark Miller, executive vice president of the Bank of Boston, offered to lead the effort on mortgage lending. Richard Driscoll, chairman of The Bank of New England, who had been active in the housing issues, volunteered to work on affordable housing. Pollard assumed responsibility for banking services. Finally, Shawmut Bank's president, John P. Hamill, took the lead on small-business lending.

Further Government Pressure. On several fronts, regulatory pressures concerning community banking practices were mounting.

While the Boston Fed continued its research, Boston Mayor Ray Flynn, working through the Boston Redevelopment Agency (BRA), decided to hire Charles B. Finn of the Hubert H. Humphrey Institute of Public Affairs at the University of Minnesota. Finn's 1988 studies of home mortgage lending in Detroit[22] and Atlanta[23] heightened public awareness of discrimination in lending. Ultimately, Detroit and Atlanta financial institutions donated funds for a below-market-rate mortgage loan pool similar to B-BURG.

1989 saw significant activity on a national level as well. In a highly visible case, the Federal Reserve Bank of Chicago employed the CRA to halt an acquisition by Continental Bank.[24] By March, the federal financial supervisory agencies completed a review of the CRA and its enforcement. The agencies stated that:

> the CRA and the implementing regulations place upon all financial institutions an affirmative responsibility to treat the credit needs of low- and moderate-income members of their community as they would any other market for services that the institution has decided to serve. As with any other targeted market, financial institutions are expected to ascertain needs and demonstrate their responses to those needs.[25]

Specific suggestions for effective programs included: more flexible lending criteria, participation in government-insured lending programs, improved advertising and marketing efforts, involvement at all levels of management, improved customer assistance, adoption of a branch closing policy (specifically appropriate notice), assistance in community development programs, establishment of a community development corporation, the funding of a small-business investment corporation, and investments in state or municipal bonds. Finally, amendments to the Financial Institutions Reform, Recovery, and Enforcement Act of 1989, clarified and strengthened the CRA reporting and evaluation process. CRA evaluations would be more detailed and publicly available. (See Exhibit 4.) Lenders would be required to provide information on the sex, race, and income of mortgage applicants, as part of their HMDA reporting. These additions permitted more thorough analysis of mortgage lending practices.

Community Groups Response. The news of the Fed study energized a number of community groups. It was just the sort of credible evidence that they needed to press their case for more community banking. There were many local community groups interested in the CRA and its interpretation. The Massachusetts Urban Reinvestment Advisory Group (MURAG) had been formed nearly 20 years earlier to focus attention on the disinvestment problem. The Dudley Street Neighborhood Initiative, a Roxbury community group, was involved in "a grassroots effort to preserve and redevelop our neighborhood for the people who live and work in it."[26] The Greater Roxbury Neighborhood Authority, Nuestra Communidad Community Development Corporation, and Urban Edge Community Development Corporation were also active. Another participant was the statewide affordable housing coalition, the Massachusetts Affordable Housing Alliance. A Boston union of hotel workers, Local 26, through

---

[22] "The Race for Money," a newspaper series printed in *The Detroit Free Press*, July 24–27, 1988.

[23] The series, "The Color of Money," was written by Bill Dedman of *The Atlanta Journal & Constitution*, May 1 thorough November 3, 1988.

[24] Bill Barnhart, "Fed Hits Continental's Civic Investment," *Chicago Tribune*, February 16, 1989, sec. 3, p. 1.

[25] Joint Statement of the Federal Financial Supervisory Agencies Regarding the Community Reinvestment Act, March 21, 1989.

[26] Dudley Street Neighborhood Initiative, *A Neighborhood Building Its Future,* 1991.

EXHIBIT 4 Amendments to the Financial Institutions Reform, Recovery, and Enforcement Act of 1989

As of July 1, 1990, CRA ratings are no longer on a numerical basis; rather they are written evaluations using a four-tier descriptive system:

Outstanding record of meeting community credit needs.
Satisfactory record of meeting community credit needs.
Needs to improve record of meeting community credit needs.
Substantial noncompliance in meeting community credit needs.

Each institution will have its performance reviewed in five major categories:

1. Ascertainment of community credit needs.
2. Marketing and types of credit extended.
3. Geographical distribution and record of opening and closing offices.
4. Discrimination and other illegal credit practices.
5. Community development.

An "outstanding" rating will be achieved only by financial institutions that demonstrate certain qualities, including leadership is ascertaining community needs, participation in community revitalization, and affirmative involvement in planning, implementing, and monitoring their CRA-related performance. Most CRA observers agree that "outstanding" ratings will be difficult to achieve.

CRA evaluations can be found at an institution's main office and designated branch in each of its local communities. They are not, however, required to provide free copies.

Source: Virginia M. Mayer, Marina Sampanes, and James Carras, *Local Officials Guide to the Community Reinvestment Act* (Washington, D.C.: National League of Cities, 1991), p. 15.

---

its subsidiary, Union Neighborhood Assistance Corporation (UNAC), was involved because of a housing trust fund benefit that had recently been granted. These community groups threatened class action suits, organized demonstrations, and submitted information to the media. Also active nationally but sited in Boston, the Reverend Charles Stith and his group, the Organization of a New Equality (O.N.E.), encouraged the efforts. No one organization or individual emerged as the leader. In addition, representing the business interests of the minority community, the Minority Developers Association took an active interest. The groups shared a common concern about the problem, while representing a diversity of interests and political perspectives.

Working toward a Solution

During the spring of 1989, industry, community groups, and government agencies worked separately. The MBA needed time to analyze the problem from the perspective of the industry as a whole and individually within each financial institution. Several of the community groups united as the Community Investment Coalition (CIC) and insisted on representation in the bankers' meetings. By early June, three forums were scheduled by the MBA, each one dealing with a facet of the problem. The Boston Fed agreed to host the forums, so all parties would feel comfortable. The MBA made an effort to be inclusive and thereby opened the forums to everyone. Of course, not all of the participants agreed with this collaborative approach. Bruce Marks of UNAC refused to attend the forums. Instead, his group organized a sit-in at the Bank of Boston.

The Forums. As Pollard entered the first forum on small-business lending, a reporter inquired, "Do you think that the banks have caused these problems?" He responded, "I do not know if the banks are part of the problem, but we are certainly part of the solution." This was the tone the MBA tried to set. The bankers and the community representatives were addressing the issues and designing solutions together. Shea of the MBA explained that the emphasis of this first forum was to explore ways "to develop jobs, incomes, stability, and savings, so that residents will be able to afford housing on truly market standards."

The second forum addressed affordable housing. Richard D. Driscoll's comments reenforced the emphasis on problem solving:

> The problem of affordable housing in our community is critical and needs more involvement by everybody, certainly by banks. . . . Everybody has to abandon old ideas about how this problem will be solved. Certainly banks have to stop saying "we've never done it this way before" or "our current policies prevent us from doing that" or "it's not my problem, let's give it to the government."[27]

In July, the third session, addressing bank services, was held. The concerns raised ranged from branch openings and closing to cashing welfare checks.

With over 90 bankers and over 100 community representatives at each of the forums, recognition of the needs of the community as well as the limitations on private organizations were acknowledged by participants. After the forums, the bankers' task forces continued to work on solutions. Yet, there were some skeptics. Peter Dreir of the Boston Redevelopment Authority (BRA) commented, "This could be a window of opportunity or it could simply be a window dressing."[28] Another doubter, Representative Joseph P. Kennedy (D–Massachusetts) stated that "While it's encouraging to see the formation of task forces, and forums . . . I still am unclear at what specific measures came out of them."[29] The MBA promised to reveal their plan and the banks' commitments to the reinvestment efforts in late September.

Negotiating a Settlement

While the bankers were drafting a plan, pressure continued to mount from the media, community groups, and politicians. The Greater Roxbury Neighborhood Authority printed and circulated their study on patterns of mortgage discrimination. Peter Dreir of the BRA continually made reference to the Finn study but failed to state when the study would be released to the public. On August 24, the Community Investment Coalition (CIC) took a stand, "calling for the infusion of $2.1 billion in private bank loans and the reopening of closed bank branches to redress years of lending bias and neglect."[30] As reported, the CIC groups "want the city's largest banks to finance the construction and rehabilitation of 12,000 housing units. They want a program of discounted mortgage rates at 5 percent and 15 more bank branches and ATMs for the

---

[27] Steven Marantz, "Bank of N.E. Official Urges More Community Lending," *Boston Globe,* June 23, 1989, p. 21.

[28] James T. Campen, "The Struggle for Community Investment in Boston," in Gregory D. Squires, ed., *From Redlining to Reinvestment: Community Responses to Urban Disinvestment* (Philadelphia: Temple University Press, 1992), p. 48.

[29] Steve Marantz, "Banks Eye Kennedy-amended Bailout Bill," *Boston Globe,* August 2, 1989, p. 25.

[30] "Roxbury Leaders Ask $2.1-B In 'Bias Loan,' " *Milford Daily News,* August 25, 1989, p. 20.

minority communities."[31] The CIC sent its 29-page analysis and plan to all of the banks in Boston. Pollard reported that in the enclosed letter the CIC stated, "While the details of the plan are open for discussion, its scope is nonnegotiable." The CIC insisted on a response by September 11 and urged that the bankers open their discussions up to CIC representatives.

Official Release of the Federal Reserve Study. On August 31, 1989, the final version of the Fed study was released. The study had compared mortgage origination patterns in predominantly black and predominantly white neighborhoods. The researchers found significantly lower mortgage activity in predominantly black neighborhoods, even controlling for income and wealth levels. The central findings were:

> Controlling for all the economic and other nonracial factors, the results suggest that neighborhoods with over 80 percent black residents would still have 24 percent fewer mortgage loans relative to the housing stock than neighborhoods with less than 5 percent black residents.[32]
>
> ... While realtors, developers, lenders, and others probably all share some responsibility for the racial pattern of mortgage activity, one group stands out as having a special role to play in correcting this situation. Not only are banks and thrift institutions central to the home ownership process, but unlike other lenders they have an affirmative obligation under the Community Reinvestment Act to help meet the credit needs of their entire community.[33]

In response to the official release of the study, Pollard maintained his early position that "if people think that somehow banks don't want to make mortgages in black areas, that couldn't be further from the truth."[34] Many bankers concurred. Some privately expressed skepticism regarding whether there was even enough good business in the urban centers for all the banks to fulfill their CRA obligations.

The conclusions of the Fed study further verified the allegations the CIC had been making over the summer. The local newspaper and television coverage continued to push the discrimination theme.

In lieu of a specific counteroffer to the CIC proposal, the MBA scheduled an open meeting on September 8. Following the meeting, the community groups hosted a meeting of their own to discuss their proposal and to negotiate the specifics of a plan. At this meeting in Roxbury, Pollard commented that "It is clear at this point that there is no single answer.... The possible solutions we have identified all depend on cooperation among bankers, government officials, and community leaders. We think we have already gone a long way and we expect more progress in the months to come."[35] Pollard went on to commit $150,000 of the MBA funds to establish a community banking council. Throughout the fall, the MBA task force meetings were open to all interested parties.

Struggling to Reach an Agreement. As the MBA worked on a four-pronged plan for community investment, BayBank Boston announced its intention to locate branches and install new ATM machines in minority neighborhoods.

[31] MaryAnne Kane, *Channel 7 WNEV TV,* August 24, 1989, transcript published by New England Newswatch (Framingham, Mass.).

[32] Katherine L. Bradbury, Karl E. Case, and Constance R. Dunham, "Geographic Patterns of Mortgage Lending in Boston, 1982–1987," *New England Economic Review,* September/October 1989, p. 21.

[33] Ibid., p. 26.

[34] Allan R. Gold, "Racial Pattern Is Found in Boston Mortgages," *New York Times,* September 1, 1989, p. A20.

[35] Media Advisory, "Massachusetts Bankers Association Testifies on Community Reinvestment Issues," September 29, 1989.

Thomas Kennedy of BayBank Boston explained:

> We were already committed to doing something in the neighborhoods of Boston. In fact, we applied to open a branch in Allston and already had approval for a branch in Jamaica Plain, which are both low- to moderate-income neighborhoods. The preliminary work had already been done. In response to the pressure, we analyzed our customers by residential zip codes. It turned out we had over 16,000 BayBank customers in the neighborhoods of Roxbury, Mattapan, and Dorchester—and they had no place to bank in their community.

Other Boston banks were developing plans to commit their personnel, funds, and branches to the MBA plan. The atmosphere was generally positive.

However, the negotiations stalled due to disagreement on the mortgage lending issue. The community groups and the bankers could not reach resolution over the mortgage rates.

The CIC, with political support in the mayor's office, demanded rates 2% below standard rates with no up-front point charges, but the bankers criticized the proposal as unsustainable in the long term. The bankers offered standard rates with two points. John Hamill of Shawmut vowed that "[w]e're 90 percent there. . . . We're going to keep working until we have something everybody is happy with."[36] Ultimately, the bankers were able to sell the community groups on market rate mortgages. They did this by addressing inequities in the loan underwriting criteria and by arranging a program to assist with downpayments. For instance, in the past, rent payments did not have the same weight as prior mortgage payments in demonstrating creditworthiness. This would be changed in the new program.

---

[36] Steven Marantz, "No Agreement on Neighborhood Lending," *Boston Globe,* December 15, 1989, p. 80.

Boston's Largest Banks (1981–1987)

Bank	Total deposits ($000)	Mortgage Loans White/Minority
The First National Bank of Boston	$7,482,003	2.1:1
Bank of New England	6,029,462	1.9:1
State Street Bank	3,983,204	*
Shawmut Bank	3,131,746	2.3:1
Boston Five	1,466,343	0.9:1
The Provident	1,146,728	4.2:1
Home Owners	1,105,742	2.6:1
United States Trust Company	886,691	1.8:1
South Boston Savings Bank	766,185	7.4:1
Neworld Bank for Savings	754,818	1.9:1
Fist Mutual of Boston	563,696	2.5:1
BayBank Boston, Harvard Trust, Norfolk	433,230	11.7:1
First American Bank	386,451	0.6:1
Capital Bank and Trust	328,718	10.2:1
Haymarket Co-Operative Bank	325,606	No mortgage loans to minority neighborhoods

* Too few mortgages to calculate ratio.

Source: Adapted from Charles Finn, "Mortgage Lending in Boston's Neighborhoods 1981–1987," December 1989.

In December of 1989, just as the final details of an agreement between the banks and the community groups were being worked out, the BRA finally released the study by Charles Finn. It again hit hard at the theme of discrimination and the special role of banks in exacerbating the problems of inner-city neighborhoods. The Finn study went beyond the Federal Reserve study in its evaluation of individual banks and BayBank stood out because of its history as a suburban bank.

The mayor and BRA officials wanted to use the Finn study to pressure the banks into a below-market-rate mortgage program. However, many observers of the summer forums and participants in the fall meetings felt that the release of the Finn study by the BRA did more harm than good, a sentiment that was captured in this cartoon.[37]

Pollard, speaking on behalf of the MBA, admitted, "We have to pause a minute to see what's happening here...the BRA study has thrown everything into confusion.... You do not want to look reactive, you want to look positive. If we don't come out with something this week it's not because we don't have it."[38] A local editorial writer wondered:

> Who figures to be hurt most by this? Who else but the people whom the program would benefit the most? As one activist put it: "The bottom line is that if this process goes by the wayside it's the black community—not some of those people who are part of the negotiations—that will suffer." Neither Mayor Flynn nor the BRA want

---

[37] Reprinted with permission from *The Boston Herald,* December 26, 1989.

[38] Steve Marantz, "Aftermath of the BRA's Mortgage Lending Report: Hub Bankers Postpone Unveiling of $1 Billion Reinvestment Plan," *Boston Globe,* December 21, 1989, p. 41.

this, we're sure — but what are they going to do to prevent it?[39]

Breaking the Stalemate. It was in this atmosphere of urgency and confusion that racial tensions were dramatically heightened in the city of Boston. In October, the police reported that Carol Stuart, a pregnant white female, had been shot and killed while driving through Mission Hill with her husband, Charles. Since the horror of that day, an investigation had begun to find the assailant, as described by Charles Stuart, "a black, with a raspy voice, high strung, wearing a black jogging suit."[40] Police were very aggressive in their tactics and incurred the anger and frustration of the black community. By early January 1990, the investigation began to focus on Charles Stuart as the murderer of his wife as a result of his leap to death off the Mystic River Bridge. Members of the city's black community demanded a public apology from Flynn for the aggressive police tactics. Flynn refused to apologize.

Revived racial tensions made it hard for Flynn's administration to take further steps to threaten the carefully negotiated MBA reinvestment plan, a plan in which many community leaders had invested a great deal of time and energy. The reinvestment plan was announced, in January 1990, at the annual Martin Luther King Day Breakfast, cosponsored by Union United Methodist Church and St. Cyprian's Episcopal Church. The MBA plan called for concerted activity on all four fronts of mortgage lending, affordable housing, economic development, and access to banking services. (See Exhibit 5 for an overview of the Massachusetts Bankers Association Community Investment Program.) Many of the programs were innovative. General Electric Credit

and Fannie Mae had agreed to insure and purchase loans made with underwriting criteria more appropriate for low- to moderate-income home buyers. The Minority Enterprise Investment Corporation (MEIC) planned to work closely with minority loan applicants to help make their businesses viable candidates for financing, blending business consultation with traditional, hard-nosed underwriting. Nearly all Massachusetts banks agreed to cash government checks even for individuals who did not have accounts at the bank. And the Massachusetts Community and Banking Council (MCBC) planned to keep alive an on-going dialogue between the community groups and the bankers.

Reactions to the MBA Plan

The community representatives were pleased with the MBA plan. Willie Jones of the CIC commented that the MBA program "should provide for the level of affordability we've been striving for."[41] At the announcement of the program, the Reverend Charles Stith, pastor of the United Methodist Church and head of Organization for a New Equality (O.N.E.), was ecstatic, exclaiming "I have never been more proud to be a citizen of this city than I am today."[42] The new year was devoted to establishing the new corporations, getting the products to the public, locating affordable housing projects, and finding sites for branch openings. Many of these activities were followed up on by the task forces, while others were up to individual banks.

BayBank Boston was satisfied with the MBA plan and its opportunity for participation. Pollard viewed it as "a permanent thing in which the funds will be replenished over and over. In the long run, it will have a more significant

[39] "The Timing Was Terrible," *The Boston Herald*, December 22, 1989, p. 34.

[40] Peggy Hernandez, "Minority Leaders in City Demand an Apology," *Boston Globe*, January 5, 1990, p. 21.

[41] Steve Marantz, "$400m Investment Plan for Hub," *Boston Globe*, January 11, 1990, p. 51.

[42] Ibid.

EXHIBIT 5 The Massachusetts Bankers Association Community Investment Program

The Massachusetts Bankers Association Community Investment Program

---

NEED: Mortgage Lending

To overcome obstacles in providing mortgages to low- and moderate-income individuals

Community Home Buyer's Program

A more flexible mortgage product insured by GE Mortgage Insurance and that would be sold to Fannie Mae

All participating banks would allocate a specific amount of funds for this program

Estimated amount to be allocated by the banks $100 million

Soft Second Product

To assist homebuyers with down payment requirements

The first mortgage would be purchased by Fannie Mae the "soft second" mortgage would be held in the bank's portfolio

---

NEED: Affordable Housing

To develop affordable housing units in low- and moderate-income communities

Massachusetts Housing Investment Corporation (MHIC)

A multibank loan consortium that would provide debt to nonprofit and for-profit affordable housing developers

Established programs
• Construction Loan Program (for construction and preservation of housing)
• Permanent Financing Program (to finance affordable rental housing)

$100 million investment by banks

Massachusetts Bankers Equity Fund

To pool the investments of the banks to provide equity to affordable housing developers

To encourage banks to make equity investments in low income housing tax credit projects

Estimated investment $100 million

NEED: Economic Development

To meet the credit needs of minority-owned businesses in order to further economic development in minority communities

Massachusetts Minority Enterprise Investment Corporation (MEIC)

A multibank community development corporation

To make equity investments or loans available to start-up or existing minority-owned businesses

Estimated investment from the banks
• $10 million in equity capital
• $50 million in lines of credit

The Commonwealth Enterprise Fund

An SBA-licensed subsidiary to establish an equity pool for minority enterprise

To establish a vehicle within which banks can invest in minority-owned businesses

---

NEED: Bank Services

To deliver bank services and products and minority, and low- and moderate-income communities

Massachusetts Community and Banking Council (MCBC)

A research and policy advisory center

To promote community investment in minority, and low- and moderate-income communities

Activities include
• Fact finding
• Community liaison
• Community outreach
• Education
• Dispute resolution

New branches and ATMs in minority, low- and moderate-income communities

All banks agreed to provide check cashing services for government checks (including welfare checks)

529

impact."[43] The BayBanks board had been following the progress throughout 1989; therefore, the board quickly approved multiple commitments. BayBanks' contributions were:

- $5 million for mortgage lending at a discounted rate.
- $10 million in equity participation for the development of affordable housing (for which the bank received tax credits).
- $2 million to Massachusetts Minority Enterprise Investment Corporation ($.5 million in equity investments and $1.5 million in loans).
- 5 branches and 25 ATMs in low- and moderate-income areas.
- Pollard would chair the Massachusetts Community and Banking Council.

As the new player in the city and in keeping with its ATM strategy, BayBank Boston had decided to take the lion's share of the MBA's promised total of nine new branches and 30 ATMs.

Members of the MBA were particularly delighted that they had avoided the temporary and potentially disastrous remedy of a below-market minority loan pool. They believed that they would avoid another B-BURG and they had not repeated what they perceived to be the mistakes made in Atlanta and Detroit. As Sheridan of the MBA commented:

> Without question, the "big bang" approach of a one-shot loan pool would have put money out on the street sooner. However, the association is convinced that if the mandate of the Community Reinvestment Act is to be taken seriously, it must be seen as a coherent, financially sound enterprise that will live on after media and even advocate attention has moved on to other things.[44]

The financial soundness of the MBA plan was crucial to the Massachusetts banks and to banking regulators. The turn of the decade brought with it a recession that hit the northeastern states particularly hard. After several years of boom, Massachusetts experienced high unemployment and a major decline in real estate values. These economic strains took their tolls on the banks. The most dramatic evidence of this was the failure of the Bank of New England, as well as many smaller banks. The Bank of New England's chairman, Richard Driscoll, who had headed the MBA task force on affordable housing, resigned from the bank while the MBA process was unfolding. Many banks were reporting losses and cutting dividends. In this environment, BayBanks, Inc., reported its first loss ever. It lost nearly $70 million in 1990. Following a rash of failures in the savings and loan industry, both banks and their regulators had a special interest in assuring that a community investment program be consistent with the safety and soundness of the financial institutions.

Second Mortgage and Home Improvement Loans
Media and advocacy attention did subside for close to a year—until the Bank of New England was to be purchased by Fleet/Norstar Financial Group. Bruce Marks of UNAC assembled documents showing that Fleet as well as other banks had financed private mortgage companies, which, in turn, charged customers interest rates well above the typical bank market rate. He alleged that Fleet was indirectly "lending at loanshark rates."[45] Not only was this usurious, according to Marks, but it led to an unfortunately high number of foreclosures.

After a 90-day moratorium on foreclosures in Suffolk and Hampden counties, the

---

[43] Steve Marantz, "Banks' $1 Billion Reinvestment Plan Called National Model," *Boston Globe,* January 15, 1990, p. 22.

[44] Statement issued by Robert K. Sheridan, president of the Massachusetts Bankers Association, August 1990.

[45] Peter Canellos and Gary Chafetz, "Mortgage Companies Got Credit from Fleet," *Boston Globe,* May 8, 1991, p. 18.

allegations had been reviewed by the federal regulators. Fleet's purchase of the Bank of New England was approved. However, this issue did not end there. Community groups demanded a more thorough investigation. Despite an aggressive advertising program, called "Setting the Record Straight,"[46] Fleet continued to be featured in the Boston press as the financier of "loanshark" loans to elderly and minority communities. Once again the Boston Fed was called on—this time to study second mortgage and home improvement lending. Its August 1991 study concluded that:

> Certain individuals have suffered great hardship, including the loss of their homes, because of burdensome second mortgages. High rates are only one dimension of the second-mortgage problem, but it is one that permits quantification. We estimate that loans with interest rates of 18 percent or more account for 1.4 percent of the nonacquisition[47] mortgages made in Suffolk county from 1987 to 1990. In the [predominantly black] neighborhoods of Roxbury and Mattapan, 5.1 percent of nonacquisition mortgages carried rates of 18 percent or more. These mortgages are supplied by a relatively small number of specialized lenders. Banks are not providers of high-rate second mortgages, although they are important suppliers of nonacquisition mortgages throughout Suffolk county. The major Boston banks have at times provided financing to some of the high-rate lenders or purchased loans from these lenders; but most of the larger high-rate lenders have many other funding sources. Finally, our survey revealed that many different lenders—banks, mortgages companies, finance companies, contractors, and

Estimates of Nonacquisition Loans in Suffolk County

Interest Rate	Total Suffolk County	Roxbury and Mattapan
18% or greater	698	207
15% to 18%	1,630	298
Less than 15%	39,581	2,147
Unidentified	9,314	1,370
Total	51,223	4,022

Source: Adopted from Table 1 of Alicia Munnell and Lynne Browne, "Second Mortgages in Suffolk County," The Federal Reserve Bank of Boston, August 14, 1991, p. 12.

individuals—operate throughout Suffolk county, offering borrowers a spectrum of rates.[48]

Media coverage expanded to cover loans made by home improvement companies as well. Several of the major Boston banks, including BayBanks, were named as financiers of questionable lenders. One television station ran a hard-hitting investigative report on the tragedies that sometimes resulted from questionable lending practices. The Massachusetts attorney general initiated a probe of the banks and their relationships with private mortgage and home improvement companies.

In October 1991, an analysis of 1990 HMDA data was released. Nineteen ninety was the first year that race, sex, and income data were reported. The data once again showed racial differences, even when income level was held constant. The release of this data made national news, with lead stories in major newspapers. Though it was unrelated to Boston's second-mortgage problem, this information simply fueled the fire.

Accused of forcing as many as 1,000 people out of their homes by "strip-mining the equity

---

[46] Doug Bailey, "Ad Campaign Responds to Critics," *Boston Globe,* June 18, 1991, p. 1.

[47] The Boston Fed defined nonacquisition mortgages as "second mortgage loans, refinancings of first mortgages, and first mortgages on properties with no existing mortgage." (Alicia Munnell and Lynn Browne, "Second Mortgages in Suffolk County: 1987–1990," The Federal Reserve Bank of Boston, August 14, 1991, p. 1.)

[48] Alicia Munnell and Lynn Browne, "Second Mortgages in Suffolk County: 1987–1990," The Federal Reserve Bank of Boston, August 14, 1991, pp. 10–11.

from minority communities,"[49] Fleet termi-nated business with 38 private mortgage com-panies. In defending Fleet Finance, the sub-sidiary involved, a spokesperson explained, "The higher the risk, the higher the rate. It's not illegal to make a profit."[50] Nonetheless, working with Mayor Flynn, Fleet agreed to establish an $11 million fund to refinance 550 cases on more favorable terms.

Employing the concept of lender liability, the attorney general threatened to investigate the banks individually. BayBanks was the major provider of financing to home improvement companies in Massachusetts. BayBanks man-agers felt that they had been careful in se-lecting the home improvement companies with which they dealt. As Pollard explained:

> The only way to control this business is on a complaint basis. BayBanks was legally bound to repair anything that broke down, to replace poor workmanship, or to complete an incom-plete project. When a home improvement sales-man carried BayBanks' paper, the consumer was protected. In general, there were no com-plaints. When we did receive two or three com-plaints from the same company, we dropped them. We policed that part of our business.

He felt that the media and community activists had overestimated the problem, at least as it related to companies funded by the banks. He also wondered why banks were being held responsible for their customers' behavior. Nonetheless, Pollard wanted to resolve this issue quickly. BayBanks entered into discus-sions with the community and the attorney general.

On February 19, 1992, the attorney general announced an agreement with BayBanks. The agreement drew on the organizations created by the MBA reinvestment plan. BayBanks created a Victim Resolution Program to be run through the recently created MCBC, improved procedures for indirect home improvement lending by offering a product directly to the consumer, committed at least $5 million to a home improvement loan program, and com-mitted $6 million in loans to another MBA-created entity, MHIC. In addition to the com-mitments made to the attorney general, BayBanks got out of the business of funding home improvement companies. The results were immediate: "[e]ven before hearing a word of the settlement, activists said BayBanks' com-bination of financial aid and corporate re-sponsibility set a new standard for other banks in Massachusetts and across the country."[51] Shortly after BayBanks announced its agree-ment, Shawmut Bank agreed to a similar reso-lution plan, facilitated by the MBA corpora-tions and council. Fleet's earlier plan was characterized by community activists as "totally inadequate . . . purely political and it flies in the face of justice and fair play."[52] In response to these comments and on further investigation, Fleet also settled with the attorney general two months later.

Continuing National Attention

In May 1992, the nation focused on urban poverty as South Central Los Angeles erupted in riots after the Rodney King verdict was announced. Despite a videotape depicting sev-eral white police officers severely beating Rod-ney King, a black male motorist whom they had stopped, the officers were found not guilty of criminal wrongdoing. The verdict fueled a sense of injustice. After the riots, the federal government began to talk more seriously about improving urban conditions. And racial

---

[49] John R. Wilke, "Back Door Loans: Some Banks' Money Flows Into Poor Areas—And Causes Anguish," *The Wall Street Journal*, October 21, 1991, p. A1.

[50] Ibid.

[51] Mitchell Zuckoff, "Shawmut Is Said to Settle over Loan Scams," *Boston Globe*, February 22, 1992, p. 1.

[52] Ibid.

discrimination became an even more prominent topic of discussion.

At the same time, the Office of the Comptroller of the Currency began an investigation
of 266 banks, all of which had shown a disparity
in their lending patterns, according to the
HMDA data. Bankers and industry experts
hoped that the result would not be further
regulations. Banks, it was felt, cannot bail out
the nation's inner cities. In a *New York Times*
editorial, Lawrence White, finance professor at
New York University, argued that enough was
enough in terms of regulations:

> The Community Reinvestment Act is at best
> obsolete.... [I]n today's competitive environ-
> ment, banks need no assistance in discover-
> ing good customers. If serving the local commu-
> nity is profitable, the law is unnecessary. If it
> is not profitable, a bank must earn extra profits
> from other activities to subsidize those losses.
> But banks and nonbank rivals have competed so
> fiercely in other financial services that extra
> profits are scarce—leaving banks with a choice
> of shirking their community reinvestment re-
> quirements or suffering losses.... If supplying
> unprofitable financial services to local companies
> and households serves a public purpose, that
> case should be made explicitly, and *public*
> resources should support those services.[53]

These concerns were raised at a time when
banking regulators were described as "schizo-
phrenic" because "[t]he Bush Administration,
fretting that tight-fisted bankers are hobbling
economic recovery, wants more aggressive lending. Congress, worried that another savings and
loan mess is about to land on it, has ordered
tighter regulation to cut risk."[54]

When Racial Disparity Persisted

Pollard was concerned about the regulatory
issues, but for the moment he had to focus
specifically on Boston. The Federal Reserve
Bank of Boston had just completed the "end
all—be all" study of mortgage lending patterns.
The researchers at the Fed had worked with
the bankers to understand the practical criteria
for evaluating a loan and they had complete
access to loan files. The methodology was
thorough. Because of their cooperation in the
study, it would be hard for the banks to ignore
the results.

Richard Syron, president of the Fed, had
called to tell Pollard that, even with all this
information, evidence of racial disparity remained. The results reflected aggregate
patterns; individual bank performance was not
studied. But there was no reason to think that
BayBank would be an exception. What held in
the aggregate probably held for BayBank Boston. The question was: What, if anything,
should he do about it?

---

[53] Lawrence J. White, "Don't Handcuff the Healthy
Banks," *The New York Times,* May 17, 1992, p. F13.

[54] Mike McNamee and Tim Smart, "The Head-Spinning
Split over Banking," *Business Week,* June 8, 1992, p. 43.

AUSTRALIAN PAPER MANUFACTURERS (A)

Ken McRae, group general manager for Australian Paper Manufacturers (APM), smiled as he re-read the headlines one winter morning in June 1990: "Report Savages PCA" and "Kayser Mill 'the dirtiest in the country.'" Accompanying articles in the *Advocate* and the *Examiner* had chronicled the toxic chemical problems that confronted the Paper Company of Australia (PCA). Although the controversy had signaled another possible opening for McRae and APM, it seemed to raise as many questions as it answered.

Just three years earlier, McRae had invaded PCA's market area, fine papers. APM was equipped with the most advanced manufacturing technology in Australia and had taken a daring marketing approach. Now, with four established fine-paper products, McRae was considering APM's next move. Should he expand APM's uncoated, fine paper capacity? How would he maintain APM's environmental record amid growing concerns over toxic chemicals, forestry, and recycling?

Australian Paper Industry Prior to 1987

Before 1987, the Australian paper industry was divided neatly into three companies.

1. Australian Newsprint Mills (ANM) supplied newsprint. Newsprint was made by a mechanical process, and, because it still contained a large proportion of the original wood, it was termed a "wood-containing" paper.
2. Australian Paper Manufacturers (APM) produced paper packaging, referred to as "paperboard." Paperboard was made using a chemical process, which eliminated all wood but the required fibers and rendered a stronger product.

3. Paper Company of Australia (PCA) dominated fine-papers. Fine-papers were also made using the chemical process. Because the chemical process eliminated all wood but the required fibers, the resulting product, when compared to newsprint, was termed "wood-free" paper. This wood-free or fine-paper was used by businesses for printing and writing, and it was divided into two types: those that had a special outer coating ("coated"), such as paper for an annual report, and those without any special coating ("uncoated"), such as copier paper. (See Figure A.)

Low average tariffs allowed imports to compete with domestic supply. The three Australian companies, however, kept to their own markets, which created cordial relations among them. In total, the three companies produced 1.7 million tonnes[1] of paper and paperboard in 1986.[2]

PCA and APM

PCA and APM were subsidiaries of major Australian corporations. Maitland Industries owned PCA and termed itself a "diversified resources group." Along with paper production, Maitland Industries operated nine mines

---

This case was prepared by Professor David Upton of the Harvard Business School.

Copyright © 1990 by the President and Fellows of Harvard College.

Harvard Business School case 691-041 (Revised 1991).

[1] A metric tonne is equal to 1,000 kilograms or about 1.1 U.S. tons.

[2] Food and Agriculture Organization of the United Nations, *Pulp, Paper and Paperboard Capacity Survey 1986–1991* (Rome: FAO, 1987), p. 94.

FIGURE A　Types of Paper and Pulping Processes

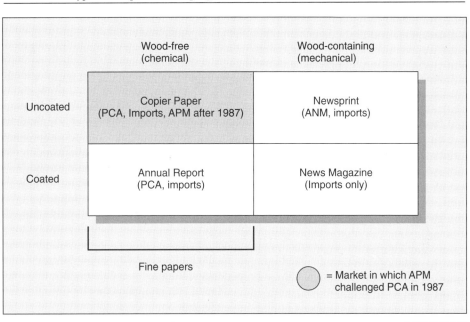

in Australia, ranging from gold and silver to copper, bismuth, and iron ore, and owned a manufacturer of industrial slurry pumps. Another Maitland subsidiary, Australian Energy Resources, was the country's largest producer of uranium and a major exporter to the United States and Europe.

PCA represented 25 percent of Maitland's sales (19.4 percent of operating profit) and dominated production of fine-papers in Australia. In 1986, PCA held 75 percent of the 179,000 ton uncoated, fine-papers market, and recorded A$495 million in total sales (A$51 million in operating profit).[3] Sales were divided roughly 60 percent and 40 percent between uncoated and coated fine-papers. Whatever PCA did not produce for the Australian market, imports gobbled up.

Amcor Limited, Australia's largest forest products and packaging company, owned APM. Amcor held extensive packaging interests throughout the world and produced metal, plastic, and paper packaging. From aluminum beverage cans and plastic jars, to fast-food containers and corrugated boxes, Amcor continued to extend its reach throughout Australia, Europe, and North America. Amcor's total sales reached A$2.4 billion in 1986, with operating profit of A$163 million. As Amcor's paper division, APM manufactured such products as cardboard consumer packages and corrugated shipping boxes. For 1986, APM recorded sales of A$600 million and operating profit of A$75 million.[4]

To enter another area of the paper industry—uncoated fine-papers—APM could draw on its strength in paperboard manufacturing. But making fine-papers required careful

---

[3] All monetary figures are in Australian dollars. Australian dollars had an approximate value of 0.8 U.S. dollars in 1989.

[4] Amcor Limited, annual report *1989,* p. 36.

attention to the manufacturing process and to growing concerns about the environment.

Making Paper

The first step in making paper and paperboard, after the wood was cut, involved "pulping." This process refined the wood so only the fibers, the substance required in paper, remained. Wood consisted of approximately 50 percent cellulose fiber, the material used in paper, 30 percent lignin, a tough, resinous adhesive that gave structural support to the tree, and 20 percent extractable oils and carbohydrates. During pulping, the cellulose fiber was separated from the other components so it could be processed further; pulping could be done either mechanically, by grinding the wood, or chemically, by boiling the wood with chemicals. Although newsprint manufacturers relied on mechanical pulping, the grinding process broke the cellulose into shorter fibers when tearing them apart and left some lignin in the resulting pulp. This created a weaker paper that turned yellow more quickly. Only products with less-rigid quality requirements—newspapers and telephone books, for example—used mechanical pulp.[5]

Chemical processes (shown in Figure B) produced much sturdier pulp, which could be used for fine-papers and packaging. Chemical reagents were added to the wood, forming soluble compounds with all of the noncellulose materials. This left a residue of cellulose less abused and purer than mechanical pulp. Two different chemical pulping methods predominated. The soda process, used by PCA at its Kayser mill in Tasmania, added caustic soda to the wood at high temperatures. The soda was then recovered as soda ash and converted back into caustic soda, using quicklime. A newer process called "kraft" used sodium sulfate as the cooking chemical, which yielded stronger pulp at a faster rate.[6] Unlike mechanical pulping, which used 90–95 percent of the wood harvested, chemical pulping used 45–50 percent.[7] Chemical pulp yielded 1.25 tonnes of paper per tonne of pulp because inert "fillers" were added in the process.

When transformed into fine-paper—the bright white type used in business and printing—chemical pulp went through an intermediate step: bleaching (see Exhibit 1). Chlorine gas and chlorine dioxide were applied to the pulp, removing the remaining lignin and leaving a pure white cellulose fiber. On average, between 50 and 80 kilograms of chlorine were used to produce one tonne of bleached kraft pulp.[8] Bleached pulp allowed producers to make a strong, bright paper that did not discolor during storage or when exposed to sunlight. It thereby satisfied the needs of paper products with high demands for purity, brightness, and permanence.[9]

Once the pulp was bleached, it was processed into "stock": a suspension of fibers and additives in water. Individual fibers of pulp were suspended in water and then "beaten" and refined to produce fibers with the proper characteristics of length, flexibility, surface area, and density. Chemicals could then be added to the stock: rosin, aluminum sulphate, or synthetics to reduce absorbency for writing papers; starch to add strength; dyes for colored paper. At the end of this

---

[5] *The Greenpeace Guide to Paper* (January 1990), pp. 4, 8.

[6] *The Kline Guide to the Paper Industry,* ed. Joan Huber, fourth edition (Fairfield, N.J.: Charles H. Kline and Company, 1980), p. 55. "Kraft" is the German word for strong.

[7] *Greenpeace Guide to Paper,* p. 7. Skogsindustrierna [the Swedish Pulp and Paper Association], *Is Bleached Paper Dangerous?* (Aeberhard & Partners Limited, 1989), p. 20.

[8] *Greenpeace Guide to Paper,* p. 13.

[9] *Is Bleached Paper Dangerous?* p. 17.

FIGURE B The Chemical Pulp Process

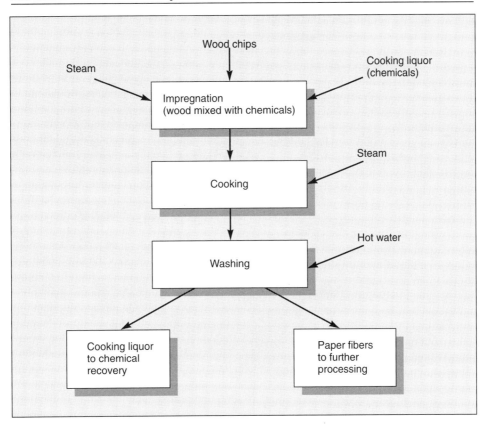

process, stock could be made into a sheet of paper.

To produce a finished sheet of paper, a paper machine had to remove water from the stock—between 100 and 500 tonnes of water for every tonne of pulp. Water was removed by three methods in sequence: first by gravity, second by squeezing, and finally by heating. In the "wet" end of the paper machine, the stock was deposited on a "wire"—a continuous belt of mesh material—and together with inclined blades of metal or plastic ("foils") underneath it, the wire drained the water from the stock. A single-wire machine, like those in all of PCA's mills, produced a paper sheet with different surface properties on each side. Newer, twin-wire machines produced paper with uniform surface properties on both sides. This double-sided, or symmetrical, paper was growing more popular; though it was unnecessary for all applications, users preferred its stability, uniformity, and flatness.

From the end of the wire, what was now a fragile paper web moved into the presses. Protected from above and below by continuous belts of felt, the paper moved through rollers, which pressed the sheet and drained water into catch basins (so the water could be used again).

EXHIBIT 1   The Bleaching Process*

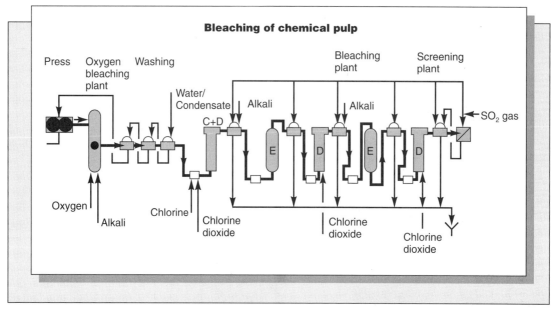

In the chemical pulp process it is impossible to remove all lignin without damaging the cellulose fibres. In the sulphate process, moreover, the pulp is coloured brown by the lignin compounds.

Paper products with very high demands on purity, brightness and permanence require 100 percent freedom from lignin.

This is the reason why chemical pulp is bleached. The introductory bleaching is called *continued delignification.*

The example in the above diagram illustrates a bleaching plant with six bleaching stages. The reaction time in the different stage varies from half an hour to a few hours:

1. Oxygen. Roughly half of the lignin is dissolved. If the delignification process is carried further, the fibres are weakened. The pulp is washed thoroughly.
2. Chlorine/chlorine dioxide (C+D). For environmental reasons more chlorine dioxide is charged at this stage: the chlorine dioxide is charged first, followed by the chlorine about 1 minute later to give the best effect (sequential charging). Steps 1 + 2 give the pulp some brightness.
3+5. The extraction stages (E) extract reaction products with alkali.
4+6. The chlorine dioxide stages (D) complete dissolving the lignin and in particular raise the brightness.

* Skogsindustrierna (The Swedish Pulp and Paper Association), *Is Bleached Paper Dangerous?* (Aeberhard & Partners Limited, 1989), p. 17. This diagram illustrates a bleaching process that includes oxygen pre-bleaching, also referred to as extended delignification.

The paper web then traveled to the "dry" end of the paper machine. There the paper crossed double rows of steam-heated, cast-iron cylinders while felt held the paper against the cylinders.

In the calendar section, the paper then got further pressed, as a set of hardened cast-iron rollers improved the surface-finish of the paper. From there the paper was wound onto a steel spool. In the final step of making paper, broadly called "finishing," large reels of paper were rewound into smaller reels, some were made into stacks of sheets (reams), and the paper was inspected.[10]

Before most paper could be used it was often "converted" into the end product. First, the paper manufacturer applied a coating appropriate to the paper's use—a pigment for fine-papers and a barrier coating for packaging materials. With packaging materials, either the primary producer, such as APM, or an independent converter would then mechanically construct the paper into products: bags, boxes, and envelopes. Fine-paper, once properly coated, inspected, and packaged, was sold to merchants, who supplied end-users.[11]

In Australia, annual consumption of fine-paper—paper made of bleached, chemical-processed pulp—rose to 358,000 tonnes in 1987. Uncoated fine-paper, such as photocopy paper, stationery, and offset printing paper, comprised 52 percent of that market, while coated fine paper, the type used in an annual report, comprised the rest. From its Kayser, Bridport, and Kiama mills, PCA could supply 230,000 tonnes of fine-papers per year, with the total divided 61 percent (140,000 tonnes) for uncoated and 39 percent (90,000 tonnes) for coated.

Paper and the Environment

When chemical pulp was bleached to produce wood-free paper, approximately 10 percent of the chlorine used combined with organic molecules from the wood, which was then discharged as effluent from the mill. Bleaching thereby produced as many as 1,000 toxic chlorine compounds called "organochlorines." Chemical pulp mills typically discharged between five and eight kilograms of these organochlorines per tonne of bleached pulp. Because the pulping process required large amounts of water to flush chemicals from the pulp, companies situated mills near rivers, lakes, and oceans; the effluent then ran directly into these bodies of water, such as Bass Strait near PCA's Kayser Mill (see Exhibit 2 for map of Australia).

Only 300 organochlorines had been formally identified, the most notorious of which was dioxin. Known most for its use in the Vietnam War, under the name Agent Orange, dioxin served as a defoliant to remove all ground growth. But dioxin had also been found to cause reproductive disorders in animals and to suppress their immune systems, leaving them more susceptible to infection. Fish found in waters off Sweden suffered reproductive and liver damage, skeletal abnormalities in offspring, and impaired immune systems—symptoms attributable, at least in part, to organochlorines released by the paper industry. Further, organochlorines were bio-accumulative: they remained in the bodies of organisms that ingested them, and contamination levels rose with every step of the food chain.[12]

Fears about dioxin's connection to pulp bleaching first arose in 1970 but gained renewed attention in 1987 when Greenpeace published *No Margin of Safety,* a report on ther United States paper industry. Greenpeace cited leaked documents from the United States Environmental Protection Agency to argue (1) that dioxin posed a far greater risk to the environment than the paper industry had been admitting and (2) that dioxin could actually be found in products using bleached pulp, such as milk cartons and sanitary napkins.[13] Organochlorines began receiving further worldwide attention in the late 1980s as pro-environment. Green parties gained strength in Scandinavia.

[10] *Note on Process Control in Pulp and Paper Making,* Harvard Business School case 687–061 (President and Fellows of Harvard College, 1987), pp. 5–10.

[11] *The Kline Guide to the Paper Industry,* p. 63.

[12] *Greenpeace Guide to Paper,* pp. 13–16.

[13] *Greenpeace Guide to Paper,* p. 17.

EXHIBIT 2 Map of Australia

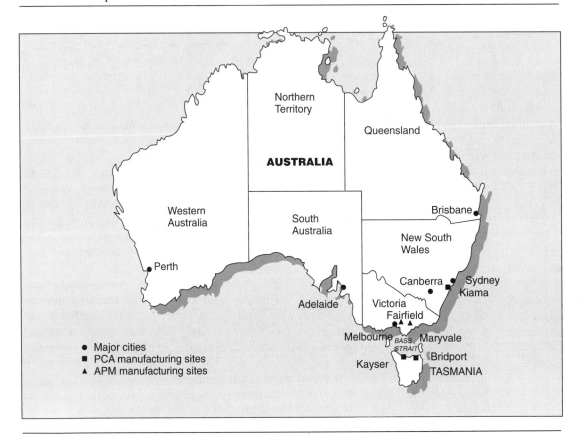

Because Finland and Sweden served as the world's number six and seven paper producers[14] as well as strongholds for the Green parties, the paper industry in those countries paid particular attention to environmental concerns, raising the level of awareness throughout the world. In Finland, environmental issues were considered so important that the paper industry had already agreed to prohibit advertising based on environmental claims. Although less advanced in its attention to environmental issues than Finland and Sweden, the Australian paper industry had responded to many of the concerns raised by the public and environmental groups.

The Australian Industry's Efforts

Both Maitland (PCA's parent) and Amcor (APM's parent) had experience responding to environmental concerns. Maitland had instituted strict environmental procedures in connection with uranium mining: to prevent potential contamination, the company collected every drop of rainwater that fell on its mines. In the 1970s, PCA had introduced a bond

---

[14] Behind the United States, Canada, Japan, U.S.S.R., and China. "World Pulp, Paper, and Board Industry at a Glance," *Pulp and Paper,* August 1988, pp. 54, 55.

writing paper from 100 percent recycled fibers, but it failed to gain market acceptance.[15] Amcor had responded to a series of concerns over packaging, ranging from the release of chlorofluorocarbons (CFCs) by aerosol cans, to the waste created with the use of polystyrene (styrofoam). Amcor's annual report was frequently prefaced by a two-page discussion of environmental issues. In addition, Amcor held international patents for Corrishell, a paper-based alternative to polystyrene for such products as fast-food containers.[16]

Organochlorines. The Australian paper industry cited studies that recorded a dioxin level in the average daily intake of food 10 times higher than in the average daily amount of paper used. APM and PCA also noted that studies had not yet provided conclusive proof linking dioxin to adverse effects on humans. Nonetheless, both companies abided by strict government standards, continually sampled emissions from their mills, and distributed pamphlets to inform consumers of the companies' environmental efforts. Rough estimates put APM's expenditures on environmental protection at A$60 million for the 1980s, compared to total capital expenditures of A$300 million.

Chlorine provided the only means for producing traditional white business paper, and, though new technologies and process modifications promised alternatives in the future, a capital-intensive industry like the pulp and paper industry would require time to implement the changes. The drastic 50 percent reduction of chlorine levels in Sweden, for example, took 10 years to implement with the technology available at the time (1979).[17] But new intermediate measures, while not the ultimate solution

environmentalists sought, could reduce the use of chlorine. Greenpeace estimated, for example, that half of all chlorine could be replaced by extending and repeating the oxygen stage of bleaching.[18] The paper produced from oxygen-bleached pulp, they asserted, could fulfill the same business requirements as chlorine-bleached paper. Environmental concerns with paper, however, extended beyond fears of dioxin to the issues of deforestation and recycling.

Deforestation. Four tonnes of wood produced one tonne of paper, and, during a period of increasing anxiety over the greenhouse effect, this seemingly wanton use of forests came under increasing scrutiny.[19] The production of one tonne of paper from discarded waste paper, when compared to production from virgin wood, used half as much energy and water. It created 74 percent less air pollution, 35 percent less water pollution, and saved the 17 pulp trees that would have been used.[20]

APM and PCA recognized the growing public interest in forest preservation and tried to inform Australians of the forestry management methods the companies used. As Australia's largest private forest plantation owner,[21] APM paid particular attention to forestry management, and PCA, with large forestry operations in Tasmania, showed similar attentiveness. Less than 30 percent of Australia's 25.6 million hectares[22] of public native forests were managed for wood production, and only about 1 percent of that managed portion was harvested in any one year.[23] To ensure future supply, both

---

[15] APPM, *Paper and the Environment* (September 1989), p. 41.

[16] Amcor Limited, annual report *1989*, p. 12.

[17] Clive Capps, "Chlorine's Bleaching Days Are Numbered," *Pulp & Paper International*, April 1990, pp. 60, 61.

[18] *Greenpeace Guide to Paper*, p. 20.

[19] The greenhouse effect refers to the warming of the earth's surface as levels of certain gases, such as carbon dioxide, increase. Trees take in carbon dioxide and replace it with oxygen, thereby serving as the earth's "lungs."

[20] *Greenpeace Guide to Paper*, p. 40.

[21] *Amcor and the Environment*, p. 3.

[22] 1 hectare = 2.47 acres

[23] Forest Industries of Australia, *Forest Facts: The Series—Overview*, March 1990.

companies had to commit themselves to re-growth programs: five eucalyptus trees planted for every one harvested, five pine trees for every four harvested.[24] Recent studies had even uncovered the advantages of managed forests, where young, active growth—which consumed high levels of carbon dioxide and released oxygen—replaced older trees that consumed less carbon dioxide, or even released it as they decayed.[25]

Although the paper industry nurtured its forests carefully and continued to conduct tree-breeding research, to generate stronger trees with improved yields and resistance to diseases, environmentalists worried about "monocultures," the dependence on one variety of tree in all replanting efforts. In contrast to an array of robust varieties that could support all forms of life and resist potential disease and soil depletion, monocultures would be unable to provide the same support to the ecosystem as natural growth and could be wiped out by a single, potent disease.

Recycling.   Australia recycled 30 percent of all recoverable paper, putting it in the same range as the United States and Finland, ahead of Canada, New Zealand, and China, and behind Sweden, Japan, and the Netherlands.[26] To recycle paper, manufacturers had to remove ink, fillers, and coating materials from the old paper. Waste paper was washed in detergent to remove the ink, and, if necessary, bleached to brighten it. High-quality white recycled paper often indicated heavy use of detergents and bleaching to transform the waste back into bright paper. Between 10 and 25 percent of collected waste paper was lost in recycling plants, most of that

fillers and coating material.[27] In addition, continued use and recycling sapped the strength of paper fibers, which could therefore be reused a maximum of 5 to 10 times. Often, companies combined virgin and recycled pulp.

Throughout the world, most paper fashionably labeled "recycled" stretched the definition somewhat. Most recycled paper contained a limited proportion of recycled fibers, and most of those came from "preconsumer" sources. Scrap from paper mills and book-printers constituted such "preconsumer" waste: it had never in fact gone through consumers. Environmentalists called special attention to "postconsumer" waste: paper collected from households and offices. Whereas the paper industry had always relied on preconsumer waste as a source of pulp, it was only just beginning to harness postconsumer waste. That in turn was creating growing demand for used paper and was providing the impetus for broader recycling efforts. Although Australia used a high percentage of postconsumer waste, inefficient collection and sorting methods, together with the lower pulp to paper yield, made it an expensive resource. One tonne of waste pulp cost A\$760 but only yielded 0.75 tonnes of recycled paper. One tonne of bleached virgin pulp cost roughly A\$1120 but yielded 1.25 tonnes of paper.

The Australian paper industry continued to address the public's concerns about environmental issues, but a basic gap separated environmental groups and the industry. Environmental groups questioned the very need for bleached, white paper. They felt that kraft pulp bleached with oxygen, rather than chlorine, provided an ivory-color paper suitable for business uses, yet gentler on the environment. Greenpeace and other groups felt that few office papers required extreme brightness. The

---

[24] *Amcor and the Environment,* p. 3.

[25] *Forest Facts: #1—The Greenhouse Effect,* March 1990. APPM, *Paper and the Environment,* p. 11.

[26] *Amcor and the Environment,* p. 4. *Greenpeace Guide to Paper,* p. 41.

[27] Here coating materials refer to those added during the "converting" stage. "Coated" fine-paper, such as that used in an annual report, could not be recycled at all.

paper industry, they felt, *created* the demand for extreme brightness, and, they argued, with some marketing attention and consumer education, paper companies could provide oxygen-bleached paper, ultimately abandon chlorine bleaching, and satisfy current business requirements with ivory-colored paper. APM and PCA both cited previous attempts to introduce less chemically-treated products into Australia and their failure to receive consumer support. As one industry document promised, "To the extent that the Australian market demonstrates a preference for off-white or unbleached products, [we are] able and pleased to meet that demand."[28]

Australians remained particularly concerned about the environment. Many considered their country a pristine frontier to be left free of the tainting influence they felt industry had brought to bear on other developed countries. While business leaders pushed for an approach that balanced economic growth and environmental protection, polls revealed that Australians favored protecting the environment at the expense of economic growth, if a choice had to be made.[29] Just over half of all Australians also reported purchasing products that did not damage the environment, with 40 percent of respondents saying that the products had been more expensive.[30]

APM Enters the Uncoated, Fine-papers Business

In 1984, APM completed a A$163 million modernization of its kraft pulp plant in Maryvale, Victoria. The improvement added 140,000 tonnes per year of kraft pulp capacity, bringing the Maryvale plant's total output to 350,000 tonnes per year. At the time, most of this pulp was used for packaging materials in one of APM's paper machines or sold on the pulp market. Pulp could generally be sold profitably on the world market, although it could be used most beneficially in the company's own machines. APM included stringent emissions and effluent controls in its improvement program. When the Australian government issued strict effluent guidelines in 1989, the Maryvale plant already met them.[31] According to the mill manager, the pulp from Maryvale contained no detectable dioxin in parts per quadrillion (10^{15}) – equivalent to the thickness of a credit card compared to the distance to the moon.

The Maryvale plant had four paper machines, and in 1986 APM turned its attention to Paper Machine 3. Originally built in 1972 to produce brown shopping bags, Machine 3 had a capacity of 31,000 tonnes per year. By the mid-1980s, though, people had stopped using these "checkout" bags (preferring plastic), and between Machines 1 and 2, the company could cover demand. This left Machine 3 ripe for transformation. APM seized the opportunity, upgraded Machine 3, and used it to take them into the heart of PCA's fine-papers market.

Between May 1986 and July 1987, APM spent A$50 million to rebuild Maryvale's Machine 3, converting it from making bag paper to producing white wood-free paper. The machine had not simply put APM next to PCA as the second domestic supplier of uncoated fine-paper.[32] It

[28] *Amcor and the Environment*, p. 6.

[29] "Economic Growth and the Environment," Business Council of Australia Environment Task Force, Melbourne, 14 June 1990. Philip McIntosh, "Most prepared to put environment ahead of growth," *Sydney Morning Herald*, 15 June 1990, p. 5.

[30] Philip McIntosh, "Most prepared to put environment ahead of growth," *Sydney Morning Herald*, 15 June 1990, p. 5.

[31] "Maryvale mill starts new pulp line," *Pulp & Paper International*, June 1984, pp. 42–43. Australian Paper Manufacturers, *APM Papers Group*, p. 18. Amcor Limited, annual report 1989, p. 17.

[32] *Pulp & Paper International*, December 1986, p. 48. "Rebuilt PM Starting Up at Maryvale," *Pulp & Paper International*, July 1987, p. 17.

also made APM the owner of Australia's largest and most technologically advanced fine-paper machine. The 70,000 tonnes per year of Machine 3 capacity gave APM the product it needed to steal from imports—the company's primary goal in entering the fine-papers market.[33] Customers had been accustomed to buying some of their paper from PCA and some from overseas, but PCA had not kept pace with the growth in demand. Although aiming to replace imports, McRae, director of marketing for APM papers group at the time, knew his toughest job lay in establishing APM's fine-papers amid a market dominated by PCA.

Ken McRae's Challenge

PCA produced three-quarters of all fine-papers consumed in Australia and even controlled 80 percent of the copier paper market, with its Prism brand copier paper. PCA owned the country's second and third largest paper merchants, Grafton Paper and PaperSource, which reinforced the company's market share. These two merchants distributed 40 percent of Australia's fine-paper and made competition with PCA a formidable task.

To steer APM around PCA's strengths and into the expanding fine-papers market, McRae designed an innovative marketing strategy, restructured the method of distribution, and plotted a careful ramp-up of demand for output. He outlined the essential elements of his plan—quality and service:

> Our technology gave us an edge in quality. We had the kraft pulping process in Maryvale, which gave us a stronger pulp than the soda process used by the competition. PCA still relied on old soda-process machines, which had been installed in the 1950s. Our paper machine, Maryvale 3, also gave us a better quality paper. It's the only twin-wire machine in Australia, a Voith duo-former, which takes water out of both sides, producing a paper with the same surface finish on both sides, unlike more traditional machines that remove water from the bottom side only, giving a different surface on one side of the sheet. With the pulping process and the paper machines PCA had, they just couldn't produce the quality of paper we could.
>
> We offered better service. You used to tell customers, "We are making product category X at a specific time, so get your order in." Now we say, "Tell us what you want, and we will make it." We attempted to bring the lead-time down so they could hold less stock. We also benefitted from having fewer subdivisions of products than PCA. We began with just three basic products. Maryvale Machine 3 was designed to make changeovers with relative ease compared to older paper machines.

McRae enhanced APM's emphasis on service by replacing merchants with direct customer contact. Paper merchants served as intermediaries between the manufacturers and customers, typically taking bulk orders, placing it with a mill, and receiving the invoice. The customer paid the mill price, while the mill paid the merchant a 3–5 percent commission. McRae described his plan:

> We went out and asked customers, "How would you like to do business directly with us?" We decided to ignore the merchants. We offered much better response to customers. We serviced everything, had a toll-free number and a computerized order-taking system. We had a simple policy: To be a direct customer, you had to buy a minimum of 500 tonnes of a single product.
>
> Merchants responded angrily. They felt we were leaving them with scraps. We asked, "How do you add value? If you add value, how come people are only paying you the mill price?" Nonetheless, we were prepared to work with them for new markets. We did need them to help us set up the distribution network.

APM wanted to deliver 95 percent of all orders on time, and, if delays arose, APM's goal was to warn customers 100 percent of the time. Toward that end, McRae reorganized APM's

---

[33] *APM Papers Group*, pp. 18–20.

TABLE A   Uncoated Fine-Papers Ramp-up (annual equivalent in tonnes)*

	8/87	11/87	6/88	8/88	3/89
APM Brands:					
PrintRight	200	4,000	10,000	12,000	17,000
DataRight	0	4,000	15,000	24,000	28,000
CopyRight	0	0	7,000	14,000	25,000
APM total	200	8,000	32,000	50,000	70,000
Imports total	46,000	36,000	32,000	24,000	22,000
PCA total	140,000	130,000	120,000	144,000	108,000
Market total	186,200	174,000	184,000	218,000	200,000

* Annual equivalent = the month's production × 12.

customer service operation. Instead of having a sales office in each of Australia's seven states, McRae situated all sales representatives and order-input clerks in the same office — the same office where production-planning people worked. APM established a nationwide toll-free number. McRae then instituted an advanced computer-based information system, which allowed APM to enter an order, assess the volume it would absorb on the machine-cycle for that month, and offer a specific date for delivery. "The intention," McRae explained, "was to do it all live with the customer, so, when the customer got off the telephone, he or she could know precisely when to expect the delivery, at least within a three-day window."

Ramp-up.   In August 1987, APM inaugurated its move into the fine-papers market. McRae developed a careful plan for ramping up to full capacity on Maryvale 3. APM intended to produce 40,000 tonnes by August 1988, starting with three crews working Monday through Friday and eventually moving to four and then five crews. Like all of Maryvale's other paper machines, Machine 3 would eventually operate 24 hours a day, 365 days a year.

APM began by selling PrintRight, an offset printing paper. "We felt it was the easiest product to make," McRae explained, "and one we could get into the marketplace fairly easily.

We wanted to get practice making that, refine things on the machine, and then go to the sheets that required greater technical expertise." Just three months later, the company introduced its continuous forms (computer) product, DataRight, which brought total annualized output to 8,000 tonnes. McRae next introduced CopyRight, APM's copier paper, in June 1988, and sales surged to the annual equivalent of 32,000 tonnes. By August 1988, Maryvale Machine 3 was producing at a rate of 50,000 tonnes per year, and by March 1989 it had reached its capacity of 70,000 tonnes per year. (See Table A.)

Markets.   Beyond ramping up to desired capacity, McRae also had to encourage consumer acceptance of APM's new product. As he put it, "We had three very different audiences, all being supplied off the one machine." CopyRight catered to the white-collar office worker; PrintRight served a blue-collar, predominantly male, audience; and DataRight was aimed at technically oriented users. Customers, however, tended to stick with the brand they were using, as much out of inertia as from brand loyalty. McRae outlined his approach:

For the offset printers, we distributed photographs on PrintRight with just a hint of color around the profile — a really difficult shot to print. We knew this would impress them, and it did indeed attract them to our product.

We talked about the technical benefit of the sheet itself when we marketed DataRight. We were selling it to people who take the paper and turn it into forms.

CopyRight had to be directed at a broader audience, one that would consume close to 85,000 tonnes in 1989, but McRae's innovative approach gained APM the acceptance and name recognition it sought.

PCA packed their copier paper in 10-ream boxes, which weighed 15 kilograms, just under the maximum of 16 kilograms allowed by the government. Although we knew it would double packaging and distribution costs, we started selling five-ream boxes, a far more manageable

weight for office workers. We also put a perforated panel into the box so people could remove the packets easily.

When we launched the product, we took out full-page advertisements in the daily newspapers. We took out ads in trade magazines for the dealers. We also advertised on the radio. In areas teeming with office workers, we handed out balloons with "CopyRight" printed on them. We wanted to get this great name "Copy-Right" recognized, so we could get the product moving.

APM spent over A$1 million to launch CopyRight, but McRae saw the introduction as well worth the expense.

We were experimenting with the market. We had to find out how much PCA's Prism name was really worth, and we wanted the

---

EXHIBIT 3   APM's Fine-Paper Production 1989

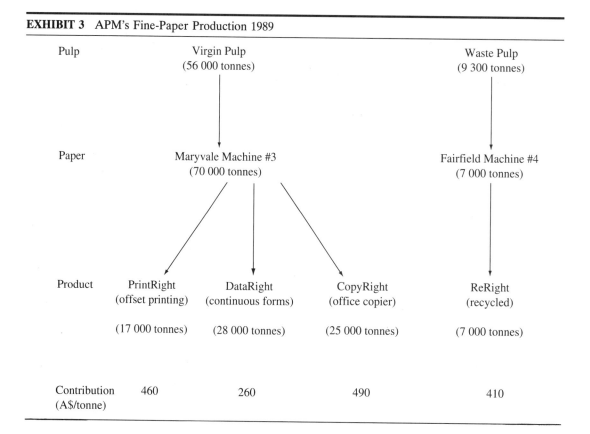

Pulp	Virgin Pulp (56 000 tonnes)			Waste Pulp (9 300 tonnes)
Paper	Maryvale Machine #3 (70 000 tonnes)			Fairfield Machine #4 (7 000 tonnes)
Product	PrintRight (offset printing) (17 000 tonnes)	DataRight (continuous forms) (28 000 tonnes)	CopyRight (office copier) (25 000 tonnes)	ReRight (recycled) (7 000 tonnes)
Contribution (A$/tonne)	460	260	490	410

market to perceive us through CopyRight. PrintRight and DataRight depended upon that market.

By the end of the first quarter of 1989, APM had established itself in the fine-papers market. The A$50 million investment in Machine 3 appeared to be paying off (see Table A and Exhibit 3).

Race to Expand

The uncoated fine-papers market was projected to grow at 6.5 percent annually through the 1990s, leading McRae to conclude that battle lines had only just been drawn between APM and PCA.

> If either of the companies makes a *significant* commitment to expanding its capacity, the first step would be to put in a pulp mill of maybe 300,000 or 400,000 tonnes. That would have to be followed up very quickly with a paper machine, although capacity destined for the new machine could produce pulp for the market in the interim.
>
> By 1995, imports will begin to grow at the expense of domestic supply, so there's room for somebody to do it. Whoever does it will have to go in with a world-scale machine – a machine capable of making 150,000 tonnes of paper per year. Otherwise, you cannot get the economies of scale. But whoever does that will knock out competitors for a decade.

PCA's Bridport Proposal

As early as 1987, PCA had begun making plans for a kraft pulp mill of its own. The new mill, to be located in Bridport, Tasmania, was projected to have a total pulp capacity of 400,000 tonnes.[34] PCA had solicited foreign partners from Japan, Canada, and the United States to participate in the project, and, by October 1988, joined by a Canadian company, PCA had mapped out a A$1 billion proposal. The mill, geared toward domestic supply and export to Japan, promised to be the largest single manufacturing project ever undertaken by private enterprise in the country. Australia's prime minister, Bob Hawke, heralded it as a venture of "major national significance."[35]

But the Bridport mill encountered unexpected public opposition. Although financial plans were completed, environmental guidelines had not been set. Environmentalists and local residents demanded stringent regulations, and the Tasmanian government responded, outlining "nonnegotiable" standards. PCA said the regulations threatened the project, and the company listed 45 objections. The two sides narrowed their differences to four points, but they remained most opposed over dioxin. One newspaper account summarized the dispute:

> The most problematic [difference] concerned emissions of dioxin, an organochlorine by-product of the plant's bleaching process. The government said there was to be no increase in the ambient level of dioxin in the marine environment. The companies said they could not guarantee this, but, if there was an emission, it would be so small as to be harmless to the marine ecology.[36]

Political battles between the state and federal governments further complicated the dispute, and, in April 1989, under great public pressure, the project was scrapped.[37]

ReRight. Just one month later (May 18, 1989), APM introduced its newest entry in the fine-papers market, ReRight. ReRight was Australia's first stationery paper made from 100 percent recycled paper – postconsumer recycled paper that was produced without chemicals and was neither de-inked nor bleached. The World Wildlife Fund endorsed ReRight,

---

[34] "Bridport Pulp Mill Plan Dropped," *Pulp & Paper International,* May 1989, p. 21.

[35] Chris Sherwell, "Tasmanian Pulp Mill Controversy Sinks into Confusion," *Financial Times,* 15 February 1989, p. 6.

[36] Ibid.

[37] "Bridport Pulp Mill Plan Dropped." p. 21.

and the product generated significant interest and publicity. As McRae explained, however, ReRight represented only the most visible aspect of a deeper strategy.

We could see environmental concerns coming more and more to the fore—the whole thing was gathering momentum. We had an infrastructure already in place because we'd been recycling paper in Australia for 60 years, and we knew how to make recycled paper on our machines. We'd just never tried to make it for office use. As we saw the public pressure mounting for more environmentally acceptable products, we picked May 1989 as about the right time to get in and launch the paper.

We also knew that all the easy paper in Australia was already being collected for recycling. We were getting everything out of the supermarket. I think we had about the highest recycling rate in the world of used boxes from supermarkets. We were doing door-to-door collections around the metropolitan areas, and PCA had always bought a lot of the waste from printing plants. So most of the easy stuff was captured. Most of the paper used in offices, though, was going to landfill. So within a week of when we launched ReRight, we also started the "APM Office Paper Chase." We set up a collection structure for us to go into offices in all the major cities. We used this to say, "Look, if you want to use recycled paper, what you've got to do is give us your used paper, so we can turn it back into a sheet that you can use again."

We had thought the whole thing through and had a compeling story to tell. We were eliminating a lot of waste in society because this stuff normally went from the office straight into the landfill. We're now capturing it, bringing it back, and making paper out of it. In Australia, we've reduced waste and the cost of waste disposal, and we're generating more paper domestically, which means Australia doesn't have to import as much as it did previously.

McRae appeared all over the media during May, and, despite ReRight's higher cost, it grabbed a 3 percent market share (7,000 tonnes per year) of the uncoated fine-papers market.

To recoup its research and development expense, APM charged 20 percent more for ReRight than for comparable, nonrecycled paper. ReRight's immediate acceptance inspired APM to introduce ReRight-Form in the spring of 1990, a recycled computer paper.

PCA's Kayser Plant

While APM expanded its recycling efforts, PCA suffered yet another blow on the environmental front. Greenpeace released a surprise report on PCA's Kayser soda pulp mill on the coast of Tasmania, declaring it the dirtiest mill of its type in Australia. Greenpeace found Kayser discharging 11.5 tonnes of organochlorines per day into the sea, at times reaching a level 80 percent above government standards. Greenpeace also decried the presence of chloroform, a cancer-causing agent, in the effluent, and cited it as a health risk to PCA's workers. The environmental group called on the government to monitor the mill's effluent levels more closely and demanded that the company reduce its discharge of organochlorines to a maximum of one kilogram per tonne of pulp. Greenpeace also recommended complete elimination of organochlorine discharges by 1993 and asked the government to review employees' medical records to search for abnormal incidence of cancers attributable to organochlorines, such as chloroform.[38]

Though surprised by the report, PCA managers responded virtually point by point to Greenpeace. First, they disputed the figures on effluent levels. Company data, much of it based on tests by government laboratories, revealed effluent levels below legal limits. PCA further noted that chlorine bleaching met the market demand for high-quality paper and no alternative existed to produce paper of similar

---

[38] Peter Hazelwood, "Report Savages PCA" and "Greenpeace Motives Questioned," *Advocate*, 23 March 1990. Steven Dally, "Kayser Mill 'The Dirtiest in the Country,'" *Examiner*, 23 March 1990, pp. 1, 2.

quality. In response to concerns about chloroform, the company noted that it was commonly found in chlorinated drinking water and swimming pools, and that only extensive exposure to chloroform posed a health risk. The company welcomed a government inquiry and cited its ongoing A$300,000 study of the mill's environmental impact as proof of its environmental efforts. Kayser's 50-year presence in Tasmania had created no apparent effect on the marine environment, according to PCA, which was planning construction of a A$16 million plant to combat the rising level of suspended solids—pieces of wood matter—in the mill's emissions.[39]

The government responded by hiring additional inspectors to monitor pollution in the Kayser region.[40] Alan Andrews, manager of the Kayser mill, and Robert Cartmel, paper expert for Greenpeace, drew different conclusions from the Kayser controversy. Andrews criticized Cartmel's methods:

> Mr. Cartmel visited our research unit last year at the invitation of the mill and was fully briefed on the mill performance and its objectives.
>
> He went out of his way to create the impression he was a man who would give a balanced view.[41]

Cartmel believed he had indeed presented a balanced view and continued to condemn the Kayser plant: "It is a question of the shareholders accepting a lower profit margin in order to maintain the environment."[42]

McRae Looks Ahead

Encouraged by APM's success, Amcor had provided A$50 million to APM to consolidate the

investment that had carried it into fine-papers, though a return of at least 20 percent per year was expected. While larger sums could always be requested, it was understood that larger sums required more attractive returns—as had been the case when APM originally entered the market by upgrading Machine 3. Further expansion into fine-papers loomed as a possibility. Copier paper alone promised 10 percent annual growth and recycled paper continued to grow in popularity. The uncoated fine-papers market as a whole was projected to grow at a rate of 6.5 percent annually through the year 2000. "Sitting on our hands is no good. If our influence in the market declines, customers will push us around."

McRae weighed his immediate options for the capital budget:

1. The capacity of Machine 3 at Maryvale could be expanded up to 100,000 tonnes. Initial estimates put the cost of increasing from the existing capacity of 70,000 tonnes at A$35 million. McRae would have to decide how he would use this extra capacity.
2. APM was producing 7,000 tonnes of recycled paper at its Fairfield plant, and increasing capacity to 15,000 tonnes would cost A$18 million.
3. In addition to APM's recycling efforts, McRae focused on ways to reduce APM's discharge of organochlorines. APM could reduce its dependence on chlorine by substituting oxygen in one of two ways:
   a. To replace chlorine through oxygen *pre*-bleaching, APM would have to spend A$15 million in development and implementation. Oxygen pre-bleaching[43] would reduce chlorine use by 50 percent. Pulp output at Maryvale would drop by 5 percent, from 350,000 tonnes to 332,500 tonnes, but many engineers at the plant had expressed keen interest in learning

[39] "Greenpeace Pulp Claims 'Impossible,'" *Advocate,* 24 March 1990. "Greenpeace Motives Questioned," *Advocate,* 23 March 1990.

[40] Andrew Darby, "Kayser Mill Worst, Says Greenpeace," *Age,* 23 March 1990.

[41] "Greenpeace Motives Questioned," *Advocate,* 23 March 1990.

[42] "Report Savages PCA," *Adovcate,* 23 March 1990.

[43] Oxygen pre-bleaching was also known as extended delignification. See Exhibit 1.

EXHIBIT 4   Long-Term Uncoated Fine-Papers Market in Australia (000 tonnes)

Category	1986				1989				Forecast 1995
	PCA	Imports	APM	Total	PCA	Imports	APM	Total	Total
Offset printing	50	19	0	69	20	7	17	44	44
Continuous forms	40	15	0	55	37	7	28	72	78
Copier	44	11	0	55	51	8	25	84	150
Recycled	0	0	0	0	0	0	7	7	30
Total	**134**	**45**	**0**	**179**	**108**	**22**	**77**	**207**	**302**

about the technology. Pulp contribution at Maryvale was A$200 per tonne of pulp.

b. Alternatively, APM could intensify the use of oxygen *during* bleaching, which would reduce the level of chlorine by 15 percent and cost approximately A$8 million. Pulp output would be unaffected.

Environmental groups lobbied for activated sludge-treatment plants to cleanse the effluent entirely of organochlorines. All pulp mills had to be equipped with primary treatment facilities, but the industry considered secondary treatment, such as activated sludge treatment, unnecessary. Environmentalists estimated the cost of activated sludge treatment to be A$25 million for APM. While they realized the industry would likely be unreceptive to such a large expense—for equipment that contributed few tangible benefits to the company—environmentalists did not consider it a quixotic request. One environmentalist typified the rising sentiment of Australians when he noted, "How can you put a dollar value on the sensible use of the environment?"

As he read accounts of the Kayser mill controversy, McRae reflected on long-term opportunities:

If we sit still, we'll get hurt sometime before the year 2000. Whoever takes the next big step will have it made in Australia. We are looking toward putting in a paper machine of 150,000 tonnes. Whatever we don't use for uncoated papers could be our foundation for going into coated papers. We'd only have to add a coater at the end of the machine. Total investment would be A$350 million, but we'd have tremendous flexibility to alternate between coated and uncoated. Of course, this would also mean a big pulp mill, but we could financially justify new pulp capacity in any case.

If PCA decides to expand, the unknown is what they would do with the capacity they've currently got. Their machines are a lot older and less efficient than ours are. Would they build two machines or will they just put in one? And will they close down all of the inefficient machines? What will their net increase be?

Some local environmentalists invoked the popular aphorism, "Think globally, act locally,"

EXHIBIT 5 Editorial from *Pulp and Paper International* — June 1990

Chlorine Bleaching Has to Go

Drastic actions are needed if mills are to become truly environmentally friendly. Renate Kroesa of Greenpeace outlined some of the changes environmentalists would like to see the industry introduce at PPI's Market Pulp conference held in Brussels in May.

Environmentalists have difficulty understanding why industry is resisting so much the introduction of less bleached paper goods into the market, since such a move would actually provide reductions in production costs in the form of saved energy and saved bleaching chemicals.

Bleaching to a lower level would also enable the mills to close the loop, since the elimination of all chlorine bleaching would also eliminate corrosion-causing chloride ions. Such a closed-loop system would also greatly reduce the amount of fresh water needed by the mill.

Consumers are prepared to accept less bright paper products, if given the choice and if educated accordingly. Opinion polls have shown again and again that consumers are more than prepared to shop consciously and that the onus is on industry to produce such products.

Very few paper products require high brightness, high quality printing papers being one of these. Yet, as we are able to see from the example of the West German company Hannoversche Papierfabrik, even this market can be satisfied by using chlorine-free sulfite pulp.

In fact, the Swedish Chemical Inspectorate published a study last year, which investigated different kinds of paper and whether these could be produced without the use of chlorine. This government study concluded that there was not one single paper product that could not also have been produced without chlorine.

Aside from eliminating chlorine-based bleaching, it is essential that all mills install secondary treatment facilities to degrade and detoxify the remaining effluent. It is encouraging to see that Canada is now following the lead of other countries to require secondary treatment for all mills, and not only those that are located along rivers and small streams. It is less encouraging to see that Sweden, which has done so much work with regard to reducing the generation of chlorinated compounds at source, is still not forcing its mills along the Baltic Sea to employ secondary treatment.

A sophisticated effluent treatment system is also of particular importance for CTMP mills, which have benefitted greatly from the growing market demand for chlorine-free pulp, but often do not employ the kind of sophisticated secondary treatment necessary to degrade the high acute toxicity of this effluent. A newly proposed CTMP mill in Canada has promised to install the first chemical recovery for CTMP mills.

Instead of full-heartedly pursuing further development of chlorine-free bleaching technologies and the marketing of less bleached products, the industry is investing vast amounts of money in the construction of new, huge kraft mills, again designed to produce highly bleached market pulp, and again using chlorine-based bleaching technologies.

Even with technology that would guarantee AOX discharges of between 1.5 and 1.0 kg AOX/ton of pulp, the sheer size of these new mills will make them become another point source of large-scale discharges of organochlorine compounds.

At the same time, existing kraft mills use the fact that they have to install better bleaching technologies as an excuse to double the original capacity, thus offsetting any improvement with regard to the overall discharge of organochlorines.

Greenpeace views new kraft mill proposals as incompatible with the concept of sustainable development for other reasons as well. Due to their sheer size, these proposed new kraft mills will require either large scale clear-cut logging of virgin and old-growth forests or intensive tree plantations, both of which are incompatible with sustainable forest management practices. Both

EXHIBIT 5   *(concluded)*

wipe out ecosystems to replace them with monocultures.

At the same time, our waste mountains are ever growing. Many cities have recently introduced recycling programs, or will soon do so. But the collected wastepaper is already exceeding the absorption capacity of existing recycling mills. At the same time, institutions and environmental groups cannot find sufficient supplies of office paper made of recycled fibers.

There can only be one conclusion to this, and that is to build recycling mills using clean recycling technologies, and at the same time to freeze the production capacity of virgin pulp, while converting the production process to become environmentally friendly and chlorine-free.

EXHIBIT 6   Editorial from *Pulp and Paper International* — May 1990

Why We Must Win Public Support

John Luke, president and chief executive officer of US pulp and paper producer Westvaco, looks at eight environmental challenges which will confront the pulp and paper industry in the future. Besides the development for cleaner processes and better forestry, he also stresses the importance of winning public support, and the need for positive action to overcome misconceptions about the industry's environmental record. This Viewpoint is based on a speech given to the American Paper Institute's Annual Paper Week, held in New York City, USA, in March.

Looking ahead, we shall work to build as progressive an environmental record in the future as we have in the past.

First, our products will be under constant and intensive scrutiny. They must not only be safe, they must be perceived as making a positive contribution to public health and the quality of life. Our product integrity must be beyond question.

Second, our forest management will also face increasing public scrutiny. Our forest practices will have to be progressively more environmentally sensitive.

Third, our industry will have to make on-going and measurable progress in reducing pollution both in the atmosphere around our mills and in receiving waters. We will also feel pressure from the public relating to the general problems of acid rain, global warming, and toxic fear. Standards will be progressively complex and stringent, and the public more demanding.

Fourth, we will have to cope with new trace chemical challenges as advancing analytical technology identifies them and as they are cast in the role of undermining human health. We will face these trace chemicals alarms in our products, in our effluents, in our solid waste disposal, and throughout our mills.

Fifth, we will face growing emphasis on "environmental aesthetics" — the range of public nuisance factors which may not represent an actual threat to our natural environment, but which are perceived as having an impact on the quality of life.

Sixth are environmental accidents. The running aground of the oil tanker Valdez in Alaska is fresh in everyone's mind, and both the public and the media will be intolerant of future accidents.

Seventh is the growing pressure for environmental codes of conduct and responsibility. The momentum for these is increasing and each of us must decide whether to react to the calls of others or to take a lead in formulating our own codes. We have decided to take a lead at Westvaco. We have formed a new committee of our board of directors, called the Committee on the Environment. It meets each quarter, and we feel that it is a constructive response to the developing environmental climate.

EXHIBIT 6 *(concluded)*

Eighth, our environmental success in the future is going to depend on how ably we manage our effluents, on how effectively we earn support for our progress, and on how we work for sound environmental policy.

Looking at these eight factors, we know that we can manage our effluents, but developing broad public support is a newer dimension to the problem. It will mean taking steps with all of our constituencies—our employees, local communities, the media, and our elected representatives at all levels. Our progress has to be recognized and not diminished by emotion and misrepresentation on the part of activists. The industry alone has the responsibility for providing the perspective, the facts, and the balance necessary for clear thinking and clear action on the public's part.

The dimension of environmental policy is also new. It is critical that we help shape an environmental policy which is responsive to genuine risk and which protects the natural environment and human health, with sound science

and regulatory reason as its foundation. This is essential to the future of our industry, and it is equally essential to the competitive position of all U.S. industry in the world economy.

These new environmental dimensions are going to be just as important as the degree of measurable environmental progress we are able to accomplish. Our reputation will be the result of our actual environmental performance and the public's perception of that performance.

In the U.S.A., we are complying with the most stringent environmental requirements in the world. No other country's paper industry has made the progress which we have made in environmental improvement.

But we now face an even more challenging environmental future, which will require us to be outspoken about our performance and to work with skill and determination to help the nation adopt soundly based environmental policies. That is what it will take to stay on the environmental high ground.

---

to argue against *any* expansion of the Australian paper industry. To preserve the earth's environment, they felt, paper use worldwide had to decrease. Environmental groups throughout the world advocated a hierarchy of measures to protect the environment: *reduce* first, *reuse* second, and *recycle* third.

McRae put down the accounts of the Kayser affair and turned to the June issue of *Pulp and Paper International* (see Exhibit 5). Despite APM's stunning success in fine-papers, McRae knew he would have to chart APM's future course very carefully.

EXHIBIT 7 Steps in the Pulp and Paper Chain for Fine Paper

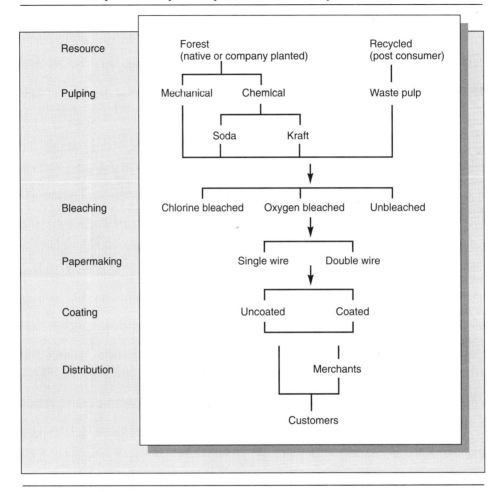

EXHIBIT 8 Precautionary Principle

The Nordic Council's Conference on Pollution of the Seas* adopted this principle as its standard for environmental protection:

> The need for an effective precautionary approach, with that important principle intended to safeguard the marine ecosystem by, among other things, eliminating and preventing pollution emissions where there is reason to believe that damage or harmful effects are likely to be caused, even where there is inadequate or inconclusive scientific evidence to prove a causal link between emissions and effect.

* The 1989 conference included members of parliament from Belgium, Canada, Czechoslovakia, Denmark, the Federal Republic of Germany, Finland, the German Democratic Republic, Iceland, Ireland, the Netherlands, Norway, Poland, Sweden, Switzerland, the U.S.S.R., the United Kingdom, the Faeroe Islands, and Greenland.

LOTUS MARKETPLACE:HOUSEHOLDS

If you market this product, it is my sincere hope that you are sued by every person for whom your data is false, with the eventual result that your company goes bankrupt.

Electronic mail message to Jim Manzi[1]

This electronic mail message was among the 30,000 that Lotus Development Corporation had received in the nine months since its April 9, 1990, new product announcement of Lotus MarketPlace:Households, a compact disk database of 80 million U.S. households for use on the Apple Macintosh personal computer. Designed as part of a family of tools to make it easy for businesses to target customers, MarketPlace:Households paralleled MarketPlace:Businesses, a database of information on 9 million businesses.

Lotus developed the household database in an unusual alliance with the consumer credit bureau and information services company, Equifax, Inc. Lotus provided software and technical expertise, along with a distribution system, while Equifax supplied information and expertise on information collection and analysis. The union brought together two very different companies and industries. Lotus, like the software industry, was young and fast paced, while Equifax was older and more conservative. But both companies saw themselves as technology leaders committed to responsible information practices and principles.

The proposed household database and software package would allow small businesses to buy targeted mailing lists (minimum 5,000 names total) for direct mail marketing. The data fields on the disc included name, address, age, gender, marital status, estimated household income, lifestyle (50 categories, including "inner-city singles," "mobile home families," "accumulated wealth," etc.), and buying propensity for more than 100 specific products (including cloth diapers, luxury cars, frozen dinners, etc.). Although lists of names and addresses could be defined and generated using any of these criteria, users could obtain only names and addresses from the product.

Unlike Lotus, Equifax had not received extensive electronic mail. However, several organizations, including the American Civil Liberties Union, had earlier, when contacted by Equifax, expressed concerns that the proposed product represented an invasion of personal privacy. In the fourth quarter of 1990, with MarketPlace scheduled for shipment in the spring of 1991, Lotus and Equifax managers undertook a very intensive reevaluation of the privacy issue. In a number of strategic sessions they considered how to respond to the privacy concerns.

Background

Lotus Development Corporation

Lotus Development Corporation, the software company developing MarketPlace, was headquartered in Cambridge, Massachusetts. It had become a dominant player in the

---

[1] Mary J. Culnan, "The Lessons of the Lotus MarketPlace: Implications for Consumer Privacy in the 1990s," paper presented at the Conference on Computers, Freedom, and Privacy, March 1991.

This case was written by Professor Lynn Sharp Paine of the Harvard Business School.

Copyright © 1991 by the President and Fellows of Harvard College.

Harvard Business School case 392-026 (Revised 1993).

EXHIBIT 1 Lotus Development Corporation Consolidated Statements of Operations, Year Ended December 31 (in thousands, except per share data)

	1989	1988	1987
Net sales	$556,033	$468,547	$395,595
Cost of sales	104,949	90,825	68,676
Gross margin	451,084	377,722	326,919
Operating expenses:			
Research and development	94,343	83,837	58,420
Sales and marketing	221,745	170,750	126,848
General and administrative	61,078	54,124	46,546
Total operating expenses	$377,166	$308,711	$231,814
Operating income	$ 73,918	$ 69,011	$ 95,105
Interest income, net	$ 5,644	$ 9,568	$ 3,960
Other income, net	5,389	1,295	3,853
Income before provision for income taxes	$ 84,951	$ 79,874	$102,918
Provision for income taxes	16,990	20,949	30,875
Net income	$ 67,961	$ 58,925	$ 72,043
Net income per share	$ 1.61	$ 1.29	$ 1.58
Weighted average common and common equivalent shares outstanding	$ 42,301	$ 45,551	$ 45,720

Source: Lotus Development Corporation, annual report, 1989

business applications segment of the personal computer software market in January 1983 with the introduction of its first product, Lotus 1-2-3, a spreadsheet software package. Like most software companies, Lotus was founded by a "techie" entrepreneur, Mitchell Kapor, a co-author of 1-2-3. However, in 1990, it was being run by a marketing executive, Jim Manzi. A former consultant with McKinsey and Company, Manzi joined Lotus in 1983 as a marketing director and quickly rose to president in 1984. Kapor's involvement in Lotus ended in 1986 when Manzi became CEO and chairman.

As Lotus entered 1990, most of its revenues of $556 million derived from sales of its spreadsheet product, 1-2-3, although the company also sold business graphics and database management products (see Exhibit 1). The

company's stated product strategy as it entered the new year was to further develop these three core software business applications. Market-Place came under a fourth area, CD-ROM (compact disk read-only memory) products, a smaller business at Lotus but one expected to provide added value.[2]

Lotus had been one of the first companies in the CD-ROM market and its Lotus One Source had the largest share of PC-based business financial information products. One Source consisted of six products: investment, corporate, banking, private, international, and mergers and acquisitions. Three international versions were introduced in February 1990 and

_____

[2] Lotus Development Corporation, annual report for fiscal year ending December 31, 1989.

Lotus planned to continue expanding the number of databases it offered on CD-ROM.[3] Although the market for CD-ROM products had looked promising for several years, sales were still limited as few companies had yet invested in optical read-only disc drives (total unit shipments in 1989 were 140 thousand versus the 20 million PCs sold).[4] Lotus manufactured its CD-ROM products at the company's manufacturing facility in Cambridge. Although most Lotus products were sold either directly to resellers or to distributors selling to resellers, One Source was sold directly to customers by specialized sales forces.[5]

In March 1990, as a first step toward its product strategy, Lotus reorganized its 2,800 employees into four operating units as follows: the software business group, the international business group, the software consulting business, and the information services group (whose responsibilities included CD-ROM products). By mid-year, Lotus had expanded its spreadsheet franchise with introductions of 1-2-3 for non-PC markets. In addition, the company was looking at expanding into network operating system software through a merger with Novell, Inc., manufacturer of Net-Ware. In May, however, the proposed merger fell through and, instead of becoming the world's largest personal computer software company, Lotus was back to relying on 1-2-3.

Personal Computer (PC) Software Industry

During its first six years, Lotus had dominated the personal computer software industry with its virtual ownership of the spreadsheet category. However, by 1990, other U.S. companies had gained share at Lotus's expense. Microsoft,

EXHIBIT 2	1989 Worldwide Sales of PC Software ($ in millions)
	Amount
Applications	$4,100
Systems	1,820
Entertainment	1,670
Education	325
Total	$7,915

Source: Compiled by casewriter from Karen Juliussen and Egil Juliussen, *The Computer Almanac 1991* (New York: Simon & Schuster, 1990), p. 10.28.

Lotus's main competitor, had surpassed Lotus as the market leader in PC software in 1988. In 1990 Microsoft was not only far larger but better positioned, with a wide range of products beyond applications software.

Worldwide sales of PC software had reached $6.8 billion in 1990. Still quite young and dominated by U.S. companies, the industry was highly fragmented and experiencing fast growth. Applications software, Lotus's product focus, comprised a little over half the market, with systems software and entertainment software the next largest segments (see Exhibit 2).[6] Within the applications software segment, word processing commanded the largest share, with spreadsheets a close second. However, the spreadsheet category was fairly mature and growing at a slower pace than newer segments like graphics and other productivity tools (see Exhibit 3).[7]

Equifax

Equifax, Lotus's partner in developing Market-Place:Households, was the leader of the $900

[3] Lotus Development Corporation, Form 10-K for the fiscal year ended December 31, 1989.

[4] Karen Juliussen and Egil Juliussen, *The Computer Industry Almanac 1991* (New York: Simon & Schuster, 1990), pp. 10.13, 10.26.

[5] Ibid.

[6] Karen Juliussen and Egil Juliussen, *The Computer Industry Almanac 1991,* (New York: Simon & Schuster, 1990), p. 10.28.

[7] Ibid.

EXHIBIT 3   PC Application Software Sales, 1989 versus 1988 ($ in millions)

	1988 $ Sales	1989 $ Sales	%Δ
Word processing	$495	$650	+31%
Spreadsheets	473	540	+14
Graphics	256	361	+41
Other productivity	355	440	+24

Source: Compiled by casewriter from Karen Juliussen and Egil Juliussen, *The Computer Almanac 1991* (New York: Simon & Schuster, 1990), p. 10.28.

million industry in providing personal credit information.[8] The company was founded in 1899 in Atlanta, Georgia, as the Retail Credit Company. C.B. Rogers, Jr., president and CEO, had joined the company in October 1987 after 33 years at IBM, where he had spent many years in the Information Systems Group. In Rogers's two years at Equifax he had seen it grow 25 percent to $840 million in sales (see Exhibit 4).[9] Equifax's annual return to investors had averaged 30.9 percent throughout the 1980s, ranking it first among the 100 diversified service companies on *Fortune's* Service 500.[10]

Much of Equifax's recent growth had come through the acquisition of regional credit bureaus. The company's 12,700 employees worked in 45 company-owned and 200 affiliated credit bureaus as well as several hundred offices that provided information services to insurance companies.[11] These facilities were spread across the United States and Canada. Equifax's U.S. credit reporting network provided credit histories on an estimated 150 million Americans for the company's two operating units, Credit and

Marketing Services, and Insurance and Special Services. These units, in turn, provided information services to credit grantors and insurance companies.

Marketing Decision Systems at Equifax, the provider of information and data collection expertise for the proposed Lotus Market-Place:Households, helped companies identify and market their products to targeted consumer groups. In addition to providing traditional market research, such as focus-group interviews and mall-intercept surveys, it offered marketers the use of its massive consumer information database.

The consumer information compiled in the Equifax Consumer Marketing Database (ECMD) was collected from a variety of sources. The database included indicators of the recency and frequency of a consumer's financial activity. These indicators were based on data (not available on ECMD) on the consumer's purchase and payment history acquired from banks and other credit grantors. The U.S. census provided demographic data and the U.S. Postal Service licensed Equifax to use its National Change of Address service. Equifax purchased public records of drivers' license data and sourced data on mail order buyers, motor vehicle purchases, and children from other direct mail companies (see Exhibit 5). Uses of the ECMD ranged from simply renting a mailing list to analyzing various combinations of data to predict product pur-

---

[8] Company and analyst reports for TRW, Trans Union, and Equifax.

[9] Equifax, annual report for the fiscal year ending December 31, 1989.

[10] Laurie Kretchmar, "How to Shine in a Sullied Industry," *Fortune,* February 24, 1992.

[11] Ibid.

EXHIBIT 4 Financial Highlights—Equifax Inc. ($ in thousands, except per share amounts)

	Year Ended December 31						
	1989	1988	1987	1986	1985	1984	1983
Operating revenue	$840,283	$743,078	$670,007	$635,076	$564,270	$466,057	$435,707
Income from continuing operations before income taxes:							
Before gain	58,711	58,046	56,378	46,636	40,320	33,223	30,657
Gain on sale of businesses	1,384	–	–	–	–	–	2,228
Total	$ 60,095	$ 58,046	$ 56,378	$ 46,636	$ 40,320	$ 33,223	$ 32,885
Provision for income taxes	24,432	24,090	25,822	21,025	17,897	14,510	14,646
Income from continuing operations before cumulative effect of the change in accounting for income taxes	35,663	33,956	30,556	25,611	22,423	18,713	18,239
Loss from discontinued operation	–	–	–	–	(4,061)	(94)	(488)
Income before cumulative effect of the change in accounting for income taxes	$ 35,663	$ 33,956	$ 30,556	$ 25,611	$ 18,362	$ 18,619	$ 17,751
Cumulative prior years' effect of the change in accounting for income taxes	–	5,400	–	–	–	–	–
Net income	$ 35,663	$ 39,356	$ 30,556	$ 25,611	$ 18,362	$ 18,619	$ 17,751
Per common share:							
Income from continuing operations	0.73	0.73	0.71	0.60	0.52	0.44	0.43
Loss from discontinued operation	–	–	–	–	(.09)	–	(.01)
Cumulative prior years' effect of the change in accounting for income taxes	–	0.12	–	–	–	–	–
Net income per common share	0.73	0.85	0.71	0.60	0.43	0.44	0.42
Income from continuing operations per dollar of operating revenue	0.042	0.046	0.046	0.040	0.040	0.040	0.042
Dividends paid	21,084	17,978	14,969	13,576	12,432	11,569	10,233
Per common share	0.43	0.39	0.35	0.318	0.291	0.271	0.242
Percent of income from continuing operations	59%	53%	49%	53%	55%	62%	56%
Additions to retained earnings from operations	14,579	21,378	15,587	12,035	5,930	7,050	7,518
Number of shareholders of record	5,369	5,217	5,035	4,755	4,279	4,200	4,301
Number of employees	12,714	12,275	10,767	11,082	10,667	9,582	9,477

Note: All share and per share data has been restated to reflect a two-for-one common stock split effective December 18, 1989.

Source: Equifax, Inc., annual report, 1989.

EXHIBIT 5   Equifax Consumer Marketing Database

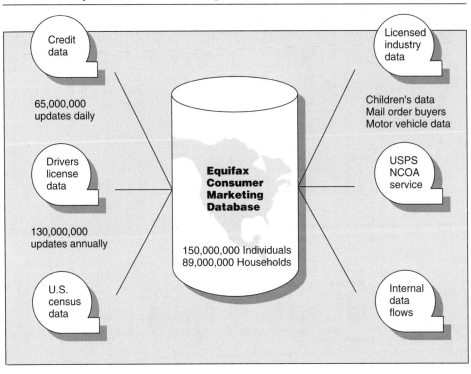

Credit Bureau Industry

Equifax competed in two industries: the credit bureau industry and the mailing list industry. In 1990, it was one of three large companies providing consumer credit reports. TRW Credit Data, and Trans Union Corporation, like Equifax, owned databases on virtually every U.S. household. These three companies issued a combined annual total of approximately 450 million reports to credit grantors based on this data. Public records of financial items like bankruptcies and foreclosures were combined with customer information from banks, stores, and other credit grantors

chase interest through statistical modeling techniques.

to generate reports on individual consumers.[12]

The credit bureaus' collection and use of information about consumers was regulated by a number of state laws and by the 1970 Fair Credit Reporting Act (FCRA) which required

> consumer reporting agencies [to] adopt reasonable procedures for meeting the needs of commerce for consumer credit, personnel, insurance, and other information in a manner which is fair and equitable to the consumer, with regard to the confidentiality, accuracy, relevancy, and proper utilization of such information in accordance with the requirements of this title.[13]

---

[12] Associated Credit Bureaus 1989 data.
[13] Fair Credit Reporting Act, 15 U.S.C.S. §1681 (b) (199).

Enforced by the Federal Trade Commission (the FTC), the FCRA limited the circumstances under which credit bureaus could share consumer information. Without a consumer's written authorization, information could only be shared with those who had "legitimate business need for the information in connection with a business transaction involving the consumer."[14]

In the fall of 1989, legislation had been introduced to review and amend the FCRA. In an oversight hearing before the House Subcommittee on Consumer Affairs and Coinage on September 13, public officials and consumer advocacy groups testified that the FCRA was no longer sufficient to protect consumers' personal privacy given the technological advances since 1970. Witnesses complained that consumers were in the dark about the sources of information for credit reports. They were also concerned that there were few controls over who could access the data.

Following the hearing, several bills were introduced to amend the FCRA. One bill proposed the establishment of a Data Protection Board to oversee the use of personal information by private and public institutions.[15] The most comprehensive, introduced on March 7, 1990, required that people supplying information to credit bureaus inform consumers of their activities. It also prohibited reporting agencies from using their data to develop lists for "pre-screening"[16] purposes unless consumers had been given an opportunity to "opt-out" by removing their names from the data base. On June 12, 1990, the subcommittee heard testimony providing suggestions for improving the bill. Several recommendations focused on how to allow consumers to remove their names from credit report-based mailing lists. The American Civil Liberties Union (ACLU) and other consumer advocacy groups claimed that, without this feature, these mailing lists were illegal under the FCRA.

The FTC was at this time working to clarify its interpretation of the current FCRA. On May 4, 1990, the FTC issued a commentary on the FCRA, which addressed the topic of prescreening. The FTC took the position that prescreening for making offers of credit, but not for issuing invitations to apply for credit, were permissible under current law.[17]

In response to growing attention to credit bureau practices, the International Credit Association (ICA) sponsored a Credit Industry Forum on Privacy in February 1990. This conference, a first for the industry, was well attended by industry members and government representatives (including the director of the U.S. Office of Consumer Affairs; a member of the House Subcommittee on Consumer Affairs and Coinage; the associate director for credit practices of the Bureau of Consumer Protection; and staff from the Federal Trade Commission). Dr. Alan Westin, a well-known privacy expert and professor at Columbia University, represented the consumer's point of view.

Mailing List and Direct Marketing Industries

By 1990, all three major credit bureaus had been in the mailing list business for three years. (They had provided pre-screening services since before 1970.). This industry, like the credit bureau industry, was dominated by three

---

[14] 15 U.S.C.S. §1681(b)(3)(E).

[15] U.S. Congress, House, *Data Protection Act of 1989,* 101st Cong., 1st session, 1989.

[16] The bill defined pre-screening: "When a reporting agency edits or compiles for its customer a list of consumers who meet some set of credit worthiness criteria provided by the customer who will use the list to solicit consumers for its product." *Congressional Record,* July 31, 1990, E 2555.

[17] 55 Fed. Reg. 18804 (May 4, 1990).

large companies, with electronic databases on nearly every U.S. household. R.L. Polk, Donnelly Marketing, and R.R. Donnelly & Sons generated annual sales between $150 million and $250 million from selling households' addresses and data (phone numbers, estimated income, purchasing habits, etc.).[18] In addition, there were many hundreds of small companies providing direct marketers with specialized lists (new parents, birthday club members, pet owners, etc.). In 1990 the total industry was estimated at $1.23 billion annually in list sales.[19]

Equifax operated as both a list owner and a list manager, since it both owned data and also promoted its usage. A company doing a direct marketing campaign could either contact Equifax directly to rent a list or go through a list broker.[20] Few list brokers rented lists of fewer than 5,000 names. To protect against objectionable or illegal offers, list owners usually reviewed a sample of the proposed mailing and seeded names and addresses in the list. Seeding was also used to monitor compliance with the list usage agreement. Lists were generally rented on a one-time-usage basis, and a renter could do repeat mailings only to consumers responding to its initial mailing. In the case of MarketPlace, buyers would own all the names purchased, could purchase in increments smaller than 5,000, and would be able to use the names as frequently as desired.

The average cost to rent a mailing list of consumers in 1990 was about $78 per 1,000 names.[21] The more detailed a list's category selectors, the higher the rental price. At the very high end of the market, several companies offered detailed databases in conjunction with software packages for modeling the data.

Donnelly Marketing Information Services (a subsidiary of the Dun & Bradstreet Corporation) offered companies this type of product. This product, called "Conquest," used modeling techniques to identify the most suitable market segments and geographical areas for a given product. The databases of information, stored on compact disc, included U.S. household demographics, Nielsen scanner data on product purchases, economic and lifestyle data, Arbitron data on media viewership, Simmons data on product usage, census data, business data, and Donnelly's Market Potential Database (total and per household expenditures on 250 product groups).[22] The cost to buy Conquest ranged from $35,000 to $70,000 per year. By January of 1990, Donnelly had installed more than 300 systems for packaged goods marketers, retailers, media buying services, media companies, and advertising agencies.[23] Although the initial investment was high, even national, mass marketers found it more cost effective to target customers than to use mass mailings or mass media due to rising media costs, consumer fragmentation, and the need for competitive differentiation.

Although Equifax's Marketing Decisions Systems did not offer as many databases as Conquest, its customers in 1990 received the most up-to-date data available and were offered a range of list selection options. Equifax sold a list called the "Powerhouse," which included all information in the ECMD. The data covered 121 million individuals in 89 million households. Powerhouse offered buyers highly specific targeting capability. The tar-

---

[18] Michael W. Miller, "Hot Lists: Data Mills Delve Deep to Find Information about U.S. Consumers," *The Wall Street Journal,* March 14, 1991, p. A1.

[19] *Direct Marketing Magazine,* "List Industry Overview," August 1991, p. 46.

[20] Since there were numerous companies offering many different kinds of lists, list brokers helped marketing companies identify the appropriate list and then arranged its rental.

[21] *Direct Marketing Magazine,* "Worldwide List Price Index," August 1991, p. 14.

[22] Wally Wood, "Tools of the Trade," *Marketing and Media Decisions,* June 1988, p. 148.

[23] Wood, "Tools of the Trade," January 1990, p. 152.

geting choices included household income, demographics, special selects (telephone numbers, children in the household, etc.), shopping psychographics (nine distinct types), and purchasing power indices (see Exhibit 6). Within the purchasing power index marketers were offered MicroVision©, a "micro-geographical consumer targeting system . . . at the Zip + 4 level of geography . . . [that] can precisely identify the profile, purchase behavior and lifestyles of . . . customers . . . based on individual and census data. [MicroVision© would] accurately target as few as ten households."[24]

Regulation of Direct Mailing

Unlike credit bureaus, direct marketers were self-regulated in 1990. The Privacy Act of 1974 had created a commission charged with examining practices of agencies and businesses dealing with personal information, including the direct marketing and mailing list industries.[25] The commission had determined as of the mid-1970s that these two industries were not endangering personal privacy, but they recommended that the issue be examined again in the future.

The commission had directed these industries to monitor their practices and cited the need for a mechanism allowing consumers to remove their names ("opt-out") from direct marketing lists. In response, the Direct Marketing Association (DMA), the trade group representing mailing list companies as well as users of mailing lists, had established guidelines for ethical business practices. These guidelines had been periodically updated and expanded during the succeeding 15 years. By joining the DMA, members agreed to abide by the guidelines. Articles 32 and 33 in the DMA's handbook stated:

Article #32 Customers who provide data that may be rented, sold or exchanged for direct marketing purposes periodically should be informed of the potential for the rental, sale or exchange of such data. Marketers should offer an opportunity to have a consumer's name deleted or suppressed upon request. . . .
Article #33 . . . Information and selection criteria that may be considered to be personal and intimate in nature by all reasonable standards should not provide the basis for lists made available for rental, sale, or exchange when there is a reasonable expectation by the consumer that the information will be kept confidential. [DMA Guidelines for Ethical Business Practice, p. 13.]

The DMA also created a service to assist in removing names from national lists and all DMA member companies developed name removal options.

The credit bureaus' entry into the mailing list business followed on their development of pre-screening and targeting techniques for credit grantors. The credit bureaus realized that data techniques developed in this context could be used in many others as well. Moreover, direct marketing had grown in the 1980s (21.94 million 1989 advertising dollars versus 7.59 million 1980 advertising dollars).[26] However, the credit bureaus' entry had caused some industry concern since the credit bureaus' lists were generated, in part, from consumer credit information. In a May 1989, *Direct Marketing Magazine* article, Roy Schwedelson, CEO of a leading list management and list brokerage firm, stated his concern about credit bureaus' use of personal information to compile mailing lists for sale:

> When a consumer goes to a bank to file a credit application, they give information of the highest sensitive matter to the banker. . . . The

---

[24] Equifax Marketing Decision Systems.
[25] Privacy Act, Public Law 93-579, December 31, 1974 (88 Stat. 1896).

[26] *"An Overview of Direct Marketing and Direct Response Advertising,"* New York, Direct Marketing Association, 1990, p. 61.

EXHIBIT 6 Power House (U.S. Household Consumer Base)

Power Lists for the 1990s

89,881,925 Households with 12-month Credit Activity Through December 1989

This 12-month credit activity file consists of 89 million households and 121 million individuals, *priced at the cost of compiled lists.* Target your market precisely utilizing Equifax's comprising a menu of demographic and psychographic selections including: Equifax Power Selects, Income, Exact Age, Sex, Marital Status, Dwelling Unit Type, Presence of Children within Age Ranges, Length of Residence, and Mail Order Buyer information. Selections are available by Head of Household and/or Spouse.

Power Selects

Household Income

$10/M	
$15,000 and under	
15,000–19,999	
20,000–24,999	
25,000–34,999	
35,000–49,999	
50,000–74,999	
75,000–99,999	
100,000 +	

Buyability $5/M

Relative Level of
Spending Power:
High
Above average
Average
Below Average
Low

Shopping
Psychographic
Lifestyle $10/M
Prestige Shoppers
Where America Shops
Value Conscious
Flexible Shoppers

Presence of Credit Card

Bank/HOH	$10/M
Bank/Spouse	$10/M
Retail/HOH	$ 5/M
Retail/Spouse	$ 5/M
Total Accounts Held	$ 5/M

Credit Card Activity
$5/M
Relative Level of
Account Activity:
High
Above average
Average
Below average
Low

VISION© Target
Marketing System[a]

VISION® Licensees	$ 5/M
Others	$10/M

Demographics

Exact Age	$ 5/M
Gender	$ 3/M
Marital Statu	$ 3/M
Dwelling Unit Type	$ 3/M
State, SCF, Z	$ 3/M
Census Geogra	$ 1/M

Special Selec

Telephone Num	$ 20/M
Children in H	$8.5/M
Children by A Group	$ 10/M
0–6 year	
7–12 year	
13–18 year	
Mail Order Bu	$ 10/M
Mail Order Re	$ 10/M
Home Ownershi	$ 4/M
Number of Adu	$ 2/M
Length of Res	$ 2/M

EXHIBIT 6 *(concluded)*

Pricing

Maximum Charge (Special Selects)
Without Phone Number: $25/M
With Phone Number: $35/M

Activity Surcharge

≤ Three Months	≤ Six Months
$20/M	$10/M

Selection Cap charges exclude
Special Selects and VISION® Selects
2nd Usage: 1.5 × original retail
3rd Usage: 2 × original retail
12-Month unlimited usage: 2.5 × original retail

Base Charge

0–4.9MM	5–9.9MM	10–14.9MM	15MM +
$35/M	$30/M	$25/M	$20/M

Selection Cap

0.49MM	5–9.9MM	10–14.9MM	15MM +
$25/M	$20/M	$15/M	$10/M

Updates
Quarterly: $35/M
Minimum Charge: $250

Net-Name   85% arrangement on 50,000 and over. Running charge $5/M. $1/M

Key Coding   4 + Up Cheshire: N/C   Magnetic Tape: $20 Each   Pressure Sens $6/M

Format   **Call (404) 740-4960 or 1-800-877-5560 for Complete Details**

Source: Equifax Marketing Decision Systems.

consumer has an implied confidentiality pact with their banker . . . not to use this information for any other purpose but credit checking. Consumers should be allowed to have a negative option clearly available to them—the consumer's right to prohibit disclosure. Unfortunately, TRW cannot offer this negative option in an open and clear form. They can't do this because the banks would balk and most consumers would balk. It flies in the face of TRW's primary business. And that's why this data is not an informational list medium. It's not usable data, regardless of its potential value.[27]

The credit bureaus maintained that they were acting within the bounds of the FCRA, because they didn't give out specific financial data but used the data to sort consumers into groups. A company buying a list from a credit bureau never knew the details behind the list. The bureaus argued that their use of the information to create lists came under the FCRA definition of a "legitimate business need." One commentator, writing in *Direct Marketing Magazine,* claimed that the right to free speech protected credit bureaus providing lists to direct marketers.[28]

Lotus MarketPlace:Households

The Product

Development. The plan for a desktop marketing product for small business had emerged from initial discussions between Lotus and Equifax in the second half of 1988. The original idea had focused on assisting small business more with marketing analysis than with direct marketing.[29] By December 1990, Lotus and Equifax had been working on

MarketPlace:Households for about two years. About 40 people were working on the project. Significant out-of-pocket costs had been incurred during this period. Since MarketPlace was a revolutionary product, it was hard to predict a payback timetable, but all involved in the project were optimistic about its ultimate success.

Marketing. MarketPlace:Households and Businesses were primarily targeted at smaller companies. Lotus estimated that all businesses in 1990 were spending $400 million annually on electronic sources of information.[30] MarketPlace would give small businesses and nonprofit organizations up-to-date data and the ability (already available to large companies through products like Conquest) to quickly and easily identify prospective consumer and business customers. A manual that accompanied the demonstration model of MarketPlace: Households pointed out its value for small businesses:

> To survive and grow, small businesses need to be able to identify and reach potential and new customers. Direct marketing is one of the key tools for accomplishing this goal. Before Lotus MarketPlace:Households, only large businesses with an abundance of resources could participate in direct marketing. It was cost prohibitive for small businesses to utilize direct marketing.

The data to be supplied on MarketPlace: Households was based on the Equifax Consumer Marketing Database, including Micro-Vision.© Shopping psychographics were not included in the final design. Buyers would have the flexibility to view, edit, and customize the data before their initial purchase (see Exhibit 7). The charge for the software package would be a minimum $695, which included an initial 5,000 records. Lotus planned to use a metering

---

[27] Roy Schwedelson, "Privacy vs. Free Speech," *Direct Marketing Magazine,* May 1989, p. 44.

[28] Roberet J. Posch, Jr., "Privacy vs. Free Speech," *Direct Marketing Magazine,* May 1989, p. 42.

[29] "Lotus MarketPlace:Households—A Case Study in Corporate Social Responsibility," attachment B to statement of John Baker, *Hearing on Public and Corporate Attitudes on Privacy,* House Subcommittee on Government Information, Justice, and Agriculture (April 10, 1991).

[30] Jim Manzi statement, Lotus MarketPlace News Conference, January 23, 1991.

EXHIBIT 7 Lotus MarketPlace:Households Prospect Profile Examples

---

Washington, D.C. Art Gallery Owner

A Washington, D.C. art gallery owner is looking to expand her base of customers. Art is not a product selection in MarketPlace, so she must find other criteria to target potential customers.

List Definition:

- Location. The gallery owner combs her current customer file to find out that most live in Prince George's County, Maryland, which contains several suburbs of Washington, D.C.

- Household income. Her current customers have a household income of at least $100,000.

- Product selection. Art isn't listed as a choice, but other luxury items are: champagne, for instance, or luxury cars. She selects all lifestyles with a strong likelihood to buy these items.

Portland Community College

A Portland, Oregon, community college wants to find prospects for a new group of night classes designed for young adults who want to develop their management skills.

The school can target adults through several methods. One possible choice is:

List Definition:

- Location. The school targets homes within a 20-mile radius of the school, by zip code.

- Age. The school selects people under age 29.

- Lifestyle codes. The school selects several lifestyle codes that are appropriate, such as those in the Mainstream Singles category.

- Product selection. The school builds a second list, selecting products that may indicate an interest in education, such as books, and merges the second list with the first.

Source: Lotus MarketPlace, "The Lotus Desktop Marketing Advantage," 1990, pp. 13, 14.

---

system to count the names purchased as users bought lists of varying sizes. Additional records would cost $400 per 5,000 names. If customers wanted additional records after their initial purchase, they could call Lotus for a meter refill. Purchasers were to be offered a quarterly data update subscription for $200 per year.

Privacy Protection Mechanisms. Planners had focused on privacy and other social impacts of the product early in the development process. The political environment and the on-going

debate about credit bureau mailing lists had made social considerations even more important than usual. Dr. Alan Westin,[31] a national authority and Equifax's regular adviser on privacy matters, provided valuable input on privacy protection during the development of MarketPlace:Households.

---

[31] Dr. Alan Westin had helped draft the federal Privacy Act of 1974 as well as portions of the 1970 Fair Credit Reporting Act.

Like most companies considering a new product introduction, Lotus and Equifax tested the product concept for MarketPlace with several consumer focus groups during the development process. In addition to looking for input on specific performance features, they were interested in learning consumers' attitudes on privacy.

> The focus groups . . . initially expressed reservations about having information they considered to be personal made available to any legitimate small business with a computer. However, . . . they were comfortable with the idea once they understood that no actual detailed personal financial information appears in Lotus MarketPlace, and that they could opt-out of MarketPlace.[32]

On announcing MarketPlace in April 1990, Lotus and Equifax brought representatives of the DMA, including the director of its ethics and consumer affairs committee, to Boston to review the product. These industry experts identified three problems with MarketPlace. First, they were concerned that consumers did not have enough ability to opt-out, which was a key DMA guideline for mailing list practices. Second, they thought that there needed to be a strict policy for screening buyers. Presumably, most mailing list managers and brokers provided this function by reviewing a sample mailing piece before supplying a list. Since MarketPlace buyers owned their list, the DMA felt it was critical to confirm that all buyers were legitimate and reputable businesses. Their third issue focused on marketing: How would consumers perceive MarketPlace and how did Lotus and Equifax plan to educate them?[33]

In response to the DMA's concerns, Lotus and Equifax changed some features and built in more privacy controls as they finalized MarketPlace. Working with Dr. Westin, they developed 12 privacy controls in total. The five areas addressed by these controls included:

1. **Access to the data:** Lotus and Equifax planned to screen purchasers to limit access to the data only to legitimate companies (no individuals), who would purchase the discs directly from Lotus and sign a form agreeing to use the data only as spelled out by Lotus. For example, the agreement prohibited use of the data to generate mailings for lotteries, speculative real estate investments, misleading offers, pornographic materials, or computer-driven telephone solicitations.
2. **Excluded data:** No actual detailed purchase history, telephone numbers, or personal financial data (such as income or credit data) would be included on the discs.
3. **Controls built into the product:** All included data would be encrypted to ensure the physical security of the data[34] and users would not be able to look up a specific name or see addresses on the screen. To print out, a minimum number of names would need to be selected and no selection criteria (financial, demographic or lifestyle) would print, only names and addresses. Like most mailing lists, MarketPlace would have decoy names seeded throughout the database to monitor for adherence to the terms of the software license agreement and for ethical use of lists.

---

[32] Consumer Privacy Protection, Lotus MarketPlace: Households.

[33] Lorna Christie (director of the Direct Marketing Association Ethics and Consumer Affairs Committee), telephone interview with the author April 1991.

---

[34] Encryption is a process that scrambles and condenses the data into a series of coded numbers. Anyone who succeeded in breaking into MarketPlace would find individual names and addresses followed by a series of eight single- and double-digit numbers.

4. **Ability to opt-out:** Consumers could choose to exclude their names by contacting the DMA, Equifax, or Lotus.

5. **Enforcement:** Consumers could address questions, concerns, and complaints to the Equifax Office of Consumer Affairs which reported to the president. Lotus and Equifax would take legal action against anyone disobeying the rules for proper use.

Materials distributed with the product explicitly mentioned Lotus' and Equifax's commitment to enforcing legal and ethical use of the software and data and included the Direct Marketing Association's guidelines for ethical business practice.[35]

Information Standards at Equifax

At the same time MarketPlace was being developed, Equifax was taking a broader look at its relationship with consumers. In March 1989 Equifax published a statement of its Fair Information Practices (see Exhibit 8). A

---

[35] Lotus MarketPlace, "The Lotus Desktop Marketing Advantage," 1990, pp. 45–55.

EXHIBIT 8 Information Policies

Equifax provides a wide range of consumer and business information services for decision makers. As the corporate name implies, the company realizes and accepts its responsibilities for equity and fairness in its handling of factual data; first, to the person applying for the benefit; secondly, to the evaluator or risk taker; and finally, to the public at large.

The company's commitment to integrity in the information industry must take primacy. Therefore, Equifax believes:

- Every person has a right to be considered for credit, insurance, employment and other benefits on his/her own merits.
- Every person who seeks to qualify for a transaction should be treated with respect and fairness.
- Every person has a right to know what information has been reported on him/her so that its accuracy can be assured, corrected or explained as needed in fairness to all involved.
- Every person has a right to personal privacy consistent with the demands and requests he or she makes of business.
- Every person is entitled to have this privacy safeguarded through the secure storage and careful transmittal of information.

March 1989

J.V. White
Chairman of the Board

Source: *The Equifax Report on Consumers in the Information Age,* 1990. Reprinted with permission of Equifax, Inc., 1600 Peachtree Street, Atlanta, Georgia 30302.

statement from Equifax's management summarized the company's view:

> As we looked at the ways information technology has developed and is making possible more extensive and sophisticated uses of consumer information, it became clear to us that information integrity and confidentiality is our company's most important asset. Accordingly, we launched a number of initiatives . . . to ensure that our corporate policies, practices, and systems fully support the singular objective of preserving effective information standards.[36]

Management thought it important to have accurate, well-documented information on consumer attitudes and later that year decided to sponsor a national survey of consumer attitudes on privacy. In 1990, Louis Harris & Associates (Harris) and Dr. Alan Westin interviewed a cross section of the public and a sample of leaders in privacy intensive industries (insurance, credit granters, banks, and direct marketers) to explore their attitudes towards current uses of personal information. To determine changes in attitudes, Harris compared the 1990 responses, where applicable, with results of a 1978 survey.[37]

In 1990, Harris found that significantly more Americans had a general concern about threats to personal privacy than they did in 1978 (79 percent versus 64 percent) and a majority felt that Americans had lost control over how personal information was circulated and used by companies.[38] When asked about the use by direct marketers of mailing lists based on consumer characteristics, 69 percent of respondents felt it was a bad thing and 86 percent were somewhat to very concerned about it.[39] Hypothesizing that the public didn't fully understand the direct marketing industry, Harris developed a new series of questions that "balanced the benefits gained by direct marketers and credit card issuers with the benefits gained by consumers."[40] More than 65 percent of the respondents found direct marketing/mailing list practices acceptable when questioned this way (see Exhibit 9).

Dr. Westin, in his introduction to the survey results, released in June 1990, commented on the direct marketing issue as follows:

> The compilation by list brokers and marketing companies of names, addresses, and consumer characteristics (type of car owned, neighborhood lived in, charge card used, publications subscribed to, etc.) troubles many consumers. . . .
>
> However, a very large public majority would consider it acceptable for original information collectors to furnish names and addresses of persons who meet criteria as prospects for direct marketers to use in making offers to consumers if three conditions are met:
> 1. Only broad categories of consumers are identified to marketers (e.g., ranges of income, not detailed financial status).
> 2. Consumers can opt out of having their names furnished by the original collector or can have their names removed from mailing list databases.
> 3. Such lists will not be used to screen out or deny consumers a benefit or opportunity they apply for.[41]

In reporting on the year-long project, Equifax's CEO told shareholders at the annual meeting on April 25, 1990:

> During 1989, we recognized fully that our activities supporting our goals of market leadership

---

[36] "The Equifax Report on Consumers in the Information Age," (hereafter, "The Equifax Report") A national opinion research survey conducted for Equifax by Louis Harris & Associates and Dr. Alan F. Westin, 1990, p. II. By permission of Equifax, Inc., 1600 Peachtree St., Atlanta, GA 30309.

[37] "The Dimensions of Privacy," A National Opinion Research Survey of Attitudes toward Privacy. A Louis Harris & Associates, Inc., survey for Sentry Insurance, 1978.

[38] "The Equifax Report," p. V.

[39] Ibid., p. VI.

[40] Ibid., p. 71.

[41] Ibid., p. XXIV.

EXHIBIT 9   The Equifax Report on Consumers in the Information Age

First Series of Questions

Whether Lists of Consumer Characteristics Should be Sold: Public

Businesses marketing goods and services directly to consumers are now able to buy from mailing list-making companies information about your consumer characteristics—such as your income level, residential area, and credit card use—and use such information to offer goods and services to you. Do you feel this is a good or bad thing?

	Total Public (%)
Base: 2,254	
Good thing	28%
Bad thing	69
Not sure	3

Level of Concern with Selling Lists of Consumer Characteristics: Public

How concerned are you about this—are you very concerned, somewhat concerned, not very concerned, or not at all concerned?

	Total Public (%)
Base: 2,254	
Very concerned	40%
Somewhat concerned	46
Not very concerned	10
Not at all concerned	4
Not sure	*

* Less than 0.5%.

Whether Use of Consumer Information by Direct Marketers Is Acceptable: Public and Direct Marketing

Some companies want to identify consumers with a certian income and a good credit history, to send them an offer for a premium credit card or a product. They ask credit reporting bureaus to screen their computerized files for those who meet the requirements and then supply just the consumer's name and address. However, they do not get the consumer's advance permission. Do you feel this practice is acceptable or is not acceptable?

	Total Public (%)	Direct Marketing (%)
Base:	2,254	150
Is acceptable	23%	75%
Is not acceptable	76	21
Not sure	1	3

EXHIBIT 9 *(continued)*

Second Series of Questions

Whether Use of Names and Addresses by Direct Marketers Is Acceptable: Public

Increasingly, companies are marketing goods and services directly to people by mail. Some reasons for this trend are that many people have less time to shop or they prefer to make shopping decisions at home. Also, companies are trying to reduce ther costs of advertising and selling in stores, and they find direct marketing can reduce their expenses and their product prices.

Companies try to learn which individuals and households would be the most likely buyers of their products or service. They buy names and addresses of people in certain age groups, estimated income groups, and residential areas with certain shopping patterns so they can mail information to the people they think will be most interested in what they are selling. Do you find this practice acceptable or unacceptable?

	Base	Acceptable (%)	Unacceptable (%)	Not Sure (%)
Total Public	2,253	67%	31%	2%
Sex				
Male	1,018	67	30	2
Female	1,235	67	31	2
Age				
8–29 years	505	79	20	1
30–49 years	990	70	28	2
50 years and over	734	54	42	4
Education				
Less than high school	264	62	35	3
High school graduate	794	69	30	2
Some college	570	67	31	3
College graduate	357	75	24	1
Postgraduate	253	64	34	2
Race				
White	1,934	66	31	2
Black	186	70	27	3
Hispanic	133	69	29	2
Household Member				
Bought/responded to credit offer by mail	883	76	23	1
Hasn't bought/responded to credit offer by mail	1,345	61	36	3

Whether Use of Names and Addresses by Direct Marketers Is Acceptable with Protective Measures: Public

If *(read each item)* people not wanting to receive these offers by mail could have their names excluded, would this use of names and addresses be acceptable or unacceptable to you?

EXHIBIT 9   *(concluded)*

	Total Public (%)
People not wanting to receive these offers by mail could have their names excluded	
Acceptable	88%
Unacceptable	10
Not sure	1
You could be sure that no personal financial information was provided to the company	
Acceptable	75%
Unacceptable	22
Not sure	3

Whether Use of Credit Records for Prescreening Is Acceptable: Public

Credit card issuers also market directly to consumers. To make sure they send information only to people who qualify, they ask credit bureaus to tell them which individuals meet their credit standards before they send a credit offer. Is this practice acceptable or unacceptable to you?

	Base	Acceptable (%)	Unacceptable (%)	Not Sure (%)
Total Public	**2,253**	**66%**	**32%**	**2%**
Sex				
Male	1,018	68	30	2
Female	1,235	64	35	1
Age				
8–29 years	505	70	29	1
30–49 years	990	63	36	1
50 years and over	734	66	31	3
Education				
Less than high school	264	67	30	3
High school graduate	794	67	32	1
Some college	570	65	34	1
College graduate	357	64	35	*
Postgraduate	253	64	34	2
Race				
White	1,934	66	32	2
Black	186	61	37	2
Hispanic	133	73	26	*
Household Member				
Bought/responded to credit offer by mail	883	69	31	1
Hasn't bought/responded to credit offer by mail	1,345	64	34	2

* Less than 0.5%.

Source: *The Equifax Report on Consumers in the Information Age,* 1990. Reprinted by permission of Equifax, Inc., 1600 Peachtree Street, Atlanta, Georgia 30302.

and technological innovation must be balanced with a commitment to protecting our most important asset — the confidentiality of information.

Industry and Consumer Response to MarketPlace:Households

When Lotus and Equifax announced Market-Place in April 1990, it was in an environment of renewed interest in privacy. In addition to governmental attention to privacy, "there were unmistakable signs of public nervousness that some technologically enhanced consumer information services might be crossing the line into unacceptable intrusions on personal privacy."[42] Feature articles in leading journals (*Business Week, U.S. News and World Report,* etc.) and on network television alerted consumers to the use of their personal information by direct marketing companies. Information they supplied for the purpose of obtaining credit, employment, insurance, and the like was being used, without their consent, to develop psychographic profiles for target marketing companies.

Robert E. Smith, editor of the *Privacy Journal* and a leading privacy advocate, learned about Lotus MarketPlace in April from an issue of the *Friday Report,* a DMA publication. He alerted Marc Rotenberg, director of the Washington, D.C., office of Computer Professionals for Social Responsibility, and another privacy defender. In May, Rotenberg, in testimony supporting the creation of the Data Protection Board before Representative Bob Wise's Government Information Subcommittee, pointed to MarketPlace as an example of new privacy problems in the private sector. In the summer of 1990, Rotenberg and Smith began a coordinated effort opposing MarketPlace.[43]

Opposition to MarketPlace focused on two features. Opponents objected to the contents of the database, because it entailed secondary use of personal information without the individual's consent and provided no mechanism for opting out. Also, they found the use of desktop technology threatening, since it meant MarketPlace lacked the controls of a centralized mailing list database. The risk of unauthorized use and misuse was thought to be greater with desktop distribution of data.

In response to the mounting opposition to MarketPlace, the project manager (also a lawyer) contacted different privacy advocates in the summer of 1990 to set up "informational" meetings. Janlori Goldman, director of the ACLU Project on Privacy and Technology, met with Equifax and Lotus representatives on August 31. The makers of MarketPlace intended to explain the product's privacy mechanisms and dispel Goldman's fears. However, the detailed information on MarketPlace only heightened Goldman's anxiety.[44] Similar meetings with the other privacy advocates had the same results. Several meetings followed in the fall as Equifax and Lotus attempted to address the privacy issue by building further controls into MarketPlace, including a list of privacy principles to accompany demo copies of the product (see Exhibit 10). In late 1990, Goldman's objection to MarketPlace had not gone away. She did not consider the MarketPlace opt-out mechanism sufficient to satisfy the requirements of the FCRA, since the name of a consumer who requested to be removed would still exist on all discs sold prior to the request and up until an updated version was released.[45]

In late 1990, Rotenberg was preparing a paper for submission to the Association for

---

[42] "The Equifax Report," p. XIX.

[43] Robert E. Smith, telephone interview with the author, April 1991.

[44] Janlori Goldman, telephone interview with the author, April 1991.

[45] Ibid.

EXHIBIT 10 Privacy Principles

An integral part of Lotus MarketPlace:Households' development was a set of Privacy Principles written and incorporated into the initial product plans. It constitutes the basis of the product.

1. Equifax and Lotus believe that organizations in the information industry have a responsibility to protect the privacy rights of consumers.
2. At the same time, consumers want opportunities to learn about new products and services, and to exercise their options to buy or not to buy those offerings.
3. Some consumers may be concerned when their names and addresses are forwarded to mailing list compilers and brokers. Providing a well-publicized and practical procedure for meeting these concerns is a privacy protection obligation of responsible companies, and Equifax and Lotus accept this obligation.
4. Direct marketing involves the use of information from many sources. It is our objective to increase levels of consumer participation, including the consumer's ability to express the desire not to receive information generated by Lotus MarketPlace or other direct marketing products.
5. Information companies have a responsibility to guard against misuse of mailing lists they compile, sell, or use for purposes that will be offensive, distasteful, or misleading to many consumers. They also, however, have a duty not to become censors of what are acceptable or unacceptable messages for responsible business advertisers, publications, or nonprofit organizations to put foward in our society—except in clear and well-defined instances, including fraudulent or misrepresented offers.

Source: Company document.

Computing Machinery (ACM) Committee on Scientific Freedom and Human Rights. He recommended the ACM oppose the product, based on the fact the information was acquired indirectly and the subjects did not consent to the use of the information in this way. He argued that, although many list companies do the same, they do not make so much personal information directly available to so many. Smith, Rotenberg, and Goldman argued that individuals should have a legally enforceable right to control the use of consumer and personal data.

Meanwhile, opposition by consumers was mobilized on the "net"—public computer networks, bulletin boards, and conferences. The number of people wishing to remove their names was increasing. (Each removal cost the company about $1.) A November article on MarketPlace in *The Wall Street Journal* got posted on the electronic bulletin boards at computer companies as an industry newsclip. As the article was forwarded through the system, comments were appended urging readers to write letters of protest. This campaign resulted in the 30,000 letters Lotus received via electronic mail. Although 30,000 consumers represented only 0.025 percent of the population included in MarketPlace's files, the letters threatening a boycott came from Lotus's customer base. In response to the electronic debate, Lotus issued a statement defending the product on the Computers and Society public conference.

As Lotus and Equifax managers considered their next steps in November and December 1990, they reflected on the misconceptions surrounding MarketPlace:Households. Although

Dr. Westin considered "the critics' objections ... off base,"[46] perhaps the intensity of the

public's privacy concerns had been underestimated. In any event, it seemed clear that many consumers and critics did not understand the technology, the privacy safeguards, or the benefits of the product.

---

[46] John R. Wilke, "Lotus Product Spurs Fears about Privacy," *The Wall Street Journal,* November 13, 1990, p. B1.

BRIBERY AND EXTORTION IN INTERNATIONAL BUSINESS

The following caselets have been disguised, but reflect actual events with which I am familiar or which have been reported in the press.

1. You are in charge of trying to secure a contract for the sale of U.S. telecommunications equipment worth about $40 million to the communications and transport ministry of a Latin American country with a military government. European firms are also eager for the contract. Quality differences in the products of the various suppliers are not important. A local accountant, who has helped you with government negotiating in the past, suggests to you that the company might receive the contract if it were to be willing to deposit $2 million in the Swiss bank account of the general in charge of the ministry.

2. You are responsible for negotiating with an African government under the terms of which your company would build and operate a battery plant in the country. You have U.S. counsel and know a local law firm with two Harvard-trained principals. However, other Americans who have successful investments in the country suggest that you hire the local

Speaker of the House, who is a lawyer, to help represent you in the negotiations. You are aware that the House must eventually approve the agreement you negotiate.

3. Your U.S. company has a major petroleum investment in a non-Arab oil country. All foreign investors have been notified that their contracts (covering taxes, royalties, and so on) will be reviewed in the light of events in other countries. A lawyer, who is the brother of the vice president, offers his services to your firm in the upcoming renegotiations. The proposed fees are about 25 percent higher than those that might be asked by a U.S. law firm.

4. You have just been put in charge of a U.S. subsidiary in a developing country and have discovered that the previous manager has been paying $40 to immigration officials each time the residence permit of U.S. employees is to be extended. There is no official basis for the charge and it has been paid each time in cash. You are told other foreign companies and even private U.S. foundations pay similar fees.

5. You are vice president for international operations of a U.S. company. One of your new managers of a rapidly expanding subsidiary in a developing country reports the following experience: A tax collector visited the firm with a bill for the firm's annual income tax. Although the bill seemed a bit high, based on the accounts earlier submitted to the government,

---

This case was prepared by Professor Louis T. Wells of the Harvard Business School.

Copyright 1979 by the President and Fellows of Harvard College.

Harvard Business School case 380-087.

the manager told the collector that he would authorize a check to the Treasury. The collector pointed out that the total due could be discussed and he was sure that some less-costly arrangement could be worked out. The manager replied that he preferred to accept the Treasury's calculation and had a check made out. Two weeks later, the manager receives a registered letter from the collector saying that an error had been made and that the company owed about 35 percent more. A bill was enclosed, but the letter mentioned that the tax collector would be happy to discuss the matter further.

6. You are the U.S. manager of a local subsidiary in a developing country. As you are leaving the country for a brief visit to headquarters, the clerk at the counter for the local airline you are using points out that you have overweight luggage. (This was no surprise to you, since you are carrying home Christmas presents for your and your wife's families, but you know some international airlines have dropped the weight limit or would simply overlook the small amount of excess weight). You ask the charge and hear that it is $75. When you look hesitant, the clerk suggests that $5 might actually take care of the matter.

7. You are on a consulting trip to a Latin American country and discover a very fine suit in a smart downtown shop. You ask about the price and discover that it is 9,000 pesos. The clerk explains that that would be $75, if you will pay in dollars. You realize that it is $300 at the official rate of exchange that you encountered at the airport and at banks.

8. The American manager of one of your Latin American subsidiaries has been kidnapped by a leftist political group. You are informed that he will be released unharmed if you will have your company run an ad in the local newspaper presenting the group's criticism of the government in power, if you will provide $100,000 of food for distribution to the poor, and if you pay $1 million in ransom to the group. You discover that the ransom payment would be illegal in the country.

RU 486 (A)

In late October 1988, Edouard Sakiz, chairman of the French pharmaceutical company Groupe Roussel UCLAF, faced several decisions about RU 486, a new drug the company had developed. When used in conjunction with another drug, RU 486 was 90 to 95 percent effective in causing a miscarriage in the first five weeks of a pregnancy. The drug also had

Christopher Sturr prepared this case under the direction of Professor Joseph L. Badaracco, Jr.

Copyright © 1990 by the President and Fellows of Harvard College.

Harvard Business School case 391-050 (Revised 1991).

properties that could make it effective for treating several serious illnesses.

Sakiz had to decide whether to market the drug in France and in China and how to do so. Both countries had already given Roussel UCLAF approval to sell RU 486. Sakiz also had to decide whether to seek approval from the Food and Drug Administration to sell the drug in the United States.

The Development of RU 486

RU 486 was developed as a result of a joint effort of private industry and members of the medical and scientific communities. In addition, the personal efforts of one man, Etienne-Emile Baulieu, were critical. Baulieu, a medical doctor by training, was a highly successful research biochemist and a specialist in the study of steroid hormones. He had long been affiliated with INSERM (the National Institute of Health and Medical Research), a laboratory run by the French government, and he also taught biochemistry at the university level and consulted for pharmaceutical companies.

Baulieu made his mark early with the discovery in 1959 of soluble steroids secreted by the adrenal glands, a breakthrough that led to advances in the treatment of adrenal cancer. Later, Baulieu worked with Gregory Pincus, a biochemist at Boston University who played a major role in the development of the contraceptive pill. Baulieu was involved in the testing of the pill and later served on a World Health Organization committee on contraception.[1] Pincus helped Baulieu secure funding from the Ford Foundation for research at INSERM.[2] This work led ultimately to the development of RU 486.

Methods of birth control, such as the rhythm method, oral contraceptives, and IUDs, depend on knowledge about physiological events during a woman's menstrual cycle and the ways hormones trigger these events. The rhythm method is preferred by women who oppose the use of other contraceptive methods, for religious or other reasons. It makes no use of scientific innovations per se but, rather, seeks to take advantage of the temporary incapacity of the uterus to receive fertilized eggs early in a menstrual cycle.[3]

Oral contraceptives—commonly called "the pill"—usually work by suppressing the hormones that trigger the production and release of an egg. (Some forms of the pill permit a sperm to fertilize an egg but then prevent the fertilized egg from implanting on the wall of the uterus where it would continue development.) The contraceptive pill is almost 100 percent effective when used as directed. However, many side effects have been attributed to the increased levels of estrogen the pill induces. Minor side effects include nausea, weight gain, bleeding, and migraine headaches. Major side effects include blood clots, heart attack, benign liver tumors, elevation of blood sugar levels, and increased susceptibility to some kinds of cancer.

Another method of fertility control, the intrauterine device, or IUD, functions mechanically, rather than chemically. An IUD is a semipermanent implant in the wall of the uterus. This foreign object changes the uterus in several ways that prevent a fertilized egg from being implanted on the wall of the uterus. IUDs can have serious side effects, including infections that can lead to infertility. Because of these risks, IUDs are illegal in many countries, and pharmaceutical companies that produced the IUDs that led to infection have faced costly lawsuits.

Baulieu's research focused on the way a woman's body receives messages from reproductive hormones, particularly the hormone progesterone. In 1970, Baulieu successfully isolated the receptors in the cells of the uterus that receive messages from progesterone. His research team then began searching for a chemical that would keep these receptors from getting the hormone's signals to prepare the uterus to receive and nurture an embryo.[4]

Soon, Baulieu's efforts were joined by chemists at Roussel UCLAF, which was a leader

---

[1] Steven Greenhouse, "A New Pill, A Fierce Battle," *New York Times Magazine,* February 12, 1989, p. 23.

[2] Jeremy Cherfas and Joseph Palca, "The Pill of Choice?", *Science,* September 22, 1989, p. 1324.

[3] *Contraception at UHS* (Harvard University Health Services, September 1989), p. 37.

[4] Jeremy Cherfas, "Etienne-Emile Baulieu: In the Eye of the Storm," *Science,* September 22, 1989, pp. 1323–4.

among pharmaceutical companies working in steroid biochemistry. The company's chemists tested a variety of molecules and in 1978 created a synthetic steroid whose chemical structure closely resembled progesterone. This molecule, it seemed, might "trick" the progesterone receptors in the uterus and halt further production of progesterone. This would cause the lining of the uterus to break down and be expelled, as in normal menstruation. If a fertilized egg were attached to the lining, it, too, would be expelled. Roussel UCLAF registered the synthetic steroid as RU 38486.

Since the full role of progesterone in reproduction remained unclear, testing of RU 486 was necessary to confirm Baulieu's suspicion that blocking progesterone would terminate a pregnancy. Initial tests on monkeys confirmed that progesterone was necessary for the maintenance of an embryo.[5] The first test of RU 486 on human subjects was done in collaboration with a professor of medicine at the University Hospital of Geneva. Eleven women who were in the first trimester of pregnancy and wanted abortions were administered doses of RU 486 over four days. Nine of the women aborted successfully; the other two had successful surgical abortions.[6] A subsequent study involved 100 women desiring abortions who were referred to researchers within 10 days of an expected missed period. The women took various doses of RU 486 over various time periods. The drug caused abortions for 85 of the women, though a minority of them experienced complications, including heavy uterine bleeding, nausea, fatigue, and uterine contractions more painful than those in normal menstruation.[7]

The success rate of 85 percent was considered too low, so the researchers decided to give women RU 486 along with a small dose of synthetic prostaglandin, a reproductive hormone that induces contractions of the uterus. Subsequent studies showed that this combined treatment would raise the success rate of both drugs and diminish side effects of each. RU 486 blocks the normal effect of progesterone on the uterus and prevents it from accepting or sustaining an embryo; prostaglandin encourages the uterus to contract and expel its contents. This method, a combined dose of RU 486 and synthetic prostaglandin, was ultimately adopted for the use of RU 486.[8]

The testing of RU 486 revealed that the drug had other properties. It also blocked the receptors for the glutocorticoid hormone. This suggested the drug could be used to treat Cushing's syndrome (a life-threatening disease), certain kinds of breast cancer, and certain benign brain tumors.[9]

The early tests also suggested that RU 486 might be used as a form of birth control with similarities to the contraceptive pill. The earliest tests on monkeys showed it to be 100 percent effective in preventing pregnancy if taken once a month. If a woman were not pregnant, taking RU 486 could induce menstruation. If a woman were pregnant, RU 486 would end the pregnancy. Baulieu and others had expressed the hope that RU 486 might someday be commonly used as a "once-a-month pill."[10] In commenting on the possible

---

[5] Beatrice Couzinet, Nelly Le Strat, André Ullmann, Etienne-Emile Baulieu, and Gilbert Schaison, "Termination of Early Pregnancy by the Progesterone Antagonist RU 486 (Mifepristone)," *New England Journal of Medicine* 315:25 (December 18, 1986), pp. 1565–70.

[6] W. Hermann, R. Wyss, A. Riondel, D. Philibert, G. Teusch, E. Sakiz, E.-E. Baulieu, "Effet d'un stéroïde antiprogestérone chez la femme: interruption du cycle menstruel et de la grossesse au début," *Comptes Rendues des Scances de l'Academie des Sciences* [iii] 294 (1982), pp. 933–38.

[7] Ibid.

[8] Ibid.

[9] Cherfas et al., p. 1322.

[10] Ibid.

uses of RU 486, an article in the *New England Journal of Medicine* stated:

> Demographic surveys estimate that there are approximately 90 million births worldwide each year and 40 to 50 million abortions. . . . Thus, unfortunately, in the last quarter of the 20th century, abortion, with its risks and sequelae, is the most widely used method of fertility regulation. The need for a safe, convenient, and effective method of preventing or terminating pregnancy is obvious.[11]

Some doctors predicted that within a decade RU 486 or a pill like it could be used for a third of France's abortions.

Baulieu held similar beliefs, saying:

> I want to help women. I have not dedicated my life to abortion. I am not antichildren. I have three children and seven grandchildren. But women die in botched abortions. Two hundred thousand every year. RU 486 can save them.[12]

Baulieu viewed RU 486 not primarily as a new abortion technology but as an advance in fertility control. RU 486 resembled other methods of fertility control that manipulated hormones. Like some of these methods, RU 486 functioned *after* a fertilized egg had implanted in a woman's uterus and had begun to develop. Baulieu preferred to call the pill a "contragestive," a way of halting gestation, not an "abortificant." He said, "I resent it when people present the very early interruption of pregnancy as killing a baby, morally or physically."

Roussel UCLAF

Roussel UCLAF was partially owned by Hoechst, the German pharmaceutical and chemical conglomerate. Hoechst owned 54.5 percent of the company. The French government

---

[11] Couzinet et al., p. 1565.

[12] Jeremy Cherfas, "Etienne-Emile Baulieu: In the Eye of the Storm," *Science,* September 22, 1989, p. 1323.

EXHIBIT 1   Hoechst AG: Basic Financial Data ($ in millions)

	1986	1987
Sales	$17,518	$20,531
Net income	645	849
Profit margin (%)	3.7	4.1
Capital spending	1,235	1,330
R&D	986	1,232
Employees	181,000	168,000

Source: *Chemical and Engineering News,* June 18, 1990. p. 75

owned another 36.25 percent. Hoechst had made its first investment in Roussel UCLAF in 1968 because it was attracted by the firm's creative R&D in biochemistry. In 1987, Hoechst was the fourth largest chemical company in the world, as measured by sales, and the seventh largest pharmaceutical company. (See Exhibit 1.)

Roussel UCLAF was the third largest chemical-pharmaceutical company in France and the 42nd largest in Europe. It specialized in steroids and related drugs, so the research and marketing of RU 486 fell within its company's area of expertise. Health care products were its main business, but roughly a third of its sales came from chemicals, pesticides and insecticides, veterinary products, and nutrition products. The company's profits had been weak in recent years, in part because of French price controls and competition from generic drugs. In early 1988, Banque Paribas Capital Markets had advised its clients to reduce their holdings of Roussel UCLAF shares. (See Exhibit 2.)

Two-thirds of Roussel UCLAF's sales were made outside France. Its U.S. sales amounted to approximately $120 million, or roughly 7 percent of its total sales of $1.7 billion, and they had been growing rapidly. The company's health care sales in the United States were made through Hoechst Roussel UCLAF Pharmaceuticals, which was majority-owned by Hoechst.

EXHIBIT 2   Roussel UCLAF: Basic Financial Data ($ in millions)

	1983	1984	1985	1986	1987
Sales	$1,217	$1,243	$1,314	$1,480	$1,611
Net income*	43	52	56	47	31
Funds from operations	87	100	128	104	98
R&D	99	108	129	171	203
New fixed assets and investments	66	82	75	110	93
Stockholders' equity	448	338	477	517	658
Employees, at year-end	17,003	17,266	17,830	16,322	14,786

Note: Roussel UCLAF financial data is reported in French francs and was converted into dollars using the average exchange rate for each year. The ratio of FF to $ was 7.62 in 1983, 8.74 in 1984, 3.99 in 1985, 6.93 in 1986, and 6.01 in 1989.
* Excluding capital gains.

Source: Roussell UCLAF annual reports.

Roussel UCLAF's involvement with RU 486 was due largely to the company's chairman, Edouard Sakiz. At the age of 20, Sakiz left his native Turkey to study medicine in Paris, and he soon became involved in research on hormones. A journalist described Sakiz as "a sensitive, courteous man" who had "flourished in the rarified environment of academia."[13] As a skilled endocrinologist, Sakiz was involved in the discovery of the steroid molecule which constitutes RU 486 and in its earliest testing. Though he was chairman of Roussel UCLAF at the time, Sakiz joined Baulieu in signing the article that announced to the medical and scientific communities the results of the first tests of RU 486.

During his mid-20s, Sakiz became a research assistant to a leading French biochemist at an elite research institute. He had published many scientific papers and served as Roussel UCLAF's research director before he became its chairman. Sakiz was also a personal friend and former classmate of Etienne-Emile Baulieu. During the 1960s,

after Sakiz had returned to France from an academic appointment in the United States, Baulieu recommended him for his first post at Roussel UCLAF, as director of biological research. Sakiz in turn played a role in Baulieu's appointment as a consultant to the company in the late 1960s, and he later encouraged the transfer of Baulieu's research on progesterone receptors to its labs. Since the mid-1960s, Baulieu had been an "independent and exclusive" consultant to Roussel UCLAF.

Sakiz and Baulieu shared a long-standing interest in reproductive technology. In Sakiz's case, this interest had a corporate side: he remembered Roussel UCLAF's decision in the 1960s not to produce the contraceptive pill, even though it fell clearly within the company's capabilities. The decision was the result of resistance to the pill in France. Sakiz later commented: "We lost the market for contraceptives even though we were the most important steroid company in the world. And now contraceptives are considered natural; they aren't at all controversial."[14]

[13] Steven Greenhouse, "A Fierce Battle," *New York Times Magazine,* February 12, 1969, p. 24.

[14] Greenhouse, p. 24.

Early Opposition to RU 486

Pressure against Roussel UCLAF for involvement with RU 486 began long before the French government approved the sale of the drug. In February of 1988, more than seven months earlier, the *New York Times* reported that U.S. companies had been threatened with boycotts if they sold or conducted research on abortion-inducing drugs like RU 486. The paper also reported that representatives of Hoechst-Roussel UCLAF, the American subsidiary of Roussel UCLAF's parent company, had stated that their company would not seek approval for RU 486 from the Food and Drug Administration.[15] A company official had said: "We're not in that business—we don't want to get into it."

Protests soon reached Roussel UCLAF. By June 1988, Sakiz was receiving threatening letters every day. Some said "Assassins, stop your work of death" or "your pill kills babies and you will suffer the consequences." Opponents of abortion had also begun to picket the company's headquarters on the Boulevard des Invalides in Paris, sometimes marching just below the window of Sakiz's office. The company also received bomb threats; anti-abortion groups and Catholic hospitals in France said they would stop buying Roussel UCLAF and Hoechst products if the company marketed RU 486; and protesters handed out leaflets calling RU 486 a "chemical weapon" that would "poison the still-tiny children of a billion third world mothers." Some opponents of RU 486 emphasized that before and during World War II Hoechst was a leading member of German chemical industry conglomerate that manufactured cyanide gas for the Nazi gas chambers. Some protesters compared RU 486 to the Holocaust: "You are changing the uterus into

a death oven," some charged. Sakiz believed these personal challenges and indictments were taking a toll on the morale of Roussel UCLAF's employees.[16]

The chairman of the Hoechst Group, Wolfgang Hilger, had stated that an abortion pill would violate the support for life expressed in Hoechst's corporate credo, and Hilger was personally opposed to abortion. Nevertheless, he had stated in 1988 that "Hoechst subsidiaries are active worldwide under their own responsibilities and at their own initiative within the framework of shared goals."[17] In 1988, West German law permitted abortions only when a pregnant woman's life was threatened, when the pregnancy resulted from rape or incest, or if birth could create severe social and economic hardship. Violators of the law faced heavy fines.

There was also opposition to RU 486 within Roussel UCLAF. On June 23, 1988, a rally of hundreds of anti-abortion protesters took place in front of Roussel UCLAF's headquarters during the company's annual meeting. The highlight of the meeting was to have been Sakiz's announcement of a significant improvement in profits, but the protests and discussions of RU 486 eclipsed the announcement. Xavier Dor, a member of the Roussel UCLAF's board of directors who opposed abortion, made the new drug the focus of the meeting.

Other foes of RU 486 inside the company said they opposed selling the pill because of the boycott threat. (Hoechst sales in North America, principally the United States, exceeded $5 billion in 1988 and represented a quarter of the company's world sales and profits. Forty percent of these sales were fibers; the rest were chemicals, pharmaceuticals, and plastics.) Two of the RU 486 opponents were members of Roussel UCLAF's five-person

---

[15] Gina Kolata, "Boycott Threat Blocking Sale of Abortion-Inducing Drug," *The New York Times,* February 22, 1988, p. A1.

[16] Greenhouse, p. 24.
[17] Roussel UCLAf UCLAF annual report, 1988, p. 6.

Executive Committee. One was about to re-tire, but the other, Alain Madec, was 43 years old and the third-ranking executive at the company.[18]

The situation grew more complex on September 18, 1988, when the government of China gave approval for marketing RU 486. This was first step in an arrangement Roussel UCLAF had made with the World Health Organization for distribution of RU 486 at cost to Third World countries. China wanted RU 486 as part of its population control program. The country's population was already 1.1 billion, and Chinese demographers described the early 1990s as "the Himalayas of population growth" because 150 million women, born in a baby boom during the 1960s, would reach their prime child-bearing age. (China's leader at the time, Mao Zedong, had opposed birth control, calling it "bloodless genocide encouraged by China's enemies.") The country's decade-old "one couple, one child" policy seemed to be failing, even though contraceptives, abortions, and sterilization were available at no cost, and living, housing, and education policies favored couples who followed the one-child rule. China seemed unlikely to meet its national goal of a population no greater than 1.2 billion in the year 2000.

On September 23, Claude Evin, the French minister of health, approved a trial period of sale for RU 486. The French government would fully fund the distribution of the pill to certain approved clinics throughout France, where women seeking abortions could obtain free treatment with the drug.

French law permitted abortions during the first three months of pregnancy in cases of "distress." In practice, this was a policy of abortion on request, since a woman decided whether she met the "distress" condition and did not need legal or medical permission for an abortion. After three months, abortion was allowed only if a woman's life or physical health was at stake or if there was a risk of fetal handicap. Approximately 160,000 abortions were carried out in France during 1987. Abortions cost roughly $200 and were available at nearly 800 authorized clinics. The government reimbursed 80 percent of the cost. Roussel UCLAF expected the government to pay it $52 for the three RU 486 pills each woman would take.

The ministry of health had approved the distribution and marketing of RU 486 with prostaglandin under strict procedures, comparable to those for narcotics distribution. Each package would be numbered, distribution was to be limited to authorized hospitals and clinics, and a special register would record the name of physicians and patients. Women would make four medical visits to use RU 486. The first was simply to request an abortion, since French law required a woman to wait one week between a request and an abortion. On the second visit, a woman would take three tablets of RU 486. On the third, 36 to 48 hours later, she would receive prostaglandin by injection or suppository and then rest for two to three hours before returning home. Eighty percent of the women would expel the embryo—roughly the size of a pea—during the next 24 hours. Two-thirds of the women would have bleeding heavier than in their normal periods.

About a week later, the abortion would be confirmed during a final visit. If RU 486 had not worked, a surgical abortion would be performed, because of the possibility of birth defects. RU 486 could be used only during the first five weeks of pregnancy, or up to about three weeks after a woman has missed a period. (After this point, natural progesterone in the uterus seemed likely to keep the pill from working.)

Sakiz had hoped that the protests against the pill were aimed mostly at preventing government approval of the drug's sale. Instead,

---

[18] Ibid.

during the month after the French government's decision, the protests from opponents of abortion increased. The Catholic Church publicly opposed RU 486. Jean-Marie Lustiger, then the Archbishop of Paris, said the pill was "extremely dangerous." In making his decisions, Sakiz also had to consider factors outside France, particularly in the United States.

Abortion in the United States

Until the late 1960s, when many states rewrote their abortion laws, abortion was illegal in the United States. In 1973, the Supreme Court ruled in its landmark *Roe* v. *Wade* decision that state governments could not prohibit abortions during the first three months of pregnancy and could regulate it in the following months. After the decision, there emerged a "pro-life" political movement of people opposed to abortion, and it came to wield considerable political force. President Reagan opposed abortion, but his administration, which produced three new Supreme Court justices, did not overturn *Roe* v. *Wade*. Only one Supreme Court decision, *Webster* v. *Reproductive Health Services* in 1989, was thought to have weakened the rights granted by *Roe* v. *Wade,* because it gave states broader rights to limit abortion.

The strategy of the right-to-live movement involved political lobbying against abortion rights legislation, as well as direct confrontational action aimed at preventing abortions or ostracizing women who had them and doctors who performed them. The anti-abortion movement gained exposure in the media through the picketing of abortion clinics and offices of doctors who perform abortions, civil disobedience, and, on occasion, the bombing of abortion clinics. Pro-life activists also produced and distributed films like *The Silent Scream,* which graphically depict what happens to an embryo or fetus during an abortion.

Supporters of abortion rights responded with vigorous political efforts, including lobbying for pro-abortion legislation, marches for abortion rights that had drawn hundreds of thousands of people, and counterdemonstrations at sites where right-to-life protesters were picketing. The Supreme Court's *Webster* decision, and the possibility of a reversal of *Roe,* posed a new challenge for the pro-choice movement and seemed to have reinvigorated it.

The United States had one of the highest abortion rates of all developed countries. Each year, approximately 28 of every 1,000 women of child-bearing age had abortions. Since the late 1960s, more than 24 million legal abortions had been performed in the United States. These represented approximately one-quarter of all pregnancies.[19] The number of abortion providers had been declining since 1985,[20] and doctors who provided abortions were distributed unevenly. In 1985, 82 percent of counties in the United States had no doctors who performed abortions, even though these counties accounted for 30 percent of women of child-bearing age. Only 2 percent of abortions in the mid-1980s took place outside of metropolitan areas.

A *New York Times* article describing the obstetricians and gynecologists opposed to abortions quoted Dr. Curtis E. Harris, the head of the American Academy of Medical Ethics, an organization that favored restrictions on abortion. She called abortion "a real contradiction since most gynecologists work to bring a child into the world in a healthy state."[21] Other doctors had been intimidated by vocal public opposition to abortion. Facing picketing, harassment, and occasional acts of violence, some doctors who did not oppose abortions in principle declined to perform them. Several

---

[19] Alan Guttmacher Institute, "Facts in Brief: Abortion in the United States" (two-page pamphlet), 1990.

[20] Ibid.

[21] Gina Kolata, "Under Pressures and Stigma, More Doctors Shun Abortion," *The New York Times,* January 18, 1990, p. A1.

doctors quoted in the article stated that the medical community ostracized doctors who perform abortions. The article said one doctor feared that her two-year-old son would be taunted and thought she would lose patients who came to her for gynecological care if she performed abortions. Some doctors who believed that abortions should be available felt ambivalent about performing them themselves, because of the strong emotions aroused.

Dr. Louise Tyrer, of Planned Parenthood, offered another explanation for the decreasing interest in performing abortions: "The older doctors like myself who used to see women by the hundreds in hospitals suffering complications of illegal abortions and even dying were highly motivated to change that." Younger doctors, she said, "have not seen any of that — they're not aware of the horrors."[22]

One gynecologist, who believed that abortions should be legal and available, said that "as long as there is someone else to provide abortions, I'd rather not do it."

Regulation and Litigation in the United States

Some observers stressed that factors other than the abortion controversy had also contributed to the unavailability of drugs like RU 486. The pharmaceutical firm Upjohn, for example, denied that it had stopped its fertility research because it feared boycotts. A spokesperson said the company had halted this work for two reasons: "an adverse regulatory climate in the United States . . . and a litigious climate. Litigation is terribly expensive, even if you win."[23]

A drug can be marketed in the United States only if the Food and Drug Administration (FDA) approves it. Both RU 486 and its accompanying synthetic prostaglandin required FDA approval. (The prostaglandins already approved by the FDA were natural prostaglandins and were not strong enough for use with RU 486.) According to the provisions of the Food and Drug Act of 1962, the FDA was required to approve only drugs that were demonstrated, through extensive and documented testing, to be "safe and effective" for their intended purpose. The drug-approval process, from research to approval, took 6 to 10 years. Furthermore, only a fifth of drugs for which Investigational New Drug Applications were submitted were eventually approved.

Groups concerned with AIDS had recently succeeded in getting the FDA to allow drugs that were available abroad but not approved by the FDA to be imported through the mail for personal use by people with "life-threatening conditions like AIDS and cancer."[24] On September 26, 1988, wary that this directive could be applied to RU 486, Burtin I. Love of the FDA clarified the new rule with this statement:

> "RU 486" or "Mifepristone" manufactured by Roussel UCLAF Laboratories, Paris, France, has been approved in France and in China. The drug is used to induce abortion and can be used up to 49 days after a woman's last menstrual period.
>
> This drug will not be allowed entry under the "Pilot Guidance for Release of Mail Importations" issued on July 20, 1988, because it does not meet the criteria in the policy statement.[25]

The federal government had been strongly influenced by the politics of abortion. This was especially true during the Reagan administration, which staunchly opposed abortion. From

---

[22] Ibid.

[23] Ibid, and Kolata, "After Large Study of Abortion Pill, French Maker Considers Wider Sale," *The New York Times,* March 8, 1990, p. 1.

[24] Food and Drug Administration, "Pilot Guidance for Release of Mail Importations" (FDA policy directive), July 20, 1988.

[25] Food and Drug Administration, "RU 486" (FDA Import Bulletin 66–B13), September 26, 1988.

the beginning of Reagan's first term, the government had prohibited federal funding of research relating to abortion. Anti-abortion members of congress had already focused on RU 486. Representative Robert Dornan of California wrote a "Dear Colleague" letter to members of the House entitled "Death Pill." In the letter, Dornan wrote: "The proponents of abortion want to replace the guilt suffered by women who undergo abortion with the moral uncertainty of self-deception. Imagine, with the 'death pill,' the taking of a pre-born life will be as easy and as trivial as taking aspirin."[26] Dornan also offered an amendment to a Health and Human Services Appropriations Bill, which would have prohibited FDA funding for testing of what he called RU 486—The "Death Pill." The amendment did not pass.

The anti-abortion movement in the United States had also influenced international organizations. In 1985, the Agency for International Development withheld $10 million from a United Nation's agency that had funded birth control programs in China, where many abortions occurred during the last three months of pregnancy, sometimes against a woman's wishes. The United States did not contribute to the World Health Organization's special program on human reproduction, and the director of the WHO feared the United States would stop supporting other WHO programs if the organization conducted research on RU 486.

Abortion-Related Research in the United States

Many observers believed that the anti-abortion movement had discouraged pharmaceutical companies from producing abortion-inducing drugs. The *New York Times* reported in early 1988 that: "National Right-to-Life and other groups opposed to abortion have served notice to drug companies that if any company sold an abortion-inducing drug the millions of Americans who oppose abortion will boycott all the company's products."[27]

Several pharmaceutical companies had already faced boycotts because of research on or marketing of abortion-related drugs. The National Right-to-Life group had called on its members to boycott the Upjohn Company of Kalamazoo, Michigan, because it sold three such drugs.[28] In 1985, after a two-year boycott by members of National Right to Life, fertility research in Upjohn's labs ceased altogether.

Winthrop Sterling USA of New York had developed a drug called "Epostane," which has abortive properties similar to those of RU 486. A spokesman for Sterling said the company had no plans to market Epostane, because it would not be "consistent with Sterling's strategic goals." John Wilke, president of the National Right to Life Committee, had said that Sterling was in communication with the NRL and

> has given us written assurances that they are removing this drug from the scene completely. They will not do any more research on it. They will not give or sell the license for it to any other company. They will not allow any other research to be done on the drug. In effect, it has been put in a deep freeze. For this, we are deeply grateful to the Winthrop Sterling Drug Company and to its owner, Eastman Kodak.[29]

The caution these companies showed was, in a sense, industrywide. The Pharmaceutical Manufacturers Association, which develops positions on public policy issues affecting the industry, had no policies on abortion-inducing

---

[26] Robert K. Dornan, "Death Pill" ("Dear Colleague" letter to members of Congress), July 29, 1986.

[27] Gina Kolata, "Boycott Threat Blocking Sale of Abortion-Inducing Drug," *The New York Times,* February 22, 1988, p. A1.

[28] John C. Wilke, "Abortion Drugs—What's the Situation Now?", *National Right-to-Life News,* January 22, 1989, p. 3.

[29] Ibid.

drugs and said it was not an industrywide matter.[30]

While abortion remained a divisive political issue in the United States, there were indications that anti-abortion sentiment was waning. Many political candidates, including a number of Republicans, had shifted their views in a pro-choice direction. A Harris poll had found that 59 percent of those polled said they would favor "a new birth control method ... to terminate unintended pregnancy in its first few weeks by taking a pill." Thirty-three percent opposed the "new method," and 8 percent were unsure.

The "adverse regulatory climate" and the "litigious climate" cited by Upjohn also described the U.S. context for the development and marketing reproduction-related drugs. Of 17 major companies doing research on contraceptives before the 1980s, only one, Ortho Pharmaceutical Corporation, was continuing the research in the late 1980s. No new contraceptive methods had been introduced in the United States in the 30 years since the introduction of the oral contraceptive pill and intrauterine devices. Only two pharmaceutical companies still sold IUDs and many doctors refused to prescribe them.[31]

In November 1989, the World Bank and the International Planned Parenthood Federation issued a joint statement criticizing the lack of leadership the United States had shown in developing of contraceptives. Barber Conable, president of the World Bank, cited an "ideological hangup" in the federal government as the reason the government had not funded international family planning programs.[32]

Similarly, a panel formed by the National Academy of Sciences concluded:

- That the slowing pace of research in the development of contraceptives has left the United States far behind Europe.
- That the number and kind of contraceptives available to people in the United States has not changed substantially in 30 years (since the introduction of the oral contraceptive and the IUD).
- That the abortion rate, and the number of people who are choosing sterilization early in their reproductive lives, are increasing.
- That there are "shortcomings of existing products, including characteristics related to health risks, effectiveness, and convenience as well as to other user preferences."[33]

According to the report, the groups particularly ill-served by these methods were teenagers and people in their early 20s. Available methods did not take account of behavioral difficulties that made even slightly inconvenient methods ineffective for this age group. Also, women who could not use a particular effective method for health reasons—many women cannot safely take the pill—had few alternatives left. The report's "wish list" included RU 486, as well as contraceptive vaccines, long-acting implantable steroids, reversible male and female sterilization, new spermicidal agents with antiviral properties, new methods for ovulation prediction and self-detection, and methods interfering with spermatogenesis.[34]

Opponents of abortion criticized the report. The legal director of the NRL said his group believed the report was part of a national campaign by abortion rights activists and family planning organizations to get abortion drugs on

[30] Ellen Benoit, "Why Nobody Wants $1 Billion: How a Small Band of Activists Has Intimidated Some of the World's Biggest Companies," *Financial World,* June 27, 1989, p. 35.

[31] "Birth Control Group Urges More Research," *Boston Globe,* January 30, 1980, p. 8.

[32] Ibid.

[33] Luigi Mastroianni et al., "Development of Contraceptives—Obstacles and Opportunities," *New England Journal of Medicine,* 322, no. 7 (February 15, 1990); pp. 482–4.

[34] Ibid.

the market in the United States, particularly RU 486.[35] Moreover, another NRL report expressed concern for the safety of RU 486 for "anemic, malnourished women" in developing countries who might be given the drug under Roussel UCLAF's agreement with the WHO. The report said "the company is promoting this drug as safe, but we don't have any idea of what the long-term effects will be."[36]

Safety concerns were shared by some supporters of abortion rights. A discussion paper for the board of directors of the National Women's Health Network, a women's advocacy group, asked whether current studies actually showed that RU 486 was safe and whether in the long run it would be proven safer than currently accepted techniques.[37] The paper also noted that the pill and the IUD turned out to have serious, unanticipated side effects.

In September 1988, when Sakiz had to make several critical decisions about RU 486, the drug had not been tested under any of the FDA's procedures. Drugs submitted to this process typically had to be introduced by a pharmaceutical company, by the National Institutes of Health or some other federal institution, or by private institutions. Since federal funds could not be used for abortion-related research, Roussel UCLAF would have to reverse its policy and seek approval itself or permit other groups to submit RU 486 pill for approval.

---

[35] Ibid.
[36] Kolata, March 9, 1990.

[37] Cindy Pearson, "RU 486: What Will It Mean for the Women's Health Movement?" (three-page discussion paper for the board of directors of the National Women's Health network), November 12, 1988.